2001

THE RIGHT TO

2001 Cumulative Supplement

This supplement supersedes all previous supplements.

THE RIGHT TO DIE
Second Edition
VOLUMES 1 AND 2

2001 Cumulative Supplement

ALAN MEISEL

KATHY L. CERMINARA

ASPEN LAW & BUSINESS
A Division of Aspen Publishers, Inc.
Gaithersburg   New York

This publication is designed to provide accurate and authoritative information in regard to the subject matter covered. It is sold with the understanding that the publisher is not engaged in rendering legal, accounting, or other professional services. If legal advice or other professional assistance is required, the services of a competent professional person should be sought.

—From a *Declaration of Principles* jointly adopted by
a Committee of the American Bar Association and
a Committee of Publishers and Associations

About Aspen Law & Business

Aspen Law & Business—comprising the former Prentice Hall Law & Business, Little, Brown and Company's Professional Division, and Wiley Law Publications— is a leading publisher of authoritative treatises, practice manuals, services, and journals for attorneys, financial and tax advisors, corporate and bank directors, and other business professionals. Our mission is to provide practical solution-based, how-to information keyed to the latest legislative, judicial, and regulatory developments.

We offer publications in the areas of banking and finance; bankruptcy; business and commercial law; construction law; corporate law; pensions, benefits, and labor; insurance law; securities; taxation; intellectual property; government and administrative law; real estate law; matrimonial and family law; environmental and health law; international law; legal practice and litigation; and criminal law.

Other Aspen Law & Business products treating medicolegal and malpractice issues include:

Anatomy and Physiology for Lawyers
Attorney's Guide to Oncology Cases
Dental Malpractice: Legal and Medical Handbook
Emergency Medicine Malpractice
Head Trauma Cases
Obstetric and Neonatal Malpractice: Legal and Medical Handbook
Pharmacy Malpractice: Law and Regulation
Preparing Orthopedic Disability Cases
2001 Medical Malpractice Update

ASPEN LAW & BUSINESS
A Division of Aspen Publishers, Inc.
A Wolters Kluwer Company
www.aspenpublishers.com

CONTENTS

Sections listed below appear only in the supplement and not in the main volume.

CONTENTS

PREFACE

Over the last year, more regulatory attention was paid to appropriate pain management and palliative care, and significantly, the country saw the first state medical board disciplinary action against a physician for undertreating pain, in Oregon. Beginning January 1, 2001, the Joint Commission on Accreditation of Healthcare Organizations will require physicians to better document their pain treatment decisions, a move that may prompt institutional encouragement of appropriate pain management among physicians and other medical staff. See § 1A.9 of this supplement for further details.

Physician-assisted suicide and euthanasia generated headlines once again, and prompted activity both in the United States and in other countries. Federal legislative efforts to override Oregon's legalization of physician-assisted suicide continued as Congress once again attempted to pass legislation making it illegal under federal law to use controlled substances in physician-assisted suicide. In Oregon, the Oregon Health Division released its second annual report on deaths occurring pursuant to the Oregon Death With Dignity Act. In Australia, Dr. Philip Nitschke is conducting voluntary euthanasia clinics for persons who wish to commit suicide. Meanwhile, although Azerbaijan's new draft criminal code punishes euthanasia, France, Belgium, and the Netherlands considered lifting their official bans on it. In the Netherlands, this would result in an affirmative legalization of practices that have been occurring without prosecution in any event, despite technically violating the law.

Judicial activity over the issue of physician-assisted suicide also continued in the United States, as discussed in §§ 1A.9, 1A.10, and 18.22 of this supplement. For example, a retired judge in Colorado asserted a unique First Amendment argument in an unsuccessful attempt to invalidate that state's statute criminalizing suicide assistance. Additionally, the Superior Court of Alaska ruled that mentally competent, terminally ill adults in that state have a constitutional privacy interest in making end-of-life decisions, but determined that the state's law prohibiting assisted suicide nevertheless was constitutional. The Alaska Supreme Court will review the decision.

The more traditional end-of-life areas of withholding and withdrawal of treatment underwent only some tweaking at the margins this year. Judicially, the most significant decisions are being reviewed by higher courts, most specifically one in California in which an appellate court, approving withdrawal of a feeding tube, refused to require clear and convincing evidence that the non-PVS patient would have requested withdrawal of treatment. The California Supreme Court has superseded this opinion pending its decision of the appeal, so this case is one to watch over the coming year. Legislatively, states continued to refine their existing statutes governing advance directives, DNRs, and surrogate decision-making standards. California, for example, reorganized and combined several disparate statutory end-of-life provisions and authorized use of a combined advance directive form, and both Texas and West Virginia amended their statutory schemes to a great extent.

A synopsis of significant new developments and a jurisdiction-by-jurisdiction list of developments in various states' laws appear in §§ **1A.9** and **1A.10** and **Table 1–1.**

Kathy L. Cerminara is happy in this supplement to join in a project in which she was involved even at the beginning. Thank you, Alan.

Pittsburgh, Pennsylvania   ALAN MEISEL
November 2000

Ft. Lauderdale, Florida   KATHY L. CERMINARA
November 2000

ACKNOWLEDGMENTS

We are grateful to Shannon Duff, Melissa J. Hogan, Daniel O. Klinedinst, Terry Roberts, Rupasri Sikdar, Rachel Turner, and Jan O. Wenzel, who assisted us in the preparation of this supplement.

VOLUME 1

CHAPTER 1A (NEW)

INTRODUCTORY CHAPTER
OF
NEW DEVELOPMENTS

§ 1A.1 Overview of 1995–1996 Developments

Although there has been a noticeable slowing of litigation and legislation over conventional right-to-die issues, nonetheless, there have been some very important developments. However, the truly astounding developments have been in the area of actively hastening death, or physician-assisted suicide as it is more commonly called.

Decisionmaking Standards for Incompetent Patients. Perhaps the most significant is the decision of the Michigan Supreme Court in *Martin v. Martin* holding that, at least in the case of a nonterminally ill patient, there must be "clear and convincing evidence of the patient's actual preferences" to life-sustaining medical treatment.[1]

Civil Liability and Futility. There have also been some interesting and potentially important decisions dealing with civil liability for not honoring a request to forgo life-sustaining treatment[2] and civil liability for terminating treatment allegedly without proper authorization to do so, or so-called futility cases.[3] Another important case raising a civil liability issue is the Minnesota case *Lundman v. McKown,* upholding an award of damages for the death of a child treated by Christian Science practitioners, a decision in which the United States Supreme Court denied *certiorari.*[4]

Religious Right to Refuse Treatment. *Lundman* is also a part of the continuing debate over a right to refuse treatment based on religious belief, as are the *M.N.* case from Florida and *Vega* case from Connecticut.[5]

---

[1] See § **1A.2.**

[2] See § **1A.2** for the latest developments in the *Anderson* case in Ohio.

[3] See *Velez* (Georgia), *Lebreton* (Louisiana), and *Gilgunn* (Massachusetts) in § **1A.2.**

[4] *Lundman* is also discussed in § **1A.2.**

[5] See § **1A.2.**

NEW DEVELOPMENTS

Prisoners' Right to Refuse Treatment. In this very slowly developing area, there have recently been three cases, *Singletary* in Florida, *Schuetzle* in North Dakota, and *Laurie* in Rhode Island. These cases demonstrate the difficulty of line-drawing, specifically between refusal of treatment and prisoner protests, an issue that will be especially problematic if physician-assisted suicide is legalized.

Advance Directives. Three states, Delaware, Maine, and New Mexico, adopted versions of the Uniform Health-Care Decisions Act.[6]

Do-Not-Resuscitate. Three more states have enacted or amended do-not-resuscitate legislation, bringing the total number of states with such statutes to 26.[7]

Physician-Assisted Suicide. The most important developments were, within a one-month period, the decisions of two United States Courts of Appeals, the Second and Ninth circuits, in the *Quill* and *Compassion in Dying* cases, holding unconstitutional, respectively, the New York and Washington criminal prohibitions on assisted suicide as they applied to physicians aiding terminally ill patients. Although decided on different grounds—*Quill* holding that the New York statute denied equal protection, and *Compassion in Dying* holding that the Washington statute denied due process—the sympathetic tone of the two opinions toward the plight of suffering terminally ill patients was remarkably similar. Both states filed petitions for *certiorari,* and the Supreme Court has granted them.[8]

An equally important event was the third acquittal of Dr. Jack Kevorkian by a Michigan jury for aiding terminally ill patients in actively ending their lives. Of the three prosecutions, this was probably the firmest one; nonetheless, the jury refused to convict. Thus, regardless of what the courts do, including the United States Supreme Court, it is possible that physician-assisted suicide will ultimately become accepted by force of popular opinion.

One manifestation of popular opinion is jury verdicts; another is referenda. The Oregon initiative legalizing physician-assisted suicide enacted in 1994, Measure 16, was enjoined by the federal district court in the *Lee* case. The temporary injunction issued in 1994 was made permanent in 1995 and has been appealed to and argued before the Ninth Circuit, the same court to declare unconstitutional Washington's prohibition on physician-assisted suicide, in an opinion that specifically rejected the *Lee* holding.[9]

---

[6] See Chs. 11, 12, and 14 in this supplement.

[7] See § **9.8,** Table 9–1, in this supplement.

[8] Both cases are summarized in this chapter and discussed more extensively in § **18.22** in this supplement.

[9] *Lee* is discussed in § **1A.2.**

Finally, outside the United States, the Northern Territory of Australia enacted legislation in 1995, effective July 1, 1996, legalizing physician-assisted suicide. Litigation has slowed the actual implementation of this legislation. The Northern Territory Supreme Court upheld the validity of the legislation in a July 24, 1996, decision, but the region's medical association planned to appeal the ruling to the High Court of Australia. The final copy of the regulations for the act have been posted to the NT Legislative Assembly website at <http://www.nt.gov.au/lant/rotti/termill.html>.

§ 1A.2   Jurisdiction-by-Jurisdiction Developments in 1995–1996

California

Statutes

Cal. Probate Code §§ 4600–4806 (health care power of attorney).

Cases

Rains v. Belshe, 38 Cal. Rptr. 2d 185 (Ct. App. 1995).

Rains v. Belshe is the first case to challenge the constitutionality of nonjudicial decisionmaking about medical treatment. California enacted a statute affirmatively recognizing the legitimacy of certain aspects of the medical decisionmaking process—not just life-sustaining medical treatment but all medical treatment—proceeding without judicial involvement. Specifically, the statute, California Health & Safety Code § 1418.8, permits determination of incompetence and designation of a surrogate to be made for nursing home residents by the patient's physician in conjunction with review by an "interdisciplinary review team" and a "patient representative."

The statute was challenged as constituting an invasion of constitutionally protected privacy and due process rights. The trial court held that the statute was unconstitutional, and the state appealed. However, before the appeal was decided, the statute was amended, and on the basis of the amended statute, the California Court of Appeal reversed, rejecting the challenges to the statute.

The portion of the decision based on the right to privacy is quite confused because the court intermingles the two different constitutional concepts of privacy—privacy as autonomy and informational privacy. The court never clearly states the nature of the plaintiff's claim as to why the statute is an unconstitutional violation of privacy. At some points its discussion implies that the claim of invasion of privacy arises from the disclosure of confidential information about the patient's medical condition and at other times, that it arises from an alleged statutory usurpation of the patient's right to determine his own treatment course by giving or withholding informed consent. The decision is also muddied by the intermixture of state and federal constitutional analyses, although the decision "rests in large part on a claim of unconstitutionality based upon the right of privacy under the California Constitution."[10]

The decisions on due process are somewhat clearer. The petitioner's claims of unconstitutionality are twofold: first, that the nonjudicial determination of incompetence violates due process, and second, that the absence of procedural protections such as notice, an independent decisionmaker, testimony, cross-examination, a written statement by the fact finder, and a surrogate whose sole allegiance is to the patient also constitute violations of due process. Drawing on well-established United States Supreme Court precedents—primarily *Washington v. Harper*,[11] but also *Youngberg v. Romeo*[12] and *Parham v. J.R.*,[13]—(as well as California precedents) holding that determinations about medical treatment for incompetent patients need not always be made in a judicial setting to pass constitutional muster, and that adequate due process can be accorded in such situations by physicians and other nonjudicial decisionmakers, the court had no difficulty sustaining the validity of the statute.

Connecticut

Cases

Stamford Hospital v. Vega, 674 A.2d 821 (Conn. 1996).

The facts of the *Vega* case present a conventional refusal of a blood transfusion by a member of the Jehovah's Witness religious faith. However, the holdings in the dictum in the case are unusual, if not novel.

At the time of admission for childbirth, the patient and her husband had signed a release requesting that no blood or its derivatives be administered. Some time after giving birth in an uncomplicated procedure, Mrs. Vega began to hemorrhage severely. Her doctor recommended a D&C, to which the patient consented, but without the administration of blood. She again signed a release, and the procedure was performed without a blood transfusion. However, the procedure was unsuccessful, and Mrs. Vega continued to bleed. Her doctors tried a number of alternatives to the use of blood, but her condition continued to worsen, and she eventually had to be put on a respira-

---

[10] 38 Cal. Rptr. 2d at 192.

[11] 494 U.S. 210 (1990).

[12] 457 U.S. 307 (1982).

[13] 442 U.S. 584 (1979).

tor in an intensive care unit. At this point, her doctors, who had been unusually solicitous of her religious objection to blood transfusions, feared for her life and thus sought a court order.

Rather than just issuing it as many judges would do, the judge held an emergency hearing in the middle of the night at the hospital. As might be expected with middle-of-the-night hearings in hospitals, there were some procedural irregularities, which, while not fatal to the outcome of the case, did not meet with unalloyed approval by the Connecticut Supreme Court. The hearing began before the patient's attorney arrived; her husband was appointed her guardian ad litem; the court granted the hospital's request for an injunction permitting it to administer blood transfusions to her but then stayed the order until Vega's attorney arrived and was given a chance to present additional evidence. At 6:20 A.M., the court reinstated its judgment permitting the hospital to administer blood transfusions. Mrs. Vega was given blood transfusions and recovered.

The Connecticut Superior Court affirmed without opinion, and the Supreme Court reversed, continuing the trend of permitting the refusal of lifesaving treatment even when health could almost certainly be restored.[14] It rejected the argument, as other courts have begun to,[15] that the patient's refusal of treatment could be overridden because of the interest of her newborn child in having two parents, or even one parent.

To this point there is nothing particularly remarkable about the decision. What is unusual is the court's extended discussion of the issue of standing, the related discussion about state interests, and the implications for due process. For decades, hospitals and physicians have been taking it on themselves to seek court orders to treat patients who have refused a treatment the administration of which would almost certainly save the patients' lives. It was assumed without question that hospitals were morally, if not legally, required and had standing to do so. This was called into question, however, in 1993 by the Florida Supreme Court in *In re Dubreuil*,[16] in which the court held that it is not the hospital's obligation to petition for a judicial hearing in such cases. The burden is on the state to do so, not the hospital, primarily because it is a *state* interest that is being asserted, and the hospital discharges any responsibility it might have by notifying the state attorney.[17]

The Connecticut Supreme Court came to a somewhat different conclusion. It held that the hospital had no duty to assert a state interest, and indeed had no standing to do so "because to permit such a facility to do so would: (1) contravene the usual rule against vicarious third party standing; [citation omitted] and (2) place the facility in an inherently conflicted posi-

---

[14] See § **8.13** in the main volume.

[15] See § **8.17** in the main volume.

[16] 629 So. 2d 819 (Fla. 1993).

[17] See §§ **5.11** and **8.17** in the main volume.

tion of opposing its patient's competently expressed desires."[18] However, this did not end the inquiry because the court held that the hospital had its own interests in the case and therefore had standing to assert *them*. These interests are not unlike the interests conventionally said to belong to the state.

However, the Connecticut court refused to consider whether the state actually had any interests in matters of this kind because the state was not a party to the case and the issue was not properly presented.[19] The court characterized the hospital's interests as "ensuring that the integrity and ethical standards of the medical profession be maintained" and "receiving official guidance in resolving the wrenching ethical dilemma it faced."[20] Furthermore, as a practical matter, these issues, whether characterized as state interests or private interests, could only be raised by the hospital, given the exigent nature of the situation:

> Conferring standing only on the state and denying it to the hospital . . . would have effectively insulated the patient's choice from any official scrutiny because, as the facts indicate here, it would have been extremely difficult for the state to initiate judicial proceedings in time to do any good, and even if the state could have done so, it would likely have been unfamiliar both with the medical options available and with the facts and circumstances surrounding the patient's desires. The hospital was, as a practical matter, the best informed and most feasible candidate, under these circumstances, to set the judicial machinery in motion.[21]

This undeniably accurate conclusion calls into question the reasoning of the Florida Supreme Court in *Dubreuil*.

Delaware

Statutes

Del. Code Ann. tit. 16, §§ 2501–2517 (living will, health care power of attorney, surrogate decisionmaking).

Cases

In re Tavel, 661 A.2d 1061 (Del. 1995).

The Delaware Supreme Court affirmed a trial court proceeding authorizing the guardian (daughter) of an elderly nursing home patient to terminate

---

[18] Stamford Hosp. v. Vega, 674 A.2d 821, 829 (Conn. 1996).

[19] *Id*. at 826.

[20] *Id*. at 829–30.

[21] *Id*. at 830.

tube-feeding. The patient, a woman in her 90s at the time of trial, had been unconscious—just what her diagnosis was is not entirely clear; one physician described it as "a 'coma vigil,' a form of persistent vegetative state"[22]—for about three years. The court held that in decisions of this kind, there must be clear and convincing evidence of either the patient's actual or probable wishes to forgo treatment. Although not nearly as clear about the difference between a substantive standard and an evidentiary standard as is desirable,[23] the court at least seemed aware of the difference. Thus, although it stated that the trial court "was correct to apply the clear and convincing standard to this case involving issues concerning Mrs. Tavel's right to withhold or withdraw treatment,"[24] it was referring to the correct evidentiary standard. The proper substantive standard for the surrogate to follow is the substituted judgment standard, which does not require knowledge of the patient's actual wishes. The court also addressed the proper role of the guardian ad litem.

Florida

Statutes

Fla. Stat. Ann. § 401.45(3) (do-not-resuscitate).

Cases

Singletary v. Costello, 665 So. 2d 1099 (Fla. Dist. Ct. App. 1996).

This is a case involving a hunger strike by a prisoner, against whom the prison authorities brought an action to compel force-feeding. He then sought a declaratory judgment permitting him to continue the hunger strike free from, as he styled it, "medical intervention." The trial court granted an injunction against the force-feeding, and the district court of appeals affirmed.

The court analyzed this case as a simple treatment-refusal case. Relying on *Cruzan* and the Florida constitutional right of privacy, it held that the state must demonstrate a compelling state interest in overcoming the right to refuse treatment and that the state interest must be narrowly tailored to accomplish only that interest. It analyzed a number of state interests—preservation of life, prevention of suicide, and prison discipline—and concluded that none were compelling.

What is unusual about this case is that the court regarded it as a case of refusal of medical treatment rather than, as most courts have, a prison disci-

---

[22] 661 A.2d at 1065.

[23] See § **5.62** in the main volume.

[24] 661 A.2d at 1070.

pline case.[25] In so doing, the court gave greater weight to the prisoner's interests, and less to the state's, than might otherwise have been the case. The court concluded that the prison authorities produced no evidence "that Costello's actions undermined the security, safety or welfare within the prison."[26] However, it tacitly admitted that there might be cases in which the evidence was otherwise and concluded that its "resolution of this case should not be interpreted as universally holding that a prison inmate has the right to starve to death."[27]

For other new cases involving prisoners, see the North Dakota case, *State v. Schuetzle,* and the Rhode Island case, *Laurie v. Senecal,* discussed in this section.

M.N. v. Southern Baptist Hospital of Florida, Inc., 648 So. 2d 769 (Fla. Dist. Ct. App. 1994).

A trial court granted a hospital's petition requesting authority to administer blood transfusions to an eight-month-old suffering from leukemia over the parents' objections, which were based primarily on religious grounds but also on the ground that the treatment would cause the baby undue suffering. The appeals court reversed and remanded because it was not clear whether the trial court considered all competing interests. The court held that the parents have a fundamental privacy and liberty interest to refuse treatment on their child's behalf that may be overcome only by a compelling state interest.[28]

Georgia

Cases

Edwards v. Shumate, 468 S.E.2d 23 (Ga. 1996).

Edwards presents an interesting twist on an old undercurrent in end-of-life decisionmaking: the fear that heirs will seek to hasten the death of the patient for their own benefit.[29] The patient in this case, Mr. Cornwell, had originally executed a will leaving his entire estate to certain nieces and nephews. Some time later, he and his siblings—who had identical wills—drew closer to a deacon in their church and his wife, Mr. and Mrs. Shumate. Eventually, Mr. Cornwell amended his will to disinherit his relatives and to leave his entire estate to the Shumates, who eventually became his caretakers.

---

[25] See § **8.19** in the main volume.

[26] 655 So. 2d at 1109.

[27] *Id.*

[28] See § **15.2** in the main volume.

[29] See § **5.35** in the main volume.

Mr. Cornwell survived his siblings and inherited their estates. A few years later, Mr. Cornwell suffered a stroke and was admitted to the hospital. Based in part on the representations of Mr. Shumate that Mr. Cornwell did not want CPR, and based in part on the patient's personal physician's knowledge of the close relationship between Mr. Shumate and the patient, the attending physician wrote a DNR order as he had authority to do under the Georgia DNR statute.[30] The patient's condition improved considerably, and he regained consciousness. However, several days later he suffered an unexpected cardiac arrest, was not resuscitated because of the DNR order, and died.

The patient's disinherited nieces and nephews brought suit to disqualify Mr. Shumate from inheriting under the will—which would have made them the heirs—on the ground that he had procured the death of the decedent and thus under the Georgia slayer's act was barred from inheriting. For a number of reasons, the court affirmed the trial court's grant of summary judgment to Mr. Shumate on this claim. The most general reason was that Mr. Shumate did not "misle[a]d hospital personnel or the attending physician so as to obtain a DNR order."[31] More specifically, he had informed hospital personnel and the attending physicians that was a friend of Mr. Cornwell and that he had only a general power of attorney.

An interesting omission, probably because it was not relevant to the claim by the former heirs, was any discussion of whether or not, once regaining consciousness, the patient also regained decisionmaking capacity. The opinion states that the patient's "[m]ental status had much improved and patient was communicative and was quite bright and alert."[32] That being the case, the physicians should have consulted him about whether or not he wished to be resuscitated if he suffered a cardiac arrest.

Although not so holding, this case seems to give tacit approval to the possibly not uncommon practice of recognizing a close friend of a patient as a lawful surrogate.[33] The case for this is bolstered, however, by the fact that the patient's physician was aware of the important caretaking role that the friend played, the seeming importance of this to the patient, and the fact that the friend was the patient's agent under a power of attorney, though not a health care power of attorney, facts that will not always be present.

Novak v. Cobb County-Kennestone Hospital Authority, 74 F.3d 1173 (11th Cir. 1996), *aff'g* 849 F. Supp. 1559 (N.D. Ga. 1994).

This was a civil rights action against a hospital, hospital official, doctors, and attorneys resulting from a court-ordered blood transfusion. The patient was a 16-year-old boy who was seriously injured in an automobile accident.

---

[30] See § **9.9** in the main volume.

[31] 468 S.E.2d at 27.

[32] *Id.* at 26.

[33] See § **5.21** in the main volume and this supplement.

As a Jehovah's Witness, he repeatedly refused to consent to a blood transfusion, as did his father, who did, however, consent to the performance of surgery without a blood transfusion. Sometime after the surgery, the seriousness of his condition led the doctors to recommend a blood transfusion, which was again refused. Eventually, the orthopedic surgeon brought the situation to the attention of the hospital administration and its attorneys because he believed that the patient was in imminent danger of dying. A hearing was eventually held at the bedside, and the judge issued an order permitting the transfusions. The transfusion was administered with the patient being "physically restrained."[34] The patient survived and was discharged.

His parents then brought suit under 42 U.S.C. § 1983 for violation of the child's and their civil rights and brought state tort actions. The trial court granted summary judgment to the defendants holding that the *ex parte* hearing did not violate procedural due process and that ordering the transfusion did not violate substantive due process. Further, the court held that there was no evidence of a conspiracy among the state and private actors necessary to impose § 1983 liability on the private actors.[35] Finally, the court concluded that there was no constitutional right of a "mature minor" to refuse medical treatment.[36] In the present case, the United States Court of Appeals for the Eleventh Circuit affirmed the grant of summary judgment.

Velez v. Bethune, 466 S.E.2d 627 (Ga. Ct. App. 1995).
This futility case is summarized below in this supplement.[37]

Hawaii

Statutes

Haw. Rev. Stat. § 321-229.5 (do-not-resuscitate).

Illinois

Cases

In re Austwick, 656 N.E.2d 773 (Ill. App. Ct. 1995).
Austwick raises the issue of the writing of a DNR order for a patient who lacks decisionmaking capacity.[38] The patient was adjudicated a "dis-

---

[34] Novak v. Cobb County-Kennestone Hosp. Auth., 849 F. Supp. 1559, 1564 (N.D. Ga. 1994).

[35] See § **17.20** in the main volume.

[36] See § **15.3** in the main volume.

[37] See § **19.2** in this supplement.

[38] See § **9.9** in the main volume.

abled person" according to Illinois statutory procedures. The Public Guardian was appointed as the plenary guardian of her person and estate. About a year later, an attorney for the Public Guardian visited her, explained what a DNR order was, and asked if she wanted one. She said that she did, and a few months later the Public Guardian authorized her attending physician to write the DNR order in her nursing home medical chart. About a year later, the patient petitioned the probate court to have the order terminated, and she requested the removal of the Public Guardian because of his failure to comply with the procedures in the Health Care Surrogate Act when consenting to the DNR, namely, that she did not lack decisional capacity. The trial court ordered that the DNR order be removed.

The Appellate Court of Illinois held that the Public Guardian had no authority to consent to a DNR order on Mrs. Austwick's behalf because her adjudication as a disabled person under the Probate Act does not overcome the presumption under the Health Care Surrogate Act that she has decisional capacity.[39] The Health Care Surrogate Act authorizes a surrogate to forgo life-sustaining treatment for a patient only when the patient lacks decisional capacity and has a qualifying condition. When the patient has decisional capacity, she must personally provide consent to forgoing life-sustaining treatment.[40]

Iowa

Statutes

Iowa Code Ann. § 707A.1-.3 (assisted suicide).

Louisiana

Statutes

La. Rev. Stat. Ann. § 14:32.12 (assisted suicide).

Cases

Lebreton v. Rabito, 650 So. 2d 1245 (La. Ct. App. 1995).
    The adult daughter of the patient, from whom life-sustaining medical treatment had been removed, brought an action alleging that the attending physician had terminated life-sustaining treatment without proper consent—and, indeed, over the refusal of one authorized under the surrogate decision-

---

[39] See §§ **4.11–4.19** in the main volume.

[40] See §§ **10.7, 11.9, 12.16,** and **12.17** in the main volume.

making provisions of the living will statute to make medical decisions for the patient. The trial court dismissed the complaint on the basis that this was a medical malpractice action and thus, by statute, it first had to be considered by a medical review panel. The Louisiana Court of Appeal reversed and reinstated the complaint, holding that it was not an action for medical malpractice but rather for wrongful death and survival.

Although not labeled as a "futility" case,[41] this in essence is what the case alleges, and for this reason the case bears further watching.

Perrier v. Bistes, 650 So. 2d 786 (La. Ct. App. 1995).

The siblings of a patient, who died when a physician terminated life support pursuant to the authorization of the patient's husband, brought suit alleging that the husband, his siblings who were his sole heirs, and the physician engaged in "an intentional, unjustified killing," and as a consequence, under Louisiana statutory law, the husband was barred from inheriting his wife's estate. The court affirmed the trial court's dismissal of the claim on the ground that this interpretation of the events is "inconsistent with the legislative intent" of the statute. As a dissenting judge pointed out, however, the majority failed to examine the fundamental issue, which was whether the husband was substantively empowered under Louisiana law to authorize termination of life support; in other words, the court failed to inquire whether the substantive standard for decisionmaking for an incompetent patient had been met.[42]

Maine

Statutes

Me. Rev. Stat. Ann. tit. 18-A, §§ 5-801 to -817 (living will, health care power of attorney, surrogate decisionmaking).
Me. Rev. Stat. Ann. tit. 24, § 2905 (surrogate decisionmaking).

Maryland

Statutes

Md. Code Ann., Health-Gen. §§ 5-601 to -618, *as amended by* Md. H.B. 1361 (enacted May 14, 1996) (living will, health care power of attorney).

---

[41] See **Ch. 19** in the main volume.
[42] See **Ch. 7** in the main volume.

Massachusetts

Cases

Gilgunn v. Massachusetts General Hospital, No. SUCV92-4820 (Mass. Super. Ct. Suffolk County, Apr. 21, 1995).
This futility case is summarized below in this supplement.[43]

Michigan

Statutes

Mich. Comp. Laws §§ 333.1051–.1067 (do-not-resuscitate).
Mich. Comp. Laws Ann. § 399.20192 (do-not-resuscitate).

Cases

Martin v. Martin, 538 N.W.2d 399 (Mich. 1995), *cert. denied,* 116 S. Ct. 912 (1996).
Martin is an extremely important case in at least two respects: the first is the patient's condition, and the second is the substantive decisionmaking standard that the court applied. Unlike most right-to-die cases previously litigated at the appellative level, Martin was not terminally ill nor permanently unconscious. However, his injuries so profoundly impaired his cognitive functioning that it was unclear whether he had any contact with his environment. This uncertainty marks the difference between his condition and PVS patients. As to PVS patients, there is no doubt that they lack any contact with their environment.[44] However, as in a PVS, there was a consensus among the medical experts that Martin's "condition and cognitive level of functioning will not improve in the future."[45]
In 1987, Martin suffered severe head injuries in an automobile accident, which "significantly impaired his physical and cognitive abilities, left him unable to walk or talk, and rendered him dependent on a colostomy for defecation and a gastrostomy tube for nutrition."[46] Five years after the accident, while being treated for an obstructed bowel, his wife consulted the hospital's bioethics committee to determine whether life-sustaining medical treatment should be withdrawn. The committee concluded that withdrawal of tube-feeding "was both medically and ethically appropriate, but that court autho-

---

[43] See § **19.2** in this supplement.

[44] See § **9.53** in the main volume.

[45] 538 N.W.2d at 404.

[46] *Id*. at 402.

rization would be required before the hospital would assist in the procedure."[47] His wife then instituted judicial proceedings to terminate tube-feeding, which was opposed by the patient's mother and sister. The trial court ultimately denied the petition, a decision that was reversed and remanded by the Michigan Court of Appeals.[48]

The Michigan Court of Appeals instructed that on remand, the trial court must make more specific findings on the patient's capacity to make a decision to forgo treatment and on his treatment preferences and best interests. If there was clear and convincing evidence of the patient's actual preferences, they would govern; otherwise, the decision on whether to withhold treatment could be made by the surrogate.

On remand, a number of physicians testified, and there was substantial agreement that Martin could only understand very short and simple questions because of his inability to retain information. As a result, they agreed that he was incapable of processing the information necessary to fully understand his condition, and thus that he did not possess decisionmaking capacity.[49] In addition to the medical testimony, there was testimony about Martin's preferences concerning treatment. The Michigan Supreme Court summarized this testimony by stating that "[p]revalent throughout Michael's statements is the preference not to be maintained in a condition where he was incapable of performing basic functions such as walking, talking, dressing, bathing, or eating, and, instead, was dependent upon others or machines for his basic needs."[50] On the basis of this evidence, the trial court determined that there was clear and convincing evidence that Martin had, prior to suffering his injuries, "expressed a medical preference to decline life-sustaining medical treatment under the circumstances presented," and the court of appeals affirmed[51] because "Martin's present condition fit squarely within the parameters that Mr. Martin specifically described."[52]

In this latest opinion, the Michigan Supreme Court reversed, holding that tube-feeding could not be withdrawn because the circumstances of Martin's situation were not those contemplated by him in his pre-injury statements. The bulk of the opinion was consistent with all aspects of the accepted national consensus about forgoing life-sustaining treatment[53] save one: the substantive standard to be applied for decisionmaking for patients who lack decisionmaking capacity. In this regard, the consensus subscribes to the sub-

---

[47] *Id.*

[48] Martin v. Martin, 504 N.W.2d 917 (Mich. Ct. App. 1993).

[49] 538 N.W.2d at 403.

[50] *Id.* at 404.

[51] *See* Martin v. Martin, 517 N.W.2d 749 (Mich. Ct. App. 1994).

[52] 538 N.W.2d at 404.

[53] See § **2.2** in the main volume.

stituted judgment standard, namely, that a surrogate may authorize the forgoing of life-sustaining treatment if there is clear and convincing evidence that the patient's actual or *probable* wishes were for treatment to be forgone.[54] The Michigan court became the third state—along with Missouri and New York—to depart from this aspect of the consensus, though seemingly limited to the facts of this case, requiring instead that there be clear and convincing evidence of the patient's *actual* wish (the "subjective standard") to forgo life-sustaining treatment,[55] because it best promotes patient self-determination. Unlike many other state courts that had joined the consensus, however, the court did recognize the difference between the evidentiary standard ("clear and convincing evidence") and the substantive standard ("actual wishes" versus "probable wishes"):

> [W]e view the clear and convincing standard not as a decision-making standard, but as an evidentiary standard of proof that applies to all decisions regarding termination of treatment, regardless of the decision-making standard employed. In right to die cases, if intent to withdraw life prolonging medical procedures is determinative of the case, then there must be "clear and convincing evidence" of that intent. If "best interests" of the patient is determinative of the case, then there must be "clear and convincing evidence" that discontinuance of medical procedures best serves the interests of the patient.[56]

Finally, it is essential to note that the court intimated that the holding—that is, the subjective standard—might not apply to patients more seriously injured than Martin, specifically, patients in a PVS.[57]

Minnesota

Cases

Lundman v. McKown, 530 N.W.2d 807 (Minn. Ct. App. 1995), *cert. denied,* 116 S. Ct. 814 (1996).
   Lundman is a negligence action by the father and sister of a boy against the mother, the stepfather, and Christian Science practitioners for the wrongful death of the boy resulting from diabetic ketoacidosis treated by Christian Science rather than by conventional medical means. This most significant aspect of this case is that the Minnesota Court of Appeals upheld the jury verdict (in excess of a million dollars in compensatory damages) against sev-

---

[54] See § **7.7** in the main volume.

[55] See § **7.5** in the main volume.

[56] 538 N.W.2d at 406 n.12 (citing first edition of this treatise). See § **5.62** in the main volume.

[57] *Id.* at 408–09.

eral of the parties, and the United States Supreme Court declined to review the case.[58]

The court refused to uphold the award of compensatory damages against the *church*. The basis for doing so, however, had nothing to do with religious freedom. The court overturned the imposition of liability against the church itself (as opposed to its agents) in part on the ground that the church merely espoused religious beliefs but did not *act* in such a way as to adversely affect the boy's well-being.[59] The court also reversed the $9 million *punitive* damages award against the First Church of Christ, Scientist (as the church is formally known), on the ground that the church was not involved in the treatment of the child. Also, at least on the facts of this case, the imposition of punitive damages would interfere with the free exercise of religion. Although "not grant[ing] churches and religious bodies a categorical exemption from liability for punitive damages," the church's involvement in the case consisted of the "espousal of spiritual treatment" which is "entitled to substantial free exercise protection."[60]

The court affirmed the jury verdicts against the boy's mother, stepfather, and Christian Science practitioners on well-accepted negligence principles. It specifically refused to hold that the religious freedoms guaranteed by the Minnesota and United States Constitutions preclude an award of compensatory damages. The primary basis for the holding is the well-accepted constitutional principle that

> [a]lthough one is free to believe what one will, religious freedom ends when one's conduct offends the law by, for example, endangering a child's life. *Cantwell v. Connecticut,* 310 U.S. 296 (1940). . . . Courts have consistently distinguished between the absolute liberty to believe (which the government may not restrict) and the limited liberty to act in furtherance of religious belief (which the government may reasonably restrict).[61]

The court did recognize that religiously-motivated conduct enjoys some constitutional protection, but concluded that the state had a compelling interest—namely, saving the life of a child—in restricting the conduct in question, and that it had used the least restrictive alternative in so doing.[62]

The court also rejected the claim that the award of compensatory damages was precluded by due process, specifically, by the lack of notice that such

---

[58] In a prior related case, State v. McKown, 475 N.W.2d 63 (Minn. 1991), an indictment for manslaughter was dismissed as violating the parents' due process rights because the statute failed to give fair notice of the prohibited conduct.

[59] 530 N.W.2d at 825–26.

[60] *Id.* at 816.

[61] *Id.* at 817.

[62] *Id.* at 818–19.

liability could exist. The right of fair notice is far less onerous in common-law civil actions than in criminal actions:

> It should not be a surprise when a rule of common law is first applied retro-spectively as, to a degree, we do in this case. That the rights awarded and obligations imposed in this case may not have been perfectly perceived yester-day is of little constitutional concern. Even if some rights and obligations were recognized here for the first time, we would still have no concern about consti-tutionality.[63]

In addition, the court held that there was fair notice in fact because "[t]here is . . . substantial precedent for overriding religious belief in matters of health—and liability should have been foreseen."[64]

Lundman, though a different sort of case than most involving religious principles in medical decisionmaking, is consistent with the general trend of recognizing that religious principles are not determinative of rights to make medical decisions. An increasing body of cases, primarily involving Jehovah's Witnesses, demonstrates that the legal right to refuse treatment does not arise from religious belief but is of more general application.[65] *Lundman* simply adds a complementary note, namely, that responsibility for the conse-quences of medical decisionmaking is not excused by religious belief.

Nevada

Statutes

Nev. Rev. Stat. Ann. § 449.670 (assisted suicide).

New Mexico

Statutes

N.M. Stat. Ann. §§ 24-7A-1 to -18 (living will, health care power of attor-ney, surrogate decisionmaking).

New York

Cases

In re Barsky (Kyle), 627 N.Y.S.2d 903 (Sup. Ct. Suffolk County 1995).

---

[63] *Id.* at 819.

[64] *Id.*

[65] See §§ **2.9** and **9.3** in the main volume.

The patient, Kyle, had been adjudicated incompetent and had no living relatives. After she suffered a heart attack or stroke, her guardian petitioned the court for an expansion of his powers to include the authority to decline the implantation of a feeding tube. He based his petition on conversations with the patient that led him to conclude that the feeding tube would not be reflective of her "best interests or desires as to preserving her personal dignity."[66] The court held that the evidence that the guardian provided did not meet the standard of "clear and convincing evidence that such a decision is consistent with what the patient would have directed if able to make and express a determination"[67] as set forth in *In re Westchester County Medical Center (O'Connor).*[68]

In re Long Island Jewish Medical Center (Baby Doe), 641 N.Y.S.2d 989 (Sup. Ct. Queens County 1996).

This is the first case to litigate the provision of New York law requiring that hospitals, when determining a patient to be dead by brain-death standards, make "reasonable accommodation" to the religious or moral views of the patient about the validity of the brain death as a standard for determining death.[69] The court held that although the hospital had not complied with that portion of the regulation requiring hospitals to have a policy on reasonable accommodation, the hospital nonetheless had complied with the substance of the religious accommodation requirement. This case is discussed below in this supplement.[70]

Finn v. Leonard "C", 634 N.Y.S.2d 262 (App. Div. 1995), *modifying and aff'g In re Finn,* 625 N.Y.S.2d 809 (Sup. Ct. Albany County 1995), *leave to appeal denied,* 665 N.E.2d 661 (N.Y. 1996).

The patient in this case was a 67-year-old profoundly mentally retarded man, residing in a community-based facility for which state officials had responsibility. His sister, who was his legal guardian, requested that a DNR order be written although "he was not suffering from any life-threatening illness" because "she was concerned about [his] quality of life if he suffered a cardiac arrest and was resuscitated."[71] A DNR order was written by his personal physician. Thereafter, the patient was examined by a state physician who concluded that a DNR order was not warranted, and the state brought an

---

[66] 627 N.Y.S.2d at 905.

[67] *Id.*

[68] 531 N.E.2d 607 (N.Y. 1988). See §§ **7.4** and **7.5** in the main volume.

[69] *See* N.Y. Dep't of Health Regulation, N.Y. Comp. Codes R. & Regs. tit. 10, § 400.16(e)(3).

[70] See § **9.48** in this supplement.

[71] 634 N.Y.S.2d at 263.

action to rescind the DNR order. The trial court agreed that the statutory criteria for the issuance of a DNR order were not met because there was "no evidence" that the patient's medical condition would make resuscitation "medically futile" as required by the statute.[72] The trial court went further, declaring that the provision of the statute under which the order was issued was unconstitutionally vague.

The appeals court affirmed on the basis of lack of evidence to support the conclusion that resuscitation would be futile as defined by the statute. However, it concluded that the trial court should not have reached the issue of constitutionality of the statute and vacated the declaration of unconstitutionality.

Quill v. Vacco, 80 F.3d 716 (2d Cir. 1996), *rev'g Quill v. Koppell,* 870 F. Supp. 78 (S.D.N.Y. 1994), *cert. granted,* 1996 WL 282544, 65 U.S.L.W. 3052 (U.S. Oct. 1, 1996) (No. 95-1858).

The United States Court of Appeals for the Second Circuit reversed the decision of the district court that upheld the constitutionality of New York's statutory prohibition on assisted suicide. The Second Circuit decision held that the statute constituted a denial of equal protection in that it permitted terminally ill patients to hasten their deaths by withholding or withdrawing life-sustaining medical treatment but denied them the right to hasten their deaths when they were not being kept alive by medical means. This case is summarized below in this supplement.[73] Also see the Washington case of *Compassion in Dying,* noted below in this section.

Williams v. Bright, 632 N.Y.S.2d 760 (Sup. Ct. N.Y. County 1995), *rev'd,* 658 N.Y.S.2d 910 (App. Div. 1997).

The plaintiff in this case was seriously injured in an automobile accident when the car in which she was a passenger was struck by a car driven by one of the defendants. Plaintiff suffered multiple fractures, for which the "normal treatment" was surgery accompanied by blood transfusions, which the plaintiff rejected because she was a member of the Jehovah's Witness religious faith. She eventually was treated with less invasive, but less effective procedures, without blood transfusions. As a consequence, the expert testimony was that plaintiff "would within three to four years become wheelchair bound or bedridden for the balance of her life and would require substantially increased medical and hospital services and home care."[74]

The defendant claimed that the plaintiff's damages should be limited by her failure to mitigate damages by undergoing the normal medical treatment, and that if damages were not mitigated, "the court would be giving a prefer-

---

[72] 625 N.Y.S.2d at 812.

[73] See § **18.22** in this supplement.

[74] 632 N.Y.S.2d at 763.

ence to a party who is excused from a duty to mitigate as a result of her religion."[75] Nonetheless, the trial court charged that the jury was not

> to consider the validity or reasonableness of her religious beliefs. . . . You have to accept as a given that the dictates of her religion forbid blood transfusions. And so you have to determine in assessing the question of damages, damages past and damages future, whether she, Mrs. Robbins, acted reasonably as a Jehovah's witness in refusing surgery which would involve blood transfusions. Was it reasonable for her, not what you would do—or your friends or family— was it reasonable for her, given her beliefs, without questioning the validity or the propriety of her beliefs.[76]

The trial judge wrote an opinion explaining the basis for the charge. Although a very discursive analysis, the court did seem to get the result right. The opinion takes somewhat of a "shotgun" approach. One of the bases for its ruling was a line of cases in the United States Supreme Court dealing with whether or not individuals could be penalized for taking action motivated by conscientiously held religious beliefs. The court concluded on this point that

> [i]t should now be abundantly clear, under *Sherbert* [*v. Verner,* 374 U.S. 398 (1963), [*Wisconsin v. Yoder,* 406 U.S. 205 (1972)], and their progeny, as reaffirmed by the Religious Freedom Restoration Act [42 U.S.C.A. §§ 2000bb *et seq.*], that "to condition the availability of benefits upon . . . [plaintiff's] willingness to violate a cardinal principle of her religious faith effectively penalizes the free exercise of her constitutional liberties." Sherbert v. Verner, 374 U.S., at p. 406.[77]

However, the court also grounded its decision on generally accepted common-law tort principles, namely, the so-called egg-shell skull or thin skull cases, or the more generalized label of the defendant's "taking the plaintiff as he finds her," or from a more conceptual perspective, the age-old tort problem of scope of liability often discussed under the heading of "proximate cause."[78] Regardless of how one phrases this, the court's conclusion that the long- and firmly held religious conviction precluding blood transfusion is as much a part of a plaintiff's character as a physical disability or a high income level, both of which would also affect the amount of damages a defendant might be required to pay, seems sound.

The common-law basis is a better one because it avoids constitutional issues, especially one so contentious and problematic as the entanglement of

---

[75] *Id.* at 762.

[76] *Id.* at 763–64.

[77] *Id.* at 768.

[78] *See generally* W.P. Keeton et al., Prosser and Keeton on the Law of Torts § 43, at 290–93 (5th ed. 1984).

church and state. However, the court did not completely avoid the problems of free exercise and establishment because it grounded the decision on the fact that the patient's beliefs were religious ones rather than on the fact that they were firmly held. The court could have reached the same result on the latter basis, and there is support in New York law (and elsewhere) for it to have done so. In *Fosmire v. Nicoleau,*[79] the New York Court of Appeals upheld the right of a Jehovah's Witness to reject a blood transfusion, basing its decision not on the fact that the patient was a Jehovah's Witness but on the common-law right of self-determination.[80] The failure to take this route is odd not only because of the ability to avoid the religious issue, but also because the court was plainly aware of *Fosmire* as evidenced by its citation of that case for another point.

North Carolina

Cases

First Healthcare Corp. v. Rettinger, 467 S.E.2d 243 (N.C. 1996), *rev'g* 456 S.E.2d 347 (N.C. Ct. App. 1995).

This case nicely illustrates how difficult it can be to put any teeth into the right to die.[81] Courts have been notoriously unwilling, in the end-of-life context, to permit the recovery of damages for the provision of nonconsensual treatment.[82] In addition, a suit for damages will not be particularly useful if the patient is not suffering a great deal between the time that the forgoing of treatment was authorized and the time of death. Consequently, some litigants have begun to explore the possibility of refusing to pay for treatment and services rendered during this period of time, but they too have not been particularly successful.[83]

This was the tack taken in *Rettinger,* but it too did not succeed. Mr. Rettinger was a nursing home resident suffering from Parkinson's disease. At least six years prior to entering the nursing home, he executed a statutory living will—in which he "stated that he did not wish his life to be prolonged by 'extraordinary means if [his] condition [was] determined to be terminal and incurable.'"[84] A copy of the living will was placed in his medical record at the nursing home.

---

[79] 551 N.E.2d 77 (N.Y. 1990).

[80] See §§ **2.9, 8.14,** and **9.3** in the main volume.

[81] It also illustrates how difficult it can be to have one particular form of treatment—a feeding tube—terminated in a nursing home, an issue discussed in § **9.40** in the main volume and this supplement.)

[82] See **Ch. 17.**

[83] See § **17.4** in the main volume.

[84] 456 S.E.2d at 348.

During a hospitalization, a nasogastric tube was inserted to facilitate the administration of medications. When Mr. Rettinger returned to the nursing home, he was, according to his wife, "'bedridden, lying in a fetal position, unable to move and unable to communicate.'"[85] The NG-tube was not removed because the nursing home "had a policy of not removing nasogastric tubes 'if to do so would likely cause a patient to starve or dehydrate to death.'"[86] Mrs. Rettinger then attempted to have her husband designated "DNR," but "because she amended the form to request that no nasogastric tube be used, [the nursing home] returned the form as invalid."[87] She then failed in her attempt to have him transferred to another nursing home and in her attempt to take him home, the latter because the nursing home "staff told her she could not, 'apparently because they felt [she] was not able to care for him.'" The nursing home ultimately stated that it would agree to the removal of the NG-tube only if there were a court order or "the requirements of [the living will statute] were satisfied."[88]

Mrs. Rettinger set about to do the latter. Thereafter, the facts are in dispute about what happened or did not happen, or perhaps more correctly, there was a dispute about whether the facts were in dispute. Mrs. Rettinger eventually sought a court order to have treatment terminated, which was issued. After Mr. Rettinger's death, the nursing home sought payment of an outstanding balance, and Mrs. Rettinger refused to pay the almost $15,000 charged for the period from when judicial proceedings to terminate treatment were initiated until the time when Mr. Rettinger died. The nursing home eventually brought suit; the trial court granted summary judgment for the plaintiff nursing home, finding that there were no genuine issues of material fact; the North Carolina Court of Appeals reversed, with two judges holding that there were material facts in dispute and one judge disagreeing; and the North Carolina Supreme Court reversed in a one-sentence per curiam opinion adopting the opinion of the dissenting court of appeals judge.

A close reading of the majority and dissenting court of appeals' opinions still does not make it simple to determine just what the facts were, what their time sequence was, and what the judges were relying on in rendering their opinions. It seems, however, the dissenting judge in the court of appeals—and hence the supreme court, which adopted his opinion—were bent on honoring form over substance. They relied heavily on the allegations that the doctors had not complied with the literal requirements of the living will statute. By contrast, the majority in the court of appeals appear to have concluded that because two doctors agreed—as the statute required—that the

---

[85] *Id.*

[86] *Id.*

[87] *Id.*

[88] *Id.*

patient be in a terminal condition or incurable, there had been compliance with the statute.

In truth, the judges did not really reach these conclusions because they were deciding merely whether material facts were in dispute. The fact that they disagreed as strongly as they did about facts is some indication of the facts not being undisputed. Thus, on this basis alone it would have done more justice for the case to have been permitted to go to trial. Moreover, the dissenting judge relied not merely on affidavits but also on the medical record to establish that, in his view, there were no genuine issues of material fact.[89] Medical records, however, are evidence, and thus subject to the form of scrutiny normally reserved for trial and not for a decision on the pleadings.

Finally, even if the complaint had been reinstated and even if the facts most favorable to Mrs. Rettinger had been proved, the opinion of the court of appeals majority would have presented an obstacle to full recovery. When Mr. Rettinger was admitted to the nursing home, Mrs. Rettinger executed an agreement "to pay for all services rendered to her husband. The agreement contains no language stating that Mrs. Rettinger would only pay for services she authorized."[90] Consequently, if the jury were to find in her favor, she would still be liable for the costs until the date he would have died, which would have been some time after treatment was terminated.

North Dakota

Cases

Gabrynowicz v. Heitkamp, 904 F. Supp. 1061 (D.N.D. 1995).

Gabrynowicz is a case testing the validity of a provision in the North Dakota advance directive statute limiting the implementation of advance directives for pregnant women, a common feature of advance directive statutes.[91] The state argued that although an advance directive need not conform exactly to the statutory form, for an advance directive to be enforceable it must be, in the terms of the statute, "'substantially' in the form set out in the statute.'"[92] Although the district court "acknowledge[d] that the challenged statutes raise constitutional questions,"[93] it held that the case was not ripe for adjudication and therefore refused to rule on them.

---

[89] 456 S.E.2d at 352.

[90] *Id.* at 351.

[91] See §§ **11.11** and **12.27** in the main volume.

[92] 904 F. Supp. at 1062 (citing N.D. Cent. Code § 23-06.4-03(3)).

[93] *Id.* at 1064.

State v. Schuetzle, 537 N.W.2d 358 (N.D. 1995).

This is an action to compel a prisoner to take insulin for diabetes. The prisoner was determined by a psychiatrist to be competent and nonsuicidal. He refused to eat (which he later changed his mind about) or to take insulin because, according to the psychiatrist, he "is a very stubborn, angry man who because of his life sentence . . . has very little to lose and thus has asserted his control."[94] The expert evidence was that he was unable to control his diabetes without insulin, that prolonged "refusal to take insulin would increase his risk of heart attack, diabetic coma, kidney failure, eye problems, pain and numbness, and premature death at some point in the future," and that untreated diabetes could increase the likelihood of "extremely costly" cardiac bypass surgery and renal dialysis at some future time.[95]

The trial court ordered the administration of insulin, finding that the prisoner's refusals of treatment were "an attempt to manipulate the system and an act of blackmail against prison officials" for actions they had taken concerning his employment outside the prison and his housing. The North Dakota Supreme Court affirmed on the ground that the state's interest in the orderly administration of prisons outweighed the individual's interests in refusing medical treatment.[96]

For other new cases involving prisoners, see the Florida case, *Singletary v. Costello,* and the Rhode Island case, *Laurie v. Senecal,* discussed in this section.

Ohio

Cases

Anderson v. St. Francis-St. George Hospital, No. C-930819, 1995 WL 109128 (Ohio Ct. App. Mar. 15, 1995), *reversed,* 671 N.E.2d 225 (Ohio 1996).

Anderson is a suit for damages by the estate of a deceased patient, Edward Winter, against the hospital whose employees administered cardiopulmonary resuscitation to him despite the patient's prior competent refusal and his attending physician's having written a DNR order. The trial court granted summary judgment to the hospital, but in *Anderson v. St. Francis-St. George Hospital,*[97] the Ohio Court of Appeals reinstated two of the three causes of action and remanded for trial. Although refusing to establish a new cause of

---

[94] 537 N.W.2d at 359.

[95] *Id.*

[96] See § **8.19** in the main volume.

[97] 614 N.E.2d 841 (Ohio Ct. App. 1992) (*Anderson I*).

action for "wrongful living," the court held that the claims for battery and negligence should go forward.[98]

After the first remand, the trial court granted the hospital's new motion for summary judgment on the ground that the estate could not, as a matter of law, prove any actual damages. The estate again appealed, and the court of appeals again reversed.[99] The Ohio Supreme Court has granted a discretionary appeal.[100]

Although the court held in *Anderson I* that there could be no recovery for damages for wrongful living—by which it meant that "he cannot recover general damages just for finding himself still alive after unwanted resuscitative measures"[101] the *Anderson II* court reiterated that there were still potentially other recoverable damages for the battery and negligence claims, as it had held in *Anderson I*. Because Winter had given "express directives for his medical care which were ignored, either negligently or intentionally . . . the issue in this case is what compensable damages arise from the violation of a competent adult patient's right to refuse treatment."[102]

However, for there to be recovery, the court stated that the jury must find that "there is . . . [a] causal relationship between the unwanted resuscitative efforts and Winter's adverse health consequences."[103] The court was correct in reinstating the causes of action. However, it placed unwarranted fetters on a finding of liability and damages through the causation requirement. It is correct that in a negligence claim there must be proof of damages and proof that they were caused by the unwanted resuscitation. However, the unwanted resuscitation, per se, should give rise to damages in battery.[104]

Oklahoma

Cases

Edinburgh v. State, 896 P.2d 1176 (Okla. Crim. App. 1995).

Edinburgh is prosecution for mercy killing against a family member of a terminally ill individual. He was convicted of murder and sentenced to life imprisonment; prosecution in situations of this sort is extremely rare and serious punishment even rarer.[105] There are two likely reasons for this. The

---

98 See § **17.4** in the main volume.

99 Anderson v. St. Francis-St. George Hosp., 1995 WL 109128 (Ohio Ct. App. Mar. 15, 1995) (*Anderson II*).

100 Anderson v. St. Francis-St. George Hosp., 652 N.E.2d 800 (Ohio 1995).

101 *Anderson II,* 1995 WL 109128, at *3.

102 *Id.*

103 *Id.* at * 5.

104 See §§ **17.2–17.4** in the main volume and § **17.4** in this supplement.

105 See § **18.17** in the main volume.

first is that there was strong evidence that the terminally ill victim had a strong desire to live and thus that the killing was nonconsensual. The second was that witnesses testified that the deceased and the defendant "'couldn't get along' and 'were at each other all of the time,'" and that the defendant said he was "tired of taking care of sick people, that it was dragging his life down and that he wished 'they' would go on and die and have it over with." Another witness testified that about two weeks before the killing, the defendant said that "'one of these days I'll kill the old bastard and I'll own the whole place down there.'"[106]

The Oklahoma Supreme Court rejected the defendant's claim that he was assisting suicide, which is a lesser crime, and not committing murder. The defendant contended that the deceased "'while mentally able to decide his own fate, is too debilitated to be physically able to perform the overt act of self-killing and must depend upon his assistant to perform that act at his request.'"[107] The court held that, as courts in other states have held, there is a distinction between mercy killing and assisting suicide, and that where, as here, "the defendant proximately causes the defendant's death he can be held liable for homicide."[108]

Oregon

Statutes

1995 Or. Rev. Stat. §§ 677.470–.485 (intractable pain).

Cases

Lee v. Oregon, 891 F. Supp. 1429 (D. Or. 1995).

The federal district court issued an order making permanent the preliminary injunction issued in Lee v. Oregon.[109] The hint that the court gave in its opinion on the preliminary injunction that it would ultimately find the statute unconstitutional was ultimately borne out. The court found the Death With Dignity Act unconstitutional on equal protection grounds. Its general basis for so finding was that the Act "singles out terminally ill persons who want to commit suicide and excludes them from protection of Oregon laws that apply to others,"[110] primarily the protections accorded terminally ill persons whose deaths are hastened by forgoing life-sustaining treatment.

---

[106] 896 P.2d at 1178.

[107] *Id.*

[108] *Id.* at 1180.

[109] 869 F. Supp. 1491 (D. Or. 1994), discussed in **§ 18.23** in the main volume.

[110] 891 F. Supp. at 1438.

For two reasons, the ultimate status of the Oregon Death With Dignity Act remains to be seen. First, the equal protection basis for decision can be changed through further legislation according those terminally ill patients who wish to hasten their dying through assisted suicide the same protections the court found lacking. This, of course, still leaves the Act susceptible to challenge on other constitutional grounds, most notably due process, which the court declined to reach. Second, the holding was based in significant part on *Compassion in Dying v. Washington,*[111] an opinion that was superseded by a decision of the Ninth Circuit en banc.[112] The latter, controlling opinion, states that Judge Hogan, who authored the *Lee* opinion, "clearly erred. *Lee* not only does not aid us in reaching our decision, it is directly contrary to our holding."[113] However, the status of *Compassion in Dying v. Washington* is itself uncertain as the state of Washington has been granted certiorari in the United States Supreme Court.

Pennsylvania

Cases

In re Fiori, 673 A.2d 905 (Pa. 1996).

Although a handful of reported trial court decisions on end-of-life decisionmaking had been rendered in Pennsylvania beginning in 1973,[114] none had reached the appellate courts until *Fiori* did in 1993. Two judges of the three-judge superior court panel wrote an opinion constituting a major departure from the legal consensus[115] that has developed in other jurisdictions since the *Quinlan* case.[116] The major point of departure was the holding that in the absence of an advance directive, the termination of life support (at least for patients in a persistent vegetative state) must occur under the auspices and with the approval of a court. It also held that the trial court must apply a "hybrid 'best interests' and 'clear and convincing' evidence approach" — a hitherto unknown standard — and the opinion placed great reliance on the advance directive statute, despite the fact that the patient had no written or even oral advance directive, unlike almost all other appellate courts, which have concluded that advance directive statutes merely provide a mechanism for the implementation of rights having an independent existence in the common law or in state or federal constitutions.[117] The superior court granted an

---

[111] 49 F.3d 586 (9th Cir. 1995).

[112] Compassion in Dying v. Washington, 79 F.3d 790 (9th Cir. 1996).

[113] *Id.* at 838.

[114] See **Table 1–1.**

[115] See § **2.2** in the main volume.

[116] *In re* Fiori, 1993 WL 471460 (Pa. Super. Ct. Nov. 16, 1993).

[117] See § **10.14** in the main volume.

en banc rehearing and reversed, with the dissenting judge of the three-judge panel authoring the majority opinion, which essentially affirmed the national consensus about the law governing end-of-life decisionmaking.[118]

The Pennsylvania Supreme Court unanimously affirmed the superior court holding. It issued a relatively brief opinion that did little more than affirm the national consensus. It should be noted, however, that the holding is very narrow. The court stated that it was merely addressing decisionmaking for patients in a persistent vegetative state without an advance directive. The important, though certainly not startling, highlights of the holding were that a decision to forgo life-sustaining treatment should be made by close family members, based on the substituted judgment standard, which could be applied by determining the patient's probable wishes if his actual wishes were not known. Judicial oversight of the decisionmaking process is not routinely required; in fact, it should be limited to resolving disputes. Finally, the court made clear that the advance directive statute applies only to persons with an advance directive issued pursuant to the statute.

Rhode Island

Statutes

R.I. Gen. Laws §§ 23-4.10-1 to -12 (health care power of attorney).

Cases

Laurie v. Senecal, 666 A.2d 806 (R.I. 1995).

Senecal was a prisoner who was refusing to eat because "he no longer desired to live because of the stigma of his conviction for first-degree sexual assault upon a minor female."[119] He was not suffering from any illness or injury. He was determined to be competent, and his decision was considered "knowing and voluntary." The trial court refused to issue an order permitting force-feeding, based on a 14th Amendment right of privacy to end his life. The Rhode Island Supreme Court reversed on the ground that this constituted suicide, which the state has an interest in preventing. It quoted *Cruzan v. Director,* to the effect that "'[w]e do not think a State is required to remain neutral in the face of an informed and voluntary decision by a physically able adult to starve to death.'"[120] The court distinguished *Thor v. Superior Court*[121] on the ground that the prisoner there was exercising his right to refuse medical treatment for a then-existing medical condition.

---

[118] *In re* Fiori, 652 A.2d 1350 (Pa. Super. Ct. 1995).

[119] 666 A.2d at 807.

[120] *Id.* at 808 (quoting Cruzan v. Director, 497 U.S. 261, 280 (1990)).

[121] 855 P.2d 375 (Cal. 1993), discussed in § **8.19** in the main volume.

For other new cases involving prisoners, see the Florida case, *Singletary v. Costello,* and the North Dakota case, *State v. Schuetzle,* discussed in this section.

South Carolina

Statutes

S.C. Code Ann. §§ 44-78-10 to -65 (do-not-resuscitate).

Texas

Statutes

Tex. Health & Safety Code §§ 674.001–.024 (do-not-resuscitate).

Tennessee

Statutes

Tenn. Code Ann. §§ 68-140-601 to -604, *as amended by* Tenn. S.B. 2743 (enacted May 15, 1996) (do-not-resuscitate).

Utah

Statutes

Utah Code Ann. §§ 75-2-1105, -1107.

Washington

Cases

Compassion in Dying v. Washington, 79 F.3d 790 (9th Cir. 1996) (en banc), *aff'g* 850 F. Supp. 1454 (W.D. Wash. 1994), *cert. granted sub nom. Washington v. Glucksberg,* 1996 WL 411596, 65 U.S.L.W. 3085 (U.S. Oct. 1, 1996) (No. 96-110).

The United States Court of Appeals for the Ninth Circuit issued an en banc decision affirming the judgment of the district court holding unconstitutional Washington's statutory prohibition on assisted suicide. A three-judge panel of the court of appeals had previously reversed the trial court's decision.[122]

---

[122] *See* Compassion in Dying v. Washington, 49 F.3d 586 (9th Cir. 1995). This case is summarized in § **18.22** in this supplement. Also see the New York case of *Quill v. Vacco,* discussed above.

Wisconsin

Statutes

Wis. Stat. Ann. §§ 154.01–.29 (do-not-resuscitate, living will).

§ 1A.3   Overview of 1996–1997 Developments

Physician-Assisted Suicide.   Without a doubt, the most important developments in the last year have been in the area of physician-assisted suicide, with the two United States Supreme Court decisions, *Washington v. Glucksberg*[123] and *Vacco v. Quill*,[124] at the top of the list. However, in light of the fact that the Supreme Court refused to hold that state statutes criminalizing assisted suicide are unconstitutional, the Florida Supreme Court's decision in *McIver v. Krischer*[125] takes on added importance. After the United States Supreme Court's decisions, one important avenue to the legalization of physician-assisted suicide is to raise claims that statutory prohibitions violate state constitutional safeguards. Florida's constitution has an express right of privacy that has been repeatedly and broadly construed in end-of-life cases to permit the forgoing of treatment. Thus, the rebuff by the Florida Supreme Court might presage similar treatment by other state courts.

In addition to these landmark cases, there were three other challenges to the constitutionality of state statutes prohibiting physician-assisted suicide. Two failed[126] and one succeeded.[127] The federal constitutional claim in the latter case, however, relied so strongly on the Ninth Circuit's *Compassion in Dying* opinion that was reversed by the Supreme Court in *Glucksberg* that it is certain that this decision also will not stand. The court also rejected a challenge based on the California constitution because a state court had previously rejected such a claim[128] and "there is no persuasive authority to believe

---

[123] 117 S. Ct. 2258 (1997). See § **18.22** in this supplement.

[124] 117 S. Ct. 2293 (1997). See § **18.22** in this supplement.

[125] 697 So. 2d 97 (Fla. 1997). See § **18.22** in this supplement.

[126] Kevorkian v. Thompson, 947 F. Supp. 1152 (E.D. Mich. 1997); People *ex rel.* Oakland County Prosecuting Attorney v. Kevorkian, 534 N.W.2d 172 (Mich. Ct. App. 1995), *appeal denied,* 549 N.W.2d 566 (Mich.), *cert. denied sub nom.* Kevorkian v. Michigan, 117 S. Ct. 296 (1996).

[127] Kevorkian v. Arnett, 939 F. Supp. 725 (C.D. Cal.), *cert. denied sub nom.* Lundgren v. Doe, 117 S. Ct. 413 (1996).

[128] Donaldson v. Van de Kamp, 4 Cal. Rptr. 2d 59 (Ct. App. 1992).

that the California Supreme Court would hold otherwise if directly presented with the issue."[129]

Liability for Nonconsensual Treatment.   A number of cases addressed the issue of whether or not liability may be imposed on health care providers for the rendition of life-sustaining medical treatment to patients without their consent or over their express refusal. Patients or their representatives were rebuffed, for all intents and purposes, at every turn to the point where one is left to wonder whether there is any effective retrospective mechanism for enforcement of the right to forgo life-sustaining treatment.

Courts held that there is no right of action based on the Patient Self-Determination Act,[130] under a state surrogate decisionmaking statute,[131] and on a common-law theory of negligence,[132] and that although there is a right of action on a battery theory, damages are limited to those arising directly from the battery and excluding consequential damages.[133]

Futility.   The last significant set of developments was in the area of futile medical treatment. Probably the most important of the three cases dealing with futility is *Bryan v. Rectors & Visitors of the University of Virginia*,[134] in which the Fourth Circuit declined to extend the reach of EMTALA as it was construed in the *Baby "K"* case.[135] This case is discussed in § **19.17** in this supplement.

A close second in terms of importance, however, is the *Rideout* case,[136] which is still in pretrial proceedings. The rulings on motions to dismiss suggest that the defendants are going to have an uphill battle to prevail. However, if they do prevail, it will likely be because of the manner in which life-sustaining medical treatment was stopped over the protests of the patient's parents rather than for failure to provide requested treatment.

---

[129] 939 F. Supp. at 732.

[130] *See* Asselin v. Shawnee Mission Medical Ctr., Inc., 894 F. Supp. 1479 (D. Kan. 1995).

[131] *See* Ficke v. Evangelical Health Sys., 674 N.E.2d 888 (Ill. App. Ct. 1996). See § **17.19** in this supplement.

[132] *See* Anderson v. St. Francis-St. George Hosp., 671 N.E.2d 225 (Ohio 1996); Allore v. Flower Hosp., No. L-96-329, 1997 WL 362465 (Ohio Ct. App. June 27, 1997). See § **17.12** in this supplement.

[133] *See* Anderson v. St. Francis-St. George Hosp., 671 N.E.2d 225 (Ohio 1996); Allore v. Flower Hosp., No. L-96-329, 1997 WL 362465 (Ohio Ct. App. June 27, 1997). See § **17.4** in this supplement.

[134] 95 F.3d 349 (4th Cir. 1996).

[135] *In re* Baby "K," 16 F.3d 590 (4th Cir. 1994).

[136] Rideout v. Hershey Medical Ctr., 16 Fiduc. Rep. 2d 181 (C.P. Dauphin County, Pa. 1995). See § **19.2** in this supplement.

A Nebraska case[137] appears to be the first reported case in which a court has ordered the termination of treatment over family protests and has been upheld on appeal. Finally, a Massachusetts case[138] might be considered a futility case simply because the surrogate wanted to continue treatment over the attending physician's recommendation to the contrary. However, this was only an incidental part of the case. The central issue was the qualifications to serve as a surrogate.

§ 1A.4   Jurisdiction-by-Jurisdiction Developments in 1996–1997

United States

Statutes

Assisted Suicide Funding Restriction Act, 42 U.S.C.A. §§ 14,401–14,408 (ban on federal funding for physician-assisted suicide).

Cases

Washington v. Glucksberg, 117 S. Ct. 2258 (1997).
Vacco v. Quill, 117 S. Ct. 2293 (1997).
These cases challenging, respectively, the constitutionality of the Washington and New York statutes making assisted suicide a crime are discussed in **§ 18.22** in this supplement.

Alabama

Statutes

Ala. Code §§ 22-8A-1 to -10, *as amended by* Ala. H.B. 553 (enacted Apr. 15, 1997) (health care power of attorney; surrogate decisionmaking).

Arizona

Statutes

Ariz. Rev. Stat. Ann. §§ 36-3201 to -3262, *as amended by* Ariz. S.B. 1328 (enacted Apr. 24, 1994), Ariz. H.B. 2023 (enacted Apr. 17, 1995), and Ariz. H.B. 2315 (enacted May 1, 1996) (living will amendments).

---

[137] Tabatha R. v. Ronda R., 564 N.W.2d 598 (Neb. 1997). See **§ 19.2** in this supplement.
[138] *In re* Mason, 669 N.E.2d 1081 (Mass. App. Ct. 1996). See **§ 19.2** in this supplement.

California

Statutes

Cal. Health & Safety Code § 1418.8, *as amended by* Cal. S.B. 1848 (enacted July 3, 1996) (health care power of attorney amendments).

Cases

Wendland v. Superior Court, 56 Cal. Rptr. 2d 595 (Ct. App. 1996).
The court held that counsel must be appointed for the patient/conservatee in an action brought by the patient's wife/conservator seeking to terminate nutrition and hydration, which was opposed by the patient's mother and sister.

Kevorkian v. Arnett, 939 F. Supp. 725 (C.D. Cal. 1996).
This case challenging the constitutionality of the California statute making assisted suicide a crime is discussed in § **18.22** in this supplement.

Delaware

Cases

In re Gordy, 658 A.2d 613 (Del. Ch. 1994).
This case contains an unusual fact situation, as far as the reported cases go, but it may in fact be a fairly common situation. The patient was a 96-year-old woman suffering from Alzheimer's disease and from "the physical losses and inabilities that normally accompany very great age."[139] She had "a very difficult time eating solid food and state[d] that she is not hungry."[140] Consequently, it was proposed that she have a feeding tube implanted.

Mrs. Gordy's oldest son petitioned to be appointed her guardian with authority to deny permission for the feeding tube. The state attorney general intervened, seeking to require the son to consent to the tube's implantation. The court granted the son's petition to be appointed guardian and directed that he make a decision about the feeding tube on the basis of a best interests standard.

The odd part about this case is the manner in which the court described the best interests standard: "In attempting to meet the best interest standard in the context of health care decisions especially, a guardian is obligated to give consideration to the views of the ward herself, if the ward is in a position to

---

[139] 658 A.2d at 618.
[140] *Id.* at 615.

consider such matters rationally (as she ordinarily will be where a guardianship is necessitated only by physical incapacity)."[141] The standard labeled as a best interests standard sounds very much like a substituted judgment, or even a subjective, standard. This oddity can only be explained by the second part of the above-quoted statement—namely, that the patient is only physically incapacitated.

The court had previously determined that Mrs. "Gordy has suffered some loss of cognitive ability in recent years, but continues to be sufficiently alert to engage in conversation with her sons, who regularly visit her, and with medical and nursing staff."[142] The court felt that "the testimony that Mrs. Gordy has lost a great deal of her cognitive competency is strong, and the seriousness of her decision is such that the effects of that loss should be carefully considered."[143] Nonetheless, the court found that Mrs. Gordy was "capable of giving informed consent."[144] Thus, it makes sense for the guardian, in making his decision, to rely on the express views of the patient.

The problem with this case, however, is that if the patient was competent, the guardian should not have had the authority to make medical decisions for her. The meaning of being competent is that one possesses the authority to make one's own decisions. If she was not competent, then it was appropriate for the guardian to make decisions, and to consider her prior and even her contemporaneous views; but this is not a best interests standard as that standard is traditionally defined.[145]

Another twist on this case is that the patient had executed a living will in which she had made it more than usually clear that she did not ever want a feeding tube inserted. If the patient lacked decisionmaking capacity, the living will should have decided the matter and no guardianship proceeding should have been necessary. That it was is evidence of the extreme unwillingness of nursing homes to permit residents to die from forgoing artificial nutrition and hydration.[146] Again, the court proceeded in an unusual, though reasonable, fashion, holding that the existence of a living will provided evidence of the fact that the patient's current statements about not wanting a feeding tube were to be credited because they were consistent with her long-standing views on the subject.

In re Holmes, C.M. No. 8066-NC, 1996 WL 633309 (Del. Ch. Oct. 30, 1996).

---

[141] *Id.* at 619.

[142] *Id.* at 615.

[143] *Id.* at 617.

[144] *Id.*

[145] See §§ **7.12–7.25** in the main volume and this supplement.

[146] See § **9.40** in the main volume.

This is a proceeding to appoint a guardian for a woman suffering from Alzheimer's disease necessitated by disagreement among her 16 children about whether she ought to be placed in a nursing home or attend a day-care facility and receive home health care services at night. The court held that this is the kind of decision that is best made by the family, but where there is intractable disagreement the court will decide, using a best interests standard.

Florida

Statutes

Fla. Stat. Ann. §§ 765.101–.401, *as amended by* Fla. H.B. 903 (enacted May 15, 1996) (living will and health care power of attorney amendments).

Cases

Harrell v. St. Mary's Hospital, Inc. 678 So. 2d 455 (Fla. Dist. Ct. App. 1996).
   Harrell follows and essentially reaffirms the holding in *In re Dubreuil*, 629 So. 2d 819 (Fla. 1993), that it is not the responsibility of a Florida hospital—indeed it is impermissible for a hospital—to petition for an order to administer a blood transfusion to a member of the Jehovah's Witness religious faith who has refused one. Rather, the proper procedure is for the hospital to notify the state attorney. It is then a matter solely within the discretion of the state attorney to initiate or refuse to initiate proceedings to obtain an order to administer a blood transfusion. As long as the patient is competent and has been provided with information adequate to obtain informed consent or refusal and the hospital acts in good faith, the hospital is immune from liability for respecting the patient's refusal of treatment. If the hospital wishes to override the refusal, it does have a duty to notify the state attorney and other "interested third parties known to the health care provider"; but the court does not specify who those third parties might be.
   What is interesting and especially significant about both of these cases is that the patients were pregnant. Thus, the fact that the hospital or the physician has obtained the informed refusal of a competent patient does not guarantee that the societal interest in the well-being of the fetus or child has been adequately protected. Neither court commented on this directly, though *Harrell* does acknowledge the existence of state interests that must be taken into account, though without specifying what those interests are.[147]

McIver v. Krischer, 697 So. 2d 97 (Fla. 1997).

---

[147] 678 So. 2d at 456.

McIver was a challenge to the Florida statute criminalizing assisted suicide. The Florida Supreme Court held that the statute did not violate the state constitutional protection of privacy.

This case is discussed in § **18.22** in this supplement.

Guam

Statutes

10 Guam Code Ann. §§ 91,100–91,117 (living will).

Illinois

Cases

Ficke v. Evangelical Health Systems, 674 N.E.2d 888 (Ill. App. Ct. 1996).

This is a suit by the family of a deceased patient against the hospital that treated her for damages for purportedly failing to inform them of the patient's rights under the Illinois surrogate decisionmaking statute, which resulted in her being treated and which caused her injuries. Had they been aware of the statute's provisions, they would have exercised their authority to discontinue life-sustaining medical treatment.

This case is discussed in § **17.19** in this supplement.

Indiana

Statutes

Ind. Code Ann. §§ 35-42-1-2, -2.5 (intractable pain).

Iowa

Statutes

Iowa Code Ann. §§ 707A.1–.3 (intractable pain).

Kansas

Cases

Asselin v. Shawnee Mission Medical Center, Inc., 894 F. Supp. 1479 (D. Kan. 1995).

The court held that there is no right of action, express or implied, by an individual who claims to have suffered injuries because of a failure on the part of hospital employees to comply with what is popularly known as the Patient Self-Determination Act, 42 U.S.C. § 1395cc(f)(1)(A), (2)(A).

Kentucky

Statutes

Ky. Rev. Stat. Ann. §§ 216.300–.308 (intractable pain).

Massachusetts

Cases

In re Mason, 669 N.E.2d 1081 (Mass. App. Ct. 1996).

The fact situation, or something reasonably close to it, in *Mason* is one that probably occurs fairly frequently in clinical practice but is rarely litigated, at least to the appellate level. The general issue is whether a family member who is acting as surrogate has the qualifications to do so.

The specific facts are that the patient's son was acting as her surrogate. At one point, he was appointed as her temporary guardian for medical decision-making purposes, but the guardianship lapsed before the events in question. The relationship between the son and the health care personnel in the hospital where his mother was a patient was evidently very contentious, and the court portrays the son as being entirely to blame. He is described in the opinion as being "disruptive of hospital schedules, abusive to medical personnel, and overly quick to allege neglect and maltreatment of his mother"[148] and

> of the view that he is the only person capable of implementing a suitable treatment program for his mother, . . . "not a good listener," . . . "hostile toward" his mother's caretakers and often behaves in a "belligerent or inappropriate manner toward them," his decisions concerning his mother, although well-motivated, are not always sound, health care providers have declined to take on the mother as a client or patient because of Joseph's behavior, he argues with health care providers, and attempts "to micromanage every aspect of his mother's life and care," he "has difficulty accepting the change in his mother's health status and is experiencing a lot of denial about the deterioration in his mother the past year," he is too "combative" to work with, and he does not have the "objectivity necessary to be the substitute decision maker for his mother."[149]

---

[148] 669 N.E.2d at 1083.

[149] *Id.* at 1085.

He sought to assert his authority to make decisions on her behalf after the expiration of the temporary guardianship and, in addition to whatever common-law authority he might have, on the basis of two health care powers of attorney, one of which he wrote and signed for his mother on the authority that he purported to have under a general durable power of attorney, and the other of which he claimed his mother had signed but which the court intimated, without deciding, was of dubious authenticity.

Based on his inability to function appropriately as a surrogate, the court denied him the legal authority to act as surrogate and granted the hospital's motion to enter a DNR order that was medically determined to be in the patient's best interests.

There are two other noteworthy facets to this case. The first is the resemblance that it bears to *Gilgunn v. Massachusetts General Hospital*,[150] in which treatment was withheld from a patient under circumstances not too dissimilar from those in *Mason*. *Gilgunn* was a suit for damages, treatment having been withheld without a prior court order. The patients in both cases were in the same hospital, and it is reasonable to conclude the hospital learned a lesson from *Gilgunn* — namely, that when treatment is sought to be withheld over the vehement protests of a close family member, prior judicial authorization is probably the prudent course to take.

Second, the holding of *Mason* is premised on the conclusion that the son who sought to act as surrogate had forfeited the authority to so act because he had not acted on a "true assessment of [patient's] best interests."[151] In Massachusetts, however, the governing standard for decisionmaking for an incompetent patient is a substituted judgment standard, and the courts have clearly rejected the use of a best interests standard. Had the court applied a substituted judgment standard, the outcome might well have been the same. On the other hand, had the court sought to determine the patient's wishes, as it would have had to do under a substituted judgment standard, it might have determined that not only the son but also the patient did not want a DNR order written. Had that been the case, the facts would have had the making of a classic futility case had the hospital sought a DNR order anyway.[152]

Michigan

Statutes

Mich. Comp. Laws Ann. § 752.1027 (intractable pain).

---

[150] No. SUCV92-4820 (Super. Ct., Suffolk County, Mass., Apr. 21, 1995), discussed in § **19.2** in this supplement.

[151] *Mason,* 669 N.E.2d at 1085.

[152] See **Ch. 19** in the main volume and this supplement.

Mich. Comp. Laws Ann. §§ 333.5651–.5661, .16221, .16226 (assisted suicide).

Cases

Kevorkian v. Thompson, 947 F. Supp. 1152 (E.D. Mich. 1997).

Dr. Kevorkian and a woman seeking to avail herself of his service of assisting patients in committing suicide brought an action to declare unconstitutional the Michigan law criminalizing assisted suicide. The court rejected the essence of the plaintiffs' claims and issued a narrow injunction against prosecution for assisted suicide during a period of time in which the law in Michigan was uncertain. This case is discussed in § **18.22** in this supplement.

People ex rel. Oakland County Prosecuting Attorney v. Kevorkian, 534 N.W.2d 172 (Mich. Ct. App. 1995), *appeal denied,* 549 N.W.2d 566 (Mich.), *cert. denied sub nom.* Kevorkian v. Michigan, 117 S. Ct. 296 (1996).

This case affirmed a 1991 Michigan trial court injunction barring Dr. Kevorkian from using his "suicide machine" because recourse to criminal sanctions would be inadequate to prevent him from committing unlawful and unethical acts.[153]

Nebraska

Cases

Tabatha R. v. Ronda R., 564 N.W.2d 598 (Neb. 1997), *modified,* 566 N.W.2d 782 (Neb. 1998).

This appears to be the first reported case in which a court ordered the termination of treatment over family protests (but was reversed on appeal). The case is discussed at greater length in § **19.2** in this supplement.

Nevada

Statutes

Nev. Rev. Stat. §§ 450B.400–.590 (do-not-resuscitate).

Attorney General's Opinion

Nev. Op. Att'y Gen. No. 97-08, 1997 WL 133532 (1997).

---

[153] See § **18.22** in the main volume and this supplement.

This was an opinion advising about a DNR order for a child who was a ward of the state. The opinion analyzes the situation according to three different factual scenarios: (1) where there is agreement between the parent and the expert medical evidence that a DNR order is appropriate; (2) where the expert medical evidence recommends a DNR order as being in the child's best interests, and a parent cannot be located; and (3) where the parent or legal guardian objects to the entry of a DNR order.

The Nevada Attorney General advised that in the first type of case, the state's child welfare agency, the Division of Child and Family Services, should present the expert evidence to the court and the court should decide. In the second type of case, it is preferable to obtain a court order for the DNR order to be written and implemented. However, if the court refuses to order the DNR directly, Nevada statutes empower the court to authorize the child welfare agency to consent to the treating physician's decision to place a DNR order. Finally, in the third kind of case, the Attorney General advised that the court has the authority under Nevada statutes to authorize a DNR order "although the court's footing may be decidedly less firm." However, before bringing this kind of case to court, the child welfare agency should give "tremendous deference" to the parents' views, though parents do not have an absolute veto power.

The final issue that the opinion addressed was the effect of a DNR order on Medicaid funding, concluding that "[i]t does not appear that a DNR order will have any impact on federal funding to Medicaid."

New Jersey

Cases

In re Roche, 687 A.2d 349 (N.J. Super. Ct. Ch. Div. 1996).

The patient suffered from senile dementia and lived in a nursing home. She had been adjudicated incompetent to make medical decisions but subsequently executed an advance directive stating her wish not to receive CPR or artificial nutrition and hydration. Two witnesses, who were present when the advance directive was executed and one of whom was the patient's guardian, believed that the patient understood what she was doing. The director of the nursing home, a physician who had examined her about six weeks prior to the execution of the advance directive, also claimed that the patient understood the nature and effect of the advance directive. It would be interesting to know, but the case report does not state, whether the impetus for the execution of the advance directive came from the patient, from the guardian, or possibly from some other person, such as an employee of the nursing home.

The guardian, who was an employee of the New Jersey Office of Public Guardian, because of the prior adjudication of incompetence, brought an action to determine the validity of the advance directive. The court held that it was not enforceable, basing its decision predominantly on the language of the New Jersey advance directive statute. The statutory language that the court referred to was the provision allowing "'competent adults to plan ahead for health care decisions through the execution of advance directives,'"[154] and the sections authorizing a "declarant" to execute an advance directive at any time.[155] The legislation defines *declarant* as "a competent adult who executes an advance directive."[156] Even though the statute permits an incompetent to suspend or reinstate a suspended advance directive,[157] incompetents "are excluded from executing a subsequent advance directive"[158] because only a declarant, who must be a competent person, may make an advance directive. Consequently, the court held that the advance directive was invalid.

This holding might, however, be termed a pyrrhic defeat because the court also held that although the advance directive was "not of binding effect on health care providers,"[159] it could, should the occasion ever arise, be used as evidence of the patient's wishes. Under the *Conroy* case,[160] "the guardian of an incompetent [may] consider a wide variety of types of information in ascertaining the subjective intent of the ward with respect to a particular medical decision. . . . [If] the incompetent clearly understood the nature and effect of the advance directive at the time it was executed, this document may be considered as evidence of the incompetent's subjective intent."[161]

New York

Cases

In re Matthews, 650 N.Y.S.2d 373 (App. Div. 1996).

In a case of substantial significance in New York, the Supreme Court Appellate Division issued a ruling helping to clarify the standard for decisionmaking by surrogates for incompetent patients. The leading New York right-to-die cases — *Eichner v. Dillon, In re Storar, In re Westchester County Medical Center (O'Connor),* and *Elbaum v. Grace Plaza of Great Neck, Inc.* — make it very clear that life-sustaining medical treatment cannot be with-

---

[154] *In re* Roche, 687 A.2d 349, 352 (N.J. Super. Ct. Ch. Div. 1996) (citing N.J. Stat. Ann. § 26:2H-54(c)) (emphasis added).

[155] N.J. Stat Ann. § 26:2H-56.

[156] *Id.* § 26:2H-55.

[157] *Id.* § 26:2H-57(d).

[158] 687 A.2d at 354.

[159] *Id.*

[160] *In re* Conroy, 486 A.2d 1209 (N.J. 1985).

[161] 687 A.2d at 354.

held or withdrawn unless there is clear and convincing evidence that the patient made such a decision before losing decisionmaking capacity. To put it another way, the New York courts have rejected the majority substituted judgment standard rule that permits a surrogate to determine if a now-incompetent patient would have wanted life-sustaining treatment forgone.

The *Matthews* court issued an important clarification of the New York rule, though one that had been in the making since before the first New York right-to-die case. In *Matthews,* the parents of a 28-year-old institutionalized mentally retarded man resisted the institution's petition to have a feeding tube implanted in him on the ground that he was able to adequately eat orally and that this activity was important to maintaining his ability to socialize with others and hence was an important aspect of his dignity. The court sided with the parents, reversing the trial court's granting of such an order, on the ground that the parents were not seeking to allow the patient to die but were merely making a choice among reasonable alternatives supported by a licensed physician.

In so doing, the court clearly distinguished between a "right-to-die case"—a case in which the surrogate sought to withhold or withdraw treatment and allow the patient to die—and a case of this sort involving a choice of medical treatments, neither of which was calculated to result in death, following earlier New York Court of Appeals' cases —*In re Hofbauer*[162] and *Weber v. Stony Brook Hospital*[163]—in which parents sought not to allow their children to die by forgoing treatment but to choose a treatment different from the one someone else thought preferable. The court was also guided by the holding in *In re Storar*[164] in which the mother, who was the guardian of an adult mentally retarded man, sought to allow him to die by forgoing treatment and in which the court rejected her effort to do so because "a parent 'may not deprive a child of lifesaving treatment, however well intentioned.'"[165] The court distinguished *Storar,* quoting it for the proposition that "'it is not for the courts to determine the most "effective" treatment when the parents have chosen among reasonable alternatives.'"[166]

Estate of Rozewicz v. New York City Health & Hospitals Corp., 656 N.Y.S.2d 593 (Sup. Ct. N.Y. County 1997).

In *Rozewicz,* a member of the Jehovah's Witness faith died after a physician allegedly committed malpractice and the patient refused a blood transfusion needed to deal with the injuries caused thereby. The trial court refused

[162] 411 N.Y.S.2d 416 (App. Div. 1978), *aff'd,* 393 N.E.2d (N.Y. 1979).

[163] 456 N.E.2d 1186 (N.Y. 1983).

[164] 420 N.E.2d 64 (N.Y. 1981).

[165] *In re* Matthews, 650 N.Y.S.2d 373, 377 (App. Div. 1996) (quoting *In re* Storar, 420 N.E.2d 64 (N.Y. 1981)).

[166] *Id.*

to charge the jury on mitigation of damages principles, instead charging that if the jury determined that the defendant/physician was negligent, it should reduce the damages to which the plaintiff was entitled by the degree to which she assumed the risk of her injuries by refusing a blood transfusion. In so holding, the court followed the leading case, and one of the very few cases in this area, *Shorter v. Drury.*[167]

Vacco v. Quill, 117 S. Ct. 2293 (1997).

This case challenging the constitutionality of the New York statute making assisted suicide a crime is discussed in **§ 18.22** in this supplement.

Ohio

Statutes

Ohio Rev. Code Ann. §§ 2133.11, .12 (intractable pain).

Cases

Anderson v. St. Francis-St. George Hospital, 671 N.E.2d 225 (Ohio 1996).

The *Anderson* case has been making its way up and down in the Ohio courts since 1992. The Ohio Supreme Court has now had the final word in the case, and it is a discouraging one for those who believe that health care professionals are frequently reluctant to adhere to patients' wishes, whether expressed contemporaneously or anticipatorily through an advance directive (including a health care power of attorney or do-not-resuscitate order or directive), and that a cause of action for damages for ignoring a patient's wishes is an important tool for implementing patient autonomy.

The Ohio Court of Appeals had twice held that the estate of a man whose DNR order had been ignored stated a cause of action against the hospital for damages for negligence or battery. The Ohio Supreme Court agreed that a cause of action was stated for battery but limited the recovery to nominal damages, unless the battery itself, as opposed to the consequences of the battery, harmed the patient. The court refused to permit recovery for negligence on the ground that the patient would have suffered the same consequential harm even if the DNR order had not been ignored, and thus there was no proximate cause.

This case is discussed in **§ 17.12** in this supplement.

Allore v. Flower Hospital, No. L-96-329, 1997 WL 362465 (Ohio Ct. App. June 27, 1997).

---

[167] 695 P.2d 116 (Wash.), *cert. denied,* 474 U.S. 827 (1985), discussed in **§ 17.16** in the main volume.

Either it is more difficult to get Ohio health care providers to honor patients' advance directives, or Ohio families of deceased patients whose advance directives have been ignored are more litigious than those in other states. In any event, less than a year after the *Anderson* decision, the Ohio Court of Appeals was confronted with a similar case. Here, however, an advance directive (living will and health care power of attorney) was either intentionally or negligently overlooked.

Mr. Allore was admitted to the defendant hospital, and at the time of admission he executed a living will and health care power of attorney. The living will "directed his attending physician to administer no 'life-sustaining treatment' in the event that the decedent suffered from a 'terminal condition' or was in a 'permanently unconscious state.'"[168] He was discharged from the hospital but was readmitted several weeks later. At the time of the latter admission

> Dr. Ali entered the following relevant orders into Frank Allore's chart: ". . . In the event of cardiac standstill, ventricular fibrillation or respiratory arrest, resuscitation measures are to be initiated immediately using ACLS protocols (With attention to written code status orders). . . . The physician will be notified immediately of any emergency interventions by nursing personnel."[169]

At the time of Mr. Allore's first admission, "[b]oth Flower Hospital and Dr. Ali were aware of the existence of the living will and power of attorney."[170] Within the space of less than three hours, Mr. Allore began suffering severe respiratory distress and was transferred to an ICU and intubated. He died less than a day later.

The estate brought suit, alleging among other claims that the hospital was negligent in disregarding Mr. Allore's advance directives and that the treatment constituted a battery. The appeals court upheld the trial court's grant of summary judgment for the hospital, and one ground for so doing was the *Anderson* case. However, the court also concluded that because of the emergency nature of the situation, the doctors and nurses were free to ignore his advance directive because of the existence of implied consent to treat in an emergency. They distinguished the *Leach* case,[171] which had held that a patient's prior instructions that she did not want treatment governed in an emergency, on the ground that the patient, before losing decisionmaking capacity and before the emergency arose, "expressly refused life support

---

[168] Allore v. Flower Hosp., No. L-96-329, 1997 WL 362465, at *1. (Ohio Ct. App. June 27, 1997).

[169] *Id.* at *1–*2.

[170] *Id.* at *1.

[171] Estate of Leach v. Shapiro, 469 N.E.2d 1047 (Ohio Ct. App. 1984).

measures" and "health care providers were fully apprised of her wishes."[172] By contrast, in *Allore,* there was no evidence that the health care professionals who actually treated the patient knew of his advance directives. This, however, overlooks the question of whether they have a legal duty to know of the advance directives, especially in light of the Patient Self-Determination Act,[173] and thus were negligent for not knowing of their existence. The court dealt with this obliquely by concluding that the fact that Dr. Ali's affidavit admits that he did not inform any other health care professional of the existence of Mr. Allore's advance directives "is insufficient to create a genuine issue of material fact as to whether" the nurse and doctor who intubated Mr. Allore were aware of his previously expressed wishes to forgo such treatment.[174]

Oregon

Statutes

Or. Rev. Stat. § 677.475(1) (intractable pain).

Cases

Lee v. Oregon, 107 F.3d 1382 (9th Cir. 1997).
   Lee is a challenge to the constitutionality of the Oregon referendum legalizing physician-assisted suicide.[175] Shortly after enactment, its implementation was enjoined by the federal district court for violating the Fourteenth Amendment's guarantee of equal protection.[176] However, in 1997, the Ninth Circuit vacated and remanded the decision because the plaintiffs lacked standing, as they had failed to establish actual injury.[177] The plaintiffs' application for certiorari[178] was not ruled on in the Supreme Court's 1996 Term, but was denied in October 1997.[179]

---

[172] *Allore,* 1997 WL 362465, at ˙6.

[173] See § **10.21** in the main volume and this supplement.

[174] 1997 WL 362465, at ˙6.

[175] Oregon Death with Dignity Act, Or. Rev. Stat. §§ 127.800 *et seq.* (1996).

[176] *See* Lee v. Oregon, 891 F. Supp. 1439 (D. Or. 1995).

[177] Lee v. Oregon, 107 F.3d 1382 (9th Cir. 1997).

[178] *See* Lee v. Harcleroad, 118 S. Ct. 328 (1997).

[179] *See* Lee v. Harcleroad, 118 S. Ct. 328 (1997).

NEW DEVELOPMENTS

Pennsylvania

Cases

Rideout v. Hershey Medical Center, 16 Fiduc. Rep. 2d 181 (C.P. Dauphin County, Pa. 1995).

    Rideout is a futility case seeking damages against defendants who terminated life support from a child over her parents' protests. The case has far more likelihood of success than have other futility cases, but not so much on the claim that the parents had a right to continue to have their child treated but for the emotional distress that is alleged to have been caused by the *manner* in which life support was terminated and the decision was made to terminate it.

    Rideout is discussed primarily in § **19.2,** and also in §§ **17.4, 17.7, 17.15A,** and **17.20,** in this supplement.

Puerto Rico

P. R. Laws Ann. tit. 33, § 4009 (assisted suicide).

Rhode Island

Statutes

R.I. Gen. Laws §§ 11-60-1 to -5 (intractable pain; assisted suicide).

South Dakota

Statutes

S.D. Codified Laws Ann. § 22-16-37 (intractable pain).

Virginia

Statutes

Va. Code Ann. §§ 18.2-76.3, -76.4 (intractable pain; assisted suicide).
Va. Code Ann. § 54.1-2982, -2901, 63.1-174.3 (DNR amendments).

Cases

Bryan v. Rectors & Visitors of the University of Virginia, 95 F.3d 349 (4th Cir. 1996).

In this case, the United States Court of Appeals for the Fourth Circuit declined to extend the reach of EMTALA as it was construed in *Baby "K"* to include a DNR order written against the wishes of a patient's family, leading to the patient's death.

This case is discussed in § **19.17** in this supplement.

Washington

Cases

Washington v. Glucksberg, 117 S. Ct. 2258 (1997).

This case challenging the constitutionality of the Washington statute making assisted suicide a crime is discussed in § **18.22** in this supplement.

Wisconsin

Statutes

Wis. Stat. Ann. §§ 154.17–.29 (do-not-resuscitate).

Cases

Edna M.F. v. Eisenberg, 563 N.W.2d 485 (Wis. 1997), *cert. denied sub nom.* Spahn v. Wittman, 1997 WL S92177 (Nov. 3, 1997) (No. 97-437).

This case is another that expresses serious reservations about the use of the substituted judgment standard. Although not purporting to overrule or modify the prior case law as expressed in *L.W. v. L.E. Phillips Career Development Center,*[180] in reality it appears to do so.

The patient in *Edna M.F.* was a 71-year-old woman with Alzheimer's disease. Her sister, who had previously been appointed her guardian, sought to have her tube-feeding discontinued. The nursing home's ethics committee agreed to approve the request if other family members would go along with it, but one niece declined to do so. The guardian then sought judicial authorization to terminate tube-feeding, which was denied.

The Wisconsin Supreme Court affirmed the denial of the guardian's request. It held that, absent clear and convincing evidence of the patient's previously stated wishes, the *L.W.* case permitted the termination of tube-feeding only if the guardian determined that it was in the patient's best interests to do so, and if the patient was in a persistent vegetative state (PVS). In this case, there was insufficient evidence of the patient's desires and the patient was not in a PVS.

---

[180] 482 N.W.2d 60 (Wis. 1992).

There are some very troubling aspects of this opinion, some of which are discussed in the concurring opinions of Chief Justice Abrahamson and Justice Bablitch. The most fundamental one, which is not discussed in the concurring opinions either, probably because these concurring justices were in agreement with the majority on this point, is that the court gives persistent vegetative state talismanic significance in end-of-life decision-making in Wisconsin.

The court's stated rationale is "the interest of the state in preserving human life and the irreversible nature of the decision to withdraw nutrition from a person."[181] The implicit rationale, however, seems different, and far weaker—namely, that "people in a PVS do not feel pain or discomfort," but because the patient here is not in a PVS, she "could . . . likely feel the pain and discomfort of starving to death."[182] The difficulty with this rationale is that the medical evidence is, at worst, mixed about whether patients who die when nutrition and hydration is forgone experience pain or discomfort. Furthermore, analgesia could be supplied so that if pain is a concomitant of termination of nutrition and hydration, it would not be perceived by the patient.[183]

Another difficulty that this holding overlooks is that a guardian is permitted to find that it is not in a patient's best interests to be kept alive by tube-feeding if the patient is in a PVS, yet a patient in a PVS can experience nothing and can be said to have no interests. For this reason, the New Jersey Supreme Court has permitted the use of a best interests standard in a case such as *Edna M.F.*, but rejected the application of this standard for patients in a persistent vegetative state.[184]

Chief Justice Abrahamson's concurring opinion reads the majority opinion as interpreting *L.W.* to reject the substituted judgment standard in any circumstances. Her opinion contends that this is not the proper reading of *L.W.*[185] and that if the court wishes to modify or expand *L.W.*, it "should do so only with the benefit of full adversarial briefing in a case presenting a real controversy framed by adversarial parties."[186] Another important point in her opinion concerns the way the ethics committee functioned in this case.

Justice Bablitch's concurrence takes the majority to task for not establishing standards for independent experts who are to determine whether or not the patient is in a PVS. Given the determinative role of PVS vel non,

---

[181] Edna M.F. v. Eisenberg, 563 N.W.2d 485, 490 (Wis. 1997).

[182] *Id.*

[183] See § **9.39** in the main volume.

[184] *See In re* Conroy, 486 A.2d 1209 (N.J. 1985).

[185] 563 N.W.2d at 493–94 (Abrahamson, C.J., concurring).

[186] *Id.* at 495.

he is more than justified in his concern. Ordinarily, the worry is that people are misdiagnosed as being in a PVS when they are not; here the concern is that the patient was misdiagnosed as not being in a PVS when she
might have been, thus denying "important constitutional rights" to the
patient.[187] In fact, the patient was diagnosed as being in a PVS soon after
the Wisconsin Supreme Court's decision, and the feeding tube was then
removed.[188]

§ 1A.5   Overview of 1997–1998 Developments

Physician-Assisted Suicide

Physician-assisted suicide continues to be the most debated aspect of end-of-
life decisionmaking. One of the major consequences of the June 1997 United
States Supreme Court decisions on the constitutionality of state legislative
prohibitions on physician-assisted suicide[189] has been increased discussion—
and action to implement the discussion—of the importance of providing terminally ill patients with adequate treatment for pain. The literature on
physician-assisted suicide is vast and continues to grow at a seemingly expo-
nential rate.[190] Public support for the legalization of physician-assisted suicide, as measured by opinion polls, continues to remain high.[191] Some groups
of doctors are issuing guidelines for the conduct of physician-assisted suicide.[192] One group was motivated to do so by the legalization of physician-
assisted suicide in Oregon.[193] Guidelines have also been written in

---

[187] *Id.* at 498 (Bablitch, J., concurring).

[188] Mary Zahn, *For Edna, A Life and Prolonged Death,* Milwaukee Journal Sentinel, Nov. 2,
1997, at 1 (1997 WL 12753311).

[189] See § **18.22** in this supplement.

[190] See **Chapter 18** bibliography in the main volume and this supplement.

[191] *See Poll Examines Adults' Innermost Feelings About Life's End,* N.Y. Times, Dec. 6,
1997, at A8 (nat'l ed.) (one-third of 1,212 adults in a random, nationwide Gallup telephone survey favored legalization of physician-assisted suicide "'under a wide variety of
circumstances'"; another one-third favor legalization "'only in a few cases'"; and one-
third oppose it under all circumstances); *Conn. Poll Shows Some Support for Assisted
Suicide,* Am. Med. News, May 4, 1998, at 11 ("70% would support legislation allowing
doctors to assist in suicide if a patient were close to death and at least two doctors
agreed").

[192] *See generally* Stolberg, *Considering the Unthinkable: Protocol for Assisted Suicide,* N.Y.
Times, June 11, 1997, at A1 (nat'l ed.).

[193] *See* Kathleen Haley & Melinda Lee, eds., The Oregon Death with Dignity Act: A
Guidebook for Health Care Providers (1998). *See also Hospital Sets Policy on Assisted
Suicide,* Am. Med. News, Apr. 13, 1998, at 39 (permitting nonemployee physicians to par-
ticipate in physician-assisted suicide but prohibiting hospital employees from doing so).

California,[194] where physician-assisted suicide is not legal but perhaps is practiced with some frequency anyway.

In the legal realm, a number of states have enacted legislation to encourage physicians to prescribe medication for pain relief and other palliative measures, bringing the total with such legislation to near 20.[195]

Developments in Oregon.   In the November 1997 election, Oregon voters reaffirmed their support of the 1994 referendum legalizing physician-assisted suicide by a 60 to 40 percent margin,[196] significantly in excess of the original slim margin of approval. When it became clear that the probability of legalized physician-assisted suicide actually occurring was now virtually certain, almost every important interest group tried to get into the act. Oregon legislative leaders quickly considered and then backed away from the idea of calling a special session of the legislature[197] to fine-tune such issues as residency requirements and immunity for pharmacists.[198] The Oregon Pharmacy Board adopted a temporary rule stating that "a prescription issued pursuant to the Oregon Death with Dignity Act shall be in writing and signed by the physician with the words 'This prescription is pursuant to ORS 127.800 — 127.897' [the Death with Dignity Act] on the face of the prescription."[199] A few months later, a lawsuit was commenced by the Oregon Medical Association[200] challenging the validity of this rule. This suit was settled, and the Pharmacy Board's rule was replaced by a Board of Medical Examiners' rule[201] requiring that physicians who prescribe medications pursuant to the Death with Dignity Act either dispense the medications themselves (if the physician is registered as a dispensing physician with the Board), or "with the patient's consent" inform the pharmacist of the purpose of the prescrip-

---

194   *See* S. Heilig et al., *Physician-Hastened Death Advisory Guidelines for the San Francisco Bay Area from the Bay Area Network of Ethics Committees,* 166 Western J. Med. 370 (1997); F. Marcus, *The Northern California Conference for Guidelines on Aid-in-Dying: Introduction,* 166 Western J. Med. 379 (1997); E. Young et al., *Report of the Northern California Conference for Guidelines on Aid-in-Dying: Definitions, Differences, Convergences, Conclusions,* 166 Western J. Med. 381 (1997).

195   See **Table 9-1A** in this supplement.

196   Timothy Egan, *In Oregon, Opening a New Front in the World of Medicine,* N.Y. Times, Nov. 6, 1997, at A1.

197   Brad Cain, *Lawmakers Drop Idea of Session on Suicide Law,* Associated Press, Nov. 7, 1997 (1997 WL 2560798).

198   Gail Kinsey Hill, *Legislators Discuss Special Session,* Oregonian (Portland), Nov. 6, 1997, at A1.

199   Or. Admin. R. 855-041-0065. *See generally* Patrick O'Neil, *Pharmacy Board Requires Notification,* Oregonian (Portland), Nov. 7, 1997, at A14.

200   Patrick O'Neil, *Physicians Appeal Rule on Suicide Medicines,* Oregonian (Portland), Jan 9, 1998, at D1.

201   Or. Admin. R. 847-015-0035 (final review, July 17, 1998).

tion. The rule does not state what is to occur if the patient refuses to consent to release this information to the pharmacist.

At about the same time, the director of the United States Drug Enforcement Administration ruled that it would be a violation of the federal Controlled Substances Act for any physician, including those in Oregon, to dispense controlled substances for the purpose of aiding a patient to end his own life.[202] However, the DEA director neglected to consult with his boss, Attorney General Reno, who commenced a study of the action and concluded that the DEA director had not acted in keeping with the congressional purpose in enacting the Controlled Substances Act (to prevent trafficking in illegal drugs and abuse of legitimate drugs). Reno concluded that the Controlled Substances Act did not support a ban on the use of legitimate drugs for an approved medical purpose.[203]

Within hours of the Attorney General's decision, bills were introduced in the House[204] and Senate[205] to block the use of controlled substances for use in physician-assisted suicide, euthanasia, or mercy killing.[206] However, prominent opponents of physician-assisted suicide, including Oregon's Governor Kitzhaber and Senator Wyden, opposed federal intervention to impede the Oregon statute, whether by the DEA[207] or by federal legislation.[208] Even the American Medical Association, one of the most outspoken and influential organizations on record as opposing the legalization of physician-assisted suicide, concurred in the opposition to federal intervention.[209] Hearings were held on these bills in the summer of 1998.

In Oregon, the state approved payment for physician-assisted suicide for Medicaid beneficiaries.[210]

And finally, although "no one is rushing in Oregon to use the new law,"[211] physicians prescribed lethal doses of medication to terminally ill patients on

---

[202] Steve Suo & Erin Hoover, *DEA Deems Suicide Law Illegal,* Oregonian (Portland), Nov. 8, 1997, at A1.

[203] *DEA Won't Sanction Oregon Physicians Who Participate in Lawful Assisted Suicides,* 7 Health L. Rep. (BNA) 958 (June 11, 1998).

[204] H.R. 4006, 105th Cong. (1997).

[205] S. 2151, 105th Cong. (1997).

[206] *See* Michael J. Sniffen, *Reno Won't Block Oregon's Assisted-Suicide Law,* Associated Press, June 5, 1998.

[207] Jim Barnett, *Utah Sen. Hatch Vows to Fight Oregon's Assisted Suicide Law,* Oregonian (Portland), Nov. 10, 1997, at A1.

[208] Erin Hoover Barnett, *Congress to Open up Debate on Assisted Suicide,* Oregonian (Portland), July 9, 1998, at B1.

[209] Diane M. Gianelli, *Aid Suicide, Lose DEA License,* Am. Med. News, July 27, 1998, at ____.

[210] *Oregon Lets State Pay for Suicides,* N.Y. Times, Feb. 27, 1998, at A10 (nat'l ed.).

[211] Timothy Egan, *No One Rushing in Oregon to Use a New Suicide Law,* N.Y. Times, Mar. 15, 1998, at 14 (nat'l ed.)

10 occasions as of August 1998. Eight patients actually died from the prescribed overdose; the other two died naturally before being able to take the medications.[212]

Prosecutions of Health Professionals.   Oregon is not the only place in which controversy about physician-assisted suicide has spilled over into the realm of law. Either there is a growing number of prosecutions of physicians and laypersons for assisted suicide (and mercy killing) of the terminally ill, or these events are being reported more frequently and more prominently. If the latter is the case, it probably results from the increased public debate about assisted suicide. In the last year or two, there have been a handful of criminal prosecutions of doctors in the United States and Canada. More often than not, one or more of the officials in the criminal justice system has shown leniency toward the involved physicians. In one of the two cases in which physicians were sentenced to imprisonment, a Canadian physician was released on bail pending appeal of a 2-year sentence on a charge carrying a maximum of 14 years.[213] In the other case, an American physician was paroled after serving only 1 year of a 5- to 20-year sentence,[214] and had his conviction reversed on appeal.[215]

Florida.   Dr. Ernesto Pinzon-Reyes was acquitted of first-degree murder charges after a month-long trial in June 1997.[216] The charges arose from Pinzon's administration of morphine, Valium, and potassium chloride to a lung cancer patient whose family had asked the doctor to reduce the patient's suffering.[217] The patient died within an hour of the injections. Pinzon's license to practice medicine was suspended for two years by the state medical board. In December 1997, the state board of medicine ruled 7–6 that Pinzon could resume his medical practice.[218]

---

[212] *8 Deaths Linked to Oregon Suicide Law,* L.A. Times, Aug. 19, 1998, at A5. Joseph B. Frazier, Health Officials Say 10 People Have Used Oregon's Assisted Suicide Law, Associated Press, Aug. 18, 1998. Erin Hoover, Doctor Comes Forward in 4th Assisted Death, Portland Oregonian, June 7, 1998, at C1.

[213] Henry Hess, *A Toronto-Based AIDS Doctor Has Become the First Canadian Physician to Be Convicted of Helping a Patient Commit Suicide,* Globe & Mail (Toronto), Dec. 23, 1997, at 1.

[214] Alan Bavley, *Now Paroled, Doctor Appeals Verdicts: Murder, Attempted Murder Convictions Involved Two Patients in Northwest Kansas,* Kansas City Star, Dec. 21, 1997, at A1.

[215] State v. Naramore, 965 P.2d 211 (Kan. Ct. App. 1998).

[216] *Acquitted Doctor Gets Board's OK to Practice,* Sun-Sentinel (Ft. Lauderdale, Fla.), Dec. 7, 1997, at 10B.

[217] *Jury Slams Medical Community After Acquitting a Doctor of Murder, Jurors Call for Reforms on How Pain Is Treated,* Orlando Sentinel, June 28, 1997, at D1.

[218] *Acquitted Doctor Gets Board's OK to Practice,* Sun-Sentinel (Ft. Lauderdale, Fla.), Dec. 7, 1997, at 10B.

Kansas.   Dr. Stan Naramore was convicted of second-degree murder and attempted first-degree murder for his treatment of two elderly patients in August 1992.[219] Complaints to the administrator of the hospital in which both patients died led to internal hospital investigations resulting in the suspension of the doctor's privileges. The Kansas Board of Healing Arts and the Kansas Board of Investigation began investigations, which eventually led to the doctor's criminal prosecution and conviction. Dr. Naramore was sentenced to 5 to 20 years in prison. He served about one year in a maximum-security correctional facility and was paroled on his first attempt,[220] and the conviction was eventually overturned.[221]

Michigan.   Dr. Jack Kevorkian continues to aid people in ending their lives with relatively little governmental interference, despite the fact that the Michigan Supreme Court has ruled that one who assists another in suicide is subject to prosecution in Michigan.[222] The number of persons whom Dr. Jack Kevorkian has assisted in ending their lives surpassed 100 in April 1998.[223] Concern is increasingly expressed in the press that a significant number of people whom he has helped were not in the final stage of a terminal illness and that these people were suffering from chronic, though serious, disabilities for which some form of relief from pain, depression, or other forms of suffering, short of ending their lives, might have been available and effective. Among the more bizarre occurrences in Dr. Kevorkian's history of aiding suicide is the case in which he removed the kidneys of the person whose suicide he assisted so that they could be donated for transplantation. This person was at least the third quadriplegic aided by Dr. Kevorkian in committing suicide.[224] Future prosecution of Dr. Kevorkian might be more successful under a new statutory prohibition on assisted suicide enacted in Michigan and effective September 1, 1998.[225]

Washington.   Dr. Eugene Turner faces possible criminal charges resulting from his actions in connection with an attempted resuscitation of a child in a hospital emergency room. The resuscitation was unsuccessful and the child's parents agreed to permit the termination of life support. Then the child was pronounced dead. A short while later, a nurse noticed that the child was turning

---

[219] Alan Bavley, *Now Paroled, Doctor Appeals Verdicts: Murder, Attempted Murder Convictions Involved Two Patients in Northwest Kansas*, Kansas City Star, Dec. 21, 1997, at A1.

[220] *Id.*

[221] State v. Naramore, 965 P.2d 211 (Kan. Ct. App. 1998).

[222] *See* People v. Kevorkian, 527 N.W.2d 714, 738 (Mich. 1994), *cert. denied sub nom.* Kevorkian v. Michigan, 115 S. Ct. 1795 (1995), discussed in § **18.17** in the main volume.

[223] *Kevorkian Deaths Total 100*, N.Y. Times, Mar. 15, 1998, at 14 (nat'l edition).

[224] David Shepardson, *Kevorkian Harvests Kidneys in Assisted Suicide*, Detroit News, Jun. 8, 1998, at A1.

[225] *See* 1997 Mich. Pub. Acts S.B. 200.

pink and gasping for air. Dr. Turner continued working on the child for another two hours, at which point he is alleged to have manually obstructed the child's airway by placing his hand over the child's mouth and pinching the nose.[226] So far Dr. Turner has been sanctioned by the medical examiners board and has had his license restricted so that he cannot make decisions about when to end resuscitation efforts.[227]

Nova Scotia. Dr. Nancy Morrison was charged with first-degree murder after administering nitroglycerine and potassium chloride to a terminally ill patient in Halifax. After the patient was taken off life support at his family's request, Morrison is alleged to have administered large doses of medications that caused his death. Dr. Morrison maintained she was trying to ease the patient's suffering and that his death was an unintended result. The charges against Dr. Morrison were dismissed after a preliminary hearing.[228] However, the prosecutor intends to petition the Nova Scotia Supreme Court to reinstate the manslaughter charge against Dr. Morrison.[229]

Ontario. In Toronto, Dr. Maurice Genereux pleaded guilty in January 1998 to two counts of assisting suicide.[230] He was sentenced to two years less one day for an offense that carries a maximum penalty of fourteen years imprisonment, and was released on bail pending appeal of the sentence. Dr. Genereux prescribed lethal doses of Seconal to two patients knowing that the patients intended to commit suicide. One patient survived, but the other succeeded in killing himself. Dr. Genereux falsified the death certificate of this patient, listing the cause of death as pneumonia and AIDS. Both patients suffered from HIV, but had not yet developed AIDS.[231]

In addition to these arguably good faith actions, there have also been some reported instances of health care professionals who have run amok and killed large numbers of terminally ill patients. It is very important to distinguish these cases from assisted suicide and even from active euthanasia. Most fundamentally, these cases are different because the termination of life is not requested by the patient. It is not consensual, voluntary, or informed.

---

[226] *Doctor: Baby Was Brain Dead on Arrival,* Seattle Times, Feb. 4, 1998, at B3.

[227] James Burke, *Doctor Restricted After Baby's Death,* Seattle Times, Feb. 24, 1998, at B1.

[228] Kevin Cox, *Murder Charges Against Halifax Doctor Dismissed: Discharge Reopens Issue of Treating Dying Patients,* Globe & Mail (Toronto), Feb. 20, 1998, at 1.

[229] Kevin Cox, *Crown Wants Morrison Case to Proceed: Ruling in Patient's Death "Bad in Law"* Globe & Mail (Toronto), June 6, 1998, at 1.

[230] Henry Hess, *Doctor Jailed Two Years for Helping Man Kill Himself,* The Globe & Mail (Toronto), May 14, 1998, at 1.

[231] Henry Hess, *A Toronto-Based AIDS Doctor Has Become the First Canadian Physician to Be Convicted of Helping a Patient Commit Suicide,* Globe & Mail (Toronto), Dec. 23, 1997, at 1.

California.   Respiratory therapist Efren Saldivar confessed to police that he killed between 40 and 50 patients. Saldivar stated that he killed the patients either by cutting off their oxygen supply or by injecting them with the muscle relaxants Pavulon or succinylcholine chloride.[232] Saldivar subsequently recanted his confession.[233] The forensic evidence of these crimes could be difficult to uncover, because there will be no chemical evidence of suffocation and succinylcholine breaks down very quickly.

Florida.   The medical examiner in Volusia County is investigating the deaths of 15 to 20 terminally ill patients on the suspicion that some of the patients were murdered by overdoses of morphine.[234]

Indiana.   A former nurse, Orville Lynn Majors, was arrested for murdering six patients after an investigation showed a drastic increase in the number of patient deaths between 1993 and 1995 when Majors was on duty. Additional evidence leading to his arrest included potassium chloride and syringes found in his home; an eyewitness claimed that Majors gave her mother an injection and that within a minute the patient died.[235]

Prosecutions of Laypersons.   In addition to prosecutions of physicians and other health care professionals, there have also been a number of prosecutions in the United States and Canada of laypersons—usually relatives—for assisting in the suicide or mercy killing of a terminally ill person.

California.   James Guthrie was charged with manslaughter for bludgeoning his terminally ill mother to death. His mother suffered from lung cancer and had refused life support. Guthrie brought a metal pipe, wrapped in tape and a sock, into the hospital room and hit his mother on the back of the head. She died three days later. Although the charge of manslaughter carries a maximum penalty of 12 years, Guthrie was sentenced to time served, 2,000 hours of community service, and a $200 fine.[236]

Charles Bauld of San Francisco was charged with homicide for the beating death of his bedridden, diabetic wife. Bauld beat his wife with a dumbbell.

---

[232] Julie Marquis & Jill Leovy, *Investigators Face Difficult Forensic Task,* Los Angeles Times, March 29, 1998, at A1.

[233] Scott Glover, *Police Prepare to Exhume Bodies in Hospital Probe Inquiry: About a Dozen Deceased Patients of the Glendale Facility Are Expected to Be Examined in Investigation of Possible Victims of Efren Saldivar, Sources Say,* Los Angeles Times, June 3, 1998, at B3.

[234] Phil Long, *Deaths of Terminally Ill Under Investigation,* Miami Herald, May 16, 1998, at 1.

[235] Judy Pasternak, *Deaths at Hospital Roil Rural County Crime: Some Say Ex-Nurse Killed. For Others, the Issue Isn't So Clear,* Los Angeles Times, Dec. 31, 1997, at A1.

[236] Geoff Boucher, *Man Who Killed His Ailing Mother Freed After 10 Months,* Los Angeles Times, Apr. 24, 1998, at A1.

The wife was found dead with a plastic bag over her head. Evidence at the scene suggested that she had resisted her husband's efforts to kill her.[237]

Florida. Mr. McIlroy was terminally ill with leukemia and had attempted to end his own life through a drug overdose, which made him vomit and left him too weak to accomplish his goal. He then enlisted his wife's assistance in sprinkling 50 capsules of Seconal on a bowl of ice cream which he ate, causing his death.[238] Mrs. McIlroy faces a possible charge of manslaughter for assisting suicide.

Nebraska. James Hall was charged with aiding or abetting the suicide of a neighbor by supplying the shotgun the neighbor used to kill himself. The trial court dismissed the charges because the state failed to prove that Hall aided or abetted the suicide, and the Nebraska Supreme Court declined to review the case. Hall was the first person prosecuted under the 18-year-old statute.[239]

New York. Following his wife's request (she was paralyzed from the neck down from Lou Gehrig's disease), John Bement gave her a mixture of pain medication, vodka, and pudding. After she became semiconscious, he put a plastic bag over her head. Bement was convicted of second-degree manslaughter, for which the maximum penalty is 15 years.[240] However, Bement was sentenced to a 2-week prison sentence followed by probation for 5 years and 400 hours of community service.[241]

Manitoba. A 79-year-old man, Bert Doerksen, was charged with assisting the suicide of his wife, who suffered from chronic back pain and had taken morphine for the last 15 years. Mr. and Mrs. Doerksen sealed the garage of their home with tape and Mrs. Doerksen asphyxiated herself.[242] When paramedics arrived to resuscitate her, Mr. Doerksen produced her health care directive, which stated that she wished not to be resuscitated. He faces a charge of assisting suicide, which carries a maximum sentence of 14 years.

Saskatchewan. Robert Latimer was convicted of second-degree murder for killing his 12-year-old daughter, who suffered from cerebral palsy and

---

[237] Ray Delgado, *Suicide Try Follows Alleged Euthanasia: Man Says He Beat Wife to Death Before Jumping from Second Floor,* San Francisco Chronicle, Apr. 24, 1998, at A7.

[238] Kevin Krause & Diane C. Lade, *Wife Focus in Assisted Suicide, Police to Turn Over Findings to State Attorney's Office,"* Sun-Sentinel (Fort Lauderdale, Fla.), Dec. 31, 1997, at 1A.

[239] Todd Cooper, *Court Won't Review Law on Suicide,* Omaha World-Herald, Jan. 28, 1998, at 24 (sunrise ed.).

[240] Carolyn Thompson, *Man Found Guilty of Manslaughter in Assisted Suicide,* Associated Press, Feb. 20, 1998 (1998 WL 6642502).

[241] Carolyn Thompson, *Man Convicted for Helping Suicide,* Associated Press, May 12, 1998 (1998 WL 6664096).

[242] David Roberts, *Husband Defends Helping Elderly Wife End Life: First Manitoban Charged with Aiding Suicide Says Spouse Wanted Unrelenting Pain to Stop,* Globe & Mail (Toronto), Feb. 27, 1998, at A4.

acute pain from a displaced hip, with carbon monoxide from his truck. The child could not walk or feed herself, and was unable to speak, but her condition was not terminal. She was able to communicate with persons close to her, but there was no evidence that she ever expressed the wish for her life to be ended. Although this offense carries a 25-year mandatory minimum sentence, the trial judge granted Latimer a constitutional exemption to the sentence, the first ever in a murder case, reducing it to 2 years because he was convinced that Latimer had acted out of compassion.[243] Motivated by the outcome of the Latimer case, an effort was made to introduce a bill in the House of Commons for the purpose of engendering a public debate on physician-assisted suicide. However, the effort was defeated by a vote of 169–66.[244]

Legislative Efforts to Legalize Assisted Suicide.   There have been numerous efforts to enact legislation dealing with assisted suicide, and these efforts are likely to continue.[245] Some of the bills have sought to make assisted suicide a crime, and these are noted in **Table 18-1** in this supplement. Other bills were introduced in almost half the state legislatures between mid-1997 and mid-1998 to legalize assisted suicide, but none have been enacted.

Michigan.   The most promising effort to legalize physician-assisted suicide is a Michigan referendum scheduled for November 3, 1998, on whether to legalize physician-assisted suicide for a terminally ill, mentally competent adult.[246]

Hawaii.   Also, in Hawaii, the governor's "Blue Ribbon Panel on Living and Dying with Dignity" submitted its report. Thereafter, the governor announced that he would submit the issue of physician-assisted suicide to the legislature in the spring of 1999.[247]

Other Countries.   The debate about the legality of physician-assisted suicide also continues in countries other than the United States and Canada. In Australia, after the Northern Territory's statutory legalization of physician-assisted suicide, effective July 1, 1996,[248] Dr. Philip Nitschke, practicing near Darwin, aided at least four terminally ill patients in committing suicide

---

[243] Barry Siegel, *Girl's Tragic Death Moves Judge, Jury to Look Beyond the Law: In Emotional Mercy-Killing Case, the Big Questions Ultimately Gave Way to What They Saw as the Greater Good,* Los Angeles Times, Dec. 25, 1997, at A5.

[244] *Bill to Revive Euthanasia Debate Dies,* Associated Press Political Service, Mar. 25, 1998, 1998 WL 7399445.

[245] *See generally* Diane M. Gianelli, *Comfort, Aid for the Dying—California, Other States May Copy Oregon's Assisted-Suicide Law,* Am. Med. News, Dec. 15, 1997, at 3.

[246] *Governor Signs Bill Banning Assisted Suicide, But Ballot Question May Supersede New Law,* 7 Health L. Rep. (BNA) 1226 (1998).

[247] *Hawaii Governor to Put Euthanasia Before Legislature,* CongressDaily/A.M. June 15, 1998.

[248] See § **1A.1** in this supplement.

between September 1996 and March 1997.[249] In March 1997, the Australian Parliament enacted legislation overriding the territorial law, but this has not deterred Dr. Nitschke's efforts.[250]

Argentina. In Argentina, in a survey of 407 doctors under the age of 34 who have practiced medicine for less than 10 years, about 25 percent (97) supported the legalization of physician-assisted suicide and almost two-thirds (257) supported active euthanasia for terminally ill patients unable to request or consent to it; 162 had already taken such actions.[251]

England. The manslaughter conviction of Julie Watts, for killing her severely handicapped daughter, was overturned. The daughter, born with a rare skull deformity that left her brain-damaged, partially sighted, deaf, and unable to breathe or eat without help, died when her tracheotomy tube came out. Her mother was present at the time and did not replace the tube. The appeals court found that the trial judge had incorrectly instructed the jury because there was no direct evidence that Mrs. Watts had removed the tube.[252]

Dr. Michael Moor was charged with killing an elderly cancer patient.[253] An investigation into this death began when Dr. Moor claimed that he had helped as many as 150 patients die during the past 30 years. This claim was made in conjunction with another by Dr. Michael Irwin, chairman of the Voluntary Euthanasia Society and former medical director of the United Nations, that he had administered fatal doses of medication to about 50 patients during his 40-year career.[254]

Debate over euthanasia was given further impetus when Reverend Brian Anderson admitted to having been present at over 20 mercy killings.[255]

Civil Legislation to Prevent Assisted Suicide. Perhaps the most interesting legislation dealing with assisted suicide is that enacted in a few states[256] which attempts to prevent assisted suicide not by criminalizing it but by providing civil penalties and a means of obtaining injunctive relief.

---

[249] See § **18.24** in this supplement.

[250] *See* Rohan Sullivan, *Storm Over Assisted Suicide Hits Australia,* San Diego Union-Tribune, Feb. 14, 1998, at A22; David W. Kissane, Annette Street, & Philip Nitschke, *Seven Deaths in Darwin: Case Studies Under the Rights of the Terminally Ill Act, Northern Territory, Australia,* 352 Lancet 1097 (1998).

[251] Pablo Przygoda et al., *Letter to the Editor,* 316 Brit. Med. J. 71 (1998).

[252] *Mother Wins Appeal Against Manslaughter Conviction,* BBC, May 18, 1998.

[253] Clare Dyer, *Newcastle GP Charged with Murder,* 316 Brit. Med. J. 1849 (1998).

[254] Clare Dyer, *Two Doctors Confess to Helping Patients to Die,* 315 Brit. Med. J. 205 (1997).

[255] Mark Austin, *Church of England Minister Admits He Was Present at 20 Mercy Killings,* Sunday Times of London, Dec. 28, 1997 (home news).

[256] See § **18.26** in this supplement, discussing the enactment of such legislation in Kansas, Oklahoma, and Virginia.

Statutory Enactments

There has been a noticeable slowing of adoption of end-of-life legislation. Although legislatures have engaged in a significant amount of tinkering with existing advance directive, surrogate decisionmaking, DNR, and intractable pain statutes, there have been very few entirely new enactments. DNR legislation was adopted in Michigan, Ohio, and Oklahoma[257]; Mississippi adopted the Uniform Health-Care Decisions Act.[258] Several states—California, Indiana, Kentucky, Minnesota, Ohio, Oklahoma, Oregon, Rhode Island, West Virginia, and Virginia—either enacted or amended intractable-pain legislation,[259] and a number of other state legislatures enacted statutes or passed resolutions to study the problem of inadequate treatment of intractable pain.

Administration of Advance Directives
and Undue Influence

It seems reasonable that there should begin to be litigation about advance directives, as they become more common in general and more common among those who actually find themselves in end-of-life decisionmaking situations. The Smith case[260] in Massachusetts presented the question of whether guardians designated by the principal in his power of attorney had a conflict of interest; the *Goldman* case[261] concerned the enforceability of an out-of-state advance directive. In the *Blackman* case[262] in New York, the court was faced with the issue of whether a competent patient's decision was voluntary or was unduly influenced by a family member. These and related issues arise with great frequency in clinical settings but are rarely litigated. Taking some of these cases to court might provide guidance to clinicians and their attorneys about the appropriate resolution of these issues.

Jehovah's Witnesses

Several landmark cases involving the refusal of blood transfusions by Jehovah's Witnesses have been decided in the last decade or decade and a

---

[257] See **Table 9-1** in this supplement.

[258] *See* 1998 Miss. Laws ch. 542 (H.B. 546).

[259] See **Table 9-1A** in the supplement.

[260] *In re* Smith, 684 N.E.2d 613 (Mass. App. Ct. 1997), discussed in § **1A.6** in this supplement.

[261] *In re* Goldman, 18 Fiduc. Rep. 2d 79 (C.P. Northampton County, Pa. 1997), discussed in § **1A.6** in this supplement.

[262] Blackman v. New York City Health & Hosps. Corp., 660 N.Y.S.2d 643 (Sup. Ct. Kings County 1997), discussed in § **1A.6** in this supplement.

half.[263] Some have involved pregnant patients, but none has squarely raised the question of whether a transfusion could be required if it was said to be necessary to maintain the fetus's survival. In *In re Fetus Brown*,[264] the trial court ordered a transfusion of a pregnant mother, who had to be forcibly restrained. The Illinois Appeals Court reversed, holding that the state's interest in protecting a viable fetus did not outweigh the mother's right to refuse treatment.[265]

§ 1A.6   Jurisdiction-by-Jurisdiction Developments in 1997–1998

California

Statutes

Cal. Health & Safety Code 124960, 124961 (intractable pain).

Illinois

Cases

In re Fetus Brown, 689 N.E.2d 397 (Ill. App. Ct. 1997), appears to be the first instance of an appellate court's recognition of the right of a pregnant Jehovah's Witness to refuse a blood transfusion alleged to be necessary not only to save the life of the mother but of the fetus too. The mother, Darlene Brown, underwent surgery in her 35th week of pregnancy to remove a urethral mass. During the surgery, she lost enough blood that the surgeon ordered a blood transfusion. She had not previously told the doctor that she was a Jehovah's Witness, but was conscious when the blood transfusion was ordered and refused it. The doctors were able to complete the surgery and control the bleeding without the transfusion.

However, after the surgery, the mother's hemoglobin level became dangerously low, posing a grave risk with only a 5 percent chance of survival for both the mother and the fetus. After considerable consultation by the attending physician with specialists about other possible treatments, the state was notified, and it petitioned for temporary custody of the fetus. The trial court awarded custody to the hospital "with the right to consent to any and all blood transfusions for Darlene Brown when advised of such necessity by any

---

[263] See § **2.9** in the main volume.

[264] 689 N.E.2d 397 (Ill. App. Ct. 1997).

[265] See § **1A.6** in this supplement.

attending physician."[266] According to the Browns' later pleadings, when transfusions were recommended, "Darlene Brown tried to resist the transfusion and the doctors 'yelled at and forcibly restrained, overpowered and sedated' her."[267] The baby was delivered a few days later and was healthy.

After the trial court vacated the temporary custody order, Brown appealed. The Appellate Court of Illinois held that the trial court had erred in appointing a temporary guardian with the power to order blood transfusions. The court relied heavily on *In re Baby Boy Doe*,[268] which had held that trial courts

> should not engage in a balancing of the maternal and fetal rights such that "a woman's competent choice in refusing medical treatment as invasive as a cesarean section during her pregnancy must be honored, even in circumstances where the choice may be harmful to her fetus. . . . [A] woman's right to refuse invasive medical treatment, derived from her rights to privacy, bodily integrity, and religious liberty, is not diminished during pregnancy. The woman retains the same right to refuse invasive treatment, even of lifesaving or other beneficial nature, that she can exercise when she is not pregnant. The potential impact upon the fetus is not legally relevant; to the contrary, the Stallman court explicitly rejected the view that the woman's rights can be subordinated to fetal rights."[269]

In light of this holding, the state argued not that the mother's right to refuse treatment should be balanced against the *rights* of the fetus, but that the mother's right should be balanced against the *state's interest* in the viable fetus.[270] The court first acknowledged that the mother's right to refuse treatment was based on Illinois common law, fourteenth amendment due process rights, and the first amendment right of religious freedom.[271] However, this right must be balanced against the usual litany of state interests,[272] none of which was found to overcome the patient's right to refuse treatment. The countervailing state interest most likely to outweigh the patient's right—the impact upon third parties—was not supported by the record, which indicated that the mother's parents and her husband and his parents would provide adequate support to their children. The court did not consider the fetus under this heading, presumably because, at the time of the hearing and the transfusion, the fetus was not a legally cognizable person.

Thus, the determinative issue was whether the state's interest in protecting a viable fetus outweighed the mother's right to refuse treatment. The court

---

[266] 689 N.E.2d at 400.

[267] *Id.*

[268] 632 N.E.2d 326 (Ill. App. Ct. 1994).

[269] *Id.* at 330, 332.

[270] 689 N.E.2d at 401–02.

[271] Id. at 402.

[272] See §§ **8.15–8.19** in the main volume and this supplement.

held that it did not. Relying on *Planned Parenthood v. Casey*,[273] the court acknowledged that the state has an important and legitimate interest, which becomes compelling at viability, and that the state may restrict abortion at this point and afterward.[274] Nonetheless, this interest does not outweigh the mother's interest in bodily integrity. Central to this conclusion is the court's recognition that a blood transfusion is not a "'relatively noninvasive and risk-free procedure'" as the *Baby Boy Doe* court had concluded.[275]

Kentucky

Statutes

Ky. Rev. Stat. Ann. §§ 311.621–.643, 386.093 (amending advance directive statute and related portions of guardianship statute).

Massachusetts

Cases

In re Smith, 684 N.E.2d 613 (Mass. App. Ct. 1997), raises issues that lurk in the background of many instances of end-of-life decisionmaking but rarely surface in litigation. Smith, through a durable power of attorney, appointed two business associates to be his attorneys-in-fact, and to serve as his guardians should guardianship ever be needed. In fact, it was needed when Smith later suffered from advanced Parkinson's disease with dementia.

When he became seriously disabled, Smith's wife petitioned for the appointment of her daughter and a family friend to serve as Smith's co-guardians. It is possible that she was unaware of the existence of the durable power of attorney.[276] The probate court appointed them temporary guardians. Thereafter, the attorneys-in-fact learned of the proceedings, filed objections, and petitioned to be appointed guardians. At the hearing on the objections and permanent guardianship, little evidence was adduced, but unsubstantiated allegations were made about the unfitness of one of the attorneys-in-fact to serve as guardian. The trial judge abruptly terminated the hearing and appointed Smith's daughter and friend as guardians. The basis for the decision was that because both attorneys-in-fact were officers and directors of the corporation of which Smith was the majority shareholder, "'[g]ranting them a guardianship over [James Smith] . . . would create a conflict of interest and

---

[273] 505 U.S. 833 (1992).

[274] 689 N.E.2d at 404.

[275] *Id*. at 405, quoting *In re* Baby Boy Doe, 632 N.E.2d at 333.

[276] 684 N.E.2d at 615 n.15.

give [both men] an undue advantage' sufficient to disqualify them from serving as Smith's guardians."[277]

On appeal, by the attorneys-in-fact, the court held that

> when a principal has nominated his future guardian by durable power of attorney and protective fiduciary proceedings are thereafter commenced, the Massachusetts Uniform Durable Power of Attorney Act . . . mandates that the Probate Court make its appointment in accordance with the nomination in the absence of good cause [for] disqualification.[278]

In reaching this conclusion, the court invoked the purpose of the legislation and looked to accepted rules of statutory construction. The statute was specifically intended to obviate the need for guardianship proceedings.[279] The statute was clearly designed to enhance and provide a mechanism for the effectuation of individual autonomy.[280] Finally, the statute contains mandatory language stating that the court "shall" appoint as guardian the person nominated in a durable power of attorney if a guardianship proceeding is initiated for one who has executed such an instrument.[281] Only if the court is presented with competent evidence that would disqualify the attorney-in-fact from serving as guardian may the principal's wishes be overlooked.[282]

The court concluded that although the probate judge had not relied on these allegations, he had based his decision on the fact that the attorneys-in-fact were officers and directors of the corporation and that this alone created a conflict of interest sufficient to disqualify them from serving. The appeals court held that there must be evidence of an actual conflict of interest to remove a fiduciary, and that here there was none. Indeed, the fact that the principal had nominated them as guardians, with full awareness of their involvement in the corporation, demonstrated that "[t]here was no inherent conflict of interest in these circumstances. . . . [T]he mere possibility that future conflicts might arise as a result of [the guardians'] dual roles is [not] sufficient to disqualify them from serving as Smith's guardians."[283]

---

[277] *Id*. at 615.

[278] *Id*. at 616.

[279] *Id*. ("[T]he 'dominant idea was that durable powers would be used as alternatives to court-oriented, protective procedures' such as guardianships. Uniform Durable Power of Attorney Act, Prefatory Note, 8A U.L.A. 310 (1993)").

[280] 684 N.E. 2d at 616–17.

[281] *Id*. at 616.

[282] *Id*. at 617.

[283] *Id*. at 619.

Maryland

Statutes

Md. Code Ann., Health Gen. § 5-608(d)(1) (amendments to DNR).

Michigan

Statutes

Mich. Comp. Laws Ann. §§ 333.1051–1067 (99supp) (DNR).

Minnesota

Statutes

Minn. Stat. Ann. 152.125 (intractable pain).

Senate File 2050 (enacted April 21, 1998) (amendments to health care power of attorney).

Mississippi

Statutes

Miss. Code Ann. §§ 41-41-201 to -229 (advance directives).

Nevada

Statutes

Nev. Rev. Stat. §§ 450B.400–.590 (DNR).

New York

Cases

Afentakis v. Memorial Hospital, 667 N.Y.S.2d 602 (Sup. Ct. N.Y. County 1997). This case was filed by the wife of a man who had died in the defendant hospital, seeking damages for the loss of dignity to which he had been subjected in the process of dying from brain cancer. The complaint was styled as a cause of action for breach of the "right to dignity," but in recognition of the weakness of their pleading, plaintiff's counsel admitted that the claim was "'quite similar to or may be just another way of articulating a claim for negligent infliction of emotional distress.'"[284]

In fact, the court treated the suit as one for negligent infliction of emotional distress. And while advocating that dying patients be treated in a dignified manner, the judge dismissed the suit for failure to plead or prove the minimum requisites of such a claim: namely, both physical injury and emotional injury attributable to the doctors' conduct and departure from accepted practice. To permit such a claim to go forward without proof of the elements of negligent infliction of emotional distress would require courts "to attempt to dictate a standard of care relating to such an abstraction as the precise quantum of respect and consideration which should be accorded hospital patients by hospital and their staffs, or to arbitrate the complex emotional response a patient's terminal illness is likely to invoke in their caretakers," a task for which courts are unsuited.[285]

On its surface, *Blackman v. New York City Health & Hospitals Corp.*, 660 N.Y.S.2d 643 (Sup. Ct. Kings County 1997), is a simple case involving a treatment refusal by a competent, elderly patient. However, it also raises and addresses an issue that must frequently occur in many cases involving treatment refusal by competent patients: namely, the legitimacy of influence by family members on patients' decisions. This issue is especially timely in light of the concern expressed by opponents of the legalization of physician-assisted suicide that patients will be pressured by family members to request assisted suicide.

In this case, the patient was hospitalized for the treatment of pneumonia and was being treated by a "ventilator . . . connected to her orally by means of an endotracheal tube" and by a nasogastric feeding tube, the latter of which was replaced by an intravenous line. Her doctors wanted to perform a tracheostomy for the ventilator, which would have allowed her to experience less discomfort, take nourishment by mouth, and eventually be weaned from the ventilator. On at least two occasions she gave consent for the tracheostomy, but then withdrew it before the surgery could be performed. The doctors believed that the patient was not competent and that she was being unduly influenced in her decisionmaking by her grandson, who was also her health care proxy; therefore, they objected to her petition requesting a judicial order forbidding the surgery.

The two psychiatrists who examined her (one at the hospital's behest), as well as the trial judge who met with the patient, concluded that she possessed decisionmaking capacity:

---

[284] 667 N.Y.S.2d at 603.

[285] *Id.* at 604.

[S]he was alert and lucid. She was aware of who The Court was, the reason for its being there at that time, and the nature of the proceedings. She answered all questions under oath. When asked if she understood that she would die if the food tube and respirator were removed, she wrote "It is a living death now. I will take that chance". She stated that she was advised of the consequences, and that she had been advised that she would be able to eat at some time after she had the tracheostomy. When asked if she wanted to live or die, she wrote "I will take that chance", and further wrote "no" when asked if she would consent to an operation that would make it possible for her to eat and stay alive.[286]

Consequently, the court entered an order granting the patient's request that the hospital be directed to withhold all medical treatment except what was needed to keep her comfortable and to alleviate pain.

On an issue that is rarely discussed in end-of-life judicial opinions, the court also addressed the hospital's concern that the patient's grandson was exerting undue influence on the patient. As the patient had been hospitalized for several weeks, with her grandson visiting frequently, hospital personnel drew this conclusion from repeated interactions and a variety of events rather than from a particular incident, yet one specific example does illustrate the hospital's concern. In the evaluation by the psychiatrist selected by the petitioner to evaluate the patient, she mistook the psychiatrist for her grandson; when the psychiatrist asked her why she had changed her mind about having the tracheostomy, she wrote "'because that is what you [meaning her grandson] wanted.'"[287]

The psychiatrist selected by the hospital to evaluate the patient felt that she had "'spilled the beans'" in this incident. Nonetheless, "he did not believe that there was anything unethical in family members counseling one another."[288] Nor did the court. It observed that although the role of the grandson and a friend of his could not be ignored, in terms of their influence on the patient in her depressed and sometimes confused state, "there is no showing of irresponsibility, overreaching, or financial gain on either of their part."[289] The court echoed the psychiatrist's observation that "there is nothing unethical where one family member counsels another."[290]

The court appeared unconcerned about the grandson's influence for two reasons. First, the judge was convinced that the grandson had merely made his opinions known to the patient, and that her "decision is the product of her own mind."[291] Second, hospital personnel had attempted to influence her in

[286] 660 N.Y.S.2d at 647.

[287] *Id.* at 647.

[288] *Id.*

[289] 660 N.Y.S. 2d at 649.

[290] *Id.*

[291] *Id.*

the opposite direction. This, and the failure to counsel her as to the quality of life that she was likely to experience if she did undergo the tracheostomy, contributed to her confusion and ambivalence. Indeed, the court seemed to find the behavior of hospital personnel more objectionable than the grandson's. Once she arrived at her decision, "Respondents had the clear duty to honor this decision and not tax her, her family, and her resources by opposing this application, since 'no person or court should substitute its judgment as to what would be an acceptable quality of life for another.'"[292]

Thus, though not discussing what might constitute undue influence by a family member over a patient's decisionmaking about end-of-life care, the court made it clear that a family member's expression of his or her views to the patient, even repeatedly, did not constitute undue influence.

Ohio

Statutes

Ohio Rev. Code Ann. 2133.02 (amendments to DNR).
Ohio Rev. Code Ann. 2133.11, 2133.12 (intractable pain).
Ohio Rev. Code Ann. 4731.052 (intractable pain)

Oklahoma

Statutes

Okla. Stat. Ann. tit. 63, §§ 3131.1–14 (DNR), as amended by S.B. 840 (1998).
Okla. Stat. Ann. tit. 63, § 3141.4 (intractable pain).

Pennsylvania

Cases

In re Goldman, No. 1997-1368 (C.P. Northampton County, Pa. 1997). The patient in this case was an 80-year-old woman with Alzheimer's disease, who had developed an ulcer on her leg that required antibiotics and whirlpool treatment. Prior to losing decisionmaking capacity, she had executed in California (where she then lived) a durable power of attorney giving her daughter authority to make health care decisions for her, including end-of-life decisions. There were also some instructions in the document in the nature of a living will, which she requested guide her attorney in fact. On the basis of

---

[292] *Id.,* quoting *In re* Westchester County Medical Ctr. (O'Connor), 531 N.E.2d 607, 613 (N.Y. 1988).

this document and knowledge of her mother's wishes, the daughter refused to authorize the antibiotics and whirlpool treatments.

As a consequence of the daughter's refusal, a petition was filed for the appointment of a guardian. The court appointed someone else guardian to consent to the antibiotics and whirlpool treatments, but appointed the daughter guardian for all other purposes. The court refused to permit the antibiotics and whirlpool to be withheld, on the basis that it would offend the ethical integrity of the "medical community" because they are a "minimally intrusive regimen."[293] However, amputation of the patient's leg above the knee "would not negatively impact on the ethical integrity of the medical community" because it "is such a profound invasion of her body." Without saying so, this court appears to have reverted to use of the ordinary/extraordinary distinction, which has long been discredited in law.[294]

The patient had executed a durable power of attorney for health care in California when she lived there, prior to losing decisionmaking capacity. This document gave her daughter plenary authority to make medical decisions for the patient. The court refused to enforce it because it did not conform to the requirements of the Pennsylvania advance directive statute, but it acknowledged that the daughter had common-law authority to act as surrogate, and it was on this basis that it appointed her guardian to make decisions about all other forms of treatment.

Rhode Island

Statutes

R.I. Gen. Laws §§ 5-37.4-1 to -3 (intractable pain).
R.I. Gen. Laws § 23-4.11 (making technical amendments to advance directive statute).

Virginia

Statutes

Va. Code Ann. §§ 18.2-76.3, -76.4 (civil assisted suicide legislation).
Va. Code Ann. 54.1-3408.1 (DNR).

---

[293] Slip op. at 9.
[294] See § **8.8** in the main volume.

West Virginia

Statutes

W. Va. Code §§ 30-3A-1 to -4 (intractable pain).
Senate Bill 318 (enacted April 12, 1997) (to be codified as W. Va. Code §§ 16-306-2, -3, -5, -7) predominantly makes technical changes to the surrogate decisionmaking statute. However, the legislation expands the process for challenging the selection of a surrogate and for decisions made by the surrogate.

Wisconsin

Statutes

Wis. Stat. Ann. §§ 3087S.154.225 (amends DNR statute to permit guardians of a principal either to grant or to revoke a DNR order).
Wis. Stat. Ann. §§ 243.07, 243.10 (makes minor amendments to the health care power of attorney statute).

§ 1A.7   Overview of 1998–1999 Developments

Termination of Life Support

One of the most surprising events of the past year is the "Hugh Finn" case in Virginia. This case is a stark reminder that although there may be a consensus about the law governing the termination of life support,[295] approximately half the states still have no definitive judicial decision on the subject; each time a case arises in one of these states, all bets are off as to how the trial courts, and indeed the appellate courts, will rule.

Mr. Finn, age 44, was in a persistent vegetative state as the result of a 1995 automobile accident. After three years in this condition, his wife sought to have his feeding tube removed. Permission was granted by a trial court to do so, but the state attempted to intervene to prevent the action after being contacted by some family members who opposed the action, claiming that Finn was not in a persistent vegetative state.[296] Although the family eventually withdrew their objections and the trial court denied the state's motion for

---

[295] See §§ **2.2–2.5** in the main volume and this supplement.

[296] Brooke A. Masters, *Family's Life-and-Death Battle Plays Out in Court,* Washington Post, Sept. 9, 1998, at A-1, 1998 WL 16554764.

a temporary restraining order, state officials (including the governor, who took an extreme interest in the case) pursued an appeal.[297]

The Virginia Supreme Court rejected the governor's attempt to have the feeding tube continued. The case was somewhat of a political football for two months during the election season.[298] In addition, the trial court ordered the state and the governor to pay Mrs. Finn $13,000 for court costs and attorney's fees for having filed a frivolous lawsuit to stop the termination of life support.[299] The Virginia Supreme Court overturned the award of court costs and attorneys' fees.[300] In addition, "[d]espite intensive lobbying by the governor and his staff, a majority of Republicans [in the Virginia legislature] deserted [the governor] and joined Democrats in approving a payment of $48,000 for the widow, plus $10,000 for one of Hugh Finn's brothers."[301] The governor eventually dropped his efforts to deny the payment to the Finns.[302]

One of the stranger right-to-die cases in the last year revolved around the request of a Florida woman, Georgette Smith, who was shot by her 68-year-old mother and paralyzed from the neck down, to have her life support terminated. The hospital where she was a patient refused to disconnect her life support, and she was forced to bring suit against the physicians to do so. In some respects, this case illustrates even more than the Finn case the difficulty of implementing the right to die, because Florida, unlike Virginia, has solid case law holding that there is a right to refuse life-sustaining medical treatment even if one is not terminally ill.[303] The trial court granted Ms. Smith's request, but stayed its implementation for a day so that she could cooperate with prosecutors in building a case against her mother.[304] However, the prosecutor eventually decided not to bring charges against the frail,

---

[297] Gilmore v. Annaburg Manor Nursing Home, Chancery No. 44386 (Va., filed Oct. 2, 1998). *See also* Irvin Molotsky, *Wife Wins Right-to-Die Case; Then a Governor Challenges It,* N.Y. Times, Oct. 2, 1998, at A1, 1998 WL 5429395.

[298] *Doctors Properly Removed Feeding Tube, Followed Virginia's Health Care Decisions Act,* 7 Health L. Rep. (BNA) 1645 (1998); R.H. Melton and Brooke A. Masters, *Court Rejects Gilmore's Bid to Overturn Finn Ruling; Family Decision Stands to Let Newscaster Die,* Washington Post, Oct. 3, 1998, at C1, 1998 WL 16559882.

[299] Stephen Dinan, *Finn Case Judge Faults Gilmore, Rules State, Governor Owe Costs,* Washington Times, Nov. 26, 1998, at C4, 1998 WL 3464774.

[300] Gilmore v. Finn, 527 S.E.2d 426 (Va. 2000).

[301] Donald P. Baker and R.H. Melton, *Va. General Assembly Ends Its Surplus-Driven Session,* Feb. 28, 1999, at C1, 1999 WL 2203109.

[302] Donald P. Baker, *Gilmore Drops Bid to Block Finn Payment,* Washington Post, Mar. 27, 1999, at B1, 1999 WL 2207678.

[303] *See, e.g., In re* Dubreuil, 629 So. 2d 819 (Fla. 1993).

[304] Rick Bragg, *A Family Shooting and a Twist Like No Other,* N.Y. Times, May 19, 1999, at A1 (nat'l ed.). *See also* Rick Bragg, *Woman Shot by Mother Is Allowed to Die,* N.Y. Times, May 20, 1999, at A18 (nat'l ed.).

elderly woman because "'deteriorating health, and her relationship to the victim, do not provide an appropriate circumstance' for a murder charge."[305]

Physician-Assisted Suicide

Physician-assisted suicide continued to be a major topic of debate in 1998 and 1999. Efforts to legalize it through litigation have slowed down considerably, with only one case having been filed.[306] However, numerous bills have been introduced in state legislatures to legalize it, and a referendum to do so failed in Michigan by a 2-1 ratio.[306.1]

Developments in Oregon.   The initial efforts to halt the implementation of the 1994 Death with Dignity Act ran out in October 1997, when the United States Supreme Court denied certiorari.[307] A little more than a week later, the Oregon voters turned back an effort to repeal the statute. Thereafter, legalized physician-assisted suicide began to occur in Oregon. However, the judicial challenges to the statute did not end until almost a year later, when the district court judge who had presided over litigation seeking to declare the statute unconstitutional ruled that the plaintiffs lacked standing even under their amended claim.[308]

The state health division, as required by the Death with Dignity Act, issued a report in early 1999 summarizing the experience with the statute to the end of 1998.[309] In brief, the state health division received information on 23 persons who had received prescriptions for lethal medications. Of these, 15 died after taking the medications, 6 died from their underlying illnesses, and 2 had not taken the lethal medications. Of the patients who took the lethal medications, 8 were male and 7 were female; all were white; and 13 were dying from cancer.

---

[305] Rick Bragg, *Woman Avoids Murder Charge Over Daughter,* N.Y. Times, May 26, 1999, at A22 (nat'l ed.).

[306] Sampson v. Alaska, No. 3AN-98-11288-CIV (Alaska Super. Ct., filed Dec. 15, 1998), *reported in* 7 Health L. Rep. (BNA) 2040 (Dec. 24, 1998).

[306.1] Charlie Cain and Tim Kiska, *Proposal B: Assisted suicide: Religion key factor in defeat,* Detroit News, Nov. 4, 1998, at A6, 1998 WL 3843605, *discussing* Terminally Ill Patient's Right to End Unbearable Pain and Suffering Act, 1997 Mich. V.2, 89th Leg., 1998 Reg. Sess., Ballot Measure 2, Proposal B.

[307] Lee v. Harcleroad, 118 S. Ct. 328 (1997).

[308] *See* Lee v. Oregon, No. 94-6467-HO (D. Or., Sept. 22, 1998), *reported in* 7 Health L. Rep. (BNA) 1554 (Oct. 1, 1998).

[309] *See* Oregon Health Division; "Oregon's Death with Dignity Act: The First Year's Experience," <http://www.ohd.hr.state.or.us/cdpe/chs/pas/ar-index.htm>. *See also* Arthur E. Chin et al., *Legalized Physician-Assisted Suicide in Oregon—The First Year's Experience,* 340 New Eng. J. Med. 577 (1999).

Chin and colleagues compare these 15 patients with a control group of individuals who died from similar illnesses but did not receive prescriptions for lethal medications. Despite the concerns that patients who opted for a lethal prescription would be disproportionately poor, elderly, female, and from racial minorities, they found that the patients who took the lethal medications and the controls were similar with regard to sex, race, urban or rural residence, level of education, health insurance coverage, and hospice enrollment; and that neither the patients nor the control group members expressed concern about the financial impact of their illness. Furthermore, despite the concern that physician-assisted suicide would be used instead of adequate palliative care, the preliminary results show the opposite: namely, that 15 control patients expressed concern about inadequate control of pain, but only one patient who took lethal medication did. Concerns were also previously expressed that physician-assisted suicide would be more likely to be utilized by individuals who were isolated; in fact, the study found that the control patients were more likely to have been married at some time. Finally, the patients who took lethal overdoses were more likely to be concerned about loss of autonomy or control of bodily functions than the control patients.

The Oregon legislature amended the Death with Dignity Act in 1999.[310] The amendments do little more than clarify the original enactment. Some of the more far-reaching provisions, such as permitting pharmacists to refuse to fulfill a lethal prescription for reasons of conscience, were defeated.[311] The definitional sections clarify that an "adult" is a person 18 years of age or older[312] and that pharmacists fall within the definition of *health care provider*.[313] The responsibilities of attending physicians are expanded and clarified. One important new responsibility is to counsel patients "about the importance of having another person present when the patient takes the medication . . . and of not taking the medication in a public place. . . ."[314]

Attending physicians are also expressly authorized to dispense the lethal medications rather than having a pharmacist do so.[315] An interesting omission is the bill's failure to address the issue of whether the attending physician must inform the pharmacist of the purpose of the prescription. A new statutory provision blandly states that the attending physician is required to "[c]ontact a pharmacist and inform the pharmacist of the prescription"[316] and

---

[310] *See* 1999 OR. S.B. 491 (effective June 30, 1999).

[311] Jeff Mapes, *House Votes Against Pharmacists in Ethical, Religious Case—Critics Say HB2010 Could Make It Hard for Women in Rural Areas to Get Emergency Contraception Drugs,* Oregonian, May 18, 1999, at B6.

[312] Or. Rev. Stat. § 127.800, 1.01(1).

[313] *Id.* § 127.800, 1.01(6).

[314] *Id.* § 127.815, 3.01(g).

[315] *Id.* § 127.815, 3.01(L).

[316] *Id.* § 127.815, 3.01 (L)(B)(i).

to "[d]eliver the written prescription personally or by mail to the pharmacist, who will dispense the medications to either the patient, the attending physician or an expressly identified agent of the patient."[317] However, to the extent that this procedure varies from the ordinary procedure for prescribing medications, the pharmacist may be readily able to infer the purpose of the prescription even without an express statement of its purpose.

To address the concerns that have been raised that people will be motivated by depression to seek a physician's assistance in ending their lives, the bill adds "depression causing impaired judgment" to the generic "psychiatric or psychological disorder" that the attending physician must determine the patient does not have before medications may be prescribed for ending life in a "dignified and humane manner."[318]

Another concern about the statute has been that although its provisions are limited to Oregon residents, there is no definition of *residence*. The bill adds four "factors demonstrating Oregon residence" and states that they "include but are not limited to:

Possession of an Oregon driver's license;

Registration to vote in Oregon;

Evidence that the person owns or leases property in Oregon;

Filing of an Oregon tax return for the most recent tax year."[319]

The bill also adds an important new reporting requirement: any health care provider who dispenses medication under the statute must file a copy of the dispensing record with the state health division.[320]

Finally, the bill adds several provisions expanding immunities. First, it permits a health care provider to prohibit another health care provider from participating in assisted suicide on the premises of the first health care provider if prior notice of such prohibition has been given.[321] Presumably this affects primarily physicians in hospitals or clinics and pharmacists, and is probably the most far-reaching aspect of the amended legislation. If a health care provider violates this prohibition, the provider issuing the prohibition may impose sanctions on the prohibited health care provider, including:

---

[317] *Id.* § 127.815, 3.01 (L)(B)(ii).

[318] *Id* § 127.825, 3.03.

[319] *Id.* § 127.860, 3.10.

[320] *Id.* § 127.865, 3.11.

[321] *Id.* § 127.885, 4.01(5)(a).

[322] *Id.* § 127.885, 4.01(5)(b)(A).

- loss of medical staff privileges[322]
- termination of a lease or other property contract[323]
- termination of employment contract if prohibited provider acts in course of employment as employee or independent contractor of prohibiting party.[324]

However, even if prohibited from doing so under one of the preceding provisions, a health care provider may participate in an assisted suicide under the statute if it is done outside the course of employment.[325] Further, any health care provider sanctioning another must follow due process[326]—the provisions of which, however, are not defined.

Efforts to make legalized physician-assisted suicide more difficult to obtain did not end with this legislation. The Republican-controlled Oregon Senate, in a direct challenge to the Democratic governor, who is a physician who supports legalized physician-assisted suicide, approved a spending plan that eliminates state Medicaid funds for abortion and physician-assisted suicide. The governor said he would veto the party-line general-fund proposal.[327]

Federal Legislation.   Although the federal legislative attempts to prevent the use of controlled substances in physician-assisted suicide that is legal under state law (specifically in Oregon)[328]—the Lethal Drug Abuse Prevention Act of 1998—failed in the 105th Congress, legislation with the same goal was introduced in the 106th Congress,[329] and hearings on these bills were proceeding in the summer of 1999 as they did in the previous summer. Some of the groups—National Hospice Organization, American Academy of Pain Management, American Society of Anesthesiologists, American Medical Association—that opposed the 1998 legislation are supporting the new version. The National Hospice Organization is supporting the bill because it no longer contains a provision for a board or committee that would report on physicians' activities and potentially wrongly accuse doctors of assisted suicide when patients die after receiving pain medication.[330]

---

[323] *Id.* § 127.885, 4.01(5)(b)(B).

[324] *Id.* § 127.885, 4.01(5)(b)(C).

[325] *Id.* § 127.885, 4.01(5)(b)(C)(i).

[326] *Id.* § 127.885, 4.01(5c).

[327] Paul Neville, *Human Resources Budget Cuts Abortion, Suicide Funds*, Eugene Register-Guard, Jul. 21, 1999, at ___.

[328] See § **1A.5** in this supplement.

[329] *See* Pain Relief Promotion Act of 1999, H.R. 2260, 106th Cong., 1st Sess. (1999); S. 1272, 106th Cong., 1st Sess. (1999).

[330] John Hughes, *Nickles, Lawmakers Renew Fight Against Assisted Suicide,* Associated Press, Jun. 17, 1999.

Prosecutions for Assisted Suicide and Mercy Killing

The prosecution of health professionals and laypersons for aiding suicide or mercy killing of terminally ill patients continues to occur. It is difficult, if not impossible, to know what the rate is and whether it is increasing, but judging by the number of reported instances in the media, which presumably is the tip of the iceberg, there are probably a considerable number of assisted suicides and mercy killings.[331] However, there are very few convictions and very few imprisonments.

Health Care Professionals.

United States. The only conviction in the United States this year of a health care professional for mercy killing to make it into the official case reports is *State v. Naramore.*[332] However, the conviction was reversed on appeal.[333]

Although not yet at the appellate level, the conviction of Dr. Jack Kevorkian for murder is certainly better known. After claiming to have aided more than 130 individuals to end their own lives,[334] Dr. Kevorkian personally administered a lethal injection to a patient on a nationally televised program,[335] virtually challenging prosecutors to prosecute him for murder after failing to convict him on a number of occasions for aiding suicide. The prosecutors took up the challenge and obtained a conviction for second-degree murder,[336] after Kevorkian defended himself and put on an extremely weak defense.[337] Kevorkian is currently in prison on a 10- to 15-year sentence, while seeking a new trial on the ground that the attorney who represented him in his trial before he took over his own defense committed errors.[338]

In the case of Dr. Eugene Turner, a pediatrician in Port Angeles, Washington, who was accused of holding his hand over the nose and mouth

---

[331] *See generally* Jennifer Steinhauer, *Was It an Act of Mercy or Murder?—Manslaughter Arrest Puts a Spotlight on Assisted Suicide Pacts,* N.Y. Times, Oct. 17, 1998, at A14 (nat'l ed.).

[332] 965 P.2d 211 (Kan. Ct. App. 1998).

[333] See § **1A.8** in this supplement.

[334] Pam Belluck, *Kevorkian Is Found Guilty of Murdering Dying Man,* N.Y. Times, Mar. 27, 1999, at A1 (nat'l ed.).

[335] Pam Belluck, *Prosecutor to Weigh Possibility of Charging Kevorkian,* N.Y. Times, Nov. 23, 1998, at A12; Caryn James, *"60 Minutes," Kevorkian and a Death for the Cameras,* N.Y. Times, Nov. 23, 1998, at A12.

[336] *Id.*

[337] Pam Belluck, *Kevorkian Stumbles in His Self-Defense— Doctor's Lack of Legal Skill Becomes Evident in His Murder Trial,* N.Y. Times, Mar. 24, 1999, at A17 (nat'l ed.).

[338] James A. McClear, *Court Gets Appeal for New Kevorkian Trial—Lawyer Blames Ex-counsel Gorosh for Former Doctor's Prison Term,* Detroit News, Jun. 3, 1999, at D4.

of an infant to stop its breathing,[339] and who was charged with second-degree murder, the prosecutor dropped the charges. However, Turner still faces a hearing before the State Medical Quality Assurance Commission for alleged unprofessional conduct[340]; he has also surrendered his hospital privileges, and faces a $1.5 million lawsuit by the baby's parents.[341]

United Kingdom. The most noteworthy case in the United Kingdom was that involving Dr. John Moor, who was charged with murdering 85-year-old George Liddell, who suffered from colon cancer. Moor was acquitted.[342] He was the first general practitioner to face a charge of murder under such circumstances.[343] Moor denied murdering Liddell, but admitted that he has helped about 300 terminally ill people die during his 30 years of practicing medicine.[344] Liddell's family stated that only after he was screaming in agony did Moor give him "considerable quantities of morphine" to relieve the pain. Although the patient died, Dr. Moor says he did not want it to occur, but when administering that dosage of morphine there is a thin line between comfort and death.[345] Moor was arrested after speaking out in favor of euthanasia and claiming to have helped take patient's lives. His comments came after the publication of a controversial article about euthanasia in the Sunday *Times* by another doctor.

Canada. The prosecutor in the case of Dr. Nancy Morrison, accused of administering lethal medications to a terminally ill patient in Halifax, Nova Scotia, eventually dropped efforts to prosecute after the charges were dropped at a preliminary hearing.[346] However, Dr. Morrison was reprimanded by the Nova Scotia College of Physicians and Surgeons, which ruled that her action in Mills's death was not acceptable to the medical profession.[347] Morrison has since said she is sorry for "hastening" the death of a terminally ill man, and by accepting the reprimand admits that she acted "outside the accepted standards of medical care."[348]

---

[339] See § **1A.5** in this supplement.

[340] *Special Prosecutor Will Take Physician to Trial,* Associated Press, Dec. 4, 1998.

[341] *Charge Dropped in Washington Baby Death,* Associated Press, Feb. 1, 1999.

[342] Clare Dyer, *GP on Trial for Murder,* 318 Brit. Med. J. 1095 (1999).

[343] Paul Wilkinson, *Cheers as GP Is Cleared of Murdering Patient,* Times, May 12, 1999, at ___.

[344] *Murder Case GP "Said He Helped 300 Patients Die,"* Daily Telegraph, Apr. 17, 1999, at 17.

[345] *Id.*

[346] *Prosecutor Drops Case Against Doctor,* UPI, Dec. 11, 1998.

[347] *Nova Scotia Doctor Gets Reprimand,* UPI, Mar. 3, 1999.

[348] *"Remorseful" Doctor Admits Hastening Death was Wrong, Lethal Injection Was Mistake,* National Post, Mar. 31, 1999, at ___.

Prosecutions of Laypersons.   It appears that there is a greater number of investigations and prosecutions of laypersons for assisted suicide and mercy killing than of health care professionals. Health care professionals, especially physicians, are better able to conceal their role in ending a terminally ill person's life or to pass it off as the consequence of medications used for the treatment of pain. Laypersons—usually close family members—of necessity sometimes resort to more violent means of ending life, are not able to sign death certificates, and are not as easily able to obtain prescription medications.

There do not appear to be any reported American appellate cases involving assisted suicide or mercy killing by laypersons. However, news accounts seem to occur at least weekly around the country, ranging from a veterinarian in New York City who administered a lethal dose of medication to a friend dying of cancer[349] to a man who shot his wife whom he believed to be dying of cancer.[350] In a well-publicized Canadian case, the Saskatchewan Supreme Court overturned the 2-year prison sentence of Robert Latimer for the mercy killing of his 12-year-old daughter, and imposed instead a life sentence with no chance of parole for 10 years.[351]

Civil Legislation to Prevent Assisted Suicide.   Two more states— Maryland and North Dakota—have joined the three that already have civil legislation that attempts to deter assisted suicide through injunctive relief and the imposition of professional discipline if the aiding party is a health care professional.[352]

Futility

There have been two notable futility cases in the last year. One is a reported case; the other is still at the trial level. In *Causey v. St. Francis Medical Center,*[353] the Louisiana Court of Appeals held that physicians have no obligation to provide treatment that is "medically inappropriate."[354]

In the unreported case, the patient, Shirron Lewis, at the time of trial in May 1999, was a 20-month-old boy who was said to be in a persistent vegetative state, allegedly as a result of being beaten by his father, who was

---

[349] Randy Kennedy, *Veterinarian Is Charged in His Receptionist's Assisted Suicide,* N.Y. Times, Oct. 15, 1998, at A27 (nat'l ed.).

[350] *Autopsy Finds No Cancer in Woman Shot by Husband,* N.Y. Times, Feb. 9, 1999, at A15 (nat'l ed.).

[351] Anthony DePalma, *Light Sentence in Mercy Death Is Overturned in West Canada,* N.Y. Times, Nov. 24, 1998, at A8 (nat'l ed.).

[352] See § **18.26** in this supplement.

[353] 719 So. 2d 1072 (La. Ct. App. 1998).

[354] *Id.* at 1075, discussed in § **19.2** in this supplement.

imprisoned awaiting trial on a charge of attempted murder for having shaken the boy violently enough to cause the injuries. The hospital and child welfare authorities sought to remove life support, but both parents resisted the recommendation, purportedly for religious reasons.[355] The only similar reported case is *Tabatha R. v. Ronda R.*,[356] in which the Nebraska Supreme Court reversed and remanded the trial court's order, authorizing the termination of life support under virtually identical circumstances, for a new hearing according appropriate due process, because the termination of life support would be tantamount to a termination of parental rights.

Civil Liability

There have been a relatively large, though still small in absolute terms, number of cases attempting to recover damages for the administration of life-sustaining medical treatment refused by the patient or the patient's surrogate.[357] Although the results are mixed, the important point to be extracted from these cases, which are probably the tip of an iceberg, is that there seems to be a continuing reluctance on the part of physicians to honor advance directives and the requests of competent patients to refuse treatment.

---

[355] Jennifer Brown, *Judge Ruling on Boy's Life Support*, Pittsburgh Post-Gazette, May 26, 1999, at B6; Rachel Scheier, *Battle Over Boy's Life Support Has Court on Ethical Cutting Edge*, Philadelphia Inquirer, May 25, 1999, at Al.

[356] 564 N.W.2d 598 (Neb. 1997), discussed in § **19.2** of this supplement.

[357] **CA:** Duarte v. Chino Community Hosp., 85 Cal. Rptr. 2d 521 (Ct. App. 1999) (holding statutory immunity conferred by California health care power of attorney statute applies to decision made by surrogate not appointed pursuant to a health care power of attorney), discussed in § **17.24** in this supplement.

  IL: Gragg v. Calandra, 696 N.E.2d 1282 (Ill. App. Ct. 1998) (holding cause of action stated for intentional infliction of emotional distress for nonconsensual treatment arising from failure to honor living will), discussed in § **1A.8** in this supplement.

  MA: *In re* Shine v. Vega, 709 N.E.2d 58 (Mass. 1999) (reinstating causes of action based on failing to honor request of allegedly competent patient not to be intubated), discussed in § **17.16** in this supplement.

  MD: Wright v. Johns Hopkins Health Sys. Corp., 728 A.2d 166 (Md. 1999) (affirming dismissal of claims for unauthorized resuscitation of patient), discussed in §§ **9.6** and **17.19** in this supplement.

  TX: Stolle v. Baylor College of Med., 981 S.W.2d 709 (Tex. Ct. App. 1998) (affirming dismissal of claims for unauthorized resuscitation of handicapped newborn infant), discussed in § **17.24.**

  WA: Branom v. State, 974 P.2d 335 (Wash. Ct. App. 1999) (affirming dismissal of claims for failure to obtain informed consent and for negligent infliction of emotional distress arising out of treatment provided to handicapped newborn infant against parents' wishes), discussed in § **1A.8** in this supplement.

Intractable Pain Legislation

Three more states—Arkansas, Maryland, and New Mexico—have enacted statutes intended to encourage physicians to treat the intractable pain of the terminally ill without being deterred by the threat of legal penalties if the pain medication contributes to the patient's death.[358] Whether these statutes will accomplish their goal, however, is open to significant question.[359]

DNR Legislation

Two additional states (Indiana and Louisiana) enacted DNR legislation, and five others (Florida, Nevada, Oklahoma, Texas, and Virginia) amended existing legislation.[360]

Advance Directive Legislation

There was not a great deal of legislation concerning advance directives in 1998–1999. A few states (Arkansas, Hawaii, Michigan, Minnesota, and Texas) enacted amendments—sometimes entirely replacing the statute—to their existing statutes.[361]

Mental Health Advance Directives.   Over the past few years, a number of states have adopted "mental health advance directives," which are statutes permitting individuals to make an advance directive concerning what kind of mental health treatment they wish to have if they subsequently become mentally ill and unable to make decisions about their treatment at that time. **Section 12.29A** of this supplement discusses these statutes.

§ 1A.8   Jurisdiction-by-Jurisdiction Developments in 1998–1999

Arkansas

Statutes

1999 Ark. H.B. 1298, Act 394 of 1999, § 1(D) (assisted suicide; intractable pain).

---

[358] See **Table 9-1A** in this supplement.
[359] See § **9.38** in this supplement.
[360] See § **9.8** *et seq.* in this supplement.
[361] See **chs. 11** and **12** in this supplement.

1999 Ark. Acts 1448 (health care power of attorney).

California

Cases

Duarte v. Chino Community Hospital, 85 Cal. Rptr. 2d 521 (Ct. App.), *review denied* (Sept. 1, 1999).

Duarte holds that the statutory immunity conferred by the California health care power of attorney statute applies to a decision made by a surrogate not appointed pursuant to a health care power of attorney. This case is discussed in § **17.24** in this supplement.

Florida

Statutes

Fla. Stat. Ann. § 401.45(5)(c) (DNR, advance directives, surrogate decision-making amendments).

Hawaii

Statutes

1999 Haw. Sess. Laws 169 (advance directives).

Illinois

Cases

Gragg v. Calandra[362] is a case that spiraled out of control. Surgeons first performed surgery on the patient, alleged by his daughter to be nonconsensual, and then continued to provide life support and to refuse to honor the patient's living will. In the process, the defendants are alleged to have repeatedly accused the patient's wife and daughter, in a public area in the presence of others, of trying to kill the patient by requesting the termination of life support.

The court held that the trial court erred in dismissing the plaintiff's count for intentional infliction of emotional distress; under these facts, "there was a high probability that severe emotional distress would follow, but defendants consciously disregarded it."[363]

---

[362] 696 N.E.2d 1282 (Ill. App. Ct. 1998).

[363] *Id.* at 1289.

Indiana

Statutes

Ind. Code Ann. §§ 16-36-5, added by 1999 Ind. Acts 262 (DNR).

Iowa

Cases

Polk County Sheriff v. Iowa District Court[364] held that a pretrial detainee suffering from kidney failure could not refuse life-saving kidney dialysis. Although recognizing a qualified liberty interest in refusing treatment, the court held that this interest was overcome by the combined weight of several countervailing state interests: namely, the state interest in the preservation of life when life can be saved; the interest in the protection of minor children; the interest in the ethical integrity of the medical profession; and, most notably, the state's interest in maintaining prison security, order, and discipline. The opinion was strongly deferential to and was heavily influenced by testimony of the jailer and the sheriff who transported the prisoner from jail to the hospital for dialysis, that

> Brown's refusal of medical treatment would require more staff supervision for Brown than for other inmates suffering, for example, from a contagious disease or mental illness. The staff would have to watch Brown closely for signs that he was going into cardiac arrest so they could rush him to the hospital. To the chief jailer, this was in his language, a "big, big" concern in light of his duty to provide medical care to every inmate.[365]

Kansas

Statutes

1997 Kan. Sess. Laws, H.B. 2531 (assisted suicide).

Cases

State v. Naramore[366] is a ground-breaking case but has received relatively little attention. It is only the second officially reported prosecution of a physician in connection with end-of-life medical treatment, coming some 15

---

[364] 594 N.W.2d 421 (Iowa 1999).

[365] *Id.* at 431.

[366] 965 P.2d 211 (Kan. Ct. App.1998).

years after the first,[367] Dr. Naramore was charged with crimes in two different cases. The Willt case, in which he was convicted of second-degree murder, is the more conventional of the two. In fact, in some respects it is more closely akin to a case of criminal negligence than murder. The other case, the Leach case in which Dr. Naramore was convicted of attempted murder, is far more significant because it involved an issue that is in the forefront of contemporary end-of-life discussions—the administration of medications for the relief of severe pain suffered by terminally ill patients.

Naramore was sentenced to concurrent terms of 5 to 20 years. Both convictions were reversed by the Court of Appeals of Kansas, though not before he had spent some time in prison, on the ground that the jury ignored "strong evidence" from "an impressive array of apparently objective medical experts, who found the defendant's actions to be not only noncriminal, but medically appropriate."[368]

The Willt Case. In the Willt case, Dr. Naramore was called to the hospital to attend to an elderly, unconscious man who had been brought to the emergency room. He attended to the man for more than three hours, trying to diagnose and treat his condition or the interaction of several conditions. Mr. Willt's condition was very grim. Dr. Naramore told the hospital administrator (Mr. White) that he thought the patient "was 'brain dead' and wanted White's opinion on removing life support. White told Dr. Naramore that if Mr. Willt was 'brain dead' and if he had a second opinion from a neurologist, then life support could be withdrawn."[369] Dr. Naramore and the hospital's administrator advised the patient's brother of the situation. The brother conferred with his minister and another family member and decided that the patient "would not want to be maintained artificially."[370]

For the next hour or so the situation was uncertain. There was some evidence that the patient was improving, but it was ambiguous and Dr. Naramore thought that what others perceived as signs of improvement were actually seizure activity. He got another doctor to give an opinion, who concluded that Mr. Willt was "gone" and that further treatment was "kind of like beating a dead horse."[371] Shortly afterward, mechanical ventilation was stopped, and the cardiac monitor showed only pacemaker activity. Six minutes later, there was no spontaneous neurological activity, no respiratory activity, and no cardiac activity. Mr. Willt was then pronounced dead.

Dr. Naramore was charged with "intentional and malicious second-degree murder" in connection with the Willt case. In effect, his judgment that Mr.

---

[367] *See* Barber v. Superior Court, 195 Cal. Rptr. 484 (Ct. App. 1983), discussed in § **18.9** *et seq.* in the main volume.

[368] 965 P.2d at 224.

[369] *Id.* at 216.

[370] *Id.* at 217.

[371] *Id.* at 217.

Willt had suffered a lethal stroke and the way he tried to deal with Willt's condition, complicated by the patient's heart disease and diabetes and the patient's neglect of both of them, were questioned by the prosecution. Based on the medical evidence, there was substantial question about whether Dr. Naramore handled the situation properly or improperly, which created more than enough reasonable doubt to lead to reversal of the criminal conviction. If anything, there was medical negligence, but that was not established by this criminal case.

It is likely that Dr. Naramore was subjected to criminal prosecution in connection with Mr. Willt's death for two reasons. One is the facts of the companion Leach case. The other, perhaps, is some of the nonmedical facts of the case. Although the court made no comment on these facts, there are two or three facts in this case that make Dr. Naramore's conduct look worse than it might really have been. The first is the overly facile, imprecise, and incorrect way in which he used the term "brain dead" to describe Mr. Willt. The second is his turning to the hospital administrator for advice on whether to terminate medical efforts. Another is the language used, not by Dr. Naramore, but by the consulting physician, that further treatment would be "like beating a dead horse." The lesson to be taken away, perhaps, is the importance of acting in as professional a manner as possible; that appearances are just as important as substance in treating patients.

The Leach Case. Mrs. Leach was a 78-year-old woman who had been suffering from cancer for a number of years. In her second or third month of hospitalization, during a visit by a few family members, a nurse told the family that the morphine patches used for pain medication seemed no longer to be adequate. What transpired thereafter is worth quoting at length.

> [The nurse] suggested calling Dr. Naramore to prescribe a stronger dose of pain medication. Dr. Naramore came to the hospital and examined Mrs. Leach. She told him she felt terrible. Dr. Naramore and the Leach family went to the hospital chapel where they could have some privacy.
>
> Dr. Naramore asked the family what they wanted to do, and Jim said he wanted his mother to have more painkillers. Dr. Naramore explained that when extra pain medication is given to a patient in Mrs. Leach's condition, it slows respiration and there is a real danger the patient can die. Mrs. Leach had developed a relatively high level of tolerance for pain medication by that time. The family discussed Mrs. Leach's living will and her desire to have no heroic measures taken to save her life, and then told Dr. Naramore to give her more pain medication.
>
> * * *
>
> Dr. Naramore gave Mrs. Leach a 4-milligram shot of Versed, a painkiller, and [5 minutes later], he gave her a 100-micromilligram shot of Fentanyl, an anesthetic. Jim [her son, who was an emergency medical technician] testified his mother's respiration slowed to a very low level. He thought she was close to death. Jim testified Dr. Naramore asked everyone to hold hands, and he

recited a poem by Robert Frost called "Into the Woods." He told them he could reverse the effects of the pain medication by giving a drug called Narcan. Jim believed Dr. Naramore had given Mrs. Leach an overdose and asked the family, "Aren't we going to reverse it?" No one answered.

At this point, Dr. Naramore prepared a syringe of morphine. Jim told him to not give his mother any more medication because he thought the injection would kill her. Bizer [a nurse] testified Dr. Naramore stated, "I'm not going to give her any more, we can reverse these effects by giving her Narcan."

Jim and Dr. Naramore went into the hallway. Jim told Dr. Naramore he was giving his mother too much medication. Jim said "Let me make one thing perfectly clear: I'd rather my mother lay there and suffer for ten more days than you do anything to speed up her death." Jim testified that Dr. Naramore told him that "it just gets terrible from here on out," and "[t]he next few days for her are just going to be absolutely terrible." Dr. Naramore complied with Jim's request to give Mrs. Leach minute amounts of morphine, and he set up an IV for a slow drip of morphine.

Dr. Naramore asked Jim, "If I continue to treat your mother, will you hold me responsible if anything happens to her?" Jim replied with a very emphatic, "Yes, I will." Dr. Naramore did not want to be further involved in the case. Jim had Mrs. Leach transported to a hospital in Goodland, Kansas, the next morning. She was given morphine injections at the Goodland hospital. She died a couple of days later, presumably from the course of the cancer.[372]

Dr. Naramore was charged with and convicted of attempted murder as a result of these events. The Kansas Medical Society and the Kansas Osteopathic Association filed extremely influential amicus curiae briefs from which the court quoted approvingly at great length. These briefs brought to the court's attention contemporary thinking about the need for palliative care for terminally ill patients suffering from great pain, the need to use pain relief medications without fear that they might inadvertently hasten the patient's death, and the fear that doctors in fact have of adverse legal consequences in such situations. However, what ultimately led to the reversal of Dr. Naramore's conviction was the significant medical testimony that what he had done was acceptable medical practice and thus the jury could not have found him guilty beyond a reasonable doubt. Although reversing on conventional evidentiary grounds and not writing a particularly expansive opinion, the case should prove somewhat helpful in further establishing the importance of the doctrine of double effect in the legal analysis of end-of-life decisionmaking.[373] Unfortunately, the lesson that physicians may take away from this case is that they risk criminal prosecution if they use large doses of pain relief medications, especially as there was not even an allegation that what Dr. Naramore did actually shortened the patient's life. After all, he was

---

[372] *Id.* at 213, 215.

[373] See § **8.7** in the main volume and this supplement.

charged only with attempted murder for administering pain relief medications, not for murder. Had the court cited the discussion of double effect and the need for adequate palliative care in the United States Supreme Court's *Vacco* decision,[374] it might have helped to neutralize this potential consequence of the Naramore prosecution.

Louisiana

Statutes

S.B. 209, 1999 Reg. Sess. (La. 1999), *codified at* La. Rev. Stat. Ann. §§ 40:1299.58.2, .58.3, and .58.7-10 (DNR).

Cases

Causey v. St. Francis Medical Center, 719 So. 2d 1072 (La. Ct. App. 1998). This futility case is summarized in § **19.2** in this supplement.

Maine

Statutes

H.P. 797, 119 Leg., 1st Reg. Sess. (Me. 1999) (surrogate decisionmaking amendments).

Cases

In re Nikolas E.[375] is not a case involving the refusal of life-sustaining medical treatment, but it does raise closely related issues. The patient, Nikolas, was a four-year-old child infected with the HIV virus. His sister had previously died from HIV. Both presumably had been infected at birth by their mother. Their family physician referred Nikolas to an infectious disease specialist for an evaluation to determine whether he should be entered into a clinical trial using a "highly aggressive" form of experimental treatment. The mother had the child seen by this physician, but declined the recommended treatment; "Based upon developments in her own illness and her experience with the drug therapy that accompanied the tragic and painful death of her daughter, the mother expressed her distrust of the drug therapy and declined to permit her son to participate at that time."[376]

---

[374] Vacco v. Quill, 117 S. Ct. 2293 (1997).

[375] 720 A.2d 562 (Me. 1998).

[376] *Id.* at 563.

After the mother's refusal, the infectious disease specialist wrote a report to Nikolas's family physician and sent a copy to the state child protective services agency, because he believed that the mother's refusal of the experimental treatment constituted child neglect. The state arranged for a consultation with another specialist, who thought that the child might benefit from the treatment but could not provide an estimate of how much benefit or how much the treatment might extend his life. He also believed "'that no child should be started on this program unless his parents are fully accepting and in support of the treatment.'"[377]

Thereafter, the state filed a petition for a child protection order, and "sought custody of Nikolas for the limited purpose of approving medical treatment for his HIV condition."[378] The trial court denied the petition, the guardian ad litem appealed, and the supreme court affirmed. The mother's decision to "'wait and see' if Nikolas's health began to deteriorate significantly before accepting treatment"[379] combined with the fact that the refusal of treatment would not lead to "an imminent t[h]reat of serious harm," meant that the mother's decision to delay treatment of AIDS did not constitute neglect. However, the court added that "[i]f the child's health should change, if the treatment efficacy should be demonstrated to be better than it is now known to be, or if better treatment options should become available, that balance could shift in favor of treatment."[380]

Maryland

Statutes

1999 Md. H.B. 496 (effective Oct. 1, 1999), to be codified as Md. Code Ann., Crimes and Punishments, art. 27, § 416 (assisted suicide; intractable pain).

Cases

Wright v. Johns Hopkins Health Systems Corporation[381] was a suit for damages against a hospital for resuscitation of a patient without his consent. The court affirmed the summary judgment for the defendants. This case is discussed in §§ **9.6** and **17.19** in this supplement.

---

[377] *Id*. at 564.

[378] *Id*. at 563.

[379] *Id*. at 567.

[380] *Id*. at 568.

[381] 728 A.2d 166 (Md. 1999).

Massachusetts

Cases

In re Rena[382] raises the issue of the refusal of a blood transfusion by a 17-year-old Jehovah's Witness who may be a mature minor, and by her parents on her behalf. The patient had lacerated her spleen in a snowboarding accident, giving rise to the need for the transfusion. She had "periodically executed a written medical directive" stating her refusal to have a blood transfusion, and had last reexecuted this document less than a month before the current issue arose. There was no question that she understood the possible life-threatening consequences of this refusal.

The patient and her parents reiterated their refusal when the blood transfusion was proposed, and the hospital sought to obtain a court order to administer the transfusion if it became medically necessary to do so. After a hearing, the trial court issued the order. On appeal, the case was dismissed as moot, the patient having been released from the hospital. Whether she received the transfusion or not is unclear from the case report.

What is significant is that the court accepted the mature minor doctrine.[383] Had the case not been moot, the court clearly would have remanded to the trial court for a finding on whether the patient was a mature minor, that is, whether she had the "maturity to make an informed choice."[384] The court also admonished the trial court for not taking the patient's own testimony in order to make a determination of what was in her best interests, and, following Massachusetts' idiosyncratic precedents,[385] set forth the test for determining best interests.[386]

In re Shine v. Vega[387] makes a rather novel claim for liability. This case is discussed in § **17.16** in this supplement.

---

[382] 705 N.E.2d 1155 (Mass. App. Ct. 1999).

[383] See § **15.3** in the main volume and this supplement.

[384] 705 N.E.2d at 1157.

[385] *See In re* Beth, 587 N.E.2d 1377 (Mass. 1992). See § **7.3** in the main volume.

[386] 705 N.E.2d at 1157:

The best interests of a child are determined by applying the same criteria applicable in substituted judgment cases, namely (1) the patient's expressed preferences, if any; (2) the patient's religious convictions, if any; (3) the impact on the patient's family; (4) the probability of adverse side effects from the treatment; (5) the prognosis without treatment; and (6) the present and future incompetency of the patient in making that decision.

[387] 709 N.E.2d 58 (Mass. 1999).

Michigan

Statutes

Mich. Comp. Laws Ann. §§ 333.16204c, 333.21052, 500.1402, 500.2212 (intractable pain).
Mich. Comp. Laws Ann. § 750.329a (assisted suicide).
Mich. Comp. Laws Ann. §§ 333.1051–.1067.
Mich. Comp. Laws § 700.496 (health care power of attorney).
Mich. Comp. Laws § 700.5501–.5513 (health care power of attorney).

Minnesota

Statutes

1999 Minn S.B. 301, 81st Reg. Sess. (living will; health care power of attorney).

Mississippi

Statutes

H.B. 865, 1999 Reg. Sess. (Miss. 1999) (surrogate decisionmaking amendments).

Nevada

Statutes

1999 Nev. A.B. 73, 70th Reg. Sess. (DNR amendments).

New Mexico

Statutes

1999 N.M. S.B. 343 (intractable pain).

New York

Cases

In re Christopher[388] illustrates how New York's theoretically stringent subjective standard for decisionmaking for incompetent patients can be applied in a manner looser than probably envisioned by the New York Court of Appeals. This case is discussed in § **7.5** in this supplement.

In re Lowe[389] was an action by the wife of an incompetent patient, who had previously appointed her as his proxy under a health care power of attorney, to be appointed her husband's guardian for the purpose of appointing a successor proxy to replace a successor proxy who had died. The court held that it did not have the authority to appoint a guardian for an individual who had already appointed a proxy, because "a guardian should be appointed only as a last resort, and should not be imposed if available resources or other alternatives will adequately protect the person."[390] Furthermore, even if it did have the authority to appoint a guardian, the guardian would not have the authority to appoint a successor proxy because "the selection of a health care agent is a strictly personal decision, which can only be made by the competent principal himself."[391]

Oklahoma

Statutes

Public Health and Safety Assisted Suicide Prevention Act, ch. 194, 1998 Okla. Sess. Law Serv., S.B. 1243 (to be codified as Okla. Stat. Ann. tit. 63, §§ 3141.1–.8) (assisted suicide).
H.B. 1381, 47th Leg., 1st Sess. (Okla. 1999) (DNR amendments).

Texas

Statutes

1999 Tex. S.B. 1260 (DNR, living will, health care power of attorney, surrogate decisionmaking).

---

[388] 675 N.Y.S.2d 807 (Sup. Ct. Queens County 1998).
[389] 688 N.Y.S.2d 389 (Sup. Ct. Queens County 1999).
[390] 688 N.Y.S.2d at 390.
[391] *Id.* at 391.

NEW DEVELOPMENTS

Cases

Stolle v. Baylor College of Medicine[392] was an action by the parents of a handicapped newborn infant to impose liability for resuscitation of the child in violation of the parents' directions to withhold life-sustaining medical treatment. The court affirmed the trial court's dismissal on the basis of the immunity provision of the state living will statute. This case is discussed in § **17.24** in this supplement.

Virginia

Statutes

1998 Va. Acts H.B. 1378, to be codified as Va. Code Ann. § 8.01-622.1 (assisted suicide).
1998 Va. S.B. 1299, to be codified as Va. Code Ann. §§ 38.2-4214, 38.2-4319, 38.2-3407.11:1 (intractable pain).
1999 Va. Acts 814, to be codified as Va. Code Ann. §§ 37.1-134.21, 54.1-2901, 54.1-2982, 54.1-2984, 54.1-2986, 54.1-2987.1, 54.1-2988, 54.1-2990 (amendments to living wills, health care powers of attorney, surrogate decisionmaking, DNR).

Washington

Cases

Branom v. State[393] raises interesting issues concerning medical decisionmaking for infants, but provides a rather mechanistic solution based primarily on the Washington medical malpractice statute.

The Branoms' baby was born with a bowel obstruction and an abnormally small head (microcephaly), indicating probable mental defects. He was transferred shortly after birth to another hospital to have surgery performed to relieve the life-threatening bowel obstruction. The parents alleged that the neonatologist who explained the surgery to them and obtained their consent failed to inform them of the baby's microcephaly (which the defendants disputed); had they been told, they claimed they would have opted not to have the surgery and would have allowed the baby to die.

The parents sued the hospital and neonatologist on a number of theories, but on appeal from the summary judgment entered against them, the parents pursued only claims of informed consent and negligent infliction of emo-

---

[392] 981 S.W.2d 709 (Tex. Ct. App. 1998).
[393] 974 P.2d 335 (Wash. Ct. App. 1999).

92

tional distress. On the informed consent claim, the court affirmed the dismissal, because the doctor was held to owe a duty to parents to obtain informed consent for treatment of their child only in their capacity as the child's representatives and not as parents qua parents, and the action before the court was brought in their own right. The dismissal of the negligent infliction of emotional distress claim was also affirmed, on the basis that the Washington statute authorizing causes of action growing out of the provision of health care does not authorize such claims, and that in any event such a claim requires that the plaintiffs (i.e., the parents) themselves have been placed in peril by the defendants' conduct, which they were not.

Perhaps the most interesting aspect of this case is an issue lurking in the background but not mentioned in the case: the effect, if any, of the Child Abuse Amendments.[394] This would appear to be a classic example of medical neglect for not providing treatment under the Child Abuse Amendments. However, the case makes absolutely no mention of this matter.

§ 1A.9   Overview of 1999–2000 Developments

Physician-Assisted Suicide

Physician-assisted suicide and euthanasia seemed to create the most headlines of all the end-of-life issues in 1999 and early 2000. In the United States courts, the Alaska Supreme Court agreed to hear an appeal of a decision by the Superior Court of Alaska in *Sampson v. Alaska*,[395] and a retired judge in Colorado asserted a unique First Amendment argument in an attempt to invalidate that state's statute criminalizing suicide assistance.[396]

Additionally, instances of assisted suicide made headlines across the world, and the issue arose for legislative and other governmental consideration in many jurisdictions.

Developments in Oregon.   In February 2000, the Oregon Health Division released its second annual report on deaths occurring pursuant to the Oregon Death With Dignity Act. According to the report, in 1999, 33 persons received prescriptions for lethal medications pursuant to the statute. Of those, 26 died after taking the medications prescribed, five died from their underlying illnesses, and two were alive as of January 1, 2000.[397]

---

[394] See § **16.9** *et seq.* in the main volume.

[395] See §§ **1A.7** and **1A.10** of this supplement.

[396] Sanderson v. State, No. 99CA0203, 2000 WL 729008 (Colo. Ct. App. June 8, 2000). See § **18.22** of this supplement.

[397] Amy D. Sullivan, et al., *Legalized Physician-Assisted Suicide in Oregon—The Second Year*, 342 New Eng. J. Med. 598 (2000).

Once again, the reasons patients give for their requests seem to contradict previously expressed concerns about pressures being brought to bear on them. Those who used their prescriptions to end their lives generally were better educated than, but otherwise demographically similar to, residents of Oregon with similar diseases who had died in 1998. All had insurance for most medical expenses, with the exception of some, such as the cost of prescriptions. They most frequently cited concern about loss of control and autonomy as motivating their decisions. There was an increase, as compared to 1998, in the percentage of patients who were concerned about inadequate pain control, but in fact palliative care was available to all patients who had requested suicide assistance. Three-quarters of them received hospice care before they died.

Federal Legislation. Efforts in Congress to override the Oregon Death With Dignity Act continued as the proposed Pain Relief Promotion Act[398] passed the House of Representatives and the Senate Judiciary Committee but then stalled in the Senate. After securing amendments at the Senate committee level,[399] and despite some opposition raised by Oregon physicians, the American Medical Association backed the measure.[400] The Board of the American Academy of Pharmaceutical Physicians, however, voted to oppose it.[401]

Oregon's U.S. senators are split on the bill, which would subject to federal prosecution physicians prescribing federally controlled substances to patients to use in causing their own deaths pursuant to the Oregon Death With Dignity Act.[402] The Oregon Health Division has indicated that it would refuse to disclose to federal drug investigators the suicide reports it collects pursuant to the law, which serve as the basis for its annual report on the practice of physician-assisted suicide in Oregon.[403]

Maine. At the time this supplement went to press, Maine voters were slated to consider a statute that would legalize physician-assisted suicide. Researchers should check that state's law for possible changes in light of that vote.

---

[398] *See* Pain Relief Promotion Act of 1999, H.R. 2260, 106th Cong., 1st Sess. (1999); S. 1272, 106th Cong., 1st Sess. (1999). *See also* S. Rep. 106-299, 106th Cong., 2d Sess. (2000) (amending proposed H.R. 2260).

[399] *See* Vida Foubister, *AMA Secures Changes to Anti-Suicide Bill*, Am. Med. News, Apr. 24, 2000, <http://www.ama-assn.org/sci-pubs/amnews/pick_00/gvsa0424.htm>.

[400] *See* Ben Fox, *Assisted Suicide on Doctor's Agenda*, Associated Press, Dec. 8, 1999.

[401] *See* AAPP Opposes Hyde-Nickels Pain Relief Promotion Act Bill; Misguided Act Will Actually Deprive Patients of Pain Relief, PR Newswire, Apr. 27, 2000.

[402] *See* John Hughes, *After Months of Indecision, Smith Backs Anti-Suicide Bill*, Associated Press, Apr. 25, 2000.

[403] *See State Says Suicide Records Off Limits to DEA*, Associated Press, Nov. 25, 1999.

Legislative Activity in Other Countries.   Several other countries this year saw some movement toward legislation addressing physician-assisted suicide or euthanasia. In the Netherlands, the Dutch parliament was set to consider a bill that explicitly would legalize voluntary euthanasia, thus instituting positive legal recognition of a practice that has occurred without prosecution there as long as physicians adhered to certain guidelines.[404] France and Belgium similarly were considering lifting their bans on euthanasia in certain cases.[405] In Australia, despite the repeal of the Northern Territory law legalizing physician-assisted suicide,[406] Dr. Philip Nitschke has established and is operating a number of "voluntary euthanasia clinics," reportedly without prosecution at the time of this writing.[407]

Conversely, Azerbaijan's new draft Criminal Code will punish "euthanasia" by three years' imprisonment.[408] The exact scope of the act is currently unclear, as it apparently defines "euthanasia" as "accelerating the death of a patient at his own request or halting the artificial maintenance of life."[409] This definition would, of course, encompass within the term "euthanasia" some activity that is more properly understood as withholding or withdrawing life-sustaining treatment.[410] Similar terminological confusion could be seen in Taiwan, where news reports indicated that the parliament had passed a draft bill "on euthanasia," but also described the bill as permitting a terminally ill patient to refuse life-prolonging intervention and instead to die naturally.[411]

High-Profile Cases of Refusal of Treatment

At least three cases of refusal of life-sustaining treatment in the United States this year have generated numerous headlines, even if they have not resulted in reported court opinions.

---

[404] *See* Richard H. Nicholson, *No Painless Death Yet for European Euthanasia Debate*, Hastings Center Report 7, May-June 2000; Anthony Deutsch, *Dutch Debate Legalized Euthanasia*, Associated Press, Sept. 24, 1999.

[405] *Id.*

[406] See § **18.24.**

[407] *See* Anne Barbeliuk, *State Okays Death Clinics*, The Mercury, Mar. 16, 2000 (Tasmania); Paul Starick, *Euthanasia Clinics 'Up to Police'*, The Advertiser, Aug. 11, 1999 (Adelaide); *First Euthanasia Clinic Now Held,* The VE Bulletin, July 1999, available at <http://www.on.net/clients/saves/cclinc.htm>. *See generally* Nadia Miraudo, *Euthanasia Is Illegal but One in Three Doctors Has Granted a Terminally Ill Person's Wish to Die*, West Australian Sunday Times, May 28, 2000; Victoria Button, *Nitschke Patients Commit Suicide*, The Age (Melbourne), Nov. 20, 1999.

[408] *Euthanasia to be Criminal Offence in Azerbaijan*, BBC News, Dec. 23, 1999.

[409] *Id.*

[410] See generally §§ **18.1, 18.3, 18.11.**

[411] *See Euthanasia Bill Passes First Stage*, Deliverance News Service, May 23, 2000.

Florida. In St. Petersburg, Florida, the husband and parents of a comatose 36-year-old woman went to court over the husband's desire to withdraw his wife's feeding tube.[412] The trial court granted the husband's request, but ordered that the tube not be removed until 30 days after exhaustion of her parents' appeals. The publicity generated by the case, however, prompted the nursing home in which the woman was a patient first to ask that she be moved and then to post security guards.[413] Later, the patient's husband attempted to move his wife to a hospice pending the outcome of her parents' appeals, but her parents opposed that move.[414] The case is on appeal.

New York. Two cities in upstate New York, Rochester and Syracuse, also saw a great deal of media coverage of refusal of treatment decisions this year. In Rochester, Bill White, a quadriplegic who had been on a ventilator for 32 years, succeeded in his quest to have the ventilator removed despite activists' protests and trips to court to attempt to block the hospital from carrying out his wishes.[415] And in Syracuse, the family of Sylvia Pouliot, who had been in a vegetative state since suffering from mumps at the age of nine months, won the right to withdraw her nutrition and hydration from a trial court judge despite opposition from the state attorney general. Ms. Pouliot died before the state appellate court could consider the attorney general's appeal of the decision.[416]

Prosecutions for Assisted Suicide and Mercy Killing

Prosecutions of both health care professionals and laypersons for assisted suicide and mercy killing continue. Some of the more notable are highlighted below.

Health Care Professionals. *New Mexico.* George Reding, a retired psychiatrist who has in the past assisted Jack Kevorkian in assisted suicides, has been charged with murder and has been sued for malpractice in the death of a 54-year-old multiple sclerosis patient.[417]

---

[412] *See Parents, Husband Battling Over Life of Comatose Woman*, Sun-Sentinel, Jan. 26, 2000.

[413] Lynn Porter, *Largo Nursing Home Agrees Not to Evict Comatose Woman*, The Tampa Tribune at 9, Mar. 3, 2000; Anita Kumar, *Publicity Leads Nursing Home to Evict Mrs. Schiavo*, St. Petersburg Times, at 1A, Feb. 25, 2000.

[414] Anita Kumar, *Parents Oppose Care at Hospice*, St. Petersburg Times, Apr. 25, 2000.

[415] *See* Patrick Flanigan, *Disabled Patient Dies on His Terms*, The Rochester News, Aug. 14, 1999.

[416] Jim O'Hara, *Right-to-Die Case ends: Sheila Pouliot Died Before a State Appeals Court Could Consider Her Case,* The Post-Standard at B1, Mar. 8, 2000.

[417] Jeremy Pawloski, *Dead Woman's Family Sues Reding*, Albuquerque Journal, Sept. 8, 1999; Brian Ballou, *Kevorkian's Aide Eludes Cops and FBI*, Detroit Free Press, Sept. 23, 1999.

Utah.   A psychiatrist was convicted of manslaughter and negligent homicide for prescribing fatal doses of morphine to five elderly patients.[418]

Australia.   In Australia's first criminal case linked to euthanasia, a urologist was charged with wilful murder after allegedly administering lethal medications to Freeda Hays, a 48-year-old kidney cancer patient.[419] The patient's brother and sister were also charged because they allegedly were present at the time the drugs were administered.[420]

Norway.   The Supreme Court of Norway upheld the murder conviction of the first Norwegian doctor tried for euthanasia. The retired physician gave a lethal dose of morphine to a multiple sclerosis patient and then demanded that he be tried. He was convicted of first-degree murder, but sentence was withheld.[421]

Laypersons. *Canada.*   The Supreme Court of Canada heard arguments regarding the sentence imposed in the case of Robert Latimer, who was twice convicted of killing his daughter, who had severe cerebral palsy, in 1993.[422] Latimer had argued that he killed his daughter to spare her from pain and from an upcoming operation, which he and his wife believed would worsen her pain. A Saskatchewan appellate court had ruled that he must serve the mandatory life sentence with no chance of parole for 10 years for second-degree murder. His lawyers argued that the trial court, which imposed a two-year sentence, one year of which was to be served in jail, had properly granted him a constitutional exemption to the mandatory sentence.[423] A decision was expected in early 2001.[424]

Licensure Proceeding for Mercy Killing

In *Gallant v. Board of Medical Examiners*, a court affirmed action taken by the Oregon Board of Medical Examiners to discipline a physician for

---

[418] *Doctor Convicted in Drug Deaths*, Associated Press, July 11, 2000.

[419] David Reardon, *Family to Face Interview Over 'Mercy Killing'*, Sydney Morning Herald, Apr. 8, 2000.

[420] Les Kennedy, *Two Accused of Wilful Murder for Sister's Hospice Death*, Sydney Morning Herald, Apr. 13, 2000.

[421] *Norway Upholds Euthanasia Conviction*, Associated Press, Apr. 14, 2000.

[422] See § **1A.5** of this supplement.

[423] *Court Hears Latimer Appeal*, The Canadian Press, June 14, 2000. *See also* Kirk Makin, *Beware Slippery Slope, Judges Warned*, The Globe and Mail, June 15, 2000 (describing arguments).

[424] Nahlah Ayed, *Latimer's Fate in Hands of Supreme Court*, The Canadian Press, June 14, 2000.

"unprofessional or dishonorable conduct" in causing a patient's death. The state licensure board formally reprimanded the physician, suspended his license for 60 days, and required him to pay costs for ordering Succinylcholine to paralyze a patient's muscles and end her respiration after she remained alive despite disconnection of a breathing tube and attempts at deactivating her pacemaker.[425]

Pain Management and Palliative Care

As noted in several places throughout this text, increased attention has been paid to pain management and the proper administration of palliative care on the heels of the Oregon Death With Dignity Act. Indeed, the increased interest in the subject may well have been propelled by that legislation, the Supreme Court's decisions in *Washington v. Glucksberg* and *Vacco v. Quill*, and the amount of publicity accorded end-of-life issues over the past decade. The years 1999 and 2000 saw more regulatory attention being paid to appropriate pain management and palliative care, as well as the first state medical board disciplinary action against a physician for undertreating pain.

As state legislatures passed intractable pain legislation,[426] Florida imposed on physicians a state statutory duty to inform patients on pain management and palliative care;[427] Congress considered the Pain Relief Promotion Act; and lawyers have urged removing legal impediments that exist to appropriate pain management. The American Bar Association's House of Delegates adopted a policy resolution supporting appropriate pain management as part of basic medical care and urging state, federal, and territorial governments to clear the way for physicians to engage in quality pain and symptom management.[428] The resolution did not expressly support or oppose any particular legislation; rather, it urged various governments to remove legal barriers to quality pain and symptom management and to recognize and support individuals' rights to be free of pain, even if the efforts to free them from pain shorten their lives.

Within health care facilities, regulatory entities began to focus more on the issue as well. Beginning on January 1, 2001, the Joint Commission on Accreditation of Healthcare Organizations will require physicians to better document their pain treatment decisions. Its new pain standards emphasize that "pain requires explicit attention," and require health care facilities to:

---

[425] Gallant v. Board of Medical Examiners, 974 P.2d 814 (Ore. Ct. App. 1999). See § **1A.10** of this supplement.

[426] See **Table 9-1A**.

[427] Fla. Stat. Ann. § 765.1103.

[428] *See* American Bar Association Commission on Legal Problems of the Elderly, *Report to the House of Delegates*, available at <http://www.abanet.org/ftp/pub/elderly/ POLICYFINAL.doc>.

—Recognize patients' rights to have pain assessed and managed;

—Screen all patients for pain and determine its nature and intensity;

—Periodically reassess patients' pain status;

—Prescribe effective pain-control medications;

—Address continued needs for pain control at discharge;

—Ensure staff competency in pain assessment and management; and

—Educate patients and their families about pain treatment.[429]

A final development in 1999 was of no little significance. The year saw the first reported instance of a medical licensure board's disciplining a physician for undertreating a patient's pain. Based on six patient complaints, three of which alleged undertreatment of pain, the Oregon Board of Medical Examiners required Dr. Paul Bilder of Roseberg, Oregon, to undergo a peer evaluation and education program and complete a course on physician–patient communication.[430] The action was apparently the first of its kind, although the Oregon board previously had indicated its intention to aggressively investigate alleged underprescribing.[431] The action was also apparently consistent with the tone of model guidelines promulgated by the Federation of State Medical Boards and adopted in many states, which are aimed at increasing patient access to pain relief.[432]

§ 1A.10   Jurisdiction-by-Jurisdiction Developments in 1999–2000

Alaska

Cases

Sampson v. Alaska, No. 3AN-98-11288CI (Alaska Super. Ct. Sept. 9, 1999), *reported in* 15 Issues in L. & Med. 199 (1999).

---

[429] Vida Foubister, *Joint Commission Increases Focus on Pain Management*, Am. Med. News, June 26, 2000. *See also Poor Pain Control No Longer Acceptable Under Joint Commission Pain Standards*, [July-Dec.] Health L. Rep. (BNA) No. 31 at 1224 (Aug. 3, 2000).

[430] *See Oregon Doctor Cited for Negligence for Undertreating Pain*, Am. Med. News, Sept. 27, 1999; *Doctor Disciplined Over Lack of Aid*, Associated Press, Sept. 2, 1999.

[431] *See Oregon Doctor Cited for Negligence for Undertreating Pain,* Am. Med. News, Sept. 27, 1999.

[432] *See id.*; <http://www.fsmb.org/pain.htm>.

In *Sampson*, the Superior Court of Alaska, Third Judicial District, joined the courts that thus far have refused to declare unconstitutional state laws prohibiting physician-assisted suicide.[433] The court rejected assertions by two patients, one with AIDS and one suffering from breast cancer,[434] that Alaska's statute criminalizing physician-assisted suicide violated state constitutional rights of liberty, privacy, and equal protection. Significantly, the court ruled that, under the Alaska constitution, "mentally competent, terminally ill adults do have an autonomy-based, non-fundamental privacy interest in making end of life decisions."[435] It ruled, however, that the state had asserted proper governmental interests aimed at the preservation of human life and the protection of vulnerable individuals.[436] Because the state interests bore "a close and substantial relationship to the legitimate goal of protecting the general health and welfare,"[437] the statute did not, in the court's view, violate either the privacy or the liberty rights embodied in the Alaska constitution.

The court also rejected the plaintiffs' equal protection argument despite finding a privacy right at stake. The plaintiffs' equal protection argument echoed that asserted in *Vacco v. Quill*,[438] except that it relied on a state constitutional right to equal protection and thus was subject to slightly different analysis. In granting summary judgment to the state on the claim, the court, like the U.S. Supreme Court in *Vacco*, relied on the distinction between acts and omissions and on a causation-based distinction between intervention to end life and withdrawal of life-sustaining treatment.[439]

In rendering its ruling, the court took pains to note that it did "not find that physician-assisted suicide should not be permitted in Alaska."[440] Rather, it noted that legalization of physician-assisted suicide should come through the legislature or through the initiative process.[441]

The Alaska Supreme Court will review the ruling.

---

[433] See **Ch. 18.**

[434] *See Alaska: Superior Court Rejects Class Action Seeking to Legalize Assisted Suicide*, 8 Health L. Rep. (BNA) 1512 (Sept. 16, 1999); *Alaska: Terminally Ill Patients Sue State for Right to Doctor-Assisted Suicide*, 7 Health L. Rep. (BNA) 2040 (Dec. 24, 1998).

[435] 15 Issues in L. & Med. at 214.

[436] *Id.*

[437] *Id.*

[438] See § **18.22** of this supplement.

[439] 15 Issues in L. & Med. at 218–19.

[440] *Id.* at 214.

[441] *Id.* at 214–15.

Arizona

Statutes

Ariz. Rev. Stat. Ann. § 36-3281 (surrogate decisionmaking).
Ariz. Rev. Stat. Ann. § 36-3231 (mental health care power of attorney).

Arkansas

Statutes

Ark. Stat. Ann. § 20-17-201 (durable power of attorney).
Ark. Stat. Ann. § 20-13-104 (assisted suicide).

California

Statutes

Cal. Bus. & Prof. Code § 2089 (palliative care).

Cases

Wendland v. Wendland (In re Wendland), 93 Cal. Rptr. 2d 550 (Ct. App. 2000), *review granted and opinion superseded* (June 21, 2000).

This case arose out of a conservator's request to withdraw a feeding tube from a patient with severe brain damage not rising to the level of a persistent vegetative state. The California Court of Appeals refused to require clear and convincing evidence that the patient would have requested withdrawal of treatment to justify a decision to withdraw life-sustaining treatment from a patient in such a condition.[442] Rather, pursuant to California's statutory scheme, it required clear and convincing evidence that the conservator had complied with the statute by acting "in good faith, based upon medical evidence and after considering the conservatee's best interests, including his likely wishes."[443] In doing so, it took pains to separate the threads of evidentiary and substantive decision-making standards.[444]

Wendland is one of only three reported cases to date[445] involving patients who were formerly competent and whose condition fell short of a persistent

---

[442] For cases holding to the contrary, *see In re* Martin, 538 N.W.2d 399 (Mich. 1995), and Matter of Edna, 563 N.W.2d 485 (Wis. 1997).

[443] *Id.* at 567.

[444] See § **5.62**.

[445] **CA:** Wendland v. Wendland (*In re* Wendland), 93 Cal. Rptr. 2d 550 (Ct. App. 2000), *review granted and opinion superseded* (June 21, 2000).

vegetative state, and probably even of being life-threatening. In *Wendland*,[446] the patient suffered brain injury in an automobile accident. After existing in a coma for 16 months, he emerged from his coma but "remain[ed] severely cognitively impaired."[447] He remained paralyzed on his right side and was unable to communicate consistently, feed himself, or control his bowels or bladder. He interacted with his environment "minimally and inconsistently."[448]

> At his highest level of functioning, he has been able to do (with repeated prompting and cuing [pointing] by therapists) such activities as grasp and release a ball, operate an electric wheelchair with a "joystick," move himself in a manual wheelchair with his left hand or foot, balance himself momentarily in a "standing frame" while grabbing and pulling "thera-putty," draw the letter "R," and choose and replace requested color blocks out of several color choices. Each activity is performed only after excruciatingly repetitive prompting and cuing by the therapists. [The patient] never smiles. What little emotion he does show is negative and combative.[449]

While emphasizing that the patient was not in a persistent vegetative state, the court refused to attach a label to his condition.[450]

After the fourth time the patient's feeding tube became dislodged, his wife refused consent for reinsertion, "stating she believed Robert would not want to go through it again."[451] A tube was nevertheless inserted "in order to maintain the status quo pending review by the hospital ethics committee."[452]

MI: Martin v. Martin, 538 N.W.2d 399 (Mich. 1995), *rev'g on other grounds*, Martin v. Martin, 517 N.W.2d 749 (Mich. Ct. App. 1994); Martin v. Martin, 504 N.W.2d 917 (Mich. Ct. App. 1993), *cert. denied*, 116 S. Ct. 912 (1996). See §§ **1A.2, 9.53** in this supplement.

WI: *See also* Edna M.F. v. Eisenberg, 563 N.W.2d 485 (Wis. 1997), *cert. denied sub nom.* Spahn v. Wittman, 522 U.S. 951 (1997) (patient with Alzheimer's disease). See § **1A.4** in this supplement.

[446] Wendland v. Wendland (*In re* Wendland), 93 Cal. Rptr. 2d 550 (Ct. App. 2000), *review granted and opinion superseded* (June 21, 2000).

[447] *Id*. at 554.

[448] *Id*.

[449] *Id*.

[450] Wendland, 93 Cal. Rptr. 2d at 555 n.6.

[451] *Id*. at 555.

[452] *Id*. Neither the ethics committee, nor the attending physician, nor the San Joaquin County patient ombudsman objected to the wife's request. *Id*. at 555 & n.8. Upon learning of the request, the patient's mother and sister filed suit in an attempt to prevent withdrawal of nutrition and hydration, prompting the patient's wife to request judicial appointment as the patient's conservator. *Id*. at 555. The patient's brother supported the patient's wife in the litigation. *Id*. at 558. See § **5.31.**

The court heard conflicting testimony about the level of the patient's cognitive functioning. While testimony indicated that the patient sometimes performed simple tasks, "[d]octors testified that, to the highest degree of medical certainty, [the patient would] never be able to feed himself, bathe himself, control his bladder or bowels, or communicate verbally or in writing."[453] Family members disagreed regarding whether the patient recognized family members when they visited him.[454] Experts "viewed Robert's activity as 'very low-level cognitive response'—like a trained response where an animal or child is trained on a primitive level to perform an action in response to a direct specific stimulus, or rote execution of exceedingly simple tasks."[455] They opined that he could survive many years but noted that he was susceptible to dental problems and respiratory or bladder infections, some of which he had already experienced.

The court ruled that California's conservatorship statute[456] permitted a conservator to withhold life-sustaining nutrition and hydration from a non-PVS patient and determined that the conservator could make such a decision based on her own good faith judgment of the patient's best interests, including his likely wishes.[457] While it required clear and convincing evidence of the conservator's having acted in good faith in the patient's best interests, it did not require proof that withdrawal of treatment was what the patient would have wanted.[458] In doing so, the court distinguished the case before it from the Michigan case of *Martin v. Martin*[459] because the California statute granted "exclusive authority" to the conservator, whereas the Michigan statute at issue in *Martin* did not do so.[460] It similarly distinguished a Wisconsin case also involving a non-PVS patient, *Edna M.F. v. Eisenberg*,[461] on a statutory basis. Ultimately, the court remanded the case to the trial court for an evidentiary hearing, the matter before it having been decided on a motion for judgment.[462]

With regard to statutory authorization of conservator action on behalf of a patient in a non-PVS condition, the *Wendland* court explained:

---

[453] Wendland, 93 Cal. Rptr. 2d at 556.

[454] *Id.*

[455] *Id.* at 557.

[456] Cal. Probate Code § 2355.

[457] Wendland, 93 Cal. Rptr. 2d at 565–67.

[458] *Id.* at 572–75. It emphasized that its decision "to apply the clear and convincing evidence standard of proof applies only where it is expected that withdrawal of medical treatment will certainly lead to death. We do not decide or suggest what standard should apply to other, less final decisions." *Id.* at 575.

[459] *See In re* Martin, 538 N.W.2d 399 (Mich. 1995).

[460] Wendland, 93 Cal. Rptr. 2d at 566–67.

[461] *See* 538 N.W.2d 399.

[462] Wendland, 93 Cal. Rptr. 2d at 580.

[W]hen courts in section 2355 cases inquire whether there is a reasonable possibility the conservatee will return to "cognitive and sapient life" before allowing a conservator to withhold life-sustaining treatment . . . , the point of the inquiry is to determine whether there is a possibility the conservatee will regain capacity to make his or her own decision. Thus, while we recognize a distinction has been made between sapience and the vegetative state . . . , we do not believe that any non-vegetative state of a conservatee removes from the conservator the statutory authority to make a decision to withhold life-sustaining treatment. We accordingly reject . . . arguments that because courts sometimes omit the word "sapient" and speak of a return to "cognitive life," sapience has no separate meaning, and the existence of any cognitive function should remove the conservatee from the conservator's power to make a decision to withdraw life-sustaining treatment. . . .

[W]hen courts in section 2355 cases inquire whether there is a reasonable possibility the conservatee will return to "cognitive and sapient life" before allowing a conservator to withhold life-sustaining treatment . . . , the point of the inquiry is to determine whether there is a possibility the conservatee will regain capacity to make his or her own decision. Thus, while we recognize a distinction has been made between sapience and the vegetative state . . . , we do not believe that any non-vegetative state of a conservatee removes from the conservator the statutory authority to make a decision to withhold life-sustaining treatment. We accordingly reject . . . arguments that because courts sometimes omit the word "sapient" and speak of a return to "cognitive life," sapience has no separate meaning, and the existence of any cognitive function should remove the conservatee from the conservator's power to make a decision to withdraw life-sustaining treatment. . . .

Moreover, the case of a non-PVS patient presents an equally compelling case for application of section 2355 as a PVS patient, because the non-PVS patient can feel pain and suffering, hence refusal to allow a surrogate to exercise the patient's right to refuse treatment may condemn the patient to prolonged suffering. (Of course, the prospect of pain after removal of the treatment is a factor to be considered in these cases as well.)[463]

Wendland has the potential to be a significant case because of the paucity of cases involving patients whose brain damage does not rise to the level of a persistent vegetative state. The impact of the court's decision is somewhat lessened, however, for two reasons. First, it is statutorily based,[464] which means the court's decision may not prove persuasive in other states with statutory schemes differing from California's. Second, the California Supreme Court has granted review of the decision and has superseded the opinion of the Court of Appeals pending its decision.

Colorado

Cases

Sanderson v. State, No. 99CA0203, 2000 WL 729008 (Colo. Ct. App. June 8, 2000).

The plaintiff in *Sanderson* raised a unique, and ultimately unsuccessful, First Amendment challenge to Colorado's statute criminalizing assisted suicide. The case is discussed in § **18.22** of this supplement.

---

463 Wendland, 93 Cal. Rptr. 2d at 565. The court had earlier noted that "[c]ase law has not made clear whether 'sapient' has any meaning distinct from 'cognitive.'" *Id.* at 562 n.5.

464 *See* Wendland v. Wendland (*In re* Wendland), 93 Cal. Rptr. 2d at 566–67.

District of Columbia

Cases

In re K.I., 735 A.2d 448 (D.C. Ct. App. 1999).

In this heart-wrenching case, the District of Columbia Court of Appeals affirmed the actions of a trial court asked by a two-year-old child's medical guardian ad litem to approve entry of a Do Not Resuscitate (DNR) order regarding the child. The court affirmed the trial court's assumption of jurisdiction over the matter, application of the "best interests of the child" standard in approving the DNR order over the child's mother's objections, and use of the clear and convincing evidentiary burden in that decisionmaking.

The child, K.I., had been born prematurely, at 26 weeks gestation.[465] Due to various medical conditions, K.I. "was required to wear a heart monitor and an apnea monitor, take medication for the lungs, and use oxygen continuously."[466] Within six months of her birth, child protective services authorities had filed a neglect petition, alleging in part that K.I.'s mother would not provide the required medical care. K.I.'s medical guardian ad litem requested issuance of a DNR order. At the time the DNR matter was heard, the Superior Court of the District of Columbia, Family Division, had already adjudicated K.I. as a neglected child and committed her to the Department of Human Services.[467] Also by the time of this hearing, K.I. had, in addition to her initial medical problems, gone into cardiac arrest, suffered hypoxia for about 25 minutes, and experienced a seven-hour seizure.[468] The court of appeals noted that, at the DNR hearing, K.I.'s treating physician "described the child's current condition [as being characterized by] no 'purposeful movements,' [and] persistent 'myochronic jerks' [involving] 'shaking of [the] arms and legs.'"[469] K.I. also "[withdrew from] pain or . . . [felt] discomfort when people [performed] interventions such as . . . when [he] attempted to place [an] IV in [K.I.'s] . . . hand, [K.I.] actually was grimacing and sort of writhing and moving around as if in discomfort."[470]

Over K.I.'s mother's objection, the trial court issued a DNR order, and the District of Columbia Court of Appeals affirmed. In doing so, the appellate court approved the trial court's assumption of jurisdiction over the neglected

---

[465] 735 A.2d at 451.

[466] *Id.*

[467] *Id.* at 457–58 (trial court memorandum opinion, attached as appendix to court of appeals opinion indicates that neglect adjudication took place on August 26, 1998, and DNR hearing took place on September 4, 1998).

[468] *Id.* at 451–52.

[469] *Id.* at 452.

[470] *Id.*

child in its role of *parens patriae*,[471] ruled that K.I.'s mother's interests in refusing entry of a DNR must yield to her child' best interests, and affirmed the court's application of the best interests standard to, and use of the clear and convincing evidentiary burden in, the matter at hand.[472]

Florida

Statutes

Fla. Stat. Ann. § 401.45 (DNR).
Fla. Stat. Ann. § 765.101 (advance directive).
Fla. Stat. Ann. § 765.302 (living will).
Fla. Stat. Ann. § 765.401 (surrogate decisionmaking).

Georgia

Statutes

Ga. Code Ann. § 31-36A-1-6-7 (surrogate decisionmaking).

Hawaii

Statutes

Haw. Rev. Stat. § 327E (advance directive).

Illinois

Statutes

Ill. Ann. Stat. ch. 755, § 40/60 (surrogate decisionmaking).

Indiana

Cases

Estate of Taylor v. Muncie Medical Investors, L.P., 727 N.E.2d 466 (Ind. Ct. App. 2000).

In *Taylor*, the Indiana Court of Appeals considered and rejected imposition of liability on a nursing home for wrongful prolongation of the life of a

---

[471] *See infra* § **2.11** and **Ch. 15.**
[472] *Id*. at 253–54.

comatose resident. It thus joined two other cases in which courts have considered and rejected recognition of claims for wrongful living or wrongful prolongation of life. For discussion of *Taylor* and those cases, see § **17.17**.

Kentucky

Cases

Woods ex rel. Simpson v. Commonwealth, No. 1998-CA-000295-DG, 1999 WL 550528 (Ky. Ct. App. 1999), *review granted and opinion withdrawn* (Apr. 12, 2000)

The Kentucky Court of Appeals this year determined that the guardian of a never-competent patient in a vegetative state could require withdrawal of life-sustaining treatment without obtaining a court order.[473] The Kentucky Supreme Court will review the decision.

Louisiana

Statutes

La. Rev. Stat. Ann. § 40:1299.58 (DNR).

Maryland

Statutes

Md. Code Ann., Health-Gen. § 5-608 (DNR).

Nebraska

Statutes

Neb. Rev. Stat. § 71-7418 (intractable pain).

New Mexico

Statutes

N.M. Stat. Ann. § 24-2D (intractable pain).

---

[473] *See* Woods *ex rel.* Simpson v. Commonwealth, No. 1998-CA-000295-DG, 1999 WL 550528 (Ky. Ct. App. 1999), *review granted and opinion withdrawn* (Apr. 12, 2000); Mark Chellgren, *Court Rules Guardians Can Pull Plug; Jurists See Decision as a Privacy Issue*, Cincinnati Enquirer, July 31, 1999, at C2.

Cases

Protection and Advocacy System, Inc. v. Presbyterian Healthcare Services, 989 P.2d 890 (N.M. Ct. App. 1999)

The opinion in *Presbyterian Healthcare Services* primarily involved standing, but the case is useful, especially in light of the dearth of case law in New Mexico, for its discussion of the Uniform Health Care Decisions Act (UHCDA) as enacted in that state. In this case, a 51-year-old man with moderate mental retardation suffered a stroke. His mother requested withdrawal of a nasogastric feeding tube, pursuant to her appointment as guardian for her son for purposes of medical decisionmaking. Protection and Advocacy System, Inc., a not-for-profit advocacy group for the developmentally disabled, petitioned the court for an order continuing nasogastric feeding.

In ruling that the advocacy group lacked standing, the court discussed in detail New Mexico's adoption of the UHCDA and noted that it accorded patients, including the developmentally disabled, both procedural and substantive protections. The advocacy group's authorization under federal law to pursue remedies on behalf of that population did not accord it standing in the sort of action it had filed in this instance.

North Dakota

Statutes

N.D. Cent. Code § 12.1-16 (assisted suicide).

Oklahoma

Statutes

Okla. Stat. Ann. tit. 47, § 6-111(a).

Oregon

Statutes

Ore. Rev. Stat. §§ 127.800 - .897 (Death With Dignity Act).

Cases

Gallant v. Board of Medical Examiners, 974 P.2d 814 (Ore. Ct. App. 1999)

In *Gallant*, the Oregon Court of Appeals displayed great deference to the self-regulation of the medical profession. *Gallant* involved a physician who engaged in active euthanasia of a 78-year-old patient who had suffered a severe brain hemorrhage. The physician had served as the patient's primary physician for six years, and he had discussed her end-of-life wishes with her on several occasions.[474] The patient had documented her desire that, "in the event that she became terminally ill, she did not want her life prolonged through artificial or extraordinary means" and had designated her daughter as her surrogate.[475] Thus, the physician ordered removal of the patient's breathing tube and prescribed Valium and morphine for pain relief. He "expected [the] patient to 'die within minutes[,]' but to his surprise, she did not."[476] Thereafter, after the patient's breathing had been described as "'agonal,'" after attempting to deactivate her pacemaker, and after repeated familial requests to end the patient's suffering, the physician approved the use of Succinylcholine to paralyze her muscles and end her respiration.[477] He "believed the use of Succinylcholine was consistent with the wishes of patient and her family."[478]

There is no indication in the reported decision that the patient's family was displeased with the physician's actions. The hospital at which he had treated the patient, however, contacted the Board of Medical Examiners (the Board) approximately three weeks after the patient's death.[479] The Board concluded that the physician's conduct had constituted "'unprofessional or dishonorable conduct'" and disciplined him by formally reprimanding him, suspending his medical license for 60 days, and ordering him to pay costs.[480] The physician appealed the decision on procedural grounds, and the Oregon Court of Appeals affirmed.[481]

The court neither discussed the patient's right to refuse treatment, nor opined on euthanasia, other than to note that the case "in no way" concerned Oregon's Death With Dignity Act.[482] The decision is interesting, however, for its rejection of the physician's argument that a clear and convincing standard of proof should apply when possible license revocation is at stake in a Board proceeding. The court balanced the private interest at stake, the risk of error, and the countervailing public interest.[483] It conceded that the physician's

---

[474] 974 P.2d at 815.

[475] *Id.* at 815 n.2.

[476] *Id.* at 815.

[477] *Id.*

[478] *Id.*

[479] *Id.*

[480] *Id.* at 816.

[481] Specifically, the court considered "whether the Board correctly applied the preponderance of the evidence standard of proof and whether the Board impermissibly allowed a disqualified Board member to participate in the deliberations of petitioner's case." *Id.* at 814.

[482] *Id.* at 814 n.1.

[483] *Id.* at 818.

interest in his right to practice was substantial, but it ruled that the risk of error was low because the Board was comprised primarily of physicians and the primary issue was the nature of the physician's conduct (professional or unprofessional), rather than whether he had acted as alleged.[484] Finally, the court ruled that the public interest was also substantial. It noted that Oregon's medical licensing statute "reflects a concern that unprofessional conduct by a physician can endanger life itself."[485] Because that potential harm was so serious, the court ruled the medical licensee should bear the risk of error in a disciplinary proceeding by having his or her possible loss of license judged by a preponderance of the evidence standard. One possible implication is that organized medicine's view of the ethics of practices such as euthanasia and assisted suicide is likely to remain a powerful factor in physicians' determining whether to engage in such practices, even if those practices often are not prosecuted in the criminal liability system.

Pennsylvania

Statutes

Pa. Cons. Stat. Ann. tit. 20, §5611 (durable power of attorney).

Cases

In re Kauffman, 20 Fiduc. Rptr. 2d 223 (C.P. Montgomery County, Pa. 2000)

In this case, the husband of a 65-year-old woman requiring ventilator support and dialysis sought to enter a DNR on her hospital records. The patient had designated her husband as both her agent under her general durable power of attorney and her proxy decisionmaker under her living will. When one of the patient's sons from an earlier marriage challenged her husband's decision, the husband sought an injunction from the Orphans' Court Division of the Court of Common Pleas of Montgomery County. The court denied the husband's request for entry of the DNR order.

There was no dispute over whether the terms of the patient's living will had been triggered in this case. Two physicians testified that the patient was in a terminal condition and that she was in a state of permanent unconsciousness, although they disagreed with regard to whether she was experiencing pain.[486]

Rather, the court based its decision in large part on the patient's unusually strongly worded living will. The patient had executed the living will, which

---

[484] *Id.* at 819.

[485] *Id.*

[486] *In re* Kauffman, 20 Fiduc. Rptr. 2d 223, 233 (C.P. Montgomery County, Pa. 2000).

she had largely personally drafted,[487] less than a month before most recently entering the hospital.[488] It stated:

> Regardless of my mental or physical condition, it is my wish to receive any and all available and medically advisable medical treatments to attempt to sustain and prolong my life and improve the quality of my life. Should these goals conflict, I direct that my proxy . . . be consulted about the decision in such circumstances.[489]

It further directed that, "[r]egardless of whether there is no reasonable expectation of . . . recovery from extreme physical or mental disability," she was to be kept alive by "medications, artificial means and 'heroic measures.'"[490] The patient specified that "in the face of impending death or a permanent coma (as well as all other circumstances)," she wished to receive, *inter alia,* "electrical or mechanical resuscitation of [her] heart when it [had] stopped beating."[491]

Additionally, all fact witnesses testifying before the court stated that the patient "was firm in her belief that she wanted to be kept alive by all means available."[492] The patient's son testified that she had "always and adamantly" believed that hope remained as long as both heart and brain functioned. Similarly, her long-time friend testified that as recently as the previous month she had asked the patient whether she wanted to give up but that the patient had responded negatively.[493]

The patient's husband, her designated proxy, testified that he had considered the advice of several doctors, nurses, and social workers; had observed her condition; and had the impression that his wife was in pain and had lost the will to live.[494] He apparently argued that the case presented an example of the type specified for proxy decisionmaking in the living will—a situation in which the patient's goals of sustaining her life and improving the quality of her life conflicted. The court, however, disagreed, ruling that the proxy's decision-making role "had not been triggered."[495] Essentially, then, it ruled that the precise terms of the advance directive, representing the patient's expressed wishes, still governed, and that proxy decisionmaker's input in balancing benefits and burdens of treatment was not yet warranted. Because

---

[487] *Id.* at 227.

[488] *Id.* at 224.

[489] *Id.* at 226.

[490] *Id.*

[491] *Id.*

[492] *Id.* at 227.

[493] *Id.*

[494] *Id.*

[495] *Id.* at 228.

it believed that the patient would not have consented to a DNR order, it refused to order the entry of one. It further ordered that "all measures, including heroic efforts, can be undertaken on her behalf in conformity with the 'balancing test' set forth in her living will declaration."[496]

Virginia

Statutes

Va. Code Ann. § 54.1-2986 (DNR).
Va. Code Ann. § 54.1-2990 (advance directive).

Cases

Gilmore v. Finn, 527 S.E.2d 426 (Va. 2000).

In *Finn*, the Virginia Supreme Court reversed an award of attorneys' fees and costs against the governor of Virginia, who had opposed withdrawal of nutrition and hydration from a patient in a persistent vegetative state. For further details about the *Hugh Finn* case, see § **1A.7.**

West Virginia

Statutes

W. Va. Code § 16-30-2-30 (advance directive).

---

[496] *Id.*

CHAPTER 1

WHAT IS THE RIGHT TO DIE?

§ 1.1 Meaning of the Right to Die

Page 3, add to footnote 1:

NY: *Cf. In re* Matthews, 650 N.Y.S.2d 373, 376 (App. Div. 1996) (case in which parents of mentally retarded man refuse to permit implantation of feeding tube "is not a 'right to die' case" but a case involving patient's "right to live with dignity and his right to make his own choice to eat in order to sustain himself").

§ 1.2 Purpose of This Treatise

Page 6, add note 12.1 reference at end of third sentence of first paragraph and add note 12.1:

[12.1]**MA:** *In re* Shine v. Vega, 709 N.E.2d 58, 59 (Mass. 1999) ("In this wrongful death case, we must resolve the conflict between the right of a competent adult to refuse medical treatment and the interest of a physician in preserving life without fear of liability.").

§ 1.4 Existing Practices

Page 11, add to footnote 28:

See The SUPPORT Principal Investigators, *A Controlled Trial to Improve Care for Seriously Ill Hospitalized Patients,* 274 JAMA 1591 (1995); Marion Danis et al., *A Prospective Study of the Impact of Patient Preferences on Life-Sustaining Treatment and Hospital Cost,* 24 Critical Care Med. 1811 (1996).

§ 1.6   Medical Attitudes

Page 14, add to footnote 37:

MA: *See, e.g., In re* Shine v. Vega, 709 N.E.2d 58 (Mass. 1999) (physician intubated competent patient despite her repeated refusals of treatment).

See Martin D. Goodman et al., *Effect of Advance Directives on the Management of Elderly Critically Ill Patients,* 26 Critical Care Med. 701 (1998); The SUPPORT Principal Investigators, *A Controlled Trial to Improve Care for Seriously Ill Hospitalized Patients,* 274 JAMA 1591 (1995); Marion Danis et al., *A Prospective Study of the Impact of Patient Preferences on Life-Sustaining Treatment and Hospital Cost,* 24 Critical Care Med. 1811 (1996).

Page 15, add note 47.1 reference at end of second sentence of first full paragraph and add note 47.1:

[47.1] David Orentlicher, *The Illusion of Patient Choice in End-of-Life Decisions,* 267 JAMA 2101, 2101 (1992) ("[T]here is increasing evidence that physician values may be a more decisive factor than patient values in [end-of-life] decisions.").

Page 15, add at end of second paragraph:

Furthermore, local professional practices may greatly influence doctors' willingness to administer or withhold life-sustaining medical treatment.[47.2] Although overtreatment is the predominant problem, undertreatment is also a problem, and sometimes the two can exist simultaneously, such as when doctors provide terminally ill patients with aggressive curative treatment but fail to provide adequate treatment for pain and related physical and psychological symptoms.[47.3]

[47.2] *See* George Anders, *ZIP Code Is a Key to Course of Terminal Care,* Wall St. J., Oct. 15, 1997, at B1 (discussing Chapter Four, "The American Experience of Death," in The Center for the Evaluative Clinical Sciences, Dartmouth Medical School, The Dartmouth Atlas of Health Care 1998; available at <http://www.dartmouth.edu/~atlas/toc98.html>).

[47.3] *See* Institute of Medicine, Approaching Death: Improving Care at the End of Life 126 & *passim* (Marilyn J. Field & Christine K. Cassel eds. 1997).

§ 1.7   Legal Antecedents and Current Status of the Right to Die

Page 19, add to Table 1–1:

UNITED STATES

Supreme Court

Vacco v. Quill, 117 S. Ct. 2293 (1997)
Washington v. Glucksberg, 117 S. Ct. 2258 (1997)

Court of Appeals—Reported

Bryan v. Rectors & Visitors of Univ. of Va., 95 F.3d 349 (4th Cir. 1996)
Compassion in Dying v. Washington, 79 F.3d 790 (9th Cir. 1996) (en banc), *aff'g* 850 F. Supp. 1454 (W.D. Wash. 1994), *rev'd sub nom.* Washington v. Glucksberg, 117 S. Ct. 2258 (1997)
Lee v. Oregon, 107 F.3d 1382 (9th Cir. 1997), *cert. denied sub nom.* Lee v. Harcleroad, 118 S. Ct. 328 (1997)
Novak v. Cobb County Kennestone Hosp. Auth., 74 F.3d 1173 (11th Cir. 1996)
Quill v. Vacco, 80 F.3d 716 (2d Cir. 1996), *rev'd*, 117 S. Ct. 2293 (1997)

District Court—Reported

Gabrynowicz v. Heitkamp, 904 F. Supp. 1061 (D.N.D. 1995)
Kevorkian v. Arnett, 939 F. Supp. 725 (C.D. Cal.), *vacated & appeal dismissed*, 136 F.3d 1360 (9th Cir. 1998)
Kevorkian v. Thompson, 947 F. Supp. 1152 (E.D. Mich. 1997)

Alaska

Appellate—Unreported (Officially)

Sampson v. Alaska, No. 3AN-98-11288CI (Alaska Super. Ct. Sept. 9, 1999), *reported in* 15 issues in L. & Med. 199 (1999)

California

Appellate—Reported

Duarte v. Chino Community Hosp., 85 Cal. Rptr. 2d 521 (Ct. App. 1999), *review denied* (Sept. 1, 1999)

Rains v. Belshe, 38 Cal. Rptr. 2d 185 (Ct. App. 1995)

Wendland v. Superior Court, 56 Cal. Rptr. 2d 595 (Ct. App. 1996)

Wendland v. Wendland (*In re* Wendland), 93 Cal. Rptr. 2d 550 (Ct. App. 2000), *review granted and opinion superseded* (June 21, 2000)

Trial—Reported

Kevorkian v. Arnett, 939 F. Supp. 725 (C.D. Cal.), *vacated & appeal dismissed,* 136 F.3d 1360 (9th Cir. 1998)

Trial—Unreported

In re Wendland, Probate No. 65669 (Super. Ct. San Joaquin County, Cal. Jan. 17, 1998)

Colorado

Appellate—Reported

Sanderson v. State, No. 99CA0203, 2000 WL 729008 (Colo. Ct. App. June 8, 2000)

Connecticut

Appellate—Reported

Stamford Hosp. v. Vega, 674 A.2d 821 (Conn. 1996)

Delaware

Appellate—Reported

In re Tavel, 661 A.2d 1061 (Del. 1995)

Trial—Reported

In re Gordy, 658 A.2d 613 (Del. Ch. 1994)

Trial—Unreported

In re Holmes, C.M. No. 8066-NC, 1996 WL 633309 (Del. Ch. Oct. 30, 1996)

District of Columbia

Appellate—Reported

In re K.I., 735 A.2d 448 (D.C. Ct. App. 1999)

Florida

Appellate—Reported

Harrell v. St. Mary's Hosp., Inc., 678 So. 2d 455 (Fla. Dist. Ct. App. 1996)
McIver v. Krischer, 697 So. 2d 97 (Fla. 1997)
M.N. v. Southern Baptist Hosp. of Fla., Inc., 648 So. 2d 769 (Fla. Dist. Ct. App. 1994)
Singletary v. Costello, 665 So. 2d 1099 (Fla. Dist. Ct. App. 1996)

Georgia

Appellate—Reported

Novak v. Cobb County Kennestone Hosp. Auth., 74 F.3d 1173 (11th Cir. 1996)
Edwards v. Shumate, 468 S.E.2d 23 (Ga. 1996)
Velez v. Bethune, 466 S.E.2d 627 (Ga. Ct. App. 1995)

Illinois

Appellate—Reported

In re Austwick, 656 N.E.2d 773 (Ill. App. Ct. 1995)
Cohen v. Smith, 648 N.E.2d 329 (Ill. App. Ct. 1995)
In re Fetus Brown, 689 N.E.2d 397 (Ill. App. Ct. 1997)
Ficke v. Evangelical Health Sys., 674 N.E.2d 888 (Ill. App. Ct. 1996), *appeal denied,* 679 N.E.2d 379 (Ill. 1997) (Table, No. 82541)
Gragg v. Calandra, 696 N.E.2d 1282 (Ill. App. Ct.), *appeal denied*, 706 N.E.2d 496 (Ill. 1998)
People v. Caldwell, 692 N.E.2d 448 (Ill. App. Ct. 1998)

Indiana

Appellate—Reported

Estate of Taylor v. Muncie Medical Investors, L.P., 727 N.E.2d 466 (Ind. Ct. App. 1999)

Iowa

Polk County Sheriff v. Iowa Dist. Court, 594 N.W.2d 421 (Iowa 1999)
Wendland v. Sparks, 574 N.W.2d 327 (Iowa 1998)

Kansas

Appellate—Reported

State v. Naramore, 965 P.2d 211 (Kan. Ct. App. 1998)

Kentucky

Appellate—Reported

Woods *ex rel.* Simpson v. Commonwealth, No. 1998-CA-000295-DG, 1999 WL 550528 (Ky. Ct. App. 1999), *review granted and opinion withdrawn* (Apr. 12, 2000)

Louisiana

Appellate—Reported

Causey v. St. Francis Med. Center, 719 So. 2d 1072 (La. Ct. App. 1998)
Lebreton v. Rabito, 650 So. 2d 1245 (La. Ct. App. 1995)
Perrier v. Bistes, 650 So. 2d 786 (La. Ct. App.), *cert. denied,* 653 So. 2d 569 (La. 1995)

Maryland

Appellate—Reported

Wright v. Johns Hopkins Health Sys. Corp., 728 A.2d 166 (Md. 1999)

Massachusetts

Appellate—Reported

Lane v. Candura, 376 N.E.2d 1232 (Mass. App. Ct. 1978)
In re Mason, 669 N.E.2d 1081 (Mass. App. Ct. 1996)
In re Shine v. Vega, 709 N.E.2d 58 (Mass. 1999)
In re Smith, 684 N.E.2d 613 (Mass. App. Ct. 1997)

§ 1.7   LEGAL ANTECEDENTS/CURRENT STATUS

Trial—Unreported

Gilgunn v. Massachusetts Gen. Hosp., No. 92-4820 (Mass. Super. Ct. Suffolk County Apr. 22, 1995)

Michigan

Appellate—Reported

Martin v. Martin, 538 N.W.2d 399 (Mich. 1995), *cert. denied,* 116 S. Ct. 912 (1996)
People *ex rel.* Oakland County Prosecuting Attorney v. Kevorkian, 534 N.W.2d 172 (Mich. Ct. App. 1995), *appeal denied,* 549 N.W.2d 566 (Mich.), *cert. denied sub nom.* Kevorkian v. Michigan, 117 S. Ct. 296 (1996)

Trial—Reported

Kevorkian v. Thompson, 947 F. Supp. 1152 (E.D. Mich. 1997)

Minnesota

Appellate—Reported

Lundman v. McKown, 530 N.W.2d 807 (Minn. Ct. App. 1995), *cert. denied,* 116 S. Ct. 814 & 828 (1996)

Nebraska

Appellate—Reported

Tabatha R. v. Ronda R., 564 N.W.2d 598 (Neb. 1997), *modified,* 566 N.W.2d 782 (Neb. 1998)

Nevada

Appellate—Reported

Board of Nursing v. Merkley, 940 P.2d 144 (Nev. 1997)

Attorney General Opinion

Nev. Op. Att'y Gen. No. 97-08, 1997 WL 133532 (1997)

WHAT IS THE RIGHT TO DIE?

New Jersey

Trial—Reported

In re Roche, 687 A.2d 349 (N.J. Super. Ct. Ch. Div. 1996)

New Mexico

Appellate—Reported

Protection and Advocacy System, Inc. v. Presbyterian Healthcare Services, 989 P.2d 890 (N.M. Ct. App. 1999)

New York

Appellate—Reported

Finn v. Leonard "C," 634 N.Y.S.2d 262 (App. Div. 1995), *leave to appeal denied,* 87 N.Y.2d 810, 665 N.E.2d 661, 642 N.Y.S.2d 859 (Mar 26, 1996) (Table, No. 95), *aff'g & modifying* 625 N.Y.S.2d 809 (Sup. Ct. Albany County 1995)
In re Matthews, 650 N.Y.S.2d 373 (App. Div. 1996), *leave to appeal denied,* 655 N.Y.S.2d 888 (N.Y. 1997) (Table, No. 47)
Vacco v. Quill, 117 S. Ct. 2293 (1997), *rev'g* 80 F.3d 716 (2d Cir. 1996)

Trial—Reported

Afentakis v. Memorial Hosp., 667 N.Y.S.2d 602 (Sup. Ct. N.Y. County 1997)
In re Barsky (Kyle), 627 N.Y.S.2d 903 (Sup. Ct. Suffolk County 1995)
Blackman v. New York City Health & Hosps. Corp., 660 N.Y.S.2d 643 (Sup. Ct. Kings County 1997)
In re Christopher, 675 N.Y.S.2d 807 (Sup. Ct. Queens County 1998)
In re Long Island Jewish Medical Ctr. (Baby Doe), 641 N.Y.S.2d 989 (Sup. Ct. Queens County 1996)
In re Lowe, 688 N.Y.S.2d 389 (Sup. Ct. Queens County 1999)
Estate of Rozewicz v. New York City Health & Hosps. Corp., 656 N.Y.S.2d 593 (Sup. Ct. N.Y. County 1997)

North Carolina

Appellate—Reported

First Healthcare Corp. v. Rettinger, 467 S.E.2d 243 (N.C. 1996), *rev'g,* 456 S.E.2d 347 (N.C. Ct. App. 1995)

North Dakota

Appellate—Reported

Gabrynowicz v. Heitkamp, 904 F. Supp. 1061 (D.N.D. 1995)
State v. Schuetzle, 537 N.W.2d 358 (N.D. 1995)

Ohio

Appellate—Reported

Allore v. Flower Hosp., No. L-96-329, 1997 WL 362465 (Ohio Ct. App. June 27), *appeal not allowed,* 685 N.E.2d 546 (Ohio 1997) (Table, No. 97-1669)
Anderson v. St. Francis-St. George Hosp., 671 N.E.2d 225 (Ohio 1996)

Oklahoma

Appellate—Reported

Edinburgh v. State, 896 P.2d 1176 (Okla. Crim. App. 1995)
Sparks v. Hicks, 912 P.2d 331 (Okla. 1996)

Oregon

Appellate—Reported

Gallant v. Board of Medical Examiners, 974 P.2d 814 (Ore. Ct. App. 1999)
Lee v. Oregon, 107 F.3d 1382 (9th Cir. 1997), *cert. denied sub nom.* Lee v. Harcleroad, 118 S. Ct. 328 (1997)

Trial—Reported

Lee v. Oregon, 891 F. Supp. 1439 (D. Or. 1995)
Lee v. Oregon, 891 F. Supp. 1429 (D. Or. 1995)
Lee v. Oregon, 1995 WL 471689 (D. Or. 1995)

Pennsylvania

Appellate—Reported

In re Fiori, 673 A.2d 905 (Pa. 1996)

Trial—Reported

In re Bracco, 15 Fiduc. Rep. 2d 173 (C.P. Bucks County, Pa. 1995)
In re Kauffman, 20 Fiduc. Rptr. 2d 223 (C.P. Montgomery County, Pa. 2000)
Rideout v. Hershey Medical Ctr., 16 Fiduc. Rep. 2d 181 (C.P. Dauphin
County, Pa. 1996)

Trial—Unreported

In re Goldman, 18 Fiduc. Rep. 2d 79 (C.P. Northampton County, Pa. 1997)

Rhode Island

Appellate—Reported

Laurie v. Senecal, 666 A.2d 806 (R.I. 1995)

Virginia

Appellate—Reported

Gilmore v. Finn, 527 S.E.2d 426 (Va. 2000)

Washington

Appellate—Reported

Branom v. State, 974 P.2d 335 (Wash. Ct. App. 1999)
Washington v. Glucksberg, 117 S. Ct. 2258 (1997), *rev'g* Compassion in
Dying v. Washington, 79 F.3d 790 (9th Cir. 1996) (en banc)

Wisconsin

Appellate—Reported

Edna M.F. v. Eisenberg, 563 N.W.2d 485 (Wis. 1997), *cert. denied sub nom.*
Spahn v. Wittman, 118 S. Ct. 372 (1997)

Bibliography

American Board of Internal Medicine. *Caring for the Dying: Identification and Promotion of Physician Competency: Personal Narratives.* Philadelphia, PA: American Board of Internal Medicine, 1996.

American Medical Association Council on Scientific Affairs. "Good Care of the Dying Patient." *Journal of the American Medical Association* 275 (1996): 474.

American Thoracic Society. "Withholding and Withdrawing Life-Sustaining Therapy." *Annals of Internal Medicine* 115 (1991): 478.

Annas, G. "The 'Right to Die' in America: Sloganeering from *Quinlan* and *Cruzan* to *Quill* and *Kevorkian*." *Duquesne Law Review* 34 (1996): 875.

Brody, H., et al. "Withdrawing Intensive Life-Sustaining Treatment—Recommendations for Compassionate Clinical Management." *New England Journal of Medicine* 336 (1997): 652.

Catholic Health Association of the United States. *Caring for Persons at the End of Life: A Facilitator's Guide to Educational Modules for Healthcare Leaders.* St. Louis, MO: Catholic Health Association of the United States, 1993.

Daar, J. "Direct Democracy and Bioethical Choices: Voting Life and Death at the Ballot Box." *University of Michigan Journal of Law Reform* 28 (1995): 799.

Davies, B., et al. *Fading Away: The Experience of Transition in Families with Terminal Illness.* Amityville, NY: Baywood, 1995.

Emanuel, E. "Cost Savings at the End of Life." *Journal of the American Medical Association* 275 (1996): 1907.

Emanuel, E., and L. Emanuel. "The Promise of a Good Death." *Lancet* 351 (1998): SH21.

Field, M., and C. Cassel, eds. *Approaching Death: Improving Care at the End of Life.* Washington, DC: National Academy Press, 1997.

Filene, P. *In the Arms of Others: A Cultural History of the Right-To-Die in America.* Chicago: Ivan R. Dee, 1998.

Garrow, D. "The Right to Die: Death with Dignity in America." *Mississippi Law Journal* 68 (1998): 407.

Goldmeier, K. Comment. "The Right to Refuse Life-Sustaining Medical Treatment: National Trends and Recent Changes in Maryland." *Maryland Law Review* 53 (1994): 1306.

Gostin, L. "Deciding Life and Death in the Courtroom: From *Quinlan* to *Cruzan, Glucksberg,* and *Vacco* — A Brief History and Analysis of Constitutional Protection of the 'Right to Die.'" *Journal of the American Medical Association* 278 (1997): 1523.

Grubb, A. "Who Decides? Legislating for the Incapacitated Adult." *European Journal of Health Law* 5 (1998): 231.

Hall, A. "To Die with Dignity: Comparing Physician Assisted Suicide in the United States, Japan, and the Netherlands." *Washington University Law Quarterly* 74 (1996): 803.

Hanafin, P. *Last Rights: Death, Dying & the Law in Ireland.* Cork, Ireland: Cork University Press, 1997.

Hanson, L., et al. "What Is Wrong with End-of-Life Care? Opinions of Bereaved Family Members." *Journal of the American Geriatrics Society* 45 (1997): 1339.

Heffner, J., et al. "Publications in Subspecialty Journals on End-of-Life Ethics." *Archives of Internal Medicine* 157 (1997): 685.

Hodgson, J. "Rights of the Terminally Ill Patient." *Annals of Health Law* 5 (1996): 169.

Jennings, B. "The Liberal Neutrality of Living and Dying: Bioethics, Constitutional Law, and Political Theory in the American Right-to-Die Debate." *Journal of Contemporary Health Law and Policy* 16 (1999): 97.

Johnson, S. "End-of-Life Decision Making: What We Don't Know, We Make Up; What We Do Know, We Ignore." *Indiana Law Review* 31 (1998): 13.

Kalt, B. "Death, Ethics, and the State." *Harvard Journal of Law & Public Policy* 23 (2000): 487.

Kapp, M. "Treating Medical Charts Near the End of Life: How Legal Anxieties Inhibit Good Patient Deaths." *University of Toledo Law Review* 28 (1997): 521.

Kübler-Ross, E. *The Wheel of Life: A Memoir of Living and Dying.* New York, NY: Simon & Schuster, 1997.

Institute of Medicine. *Approaching Death: Improving Care at the End of Life.* M. Field & C. Cassel, eds. Washington, DC: National Academy Press, 1997.

Levinsky, N. "The Purpose of Advance Medical Planning — Autonomy for Patients or Limitation of Care?" *New England Journal of Medicine* 335 (1996): 741.

Luttrell, S. "Making Decisions About Medical Treatment for Mentally Incapable Adults in the UK." *Lancet* 350 (1997): 950.

BIBLIOGRAPHY

Malloy, S. "Beyond Misguided Paternalism: Resuscitating the Right to Refuse Medical Treatment." *Wake Forest Law Review* 33 (1998): 1035.

Mehrle, J. Note. "*Degrella v. Elston:* Kentucky Supreme Court Rules on an Incompetent Patient's Right to Die." *Northern Kentucky University Law Review* 21 (1994): 449.

Michigan Commission on Death and Dying. *Final Report of the Michigan Commission on Death and Dying*. Lansing, MI: Michigan Commission on Death and Dying, 1994.

Munby, J. "Rhetoric and Reality: The Limitations of Patient Self-Determination in Contemporary English Law." *Journal of Contemporary Health Law and Policy* 14 (1998): 315.

Parker, F. "The Withholding or Withdrawal of Life-Sustaining Medical Treatment Under Louisiana Law." *Loyola Law Review* 45 (1999): 121.

Samerson, Y. *Choices for Terminally Ill Parents: A Guide for State Law Makers*. Washington, DC: American Bar Association, 1997.

Samerson, Y. "The Myth of Autonomy at the End of Life." *Villanova Law Review* 44: 577.

Samerson, Y. *The Right to Die Debate: A Documentary History*. Westport, CT: Greenwood Press, 1999.

The SUPPORT Principal Investigators. "A Controlled Trial to Improve Care for Seriously Ill Hospitalized Patients." *Journal of the American Medical Association* 274 (1995): 1591.

Zuckerman, C. *End-of-Life Care and Hospital Legal Counsel: Current Involvement and Opportunities for the Future*. New York: Milbank Memorial Fund, 1999.

Zuckerman, C., & A. Mackinnon. *The Challenge of Caring for Patients near the End of Life: Findings from the Hospital Palliative Care Initiative*. New York: United Hospital Fund of New York, 1998.

CHAPTER 2

NATURE AND SOURCES OF THE RIGHT TO DIE

§ 2.2   The Legal Consensus About Forgoing Life-Sustaining Treatment

Page 39, add to footnote 6:

IL: *In re* Fetus Brown, 689 N.E.2d 397, 401 (Ill. App. Ct. 1997).

MI: Martin v. Martin, 538 N.W.2d 399 (Mich. 1995), *rev'g* 517 N.W.2d 749 (Mich. Ct. App. 1994), *and* 504 N.W.2d 917 (Mich. Ct. App. 1993).

Page 40, add to footnote 11:

MO: Martin v. Martin, 538 N.W.2d 399 (Mich. 1995) (life-sustaining medical treatment may be forgone for incompetent, nonterminally ill patient only if there is clear and convincing evidence that he authorized the same under the circumstances that have in fact manifested themselves).

§ 2.3   —The Supreme Court's *Cruzan* Decision

Page 41, add note 14.1 reference at end of first sentence of section and add note 14.1:

[14.1] *But see* Washington v. Glucksberg, 117 S. Ct. 2258, 2269 (1997) ("[A]lthough *Cruzan* is often described as a 'right to die' case, . . . we were, in fact, more precise: we assumed that the Constitution granted competent persons a 'constitutionally protected right to refuse lifesaving hydration and nutrition.'").

Page 41, add at end of second sentence:

Subsequently, the Supreme Court denied certiorari in another right-to-die case.[16.1]

Page 43, add after carryover paragraph:

Although there may be room for a more expansive reading of *Cruzan,* this possibility was not realized in the Supreme Court's next foray into issues of

---

[16.1]   *See* Martin v. Martin, 538 N.W.2d 399 (Mich. 1995), *cert. denied,* 116 S. Ct. 912 (1996).

end-of-life decisionmaking. In *Washington v. Glucksberg*[24.1] and *Vacco v. Quill*,[24.2] the Court turned down an opportunity to extend the liberty interest recognized in *Cruzan* to permit terminally ill patients to determine the "time and manner" of their death not merely by forgoing life-sustaining treatment but also by seeking the assistance of their physician in providing them with a prescription for a lethal dose of medication—what is commonly referred to as "physician-assisted suicide."[24.3]

Proponents of physician-assisted suicide who had prevailed in the Second and Ninth Circuits on their claims that the New York and Washington statutes violated, respectively, the equal protection and due process clauses of the Fourteenth Amendment claimed that the liberty interest recognized in *Cruzan* was based on personal autonomy. The Supreme Court, however, rejected this claim, concluding that

> [t]he right assumed in *Cruzan* was not simply deduced from abstract concepts of personal autonomy. Given the common-law rule that forced medication was a battery, and the long legal tradition protecting the decision to refuse unwanted medical treatment, our assumption was entirely consistent with this Nation's history and constitutional traditions.[24.4]

Thus, this liberty interest could not be extended to include the assistance of a physician in actively aiding death because the interests involved were not implicated in the law of battery. Even though "[t]he decision to commit suicide with the assistance of another may be just as personal and profound as the decision to refuse unwanted medical treatment, . . . it has never enjoyed similar legal protection. Indeed, the two acts are widely and reasonably regarded as quite distinct."[24.5]

The broader understanding of what was at stake in *Cruzan* was supported by Justices Stevens and Breyer. Justice Stevens thought that "the source of Nancy Cruzan's right to refuse treatment was not just a common-law rule." He continued:

> Rather, this right is an aspect of a far broader and more basic concept of freedom that is even older than the common law. This freedom embraces, not merely a person's right to refuse a particular kind of unwanted treatment, but also her interest in dignity, and in determining the character of the memories that will survive long after her death. [Citation omitted.] In recognizing that the State's interests did not outweigh Nancy Cruzan's liberty interest in refusing

---

[24.1] 117 S. Ct. 2258 (1997).

[24.2] 117 S. Ct. 2293 (1997).

[24.3] See **Ch. 18** in the main volume and this supplement.

[24.4] Washington v. Glucksberg, 117 S. Ct. 2258, 2270 (1997).

[24.5] *Id.*

medical treatment, *Cruzan* rested not simply on the common-law right to refuse medical treatment, but—at least implicitly—on the even more fundamental right to make this "deeply personal decision."[24.6]

§ 2.4 —Current State of the Law: Competent Patients

Page 50, add to footnote 61:

CT: Stamford Hosp. v. Vega, 674 A.2d 821 (Conn. 1996).
IL: *In re* Fetus Brown, 689 N.E.2d 397, 402 (Ill. App. Ct. 1997).
NY: Blackman v. New York City Health & Hosps. Corp., 660 N.Y.S.2d 643 (Sup. Ct. Kings County 1997).

Page 50, add to footnote 63:

But see Rick Bragg, *A Family Shooting and a Twist Like No Other,* N.Y. Times, May 19, 1999, at A1 (nat'l ed.) (judicial order permitting removal of life support from woman shot and paralyzed by her mother, overruling hospital's refusal to do so). See **§ 1A.7** in this supplement discussing the Georgette Smith case.

Page 51, add to footnote 68:

See also Institute of Medicine, Approaching Death: Improving Care at the End of Life 126 (Marilyn J. Field & Christine K. Cassel, eds., 1997) ("Care at the end of life is characterized by overuse of care. . . . Overuse and underuse of care may occur simultaneously, for example, when futile efforts to cure are continued at the expense of efforts to relieve physical and psychological symptoms and help patients and families prepare emotionally, spiritually, and practically for death.").

Page 52, add to footnote 69:

CT: Stamford Hosp. v. Vega, 674 A.2d 821 (Conn. 1996).
FL: *But see* Harrell v. St. Mary's Hosp., Inc., 678 So. 2d 455, 456 (Fla. Dist. Ct. App. 1996) ("It is unquestioned that in considering whether

---

[24.6] *Id.* at 2306 (Stevens, J., concurring in the judgment) (quoting Cruzan v. Director, 497 U.S. 261, 289 (1990) (O'Connor, J., concurring)). *See also id.* at 2311 (Breyer, J., concurring) (disagreeing with majority that respondents' claim is for a "'right to commit suicide with another's assistance'" and asserting that proper formulation is "'right to die with dignity'").

a patient may forego medical treatment, several state interests must
be addressed.").

IL: Ficke v. Evangelical Health Sys., 674 N.E.2d 888, 889 (Ill. App. Ct.
1996).

NY: *But see* Blackman v. New York City Health & Hosps. Corp., 660
N.Y.S.2d 643, 649 (Sup. Ct. Kings County 1997) (state interests must
be balanced against patient's right to refuse treatment).

Page 52, add to footnote 71:

CT: Stamford Hosp. v. Vega, 674 A.2d 821, 832 (Conn. 1996) ("If the
common law right to refuse medical treatment, based on the doctrine
of informed consent, is entitled to respect, that respect must be
accorded when the consequences are likely to be the most serious—
in matters of life and death.").

IL: *In re* Fetus Brown, 689 N.E.2d 397, 402 (Ill. App. Ct. 1997).

§ 2.5   —Current State of the Law: Incompetent Patients

Page 53, add to footnote 74:

DE: *In re* Tavel, 661 A.2d 1061, 1068 (Del. 1995) ("[T]he constitutional
right of self-determination is not lost when an individual becomes
incompetent.").

MD: Wright v. Johns Hopkins Health Sys. Corp., 728 A.2d 166, 168 (Md.
1999) ("Under Maryland common law, a competent adult has the
right to refuse medical treatment and to withdraw consent to medical
treatment once begun. The right exists even though an individual is
unable to exercise that right for himself.").

MI: Martin v. Martin, 538 N.W.2d 399, 406 (Mich. 1995) (but only if
patient "made and communicated [decisions] before losing the capacity to make further choices")

NJ: *In re* Roche, 687 A.2d 349, 351 (N.J. Super. Ct. Ch. Div. 1996).

PA: *In re* Fiori, 673 A.2d 905, 910 (Pa. 1996) ("Courts have unanimously
concluded that this right to self-determination does not cease upon
the incapacitation of the individual.").

§ 2.6 Sources of the Right to Die

Page 55, add after first sentence of second paragraph:

One reason for this is "the principle that [courts] 'eschew unnecessary determinations of constitutional questions'."[86.1]

Page 55, add to footnote 87:

MI: Martin v. Martin, 538 N.W.2d 399, 405 (Mich. 1995) (citing first edition of this treatise).

§ 2.7 Common-Law Basis

Page 56, add note 94.1 reference at end of first sentence of section and add note 94.1:

[94.1]**MA:** *See* Norwood Hosp. v. Munoz, 564 N.E.2d 1017, 1021 (Mass. 1991) ("The right to bodily integrity has been developed . . . through the doctrine of informed consent"); *In re* Shine v. Vega, 709 N.E.2d 58, 63 (Mass. 1999).

Page 57, add to footnote 96:

CT: Stamford Hosp. v. Vega, 674 A.2d 821, 831 (Conn. 1996).
DE: *In re* Tavel, 661 A.2d 1061, 1068 (Del. 1995).
IL: Ficke v. Evangelical Health Sys., 674 N.E.2d 888, 889 (Ill. App. Ct. 1996).
LA: Causey v. St. Francis Med. Ctr., 719 So. 2d 1072, 1074 (La. Ct. App. 1998) ("The legal basis for individual autonomy is the requirement of informed consent.").
NJ: Matthies v. Mastromonaco, 733 A.2d 456, 460 (N.J. 1999) ("Eventually, courts recognized that the need for the patient's consent is better understood as deriving from the right of self-determination."); *In re* Roche, 687 A.2d 349, 351 (N.J. Super. Ct. Ch. Div. 1996).
PA: *In re* Fiori, 673 A.2d 905, 909 (Pa. 1996).

Page 57, add to footnote 97:

MD: Wright v. Johns Hopkins Health Sys. Corp., 728 A.2d 166, 168 (Md. 1999).

[86.1] Stamford Hosp. v. Vega, 674 A.2d 821, 831 (Conn. 1996).

MI: Martin v. Martin, 538 N.W.2d 399, 405 (Mich. 1995) (common-law doctrine of informed consent) (citing first edition of this treatise).
NY: Blackman v. New York City Health & Hosps. Corp., 660 N.Y.S.2d 643, 647 (Sup. Ct. Kings County 1997).

Page 58, add to footnote 103:

LA: Causey v. St. Francis Med. Ctr., 719 So. 2d 1072, 1074 (La. Ct. App. 1998) ("The legal basis for individual autonomy is the requirement of informed consent.").

Page 58, add to footnote 104:

CT: Stamford Hosp. v. Vega, 674 A.2d 821, 831 (Conn. 1996).

Page 59, replace Ohio citation in footnote 107 with:

OH: *But see* Anderson v. St. Francis-St. George Hosp., 671 N.E.2d 225 (Ohio 1996).

Page 59, add to footnote 108:

IL: *Accord In re* Fetus Brown, 689 N.E.2d 397, 402 (Ill. App. Ct. 1997).
PA: *In re* Fiori, 673 A.2d 905, 909–10 (Pa. 1996).

Page 61, add to footnote 115:

MA: *In re* Shine v. Vega, 709 N.E.2d 58 (Mass. 1999) (quoting Norwood Hosp. v. Munoz, 564 N.E.2d 1017 (Mass. 1991)).

§ 2.8   Constitutional Rights of Privacy and Liberty

Page 61, add to footnote 118:

FL: M.N. v. Southern Baptist Hosp. of Fla., Inc., 648 So. 2d 769, 771 (Fla. Dist. Ct. App. 1994) (dictum).

Page 61, add to footnote 119:

FL: M.N. v. Southern Baptist Hosp. of Fla., Inc., 648 So. 2d 769, 771 (Fla. Dist. Ct. App. 1994).

Page 62, add to footnote 121:

FL: M.N. v. Southern Baptist Hosp. of Fla., Inc., 648 So. 2d 769 (Fla. Dist. Ct. App. 1994).

NJ: *In re* Roche, 687 A.2d 349, 351 (N.J. Super. Ct. Ch. Div. 1996).

Page 62, add to footnote 122:

DE: *In re* Tavel, 661 A.2d 1061, 1068 (Del. 1995) ("The preservation of that common law right of self-determination has been implemented by the Fifth Amendment to the United States Constitution and Article I, § 7 of the Delaware Constitution.").

IL: Ficke v. Evangelical Health Sys., 674 N.E.2d 888, 889 (Ill. App. Ct. 1996). *Cf. In re* Fetus Brown, 689 N.E.2d 397, 402 (Ill. App. Ct. 1997).

Page 63, add to footnote 125:

IL: *Cf. In re* Fetus Brown, 689 N.E.2d 397, 402 (Ill. App. Ct. 1997).

PA: *See, e.g., In re* Fiori, 673 A.2d 905, 909 (Pa. 1996) ("[C]ourts should avoid constitutional issues when the issue at hand may be decided upon other grounds.").

Page 63, add to footnote 126:

See also Washington v. Glucksberg, 117 S. Ct. 2258, 2267 (1997).

Page 64, add to footnote 137:

FL: M.N. v. Southern Baptist Hosp. of Fla., Inc., 648 So. 2d 769 (Fla. Dist. Ct. App. 1994) (unclear whether federal or state constitutional right or both).

Page 65, add to footnote 141:

DE: *In re* Tavel, 661 A.2d 1061, 1068 (Del. 1995) ("The preservation of that common law right of self-determination has been implemented by the Fifth Amendment to the United States Constitution and Article I, § 7 of the Delaware Constitution.").

FL: *Cf.* Singletary v. Costello, 665 So. 2d 1099, 1103 (Fla. Dist. Ct. App. 1996) (provides greater protection to privacy than 14th Amendment due process clause).

Page 66, add to footnote 144:

See generally James Bopp & Daniel Avila, *The Due Process "Right to Life" in* Cruzan *and Its Impact on "Right-to-Die" Law,* 53 U. Pitt. L. Rev. 193 (1991).

§ 2.9   Religious Belief

Page 67, add to footnote 149:

FL: M.N. v. Southern Baptist Hosp. of Fla., Inc., 648 So. 2d 769 (Fla. Dist. Ct. App. 1994).

Page 68, add to footnote 154:

IL: *But see In re* Fetus Brown, 689 N.E.2d 397, 402 (Ill. App. Ct. 1997).

Page 68, add to footnote 156:

MN: *Accord* Lundman v. McKown, 530 N.W.2d 807, 826 (Minn. Ct. App. 1995), *cert. denied,* 116 S. Ct. 814 (1996) ("A church always remains free to espouse whatever religious belief it chooses; it is the practices of its adherents that may be subject to state sanctions.").

Page 68, add to footnote 157:

MN: Lundman v. McKown, 530 N.W.2d 807 (Minn. Ct. App. 1995) (holding First Amendment confers no immunity from civil liability for wrongful death of child resulting from parental, religiously motivated refusal of treatment).

Page 70, add to footnote 160:

CA11:   Novak v. Cobb County-Kennestone Hosp. Auth., 74 F.3d 1173 (11th Cir. 1996) (under Georgia law, 16-year-old is not a competent adult), *aff'g* 849 F. Supp. 1559 (N.D. Ga. 1994).

FL: *Cf.* M.N. v. Southern Baptist Hosp. of Fla., Inc., 648 So. 2d 769 (Fla. Dist. Ct. App. 1994) (infant; right to refuse treatment asserted by parents can be outweighed by compelling state interest).

MA: *In re* Rena, 705 N.E.2d 1155 (Mass. App. Ct. 1999) (mature minor).

Page 70, add to footnote 163:

MA: *See also In re* Rena, 705 N.E.2d 1155 (Mass. App. Ct. 1999).

§ 2.10   Statutes and Regulations

Page 71, add note 168.1 reference in line 8 after "the public policy of the state is reflected in its advance directive statute" and add note 168.1:

[168.1] **LA:** *See* Causey v. St. Francis Med. Ctr., 719 So. 2d 1072, 1074 (La. Ct. App. 1998) ("Patient participation in medical decisionmaking is now well-established. Recognizing individual autonomy and the right to self-determination, our state legislature enacted a statute granting a competent, terminally ill person the right to refuse medical treatment. La. R.S. 40:1299.58.1, *et seq*.").

Page 71, add to footnote 169:

IL: *In re* Fetus Brown, 689 N.E.2d 397, 404 (Ill. App. Ct. 1997) (relying on surrogate decisionmaking statute to find a right to forgo life-sustaining treatment); Ficke v. Evangelical Health Sys., 674 N.E.2d 888, 891 (Ill. App. Ct. 1996) (surrogate decisionmaking statute "codifies Illinois' common law and constitutional rights to forego life-sustaining treatment").

MD: Wright v. Johns Hopkins Health Sys. Corp., 728 A.2d 166 (Md. 1999) ("In addition to constitutional and common law rights to refuse life-sustaining medical procedures, an individual's ability to direct in advance his choice concerning whether to refuse life-sustaining procedures is based in" the advance directive statute).

Page 72, add to footnote 172:

IL: *In re* Fetus Brown, 689 N.E.2d 397, 404 (Ill. App. Ct. 1997) (surrogate decisionmaking statute provides basis for *competent* patient's right to forgo life-sustaining treatment, in combination with common-law right).

§ 2.11   Parens Patriae Power

Page 75, add to footnote 190:

DC: *In re* K.I., 735 A.2d 448, 454 (D.C. Ct. App. 1999) (in case of brain-damaged minor previously adjudicated as neglected, upon application by medical guardian ad litem for a DNR order, "[t]he court's exercise of its discretion as parens patriae was essential since the [District of Columbia] government took no position on the resuscitation issue and because [the child's mother and putative father] had a fundamental disagreement concerning resuscitation").

Bibliography

Bopp, J., and D. Avila. "The Due Process 'Right to Life' in *Cruzan* and Its Impact on 'Right-to-Die' Law." *University of Pittsburgh Law Review* 53 (1991): 193.

BIBLIOGRAPHY

Gostin, L. "Deciding Life and Death in the Courtroom: From *Quinlan* to *Cruzan, Glucksberg,* and *Vacco*—A Brief History and Analysis of Constitutional Protection of the 'Right to Die.'" *Journal of the American Medical Association* 278 (1997): 1523.

Padmore, S. "California's Limits on the Right to Refuse Life Saving Treatment—'No Holds Barred?' *Thor v. Superior Court,* 855 P.2d 375 (Cal. 1993) (en banc)." *Washington University Journal of Urban and Contemporary Law* 46 (1994): 369.

Post, S. "Baby K: Medical Futility and the Free Exercise of Religion." *Journal of Law, Medicine & Ethics* 23 (1995): 20.

Rillo, T. Comment. "Constitutional Law: The Limits of a Patient's Right to Refuse Medical Treatment." *Florida Law Review* 46 (1994): 347.

Rizzo, P. "Religion-Based Arguments in the Public Arena: A Catholic Perspective on Euthanasia, *Compassion in Dying v. State of Washington* and *Quill v. Vacco.*" *DePaul Journal of Health Care Law* 1 (1996): 243.

Sinclair, D. "The Obligation to Heal and Patient Autonomy in Jewish Law." *Journal of Law and Religion* 13 (1998–99): 351.

CHAPTER 3

BASIC PRINCIPLES OF MEDICAL DECISIONMAKING

§ 3.2 Introduction to the Doctrine of Informed Consent

Page 83, add note 1.1 reference at end of second sentence of second paragraph and add note 1.1 :

[1.1] **NJ:** Matthies v. Mastromonaco, 733 A.2d 456, 460 (N.J. 1999) ("Eventually, courts recognized that the need for the patient's consent is better understood as deriving from the right of self-determination.").

Page 83, add to footnote 3:

NJ: Matthies v. Mastromonaco, 733 A.2d 456 (N.J. 1999).

§ 3.3 —Competent Patients

Page 84, add to footnote 5:

MA: *See In re* Shine v. Vega, 709 N.E.2d 58, 62 (Mass. 1999) (burden of proof is on defendant to establish privilege to treat without obtaining informed consent).

§ 3.7 Conversation About Therapy: Risks versus Options

Page 88, add to footnote 31:

NJ: *But see* Matthies v. Mastromonaco, 733 A.2d 456 (N.J. 1999) (holding doctor required to disclose therapeutic options he did not recommend).

Page 89, add note 31.1 reference at end of second sentence of first paragraph and add note 31.1:

[31.1] **NJ:** Matthies v. Mastromonaco, 733 A.2d 456, 462 (N.J. 1999) ("[T]he physician, by not discussing [non-recommended] alternatives, effectively makes the choice for the patient.").

Page 89, add to footnote 32:

NJ: Matthies v. Mastromonaco, 733 A.2d 456, 463 (N.J. 1999) ("By not telling the patient of all medically reasonable alternatives, the physician breaches the patient's right to make an informed choice.").

§ 3.9   Informed Consent in Practice

Page 91, add to footnote 45:

See The SUPPORT Principal Investigators, *A Controlled Trial to Improve Care for Seriously Ill Hospitalized Patients,* 274 JAMA 1591, 1592 (1995); Marion Danis et al., *A Prospective Study of the Impact of Patient Preferences on Life-Sustaining Treatment and Hospital Cost,* 24 Critical Care Med. 1811 (1996).

Page 93, add to footnote 54:

NJ: *But see* Matthies v. Mastromonaco, 733 A.2d 456, 461 (N.J. 1999) ("In informed consent analysis, the decisive factor is not whether a treatment alternative is invasive or noninvasive, but whether the physician adequately presents the material facts so that the patient can make an informed decision.").

Page 93, add at end of section:

Although few jurisdictions have so held, the better view is that disclosure should be made even of medically acceptable alternatives even if the physician does not believe that they are advisable in this particular case[54.1] and even if the patient has refused the particular treatment.[54.2]

[54.1] **NJ:** *See, e.g.,* Matthies v. Mastromonaco, 733 A.2d 456, 462 (N.J. 1999) ("For consent to be informed, the patient must know not only of alternatives that the physician recommends, but of medically reasonable alternatives that the physician does not recommend. Otherwise, the physician, by not discussing these alternatives, effectively makes the choice for the patient. Accordingly, the physician should discuss the medically reasonable courses of treatment, including nontreatment.").

[54.2] **CA:** *See, e.g.,* Truman v. Thomas, 165 Cal. Rptr. 308 (Cal. 1980).

PRINCIPLES OF DECISIONMAKING

§ 3.15 — Elements of Disclosure

Page 96, add to footnote 65:

LA: *But cf.* Causey v. St. Francis Med. Ctr., 719 So. 2d 1072 (La. Ct. App. 1998) (no obligation to disclose medically inappropriate treatments).

NY: Blackman v. New York City Health & Hosps. Corp., 660 N.Y.S.2d 643, 649 (Sup. Ct. Kings County 1997) (hospital obligated to provide patient who is refusing treatment with information about her expected quality of life if treatment is administered).

§ 3.18 — — Voluntariness

Page 98, add to footnote 81:

NY: Blackman v. New York City Health & Hosps. Corp., 660 N.Y.S.2d 643, 649 (Sup. Ct. Kings County 1997) (merely counseling patient does not constitute undue influence as long as decision is product of patient's own mind).

Page 99, add to footnote 86:

NY: Blackman v. New York City Health & Hosps. Corp., 660 N.Y.S.2d 643, 649 (Sup. Ct. Kings County 1997) (merely counseling patient does not constitute undue influence as long as decision is product of patient's own mind).

Page 99, add to footnote 89:

DE: *Cf. In re* Tavel, 661 A.2d 1061, 1064 (Del. 1995) (patient's daughter testified she was pressured into agreeing to implantation of feeding tube).

§ 3.22   Introduction

Page 104, add to carryover paragraph:

These exceptions create situations in which physicians have a privilege to treat without satisfying the full requirements, or perhaps any of the requirements, of informed consent.[109.1]

[109.1] **MA:** *In re* Shine v. Vega, 709 N.E.2d 58, 64 n.17 (Mass. 1999) (citing W.L. Prosser & W.P. Keeton, Torts § 18, at 117–18 (5th ed. 1984).

Page 104, add to footnote 110:

MA: *In re* Shine v. Vega, 709 N.E.2d 58, 63–64 (Mass. 1999).

§ 3.23   Emergency

Page 104, add note 110.1 reference at end of first sentence of section and add note 110.1:

[110.1] **MA:** *In re* Shine v. Vega, 709 N.E.2d 58 (Mass. 1999) ("The emergency exception to the informed consent doctrine has been widely recognized and its component elements broadly described. *See, e.g.,* W.L. Prosser & W.P. Keeton, Torts § 18, at 117–118 (5th ed. 1984); Meisel, The "Exceptions" to the Informed Consent Doctrine: Striking a Balance Between Competing Values in Medical Decisionmaking, 1979 Wis. L. Rev. 413, 430–438. *See also* Restatement (Second) of Torts § 892D (1979) (emergency action without consent).").

Page 104, add to footnote 112:

MA: *In re* Shine v. Vega, 709 N.E.2d 58, 59 (Mass. 1999) ("[W]e must resolve the conflict between the right of a competent adult to refuse medical treatment and the interest of a physician in preserving life without fear of liability.").

Page 105, add to footnote 113:

MA: *But see In re* Shine v. Vega, 709 N.E.2d 58 (Mass. 1999) (emergency exception cannot be used to avoid unambiguous decision of competent patient to decline treatment, even when patient's condition is life-threatening and treatment refused by patient is likely to save patient's life).

Page 105, add to footnote 114:

MA: *In re* Shine v. Vega, 709 N.E.2d 58 (Mass. 1999) (reinstating causes of action based on failing to honor request of allegedly competent patient not to be intubated).

Page 105, add to footnote 115:

MA: *But see In re* Shine v. Vega, 709 N.E.2d 58 (Mass. 1999) (emergency exception cannot be used to avoid unambiguous decision of competent patient to decline treatment, even when patient's condition is life-threatening and treatment refused by patient is likely to save patient's life).

Page 106, add at end of section:

In re Shine v. Vega[118.1] illustrates how variable and complex the concept of an emergency can be. This case involved the treatment of a woman who was having an acute attack of asthma, which lasted over a considerable period of time, during which she was conscious the entire time and probably competent. She consented to certain types of treatment but refused others; indeed, she agreed to come to the defendant hospital emergency room only after extracting a promise that she would not be intubated. However, the attending physician ultimately determined that she needed to be intubated despite her persistent refusals and did so, ultimately leading to a suit for damages premised on a variety of theories. The Massachusetts Supreme Judicial Court reversed a jury's finding of no liability and reinstated for retrial because of erroneous instructions, largely dealing with the right to refuse treatment in an emergency.[118.2]

Bibliography

American Academy of Pediatrics, Committee on Bioethics. "Informed Consent, Parental Permission, and Assent in Pediatric Practice." *Pediatrics* 95 (1995): 314.

Katz, J. "Informed Consent—Must It Remain a Fairy Tale?" *Journal of Contemporary Health Law and Policy* 10 (1994): 69.

Wear, S. *Informed Consent: Patient Autonomy and Clinician Beneficence within Health Care.* Washington, DC: Georgetown University Press, 1998.

[118.1] 709 N.E.2d 58 (Mass. 1999).

[118.2] See § **17.16** in this supplement.

CHAPTER 4

MEANING AND EFFECT OF INCOMPETENCE

§ 4.7 —Other Related Concepts

Page 116, add to footnote 14:

IL: Ill. Ann. Stat. ch. 755, § 40/20(c).

§ 4.8 Presumption of Competence

Page 118, add to footnote 25:

NJ: *In re* M.R., 638 A.2d 1274 (N.J. 1994).

Page 118, add to footnote 26:

DE: *Cf. In re* Gordy, 658 A.2d 613, 617–18 (Del. Ch. 1994) ("Certainly on such a question the burden of proof and the burden of persuasion must be upon that party attempting to deprive another of the basic liberty entailed in one's control over the medical treatment that one undergoes.").

§ 4.9 —Triggers to Inquiry into Incompetence

Page 120, add to footnote 34:

MA: *In re* Shine v. Vega, 709 N.E.2d 58, 65 n.20 (Mass. 1999) ("A physician, and a jury, may reasonably take into account a patient's refusal to consent to life-saving medical treatment in determining whether the patient is competent to consent to or refuse treatment, but this factor is not dispositive.").

§ 4.10 —Significance of Patient Ambivalence and Vacillation

Page 122, add to footnote 41:

NY: Blackman v. New York City Health & Hosps. Corp., 660 N.Y.S.2d 643 (Sup. Ct. Kings County 1997) (depressed elderly patient who twice withdrew consent to surgery not incompetent).

Page 122, add to footnote 45:

MI: Martin v. Martin, 517 N.W.2d 749 (Mich. Ct. App. 1994), *rev'd on other grounds,* 538 N.W.2d 399 (Mich. 1995).

§ 4.12 Effect of Adjudication of Incompetence

Page 124, add to footnote 53:

IL: *In re* Austwick, 656 N.E.2d 773, 776 (Ill. App. Ct. 1995).
NJ: *In re* Roche, 687 A.2d 349, 352 (N.J. Super. Ct. Ch. Div. 1996) (quoting *In re* Conroy, 486 A.2d 1209 (N.J. 1985)) (patient adjudicated incompetent to make medical decisions in general not necessarily incompetent to make particular medical decisions).

§ 4.13 —Appointment of Guardian

Page 125, add at end of first paragraph:

A guardian should not be appointed, even for a person who lacks decision-making capacity, if that person has sought by other valid means—such as the execution of a health care power of attorney—to "'effectuate[] a plan for the management of his affairs.'"[54.1]

§ 4.15 —Guardian's Authority to Forgo Life-Sustaining Treatment

Page 126, add to footnote 63:

IL: *In re* Austwick, 656 N.E.2d 773 (Ill. App. Ct. 1995) (plenary public guardian mistakenly thought he had authority to consent to DNR order).

[54.1] **NY:** *In re* Lowe, 688 N.Y.S.2d 389, 390 (Sup. Ct. Queens County 1999).

NY: *In re* Barsky (Kyle), 627 N.Y.S.2d 903, 904 (Sup. Ct. Suffolk County 1995).

§ 4.17   — —Plenary Guardianship

Page 127, add to footnote 66:

IL: *But see In re* Austwick, 656 N.E.2d 773, 776 (Ill. App. Ct. 1995) (plenary public guardian lacked authority to consent to DNR order because patient did not lack decisionmaking capacity).

Page 128, add to footnote 68:

NY: *Cf. In re* Barsky (Kyle), 627 N.Y.S.2d 903 (Sup. Ct. Suffolk County 1995) (plenary guardian sought judicial clarification of powers in light of state's strict standard for forgoing life-sustaining treatment).

§ 4.19   — —Limited Guardianship for Medical Decisionmaking

Page 134, add to footnote 103:

NJ: *But see In re* Roche, 687 A.2d 349 (N.J. Super. Ct. Ch. Div. 1996) (quoting *In re* Conroy, 486 A.2d 1209 (N.J. 1985)) (patient adjudicated incompetent to make medical decisions in general not necessarily incompetent to make particular medical decisions).

Page 135, add after note 105 reference:

In Virginia, a guardian is authorized to make decisions regarding a ward's health, but the guardian's authority does not permit changing decisions about end-of-life care that a ward made in a valid advance directive or health care power of attorney. A guardian may petition for the appointment of a health care agent different from the one the patient appointed, but a new agent may not change the person's "directives concerning the provision or refusal of specific medical treatments or procedures."[105.1]

Page 136, add to footnote 109:

ID: *See also* Idaho Code § 66-405(8) (guardian of developmentally disabled individual may consent to forgoing life-sustaining treatment only if patient has incurable condition or is in persistent vegetative state).

[105.1] **VA:** Va. Code Ann. §§ 37.1-134.6, 37.1-137.1.

§ 4.20   Effect of De Facto Incompetence

Page 137, add note 113.1 reference after "affairs" in second sentence of first full paragraph and add note 113.1:

[113.1] **DE:** *In re* Tavel, 661 A.2d 1061, 1063 (Del. 1995) (patient's daughter "acted as her mother's de facto personal guardian after her mother's stroke").

§ 4.23   General Incompetence

Page 140, add to footnote 130:

MI: Martin v. Martin, 504 N.W.2d 917 (Mich. Ct. App. 1993), *rev'd on other grounds,* 538 N.W.2d 399, 406 n.10 (Mich. 1995) (citing first edition of this treatise).

§ 4.24   —Use in Right-to-Die Cases

Page 143, add to footnote 141:

MI: Martin v. Martin, 504 N.W.2d 917 (Mich. Ct. App. 1993), *rev'd on other grounds*, 538 N.W.2d 399, 406 n.10 (Mich. 1995) (citing first edition of this treatise).

§ 4.25   Specific Incompetence

Page 144, add to footnote 145:

MI: Martin v. Martin, 517 N.W.2d 749 (Mich. Ct. App. 1994), *rev'd on other grounds*, 538 N.W.2d 399 (Mich. 1995).

§ 4.26   The Emerging Consensus: Incompetence as Lack of Understanding

Page 146, add to footnote 155:

NY: Blackman v. New York City Health & Hosps. Corp., 660 N.Y.S.2d 643 (Sup. Ct. Kings County 1997) (patient who cannot hear, whose vision is severely compromised, who is depressed, who has twice changed her mind about treatment but who understands consequences of treatment refusal is competent).

OR: *Cf.* Or. Rev. Stat. § 127.800, 1.01(6), (7) (in statute legalizing physician-assisted suicide, "'[i]ncapable' means that in the opinion of a court or in the opinion of the patient's attending physician or consulting physician, a patient lacks the ability to make and communicate health care decisions to health care providers . . . that is based on an appreciation of the relevant facts after being fully informed . . . .").

§ 4.32   —Nature of Decision

Page 155, add to footnote 194:

See generally David Orentlicher, *The Illusion of Patient Choice in End-of-Life Decisions,* 267 JAMA 2101, 2101 (1992) ("[P]atients' preferences respected as long as the physicians thought that the patients' choices resulted in the best decisions.") (discussing Marion Danis et al., *A Prospective Study of Advance Directives for Life-Sustaining Care,* 324 N. Eng. J. Med. 882 (1991)).

Bibliography

Appelbaum, P., and T. Grisso. "Capacities of Hospitalized, Medically Ill Patients to Consent to Treatment." *Psychosomatics* 38 (1997): 119.

Appelbaum, P., and T. Grisso. "The MacArthur Treatment Competence Study, I. Mental Illness and Competence to Consent to Treatment." *Law and Human Behavior* 19 (1995): 105.

Berg, J., et al. "Constructing Competence: Formulating Standards of Legal Competence to Make Medical Decisions." *Rutgers Law Review* 48 (1996): 345.

Bradley, E., et al. "Assessing Capacity to Participate in Discussions of Advance Directives in Nursing Homes: Findings from a Study of the Patient Self Determination Act." *Journal of the American Geriatrics Society* 45 (1997): 79.

Culver, C., and B. Gert. "The Inadequacy of Incompetence." *Milbank Quarterly* 68 (1990): 619.

Donaldson, J. "Reform of Adult Guardianship Law." *University of Richmond Law Review* 32 (1998): 1273.

Fazel, S., et al. "Assessment of Competence to Complete Advance Directives: Validation of a Patient Centred Approach." *British Medical Journal* 318 (1999): 493.

Fitten L. J., et al. "Assessing Treatment Decision-Making Capacity in Elderly Nursing Home Residents." *Journal of the American Geriatric Society* 38 (1990): 1097.

Grisso, T., and P. Appelbaum. *Assessing Competence to Consent to Treatment.* New York: Oxford University Press, 1998.

Grisso, T., and P. Appelbaum. "A Comparison of Standards for Assessing Patients' Capacities to Make Treatment Decisions." *American Journal of Psychiatry* 152 (1995): 1033.

Grisso, T., and P. Appelbaum. "The MacArthur Treatment Competence Study, II. Measures of Abilities Related to Competence to Consent to Treatment." *Law and Human Behavior* 19 (1995): 127.

Grisso, T., and P. Appelbaum. "The MacArthur Treatment Competence Study, III. Abilities of Patients to Consent to Psychiatric and Medical Treatments." *Law and Human Behavior* 19 (1995): 149.

Gunn, M. "The Meaning of Incapacity." *Medical Law Review* 2 (1994): 8.

Hurme, S. "Current Trends in Guardianship Reform." *Maryland Journal of Contemporary Legal Issues* 7 (1995–1996): 143.

Janofsky, J., et al. "The Hopkins Competency Assessment Test: A Brief Method for Evaluating Patients' Capacity to Give Informed Consent." *Hospital and Community Psychiatry* 43 (1992): 132.

Kapp, M. "Assessment of Competency." In L. Carstensen, *The Practical Handbook of Clinical Gerontology.* Thousand Oaks, Cal: Sage Publications, 1996.

Kjervik, D., et al. "Decisions About Guardianship for Older Persons: Incompetency Criteria." *American Journal of Alzheimer's Care and Related Disorders and Research* (1994): 13.

Kloezen, S., et al. "Assessment of Treatment Decision-Making Capacity in a Medically Ill Patient." *Journal of the American Geriatric Society* 36 (1988): 1055.

Markson, L., et al. "Physician Assessment of Patient Competence." *Journal of the American Geriatrics Society* 42 (1994): 1074.

Marson, D., et al. "Assessing the Competency of Patients with Alzheimer's Disease Under Different Legal Standards." *Archives of Neurology* 52 (1995): 949.

Marson, D., et al. "Neuropsychologic Predictors of Competency in Alzheimer's Disease Using a Rational Reasons Legal Standard." *Archives of Neurology* 52 (1995): 955.

Marson, D., et al. "Toward a Neurologic Model of Competency: Cognitive Predictors of Capacity to Consent in Alzheimer's Disease Using Three Different Legal Standards." *Neurology* 46 (1996): 666.

BIBLIOGRAPHY

May, T. "Assessing Competency Without Judging Merit." *Journal of Clinical Ethics* 9 (1998): 247.

Mezey, M., et al. "Assessment of Decision-Making Capacity: Nursing's Role." *Journal of Gerontological Nursing* 23 (1997): 28.

Morris, G. "Judging Judgment: Assessing the Competence of Mental Patients to Refuse Treatment." *San Diego Law Review* 32 (1995): 343.

National Bioethics Advisory Commission, ed. *Research Involving Persons with Mental Disorders That May Affect Decisionmaking Capacity,* vol. I. Rockville, MD: National Bioethics Advisory Commission, 1998. <www.bioethics.gov>.

Schmidt, W. *Guardianship: Court of Last Resort for the Elderly and Disabled.* Durham, N.C.: Carolina Academic Press, 1995.

Schwartz, S. "Abolishing Competency as a Construction of Difference: A Radical Proposal to Promote the Equality of Persons with Disabilities." *University of Miami Law Review* 47 (1993): 867.

Silberfeld, M., et al. "Capacity to Complete an Advance Directive." *Journal of the American Geriatric Society* 41 (1993): 1141.

Slobogin, C. "'Appreciation' as a Measure of Competency." *Psychology, Public Policy, and Law* 2 (1996): 18.

Snyder, A. "Competency to Refuse Lifesaving Treatment: Valuing the Nonlogical Aspects of a Person's Decisions." *Issues in Law and Medicine* 10 (1994): 299.

Walkow, M. Comment. "Informed Consent—Legal Competency Not Determinative of Person's Ability to Consent to Medical Treatment—*Miller v. Rhode Island Hospital,* 625 A.2d 778 (R.I. 1993)." *Suffolk University Law Review* 28 (1995): 271.

White, B. *Competence to Consent.* Washington, D.C.: Georgetown University Press, 1994.

Wicclair, M. "The Continuing Debate over Risk-Related Standards of Competence." *Bioethics* 13 (1999): 149.

Wicclair, M. "Patient Decision-Making Capacity and Risk." *Bioethics* 5 (1991): 91.

Wilks, I. "Asymmetrical Competence." *Bioethics* 13 (1999): 154.

Wilks, I. "The Debate Over Risk-Related Standards of Competence." *Bioethics* 11 (1997): 413.

Winick, B. "Competency to Consent to Treatment: The Distinction Between Assent and Objection." *Houston Law Review* 28 (1991): 15.

CHAPTER 5

DETERMINATION OF INCOMPETENCE, DESIGNATION OF A SURROGATE, AND REVIEW OF DECISIONS

§ 5.1 The General Issue: Going to Court

Page 164, add to footnote 4:

CA: *See also* Rains v. Belshe, 38 Cal. Rptr. 2d 185 (Ct. App. 1995) (upholding constitutionality of Cal. Health & Safety Code § 1418.8, authorizing such determinations for nursing home residents to be made nonjudicially).

IL: *Cf.* Ficke v. Evangelical Health Sys., 674 N.E.2d 888, 891 (Ill. App. Ct. 1996) (surrogate decisionmaking statute "establishes a private decision-making process").

§ 5.2 Specific Procedural Issues

Page 167, add to footnote 17:

MI: Martin v. Martin, 504 N.W.2d 917 (Mich. Ct. App. 1993), *rev'd on other grounds,* 538 N.W.2d 399 (Mich. 1995).

§ 5.7 Terminology: Surrogate, Guardian, and Similar Terms

Page 170, add note 28.1 reference at end of fifth sentence of third paragraph and add note 28.1:

28.1 *But see* Fla. Stat. Ann. § 765.101(13) (using term "proxy" to refer to one "who has not been expressly designated to make health care decisions for a particular incapacitated individual, but who" is entitled to do so by virtue of

Fla. Stat. Ann. § 765.401, and using "surrogate" to refer to a decisionmaker appointed by the patient under Fla. Stat. Ann. §§ 765.201–.205).

§ 5.9   Choice of Clinical or Judicial Approach to Determining Incompetence and Designating a Surrogate

Page 173, add note 33.1 reference at end of carryover sentence and add note 33.1:

[33.1] *Cf.* Rains v. Belshe, 38 Cal. Rptr. 2d 185, 189 (Ct. App. 1995) (possibility of several-month delay in obtaining judicial decree to authorize nonemergency treatment).

§ 5.10   Customary Medical Practice in Determining Incompetence and Designating a Surrogate

Page 174, add at end of first sentence of second paragraph:

and by some legislatures.[41.1]

§ 5.11   Legal Status of Clinical Determinations of Incompetence

Page 183, add to footnote 71:

FL: *In re* Dubreuil, 629 So. 2d 819 (Fla. 1993); Harrell v. St. Mary's Hosp., Inc., 678 So. 2d 455 (Fla. Dist. Ct. App. 1996).

Page 184, add to footnote 76:

FL: Harrell v. St. Mary's Hosp., Inc., 678 So. 2d 455, 457–58 (Fla. Dist. Ct. App. 1996).

[41.1] *See, e.g.,* Cal. Health & Safety Code § 1418.8 (permitting physician of nursing home residents to determine whether resident has surrogate), *constitutionality upheld in* Rains v. Belshe, 38 Cal. Rptr. 2d 185 (Ct. App. 1995).

Page 184, add to footnote 79:

FL: Harrell v. St. Mary's Hosp., Inc., 678 So. 2d 455, 457–58 (Fla. Dist. Ct. App. 1996).

Page 185, add to footnote 81:

FL: Harrell v. St. Mary's Hosp., Inc., 678 So. 2d 455, 457–58 (Fla. Dist. Ct. App. 1996).

Page 185, add at end of first full paragraph:

The problem with this holding is that the exigencies of medical decisionmaking, especially in the case of Jehovah's Witnesses, will sometimes mean that no one will be available to raise the state's interest if the hospital cannot do so. The Connecticut Supreme Court recognized this in *Stamford Hospital v. Vega:*[81.1]

> Conferring standing only on the state and denying it to the hospital . . . would have effectively insulated the patient's choice from any official scrutiny because, as the facts indicate here, it would have been extremely difficult for the state to initiate judicial proceedings in time to do any good, and even if the state could have done so, it would likely have been unfamiliar both with the medical options available and with the facts and circumstances surrounding the patient's desires. The hospital was, as a practical matter, the best informed and most feasible candidate, under these circumstances, to set the judicial machinery in motion.[81.2]

Consequently, although not permitting the hospital to raise the state's interests in litigation (in no small part because the court had not previously recognized that the state actually has such interests), the court accorded the hospital has standing to assert its own interests—the well-being of minor children and the ethical integrity of the medical profession, which overlap with state interests should the court eventually find that they exist.

Page 185, add to footnote 84:

CT: *Cf.* Stamford Hosp. v. Vega, 674 A.2d 821, 827 (Conn. 1996) (noting "extraordinary procedural history" of case in which "hearing before the trial court took place in the middle of the night, under extreme emergency conditions that were not conducive to the ability of either party to develop fully its arguments, . . . [patient] was not represented by counsel at the outset of the hearing and, of that portion of the hearing in which her attorney was present, most was not recorded").

[81.1]   674 A.2d 821 (Conn. 1996).

[81.2]   *Id.* at 830.

§ 5.13   —In Medical Decisionmaking Generally

Page 188, add to footnote 93:

MA: *E.g., In re* Shine v. Vega, 709 N.E.2d 58, 65 (Mass. 1999) ("[J]ury should have been required to decide whether [patient] was capable of consenting to treatment, and, if not, whether the consent of a family member could have been obtained.").

Page 189, add to footnote 97:

CA10:   *But see* Jurasek v. Utah State Hosp., 158 F.3d 506 (10th Cir. 1998) (permitting administrative hearing re involuntary administration of medication to civilly committed individual).

§ 5.14   —In Right-to-Die Cases

Page 190, add to footnote 99:

DE: *Cf. In re* Holmes, C.M. No. 8066-NC, 1996 WL 633309, at *1 (Del. Ch. Oct. 30, 1996) ("decision [about whether to place patient suffering from Alzheimer's disease in nursing home or combination of day care and home nursing care] is one that is best made by the family"; but where patient's 16 children cannot agree, decision will be made by court).

PA: *In re* Fiori, 673 A.2d 905, 912 (Pa. 1996).

§ 5.15   Who May Serve as Surrogate When
Judicially Appointed

Page 195, add to footnote 133:

MA: *But see In re* Smith, 684 N.E.2d 613, 618 (Mass. App. Ct. 1997) ("when a principal has nominated his guardian by power of attorney . . . and protective proceedings are thereafter commenced, the Probate Court must, on proper petition, appoint the individual(s) nominated in the power, except for good cause or disqualification."), *construing* Mass. Gen. Laws ch. 201B, § 3(b).

Page 195, add to footnote 135:

MA: *In re* Smith, 684 N.E.2d 613, 617 (Mass. App. Ct. 1997) (when ward's preference for guardians is stated in durable power of attorney, ward's preference is critical factor in determining best interests).

Page 196, add to footnote 137:

MA: *But see In re* Smith, 684 N.E.2d 613, 617 (Mass. App. Ct. 1997) (court's equitable powers "'to act in the best interests of a person under its jurisdiction'" do not permit disregard of statutory requirements).

Page 196, add to footnote 138:

PA: *See also In re* Goldman, 18 Fiduc. Rep. 2d 79 (C.P. Northampton County, Pa. 1997) (daughter was appointed guardian to make decisions about all treatments except antibiotics, which she had refused to authorize).

Page 197, add note reference 141.1 at end of first paragraph and add note 141.1:

141.1 **MA:** *See, e.g., In re* Smith, 684 N.E.2d 613 (Mass. App. Ct. 1997).

§ 5.16   —In Right-to-Die Cases

Page 197, add to footnote 142:

DE: *In re* Gordy, 658 A.2d 613, 614 (Del. Ch. 1994) (patient's son "is an appropriate person to be granted legal power to make decisions respecting his mother's person").

MI: Martin v. Martin, 504 N.W.2d 917 (Mich. Ct. App. 1993), *rev'd on other grounds,* 538 N.W.2d 399 (Mich. 1995).

§ 5.18   —Presumption of Family Member as Surrogate

Page 199, add to footnote 154:

PA: *Accord In re* Fiori, 673 A.2d 905, 912 (Pa. 1996).

Page 199, add to footnote 156:

MA: *See, e.g., In re* Mason, 669 N.E.2d 1081, 1083, 1085 (Mass. App. Ct. 1996) (patient's son who "was disruptive of hospital schedules, abusive to medical personnel, and overly quick to allege neglect and maltreatment of his mother" and incapable of making health care decisions based on "true assessment of [patient's] best interests" is not qualified to serve as surrogate).

Page 200, add to footnote 159:

PA: *Accord In re* Fiori, 673 A.2d 905, 912 (Pa. 1996).

§ 5.19   —Rationale for Family Member
as Surrogate

Page 203, add to footnote 172:

PA: *Accord In re* Fiori, 673 A.2d 905, 912 (Pa. 1996) ("[C]lose family members have a special bond with the PVS patient.");   *In re* Goldman, 18 Fiduc. Rep. 2d 79 (C.P. Northampton County, Pa. 1997).

Page 204, add to footnote 174:

PA: *Accord In re* Fiori, 673 A.2d 905, 912 (Pa. 1996).

See generally Marion Danis et al., *Patients' and Families' Preferences for Medical Intensive Care*, 260 JAMA 797 (1988); P. M. Layde et al., *Surrogates' Predictions of Seriously Ill Patients' Resuscitation Preferences*, 4 Archives Fam. Med. 518 (1995); Daniel P. Sulmasy et al., *The Accuracy of Substituted Judgments in Patients with Terminal Diagnoses*, 128 Ann. Internal Med. 621 (1998).

Page 204, add note 174.1 reference after second sentence of first full paragraph and add note 174.1:

[174.1] **RI:** *See, e.g., In re* Jane Doe, 533 A.2d 523 (R.I. 1987) (mother of minor whose contact with daughter who had been placed with governmental child welfare department was so slight and sporadic as to disqualify mother from making decision about whether daughter should have abortion).

§ 5.21   —Friends

Page 209, add to footnote 201:

CA: Rains v. Belshe, 38 Cal. Rptr. 2d 185, 189 (Ct. App. 1995) (observing that absence of family was basis for legislature's enactment of statute authorizing decisionmaking for nursing home residents in the clinical setting by an interdisciplinary health care team, including a patient representative).

GA: *See, e.g.,* Edwards v. Shumate, 468 S.E.2d 23 (Ga. 1996).

Page 210, add at end of first sentence:

especially if the patient's physician is familiar with the friend's role as the patient's caretaker.[204.1]

Page 210, add to footnote 209:

GA: *Cf.* Edwards v. Shumate, 468 S.E.2d 23 (Ga. 1996) (tacitly approving decisionmaking by friends of the patient who the patient's personal physician knew to be their caretakers).

Page 210, add after footnote 210 reference:

Some surrogate decisionmaking statutes also recognize friends as legitimate surrogates for patients.[210.1]

Page 211, add at end of section:

Because of the uncertainty attendant to the use of a friend of the patient as a surrogate decisionmaker, a legislative declaration of the permissibility of this practice is desirable.[213.1]

§ 5.22   —Health Care Professionals; Public Guardians; Corporate Guardians

Page 212, add to footnote 217:

NV: Nev. Op. Att'y Gen. No. 97-08, 1997 WL 133532 (1997) (in absence of parents, juvenile court must make decision about DNR orders for minor child).

Page 214, add to footnote 224:

IL: *Cited in In re* Austwick, 656 N.E.2d 773 (Ill. App. Ct. 1995).

NJ: *E.g.,* N.J. Stat. Ann. §§ 52:27G-20 *et seq.* (Public Guardian for Elderly Adults Act), *construed in In re* Roche, 687 A.2d 349 (N.J. Super. Ct. Ch. Div. 1996) (public guardian appointed for institutionalized patient with senile dementia for whom there were no family members willing or able to undertake guardianship responsibility).

[204.1] *See* Edwards v. Shumate, 468 S.E.2d 23, 27 (Ga. 1996).

[210.1] See § **14.4** in this supplement.

[213.1] *See, e.g.,* Cal. Health & Safety Code § 1418.8 (authorizing decisionmaking for nursing home residents by interdisciplinary health care team, including a patient representative who may include a friend of the patient), *constitutionality upheld in* Rains v. Belshe, 38 Cal. Rptr. 2d 185 (Ct. App. 1995).

§ 5.24   Incompetence of the Surrogate

Page 216, add to footnote 235:

MA: *See, e.g., In re* Mason, 669 N.E.2d 1081, 1083, 1085, 1086 (Mass. App. Ct. 1996) (proper for hospital to seek judicial approval for entry of DNR order where family member acting as surrogate "was disruptive of hospital schedules, abusive to medical personnel, and overly quick to allege neglect and maltreatment of his mother," believed that patient's condition was "brought about by the painkillers and sedatives given her and that if these medications were stopped, his mother would improve," and was incapable of making health care decisions based on "true assessment of [patient's] best interests").

§ 5.26   Judicial Review Not Required

Page 219, add to footnote 251:

IL: *See also* Ill. Ann. Stat. ch. 755, § 40/20(b-5).

Page 220, add to footnote 255:

FL: *In re* Dubreuil, 629 So. 2d 819 (Fla. 1993); Harrell v. St. Mary's Hosp., Inc., 678 So. 2d 455 (Fla. Dist. Ct. App. 1996).
NY: *In re* Christopher, 675 N.Y.S.2d 807, 810 (Sup. Ct. Queens County 1998) ("It is indeed unfortunate that judges are called upon to play God in case by case situations. These decisions should properly be medical and personal between the patient's family and the medical profession.").
PA: *In re* Fiori, 673 A.2d 905, 912 (Pa. 1996).

Page 220, add to footnote 257:

CA: *Accord* Rains v. Belshe, 38 Cal. Rptr. 2d 185, 198 (Ct. App. 1995) (quoting *Quinlan* and upholding constitutionality of state legislation permitting decisionmaking to rest with proceeding without judicial oversight).

Page 221, add to footnote 260:

PA: *In re* Fiori, 673 A.2d 905, 913 (Pa. 1996) (rejecting "idea that courts in our society are the repository of wisdom and the only institution available to protect human life and dignity").

Page 222, add at end of section:

Another important reason for not requiring judicial review is respect for the family.[261.1]

§ 5.27   Judicial Review Not Required but Permissible

Page 222, add to footnote 262:

PA: *In re* Fiori, 673 A.2d 905, 912 (Pa. 1996).

Page 222, add to footnote 263:

CA: *E.g.,* Cal. Health & Safety Code § 1418.8(i) (court order not required but may be obtained), *constitutionality upheld in* Rains v. Belshe, 38 Cal. Rptr. 2d 185 (Ct. App. 1995).

Page 223, add to footnote 265:

PA: *In re* Fiori, 673 A.2d 905, 912 (Pa. 1996).

§ 5.30   —Disagreement Among Participants in the Decisionmaking Process

Page 227, add to footnote 294:

PA: *In re* Fiori, 673 A.2d 905, 912 (Pa. 1996).

Page 227, add to footnote 299, at end of "IN:" *entry:*

See also Estate of Taylor v. Muncie Medical Investors, L.P., 727 N.E.2d 466, 471 (Ind. Ct. App. 2000) ("When health care providers and family members disagree as to the proper course of medical treatment, they have the statutory right to go to court to resolve the dispute.") (citing *In re* Lawrance, 579 N.E.2d at 43).

§ 5.31   —Disagreement Among Family Members

Page 229, add to footnote 304:

CA: Wendland v. Superior Court, 56 Cal. Rptr. 2d 595 (Ct. App. 1996) (wife/conservator seeking to terminate nutrition and hydration

---

[261.1] *In re* Fiori, 673 A.2d 905, 913 (Pa. 1996).

opposed by patient's mother and sister; counsel must be appointed for conservatee).

DE: *In re* Holmes, C.M. No. 8066-NC, 1996 WL 633309, at *1 (Del. Ch. Oct. 30, 1996) ("decision [about whether to place patient suffering from Alzheimer's disease in nursing home or combination of day care and home nursing care] is one that is best made by the family"; but where patient's 16 children cannot agree, decision will be made by court).

MA: *Cf. In re* Mason, 669 N.E.2d 1081, 1086 n.9 (Mass. App. Ct. 1996) (where patient had three sons and the one acting as surrogate sought restraining orders to keep one brother away from the mother, failed to notify the brothers of his appointment as temporary guardian, and did not volunteer their addresses to the guardians ad litem so that they could be interviewed, he is unqualified to serve as surrogate).

PA: *In re Kauffman*, 20 Fiduc. Rptr. 2d 223 (C.P. Montgomery County, Pa. 2000) (patient's husband sought entry of DNR, but one of patient's two sons by a previous marriage opposed DNR based on the terms of patient's living will and other expressions of her wishes).

§ 5.33   — Disagreement Between Family and Treatment Team

Page 231, at end of paragraph delete period in last sentence (retaining foot-note 311) and add following text to the sentence:

or involving the court in an attempt to enforce the right to refuse treatment.[311.1]

§ 5.35   — Conflicts of Interest

Page 233, add to footnote 318:

DE: *Cf. In re* Tavel, 661 A.2d 1061, 1066 (Del. 1995) (trial court "found no reason to discredit the witnesses' testimony, particularly because [patient] had no property and there was no question of ulterior motives")

NY: Blackman v. New York City Health & Hosps. Corp., 660 N.Y.S.2d 643, 649 (Sup. Ct. Kings County 1997) (family member of compe-

---

[311.1] **IN:** Estate of Taylor v. Muncie Medical Investors, L.P., 727 N.E.2d 466, 472 (Ind. Ct. App. 2000) (refusing to recognize claim for wrongful prolongation of life "because an existing statutory remedy already protects patients' rights to refuse medical treatment and gives families the power to enforce those rights"). *See also id.* at 471.

tent patient who repeatedly expressed his view that patient should refuse treatment has not acted improperly if "there is no showing of irresponsibility, overreaching, or financial gain on either of their part" and if patient's "decision is the product of her own mind").

Page 233, add to footnote 322:

LA: Causey v. St. Francis Med. Ctr., 719 So. 2d 1072, 1074 (La. Ct. App. 1998) ("The court as the protector of incompetents . . . can override an intolerable choice by a surrogate decision-maker.").

MA: *In re* Smith, 684 N.E.2d 613 (Mass. App. Ct. 1997).

MI: Martin v. Martin, 517 N.W.2d 749 (Mich. Ct. App. 1994), *rev'd on other grounds,* 538 N.W.2d 399 (Mich. 1995).

Page 234, add to footnote 325:

GA: *See, e.g.,* Edwards v. Shumate, 468 S.E.2d 23 (Ga. 1996).

LA: *See, e.g.,* Perrier v. Bistes, 650 So. 2d 786 (La. Ct. App.), *cert. denied,* 653 So. 2d 569 (La. 1995).

Page 234, add to footnote 326:

MA: *In re* Smith, 684 N.E.2d 613 (Mass. App. Ct. 1997) (persons appointed by patient through durable power of attorney to be his guardians were not disqualified because of their being directors and officers of corporation of which patient was principal shareholder).

Page 234, add to footnote 327:

GA: *Cf.* Edwards v. Shumate, 468 S.E.2d 23 (Ga. 1996) (testamentary heirs who were not relatives of patient and who acted as surrogates did not act contrary to patient's interests).

MA: *In re* Smith, 684 N.E.2d 613 (Mass. App. Ct. 1997) (must be actual, rather than possible, conflict of interest for court to remove as surrogate proxy appointed by durable power of attorney).

Page 235, add to footnote 331:

LA: *See also* Perrier v. Bistes, 650 So. 2d 786 (La. Ct. App.), *cert. denied,* 653 So. 2d 569 (La. 1995) (siblings of patient who died when husband authorized termination of life support alleged that husband was involved in conspiracy with his siblings to end patient's life so that husband's siblings rather than patient's siblings would inherit patient's estate).

Page 236, add note 334.1 reference at end of section and add note 334.1:

334.1 **LA:** *See, e.g.,* Causey v. St. Francis Med. Ctr., 719 So. 2d 1072, 1076 n.3 (La. Ct. App. 1998) (describing surrogate's demand to continue aggressive treatment, deemed to be medically inappropriate, as abusive and inhumane).

§ 5.37   Judicial Review Required as a Matter of Course

Page 240, add to footnote 356:

MA: *In re* Mason, 669 N.E.2d 1081 (Mass. App. Ct. 1996) (citing *In re* Dinnerstein, 380 N.E.2d 134 (Mass. App. Ct. 1978); Brophy v. New Eng. Sinai Hosp., Inc., 497 N.E.2d 626 (Mass. 1986)).

Page 240, add at end of first full paragraph:

Judicial review is also appropriate if the surrogate lacks decisionmaking capacity, is unable to act in the best interests of the patient, or holds a health care power of attorney of questionable validity.[357.1]

*Page 242, add after **Minnesota** subsection:*

Nevada

An opinion of the Nevada Attorney General requires that there be a court order to enter a DNR order for a minor if there is no parent to consent to the order or if the parents object to a doctor's decision to write a DNR order.[372.1]

Page 244, add to footnote 384:

CA9:   *But cf.* Compassion in Dying v. Washington, 79 F.3d 790, 824 (9th Cir. 1996) (in case addressing the right of competent, terminally ill "victim of unmanageable pain and suffering to end his life peacefully and with dignity at the time he deems most desirable," error that ends life actually benefits individual), *rev'd sub nom.* Washington v. Glucksberg, 117 S. Ct. 2258 (1997).

[357.1] *In re* Mason, 669 N.E.2d 1081 (Mass. App. Ct. 1996).

[372.1] Nev. Op. Att'y Gen. No. 97-08, 1997 WL 133532 (1997).

DETERMINATION OF INCOMPETENCE

§ 5.40 —Florida: Blood Transfusions

Page 247, add to footnote 400:

FL: Harrell v. St. Mary's Hosp., Inc., 678 So. 2d 455 (Fla. Dist. Ct. App. 1996).

Page 248, add to footnote 406:

FL: Harrell v. St. Mary's Hosp., Inc., 678 So. 2d 455, 457 (Fla. Dist. Ct. App. 1996).

Page 248, add to footnote 407:

FL: Harrell v. St. Mary's Hosp., Inc., 678 So. 2d 455, 457 (Fla. Dist. Ct. App. 1996).

Page 248, add to footnote 408:

FL: Harrell v. St. Mary's Hosp., Inc., 678 So. 2d 455, 457 (Fla. Dist. Ct. App. 1996).

Page 248, add to footnote 410:

FL: Harrell v. St. Mary's Hosp., Inc., 678 So. 2d 455, 457–58 (Fla. Dist. Ct. App. 1996).

Page 249, add note 411.1 reference at end of first sentence of first full paragraph and add note 411.1:

[411.1] **FL:** Harrell v. St. Mary's Hosp., Inc., 678 So. 2d 455, 458 (Fla. Dist. Ct. App. 1996).

Page 249, add to footnote 412:

FL: Harrell v. St. Mary's Hosp., Inc., 678 So. 2d 455, 458 (Fla. Dist. Ct. App. 1996).

Page 249, add to footnote 416:

CT: *Cf.* Stamford Hosp. v. Vega, 674 A.2d 821, 827 (Conn. 1996) (noting "extraordinary procedural history" of case in which "hearing before the trial court took place in the middle of the night, under extreme emergency conditions that were not conducive to the ability of either party to develop fully its arguments, . . . [patient] was not represented by counsel at the outset of the hearing and, of that portion of the hearing in which her attorney was present, most was not recorded").

§ 5.41   —Illinois: Artificial Nutrition and Hydration; Minors

Page 249, add to footnote 417:

IL: Ficke v. Evangelical Health Sys., 674 N.E.2d 888, 890 (Ill. App. Ct. 1996) (implying that requirement of judicial review applies to forgoing of any form of life-sustaining medical treatment).

§ 5.41A   —Nebraska: Neglected Minors (New)

When the parents of a minor have had custody terminated, and custody is lodged in a state child protective welfare agency, judicial review may be necessary to forgo life-sustaining treatment. The Nebraska Supreme Court concluded that judicial proceedings were required to terminate life support on the petition of the state Department of Social Services in such a case because the termination of treatment was almost certain to result in the minor's death, which would "sever the relationship between the infant and the parents."[423.1] Under Nebraska statutes, termination of parental rights requires judicial approval. Thus, "the same due process must be afforded in the . . . proceeding [to terminate life support] as is required in a proceeding to terminate parental rights."[423.2]

§ 5.46   Protection Against Abuse

Page 255, add to footnote 445:

LA: Causey v. St. Francis Med. Ctr., 719 So. 2d 1072, 1076 n.3 (La. Ct. App. 1998) (surrogate's demand to continue medically inappropriate treatment constituted abuse).

See generally Institute of Medicine, Approaching Death: Improving Care at the End of Life 126 (Marilyn J. Field & Christine K. Cassel, eds., 1997) ("Care at the end of life is characterized by overuse of care. . . . Overuse and underuse of care may occur simultaneously, for example, when futile efforts to cure are continued at the expense of efforts to relieve physical and psychological symptoms and help patients and families prepare emotionally, spiritually, and practically for death.").

[423.1] Tabatha R. v. Ronda R., 564 N.W.2d 598, 605 (Neb. 1997).

[423.2] *Id.* (distinguishing Lovato v. District Court, 601 P.2d 1072 (Colo. 1979), on ground that child there was dead when order regarding termination of life support was entered).

§ 5.47 Speed and Convenience

Page 257, add to footnote 451:

CA: *Cf.* Rains v. Belshe, 38 Cal. Rptr. 2d 185, 189 (Ct. App. 1995) (noting possibility of several-month delay in obtaining judicial decree to authorize nonemergency treatment).

§ 5.49 Instituting Litigation

Page 260, add after first full paragraph:

This is a somewhat unrealistic policy, at least in the context of cases like *Dubreuil* involving acute medical emergencies. The Connecticut Supreme Court recognized this in *Stamford Hospital v. Vega*[466.1] and concluded that hospitals were justified in initiating litigation to determine whether the refusal of a blood transfusion by a member of the Jehovah's Witness faith, who was the mother of a newborn baby, could be overridden. Although the court held that the hospital had no standing to assert *state* interests, "the hospital has standing in its own right to invoke the judicial process in order to seek determinative guidance regarding its obligations in this difficult position."[466.2] These interests—not unlike those of the state[466.3]—include the hospital's "interest in ensuring that the integrity and ethical standards of the medical profession be maintained," the hospital's "interest in receiving official guidance in resolving the wrenching ethical dilemma it faced," and the practical consideration that there was no opportunity for the state to assert its own interests.[466.4]

§ 5.54 Respect for Privacy

Page 263, add to footnote 479:

See, e.g., Fort Wayne Journal-Gazette v. Baker, 788 F. Supp. 379 (N.D. Ind. 1992).

[466.1] 674 A.2d 821 (Conn. 1996).

[466.2] *Id.* at 829.

[466.3] See §§ **8.14–8.19** in the main volume and this supplement.

[466.4] 674 A.2d at 829–30.

§ 5.59   —Medical Review

Page 267, add note 509.1 reference at end of first sentence and add note 509.1:

[509.1] **GA:** *In re* L.H.R., 321 S.E.2d 716, 723 (Ga. 1984) (diagnosis of terminal illness and prognosis of persistent vegetative state must be made by attending physician and two other physicians with no interest in outcome).

NJ: *In re* Conroy, 486 A.2d 1209, 1242 (N.J. 1985) (in order to remove life-sustaining treatment from nursing home patient, attending physician and two other physicians unaffiliated with nursing home must confirm prognosis and condition).

PA: *In re* Fiori, 673 A.2d 905, 912–13 (Pa. 1996) (two physicians qualified to evaluate patient's condition, and attending physician if any, must certify that patient has been diagnosed as being in permanent vegetative state).

WA: *In re* Colyer, 660 P.2d 738, 749 (Wash. 1983) (must be a unanimous concurrence of prognosis committee consisting of no fewer than two physicians and attending physician that there is no reasonable medical probability that patient will return to a sapient state).

§ 5.61   Standard of Proof

Page 272, add to footnote 530:

DE: *In re* Tavel, 661 A.2d 1061, 1070 (Del. 1995).
MI: Martin v. Martin, 538 N.W.2d 399, 409–10 (Mich. 1995) (citing first edition of this treatise).
NY: *In re* Christopher, 675 N.Y.S.2d 807 (Sup. Ct. Queens County 1998).

Page 272, add to footnote 531:

NY: *In re* Christopher, 675 N.Y.S.2d 807, 808 (Sup. Ct. Queens County 1998) ("The evidence must be unequivocal when the decision to terminate life support is at issue.").

Page 272, add to footnote 532:

MI: *Accord* Martin v. Martin, 538 N.W.2d 399, 410 (Mich. 1995).

Page 272, add to footnote 534:

MI: Martin v. Martin, 538 N.W.2d 399, 410 (Mich. 1995).

Page 273, add to footnote 536:

MI: *See also* Martin v. Martin, 538 N.W.2d 399, 413 n.23 (Mich. 1995) (appellate court may review record not to search for new facts but to determine whether facts provide a sufficient evidentiary basis for trial court's determination that "rigorous demands of the clear and convincing standard were met").

Page 273, add to footnote 537:

MI: *Accord* Martin v. Martin, 538 N.W.2d 399, 409–10 (Mich. 1995).

Page 274, add to footnote 543:

MI: *Accord* Martin v. Martin, 538 N.W.2d 399, 409–10 (Mich. 1995).

Page 274, add to footnote 546:

CA9:   *Cf.* Compassion in Dying v. Washington, 79 F.3d 790, 824 (9th Cir. 1996) (in case addressing right of competent, terminally ill "victim of unmanageable pain and suffering to end his life peacefully and with dignity at the time he deems most desirable," error that ends life actually benefits individual), *rev'd sub nom.* Washington v. Glucksberg, 117 S. Ct. 2258 (1997).

Page 275, add to footnote 551:

MI: Martin v. Martin, 538 N.W.2d 399, 410 (Mich. 1995) (citing first edition of this treatise).

§ 5.62   —Relationship Between Evidentiary and Substantive Standards

Page 276, add at end of first paragraph:

As the Michigan Supreme Court observed, "Contrary to a growing misconception . . . we view the clear and convincing standard not as a decision-making standard, but as an evidentiary standard of proof that applies to all decisions regarding termination of treatment, regardless of the decision-making standard employed."[557.1]

[557.1] Martin v. Martin, 538 N.W.2d 399, 406 n.12 (Mich. 1995) (citing first edition of this treatise).

§ 5.62 EVIDENTIARY/SUSTANTIVE STANDARDS

Page 277, add to footnote 561:

DE: *See, e.g., In re* Tavel, 661 A.2d 1061 (Del. 1995) (holding that there must be clear and convincing evidence of the patient's actual or probable wishes).

MD: Wright v. Johns Hopkins Health Sys. Corp., 728 A.2d 166, 168 (Md. 1999).

NY: *In re* Christopher, 675 N.Y.S.2d 807, 808 (Sup. Ct. Queens County 1998) (correctly distinguishing between evidentiary and substantive standards).

Page 277, add at end of carryover paragraph:

and in determining the patient's physical condition.[562.1]

Page 277, add at end of first sentence of first full paragraph:

As the Pennsylvania Supreme Court observed, the term "clear and convincing evidence" is used in two different ways: to refer to a standard for decisionmaking for incompetent patients, but "more commonly, however, as a burden of proof. In that context, the standard refers to that quantum of evidence necessary for a party to establish a point."[562.2]

Page 278, add to footnote 568:

PA: *Accord In re* Fiori, 673 A.2d 905, 911 n.9 (Pa. 1996).

Page 279, replace footnote 575 with:

DE: *In re* Tavel, 661 A.2d 1061, 1070 (Del. 1995).

KY: *E.g.,* DeGrella v. Elston, 858 S.W.2d 698 (Ky. 1993).

MD: Mack v. Mack, 618 A.2d 744, 757 (Md. 1993) (in absence of living will or health care power of attorney, "inquiry focuses on whether [patient], while competent sufficiently had evidenced his views, one way or the other, to enable the court to determine, by clear and convincing evidence, what [his] decision would be under the present circumstances").

MI: Martin v. Martin, 538 N.W.2d 399, 406 n.12 (Mich. 1995) ("In right to die cases, if intent to withdraw life prolonging medical procedures is determinative of the case, then there must be 'clear and convincing evidence' of that intent. If 'best interests' of the patient is determinative of the case, then there must be 'clear and convincing evidence' that discontinuance of medical procedures best serves the interests of the patient.")

[562.1] *In re* Tavel, 661 A.2d 1061, 1071 (Del. 1995).

[562.2] *In re* Fiori, 673 A.2d 905, 911 n.9 (Pa. 1996) (citing Kristen L. Beebe, Comment, *The Right to Die,* 96 Dick. L. Rev. 649, 651, 665–69 (1992)).

NJ: *But see In re* Jobes, 529 A.2d 434, 451 (N.J. 1987) (when patient is in persistent vegetative state, "[t]he interested parties need not have clear and convincing evidence of the patient's intentions; they need only 'render their best judgment' as to what medical decision the patient would want them to make") (quoting *In re* Quinlan, 355 A.2d 647, 664 (N.J. 1976)).

Page 280, add to footnote 577:

IL: *In re* Austwick, 656 N.E.2d 779, 785 (Ill. App. Ct. 1995) (*Longeway* [Estate of Longeway v. Community Convalescent Ctr., 549 N.E.2d 292 (Ill. 1989)] stands for proposition that there must be clear and convincing evidence that substituted judgment standard is met).

Bibliography

Boozang, K. "An Intimate Passing: Restoring the Role of Family and Religion in Dying." *University of Pittsburgh Law Review* 58 (1997): 549.

Brock, D. "What Is the Moral Authority of Family Members to Act as Surrogates for Incompetent Patients?" *Milbank Quarterly* 74 (1996): 599.

Davies, B., et al. *Fading Away: The Experience of Transition in Families with Terminal Illness.* Amityville, NY: Baywood, 1995.

DiPaolo, S. "Getting Through the Door: Threshold Procedural Considerations in Right-to-Die Litigation." *Risk: Health Safety and Environment* 6 (1995): 59.

Fader, J. "The Precarious Role of the Courts: Surrogate Health Care Decisionmaking." *Maryland Law Review* 53 (1994): 1193.

Fraleigh, A. "Note. An Alternative to Guardianship: Should Michigan Statutorily Allow Acute-Care Hospitals to Make Medical Treatment Decisions for Incompetent Patients Who Have Neither Identifiable Surrogates Nor Advance Directives?" *University of Detroit Mercy Law Review* 76 (1999): 1079.

Freeman, I. "One More Faulty Solution Is Novelty Without Progress: A Reply to 'Medical Decision-Making for the Unbefriended Nursing Home Resident.'" *Journal of Law and Aging* 1 (1995): 93.

Gatter, R. "Unnecessary Adversaries at the End of Life: Mediating End-of-Life Treatment Disputes to Prevent Erosion of Physician-Patient Relationships." *Boston University Law Review* 79 (1999): 1091–1137.

BIBLIOGRAPHY

Gillick, M. "Medical Decision-Making for the Unbefriended Nursing Home Resident." *Journal of Law and Aging* 1 (1995): 87.

Hafemeister, T. "End-of-Life Decision Making, Therapeutic Jurisprudence, and Preventive Law: Hierarchical v. Consensus-Based Decision-Making Model." *Arizona Law Review* 41 (1999): 329.

Kapp, M. "Health Care in the Marketplace: Implications for Decisionally Impaired Consumers and Their Surrogates and Advocates." *Southern Illinois University Law Journal* 24 (1999): 1.

Koch, T. "The Gulf Between: Surrogate Choices, Physician Instructions, and Informal Network Responses." *Cambridge Quarterly of Healthcare Ethics* 4 (1995): 185.

Levine, C. and Zuckerman, C. "Hands On/Hands Off: Why Health Care Professionals Depend on Families But Keep Them at Arm's Length." *Journal of Law, Medicine & Ethics* 28 (2000): 5.

Lightfoot, R. "*Butcher v. Fashingbauer:* The 'Case' for a Surrogate Decision Maker Statute in Minnesota." *Hamline Journal of Public Law and Policy* 16 (1994): 231.

Luttrell, S. "Making Decisions About Medical Treatment for Mentally Incapable Adults in the UK." *Lancet* 350 (1997): 950.

Lynn, J., et al. "Perceptions by Family Members of the Dying Experience of Older and Seriously Ill Patients." *Annals of Internal Medicine* 126 (1997): 97.

McCrary, S.V., et al. "Questionable Competency of a Surrogate Decision Maker under a Durable Power of Attorney." *Journal of Clinical Ethics* 4 (1993): 166.

Meier, D. "Voiceless and Vulnerable: Dementia Patients Without Surrogates in an Era of Capitation." *Journal of the American Geriatrics Society* 45 (1997): 375.

Mezey, M., et al. "Assessment of Decision-Making Capacity: Nursing's Role." *Journal of Gerontological Nursing* 23 (1997): 28.

Miles, S., et al. "Advance End-of-Life Treatment Planning: A Research Review." *Archives of Internal Medicine* 156 (1996): 1062.

Miller, T., et al. "Treatment Decisions for Patients Without Surrogates: Rethinking Policies for a Vulnerable Population." *Journal of the American Geriatrics Society* 45 (1997): 369.

Pearlman, R., et al. "Spousal Understanding of Patient Quality of Life: Implications for Surrogate Decisions." *Journal of Clinical Ethics* 3 (1992): 114.

Rai, A. et al. "The Physician as a Health Care Proxy." *Hastings Center Report* 29 (Sept./Oct. 1999): 14.

Skinner, P. "Note. Tipping the Scales: How Guardianship of Brandon Has Upset Massachusetts' Balanced Substituted Judgment Doctrine. (Guardianship of Brandon, 677 N.E.2d 114, Mass. 1997)." *Boston College Law Review* 40 (1999): 969.

Stone, A. "Iatrogenic Ethical Problems: A Commentary on 'Can a Patient Refuse a Psychiatric Consultation to Evaluate Decision Making Capacity?'" *Journal of Clinical Ethics* 5 (1994): 234.

Swigart, V., et al. "Letting Go: Family Willingness to Forgo Life Support." *Heart & Lung* 25 (1996): 483.

Terry, P. et al. "End-of-Life Decision Making: When Patients and Surrogates Disagree." *Journal of Clinical Ethics* 10 (1999): 286.

Tucker, K. "Surrogate End of Life Decisionmaking: The Importance of Providing Procedural Due Process, A Case Review." *Washington Law Review* 72, no. 3 (1997): 859.

Wenger, N., and J. Halpern. "Can a Patient Refuse a Psychiatric Consultation to Evaluate Decision-Making Capacity?" *Journal of Clinical Ethics* 5 (1994): 230.

Whitton, L. "Caring for the Incapacitated—A Case for Nonprofit Surrogate Decision Makers in the Twenty-First Century." *University of Cincinnati Law Review* 64 (1996): 879.

CHAPTER 6
ETHICS COMMITTEES

§ 6.3 Legal Status of Ethics Committees

Page 289, add to footnote 23:

WI: *But cf.* Edna M.F. v. Eisenberg, 563 N.W.2d 485, 495 (Wis. 1997) (Abrahamson, C.J., concurring) (criticizing procedural informality of nursing home ethics committee because "no formal minutes or report of the meeting was produced at the hearing and . . . the committee members apparently functioned without either a shared body of rules or training in ethics").

§ 6.4 Substitute for Judicial Review

Page 294, add to footnote 53:

WI: *But cf.* Edna M.F. v. Eisenberg, 563 N.W.2d 485, 495 (Wis. 1997) (Abrahamson, C.J., concurring) (criticizing procedural informality of nursing home ethics committee because "no formal minutes or report of the meeting was produced at the hearing and . . . the committee members apparently functioned without either a shared body of rules or training in ethics").

§ 6.5 Improving the Decisionmaking Process

Page 295, add to footnote 62:

LA: *See* Causey v. St. Francis Med. Ctr., 719 So. 2d 1072, 1075 (La. Ct. App. 1998) ("The inclusion of non-medical persons on the Morals and Ethics Board signals that this is not strictly a physiological or medical futility policy, but a policy asserting values and beliefs on the worth of sustaining life, even in a vegetative condition.").

§ 6.12   Case Consultation

Page 303, add to footnote 90:

LA: *See, e.g.*, Causey v. St. Francis Med. Ctr., 719 So. 2d 1072 (La. Ct. App. 1998) (consultation to terminate "futile" medical treatment).

WI: Edna M.F. v. Eisenberg, 563 N.W.2d 485 (Wis. 1997).

Page 304, add note 95.1 reference at end of section and add note 95.1:

[95.1]**WI:** Edna M.F. v. Eisenberg, 563 N.W.2d 485, 496 (Wis. 1997) (Abrahamson, C.J., concurring) (criticizing ethics committee for "seem[ing] to understand that its function was to reach a determination that would insulate the facility from legal liability rather than the determination that best comported with medical ethics. [Footnote omitted] The focus of all participants in this fateful and difficult process should be on the propriety of taking action which will lead to a person's death.").

§ 6.16   — Institutional Protocols

Page 310, add to footnote 106:

LA: *But see* Causey v. St. Francis Med. Ctr., 719 So. 2d 1072 (La. Ct. App. 1998) (in which ethics committee's Futile Care Policy was followed but did not prevent litigation).

Page 310, add at end of first full paragraph:

The Joint Commission now also requires hospitals to have a policy broader than a DNR policy that addresses care at the end of life.[109.1] Hospitals are increasingly developing protocols to deal with termination of care thought by health care professionals to be "futile"[109.2] but demanded by patients or surrogates nonetheless.[109.3]

[109.1] Joint Comm'n on Accreditation of Healthcare Orgs., 1996 Accreditation Manual for Hospitals § RI.2.7.

[109.2] See **ch. 19** in the main volume and this supplement.

[109.3] **LA:** *See, e.g.*, Causey v. St. Francis Med. Ctr., 719 So. 2d 1072, 1075 (La. Ct. App. 1998) (hospital "had in place a Futile Care Policy which allowed for the discontinuance of medical care over and above that necessary for comfort and support if the probability of improving the patient's condition was slight and would serve only to prolong life in that condition.").

§ 6.17 —Legal Status of Institutional Protocols

Page 311, add note 116.1 reference at end of first paragraph of section and add note 116.1:

[116.1] **LA:** *See* Causey v. St. Francis Med. Ctr., 719 So. 2d 1072 (La. Ct. App. 1998) (giving credence to institutional protocol for futile treatment in part because it was drafted by ethics committee containing lay members).

Page 312, add at end of carryover paragraph:

Another example is protocols dealing with termination of "futile" medical treatment.[117.1]

Bibliography

Agich, G.J. "Authority in Ethics Consultation." *Journal of Law, Medicine and Ethics* 23 (1995): 273.

Aulisio, M., R. Arnold, and S. Youngner, eds. "Special Issue: Commentary on the ASBH Core Competencies for Health Care Ethics Consultation." *Journal of Clinical Ethics* 10: (1999): 3.

Aulisio, M., et al. "Can There Be Educational and Training Standards for Those Conducting Health Care Ethics Consultation?" in J. Monagle, and D. Thomasma, eds., *Health Care Ethics: Critical Issues for the 21st Century*. Gaithersburg, MD: Aspen Publishers, Inc., 1998.

Brennan, T.A. "Ethics Committees and Decisions to Limit Care: The Experience at the Massachusetts General Hospital." *Journal of the American Medical Association* 260 (1988): 803.

Duval, G. "Liability of Ethics Consultants: A Case Analysis." *Cambridge Quarterly of Healthcare Ethics* 6 (1997): 269.

Fost, N., and R. Cranford, "Hospital Ethics Committees: Administrative Aspects." *Journal of the American Medical Association* 253 (1985): 2687.

Hoffmann, D., et al. "Are Ethics Committee Members Competent to Consult?" *Journal of Law, Medicine & Ethics* 28 (2000): 30.

Howe, E.G. "Inner Turmoil: An Important Consideration in Conflicts of Interest." *Journal of Clinical Ethics* 6 (1995): 367.

[117.1] **LA:** *See, e.g.*, Causey v. St. Francis Med. Ctr., 719 So. 2d 1072 (La. Ct. App. 1998) (giving credence to institutional protocol for futile treatment in part because it was drafted by ethics committee containing lay members).

ETHICS COMMITTEES

LaPuma, J. "Medical Ethics: Consultations in Clinical Ethics—Issues and Questions in 27 Cases." *Western Journal of Medicine* 146 (1987): 633.

LaPuma, J., and D. Schiedermayer, "Ethics Consultation: Skills, Roles, and Training." *Annals of Internal Medicine* 114 (1991): 155.

LaPuma, J., et al. "An Ethics Consultation Service in a Teaching Hospital: Utilization and Evaluation." *Journal of the American Medical Association* 260 (1988): 808.

Leeman, C., et al. "Quality Control for Hospitals' Clinical Ethics Services: Proposed Standards." *Cambridge Quarterly of Healthcare Ethics* 6 (1997): 257.

Nelson, R., and R. Shapiro. "The Role of an Ethics Committee in Resolving Conflict in the Neonatal Intensive Care Unit." *Journal of Law, Medicine and Ethics* 23 (1995): 27.

Siegler, M., and P. Singer, "Clinical Ethics Consultation: Godsend or 'God Squad'?" *American Journal of Medicine* 85 (1988): 759.

Symposium. "Ethics Consultation Revisited." *Trends in Health Care, Law and Ethics* 10(4) (1995): 7.

Vinicky, J.K., et al. "Conflicts of Interest, Conflicting Interests, and Interesting Conflicts." *Journal of Clinical Ethics* 6 (1995): 358.

Weinstein, B. "The Possibility of Ethical Expertise." *Theoretical Medicine* 15 (1994): 61.

Wilson, R. "Hospital Ethics Committees as the Forum of Last Resort: An Idea Whose Time Has Not Come." *North Carolina Law Review* 76 (1998): 353.

Young, E. "Ethics in the Outpatient Setting: New Challenges and Opportunities." *Cambridge Quarterly of Healthcare Ethics* 6 (1997): 293.

CHAPTER 7

DECISIONMAKING STANDARDS FOR INCOMPETENT PATIENTS

§ 7.2 Hierarchy of Standards for Surrogate Decisionmaking

Page 345, add to footnote 19:

MI: Martin v. Martin, 538 N.W.2d 399, 407 (Mich. 1995) ("The best interest analysis is generally invoked, if at all, only as a secondary approach when subjective evidence of a particular patient's decision is lacking because it involves a qualitative assessment of the patient's condition, a decision the state may legitimately decline to make.").

Page 346, add to footnote 20:

MI: Martin v. Martin, 538 N.W.2d 399, 401 (Mich. 1995) ("[T]he paramount goal of our decision is to honor, respect, and fulfill the decisions of the patient, regardless of whether the patient is currently competent.").

Page 346, add to footnote 22:

MI: *But see* Martin v. Martin, 538 N.W.2d 399 (Mich. 1995), *modifying* Martin v. Martin, 504 N.W.2d 917 (Mich. Ct. App. 1993).

§ 7.3 Continuum of Substantive Standards

Page 347, add note 28.1 reference at end of first sentence and add note 28.1:

28.1 Martin v. Martin, 538 N.W.2d 399, 407 (Mich. 1995).

Page 348, add to footnote 29:

But see Martin v. Martin, 538 N.W.2d 399 (Mich. 1995), *modifying* Martin v. Martin, 504 N.W.2d 917 (Mich. Ct. App. 1993).

Page 351, add to footnote 42:

MI: Martin v. Martin, 538 N.W.2d 399 (Mich. 1995) (best interests standard undermines self-determination) (quoting Estate of Longeway v. Community Convalescent Ctr., 549 N.E.2d 292, 299 (Ill. 1989)).

Page 351, add note 42.1 reference at end of first full paragraph and add note 42.1:

[42.1] **DE:** *See, e.g., In re* Gordy, 658 A.2d 613 (Del. Ch. 1994) (purporting to apply best interests standard but defining it as a "standard that attempts in the first instance to replicate the decisions that the ward herself would make in the circumstances present, if she did not suffer from diminished mental capacity or physical incapacity").

§ 7.4   Nature of and Rationale for the Subjective Standard

Page 352, add to footnote 51:

NY: *But see In re* Christopher, 675 N.Y.S.2d 807, 808 (Sup. Ct. Queens County 1998) (correctly distinguishing between substantive decision-making standard and evidentiary standard).

Page 352, add to footnote 53:

NY: *In re* Christopher, 675 N.Y.S.2d 807, 808 (Sup. Ct. Queens County 1998) (referring to "subjective standard").

Page 355, add to footnote 66:

PA: *In re* Fiori, 673 A.2d 905, 912 (Pa. 1996) ("Were this test to be applied, all of those patients who did not have the prescience or the sophistication to express clearly and unmistakably their wishes on this precise matter would not be able to have life support removed.").

Page 356, add to footnote 73:

PA: *In re* Fiori, 673 A.2d 905, 912 (Pa. 1996) (test is "overly restrictive" because it "would thwart the PVS patient's right to determine the medical care to be received").

§ 7.5   States Requiring Subjective Standard

Page 356, add at end of first paragraph:

Some states require by statute that the subjective standard be used.[75.1]

Page 357, add to footnote 77:

See also In re Barsky (Kyle), 627 N.Y.S.2d 903 (Sup. Ct. Suffolk County, 1995).

Page 358, add note 83.1 reference at end of second sentence of first paragraph and add note 83.1:

[83.1] **NY:** *In re* Storar, 420 N.E.2d 64, 73 (N.Y. 1981) (citing *In re* Hofbauer, 393 N.E.2d 1009 (N.Y. 1979)); *In re* Matthews, 650 N.Y.S.2d 373, 377 (App. Div. 1996); Weber v. Stony Brook Hosp., 467 N.Y.S.2d 685 (App. Div.), *aff'd on other grounds,* 456 N.E.2d 1186 (N.Y. 1983).

Page 358, add at end of first paragraph:

Also, a significant factor was that Mr. Storar had "various physicians assigned by the State facility where he resided" rather than a "personal physician."[83.2] By contrast, if the surrogate of a never-competent patient rejects a treatment, and that position is supported by the patient's personal physician, a petition to override the guardian's decision "should be dismissed since this is 'a matter to be decided by the private physician with the patient's family and [petitioner] would have no power to intervene or standing to sue.'"[83.3]

Page 358, add to footnote 85:

MI: *Cf.* Martin v. Martin, 538 N.W.2d 399, 404 (Mich. 1995) (characterization of evidence of patient's wishes similar to that in *O'Connor*). *But see* Martin v. Martin, 538 N.W.2d at 419 n.38 (Levin, J., dissenting) ("In *Browning,* [568 So. 2d 4 (Fla. 1990)], the Florida Supreme Court espoused a substituted judgment standard where the patient was in a condition similar to Michael Martin's and had executed a prior directive that only arguably addressed her current condition.").

[75.1] See **§ 14.8** in the main volume.

[83.2] *In re* Storar, 420 N.E.2d 64, 69 (N.Y. 1981).

[83.3] *In re* Matthews, 650 N.Y.S.2d 373, 377 (App. Div. 1996) (citing Weber v. Stony Brook Hosp., 456 N.E.2d 1186 (N.Y. 1983)).

WI: *See also* Edna M.F. v. Eisenberg, 563 N.W.2d 485, 491 (Wis. 1997) ("The record speaks very little to what Edna's desires would be under the current circumstances. We know from the record that she was a vibrant woman, a gifted journalist, and a devout Roman Catholic. We know that she was and is loved dearly by her family and friends, and that the majority of them feel that she 'would not want to be kept alive' in this condition. We know that in 1966 or 1967 during a time of family crisis, she said that she 'would rather die of cancer than lose [her] mind.' But we do not have any clear statement of what her desires would be today, under the current conditions. Her friends and family never had any conversations with her about her feelings or opinions on the withdrawal of nutrition or hydration, and she did not execute any advance directives expressing her wishes while she was competent.").

Page 359, add to footnote 86:

MI: Martin v. Martin, 538 N.W.2d 399 (Mich. 1995) (patient's statements about not wanting treatment if "vegetative" did not contemplate the condition that he was in and are therefore not relevant).

Page 360, add to footnote 92:

DE: *Accord In re* Tavel, 661 A.2d 1061, 1065 (Del. 1995) (relying in part on testimony of patient's friends and family that she would not want to be kept alive like this, and in part on daughter's testimony "that her mother had approved of Dr. Kevorkian's actions in assisting seriously ill people commit suicide, specifically referring to his actions as 'a blessing'").

Page 362, add at end of New York subsection:

In re Christopher[99.1] is a relatively straightforward and simple case, yet important because it illustrates how New York's stringent subjective standard for decisionmaking for incompetent patients can be ameliorated in practice.

The patient was an elderly woman suffering from Alzheimer's disease. She had been in a nursing home for almost two years and was transferred to the petitioner hospital when she developed pneumonia. She was described as being bedridden, incontinent, noncommunicative, and in a fetal position. Her

---

[99.1] 675 N.Y.S.2d 807 (Sup. Ct. Queens County 1998).

son refused to permit the insertion of a feeding tube, and so the hospital petitioned for an order to permit it to do so.

The trial court denied the petition based on the son's representation of his mother's wishes. Although the son had consented to the insertion of a feeding tube during a prior hospitalization,

> [n]ow that his mother has lost all cognitive function and is in constant pain, he refuses to consent to any procedure that will prolong her life. He volunteered that his decision has nothing to do with money, since his mother's nursing home and hospital expenses are being paid by Medicare and Medicaid. The Court observed Emil's interaction with his mother and is convinced that his refusal to consent to the feeding tube stems from love and compassion. He visits his mother every day and attempts to feed her by mouth with food he brings into the hospital. The law guardian, Gary DiLeonardo, stated that he observed Emil feed his mother a piece of turkey and a strawberry. She is still able to swallow and, in fact, has gained four pounds since April 24, 1998. Her son, however, testified that she cried out in pain whenever anyone touched her or tried to move her body.[99.2]

The court acknowledged that New York's subjective standard requires clear and convincing evidence of the patient's actual wishes, but applying it to the evidence, found that the standard had been met. The specific evidence before the court was the following:

> When the son was asked whether his mother had ever expressed her wishes regarding medical treatment, if she became mentally incompetent, he related an incident that took place approximately ten years earlier. They were watching a program on television about the Von Bulow case. The screen showed Sunny Von Bulow lying in bed in a coma. Emil said to his mother "It's good to be rich in this country, Mom, because even in her condition, she still looks like a model." His mother replied, "No, [even] if you was rich, I wouldn't want to be in this condition, never." He could not remember any other conversations along this line.[99.3]

It is arguable that the evidence is not nearly as specific and "clear and convincing" as the New York Court of Appeals envisioned in its definitive pronouncement on this subject, the *O'Connor* case.[99.4] However, as long as no appeal is taken, trial courts seemingly have a great deal of latitude to apply the standard as loosely (or stringently) as they wish.

[99.2] *Id.* at 808.

[99.3] *Id.*

[99.4] *In re* Westchester County Medical Ctr. (O'Connor), 531 N.E.2d 607 (N.Y. 1988).

Page 366, add to footnote 117:

MI: *Accord* Martin v. Martin, 538 N.W.2d 399, 411 (Mich. 1995).

Page 366, add at end of section:

In 1993 and 1994, the Michigan Court of Appeals issued opinions in the case of *Martin v. Martin,* authorizing the guardian/wife of a brain-damaged, incompetent but conscious, man to terminate his tube-feeding based on the application of the substituted judgment and/or best interests standards.[118.1] On appeal, the Michigan Supreme Court held that the best interests standard was inapplicable to a patient who was conscious and not terminally ill.

On the issue of what standard *should* apply, the court was somewhat unclear because of the variety of different ways in which it characterized and labeled the standard. On balance, however, the court seems to follow the New York view, at least with respect to a patient in Martin's condition, that there must be clear and convincing evidence that the patient, before losing decisionmaking capacity, made a decision to forgo treatment under the circumstances that have in fact become manifest. For example, citing *In re Westchester County Medical Center (O'Connor),*[118.2] the court stated that "[t]he decisionmaker should examine the statement [of the patient made prior to losing decisionmaking capacity] to determine whether it was a well thought out, deliberate pronouncement or a casual remark made in reaction to the plight of another."[118.3] "Only when the patient's prior statements clearly illustrate a serious, well thought out, consistent decision to refuse treatment under these exact circumstances, or circumstances highly similar to the current situation, should treatment be refused or withdrawn."[118.4] Furthermore, the court refers to the standard that it is applying as a *subjective* standard or even a "purely subjective standard."[118.5]

The holding of this case must be understood against the facts of the case. Although there was conflicting testimony about Martin's condition, it was certain that he was not unconscious. The trial court had found, after visiting the patient, that he had moved his arm and leg on command and had appropriately responded with head nods to a series of questions.[118.6] The court left open the question whether if a patient were terminally ill or permanently unconscious, or had never previously been competent, some other, more objective, standard might apply. It specifically did not repudiate the holding

---

[118.1] *See* Martin v. Martin, 504 N.W.2d 917 (Mich. Ct. App. 1993); Martin v. Martin, 517 N.W.2d 749 (Mich. Ct. App. 1994).

[118.2] 531 N.E.2d 607 (N.Y. 1988).

[118.3] Martin v. Martin, 538 N.W.2d at 411.

[118.4] *Id.*

[118.5] *Id.* at 409.

[118.6] *Id.* at 402–03.

in *Rosebush v. Oakland County Prosecutor,*[118.7] permitting the application of the substituted judgment standard in the case of a never-competent patient.[118.8]

§ 7.6   States Preferring but Not Requiring Subjective Standard

Page 370, add to footnote 137:

CA9:   *But cf.* Compassion in Dying v. Washington, 79 F.3d 790, 824 (9th Cir. 1996) (in case addressing right of competent, terminally ill "victim of unmanageable pain and suffering to end his life peacefully and with dignity at the time he deems most desirable," error that ends life actually benefits individual), *rev'd sub nom.* Washington v. Glucksberg, 117 S. Ct. 2258 (1997).

§ 7.7   Origins and Application of Substituted Judgment Standard in Right-to-Die Cases

Page 371, add note 146.1 reference at end of first paragraph and add note 146.1:

[146.1] **DE:**   *See, e.g., In re* Tavel, 661 A.2d 1061, 1068–69 (Del. 1995) ("Under the substituted judgment doctrine, where an incompetent's wishes are not clearly expressed, a surrogate decisionmaker considers the patient's personal value system for guidance. The surrogate considers the patient's prior statements about and reactions to medical issues, and all the facets of the patient's personality that the surrogate is familiar with—with, of course, particular reference to his or her relevant philosophical, theological, and ethical values—in order to extrapolate what course of medical treatment the patient would choose.").

Page 375, replace "Fiori" citation in footnote 160 with:

PA: *In re* Fiori, 652 A.2d 1350 (Pa. Super. Ct. 1995), *aff'g* 17 D. & C.4th 558 (C.P. Bucks County Pa. 1993), *aff'd,* 673 A.2d 905 (Pa. 1996).

Page 375, add to footnote 163:

PA: *In re* Fiori, 673 A.2d 905, 911 (Pa. 1996) (substituted judgment standard intended to effectuate patient's values).

[118.7] 491 N.W.2d 633 (Mich. Ct. App. 1992).
[118.8] 538 N.W.2d at 408–09.

Page 376, delete Wisconsin citation in footnote 164.

Page 376, add to footnote 164:

DE: *In re* Tavel, 661 A.2d 1061 (Del. 1995).
MD: Wright v. Johns Hopkins Health Sys. Corp., 728 A.2d 166, 168 (Md. 1999).
PA: *In re* Fiori, 673 A.2d 905 (Pa. 1996).

Page 376, add at end of carryover paragraph:

Some states require by statute that the substituted judgment standard be used.[166.1]

Page 377, add to footnote 169:

See also Sanford Kadish, *Letting Patients Die: Legal and Moral Reflections,* 80 Cal. L. Rev. 857 (1992); Rhoden, *Litigating Life and Death,* 102 Harv. L. Rev. 357, 400 (1988).

§ 7.8   Meaning of "Substituted Judgment": Subjective or Objective?

Page 378, add to footnote 173:

DE: *In re* Tavel, 661 A.2d 1061, 1068–69 (Del. 1995).
LA: Causey v. St. Francis Med. Ctr., 719 So. 2d 1072, 1074 (La. Ct. App. 1998) ("Implicitly, the decision to refuse care is based on the patient's personal values.").

Page 378, add to footnote 174:

PA: *Accord In re* Fiori, 673 A.2d 905, 911 (Pa. 1996). *See also In re* Kauffman, 20 Fiduc. Rptr. 2d 223 (C.P. Montgomery County, Pa. 2000) (refusing entry of DNR on proxy's request based on court's belief that patient would not have consented).

Page 379, add to footnote 177:

MI: Martin v. Martin, 538 N.W.2d 399 (Mich. 1995).

[166.1] See § **14.8** in the main volume.

Page 381, add to footnote 187:

DE: *Cf. In re* Gordy, 658 A.2d 613 (Del. Ch. 1994) (purporting to apply best interests standard but defining it as a "standard that attempts in the first instance to replicate the decisions that the ward herself would make in the circumstances present, if she did not suffer from diminished mental capacity or physical incapacity").

PA: *Accord In re* Fiori, 673 A.2d 905 (Pa. 1996) (applying a substituted judgment standard to a formerly competent patient, but one whose wishes were completely unknown).

Page 383, add at end of section:

Another way in which the term *substituted judgment* is used is to describe a process rather than a substantive standard. For example, the Delaware Supreme Court explained that "[t]he term 'substituted judgment' is commonly used to describe" the process by which a guardian is able "to invoke and vicariously assert the constitutional right of an incompetent ward to accept medical care or to refuse it."[196.1]

§ 7.9   Factors to Be Considered in Applying Substituted Judgment

Page 383, add after second sentence of first paragraph of section:

Some state surrogate decisionmaking statutes also list factors surrogates should take into account in making a decision for an incompetent patient using the substituted judgment standard.[197.1]

Page 383, add to footnote 198:

PA: *See, e.g., In re* Fiori, 673 A.2d 905, 911 (Pa. 1996) ("The surrogate considers the patient's prior statements about . . . medical issues.").

Page 385, add to footnote 205:

DE: *In re* Tavel, 661 A.2d 1061, 1069 (Del. 1995).
PA: *In re* Fiori, 673 A.2d 905, 911 (Pa. 1996).

[196.1] *In re* Tavel, 661 A.2d 1061, 1068 (Del. 1995).

[197.1] See § **14.8** in the main volume and this supplement.

Page 385, add to footnote 206:

NE: Tabatha R. v. Ronda R., 564 N.W.2d 598, 603 (Neb. 1997) (evidence of bioethical considerations followed by religious group not relevant when the policy of particular health care provider not at issue).

PA: *In re* Fiori, 673 A.2d 905, 911 (Pa. 1996) ("philosophical, theological, and ethical values").

Page 385, add to footnote 207:

DE: *In re* Tavel, 661 A.2d 1061, 1069 (Del. 1995).

Page 387, add to footnote 219:

DE: *In re* Tavel, 661 A.2d 1061, 1069 (Del. 1995) ("[S]urrogate considers . . . all the facets of the patient's personality.").

PA: *In re* Fiori, 673 A.2d 905, 911 (Pa. 1996).

Page 387, add to footnote 220:

LA: Causey v. St. Francis Med. Ctr., 719 So. 2d 1072, 1074 (La. Ct. App. 1998) ("Implicitly, the decision to refuse care is based on the patient's personal values.").

Page 387, add to footnote 221:

DE: *In re* Tavel, 661 A.2d 1061, 1069 (Del. 1995) ("[S]urrogate considers the patient's prior statements about . . . medical issues.").

Page 387, add factor 23 at end of list:

23.   An unrevoked advance directive that is found to be invalid due to a technical deficiency.[221.1]

§ 7.10   Application to Never-Competent Patients

Page 388, add to footnote 227:

DC: *In re* K.I., 735 A.2d 448 (D.C. Ct. App. 1999) (two-year-old, comatose child).

NY: *In re* Matthews, 650 N.Y.S.2d 373 (App. Div. 1996).

[221.1] **IL:** Ill. Ann. Stat. ch. 755, § 40/20(b-5)(1).

Page 390, add to footnote 228:

NY: *But cf. In re* Matthews, 650 N.Y.S.2d 373 (App. Div. 1996) (when purpose in refusing feeding tube is not to allow patient to die but to allow patient to eat orally, this is permissible as choice between reasonable medical alternatives; "standards applicable to formerly competent patients is *[sic]* inapposite and the law relating to decisions as to life-sustaining treatment for infants" applies).

Page 393, add reference 258.1 at end of last full paragraph and add note 258.1:

258.1 **DPA:** *See, e.g.,* Halderman v. Pennhurst State Sch. & Hosp., 1997 WL 835412, at *7 (E.D. Pa., Dec. 23, 1997) (state and county officials ordered "to identify members of the . . . class who are capable of making their own health care decisions and to take affirmative steps to advise these individuals and members of their interdisciplinary team on any health care decisionmaking supports which are currently available"; institutionalized mentally retarded individuals "should be given every opportunity to make their own health care decisions"; state and county officials must "advise class members who are capable of making their own health care decisions on the use of advance directives for end-of-life decisionmaking").

Page 394, add to footnote 262:

CA9: *But cf.* Compassion in Dying v. Washington, 79 F.3d 790, 824 (9th Cir. 1996) (in case addressing right of competent, terminally ill "victim of unmanageable pain and suffering to end his life peacefully and with dignity at the time he deems most desirable," error that ends life actually benefits individual), *rev'd sub nom.* Washington v. Glucksberg, 117 S. Ct. 2258 (1997).

§ 7.12   Applicability to Right-to-Die Cases

Page 396, add to footnote 274:

IL: *In re* Austwick, 656 N.E.2d 784 (Ill. App. Ct. 1995).

Page 397, add to footnote 276:

DE: *In re* Gordy, 658 A.2d 613 (Del. Ch. 1994).

Page 397, add to footnote 278:

DE: *Cf. In re* Gordy, 658 A.2d 613, 618 (Del. Ch. 1994) ("The best interests of the ward is a standard that attempts in the first instance to replicate the decisions that the ward herself would make in the circumstances present, if she did not suffer from diminished mental capacity or physical incapacity.").

Page 398, add to footnote 279:

DE: *In re* Gordy, 658 A.2d 613 (Del. Ch. 1994).

Page 399, add to footnote 280:

MI: Martin v. Martin, 538 N.W.2d 399, 408 (Mich. 1995) ("[T]he facts of the present case do not require that we decide whether the state's parens patriae authority may be expansive enough to encompass a best interest analysis.").

Page 399, add to footnote 281:

DE: *Cf. In re* Gordy, 658 A.2d 613, 618 (Del. Ch. 1994) ("The best interests of the ward is a standard that attempts in the first instance to replicate the decisions that the ward herself would make in the circumstances present, if she did not suffer from diminished mental capacity or physical incapacity.").

Page 400, add at end of section:

Some states by statute permit the application of the best interests standard.[283.1]

§ 7.13   —Treatment Not Always in Best Interests

Page 401, add to footnote 284:

DE: *In re* Gordy, 658 A.2d 613, 618 (Del. Ch. 1994) ("Because our biologic life is not our only value, in considering the interests of an incompetent person, biologic life need not be the exclusive focus of the guardian's attention or of the court to which the guardian must answer.").

WI: Edna M.F. v. Eisenberg, 563 N.W.2d 485, 489 (Wis. 1997).

Page 401, add to footnote 287:

WI: Edna M.F. v. Eisenberg, 563 N.W.2d 485, 489 (Wis. 1997).

Page 402, add to footnote 291:

WI: Edna M.F. v. Eisenberg, 563 N.W.2d 485, 491 (Wis. 1997).

[283.1] See § **14.8** in the main volume.

Page 403, add to footnote 293:

WI: *But see* Edna M.F. v. Eisenberg, 563 N.W.2d 485 (Wis. 1997) (best interests standard required to remove feeding tube from patient in PVS if subjective standard cannot be met).

Page 403, add note 293.1 reference at end of second sentence of first full paragraph and add note 293.1:

[293.1] **WI:** Edna M.F. v. Eisenberg, 563 N.W.2d 485 (Wis. 1997) (always in best interests of patient to be kept alive by feeding tube if patient is not in PVS and has not provided clear and convincing evidence of wishes before losing decisionmaking capacity).

Page 404, add to footnote 299:

NY: *But see In re* Matthews, 650 N.Y.S.2d 373 (App. Div. 1996) (citing *In re* Hofbauer, 393 N.E.2d 1009 (N.Y. 1979)) (treatment recommended by a physician may be rejected if another treatment is pursued instead).

Page 405, add at end of section:

In an unusual fact situation, a Delaware trial court appointed a guardian for a woman because of her physical incapacity. She suffered from Alzheimer's disease, but the court found that the expert evidence supported a finding that she possessed decisionmaking capacity, although it might be diminished and would certainly diminish in the future. The court directed the guardian, in making a decision whether to permit the implantation of a feeding tube, to use what it termed a best interests standard. However, the manner in which the court described the standard makes it a substituted judgment, or even a subjective, standard:

> In attempting to meet the best interest standard in the context of health care decisions especially, a guardian is obligated to give consideration to the views of the ward herself, if the ward is in a position to consider such matters rationally (as she ordinarily will be where a guardianship is necessitated only by physical incapacity).[302.1]

The second part of the court's direction provides the rationale for this unusual description of the best interests standard. In fact, this patient was not mentally incapacitated to the degree that she required a surrogate decisionmaker. The only reason for the surrogate was the physical incapacity. Consequently, the court was essentially permitting the patient, herself, to decide.

[302.1] *In re* Gordy, 658 A.2d 613, 619 (Del. Ch. 1994).

§ 7.14   Benefit/Burden Approach to Best Interests

Page 405, add to footnote 305:

DC: *Cf. In re* K.I., 735 A.2d 448, 456 (D.C. Ct. App. 1999) (in case involving brain-damaged child, court determined that DNR order was in child's best interests after "balancing the burdens of continued life against the benefits and rewards of furthering life").

§ 7.16   —The *Conroy* Elaboration

Page 407, add note 317.1 reference at end of second paragraph and add note 317.1:

[317.1] **NJ:** *See In re* Roche, 687 A.2d 349, 351 (N.J. Super. Ct. Ch. Div. 1996) (construing *Conroy* as requiring patient's interest in self-determination to be balanced against patient's best interests).

§ 7.17   —Burdens

Page 409, add to footnote 332:

See also Sanford Kadish, *Letting Patients Die: Legal and Moral Reflections,* 80 Cal. L. Rev. 857 (1992).

§ 7.18   — —Pain

Page 410, add to footnote 337:

MI: *See, e.g.,* Martin v. Martin, 538 N.W.2d 399 (Mich. 1995) (disputed evidence about whether noncomatose, brain-injured patient was able to experience pain).

§ 7.19   — —Indignity

Page 412, add note 346.1 reference after first sentence of section and add note 346.1:

[346.1] **DE:** *In re* Gordy, 658 A.2d 613, 618–19 (Del. Ch. 1994) (guardian must consider views of ward about "dignity, as well as . . . ability to experience the joys and benefits of living").

Page 414, add to footnote 353:

MI: *Accord* Martin v. Martin, 538 N.W.2d 399, 419 (Mich. 1995) (Levin, J., dissenting).

§ 7.22 —Quality of Life

Page 417, add to footnote 368:

DE: *In re* Gordy, 658 A.2d 613, 618 (Del. Ch. 1994) ("We are social creatures to lesser or greater degrees concerned about others, as well as ourselves; we are concerned to advance chosen values; and we value our dignity, as well as our ability to experience the joys and benefits of living. Because our biologic life is not our only value, in considering the interests of an incompetent person, biologic life need not be the exclusive focus of the guardian's attention or of the court to which the guardian must answer.").

Page 418, add to footnote 375:

US: Washington v. Glucksberg, 117 S. Ct. 2302, 2308 (1997) (O'Connor, J., concurring):

Allowing the individual, rather than the State, to make judgments "'about the "quality" of life that a particular individual may enjoy'" [citation omitted] does not mean that the lives of terminally-ill, disabled people have less value than the lives of those who are healthy [citation omitted]. Rather, it gives proper recognition to the individual's interest in choosing a final chapter that accords with her life story, rather than one that demeans her values and poisons memories of her.

§ 7.27 The *Conroy* Subjective Standard

Page 434, add to footnote 452:

DE: *But cf. In re* Tavel, 661 A.2d 1061, 1064 (Del. 1995) (decision to permit removal of feeding tube based in part on testimony of patient's rabbi that "removing the feeding tube to permit Mrs. Tavel to die would be consistent with the tenets of Reform Judaism").

NE: Tabatha R. v. Ronda R., 564 N.W.2d 598, 603 (Neb. 1997) (evidence of bioethical considerations followed by religious group not relevant when the policy of particular health care provider not at issue).

§ 7.35 —Nonelderly Nursing Home Patients in Persistent Vegetative State: *Jobes*

Page 445, add to footnote 517:

See Edna M.F. v. Eisenberg, 563 N.W.2d 485, 496–97 (Wis. 1997) (Bablitch, J., concurring) (discussing criteria for appointment of independent experts).

§ 7.36 —Patients in Homecare: *Farrell*

Page 445, add to footnote 518:

See generally Kelli I. Stajduhar & Betty Davies, *Death at Home: Challenges for Families and Directions for the Future,* 14 J. Palliative Care 8 (1998).

§ 7.37 Critique of the New Jersey Approach

Page 448, add note 533.1 reference at end of third item in numbered list and add note 533.1:

[533.1] *See* Edna M.F. v. Eisenberg, 563 N.W.2d 485, 496–97 (Wis. 1997) (Bablitch, J., concurring) (discussing criteria for appointment of independent experts).

§ 7.40 —Providing Informed Consent

Page 450, add to footnote 541:

IL: Ill. Ann. Stat. ch. 755, § 40/25(e) ("The surrogate decision maker has the same right as the patient to receive medical information and medical records and to consent to disclosure.").

§ 7.43 —Limits Imposed by Guardian ad Litem

Page 455, add to footnote 560:

DE: *In re* Tavel, 661 A.2d 1061, 1071 (Del. 1995) ("[I]n cases where a guardian has petitioned for the termination of life support, the Court of Chancery has a duty to provide an attorney ad litem on behalf of the disabled person.").

Page 455, add to footnote 562:

DE: *In re* Tavel, 661 A.2d 1061, 1071 (Del. 1995) (role of guardian ad litem is to discern patient's actual or probable wishes, not automatically to oppose guardian's petition to forgo life-sustaining treatment).

Page 455, add to footnote 565:

DE: *In re* Tavel, 661 A.2d 1061, 1071 (Del. 1995).

Page 457, add at end of section:

In Delaware, because there is no requirement that the guardian ad litem oppose the petitioner's request to forgo life-sustaining treatment, the trial court may appoint a "life advocate" to oppose the request if there would be benefit to an adversarial hearing. "Unlike the [guardian] ad litem, the 'life advocate' would not be bound to represent the ward 'as if engaged by the ward.'"[578.1]

§ 7.44A   —Patient's Regaining Decisionmaking Capacity (New)

Finally, a surrogate also loses the authority to make decisions for a patient if and when the patient regains decisionmaking capacity. The case law is clear that competent patients retain the authority to make their own decisions. Some surrogate decisionmaking statutes expressly become effective only on a patient's loss of decisionmaking capacity,[585.1] but as to those lacking such an express provision, it is implicit that this is the case. However, both the case law and the statutes are relatively silent about the locus of decisionmaking authority if a patient regains decisionmaking capacity. What authority there is is consistent with common sense and with the underlying values at stake (patient self-determination) and purpose of surrogate decisionmaking, and therefore rightly requires that decisionmaking authority revert to the patient if he regains decisionmaking capacity.[585.2]

[578.1] *In re* Tavel, 661 A.2d 1061, 1071–72 (Del. 1995).

[585.1] See § **14.3** in the main volume.

[585.2] *See, e.g.,* Browning v. Herbert, 568 So. 2d 4, 17 (Fla. 1990) ("[A] possible challenge to a surrogate's exercise of authority would be an assertion that there was a reasonable probability that the patient would regain competency."). *Cf.* Browning v. Herbert, 543 So. 2d 258, 272 (Fla. Dist. Ct. App. 1989) ("If there is a reasonable probability that the patient will regain sufficient competency to assist in the decisionmaking process, the decision should be deferred."); Martin v. Martin, 517 N.W.2d 749, 751 (Mich. Ct. App. 1994) ("The proof must be clear and convincing that the patient does not have and will not regain the capacity of making the decision."); Martin v. Martin, 504 N.W.2d 917, 924 (Mich. Ct. App. 1993) (same); *In re* Conroy, 486 A.2d 1209, 1241 (N.J. 1985) (same).

§ 7.45   Preferences of Incompetent Patients

Page 458, add to footnote 586:

DE: *Cf. In re* Gordy, 658 A.2d 613 (Del. Ch. 1994) (although patient is currently competent, competence is somewhat compromised and is gradually being eroded by Alzheimer's disease; fact that her current expressed wishes are consistent with wishes expressed when clearly competent support son's decision consistent with these wishes).

NJ: *In re* Roche, 687 A.2d 349 (N.J. Super. Ct. Ch. Div. 1996) (patient lacking in decisionmaking capacity executed advance directive).

NY: *In re* Matthews, 650 N.Y.S.2d 373, 376 n.7 (App. Div. 1996) ("Scott, who is quadriplegic, nonverbal and incontinent, makes no other purely voluntary decision than his choice to eat.").

Page 458, after of third sentence of first paragraph:

Whether overriding the objection of an incompetent patient without some review beyond that of the attending physician is constitutional is open to question.[586.1]

Page 459, add to footnote 588:

DE: *See also In re* Tavel, 661 A.2d 1061, 1064 (Del. 1995).

Page 459, add to footnote 589:

MI: Martin v. Martin, 538 N.W.2d 399 (Mich. 1995).

Page 459, add to footnote 592:

DE: *Cf. In re* Gordy, 658 A.2d 613 (Del. Ch. 1994).

§ 7.46   —Weight to Be Accorded Preferences

Page 462, add at end of section:

If an incompetent patient executes an advance directive, the directive is not binding as such, but it is permissible for the guardian of an incompetent patient to consider an advance directive made by an incompetent patient "as

---

[586.1] **NY:** T.D. v. New York State Office of Mental Health, 650 N.Y.S.2d 173, 193 (App. Div. 1996) (administrative regulation permitting the overriding of objection of patient lacking decisionmaking capacity or minor patient by psychiatrist without notice to patient or patient's representative violated due process).

evidence of the incompetent's subjective intent. Of course, the guardian must carefully consider and weigh all other probative evidence in making such a determination."[609]

Bibliography

Alpers, A., and B. Lo. "Avoiding Family Feuds: Responding to Surrogate Demands for Life-Sustaining Interventions." *Journal of Law, Medicine and Ethics* 27 (1999): 74.

Asch, D., et al. "Decisions to Limit or Continue Life-Sustaining Treatment by Critical Care Physicians in the United States: Conflicts Between Physicians' Practices and Patients' Wishes." *American Journal of Respiratory and Critical Care Medicine* 151 (1995): 288.

Baergen, R. "Surrogates and Uncertainty." *Journal of Clinical Ethics* 6 (1995): 372.

Bishop, M. "Crossing the Decisional Abyss: An Evaluation of Surrogate Decision-Making Statutes as a Means of Bridging the Gap Between Post-Quinlan Red Tape and the Realization of an Incompetent Patient's Right to Refuse Life-Sustaining Medical Treatment." *Elder Law Journal* 7 (1999): 153.

Blustein, J. "Choosing for Others as Continuing a Life Story: The Problem of Personal Identity Revisited." *Journal of Law, Medicine and Ethics* 27 (1999): 20.

Broder, A. "'She Don't Want No Life Support.' A Summary of *Osgood* and Other Developments in Michigan Since *Martin*." *University of Detroit Mercy Law Review* 75 (1998): 595.

Callahan, D. "Terminating Life-Sustaining Treatment of the Demented." *Hastings Center Report* 25(6) (1995): 25.

Cantor, N. "Discarding Substituted Judgement and Best Interests: Toward a Constructive Preference Standard for Dying, Previously Competent Patients Without Advance Instructions." *Rutgers Law Review* 48 (1996): 1193.

Collopy, B. "The Moral Underpinning of the Proxy-Provider Relationship: Issues of Trust and Distrust." *Journal of Law, Medicine and Ethics* 27 (1999): 37.

Cranford, R. "Mary, Mary, Quite Contrary, How Was I to Know?" Michael Martin, "Absolute Prescience, and the Right to Die in Michigan." *University of Detroit Mercy Law Review* 72 (1995): 787.

---

[609] **NJ:** *In re* Roche, 687 A.2d 349 (N.J. Super. Ct. Ch. Div. 1996) (citing *In re* Conroy, 486 A.2d 1209 (N.J. 1985)).

Drane, J., and J. Coulehan. "The Best-Interest Standard: Surrogate Decision Making and Quality of Life." *Journal of Clinical Ethics* 6 (1995): 20.

Dresser, R. "Dworkin on Dementia: Elegant Theory, Questionable Policy." *Hastings Center Report* 25(6) (1995): 32.

Fenwick, A. "Applying Best Interests Standard to Persistent Vegetative State—A Principled Distortion?" *Journal of Medical Ethics* 24 (1998): 86.

Fins, J. "Commentary: From Contract to Covenant in Advance Care Planning." *Journal of Law, Medicine and Ethics* 27 (1999): 46.

Gillon, R. "Persistent Vegetative State, Withdrawal of Artificial Nutrition and Hydration, and the Patient's 'best interests.'" *Journal of Medical Ethics* 24 (1998): 75.

Hackler, C., and C. Hiller. "Family Consent to Orders Not to Resuscitate." *Journal of the American Medical Association* 264 (1990): 1281.

Hafemeister, T. "End-of-Life Decision Making, Therapeutic Jurisprudence, and Preventive Law: Hierarchical v. Consensus-Based Decision-Making Model." *Arizona Law Review* 41 (1999): 329.

Harrison, C., et al. "Should People Do unto Others as They Would Not Want Done unto Themselves?" *Journal of Clinical Ethics* 6 (1995): 14.

Hess, J. "Looking for Traction on the Slippery Slope: A Discussion of the Michael Martin Case." *Issues of Law and Medicine* 11 (1995): 105.

Hoffmann, D., et al. "How Close Is Enough? Family Relationships and Attitudes Toward Advance Directives and Life-Sustaining Treatments." *Journal of Ethics, Law and Aging* 3 (1997): 5.

Hofmann, J., et al. "Patient Preferences for Communication with Physicians about End-of-Life Decisions." *Annals of Internal Medicine* 127 (1997): 1.

Jecker, N. "Being a Burden on Others." *Journal of Clinical Ethics* 4 (1993): 16.

Kadish, S. "Letting Patients Die: Legal and Moral Reflections." *California Law Review* 80 (1992): 857.

Kapp, M. "Commentary: Anxieties as a Legal Impediment to the Doctor-Proxy Relationship." *Journal of Law, Medicine and Ethics* 27 (1999): 69.

Kirkland, L. "Family Refusal to Accept Brain Death and Termination of Life Support: To Whom Is the Physician Responsible?" *Journal of Clinical Ethics* 3 (1992): 78.

Koch, T. "The Gulf Between: Surrogate Choices, Physician Instructions, and Informal Network Responses." *Cambridge Quarterly of Healthcare Ethics* 4 (1995): 185.

BIBLIOGRAPHY

Kuczewski, M. "Commentary: Narrative Views of Personal Identity and Substituted Judgment in Surrogate Decision Making."*Journal of Law, Medicine and Ethics* 27 (1999): 32.

Loewy, E.H. "Treatment Decisions in the Mentally Impaired: Limiting But Not Abandoning Treatment." *New England Journal of Medicine* 317 (1987): 1465.

Luttrell, S., "Making Decisions About Medical Treatment for Mentally Incapable Adults in the UK." *Lancet* 350 (1997): 950.

Lynn, J., et al. "Perceptions by Family Members of the Dying Experience of Older and Seriously Ill Patients." *Annals of Internal Medicine* 126 (1997): 97.

Marzen, T. "Will the Real Michael Martin Please Speak Up! Medical Decisionmaking for Questionably Competent Persons." *University of Detroit Mercy Law Review* 72 (1995): 833.

McFadzean, J., et al. "The Dilemma of the Incapacitated Patient Who Has Previously Refused Consent for Surgery." *British Medical Journal* 315 (1997): 1530.

Meier, D. "Voiceless and Vulnerable: Dementia Patients Without Surrogates in an Era of Capitation." *Journal of the American Geriatrics Society* 45 (1997): 375.

Miller, T., et al. "Treatment Decisions for Patients Without Surrogates: Rethinking Policies for a Vulnerable Population." *Journal of the American Geriatrics Society* 45 (1997): 369.

Newton, Michael J. "Precedent Autonomy: Life-Sustaining Intervention and the Demented Patient." *Cambridge Quarterly of Healthcare Ethics* 8 (1999): 189.

O'Brien, L. "Nursing Home Residents' Preferences for Life-Sustaining Treatments." *JAMA* 274 (1995): 1775.

Post, L., J. Blustein, and N. Dubler. "The Doctor-Proxy Relationship: An Untapped Resource." *Journal of Law, Medicine and Ethics* 27 (1999): 5.

Powell, T. "Extubating Mrs. K: Psychological Aspects of Surrogate Decision Making." *Journal of Law, Medicine and Ethics* 27 (1999): 81.

Sabatino, C. "The Legal and Functional Status of the Medical Proxy: Suggestions for Statutory Reform." *Journal of Law, Medicine and Ethics* 27 (1999): 52.

Schneiderman, L., et al. "Do Physicians' Own Preferences for Life-Sustaining Treatment Influence Their Perceptions of Patients' Preferences?" *Journal of Clinical Ethics* 4 (1993): 28.

Skinner, P. "Note. Tipping the Scales: How Guardianship of Brandon Has Upset Massachusetts' Balanced Substituted Judgment Doctrine. (Guardianship of Brandon, 677 N.E.2d 114, Mass. 1997)." *Boston College Law Review* 40 (1999): 969.

Strasser, M. "Incompetents and the Right to Die: In Search of Consistent Meaningful Standards." *Kentucky Law Journal* 83 (1994–95): 733.

Sulmasy, D., et al. "The Accuracy of Substituted Judgments in Patients with Terminal Diagnoses." *Archives of Internal Medicine* 128 (1998): 621.

Swigart, V., et al. "Letting Go: Family Willingness to Forgo Life Support." *Heart & Lung* 25 (1996): 483.

Tonelli, M. "Substituted Judgment in Medical Practice: Evidentiary Standards on a Sliding Scale." *Journal of Law, Medicine & Ethics* 25 (1997): 22.

Truog, R., and J. Fackler. "It Is Reasonable to Reject the Diagnosis of Brain Death." *Journal of Clinical Ethics* 3 (1992): 80.

Yarborough, M. "Continued Treatment of the Fatally Ill for the Benefit of Others." *Journal of the American Geriatric Society* 36 (1988): 63.

Zeleznik, J., et al. "The Doctor-Proxy Relationship: Perception and Communication." *Journal of Law, Medicine and Ethics* 27 (1999): 13.

CHAPTER 8

LIMITATIONS ON THE RIGHT TO DIE

§ 8.1   Introduction

Page 466, add to footnote 2:

MD: Wright v. Johns Hopkins Health Sys. Corp., 728 A.2d 166, 168 (Md. Ct. App. 1999).

MI: Martin v. Martin, 538 N.W.2d 399, 405 n.9 (Mich. 1995) (citing first edition of this treatise).

PA: *In re* Fiori, 673 A.2d 905, 910 (Pa. 1996).

§ 8.2   Limitations on Decisions of Competent Patients

Page 470, add to footnote 15:

MI: Martin v. Martin, 538 N.W.2d 399, 408 (Mich. 1995) ("[C]learly expressed wishes of a patient, while competent, should be honored regardless of the patient's condition.") (dictum).

Page 470, add to footnote 18:

FL: *But see* Harrell v. St. Mary's Hosp., Inc., 678 So. 2d 455, 456 (Fla. Dist. Ct. App. 1996) ("It is unquestioned that in considering whether a patient may forego medical treatment, several state interests must be addressed.").

MA: *In re* Shine v. Vega, 709 N.E.2d 58, 63 (Mass. 1999) ("'[E]very competent adult has a right "to [forgo] treatment, or even cure, if it entails what for [her] are intolerable consequences or risks however unwise [her] sense of values may be in the eyes of the medical profession."'"); Norwood Hosp. v. Munoz, 564 N.E.2d 1017, 1021 (Mass. 1991) ("It is for the individual to decide whether a particular medical treatment is in the individual's best interests. As a result, '[t]he law protects [a person's] right to make her own decision to accept or reject treatment, whether that decision is wise or unwise.' Lane v. Candura, 6 Mass. App. Ct. 377, 383, 376 N.E.2d 1232 (1978).").

NY: Blackman v. New York City Health & Hosps. Corp., 660 N.Y.S.2d 643, 649 (Sup. Ct. Kings County 1997) (state interests must be weighed against competent patient's right to refuse treatment, but hospital failed to identify any state interests).

§ 8.3   Limitations on Decisions for Incompetent Patients

Page 471, add to footnote 20:

MI: Martin v. Martin, 538 N.W.2d 399 (Mich. 1995) (serious brain injury), *rev'g* 517 N.W.2d 749 (Mich. Ct. App. 1994).

§ 8.5   Act versus Omission (Killing versus "Letting Die")

Page 473, add to footnote 34:

CA9: Compassion in Dying v. Washington, 79 F.3d 790 (9th Cir. 1996) (distinction is "untenable") (citing first edition of this treatise), *rev'd sub nom.* Washington v. Glucksberg, 117 S. Ct. 2258 (1997).

Page 474, add to footnote 36:

US: *But see* Vacco v. Quill, 117 S. Ct. 2293, 2302 (1997) (state's reasons for "recognizing and acting" on distinction between actively and passively hastening death satisfy "valid and important public interests").

CA9: Compassion in Dying v. Washington, 79 F.3d 790, 822 (9th Cir. 1996) (distinction "between commission and omission . . . is a distinction without a difference"), *rev'd sub nom.* Washington v. Glucksberg, 117 S. Ct. 2258 (1997).

§ 8.7   Intended versus Unintended Consequences ("Double Effect")

Page 478, add to footnote 56:

CA9: *See* Compassion in Dying v. Washington, 79 F.3d 790, 823 n.95 (9th Cir. 1996).

Page 478, add note 56.1 reference at end of first sentence of second paragraph and add note 56.1:

[56.1] Compassion in Dying v. Washington, 79 F.3d 790, 823 (9th Cir. 1996) ("As part of the tradition of administering comfort care, doctors have been supplying the causal agent of patients' deaths for decades. Physicians routinely and openly provide medication to terminally ill patients with the knowledge that it will have a "double effect"—reduce the patient's pain and hasten his death. . . . It commonly takes the form of putting a patient on an intravenous morphine drip, with full knowledge that, while such treatment will alleviate his pain, it will also indubitably hasten his death.").

Page 478, add to footnote 58:

KS: *See* State v. Naramore, 965 P.2d 211, 214 (Kan. Ct. App. 1998) ("'Palliative care refers to medical intervention in which the primary purpose is to alleviate pain and suffering. It is sometimes referred to as having a "double effect," however, because in addition to relieving pain and suffering, the level of pain medication necessary to relieve pain may have the consequence of shortening life. Thus, the health care provider's role as healer conflicts with his or her role as reliever of suffering when increasing amounts of pain medication are required to provide comfort care, but these increasing doses may have the effect of slowing respirations and thereby hastening death.'").

Page 478, add note 58.1 reference at end of second paragraph and add note 58.1:

[58.1] *But see* G. Kolata, *When Morphine Fails to Kill,* N.Y. Times, July 23, 1997, at C-7 (reporting studies suggesting that patients on high doses of morphine develop tolerance to effect of drug on respiration and drug is not lethal for them).

Page 479, add after first sentence of first full paragraph:

The United States Supreme Court discussed the principle of double effect in *Vacco v. Quill.*[63.1] It held that although "a State may prohibit assisting suicide while permitting patients to refuse unwanted lifesaving treatment, it may permit palliative care related to that refusal, which may have the foreseen but unintended 'double effect' of hastening the patient's death."[63.2] In addition, in the process of finding a rational distinction between actively and passively hastening death, the Court blessed, or at least did not condemn, the closely

---

[63.1]   117 S. Ct. 2293 (1997).

[63.2]   *Id.* at 2301 n.11.

related practice of "terminal sedation." In this practice, a dying patient is administered an infusion of barbiturates that results in the patient's becoming comatose, and the coma is maintained by the infusion until the patient dies from the withholding of nutrition and hydration.[63.3] The rationale for the Court's acquiescence in this practice is not clear. About the only explanation is the cryptic statement that

> Petitioners insist . . . that "'[a]lthough proponents of physician-assisted suicide and euthanasia contend that terminal sedation is covert physician-assisted suicide or euthanasia, the concept of sedating pharmacotherapy is based on informed consent and the principle of double effect.'" Reply Brief for Petitioners 12 (quoting P. Rousseau, *Terminal Sedation in the Care of Dying Patients,* 156 Archives Internal Med. 1785, 1785–1786 (1996)).[63.4]

Although Justice Stevens agreed with the majority that there is a rational distinction between forgoing life-sustaining treatment (including terminal sedation) on the one hand and assisted suicide on the other, he did not believe that physician-assisted suicide would undermine the integrity of the medical profession because there is already "significant tension between the traditional view of the physician's role and the actual practice in a growing number of cases" that involve forgoing life-sustaining treatment and terminal sedation.[63.5]

Page 479, replace footnote 64 with:

CA9: Compassion in Dying v. Washington, 79 F.3d 790, 823 (9th Cir. 1996).

GA: State v. McAfee, 385 S.E.2d 651, 652 (Ga. 1989).

KS: *Accord* State v. Naramore, 965 P.2d 211, 214 (Kan. Ct. App. 1998) ("'[A] health care provider is ethically permitted, and perhaps even required, to implement pain medication and palliative care, with the consent of the patient or the patient's family, notwithstanding the potential for hastening death.'") (dictum).

NE: *See also* Neb. Rev. Stat. § 71-7418(3) ("[a] physician should be able to prescribe, dispense, or administer a controlled substance in excess of the recommended dosage for the treatment of pain").

NV: *Accord* McKay v. Bergstedt, 801 P.2d 617 (Nev. 1990).

See also **Table 9-1A.**

[63.3] *Id.*

[63.4] *Id.*

[63.5] *Id.* at 2309 (Stevens, J., concurring in the judgment). *Accord* McIver v. Krischer, 697 So. 2d 97, 110–11 (Fla. 1997) (Kogan, C.J., dissenting).

Page 480, add to footnote 67:

See Alan Meisel, *Physician-Assisted Suicide: A Roadmap for State Courts,* 24 Fordham Urban L.J. 801 (1997).

§ 8.8   Ordinary versus Extraordinary Treatment

Page 481, add to footnote 78:

PA: *In re* Goldman, 18 Fiduc. Rep. 2d 79 (C.P. Northampton County, Pa. 1997) (protection of "ethical integrity of medical community" allows court to order antibiotics and whirlpool treatments because they are a "minimally intrusive regimen").

Page 482, add to footnote 81:

CA9:   Compassion in Dying v. Washington, 79 F.3d 790, 821 (9th Cir. 1996) (distinction is "unworkable"), *rev'd on other grounds sub nom.* Washington v. Glucksberg, 117 S. Ct. 2258 (1997).

§ 8.9   Prognostic Approach: Introduction

Page 489, add to footnote 119:

MI: Martin v. Martin, 538 N.W.2d 399 (Mich. 1995), *rev'g* 517 N.W.2d 749 (Mich. Ct. App. 1994).

§ 8.10   Terminal Illness

Page 490, add to footnote 123:

MI: Martin v. Martin, 538 N.W.2d 399 (Mich. 1995) (life-sustaining treatment may be forgone for incompetent, nonterminally ill patient only if there is clear and convincing evidence of a prior decision by the patient when competent to forgo treatment under the circumstances that have come to exist, but expressing no opinion as to standard to be followed if patient is terminally ill).

Page 492, add to footnote 129:

FL: Singletary v. Costello, 665 So. 2d 1099, 1109 (Fla. Dist. Ct. App. 1996).

MI: Martin v. Martin, 538 N.W.2d 399, 408 (Mich. 1995) ("[C]learly expressed wishes of a patient, while competent, should be honored regardless of the patient's condition.") (dictum).

Page 492, add to footnote 130:

MI: Martin v. Martin, 538 N.W.2d 399 (Mich. 1995), *rev'g* 517 N.W.2d 749 (Mich. Ct. App. 1994).

Page 492, add to footnote 131:

MI: *But see* Martin v. Martin, 538 N.W.2d 399 (Mich. 1995) (state may require that incompetent patient be terminally ill or persistently vegetative for treatment to be terminated in absence of patient's own previously expressed preference for termination), *rev'g* 517 N.W.2d 749 (Mich. Ct. App. 1994), *and* 504 N.W.2d 917 (Mich. Ct. App. 1993).

§ 8.13   Lifesaving versus Life-Sustaining Treatment

Page 498, add to footnote 168:

IA: *Accord* Polk County Sheriff v. Iowa Dist. Court, 594 N.W.2d 421, 426–27 (Iowa 1999).

Page 501, add to footnote 180:

CA11: *But see* Novak v. Cobb County-Kennestone Hosp. Auth., 74 F.3d 1173 (11th Cir. 1996) (neither 16-year-old nor parents may refuse lifesaving blood transfusion).

CT: *See* Stamford Hosp. v. Vega, 674 A.2d 821 (Conn. 1996).

Page 501, add to footnote 181:

MA: *Cf. In re* Rena, 705 N.E.2d 1155 (Mass. App. Ct. 1999).

§ 8.14   Balancing Approach: Introduction

Page 502, add note 183.1 reference at end of first sentence of section and add note 183.1:

[183.1]**NJ:** *But see In re* Roche, 687 A.2d 349, 351 (N.J. Super. Ct. Ch. Div. 1996) (claiming patient's interest in self-determination must be balanced against patient's best interests).

Page 502, add to footnote 188:

CA9: *See* Compassion in Dying v. Washington, 79 F.3d 790 (9th Cir. 1996), *rev'd on other grounds sub nom.* Washington v. Glucksberg, 117 S. Ct. 2258 (1997).

Page 503, add to footnote 190:

CA9: *See* Compassion in Dying v. Washington, 79 F.3d 790, 803 (9th Cir. 1996).

Page 503, add at end of carryover paragraph:

The weighing and balancing of individual and state interests has been described as being "quintessentially a judicial role."[192.1] It is also ultimately a subjective one:

> Despite all of the efforts of generations of courts to categorize and objectify, to create multi-part tests and identify weights to be attached to the various factors, in the end balancing entails the exercise of judicial judgment rather than the application of scientific or mathematical formulae. No legislative body can perform the task for us. Nor can any computer.[192.2]

Page 503, add to footnote 194:

Overruled by In re Conroy, 486 A.2d 1209, 1224 (N.J. 1985).

Page 504, add to footnote 195:

IA: Polk County Sheriff v. Iowa Dist. Court, 594 N.W.2d 421, 427 (Iowa 1999) (including "magnitude of the invasion" in balancing process).

Page 509, add to footnote 203:

FL: *But see* Harrell v. St. Mary's Hosp., Inc., 678 So. 2d 455, 456 (Fla. Dist. Ct. App. 1996) ("It is unquestioned that in considering whether a patient may forego medical treatment, several state interests must be addressed.").

Page 509, add to footnote 219:

FL: McIver v. Krischer, 697 So. 2d 97, 102 (Fla. 1997); Singletary v. Costello, 665 So. 2d 1099, 1105 (Fla. Dist. Ct. App. 1996).
IL: *In re* Fetus Brown, 689 N.E.2d 397, 402 (Ill. App. Ct. 1997).
IA: Polk County Sheriff v. Iowa Dist. Court, 594 N.W.2d 421, 426 (Iowa 1999).

[192.1] Compassion in Dying v. Washington, 79 F.3d 790, 836 (9th Cir. 1996).
[192.2] *Id.*

MD: Wright v. Johns Hopkins Health Sys. Corp., 728 A.2d 166, 168 (Md. Ct. App. 1999).
NJ: *In re* Roche, 687 A.2d 349, 351 (N.J. Super. Ct. Ch. Div. 1996).
PA: *In re* Fiori, 673 A.2d 905, 910 (Pa. 1996).
WI: Edna M.F. v. Eisenberg, 563 N.W.2d 485, 490 n.8 (Wis. 1997).

Page 510, add at end of section:

An interesting point beginning to receive some judicial attention is who has standing to assert state interests.[223.1]

§ 8.15   State Interest in Preservation of Life

Page 510, add to footnote 225:

FL: McIver v. Krischer, 697 So. 2d 97, 103 (Fla. 1997) (distinguishing permissible forgoing of treatment from impermissible physician-assisted suicide).
MI: Martin v. Martin, 538 N.W.2d 399, 405 (Mich. 1995) (state interest in preservation of life does not come into play unless there is clear and convincing evidence that now incompetent patient wants to die).

Page 510, add to footnote 226:

CA9: Compassion in Dying v. Washington, 79 F.3d 790, 817 (9th Cir. 1996) ("Although the state's interest in preserving life may be unqualified, and may be asserted regardless of the quality of the life or lives at issue, that interest is not always controlling. Nor is it of the same strength in each case. To the contrary, its strength is dependent on relevant circumstances, including the medical condition and the wishes of the person whose life is at stake."), *rev'd sub nom.* Washington v. Glucksberg, 117 S. Ct. 2258 (1997).
CT: *Accord* Stamford Hosp. v. Vega, 674 A.2d 821, 832 (Conn. 1996).
IA: *Accord* Polk County Sheriff v. Iowa Dist. Court, 594 N.W.2d 421, 426–27 (Iowa 1999).

Page 511, add to footnote 227:

IL: *In re* Fetus Brown, 689 N.E.2d 397 (Ill. App. Ct. 1997) (competent, pregnant patient may refuse life-saving blood transfusion).

[223.1] *See* Stamford Hosp. v. Vega, 674 A.2d 821 (Conn. 1996); In re Dubreuil, 629 So. 2d 819 (Fla. 1993). See § 5.49 in the main volume and in this supplement.

Page 511, add to footnote 228:

CA9:   Compassion in Dying v. Washington, 79 F.3d 790, 820 (9th Cir. 1996) ("As the laws in state after state demonstrate, even though the protection of life is one of the state's most important functions, the state's interest is dramatically diminished if the person it seeks to protect is terminally ill or permanently comatose and has expressed a wish that he be permitted to die without further medical treatment (or if a duly appointed representative has done so on his behalf)."), *rev'd sub nom.* Washington v. Glucksberg, 117 S. Ct. 2258 (1997).

Page 511, add to footnote 230:

PA: *In re* Goldman, 18 Fiduc. Rep. 2d 79 (C.P. Northampton County, Pa. 1997) (state's interest in life would not require amputation of leg of 80-year-old patient suffering from Alzheimer's disease) (dictum).

Page 512, add to footnote 234:

PA: *In re* Fiori, 673 A.2d 905, 910 (Pa. 1996) ("The state's interest in maintaining the PVS individual in an endless twilight state between life and death is so weak that it cannot overcome the individual's right to self-determination."); *In re* Goldman, 18 Fiduc. Rep. 2d 79 (C.P. Northampton County, Pa. 1997) (state's interest in life would not require amputation of leg of 80-year-old patient suffering from Alzheimer's disease, who is neither terminally ill nor in a persistent vegetative state, because "she is significantly impaired with no prospect of recovery or regaining any part of the quality of her life . . . . She experiences dementia. She is non-communicative. Only rarely is there a flicker of possible recognition of her daughter's voice She cannot walk or care for herself. She is completely passive.") (dictum).

Page 513, add to footnote 241:

IL: *In re* Fetus Brown, 689 N.E.2d 397, 403 (Ill. App. Ct. 1997) (in determining application of state interest in preservation of life, life of patient must be taken into account, not life of fetus that patient is carrying).

Page 513, add to footnote 242:

IL: *In re* Fetus Brown, 689 N.E.2d 397, 403 (Ill. App. Ct. 1997) (although "public policy values the sanctity of life," state also has interest in protecting individual autonomy).

Page 514, add to footnote 245:

PA: *In re* Fiori, 673 A.2d 905, 910 (Pa. 1996).

§ 8.16   State Interest in Prevention of Suicide

Page 515, add to footnote 250:

CA9:   Compassion in Dying v. Washington, 79 F.3d 790, 820 (9th Cir. 1996) ("While the state's general commitment to the preservation of life clearly encompasses the prevention of suicide, the state has an even more particular interest in deterring the taking of one's own life."), *rev'd on other grounds sub nom.* Washington v. Glucksberg, 117 S. Ct. 2258 (1997).

Page 515, add to footnote 251:

CA9:   *But see* Compassion in Dying v. Washington, 79 F.3d 790, 820 (9th Cir. 1996) (prevention of suicide is primary state interest in case challenging constitutionality of statutory prohibition on assisted suicide), *rev'd on other grounds sub nom.* Washington v. Glucksberg, 117 S. Ct. 2258 (1997).

Page 516, add to footnote 252:

FL: McIver v. Krischer, 697 So. 2d 97, 103 (Fla. 1997) (distinguishing permissible forgoing of treatment from impermissible physician-assisted suicide).

PA: *In re* Fiori, 673 A.2d 905, 910 (Pa. 1996).

Page 516, add to footnote 253:

RI: *But see* Laurie v. Senecal, 666 A.2d 806, 807 (R.I. 1995) (viewing nonphysically ill prisoner's refusal to eat as suicide and therefore ordering tube-feeding of the prisoner who was refusing to eat because "he no longer desired to live because of the stigma of his conviction for first-degree sexual assault upon a minor female").

Page 516, add note 256.1 reference at end of last paragraph and add note 256.1:

[256.1] *See* Compassion in Dying v. Washington, 79 F.3d 790, 824 (9th Cir. 1996) (court unwilling to view patient's *actively* hastening death as suicide if patient is terminally ill and competent), *rev'd sub nom.* Washington v. Glucksberg, 117 S. Ct. 2258 (1997), discussed in § **18.22** in this supplement.

§ 8.17   State Interest in Protection of Third Parties

Page 516, add to footnote 257:

CA9:   Compassion in Dying v. Washington, 79 F.3d 790, 827 (9th Cir. 1996), *rev'd on other grounds sub nom.* Washington v. Glucksberg, 117 S. Ct. 2258 (1997).

IA: *Accord* Polk County Sheriff v. Iowa Dist. Court, 594 N.W.2d 421, 428 (Iowa 1999).

Page 517, add to footnote 262:

PA: *In re* Fiori, 673 A.2d 905, 910 (Pa. 1996) ("primary focus is on whether the patient has dependents who would be left emotionally and financially bereft were the patient to refuse medical treatment" (dictum).

Page 518, add to footnote 268:

CA9:   Compassion in Dying v. Washington, 79 F.3d 790, 827 (9th Cir. 1996) ("[W]itnessing a loved one suffer a slow and agonizing death as a result of state compulsion is more likely to harm than further the interests of innocent third parties."), *rev'd sub nom.* Washington v. Glucksberg, 117 S. Ct. 2258 (1997).

Page 518, add note 268.1 reference at end of first full paragraph and add note 268.1:

268.1 **IA:** *Accord* Polk County Sheriff v. Iowa Dist. Court, 594 N.W.2d 421, 428 (Iowa 1999) (in case of pretrial detainee suffering from kidney failure, "[a]lthough not controlling, we must still weigh this factor in the balance, and we do so in favor of compelling treatment").

Page 519, add to footnote 270:

CT: *Cf.* Stamford Hosp. v. Vega, 674 A.2d 821, 831 (Conn. 1996) (Although hospital's concern for welfare of newborn is "commendable," this is "simply not an issue sufficiently within the scope of the hospital's legitimate interest in providing medical care to the baby to justify disregarding Vega's clearly expressed proscription against administering blood transfusions to her").

Page 521, add to footnote 286:

CT: *Accord* Stamford Hosp. v. Vega, 674 A.2d 821 (Conn. 1996).

Page 523, add to footnote 300:

IL: *Accord In re* Fetus Brown, 689 N.E.2d 397, 404 (Ill. App. Ct. 1997) (when there is no evidence of abandonment of minor children, "the State's interest . . . is not determinative").

Page 523, add to footnote 303:

CT: *Accord* Stamford Hosp. v. Vega, 674 A.2d 821, 831 (Conn. 1996) ("[W]hether Vega's child grows up with one, rather than two, parents, or, for that matter, with no parent at all, was simply not an issue sufficiently within the scope of the hospital's legitimate interest in providing medical care to the baby to justify disregarding Vega's clearly expressed proscription against administering blood transfusions to her.").

§ 8.18   State Interest in Protection of Ethical Integrity of Medical Profession

Page 524, add to footnote 308:

CT: *Cf.* Stamford Hosp. v. Vega, 674 A.2d 821, 832 (Conn. 1996) (hospital has no "right or obligation to thrust unwanted medical care on a patient who, having been sufficiently informed of the consequences, competently and clearly declined that care").

MA: *Accord In re* Shine v. Vega, 709 N.E.2d 58, 65 n.19 (Mass. 1999) (ethical integrity of medical profession not violated by allowing competent patient to refuse treatment, even in life-threatening emergency).

Page 525, add to footnote 311:

CT: Stamford Hosp. v. Vega, 674 A.2d 821, 829-30 (Conn. 1996).

Page 526, add to footnote 316:

IL: *See also In re* Fetus Brown, 689 N.E.2d 397, 403 (Ill. App. Ct. 1997) (no compromise of professional ethics not to impose blood transfusion on unwilling, pregnant member of Jehovah's Witness faith because "the American Medical Association Board of Trustees generally recommends that '[j]udicial intervention is inappropriate when a woman has made an informed refusal of a medical treatment designed to benefit her fetus.' H. Cole, Legal Interventions During Pregnancy, 264 JAMA 2603, 2670 (1990).").

Page 528, add to footnote 322:

PA: *In re* Fiori, 673 A.2d 905, 910 (Pa. 1996).

Page 528, add to footnote 324:

CT: Stamford Hosp. v. Vega, 674 A.2d 821, 829–30 (Conn. 1996).
IL: *But see In re* Fetus Brown, 689 N.E.2d 397, 401 (Ill. App. Ct. 1997) (competent, pregnant patient may refuse life-saving blood transfusion even though it is a "'relatively noninvasive and risk-free'" procedure).
IA: *See* Polk County Sheriff v. Iowa Dist. Court, 594 N.W.2d 421, 428 (Iowa 1999) (in case of pretrial detainee suffering from kidney failure, "[p]reserving the ethical integrity of that recommendation also favors our decision to compel treatment").
NJ: John F. Kennedy Memorial Hosp. v. Heston, 279 A.2d 670 (N.J. 1971), *overruled by In re* Conroy, 486 A.2d 1209, 1224 (N.J. 1985).
PA: *In re* Goldman, 18 Fiduc. Rep. 2d 79 (C.P. Northampton County, Pa. 1997) (interest in protection of ethics of "medical community" permits administration of antibiotics and whirlpool therapy to 80-year-old patient suffering from Alzheimer's disease, but does not require amputation should that become necessary).

Page 529, add at end of section:

In contrast with forgoing life-sustaining treatment, which has almost uniformly been held not to violate professional ethics, a physician's aiding a dying patient in actively ending the patient's own life (so-called physician-assisted suicide) does violate the ethics of the medical profession.[328.1]

[328.1] **US:**   Washington v. Glucksberg, 117 S. Ct. 2258, 2273 (1997).

CA9: *But see* Compassion in Dying v. Washington, 79 F.3d 790, 827 (9th Cir. 1996) (Permitting physicians to assist terminally ill patients in actively hastening their deaths will not compromise integrity of medical profession; rather, statutes that criminalize such assistance threaten medical profession's integrity by making "covert criminals out of honorable, dedicated, and compassionate individuals."), *rev'd sub nom.* Washington v. Glucksberg, 117 S. Ct. 2258 (1997).

FL: McIver v. Krischer, 697 So. 2d 97 (Fla. 1997).

See generally American Medical Ass'n, Code of Ethics § 2.211 (1994); Council on Ethical & Judicial Affairs, American Medical Ass'n, *Decisions Near the End of Life,* 267 JAMA 2229, 2233 (1992).

§ 8.19   Other State Interests

Page 530, add to footnote 330:

FL: Singletary v. Costello, 665 So. 2d 1099, 1104 (Fla. Dist. Ct. App. 1996) ("[L]awful incarceration brings about the necessary withdrawals or limitations of many privileges and rights, a retraction justified by the considerations underlying the penal system.").

IA: Polk County Sheriff v. Iowa Dist. Court, 594 N.W.2d 421 (Iowa 1999) (holding that state interests in maintaining prison security, order, and discipline outweighed pretrial detainee's liberty interests).

ND: State v. Schuetzle, 537 N.W.2d 358, 363–64 (N.D. 1995) (prisoner's refusal of insulin for treatment of diabetes was a "blatant attempt to manipulate his placement within the prison system" and requiring him to undergo the treatment "is reasonably related to legitimate penological interests").

Page 530, add to footnote 331:

IA: Polk County Sheriff v. Iowa Dist. Court, 594 N.W.2d 421 (Iowa 1999) (pretrial detainee needed hemodialysis).

ND: State v. Schuetzle, 537 N.W.2d 358 (N.D. 1995) (diabetic refusing insulin).

Page 530, add to footnote 332:

DNY: *In re* Sanchez, 577 F. Supp. 7 (S.D.N.Y. 1983).

FL: Singletary v. Costello, 665 So. 2d 1099 (Fla. Dist. Ct. App. 1996) (hunger strike protesting punitive transfer).

RI: Laurie v. Senecal, 666 A.2d 806 (R.I. 1995) (desire to commit suicide by starvation).

Page 530, add to footnote 333:

IA: Polk County Sheriff v. Iowa Dist. Court, 594 N.W.2d 421, 427 (Iowa 1999) ("compelling [pretrial detainee] to submit to dialysis 'does not involve a situation where "heavy physical and emotional burdens" would be imposed "to effect a brief and uncertain delay in the natural process of death,"'" quoting *Myers*).

Page 532, add after carryover paragraph:

A decision of a Florida appeals court, while acknowledging the state's interest in maintaining prison discipline, raises substantial hurdles to the effectuation of that interest. In *Singletary v. Costello*,[343.1] the prisoner launched

---

[343.1] 665 So. 2d 1099 (Fla. Dist. Ct. App. 1996).

a protest against prison discipline by refusing to eat. When it became clear that he might be force-fed, he brought a declaratory judgment action to prevent the state from inserting a feeding tube in him if his life became endangered. The court held that the Florida constitutional right of privacy gave him a prima facie right not to be subjected to medical treatment without his consent and that because a feeding tube was "medical treatment," he could refuse it unless there was a compelling state interest to the contrary. The court found that the state's interest in the preservation of life was not substantial enough to warrant force-feeding and that its interest in preventing suicide was not implicated because the prisoner's intent was not to commit suicide but to protest prison conditions. Finally, it concluded that there was no evidence that the prisoner's actions would undermine prison discipline or security.

This holding is a very simplistic reading of both the cases involving hunger strikes by prisoners and the right-to-die cases. It reads the Florida constitutional right of privacy out of context, it too simply equates feeding tubes with treatment, it too readily dismisses the suicidal consequence of the prisoner's actions, it overlooks the important differences between prisoner/patients (such as Thor) and prisoner/protestors, and it undervalues the state's interest in prison discipline. The holding is plainly inconsistent with the majority trend, and it would be surprising if the case were not overturned on appeal.

In contrast with the two lines of cases is *Laurie v. Senecal*,[343.2] in which the prisoner was neither engaging in a protest as in *Myers* nor seeking relief from the suffering caused by an illness or injury as in *Thor*. Rather, the prisoner was refusing to eat because "he no longer desired to live because of the stigma of his conviction for first-degree sexual assault upon a minor female."[343.3] The court set aside the trial court's order prohibiting force-feeding, on dual grounds. First, the court viewed this as a garden-variety suicide attempt, distinguishing it from *Thor* and other cases involving the forgoing of life-sustaining treatment by individuals whose "existences . . . are physically intolerable."[343.4] Second, the prisoner's actions were "fundamentally inconsistent with imprisonment itself or incompatible with the objectives of incarceration."[343.5]

A similar, intermediate type of case is *Polk County Sheriff v. Iowa District Court*.[343.6] The prisoner was a pretrial detainee with kidney failure who needed to be transported to a hospital for dialysis. The prisoner was neither refusing dialysis as a protest of prison conditions or because of the burdens of treatment per se. Rather, his motive for refusing treatment, according to

---

[343.2] 666 A.2d 806 (R.I. 1995).

[343.3] *Id*. at 807.

[343.4] *Id*. at 809.

[343.5] *Id*. (citing Hudson v. Palmer, 468 U.S. 517 (1984)).

[343.6] 594 N.W.2d 421 (Iowa 1999).

the psychiatrist who examined him to evaluate competence, was that the prisoner found "that spending any further time in any correctional facility was unacceptable and that he was going to stop his dialysis treatment 'whether he was looking at another month, or another year, or another five years' in incarceration."[343.7] The "chief jailer" objected to honoring the refusal of dialysis, for a number of colorable reasons:

> First, the other 600 inmates would be encouraged to refuse medical treatment as an excuse to get out of jail. Second, such an order would require jail personnel to exert more eyes-on supervision. . . . [T]his level of supervision would be more than would be required for an inmate with a contagious medical condition or with a psychotic disorder.[343.8]

The court acknowledged the prisoner's liberty interest in being free from the invasion of his bodily integrity that dialysis constitutes, but concluded that the state interests in maintaining prison security, order, and discipline outweighed his liberty interests, especially in light of the relatively small magnitude of the invasion, even taking into account that "the procedure requires [his] commitment, patience, and endurance three times a week for three and one-half hours . . . ."[343.9]

The holding drew two lengthy and reasoned dissents, both of which agreed with the majority's statement of legal principles but felt that the evidence adduced in support of the state's interest was, in the words of one of the dissenting justices, "a frail reed of supposition."[343.10]

Page 533, add at end of section:

Preventing Undue Influence; Slippery Slope.   For an analysis of other state interests relevant to end-of-life decisionmaking, see discussion of *Compassion in Dying v. Washington.*[350] Although discussed in the context of physician-assisted suicide ("active" measures to hasten death), the force of the court's reasoning is that these interests are equally relevant to forgoing life-sustaining treatment ("passive" measures to hasten death).

Viable Fetus.   Numerous cases have arisen in which doctors have sought to impose medical treatment on competent, pregnant patients in order, purportedly, to save the life of the fetus.[351] Not infrequently it has been asserted that a preg-

---

[343.7]   *Id.* at 424.

[343.8]   *Id.*

[343.9]   594 N.W.2d at 427.

[343.10]   *Id.* at 434 (Snell, J., dissenting).

[350]   79 F.3d 790 (9th Cir. 1996), *rev'd sub nom.* Washington v. Glucksberg, 117 S. Ct. 2258 (1997), in § **18.22** in this supplement.

[351]   See § **9.55** in the main volume and this supplement.

nant woman's right to refuse treatment must be balanced against the viable fetus's interest in life, but *In re Fetus Brown*[352] appears to be the first in which it has been asserted that the interests of the state in the fetus must be balanced against the mother's right to refuse treatment. The state took this position because prior decisions made it difficult, if not impossible, under Illinois law to argue that the mother's and fetus's interests must be weighed against each other.[353]

The court acknowledged that "the State maintains 'a substantial interest in potential life throughout pregnancy.'"[354] However, in furthering this interest, the state may not invade the bodily integrity of the mother, even by a blood transfusion, which it found to be "an invasive medical procedure that interrupts a competent adult's bodily integrity."[355] In so concluding, the court quoted substantially from *Casey:*

> "[T]he liberty of the woman is at stake in a sense unique to the human condition and so unique to the law. The mother who carries a child to full term is subject to anxieties, to physical constraints, to pain that only she must bear. That these sacrifices have from the beginning of the human race been endured by woman with a pride that ennobles her in the eyes of others and gives to the infant a bond of love cannot alone be grounds for the State to insist she make the sacrifice. Her suffering is too intimate and personal for the State to insist, without more, upon its own vision of the woman's role, however dominant that vision has been in the course of our history and our culture. The destiny of the woman must be shaped to a large extent on her own conception of her spiritual imperatives and her place in society."[356]

Bibliography

Anscombe, G. "Action, Intention, and Double Effect." Proceedings of the American Catholic Philosophical Association 54 (1982): 12.

Arrigo, A. et al. "Symposium: Issues Concerning the Mentally Ill. Law, Ideology, and Critical Inquiry: The Case of Treatment Refusal for Incompetent Prisoners Awaiting Execution." *New England Journal on Criminal and Civil Confinement* 25 (1999): 367.

Billings, J.A., and S. Block. "Slow Euthanasia." *Journal of Palliative Care* 12 (1996): 21.

---

[352] 689 N.E.2d 397 (Ill. App. Ct. 1997).

[353] *See In re* Doe, 632 N.E.2d 326 (Ill. App. Ct. 1994), *relying on* Stallman v. Youngquist, 531 N.E.2d 355 (Ill. 1988).

[354] 689 N.E.2d at 404, quoting Planned Parenthood v. Casey, 505 U.S. 833, 876 (1992).

[355] 689 N.E. 2d at 404.

[356] *Id.,* quoting Casey, 505 U.S. at 852.

Boyle, J. "Who Is Entitled to Double Effect?" *Journal of Medicine and Philosophy* 16 (1991): 475.

Brody, H. "Commentary on Billings and Block's 'Slow Euthanasia.'" *Journal of Palliative Care* 12 (1996): 38.

Capron, A. "Borrowed Lessons: The Role of Ethical Distinctions in Framing Law on Life-Sustaining Treatment." *Arizona Law Review* (1984): 647.

Cavanaugh, T. "The Ethics of Death-Hastening or Death-Causing Palliative Analgesic Administration to the Terminally Ill." *Journal of Pain Symptom Management* 12 (1996): 248.

Cohn, F. "The Ethics of End-of-Life Care for Prison Inmates." *Journal of Law, Medicine & Ethics* 27 (1999): 252.

Dickens, B. "Commentary on 'Slow Euthanasia.'" *Journal of Palliative Care* 12 (1996): 42.

Doyal, L. "The Moral Character of Clinicians or the Best Interests of Patients? Intention Alone Cannot Determine the Morality of Actions." *British Medical Journal* 318 (1999): 1432.

Dubler, N. "The Collision of Confinement and Care: End-of-Life Care in Prisons and Jails." *Journal of Law, Medicine and Ethics* 26 (1998): 149.

Dubler, N. "The Doctor-Proxy Relationship: The Neglected Connection." *Kennedy Institute of Ethics Journal* 5 (1995): 289.

Gillon, R. "Forseeing Is Not Necessarily the Same as Intending." *British Medical Journal* 318 (1999): 1431.

Goldblatt, A. "Commentary: No More Jurisdiction Over Jehovah." *Journal of Law, Medicine & Ethics* 27 (1999): 190.

Hanser, M. "Why Are Killing and Letting Die Wrong?" *Philosophy and Public Affairs* 24 (1995): 175.

Jerdee, A. "Note. Breaking Through the Silence: Minnesota's Pregnancy Presumption and the Right to Refuse Medical Treatment." *Minnesota Law Review* 84 (2000): 971.

Kapp, M. "Treating Medical Charts Near the End of Life: How Legal Anxieties Inhibit Good Patient Deaths." *University of Toledo Law Review* 28 (1997): 521.

Levy, J. "Jehovah's Witnesses, Pregnancy, and Blood Transfusions: A Paradigm for the Autonomy Rights of All Pregnant Women." *Journal of Law, Medicine & Ethics* 27 (1999): 171.

Mount, B. "Morphine Drips, Terminal Sedation, and Slow Euthanasia: Definitions and Facts, Not Anecdotes." *Journal of Palliative Care* 12 (1996): 31.

BIBLIOGRAPHY

Nuccetelli, S. and Seay, G. "Relieving Pain and Foreseeing Death: A Paradox About Accountability and Blame." *Journal of Law, Medicine & Ethics* 28 (2000): 19.

Parker, Jr., F. et al. "Symposium: Death and Dying Behind Bars—Cross-Cutting Themes and Policy Imperatives. Informed Consent and the Refusal of Medical Treatment in the Correctional Setting." *Journal of Law, Medicine & Ethics* 27 (1999): 240.

Portenoy, R. "Morphine Infusions at the End of Life: The Pitfalls in Reasoning from Anecdote." *Journal of Palliative Care* 12 (1996): 44.

Quill, T., et al. "The Rule of Double Effect: A Critique of Its Role in End-of-Life Decision Making." *New England Journal of Medicine* 337 (1997): 1768.

Ritterspach, B. Student article. "Refusal of Medical Treatment on the Basis of Religion and an Analysis of the Duty to Mitigate Damages Under Free Exercise Jurisprudence." *Ohio Northern University Law Review* 25 (1999): 381.

Scott, R. "Autonomy and Connectedness: A Re-evaluation of Georgetown and Its Progeny." *Journal of Law, Medicine & Ethics* 28 (2000): 55.

Sulmasy, D. "Commentary: Double Effect—Intention Is the Solution, Not the Problem." *Journal of Law, Medicine & Ethics* 28 (2000): 26.

Symposium. "Death and Dying Behind Bars." *Journal of Law, Medicine & Ethics* 27 (1999): 213.

Symposium. "Appropriate Management of Pain: Addressing the Clinical, Legal, and Regulatory Barriers." *Journal of Law, Medicine & Ethics* 24 (1996): 285–368.

CHAPTER 9

APPLICATION OF RIGHT TO DIE TO PARTICULAR TREATMENTS AND ILLNESSES

§ 9.3   Blood Transfusions

Page 539, add to footnote 15:

FL: Harrell v. St. Mary's Hosp., Inc., 678 So. 2d 455 (Fla. Dist. Ct. App. 1996).

Page 540, add at end of first sentence of first full paragraph:

and Connecticut.[21.1]

Page 541, add to footnote 26:

CA11: Novak v. Cobb County-Kennestone Hosp. Auth., 74 F.3d 1173 (11th Cir. 1996) (16-year-old patient under Georgia law did not have authority to refuse treatment, nor did parents; nonemergency at time of refusal).

Page 542, add to footnote 37:

MA: *In re* Rena, 705 N.E.2d 1155 (Mass. App. Ct. 1999) (mature minor).

§ 9.4   Cardiopulmonary Resuscitation and "DNR" Orders

Page 543, add to footnote 39:

MD: *See* Wright v. Johns Hopkins Health Sys. Corp., 728 A.2d 166, 177 n.13 (Md. 1999) ("The Attorney General defines cardiac arrest as "'the sudden unexpected cessation of heartbeat and blood pressure. It leads to loss of consciousness within seconds, irreversible brain damage in as little as 3 minutes, and death within 4 to 15 minutes.'" 79

[21.1] *See* Stamford Hosp. v. Vega, 674 A.2d 821 (Conn. 1996).

Op. Att'y Gen. at 140 (quoting Office of Technology Assessment, U.S. Congress, Life-Sustaining Technologies and the Elderly 168 (1987)).").

Page 543, add to footnote 41:

LA: *See, e.g.,* Causey v. St. Francis Med. Ctr., 719 So. 2d 1072 (La. Ct. App. 1998) (attending physician believed CPR for nonterminally, but critically, ill patient, to be futile).

Page 544, add to footnote 42:

CA4:   Bryan v. Rectors & Visitors of the Univ. of Va., 95 F.3d 349 (4th Cir. 1996).
IA: *But cf.* Wendland v. Sparks, 574 N.W.2d 327 (Iowa 1998) (reversing grant of summary judgment in favor of defendant physician who failed to resuscitate patient who did not have DNR order).
MA: *In re* Mason, 669 N.E.2d 1081 (Mass. App. Ct. 1996).

Page 543, add at end of text:

A judicial order is not ordinarily needed to enter a DNR order.[42.1]

Page 545, add to footnote 45:

IA: Wendland v. Sparks, 574 N.W.2d 327 (Iowa 1998).
NV: Nev. Op. Att'y Gen. No. 97-08, 1997 WL 133532 (1997) (dealing with DNR orders for children).

Page 545, replace Ohio citation in carryover footnote 45 with:

OH: Anderson v. St. Francis-St. George Hosp., 671 N.E.2d 225 (Ohio 1996); Allore v. Flower Hosp., No. L-96-329, 1997 WL 362465 (Ohio Ct. App. June 27, 1997).

Page 546, add to footnote 56:

IA: Wendland v. Sparks, 574 N.W.2d 327, 328 (Iowa 1998) ("[A] patient, or a family member who does not wish to have the patient resuscitated, signs a 'no code' request.").

Page 546, add to footnote 57:

NC: First Healthcare Corp. v. Rettinger, 456 S.E.2d 347 (N.C. Ct. App. 1995) ("no code blue").

[42.1] See discussion of Massachusetts in **§ 5.37** in the main volume and this supplement.

Page 547, add to footnote 58:

See also Gail Gazelle, *The Slow Code—Should Anyone Rush to Its Defense?*, 338 New Eng. J. Med. 467 (1998).

§ 9.5 —Informed Consent and DNR Orders

Page 547, add to footnote 60:

LA: *See, e.g.,* Causey v. St. Francis Med. Ctr., 719 So. 2d 1072 (La. Ct. App. 1998).

Page 550, add note 68.1 reference at end of second sentence of first full paragraph and add note 68.1:

[68.1] **LA:** *See, e.g.,* Causey v. St. Francis Med. Ctr., 719 So. 2d 1072 (La. Ct. App. 1998) (surrogate's demand to continue medically inappropriate treatment constitutes abuse).

Page 550, add to footnote 69:

LA: *See, e.g.,* Causey v. St. Francis Med. Ctr., 719 So. 2d 1072 (La. Ct. App. 1998).

Page 552, add to footnote 74:

LA: *See, e.g.,* Causey v. St. Francis Med. Ctr., 719 So. 2d 1072 (La. Ct. App. 1998).

Page 553, add to footnote 81:

LA: *See, e.g.,* Causey v. St. Francis Med. Ctr., 719 So. 2d 1072 (La. Ct. App. 1998) (physician not required to disclose medically inappropriate options).

Page 553, add to footnote 84:

LA: Causey v. St. Francis Med. Ctr., 719 So. 2d 1072 (La. Ct. App. 1998).

§ 9.6   ——Case Law on Informed Consent and DNR Orders

Page 554, add to footnote 87:

CA4:   *But see* Bryan v. Rectors & Visitors of the Univ. of Va., 95 F.3d 349 (4th Cir. 1996) (holding reasoning of *Baby "K"* does not prohibit writing of DNR order), discussed in § **19.17** in this supplement.

Page 554, add new footnote 90.1 in seventh line of second full paragraph, after "benefits,":

[90.1] In *In re* Kauffman, 20 Fiduc. Rptr. 2d 223 (C.P. Montgomery County, Pa. 2000), for example, the husband of a patient sought entry of a DNR order on her hospital records after consultation with physicians, nurses, and social workers, and after considering her condition.

Page 555, add at end of section:

A different problem arose in *Wright v. Johns Hopkins Health Systems Corporation*,[93.1] in which the question was not whether CPR could be withheld but whether there was liability for administering it despite a refusal by a competent patient. The patient was terminally ill with AIDS, though not expected to die imminently. In fact, the cardiac arrest occurred after he was given a blood transfusion in anticipation of being discharged from the hospital. He had executed a living will some time before, requesting that life-sustaining procedures be withheld or withdrawn if he were terminally ill, and in the emergency room on admission to the hospital he had told the health care staff that he did not want to be resuscitated. However, when he suffered the arrest, he was resuscitated. He was later taken off life support and died, and his estate sued the hospital for the resuscitation.

The court held that the living will did not apply because the patient had not been certified by two physicians to meet the requirements of the statute for implementation of an advance directive. It also refused to hold that the oral instructions not to resuscitate constituted a basis for liability, although the Maryland advance directive statute recognizes the validity of oral advance directives, because the statutory requirements for an oral advance directive—it "must be made in the presence of the attending physician and one witness and must be documented as part of the patient's medical record"[93.2]—were also not met. The court also rejected the claim that the defendants breached a duty to record the patient's "expressed desires" in his

---

[93.1]   728 A.2d 166 (Md. 1999).

[93.2]   *Id.* at 176, citing Md. Code Ann., Health-Gen. § 506(d).

medical record, holding that "a 'generalized and open-ended desire' need not be recorded because it is not a DNR order."[93.3]

§ 9.8 — —Purpose

Page 556, add to footnote 95:

LA: *Cf.* La. Rev. Stat. Ann. § 40:1299.58.7(E) (requiring emergency medical providers to "make reasonable effort to detect the presence of a do-not-resuscitate identification bracelet").

Page 556, replace **Table 9–1** *with:*

Table 9–1

DNR Statutes

AK:	Alaska Stat. §§ 18.12.035–.100
AZ:	Ariz. Rev. Stat. Ann. § 36-3251[a.1]
AR:	Ark. Code Ann. §§ 20-13-901 to -908[c.2]
CA:	Cal. Health & Safety Code § 1569.74
	Cal. Prob. Code § 4753
CO:	Colo. Rev. Stat. §§ 15-18.6-101 to -108[a.3]
CT:	Conn. Gen. Stat. Ann. § 19a-580d
FL:	Fla. Stat. Ann. § 401.45(3)[2]
GA:	Ga. Code Ann. §§ 31-39-1 to -9[b.3]
HI:	Haw. Rev. Stat. § 321-229.5
ID:	Idaho Code §§ 39-151 to -165[b.3]
IL:	Ill. Ann. Stat. ch. 210, § 45/2-104.2[b.4]
IN:	Ind. Code Ann. § 16-36-5[c.1]
KS:	Kan. Stat. Ann. §§ 65-4941 to -4948[c.3]
LA:	S.B. 209, 1999 Reg. Sess. (La. 1999), *codified at* La. Rev. Stat. Ann. § 40:1299.58.2, .58.3, & .58.7-10[1]
MD:	Md. Code Ann., Health Gen. § 5-608[a.1.]
MI:	Mich. Comp. Laws Ann. §§ 333.1051–.1067[2.3]
MT:	Mont. Code Ann. §§ 50-10 101 to -107[b.3]
NV:	Nev. Rev. Stat. Ann. §§ 450B.400–.590[c.3], *as amended by* A.B. 73, 70th Reg. Sess. (Nev. 1999)
NJ:	N.J. Stat. Ann. § 26:2H-68[b.1]
NM:	N.M. Stat. Ann. § 24-10B-4(J)[2]
NY:	N.Y. Pub. Health Law §§ 2960–2979[b.3]
OH:	Ohio Rev. Code Ann. § 2133.02[a.1]
OK:	Okla. Stat. tit. 63, §§ 3131.1–.14[c.3], *as amended by* H.B. 1381, 47th Leg., 1st Sess. (Okla. 1999)

[93.3] *Id.* at 178.

Table 9–1 *(continued)*

DNR Statutes

PA:	Pa. Cons. Stat. Ann. tit. 20, § 5413[a,1]
RI:	R.I. Gen. Laws § 23-4.10-4[a,1]
	R.I. Gen. Laws § 23-4.11-14[a,1]
SC:	S.C. Code Ann. §§ 44-78-10 to -65
TN:	Tenn. Code Ann. § 68-11-224[b]
	Tenn. Code Ann. §§ 68-140-601 to -604
TX:	Tex. Health & Safety Code Ann. §§ 166.081-.101[6]
UT:	Utah Code Ann. § 75-2-1105.5[a,1]
VA:	Va. Code Ann. §§ 54.1-2982,[a,1] -2986, -2987.1,[a,1] -2901, 63.1-174.3[5], *as amended by* 1999 Va. Acts 814
WA:	Wash. Rev. Code Ann. § 43.70.480[a]
WV:	W. Va. Code §§ 16-30C-1 to -16[b,3]
WI:	Wis. Stat. Ann. §§ 154.17-.29[b,3]
WY:	Wyo. Stat. §§ 35-22-201 to -208[a,1]

[a] authorizes individuals to execute directive not to resuscitate

[b] authorizes physicians to issue DNR order

[c] authorizes both individuals to execute directives and physicians to issue orders not to resuscitate

[1] DNR provision in advance directive statute

[2] emergency medical services statute

[3] freestanding DNR statute

[4] applies to nursing home care

[5] applies to adult care residences

[6] Former law, Tex. Health & Safety Code Ann. §§ 674.001-.024, continued to govern for any document executed or offense committed before September 1, 1999. Any conduct under subsection (b) § 166.095 occurring before January 1, 2000, will continue to be governed by Tex. Health & Safety Code Ann. § 674.017.

*interpreted in 79 Md. Op. Att'y Gen. 137, 1994 WL 178465 (Opinion No. 94-023, May 3, 1994)

§ 9.9 — —Who Is Authorized to Execute Directive or Issue DNR Order

Page 557, delete Florida citation in footnote 97.

Page 557, replace Kansas citation in footnote 97 with:

KS: Kan. Stat. Ann. §§ 65-4941 to -4948 (allows either declarant-executed directive or physician-issued order).

Page 557, add to footnote 97:

AK: Alaska Stat. §§ 18.12.010–.100 (allows either physician-issued order or patient-issued directive).

CA: Cal. Prob. Code § 4753(b) (allows patient to execute DNR request, but a physician must also sign).

KY: Kentucky Board of Medical Licensure, Kentucky Emergency Medical Services Do Not Resuscitate Order, *adopted pursuant to* Ky. Rev. Stat. Ann. § 311.623(3) (1995) (any adult person).

LA: La. Rev. Stat. Ann. § 40:1299.58.2(5).

MI: Mich. Comp. Laws Ann. §§ 333.1053 (1), .1055 (1).

NV: Nev. Rev. Stat. Ann. § 450B.520.

OH: Ohio Rev. Code Ann. 2133.02(A)(1).

OK: Okla. Stat. tit. 63, § 3131.1 .4(A)(1).

TX: Tex. Health & Safety Code Ann. § 674.002(a) (for advance directives executed before Sept. 1, 1999); Tex. Health & Safety Code Ann. § 166.082(a) (for directives executed thereafter).

Page 557, add to footnote 98:

CA: Cal. Prob. Code § 4753(b) (allows legally recognized surrogate health care decisionmaker to issue DNR request, but it must also be signed by a physician).

FL: Fla. Stat. Ann. § 401.45(3)(a).

IN: Ind. Code Ann. § 16-36-5, 11(b).

KY: Kentucky Board of Medical Licensure, Kentucky Emergency Medical Services Do Not Resuscitate Order, *adopted pursuant* to Ky. Rev. Stat. Ann. § 311.623(3) (1995) (allows legal surrogate designated to make health care decisions to issue DNR order if person is unable to give informed consent or is a minor).

MI: Mich. Comp. Laws Ann. 333.1053(1), .1055(1) (patient advocate).

OK: Okla. Stat. tit. 63, § 3131.4(A)(2).

TX: Tex. Health & Safety Code Ann. § 674.002(e), (f) (for advance directives executed before Sept. 1, 1999); Tex. Health & Safety Code Ann. § 166.082(d), (e) (for directives executed thereafter).

WI: Wis. Stat. Ann. 154.225.

Page 558, replace Kansas citation in carryover footnote 99 with:

KS: Kan. Stat. Ann. §§ 65-4941(b)–(c) (allows either physician-issued order or patient-issued directive).

Page 558, add to footnote 99:

AK: Alaska Stat. §§ 18.12.010–.100 (either adult patient or attending physician may issue).

HI: Haw. Rev. Stat. § 321-229.5 (attending physician may issue "comfort-care only" document with patient consent).

IN: Ind. Code Ann. § 16-36-5, 12.

NV: Nev. Rev. Stat. Ann. 450B.420.

OK: Okla. Stat. tit. 63, § 3131.4(B)(2.a.) (attending physician must inform patient's representative to apply substituted judgment standard).

SC: S.C. Code Ann. § 44-78-20 (patient may request that health care provider issue DNR order).

TN: Tenn. Code Ann. § 68-140-602 (both physician and either patient or authorized surrogate must sign DNR order).

WI: Wis. Stat. Ann. § 154.19.

Page 558, replace Kansas citation in footnote 100 with:

KS: Kan. Stat. Ann. § 65-4943 (directive must be signed by declarant).

Page 558, add to footnote 100:

HI: Haw. Rev. Stat. § 321-229.5 (patient must sign document).

IN: Ind. Code Ann. § 16-36-5, 12.

NV: Nev. Rev. Stat. Ann. 450B.510 (written approval).

SC: S.C. Code Ann. § 44-78-30 (patient must request the DNR order for it to be operative).

TN: Tenn. Code Ann. § 68-140-602 (patient must sign DNR order).

WI: Wis. Stat. Ann. § 154.19(b).

Page 558, replace Kansas citation in footnote 101 with:

KS: Kan. Stat. Ann. § 65-4943(b) (directive can be signed by surrogate in declarant's presence and by declarant's express direction).

Page 558, add to footnote 101:

SC: S.C. Code Ann. § 44-78-20 (surrogate may request that physician issue DNR order).

TN: Tenn. Code Ann. § 68-140-602 (person authorized by durable health care power of attorney can sign DNR order instead of patient).

Page 558, add to footnote 102:

GA: Ga. Code Ann. § 31-39-4(e) *construed in* Edwards v. Shumate, 468 S.E.2d 23 (Ga. 1996) (physician may issue DNR order on his own if patient lacks decisionmaking capacity and there is no surrogate).

§ 9.10 — —Types of DNR Statutes

Page 559, delete Florida citation in footnote 103.

Page 559, add to footnote 103:

AK: Alaska Stat. §§ 18.12.010–.100 (living will).

AZ: Ariz. Rev. Stat. § 36-3251 (general advance directive).

CA: Cal. Prob. Code § 4753 (health care power of attorney); Cal. Health & Safety Code § 1569.74 (residential care facilities).

LA: La. Rev. Stat. Ann. § 40:1299.58.2, .58.3, and .58.7-10 (living will).

OH: Ohio Rev. Code Ann. 2133.02(A)(1) (general advance directive).

Page 559, add to footnote 104:

HI: Haw. Rev. Stat. § 321-229.5 (emergency medical services).

TN: Tenn. Code Ann. §§ 68-140-601 to -604 (emergency medical services).

Page 559, replace Kansas citation in footnote 105 with:

KS: Kan. Stat. Ann. §§ 65-4941 to -4948.

Page 559, add to footnote 105:

MI: Mich. Comp. Laws Ann. §§ 333.1051–.1067.

NV: Nev. Rev. Stat. Ann. §§ 450B.400–.590.

OK: Okla. Stat. tit. 63, §§ 3131.1–.14.

SC: S.C. Code Ann. §§ 44-78-10 to -65.

WI: Wis. Stat. Ann. §§ 154.17–.29.

Page 560, replace Kansas citation in carryover footnote 106 with:

KS: Kan. Stat. Ann. § 65-4948 (emergency medical services board may adopt rules and regulations to implement statute).

Page 560, add to footnote 106:

NV: Nev. Rev. Stat. Ann. § 450B.490 (DNR protocol to be established by health board).

SC: S.C. Code Ann. § 44-78-65 (regulations for DNR identification to be promulgated by department of health and environmental control).

§ 9.11   — —Witnesses

Page 560, replace Kansas citation in footnote 107 with:

KS: Kan. Stat. Ann. § 65-4943(d).

Page 560, add to footnote 107:

AK: Alaska Stat. § 18.12.010.
HI: Haw. Rev. Stat. § 321-229.5(a)(2).
IN: Ind. Code Ann. § 16-36-5, 11(c).
KY: Kentucky Board of Medical Licensure, Kentucky Emergency Medical Services Do Not Resuscitate Order, *adopted pursuant to* Ky. Rev. Stat. Ann. § 311.623(3) (1995) (requires either two witnesses or notary).
MI: Mich. Comp. Laws Ann. §§ 333.1053(2)(c), .1055(2)(b).
OH: Ohio Rev. Code Ann. § 2133.02(B)(1).
OK: Okla. Stat. tit. 63, § 3131.5(B).
TN: Tenn. Code Ann. § 68-140-602(3).

Page 560, add to footnote 110:

IN: Ind. Code Ann. § 16-36-5, 2.
OH: Ohio Rev. Code Ann. § 2133.02(B)(1).

Page 560, replace Kansas citation in footnote 110 with:

KS: Kan. Stat. Ann. § 65-4943(d).

§ 9.12   — —State Plan and Standardized Forms

Page 560, add to Connecticut citation in footnote 111:

CT: *See also* Conn. Gen. Stat. Ann. § 19a-580d (Department of Public Health and Addiction Services to adopt DNR protocol and DNR identification through bracelets).

Page 561, replace Florida citation in carryover footnote 111 with:

FL: Fla. Stat. Ann. § 401.45(3)(a).

Page 561, replace Kansas citation in footnote 111 with:

KS: Kan. Stat. Ann. § 65-4948 (board may adopt rules and regulations to implement act).

Page 560, add to footnote 111:

AK: Alaska Stat. §§ 18.12.035–.037 (Department of Health and Human Services to establish DNR protocol, which must be approved by State Medical Board, and DNR identification).

CA: Cal. Prob. Code § 4753(b) (Emergency Medical Services Authority to develop DNR form).

HI: Haw. Rev. Stat. § 321-229.5 (Department of Health to adopt "comfort-care only" document and identification procedures).

IN: Ind. Code Ann. § 16-36-5, 17.

KY: Ky. Rev. Stat. Ann. § 311.623(3) (Board of Medical Licensure, in consultation with the Cabinet for Human Resources, to promulgate standard DNR form and identification).

NV: Nev. Rev. Stat. Ann. § 450B.490 (DNR protocol to be established by the board).

NH: N.H. Rev. Stat. Ann. § 151-B:18 (Emergency Medical Services Medical Control Board to adopt protocol for DNR orders).

OH: Ohio Rev. Code Ann. 2133.25(A).

OK: Okla. Stat. tit. 63, 3131.5(B) ("substantially the following form").

SC: S.C. Code Ann. § 44-78-65 (Department of Health and Environmental Control to establish regulations for DNR identification).

VA: Va. Code Ann. 32.1-111.4(3).

Page 561, replace Kansas citation in footnote 112 with:

KS: Kan. Stat. Ann. § 65-4942 (prehospital DNR request form).

Page 561, add to footnote 112:

FL: *See also* Fla. Stat. Ann. § 401.45(3)(a) (requiring signature of patient's physician and patient, "or, if the patient is incapacitated, the patient's health care surrogate or proxy . . . court-appointed guardian . . . or attorney in fact").

IN: Ind. Code Ann. § 16-36-5, 15.

MI: Mich. Comp. Laws Ann. 333.1054.

Page 561, add to footnote 113:

NV: Nev. Rev. Stat. Ann. § 450B.520.

Page 562, replace Kansas citation in footnote 116 with:

KS: Kan. Stat. Ann. § 65-4946.

§ 9.13   — — Identification of Patients Having DNR Orders

Page 562, add to footnote 117:

AK: Alaska Stat. § 18.12.017 (identification card, form, necklace, bracelet).

CA: Cal. Prob. Code § 4753(b) (medallion engraved with DNR, patient identification number, and 24-hour toll-free telephone number issued pursuant to agreement with Emergency Medical Services Authority).

CT: Conn. Gen. Stat. Ann. § 19a-580d (identifying bracelets).

HI: Haw. Rev. Stat. § 321-229.5(a)(1)(C) (identifying bracelets or necklaces).

IN: Ind. Code Ann. § 16-36-5, 17(a) (necklace or bracelet inscribed with declarant's name, date of birth, and "Do Not Resuscitate").

KY: Kentucky Board of Medical Licensure, Kentucky Emergency Medical Services Do Not Resuscitate Order, *adopted pursuant to* Ky. Rev. Stat. Ann. § 311.623(3) (1995) (hospital-type bracelet for wrist or ankle).

LA: La. Rev. Stat. Ann. § 40:1299.58.3(D)(1)(b) ("The secretary of state shall issue a do-not-resuscitate identification bracelet to qualified patients listed in the registry.").

MI: Mich. Comp. Laws Ann. § 333.1057 (identification bracelet).

TX: Tex. Health & Safety Code Ann. § 674.010 (for advance directives executed before Sept. 1, 1999); Tex. Health & Safety Code Ann. § 166.090 (for directives executed thereafter).

WI: Wis. Stat. Ann. § 154.17(1) (identification bracelet).

Page 562, add to text after footnote reference 117:

Oklahoma has passed a statute permitting identification of individuals with DNR orders through decals attached to their drivers' licenses.[117.1]

Page 562, add to footnote 118:

FL: Fla. Stat. Ann. § 401.45(5)(c) ("The department . . . shall develop a standardized do-not resuscitate identification system with devices that signify, when carried or worn, that the possessor is a patient for whom a physician has issued an order not to administer cardiopulmonary resuscitation").

NV: Nev. Rev. Stat. Ann. 450B.410.

OH: Ohio Rev. Code Ann. 2133.25(A).

[117.1] Okla. Stat. Ann. tit. 47, § 6-111(a).

OK: Okla. Stat. tit. 63, 3131.12(C) (Department of Health and Human Services responsible for distribution of bracelets, necklaces, or identification cards).

§ 9.14   — —Recording Requirements

Page 562, add to footnote 119:

AK: Alaska Stat. § 18.12.035(a) (grounds for DNR order must be documented in patient's medical file).
HI: Haw. Rev. Stat. § 321-229.5.
IN: Ind. Code Ann. § 16-36-5, 16 ("Copies of the out of hospital DNR declaration and order must be kept . . . by the declarant's attending physician in the declarant's medical file").
MI: Mich. Comp. Laws Ann. § 333.1058.
OK: Okla. Stat. tit. 63, § 3131.10 (DNR order must accompany patient when transferred from care of one health care agency to another).
SC: S.C. Code Ann. § 44-78-20 (grounds for order, including date, time, and condition that led to diagnosis of terminal condition, must be established in patient's medical record).
WI: Wis. Stat. Ann. § 154.19(2)(b).

Page 562, add at end of section:

The Oklahoma statute also requires that a physician note in the medical record when an explanation has been made to the representative and family member of the nature and consequences of the decision to be made.[119.1] In addition, health care agencies are required to maintain written policies and procedures with respect to do-not-resuscitate orders, do-not-resuscitate consent forms, and certifications of physicians.[119.2]

§ 9.15   — —Minors

Page 563, add to footnote 120:

OK: Okla. Stat. tit. 63, § 3131.4(2).
WV: *See* Belcher v. Charleston Area Medical Ctr., 422 S.E.2d 827 (W. Va. 1992).

[119.1] **OK:** Okla. Stat. tit. 63, § 3131.4(B)(2.b.).
[119.2] **OK:** Okla. Stat. tit. 63, § 3131.4(B).

§ 9.17   DIAGNOSIS REQUIRED

Page 563, add to footnote 122:

OK: Okla. Stat. tit. 63, §§ 3131.4 (2).
TX: Tex. Health & Safety Code Ann. § 674.005 (for advance directives executed before Sept. 1, 1999); Tex. Health & Safety Code Ann. § 166.085 (for directives executed thereafter).

§ 9.16   — When DNR Order Is Effective

Page 564, add to footnote 128:

IN: Ind. Code Ann. § 16-36-5, 15 (date of execution; remains in effect until death or revocation).

§ 9.17   — — Diagnosis Required for Implementation of DNR Order

Page 564, add to footnote 129:

AK: Alaska Stat. § 18.12.010 (declarant must be in terminal condition and unable to make treatment decisions).
HI: Haw. Rev. Stat. § 321-229.5 (terminal condition).
IN: Ind. Code Ann. § 16-36-5, 10 (terminal conditions).
NV: Nev. Rev. Stat. Ann. § 450B.520 (terminal condition).
OH: Ohio Rev. Code Ann. § 2133.02(A)(2) (declaration must use "either or both of the terms 'terminal condition' and 'permanently unconscious state,' and shall define or otherwise explain those terms").
SC: S.C. Code Ann. § 44-78-20 (terminal condition).
TX: Tex. Health & Safety Code Ann. § 674.002 (for advance directives executed before Sept. 1, 1999); Tex. Health & Safety Code Ann. § 166.082 (for directives executed thereafter).
WI: Wis. Stat. Ann. § 154.17(4)(a).

Page 565, add to footnote 133:

IN: Ind. Code Ann. § 16-36-5, 10(2) ("resuscitation would be unsuccessful or within a short period the person would experience repeated cardiac or pulmonary failure resulting in death").
OK: Okla. Stat. tit. 63, § 3131.4(C)(2) (resuscitation "would not prevent the imminent death of the patient").
WI: Wis. Stat. Ann. § 154.17(4)(b) (resuscitation would be unsuccessful or patient would experience repeated cardiac arrest within short period before death).

Page 565, add to footnote 134:

NY: *See In re* Finn v. Leonard "C," 625 N.Y.S.2d 809 (Sup. Ct. Albany County 1995) (holding N.Y. Pub. Health Law § 2965(3)(c) unconstitutionally vague), *rev'd on other grounds*, 634 N.Y.S.2d 262 (App. Div. 1995) (trial court should not have reached constitutional issue because of alternative grounds to dispose of proceeding).

WI: Wis. Stat. Ann. § 154.17(4)(c).

§ 9.18 ——Settings in Which DNR Order May Be Implemented

Page 565, replace Florida, Kansas, and Maryland citations in footnote 135 with:

FL: Fla. Stat. Ann. § 395.1041.

KS: Kan. Stat. Ann. §§ 65-4941 to -4948.

MD: *See* Md. Code Ann., Health-Gen. § 5-608(a) (statutory provision applies to "[h]ealth care provider, other than certified or licensed emergency medical services personnel," as well as "[c]ertified or licensed emergency medical services personnel").

Page 565, add to footnote 135:

CA: Cal. Prob. Code § 4753 (DNR directive applies within or outside hospital or other health care facility).

GA: Ga. Code Ann. § 31-39-6.1(b).

IN: Ind. Code Ann. § 16-36-5 ("out of hospital").

KY: Kentucky Board of Medical Licensure, Kentucky Emergency Medical Services Do Not Resuscitate Order, *adopted pursuant to* Ky. Rev. Stat. Ann. § 311.623(3) (1995) (applies in patients' homes, in long-term care facility, during transport to or from health care facility, or in other locations outside acute care hospitals).

LA: La. Rev. Stat. Ann. § 40:1299.58.7(E) (requiring "[c]ertified emergency medical technicians and certified first responders [to] make reasonable effort to detect the presence of a do-not-resuscitate identification bracelet on the patient").

MI: Mich. Comp. Laws Ann. 333.1061.

NV: Nev. Rev. Stat. Ann. 450B.550.

OH: Ohio Rev. Code Ann. 2133.23(A).

SC: S.C. Code Ann. § 44-78-45.

TN: Tenn. Code Ann. § 68-140-603.

§ 9.18   DNR ORDER MAY BE IMPLEMENTED

TX: Tex. Health & Safety Code Ann. § 674.001-.024 (for advance directives executed before Sept. 1, 1999); Tex. Health & Safety Code Ann. § 166.081-.101 (for directives executed thereafter).

WI: Wis. Stat. Ann. § 154.19(3)(a).

Page 566, delete Florida citation in footnote 136.

Page 566, add to footnote 136:

AK: Alaska Stat. § 18.12.035(c) (health care provider other than physician must comply when presented with DNR identification, written DNR order on prescribed form, or oral DNR order directly from physician).

IN: Ind. Code Ann. § 16-36-5, 17(b).

MI: Mich. Comp. Laws Ann. 333.1063 (health professionals not liable for attempting to resuscitate declarant if they do not have actual notice of DNR order).

OH: Ohio Rev. Code Ann. § 2133.23(A) (emergency medical personnel must comply when presented with DNR identification, written DNR order, or oral directive from a physician).

TN: Tenn. Code Ann. § 68-140-602 (EMS personnel must comply when immediately presented with DNR order, patient's identity is certain, and DNR form has all legally required elements).

TX: Tex. Health & Safety Code Ann. § 674.009 (for advance directives executed before Sept. 1, 1999); Tex. Health & Safety Code Ann. § 166.089 (for directives executed thereafter).

Page 566, replace Kansas citation in footnote 138 with:

KS: *E.g.,* Kan. Stat. Ann. §§ 65-4941 to -4948 (chest compressions, assisted ventilations, intubation, defibrillation, administration of cardiotonic medications, or other medical procedure intended to restart breathing or heart functioning).

Page 566, add to footnote 138:

HI: *E.g.,* Haw. Rev. Stat. § 321-229.5 (chest compressions, rescue breathing, electric shocks, or medication, or all of these, given to restart heart if person's breathing or heart stops).

Page 567, replace Kansas citation in footnote 140 with:

KS: Kan. Stat. Ann. §§ 65-4941 to -4948.

Page 567, add to footnote 140:

CA: Cal. Prob. Code § 4753 (DNR directive applies within and outside hospital or other health care facility).
GA: Ga. Code Ann. § 31-39-6.1.
OH: Ohio Rev. Code Ann. §§ 2133.01–.26.
OK: Okla. Stat. tit. 63, § 3131.5(B) (form directive).
SC: S.C. Code Ann. § 44-78-45.
VA: Va. Code Ann. 54.1-2987.1.

Page 567, add to footnote 141:

KY: Kentucky Board of Medical Licensure, Kentucky Emergency Medical Services Do Not Resuscitate Order, *adopted pursuant to* Ky. Rev. Stat. Ann. § 311.623(3) (1995) (DNR order applies during transport to or from health care facility).
OH: Ohio Rev. Code Ann. § 2133.23(C).

Page 567, add to footnote 142:

WI: Wis. Stat. Ann. § 154.17 (applies to EMTs, first responders, and emergency health care facilities personnel).

§ 9.19 ——Consent to CPR Presumed

Page 567, replace Florida citation in footnote 143 with:
FL: Fla. Stat. Ann. § 401.45(1).

Page 567, add to footnote 143:
OK: Okla. Stat. tit. 63, 3131.4(A).

Page 568, add to footnote 145:

AK: Alaska Stat. § 18.12.080(d).
IN: Ind. Code Ann. § 16-36-5, 24 ("This chapter does not create any presumption concerning the intent of a person who has not executed an out of hospital DNR declaration").
MI: Mich. Comp. Laws Ann. § 333.1066(3).
OH: Ohio Rev. Code Ann. § 2133.24(C)(1).
VA: Va. Code Ann. § 54.1-2986(B) ("The absence of an advance directive by an adult patient shall not give rise to any presumption as to his intent to consent or to refuse life-prolonging procedures.").
WI: Wis. Stat. Ann. § 154.25(5).

Page 568, add to footnote 146:

AK: Alaska Stat. § 18.12.080(e).
MI: Mich. Comp. Laws Ann. § 333.1066(1).
NV: Nev. Rev. Stat. Ann. § 450B.590.

§ 9.20 ——Effect of DNR Directive or Order on Treatment Other Than CPR

Page 569, replace Kansas citation in footnote 148 with:

KS: Kan. Stat. Ann. § 65-4942 (prehospital DNR request form states that decision to withhold CPR will not prevent rendering of other prehospital emergency care).

Page 569, add to footnote 148:

AK: Alaska Stat. § 18.12.040(b) (DNR order does not prevent medical procedures, including nutrition and hydration, necessary for comfort care or alleviating pain).
AZ: Ariz. Rev. Stat. Ann. § 36-3251(A).
HI: Haw. Rev. Stat. § 321-229.5 (patient must still receive comfort care, including oxygen, airway suctioning, splinting of fractures, pain medicine, and other measures required for comfort).
KY: Kentucky Board of Medical Licensure, Kentucky Emergency Medical Services Do Not Resuscitate Order, *adopted pursuant to* Ky. Rev. Stat. Ann. § 311.623(3) (1995) (DNR order does not affect provision of other emergency care, including oxygen administration, suctioning, control of bleeding, administration of analgesics, and comfort care).
SC: S.C. Code Ann. § 44-78-25 (emergency medical services personnel must still provide comfort care and relieve pain and suffering of patient with DNR order).

§ 9.20A ——Effect of Pregnancy on DNR Directive (New)

Some states have legislated a position on the effect of a declarant's pregnancy upon her previously issued DNR declaration. Alaska's statute provides that the declaration is not to be given effect if it is probable that the fetus could develop to the point of live birth with continued life-sustaining measures.[148.1] Oklahoma provides that the directive is to be given no effect if the

---

[148.1] Alaska Stat. § 18.12.040(c).

declarant is known to be pregnant, and where appropriate, considering the patient's age and other relevant factors, physicians are directed to determine whether a patient is pregnant.[148.2] The constitutional validity of these provisions is subject to the same concerns as are advance directives.[148.3]

§ 9.21 ——Duty of Physicians and Nonphysicians to Comply or Transfer

Page 569, add to footnote 149:

IN: Ind. Code Ann. § 16-36-5, 13(a), (b) ("attending physician . . . may transfer the patient to another physician, who may issue an out of hospital DNR order . . . . "[I]f an attending physician, after reasonable investigation, does not find any other physician willing to honor the patient's out of hospital DNR declaration and issue an out of hospital DNR order, the attending physician may refuse to issue an out of hospital DNR order").

OH: Ohio Rev. Code Ann. § 2133.23(B) (attending physician or health care facility shall not prevent or unreasonably delay transfer).

OK: Okla. Stat. tit. 63, § 3131.8(C).

SC: S.C. Code Ann. § 44-78-45.

VA: Va. Code Ann. § 54.1-2990(A).

Page 570, add to footnote 152:

AK: Alaska Stat. § 18.12.035(c) (health care provider other than physician).

MI: Mich. Comp. Laws Ann. § 333.1061 (paramedics, EMTs, nurses, medical first responders, respiratory therapists).

NV: Nev. Rev. Stat. Ann. § 450B.550.

SC: S.C. Code Ann. § 44-78-45 (emergency medical services personnel).

TN: Tenn. Code Ann. § 68-140-603 (emergency medical services personnel).

WI: Wis. Stat. Ann. § 154.19(3) (EMTs, first responders, and emergency health care facilities personnel).

Page 570, add to footnote 153:

AK: Alaska Stat. § 18.12.035(c) (health care provider other than physician shall comply when presented with DNR identification, written DNR directive/order on prescribed form, or oral DNR order directly from physician).

[148.2] Okla. Stat. Ann. tit. 63, § 3101.8(C).

[148.3] See §§ **9.55** and **11.11.**

SC: S.C. Code Ann. § 44-78-45 (emergency medical services personnel must comply if presented with DNR order upon their arrival).

TN: Tenn. Code Ann. §§ 68-140-602 to -603 (EMS personnel must comply when presented with DNR order immediately upon their arrival, identity of patient is verified, and DNR order includes all legally required elements).

§ 9.22 — —Revocation

Page 570, replace Georgia citation in footnote 154 with:

GA: Ga. Code Ann. § 13-39-6(a) (patient may revoke through written, oral, or any other form of communication that is communicated to or in presence of attending physician, nurse, health care professional, or EMT).

Pages 570–71, add to footnote 154:

AK: Alaska Stat. § 18.12.020(a) (declarant may revoke by any manner evidencing intent to revoke).

FL: Fla. Stat. Ann. § 765.104(1).

HI: Haw. Rev. Stat. § 321-229.5 (patient may revoke verbally or by removing identifying bracelet or necklace).

IN: Ind. Code Ann. § 16-36-5, (18)(a).

KY: Kentucky Board of Medical Licensure, Kentucky Emergency Medical Services Do Not Resuscitate Order, *adopted pursuant to* Ky. Rev. Stat. Ann. § 311.623(3) (1995) (declarant may revoke by destroying DNR order form, removing DNR bracelet, or by telling EMS personnel of desire to be resuscitated).

MI: Mich. Comp. Laws Ann. § 333.1060(1) (enacted May 13, 1996) (declarant may revoke at any time and in any manner sufficient to communicate intent to revoke).

NV: Nev. Rev. Stat. Ann. § 450B.530.

OK: Okla. Stat. tit. 63, § 3131.7(A),(B).

SC: S.C. Code Ann. § 44-78-60 (patient may revoke orally to EMS personnel or destroy, obliterate, or mutilate DNR order).

WI: Wis. Stat. Ann. § 154.21(1) (patient may revoke at any time by expressing desire for resuscitation or by tampering with or destroying DNR identification bracelet).

Page 571, replace Kansas citation in footnote 155 with:

KS: Kan. Stat. Ann. § 65-4942.

Page 571, replace Georgia citation in footnote 157 with:

GA: Ga. Code Ann. § 13-39-6(b) (surrogate can revoke consent through written, oral, or any other form of communication that is communicated to or in presence of attending physician, nurse, health care professional, or EMT).

Page 571, add to footnote 157:

IN: Ind. Code Ann. § 16-36-5, (18)(b) (only if declarant is incompetent).

KY: Kentucky Board of Medical Licensure, Kentucky Emergency Medical Services Do Not Resuscitate Order, *adopted pursuant to* Ky. Rev. Stat. Ann. § 311.623(3) (1995) (surrogate may revoke orally, by destroying DNR form, or by removing DNR bracelet).

MI: Mich. Comp. Laws Ann. § 333.1060(1) (patient advocate who executed order may revoke at any time and in any manner sufficient to communicate revocation).

OK: Okla. Stat. tit. 63, § 3131.7(C), (D), (E).

TN: Tenn. Code Ann. § 68-140-603 (person acting under health care power of attorney or attending physician may request resuscitation from EMS personnel).

VA: Va. Code Ann. § 54.1-2987.1(B).

WI: Wis. Stat. Ann. § 154.225(2) (guardian may revoke by informing emergency medical technician to resuscitate, by destroying DNR bracelet, or by removing DNR bracelet); *see also* Wis. Stat. Ann. 154.25(6) (patient's guardian or health care agent may express patient's desire to be resuscitated).

Page 571, delete Georgia citation in footnote 158.

Page 572, replace Ohio citation in footnote 160 with:

OH: Anderson v. St. Francis-St. George Hosp., 614 N.E.2d 841 (Ohio Ct. App. 1992), *opinion on remand,* No. C-930819, 1995 WL 109128 (Ohio Ct. App. Mar. 15, 1995), *appeal allowed,* 652 N.E.2d 800 (Ohio 1995).

§ 9.23   — — Dispute Resolution

Page 572, add note 161.1 reference at end of first sentence and add note 161.1:

[161.1] *See In re* Finn v. Leonard "C," 634 N.Y.S.2d 262 (App. Div. 1995) (proceedings to invalidate DNR order premature because dispute resolution system not used).

§ 9.24   — —Judicial Review

Page 572, add to footnote 164:

IN: *See also* Ind. Code Ann. § 16-36-5, 22 (creating right to judicial review).

Page 572, add to footnote 165:

NV: Nev. Op. Att'y Gen. No. 97-08, 1997 WL 133532 (1997) (judicial review required for DNR order for child in absence of parental consent).

§ 9.25   — —Penalties

Page 573, add to footnote 167:

NV: Nev. Rev. Stat. Ann. § 450B.580(1)(a) (misdemeanor if emergency medical personnel willfully fail to transfer).

Page 573, add before last sentence of section:

Alaska's statute imposes a fiscal penalty for noncompliance. Physicians who fail to comply with a DNR directive or order or who fail to reasonably effectuate a transfer lose their right to compensation for any medical services rendered to the patient after the order or declaration should have become effective.[168.1] In addition, the patient's heirs may seek from the physician an exclusive civil remedy of $1,000 plus actual costs incurred because of the failure to comply.

Page 573, add to footnote 169:

AK: Alaska Stat. § 18.12.070(b) (person who conceals or damages DNR identification or declaration or falsifies revocation may be civilly liable to declarant or heirs).
IN: Ind. Code Ann. § 16-36-5, 27 (Class B misdemeanor).
LA: La. Rev. Stat. Ann. § 40:1299.58.9(A) ("civilly liable").
NV: Nev. Rev. Stat. Ann. § 450B.580(1)(c).
VA: Va. Code Ann. § 54.1-2989.
WI: Wis. Stat. Ann. § 154.29(1) (fine of not more than $500 or imprisonment for not more than 30 days, or both, for concealing, defacing, or damaging DNR identification bracelet without patient's consent).

[168.1] Alaska Stat. § 18.12.070(a).

Page 573, add to footnote 170:

IN: Ind. Code Ann. § 16-36-5, 28(a) (Class C felony).

NV: Nev. Rev. Stat. Ann. § 450B.580 (purposely concealing knowledge of revocation is a misdemeanor).

VA: Va. Code Ann. § 54.1-2989.

WI: Wis. Stat. Ann. § 154.29(2) (falsifying, forging, or transferring DNR bracelet or concealing revocation punishable by fine of not more than $10,000 or imprisonment of not more than 10 years, or both).

§ 9.26 — — Immunities

Page 574, replace Kansas citation in footnote 172 with:

KS: Kan. Stat. Ann. § 65-4944.

Page 574, add to footnote 172:

AK: Alaska Stat. § 18.12.060(a).

AZ: Ariz. Rev. Stat. Ann. § 36-3251(F).

CA: Cal. Prob. Code § 4753(a).

FL: Fla. Stat. Ann. § 401.45(3)(b).

IN: Ind. Code Ann. § 16-36-5, 20.

LA: La. Rev. Stat. Ann. § 40:1299.58.8(A)(1).

MD: Md. Code Ann., Health Gen. § 5-608(d)(1).

MI: Mich. Comp. Laws Ann.§ 333.1062.

NV: Nev. Rev. Stat. Ann. § 450B.540.

OH: Ohio Rev. Code Ann. § 2133.22.

SC: S.C. Code Ann. § 44-78-35.

TN: Tenn. Code Ann. § 68-140-604.

VA: Va. Code Ann. § 54.1-2988.

WI: Wis. Stat. Ann. § 154.23.

Page 574, replace Kansas citation in footnote 173 with:

KS: Kan. Stat. Ann. § 65-4944.

Page 574, add to footnote 173:

AK: Alaska Stat. § 18.12.060(a)(4).

LA: La. Rev. Stat. Ann. § 40:1299.58.8(A)(2).

NV: Nev. Rev. Stat. Ann. § 450B.540(2).

OH: Ohio Rev. Code Ann. § 2133.22(A)(2)(a).

VA: Va. Code Ann. § 54.1-2988.

WI: Wis. Stat. Ann. § 154.23.

Page 574, add to footnote 174:

AK: Alaska Stat. § 18.12.060(a)(2).
FL: Fla. Stat. Ann. § 401.45(3)(a).
LA: La. Rev. Stat. Ann. § 40:1299.58.8(A)(1).
NV: Nev. Rev. Stat. Ann. § 450B.540(1)(b).
OH: Ohio Rev. Code Ann. § 2133.22(A)(2)(c),(d).
VA: Va. Code Ann. § 54.1-2988.

Page 574, add to footnote 175:

AZ: Ariz. Rev. Stat. Ann. § 36-3251(F).
CA: Cal. Prob. Code § 4763(g).
LA: La. Rev. Stat. Ann. § 40:1299.58.8 (D)(1).
MD: Md. Code Ann., Health Gen. § 5-608(d)(1).
NV: Nev. Rev. Stat. Ann. § 450B.540(1)(c).
OH: Ohio Rev. Code Ann. § 2133.22(C).
SC: S.C. Code Ann. § 44-78-35.
TN: Tenn. Code Ann. § 68-140-604.
WI: Wis. Stat. Ann. § 154.23.

Page 574, add to footnote 176:

AK: Alaska Stat. § 18.12.060(b).
SC: S.C. Code Ann. § 44-78-35.
WI: Wis. Stat. Ann. § 154.23.

Page 574, add to footnote 177:

OH: Ohio Rev. Code Ann. § 2133.22(A)(2)(c), (d) ("Any person who works for the health care facility as an employee, contractor or volunteer and who participates under the direction or authorization of a physician").
OK: Okla. Stat. tit. 63, § 3131.8(A).

Page 574, add to footnote 178:

IN: Ind. Code Ann. § 16-36-5, 20.
LA: La. Rev. Stat. Ann. § 40:1299.58.8(D)(2).
MD: Md. Code Ann., Health Gen. § 5-608(d)(1).
MI: Mich. Comp. Laws Ann. § 333.1063(a).
OK: Okla. Stat. tit. 63, § 3131.8(B).
SC: S.C. Code Ann. § 44-78-35(3).
WI: Wis. Stat. Ann. § 154.23(3).

Page 574, add to footnote 179:

AK: Alaska Stat. § 18.12.060(a)(3).
NV: Nev. Rev. Stat. Ann. § 450B.540(3).
OH: Ohio Rev. Code Ann. § 2133.22(A)(3).

Page 574, add after footnote 179 reference:

Hawaii's statute is unique in that it provides immunity to health care providers, EMS personnel, or first responders who believe in good faith that the provider's own safety, the safety of others, or the provider's conscience requires that the patient be resuscitated.[179.1]

§ 9.27   — —Effect on Insurance

Page 575, add to footnote 181:

AK: Alaska Stat. § 18.12.080(b).
IN: Ind. Code Ann. § 16-36-5, 23(b).
LA: La. Rev. Stat. Ann. § 40:1299.58.10(B)(5).
MI: Mich. Comp. Laws Ann. § 333.1065 (insurer may not refuse coverage, charge a higher premium, offer different policy terms, consider current terms breached or modified, or invoke suicide exclusion because of execution or implementation of DNR order).
NV: Nev. Rev. Stat. Ann. § 450B.570(2).
OH: Ohio Rev. Code Ann. § 2133.24(B)(1)(a).
WI: Wis. Stat. Ann. § 154.25(2).

Page 575, add to footnote 182:

AK: Alaska Stat. § 18.12.080(c).
MI: Mich. Comp. Laws Ann. §§ 333.1064, .20192.
NV: Nev. Rev. Stat. Ann. § 450B.570(3).
OH: Ohio Rev. Code Ann. § 2133.24(B)(4).
WI: Wis. Stat. Ann. § 154.25(3).

Page 575, add to footnote 183:

AK: Alaska Stat. § 18.12.080(a).
IN: Ind. Code Ann. § 16-36-5, 23(a).
NV: Nev. Rev. Stat. Ann. § 450B.570(1).
OH: Ohio Rev. Code Ann. § 2133.24(A).
SC: S.C. Code Ann. § 44-78-50(C).

[179.1] Haw. Rev. Stat. § 321-229.5(b)(3).

WI: Wis. Stat. Ann. § 154.25(1).

§ 9.28   — —Access to CPR

Page 575, add to footnote 185:

FL: Fla. Stat. Ann. § 401.45(2) (hospital not liable in any action for refusing to render emergency treatment if reasonable care is exercised in determining patient's condition, appropriateness of facilities, and qualifications of personnel to render such treatment).
OK: Okla. Stat. tit. 63, § 3131.4(C).

§ 9.29   — —Portability

Page 576, add to footnote 186:

AK: Alaska Stat. § 18.12.090.
NV: Nev. Rev. Stat. Ann. § 450B.420.

§ 9.30   — —Miscellaneous Provisions

Page 576, add to footnote 188:

AK: Alaska Stat. § 18.12.100(f).
IN: Ind. Code Ann. § 16-36-5, 25.
NV: Nev. Rev. Stat. Ann. § 450B.590(2).
OH: Ohio Rev. Code Ann. § 2133.24(D).
OK: Okla. Stat. tit. 63, § 3131.13.
SC: S.C. Code Ann. § 44-78-50(A).
VA: Va. Code Ann. § 54.1-2991.

Page 576, add at end of section:

The Oklahoma statute requires the Aging Services Division of the Department of Human Services to develop and implement a statewide educational effort to inform the public of the right to accept or refuse cardiopulmonary resuscitation.[191.1]

[191.1] **OK:** Okla. Stat. tit. 63, 3131.12(D).

§ 9.32 —DNR Orders in Schools

Page 581, add at end of section:

In the year 2000, the American Academy of Pediatrics came out with a policy statement regarding DNRs in schools.[212.1] In that statement, it recommended in part that, to avoid potential confusion and best fulfill the goals of the child and his or her family, "pediatricians and parents of children at increased risk of dying in school who desire a DNR order [should] meet with school officials—including nursing personnel, teachers, administrators, and EMS personnel—and, when appropriate, the child."[212.2]

§ 9.34 Kidney Dialysis

Page 582, add to footnote 218:

IA: *Cf.* Polk County Sheriff v. Iowa Dist. Court, 594 N.W.2d 421 (Iowa 1999) (jailer feared pretrial detainee's refusal of treatment would become disruptive to jail order and discipline).

Page 583, add to footnote 222:

LA: *But see* Causey v. St. Francis Med. Ctr., 719 So. 2d 1072 (La. Ct. App. 1998) (physician authorized discontinuance of dialysis and other life-support procedures over demands of family to continue).

§ 9.36 Mechanical Ventilators

Page 587, add to footnote 242:

LA: Causey v. St. Francis Med. Ctr., 719 So. 2d 1072 (La. Ct. App. 1998).
NY: Blackman v. New York City Health & Hosps. Corp., 660 N.Y.S.2d 643 (Sup. Ct. Kings County 1997) (pneumonia).

Page 587, add at end of first sentence on page:

Perhaps this is because physicians prefer to withhold or withdraw other forms of life support.[242.1]

[212.1] American Academy of Pediatrics, *Policy Statement: Do Not Resuscitate Orders in Schools (RE9842)*, 105 Pediatrics 878 (Apr. 2000), available at <http://www.aap.org/policy/re9842.html>.

[212.2] *Id.*

[242.1] D.A. Asch & N.A. Christakis, *Why Do Physicians Prefer to Withdraw Some Forms of Life Support over Others?*, 34 Med. Care 103 (1996).

Page 587, add to footnote 245:

Ganesh Krishna & Thomas A. Raffin, *Terminal Weaning from Mechanical Ventilation,* 27 Critical Care Med. 9 (1999).

§ 9.37   Medication

Page 588, add to footnote 251:

PA: *See In re* Goldman, 18 Fiduc. Rep. 2d 79 (C.P. Northampton County, Pa. 1997) (not employing ordinary/extraordinary analysis but (1) holding that protection of "ethical integrity of medical community" allows court to order antibiotics and whirlpool treatments because they are a "minimally intrusive regimen").

§ 9.38   —Medication for Pain Relief (Palliative Care)

Page 589, add after second sentence on page:

There is rapidly accumulating evidence that there is serious undertreatment of pain and associated physical (e.g., nausea and vomiting) and psychological (e.g., fatigue, insomnia, depression) symptoms.[254.1]

Page 589, add note 255.1 reference after "palliative care plan" in third sentence and add note 255.1:

[255.1] **KS:** *See* State v. Naramore, 965 P.2d 211, 214 (Kan. Ct. App. 1998) ("'Palliative care refers to medical intervention in which the primary purpose is to alleviate pain and suffering.'").

Page 590, add to footnote 257:

KS: *See, e.g.,* State v. Naramore, 965 P.2d 211 (Kan. Ct. App. 1998) (reversing conviction of physician for attempted murder based on physician's administration of pain relief medications to terminally ill patient, and citing with approval Council on Ethical & Judicial

---

[254.1] *See generally* Institute of Medicine, Approaching Death: Improving Care at the End of Life 128 *et seq.* & *passim* (Marilyn J. Field & Christine K. Cassel, eds., 1997); The SUPPORT Principal Investigators, *A Controlled Trial to Improve Care for Seriously Ill Hospitalized Patients,* 274 JAMA 1591, 1594 (1995); Report to the Commissioner of Health, Breaking Down the Barriers to Effective Pain Management: Recommendations to Improve the Assessment and Treatment of Pain in New York State (1998).

Affairs, American Med. Ass'n, *Decisions Near the End of Life,* 267 JAMA 2229 (1992)).

Institute of Medicine, *Approaching Death: Improving Care at the End of Life* 132 (Marilyn J. Field & Christine K. Cassel, eds. 1997); Mina L. Levin et al., *Management of Pain in Terminally Ill Patients: Physician Reports of Knowledge, Attitudes, and Behavior,* 15 J. Pain & Symptom Management 27 (1998).

Page 590, add to footnote 259:

US: Washington v. Glucksberg, 117 S. Ct. 2258, 2308 (1997) (Stevens, J., concurring in the judgment) ("[P]alliative care, however, cannot alleviate all pain and suffering. *See* Orentlicher, *Legalization of Physician Assisted Suicide: A Very Modest Revolution,* 38 Boston College L. Rev. (Galley, p. 8) (1997) ('Greater use of palliative care would reduce the demand for assisted suicide, but it will not eliminate [it]'); *see also* Brief for Coalition of Hospice Professionals as Amici Curiae 8 (citing studies showing that '[a]s death becomes more imminent, pain and suffering become progressively more difficult to treat')."). *See also Glucksberg,* 117 S. Ct. at 2311–12 (Breyer, J., concurring) ("a very few individuals for whom the ineffectiveness of pain control medicines can mean, not pain, but the need for sedation which can end in a coma").

KS: *See, e.g.,* State v. Naramore, 965 P.2d 211 (Kan. Ct. App. 1998) (reversing conviction of physician for attempted murder of terminally ill cancer patient to whom he had given very large doses of medications and who "had developed a relatively high level of tolerance for pain medication").

Institute of Medicine, Approaching Death: Improving Care at the End of Life 132 (Marilyn J. Field & Christine K. Cassel, eds., 1997) ("Reviews of pain research have suggested that pain can be fairly readily relieved in approximately 70 percent to 90 percent of cancer patients."); Timothy E. Quill et al., *The Debate over Physician-Assisted Suicide: Empirical Data and Convergent Views,* 128 Ann. Internal Med. 552 (1998) (<http://www.acponline.org>); A. Jacox, D. Carr, & R. Payne, *New Clinical-Practice Guidelines for the Management of Pain in Patients with Cancer,* 330 N. Eng. J. Med. 651 (1994) (approximately 10% of cancer patients' pain cannot be adequately relieved).

Page 590, add to footnote 260:

US: Vacco v. Quill, 117 S. Ct. 2293, 2298 (1997) ("[I]n some cases, painkilling drugs may hasten a patient's death."). *See also*

Glucksberg, 117 S. Ct. at 2303 (O'Connor, J., concurring) (use of adequate pain medication may hasten death).

But see Institute of Medicine, Approaching Death: Improving Care at the End of Life 132 (Marilyn J. Field & Christine K. Cassel, eds., 1997) ("[S]tudies suggest that the high doses of opioids needed to relieve pain in certain patients rarely hasten death [citations omitted].").

Page 590, add to footnote 261:

Just as a State may prohibit assisting suicide while permitting patients to refuse unwanted lifesaving treatment, it may permit palliative care related to that refusal, which may have the foreseen but unintended 'double effect' of hastening the patient's death. See New York Task Force, When Death is Sought, supra, n. 6, at 163 ("It is widely recognized that the provision of pain medication is ethically and professionally acceptable even when the treatment may hasten the patient's death, if the medication is intended to alleviate pain and severe discomfort, not to cause death").

Vacco v. Quill, 117 S. Ct. 2293, 2301 n.11 (1997).

Page 590, add to footnote 262:

US: Vacco v. Quill, 117 S. Ct. 2293, 2298 (1997) ("[I]n some cases, painkilling drugs may hasten a patient's death, but the physician's purpose and intent is, or may be, only to ease his patient's pain."). *See also Glucksberg,* 117 S. Ct. at 2303 (O'Connor, J., concurring) ("The parties and amici agree that in these States a patient who is suffering from a terminal illness and who is experiencing great pain has no legal barriers to obtaining medication, from qualified physicians, to alleviate that suffering, even to the point of causing unconsciousness and hastening death. *See* Wash. Rev. Code § 70.122.010 (1994); Brief for Petitioners in No. 95-1858, p. 15, n. 9; Brief for Respondents in No. 95-1858, p. 15.").

Page 590, add to footnote 263:

CA: Bouvia v. Superior Court (Glenchur), 225 Cal. Rptr. 297, 306 (Ct. App. 1986) (hospital may not deny patient relief from pain and suffering because she has chosen to exercise her right to refuse medical treatment)

NY: *In re* Christopher, 675 N.Y.S.2d 807, 810 (Sup. Ct. Queens County 1998) (hospital required "to take all means necessary to ameliorate the patient's pain" that might arise from withholding tube feeding).

Page 590, delete statutory citations in footnote 263.

Page 591, add at end of first full paragraph:

A number of state legislatures have begun to enact provisions expressly authorizing physicians to prescribe adequate medications to patients for the treatment of intractable pain, thus explicitly recognizing and legitimating the principle of double effect. For example, the Minnesota statute provides that administration, prescription, or dispensation of "medications or procedures to relieve another person's pain or discomfort, even if the medication or procedure may hasten or increase the risk of death," is not abetting or aiding suicide "unless the medications or procedures are knowingly administered, prescribed, or dispensed to cause death."[267.1] See **Table 9-1A.** Other states have adopted administrative rules or guidelines.[267.2]

The problem of undermedication for pain relief will not be solved by intractable pain statutes alone. First, these statutes provide very limited protection to physicians. Some statutes provide immunity only from state licensing board disciplinary action, thus leaving physicians subject to prosecution for assisted suicide or homicide and to tort liability for wrongful death. Others exempt physicians from criminal liability, but physicians are still subject to disciplinary action by state licensing authorities and to wrongful death actions. None of the statutes do or could confer liability against violations of federal law, and thus physicians are still subject to criminal and administrative penalties for violation of the federal Controlled Substances Act.[267.3]

The Institute of Medicine has identified the following problems with intractable pain statutes:

1. [These statutes] do not, in all cases, mark a clear area of medical practice in which physicians feel free to manage their patients' pain. The more specific laws, for example those that set out detailed prescription practices, may actually afford physicians less leeway in the practice of medicine. Additionally, by carving out an area of pain treatment that is immune from medical board discipline, there may be an implication that other forms of pain treatment should be subject to disciplinary review.

2. Even the strongest intractable pain law is still limited by the term intractable. Many cases are ambiguous, and physicians may believe that they must delay opioid treatment until pain is far enough along to be called intractable.

267.1   Minn. Stat. Ann. § 609.215(a).

267.2   *See* Ann M. Martino, *In Search of a New Ethic for Treating Patients with Chronic Pain: What Can Medical Boards Do?*, 26 J.L. Med. & Ethics 332, 332 (1998) (33 states; citing D.E. Joranson and A.M. Gilston, *State Intractable Pain Policy: Current Status*, 7 APS Bull. 7–9 (no. 2, 1997)).

267.3   *See* Alan Meisel, *Pharmacists, Physician-Assisted Suicide, and Pain Control*, 2 U. Md. J. Health Care L. & Pol'y 201 (1999).

3. An additional problem arises when state laws define addiction without regard to pain management. As noted earlier, California defines addicts as "habitual users," which might include patients taking opioids for chronic pain. Such confusing definitions . . . expose physicians to the threat of medical board discipline.

4. Finally, the legal affirmations in these laws of the importance of pain control do not, in themselves, correct practice patterns or improve physician training. Laws could, however, encourage patients to expect diligence in pain relief, including use of generally effective medications. Medical boards could consider disciplining physicians who fail to apply proven methods of pain control.[267.4]

Finally, patients need to know about their right to adequate palliative care. In states where there are intractable pain statutes, the Patient Self-Determination Act[267.5] requires health care institutions covered by the act to inform patients of their state law rights to adequate palliative care.[267.6]

Thus, additional legislation beyond that of the intractable pain statutes may be required. Florida has enacted legislation providing for the education of physicians in the matter of pain management and palliative care.[267.7] This legislation also encourages health care providers to "add the assessment of pain as a fifth vital sign"[267.8] and addresses physicians' fears of liability.[267.9] To ensure that pain management education occurs, Florida also amended its license renewal statutes to allow personnel to take continuing education on

---

[267.4] Institute of Medicine, Approaching Death: Improving Care at the End-of-Life 197 (Marilyn J. Field & Cristine K. Cassel, eds., 1997).

[267.5] See § **10.21** in the main volume and this supplement.

[267.6] Erin Hoover Barnett, *Patients Must Be Told of Right to Pain Care, Agency Says,* Oregonian, Jul. 13, 1999, at A1.

[267.7] **FL:** S.B. 2228, 1999 Leg. (Fla. 1999), § 1(1)(c) ("The legislature finds that education of physicians and other health care providers is necessary to assure that patients in pain are assessed regularly and that their pain is treated aggressively without fear of undue regulatory or legal action"). *See also* Fla. Stat. Ann. § 765.102(4) ("The legislature . . . encourages professional regulatory boards to adopt appropriate standards and guidelines regarding end-of-life care and pain management, and encourages educational institutions . . . and allied health professionals to implement curricula to train such professionals to provide end-of-life care, including pain management and palliative care.").

CA: *See also* Cal. Bus. & Prof. Code § 2089 (requiring that an applicant to the profession "successfully complete a medical curriculum that provides instruction in pain management and end-of-life care," beginning with persons entering medical school on or after June 1, 2000).

[267.8] **FL:** S.B. 2228, 1999 Leg. (Fla. 1999), § 1(1)(e).

[267.9] **FL:** S.B. 2228, 1999 Leg. (Fla. 1999), § 1(1)(e) ("Such use should not be regarded as legally blameworthy, even if appropriate pain control occurs during, and so precedes the outcome of the dying process").

end-of-life and palliative health care in lieu of AIDS/HIV courses[267.10] or domestic violence courses.[267.11] Florida's legislature also has enacted a statute requiring physicians or their designees to inform their patients of pain management and palliative care options.[267.12]

Table 9—1A

Intractable Pain Statutes

AR:	1999 Ark. H.B. 1298, Act 394 of 1999, § 1(D)
CA:	Cal. Bus. & Prof. Code 2241.5
	Cal. Health & Safety Code §§ 124960, 124961
FL:	Fla. Stat. Ann. § 458.326(3)
IN:	Ind. Stat. Ann. § 35-42-1-2.5
IA:	Iowa Code Ann. § 707A.3
KY:	Ky. Rev. Stat. Ann. § 216.304
MD:	1999 Md. H.B. 496 (effective Oct. 1, 1999), *to be codified at* Md. Code Ann., Crimes & Punishments, art 27, § 416(C)
MI:	Mich. Comp. Laws Ann. §§ 752.1027, 333.5658, 333.16204c
MN:	Minn. Stat. Ann. § 609.215(3)(a)
	Minn. Stat. Ann. § 152.125
MO:	Mo. Ann. Stat. § 334.105–.107
NE:	Neb. Rev. Stat. § 71-7418
NM:	N.M. Stat. Ann. § 24-2D
NV:	Nev. Rev. Stat. Ann. § 630.3066, 633.521
NM:	1999 N.M. S.B. 343; N.M. Stat. Ann. § 24-2D
ND:	N.D. Cent. Code §§ 19-03.3-01 to -06
OH:	Ohio Rev. Code Ann. §§ 2133.11, 2133.12
	Ohio Rev. Code Ann. § 4731.052
OK:	Okla. Stat. Ann. tit. 63, § 141.4
OR:	Or. Rev. Stat. Ann. §§ 677.470–.485
RI:	R.I. Gen. Laws § 11-60-4
	R.I. Gen. Laws §§ 5-37.4-1 to -3
SD:	S.D. Codified Laws Ann. § 22-16-37.1
TN:	Tenn. Code Ann. § 39-13-216(b)(2)
TX:	Tex. Rev. Civ. Stat. Ann. art. 4495(c)
WV:	W. Va. Code §§ 30-3A-1 to -4
VA:	Va. Code Ann. § 54.1-3408.1; 1998 Va. S.B. 1299, *to be codified at* Va. Code Ann. §§ 38.2-4214, 38.2-4319, 38.2-3407.11:1

[267.10] **FL:** Fla. Stat. Ann. § 455.604(9), 458.319(4) ("a physician may complete continuing education on end-of-life care and palliative health care in lieu of continuing education in AIDS/HIV, if that physician has completed the AIDS/HIV continuing education in the immediately preceding biennium"), and 459.008(5), amended by S.B. 2228, 1999 Leg. (Fla. 1999), §§ 9, 10, 11.

[267.11] Fla. Stat. Ann. § 455.597(3).

[267.12] Fla. Stat. Ann. § 765.1103.

See generally Sandra H. Johnson, "Disciplinary Actions and Pain Relief: Analysis of the Pain Relief Act," 24 *Journal of Law, Medicine and Ethics* 319 (1996).

Page 592, add to footnote 271:

F.J. Skelly, *Painful Barriers,* Am. Med. News, May 9, 1994, at 15; F.J. Skelly, *Price of Pain Control: Is This the Risk You Face When Appropriately Prescribing Narcotics for Pain?,* Am. Med. News, May 16, 1994, at 17; F.J. Skelly, *Fear of Sanctions Limits Prescribing of Pain Drugs,* Am. Med. News, Aug. 15, 1994, at 19.

Page 592, add to footnote 272:

KS: State v. Naramore, 965 P.2d 211, 214 (Kan. Ct. App. 1998) ("'[O]ne cause of the failure of physicians to adequately control pain is fear of legal sanctions.'").

Page 592, add to footnote 274:

AR: Hollabaugh v. Arkansas State Med. Bd., 861 S.W.2d 317 (Ark. Ct. App. 1993).

FL: Hoover v. Agency for Health Care Admin., 676 So. 2d 1380 (Fla. Dist. Ct. App. 1996).

NV: *Cf.* Board of Nursing v. Merkley, 940 P.2d 144 (Nev. 1997) (nurse's employment terminated and license suspended in connection with administration of morphine for pain relief).
See also John Seiler, *The Politics of Pain Medicine: Patients and Physicians Sometimes Have to Turn a Government Gauntlet to Get Effective Treatment for Chronic Pain,* Orange County Reg., Aug. 17, 1997, at G-1 (discussing case of Virginia physician whose license and certification to prescribe Schedule II drugs were revoked for prescribing too much pain medication to terminally ill patients).

US: Washington v. Glucksberg, 117 S. Ct. 2258, 2303 (1997) (O'Connor, J., concurring):

> The parties and amici agree that in these States a patient who is suffering from a terminal illness and who is experiencing great pain has no legal barriers to obtaining medication, from qualified physicians, to alleviate that suffering, even to the point of causing unconsciousness and hastening death. See Wash. Rev. Code 70.122.010 (1994); Brief for Petitioners in No. 95-1858, p. 15, n.9; Brief for Respondents in No. 95-1858, p. 15. . . . There is no dispute that dying patients in Washington and New York can obtain palliative care, even when doing so would hasten their deaths.

See, e.g., Joannie M. Schrof, *Caught in Pain's Vicious Cycle He Helped His Patients—and Lost His License,* U.S. News & World Rep., Mar. 17, 1997, at 64 1997 WL 8331742 ("Over 100 doctors who prescribe narcotics lose their licenses each year, and 40 percent of pain specialists admit that they under-medicate patients to avoid trouble."). *See generally* Sandra H. Johnson, *Disciplinary Actions and Pain Relief: Analysis of the Pain Relief Act,* 24 J. L., Med. & Ethics 319 (1996). See § **18.22** in this supplement.

Page 592, add to footnote 275:

See also John Seiler, *The Politics of Pain Medicine: Patients and Physicians Sometimes Have to Turn a Government Gauntlet to Get Effective Treatment for Chronic Pain,* Orange County Reg., Aug. 17, 1997, at G-1 (discussing case of Virginia physician whose license and certification to prescribe Schedule II drugs were revoked for prescribing too much pain medication to terminally ill patients). *See generally* Sandra H. Johnson, *Disciplinary Actions and Pain Relief: Analysis of the Pain Relief Act,* 24 J. L., Med. & Ethics 319 (1996), *cited with approval in* State v. Naramore, 965 P.2d 211, 214 (Kan. Ct. App. 1998).

Page 592, add to footnote 276:

US: *Cf.* Vacco v. Quill, 117 S. Ct. 2293 (1997) ("There is no dispute that dying patients in Washington and New York can obtain palliative care, even when doing so would hasten their deaths."); *id.* at 2303 (O'Connor, J., concurring) ("The parties and amici agree that in these States a patient who is suffering from a terminal illness and who is experiencing great pain has no legal barriers to obtaining medication, from qualified physicians, to alleviate that suffering, even to the point of causing unconsciousness and hastening death. *See* Wash. Rev. Code § 70.122.010 (1994); Brief for Petitioners in No. 95-1858, p. 15, n. 9; Brief for Respondents in No. 95-1858, p. 15.").

KS: *But see* State v. Naramore, 965 P.2d 211 (Kan. Ct. App. 1998) (reversing conviction of physician for attempted murder of terminally ill patient to whom he administered large doses of pain relief medications).

See also U.S. Department of Justice, Drug Enforcement Administration, Physician's Manual: An Informational Outline of the Controlled Substances Act of 1970, U.S. Government Printing Office 21 (rev. ed. March, 1990) (1990 275-114—(20793)):

> Controlled substances and, in particular, narcotic analgesics, may be used in the treatment of pain experienced by a patient with a terminal illness or chronic disorder. These drugs have a legitimate clinical use and the physician should not hesitate to prescribe, dispense or administer them when they are indicated

for a legitimate medical purpose. It is the position of the Drug Enforcement Administration that these controlled substances should be prescribed, dispensed or administered when there is a legitimate medical need.

Page 592, add to footnote 277:

See also Robyn S. Shapiro, *Health Care Providers' Liability Exposure for Inappropriate Pain Management,* 24 J. L., Med. & Ethics 360 (1996).

Page 592, delete period at end of sentence in carryover paragraph and add the following:

or licensure proceedings.[277.1]

It is difficult to know the magnitude of risk of investigation or prosecution of a physician for homicide when a patient dies for whom the physician has prescribed large doses of pain control medications. Most instances of investigation or prosecution do not result in a reported appellate case, and thus obtaining accurate data is virtually impossible.[277.2] One exception is *State v. Naramore.*[277.3] A survey of prosecutors revealed a significant unwillingness to prosecute physicians for prescribing large doses of pain medication that ended the life of a terminally ill cancer patient suffering from intractable pain.[277.4] However, in this area doctors' perceptions may matter more than reality.[277.5]

[277.1]   *See* Vida Foubister, *Oregon Doctor Cited for Negligence for Undertreating Pain,* Am. Med. News, Sept. 27. 1999; *Doctor Disciplined Over Lack of Aid,* Associated Press, Sept. 2, 1999. In the proceeding described in these articles, Oregon's medical board disciplined a physician for undertreating the pain of six patients. See generally § **1A.9** in this supplement.

[277.2]   *See generally* Ann Alpers, *Criminal Act or Palliative Care? Prosecutions Involving the Care of the Dying,* 26 J.L. Med. & Ethics 308 (1998) (Table 1, at 312–13, reporting criminal investigations of physicians; Table 2, at 313–14, reporting criminal trials of physicians). *But see* Phebe Saunders Haugen, *Pain Relief for the Dying: The Unwelcome Intervention of the Criminal Law,* 23 Wm. Mitchell L. Rev. 325, 353 (1997) ("[N]o physician in the United States has ever been convicted of murder or assisted suicide for providing a patient with high doses of medication for pain relief"), citing Melissa L. Buchan & Susan W. Tolle, *Pain Relief for Dying Persons: Dealing with Physicians' Fears and Concerns,* 6 J. Clinical Ethics 53, 53 (1995); Leonard H. Glantz, *Withholding and Withdrawing Treatment: The Role of the Criminal Law,* 15 L. Med. & Health Care 231, 238–40 (1987); Sidney H. Wanzer et al., *The Physician's Responsibility to Hopelessly Ill Patients,* 310 New Eng. J. Med. 955, 956 (1984).

[277.3]   965 P.2d 211 (Kan. Ct. App. 1998) (reversing conviction), discussed in § **1A.8** in this supplement.

[277.4]   *See* Alan Meisel, Jan C. Jernigan, & Stuart J. Youngner, *Prosecutors and End-of-Life Decision Making,* 159 Archives Internal Med. 1089 (1999) (39% of respondents said they would prosecute; 36% would not; 25% undecided).

[277.5]   *See* Ann M. Martino, *In Search of a New Ethic for Treating Patients with Chronic Pain: What Can Medical Boards Do?* 26 J.L. Med. & Ethics 332, 333 (1998)

In the two cases challenging the constitutionality of state statutory prohibitions on physician-assisted suicide,[277.6] the United States Supreme Court touched on the legality of the medically appropriate use of pain medications in the terminally ill. The court's conclusion is that there are no legal barriers to such use,[277.7] but this conclusion is reached with virtually no analysis nor citation to any relevant statutes, regulations, or case law. Although this conclusion is probably correct as a matter of law, it is also hopelessly naive. One very significant barrier to terminally ill patients' obtaining adequate pain relief is the perception by many physicians that they may suffer legal penalties—such as loss of their license to practice medicine or their right to prescribe controlled substances. Another is the lack of knowledge that many physicians have that serious pain can be controlled and the techniques for doing so.

Although in most states, physicians may dispense medications for pain relief as well as prescribe them, in practice patients rely on pharmacists to dispense medications, and pharmacists are also concerned about possible legal complications arising from the dispensing of large quantities of controlled substances over long periods of time.[277.8]

Finally, there can be significant financial barriers to adequate pain management in the terminally ill. There are stringent requirements under the Medicare program to receiving hospice benefits,[277.9] and in any event these benefits are not available to patients who do not qualify for Medicare benefits.

§ 9.39   Nutrition and Hydration

Page 595, add to footnote 289:

DE: *In re* Tavel, 661 A.2d 1061, 1069 (Del. 1995) ("[R]emoval of an artificial feeding tube is not a 'death producing agent.'").

Page 598, add to footnote 307:

DE: *In re* Tavel, 661 A.2d 1061, 1066 (Del. 1995) (one neurologist testified that patient would not suffer any pain after removal of feeding

---

("[T]he regulatory risks associated with overprescribing are perceived by most physicians to be real and far greater than those associated with underprescribing.").

[277.6]   Washington v. Glucksberg, 117 S. Ct. 2258 (1997); Vacco v. Quill, 117 S. Ct. 2293 (1997).

[277.7]   *Vacco,* 117 S. Ct. at 2298.

[277.8]   *See* Alan Meisel, *Pharmacists, Physician-Assisted Suicide, and Pain Control,* 2 U. Md. J. Health Care L. & Pol'y 201 (1999).

[277.9]   *See* 42 C.F.R. 418.20–.22, .24 (1996).

tube because PVS leaves patient unable to experience emotion or feeling; another neurologist testified it was impossible to determine whether person in PVS would or would not suffer pain).

Page 598, add at end of page:

The forgoing of artificial nutrition and hydration is receiving increasing attention as a preferred means of hastening death when the alternative is physician-assisted suicide.[307.1] The United States Supreme Court expressly approved of termination of nutrition and hydration in combination with terminal sedation.[307.2]

Page 599, add to footnote 309:

DE: *In re* Tavel, 661 A.2d 1061, 1066 (Del. 1995) (accepting testimony of one neurologist because, based on AMA standards, "he had relied on respected medical authorities," and rejecting testimony of another neurologist "because he had not relied on medical authorities and because . . . [his] opinion primarily reflected his belief that a physician has a moral duty to provide nutrition under all circumstances'").

NM: Protection and Advocacy System, Inc. v. Presbyterian Healthcare Services, 989 P.2d 890, 893 (N.M. Ct. App. 1999) (noting that the Uniform Health Care Decisions Act "treats artificial nutrition and hydration just as other kinds of health care").

Page 601, add to footnote 318:

NC: First Healthcare Corp. v. Rettinger, 456 S.E.2d 347 (N.C. Ct. App. 1995).

Page 602, add to footnote 319:

DE: *In re* Tavel, 661 A.2d 1061 (Del. 1995).
MI: Martin v. Martin, 538 N.W.2d 399 (Mich. 1995).

Page 602, add to footnote 321:

NY: *In re* Christopher, 675 N.Y.S.2d 807 (Sup. Ct. Queens County 1998) (percutaneous endoscopic gastrostomy (PEG)).

[307.1] *See, e.g.,* Franklin G. Miller et al., *Voluntary Death: A Comparison of Terminal Dehydration and Physician-Assisted Suicide,* 128 Ann. Internal Med. 559 (1998).

[307.2] Washington v. Glucksberg, 117 S. Ct. 2258, 2289 (1997); Vacco v. Quill, 117 S. Ct. 2293, 2301 n.11 (1997).

Page 606, add to footnote 350:

NY: *In re* Christopher, 675 N.Y.S.2d 807 (Sup. Ct. Queens County 1998) (denying hospital's petition to insert feeding tube because of clear and convincing evidence that patient did not want it).

Page 607, add to **Table 9–2:**

Delaware
In re Tavel, 661 A.2d 1061 (Del. 1995)

Florida
Singletary v. Costello, 665 So. 2d 1099 (Fla. Dist. Ct. App. 1996)

Indiana
Estate of Taylor v. Muncie Medical Investors, L.P., 727 N.E.2d 466 (Ind. Ct. App. 2000)

Michigan
Martin v. Martin, 538 N.W.2d 399 (Mich. 1995)

New York
In re Christopher, 675 N.Y.S.2d 807 (Sup. Ct. Queens County 1998)

North Carolina
First Healthcare Corp. v. Rettinger, 467 S.E.2d 243 (N.C. 1996), *rev'g,* 456 S.E.2d 347 (N.C. Ct. App. 1995)

Pennsylvania
In re Fiori, 673 A.2d 905 (Pa. 1996)

Virginia
Gilmore v. Finn, 527 S.E.2d 426 (Va. 2000) (reversing award of attorneys' fees but recounting with approval history of case involving withdrawal of nutrition and hydration)

§ 9.40   —Nutrition and Hydration in Nursing Homes

Page 610, add to footnote 365:

NC: First Healthcare Corp. v. Rettinger, 456 S.E.2d 347 (N.C. Ct. App. 1995), *rev'd,* 467 S.E.2d 243 (N.C. 1996) (insistence on strict compliance with living will statute).

Page 611, add to footnote 371:

See generally Alan Meisel, *Barriers to Forgoing Nutrition and Hydration in Nursing Homes,* 21 Am. J.L. & Med. 335 (1995).

Page 615, add to footnote 389:

NC: First Healthcare Corp. v. Rettinger, 456 S.E.2d 347, 348 (N.C. Ct. App. 1995) (nursing home "had a policy of not removing nasogastric tubes 'if to do so would likely cause a patient to starve or dehydrate to death'"), *rev'd,* 467 S.E.2d 243 (N.C. 1996).

§ 9.41   Surgery

Page 619, add to footnote 422:

PA: *But see In re* Goldman, 18 Fiduc. Rep. 2d 79 (C.P. Northampton County, Pa. 1997) (patient with Alzheimer's disease) (dictum).

§ 9.45   —Alzheimer's Disease and Other Senile Dementias

Page 622, add note 437.1 reference after "do-not-resuscitate orders" in second paragraph, third sentence and add note 437.1:

[437.1] **PA:** *In re* Goldman, 18 Fiduc. Rep. 2d 79 (C.P. Northampton County, Pa. 1997) (guardian of patient with Alzheimer's disease has authority to consent to DNR order).

Page 622, add note 437.2 reference after "antibiotic medications" in second paragraph, third sentence and add note 437.2:

[437.2] **PA:** *In re* Goldman, 18 Fiduc. Rep. 2d 79 (C.P. Northampton County, Pa. 1997) (guardian of patient with Alzheimer's disease does not have authority to refuse antibiotics and whirlpool treatment for ulcerated leg).

Page 622, add to footnote 439:

NY: *In re* Christopher, 675 N.Y.S.2d 807 (Sup. Ct. Queens County 1998).

Page 622, add note 439.1 reference at end of fifth sentence of second paragraph and add note 439.1:

[439.1] **NY:** *See, e.g., In re* Christopher, 675 N.Y.S.2d 807 (Sup. Ct. Queens County 1998) (denying petition to insert feeding tube but requiring that patient be offered nutrition by mouth and intravenously).

Page 623, add to footnote 442:

DE: *In re* Tavel, 661 A.2d 1061 (Del. 1995).

§ 9.48   Brain Death

Page 624, add to footnote 453:

CA: *But see* Duarte v. Chino Community Hosp., 85 Cal. Rptr. 2d 521 (Ct. App. 1999) (physician would not terminate life support because patient was merely in PVS but not brain-dead).

Page 627, add to footnote 462:

Ben Dobbin, *Pregnant Brain-Dead Woman Kept Alive,* Associated Press, Sept. 27, 1997.

Page 628, add after first paragraph:

However, in the sole case raising this issue, *In re Long Island Jewish Medical Center (Baby Doe),*[465.1] the court held that the hospital was entitled to terminate life-support equipment from a brain-dead infant despite the state law requiring "reasonable accommodation of the individual's religious or moral objection to the determination [of brain death] as expressed by the individual, or by the next of kin or other person closest to the individual."[465.2] Although the hospital had not complied with that portion of the regulation requiring hospitals to have a policy on reasonable accommodation, the court found that the hospital had complied with the regulatory provision on religious accommodation because the doctors had consulted with the parents, had encouraged them to obtain a second opinion from an expert of their own choosing, and had cooperated with this expert. Furthermore, the hospital expressed a willingness and a preference to transfer the infant to a hospital of the parents' choosing, which the parents rejected. Finally, when the attending physicians "came to the conclusion that the baby was irretrievably brain

---

[465.1]   641 N.Y.S.2d 989 (Sup. Ct. Queens County 1996).

[465.2]   *Id.* at 992 (citing N.Y. Dep't of Health Regulation, N.Y. Comp. Codes R. & Regs. tit. 10, § 400.16(e)(3)).

dead, they did not simply 'pull the plug', on their own accord, but sought judicial intervention which gave the parents a forum to express their own position."[465.3] This latter statement should probably not be taken as a requirement that judicial approval be obtained in New York to terminate life support when a patient is determined to be dead by brain-death standards and there is an objection on religious grounds, but merely as further evidence that the hospital had made reasonable accommodation to the parents' religious beliefs.

Page 631, add to footnote 477:

IL: *Cf.* People v. Caldwell, 692 N.E.2d 448 (Ill. App. Ct. 1998) (defendant liable for death of woman who, while conscious, made decision to terminate life support which had been necessitated by defendant's infliction of serious injuries on her).

§ 9.53   Persistent Vegetative State; Coma; Severe Brain Damage

Page 634, add to footnote 489:

CA: Duarte v. Chino Community Hosp., 85 Cal. Rptr. 2d 521 (Ct. App. 1999).

DE: *In re* Tavel, 661 A.2d 1061 (Del. 1995).

PA: *In re* Fiori, 673 A.2d 905 (Pa. 1996).

VA: Gilmore v. Finn, 527 S.E.2d 426 (Va. 2000) (reversing award of attorneys' fees but recounting with approval history of case involving withdrawal of nutrition and hydration from patient in a persistent vegetative state).

Page 637, add to footnote 497:

DE: *See, e.g., In re* Tavel, 661 A.2d 1061, 1065–66 (Del. 1995) (One neurologist testified patient's "stroke had left her in a 'coma vigil,' a form of persistent vegetative state in which the patient has no ability to perceive or to respond. He defined a coma vigil as a 'fixed neurological state where the brain is so irreparably damaged that the patient is actually in a coma, but they appear to be awake.'"; another testified that patient "was not in a persistent vegetative state because her kidneys continued to function, her breathing was normal and because she could open and close her eyes [and she] . . . was still capable of some movement because he had pinched her toe and she had moved her leg in response.").

[465.3]   *Id.*

Page 638, add to footnote 498:

PA: *Accord In re* Fiori, 673 A.2d 905 (Pa. 1996).

Page 638, add to footnote 499:

DE: *See also In re* Tavel, 661 A.2d 1061, 1066 (Del. 1995) (neurologist testified that "people are often misled into believing that the patient's random eye movements signify that the patient is alert and responsive").

Page 640, add to footnote 509:

PA: *In re* Fiori, 673 A.2d 905, 908 n.1 (Pa. 1996).

Page 642, add at end of carryover paragraph:

Anecdotal evidence that individuals have "awakened" from a persistent vegetative state must be evaluated against the background of uncertainty in the medical profession as to what a persistent vegetative state is, the lack of sophistication of many physicians in accurately diagnosing it, and the tendency of physicians to use the term loosely to refer to any prolonged state of unconsciousness or even to syndromes that do not involve unconsciousness, such as "locked-in state."[521.1]

Page 643, add to footnote 531:

DC: *See also In re* K.I., 735 A.2d 448 (D.C. Ct. App. 1999) (not involving a mentally retarded patient, but applying best interests standard to decision to enter DNR in case of a brain-damaged, two-year-old patient who had previously been adjudicated as a neglected child).

[521.1]   *See, e.g.,* Ronald Smothers, *Injured in '88, Officer Awakes in '96—Doctors Call Man's Return from a Vegetative State a Miracle,* N.Y. Times, Feb. 16, 1996, at A8 (nat'l ed.) (doctors "have stopped short of calling the state from which he emerged a coma. Instead they have used the phrase 'persistent vegetative state' or 'locked-in state' because Mr. Dockery remained conscious, was able to breath[e] on his own and could respond with eye motions to some questions at some times."); Melinda Beck & Vern Smith, *To Him, It Was Still 1988: The "Coma Cop" Awakens—Is He Really Back? And Was He Really Gone?,* Newsweek, Feb. 26, 1996, at 56 ("Neurologists across the country didn't believe it. They said it was more likely a misnomer than a miracle. . . . There are only a handful of documented cases of patients awakening from vegetative states after more than a year, and experts concluded that Dockery hadn't been in one.").

§ 9.55   Pregnancy

Page 645, add to footnote 545:

IL: *In re* Fetus Brown, 689 N.E.2d 397 (Ill. App. Ct. 1997).

Page 650, add to footnote 578:

IL: *See also In re* Fetus Brown, 689 N.E.2d 397 (Ill. App. Ct. 1997).

Page 651, add before last paragraph on page:

In a subsequent case, *In re Fetus Brown*,[586.1] the Illinois appeals court refused to approve the administration of a blood transfusion to a competent, pregnant Jehovah's Witness, which was alleged to be necessary to save the life of both the mother and the fetus. In an attempt to circumvent the holding of Doe that the fetus's interests need not be balanced against the mother's, the state argued in Brown that the state's interests in the viable fetus's life must be balanced against the mother's interests. The court seemed to accept this argument and seemed to apply the balancing test, but when it did so, it held in favor of the mother's right to refuse treatment because it concluded that a blood transfusion was a substantial invasion of the mother's bodily integrity.[586.2] However, the court also used broad language suggesting either that the mother's refusal could never be outweighed by the state's interest in the life of the viable fetus or would be outweighed only if the treatment involved were trivial.[586.3]

Page 652, add at end of second paragraph:

Gabrynowicz v. Heitkamp[597.1] is another case testing the validity of a provision in an advance directive statute limiting the implementation of advance directives for pregnant women. Unlike *DiNino,* the state was unwilling to concede that the statutory provision could be deleted. Instead, it argued that, although an advance directive need not conform exactly to the statutory form, for an advance directive to be enforceable it must be, in the terms of the statute, "'substantially' in the form set out in the statute.'"[597.2] Although the district court "acknowledge[d] that the challenged statutes raise constitu-

---

[586.1]   689 N.E.2d 397 (Ill. App. Ct. 1997).

[586.2]   *Id.* at 405.

[586.3]   *Id.* ("[W]e hold that the State may not override a pregnant woman's competent treatment decision, including refusal of recommended invasive medical procedures, to potentially save the life of the viable fetus.").

[597.1]   904 F. Supp. 1061 (D.N.D. 1995).

[597.2]   *Id.* at 1062, (citing N.D. Cent. Code § 23-06.4-03(3)).

tional questions,"[597.3] it held that the case was not ripe for adjudication and therefore refused to rule on them.

Page 653, add to footnote 602:

CT: *Cf.* Stamford Hosp. v. Vega, 674 A.2d 821, 827 (Conn. 1996) (noting "extraordinary procedural history" of case in which "hearing before the trial court took place in the middle of the night, under extreme emergency conditions that were not conducive to the ability of either party to develop fully its arguments, . . . [patient] was not represented by counsel at the outset of the hearing and, of that portion of the hearing in which her attorney was present, most was not recorded").

Bibliography

Artificial Nutrition and Hydration

Campbell-Taylor, I., and R.H. Fisher. "The Clinical Case Against Tube Feeding in Palliative Care of the Elderly." *Journal of the American Geriatric Society* 35 (1987): 1100.

Meisel, A. "Barriers to Forgoing Nutrition and Hydration in Nursing Homes." *American Journal of Law and Medicine* 21 (1995): 335.

Miller, F., and D. Meier, "Voluntary Death: A Comparison of Terminal Dehydration and Physician-Assisted Suicide." *Annals of Internal Medicine* 128 (1998): 559.

National Conference of Catholic Bishops. "Nutrition and Hydration: Moral and Pastoral Reflections." *Journal of Contemporary Health Law and Policy* 15 (1999): 455.

Nelson, L., et al. "Forgoing Medically Provided Nutrition and Hydration in Pediatric Patients." *Journal of Law, Medicine and Ethics* 23 (1995): 33.

Rosin, A., and M. Sonnenblick, "Autonomy and Paternalism in Geriatric Medicine. The Jewish Ethical Approach to Issues of Feeding Terminally Ill Patients, and to Cardiopulmonary Resuscitation." *Journal of Medical Ethics* 24 (1998): 44.

Schaffner, K. "Recognizing the Tragic Choice: Food, Water, and the Right to Assisted Suicide." *Critical Care Medicine* 16 (1988): 1063.

[597.3] *Id.* at 1064.

BIBLIOGRAPHY

Blood Transfusions

Filkins, J. "A Pregnant Mother's Right to Refuse Treatment Beneficial to Her Fetus: Refusing Blood Transfusions." *DePaul Journal of Health Care Law* 2 (1998): 361.

Brain Death

Diamond, E.F. "Brain-Based Determination of Death Revisited." *Linacre Quarterly* 65(4) (1998): 71.

Howsepian, A. "In Defense of Whole-Brain Definitions of Death." *Linacre Quarterly* 65(4) (1998): 39.

Inwald, D. et al. "Brain Stem Death: Managing Care When Accepted Medical Guidelines and Religious Beliefs Are in Conflict." *British Medical Journal* 320 (2000): 1266.

Provisional Commission for the Study on Brain Death and Organ Transplantation. *Important Considerations with Respect to Brain Death and Organ Transplants*. Osaka, Japan: Osaka Kidney Foundation, 1994.

Shewmon, D. "'Brainstem Death,' 'Brain Death' and Death: A Critical Re-evaluation of the Purported Equivalence." *Issues in Law and Medicine* 14 (1998): 125.

Cardiopulmonary Resuscitation

American College of Surgeons. "'Do Not Resuscitate' in the Operating Room." *ACS Bulletin* (Sept. 1994): 29.

American Medical Association Council on Ethical and Judicial Affairs. "Optimal Use of Orders Not to Intervene and Advance Directives." *Psychology, Public Policy and Law* 4 (1998): 668.

Bastron, R. "Ethical Concerns in Anesthetic Care for Patients with Do-Not-Resuscitate Orders." *Anesthesiology* 85 (1996): 1190.

Casarett, D., and L. Ross. "Overriding a Patient's Refusal to Treatment after an Iatrogenic Complication." *New England Journal of Medicine* 336 (1997): 1908.

Gazelle, G. "The Slow Code—Should Anyone Rush to its Defense?" *New England Journal of Medicine* 338 (1998): 467.

Layson, R., and T. McConnell. "Must Consent Always Be Obtained for a Do-Not-Resuscitate Order?" *Archives of Internal Medicine* 156 (1996): 2617.

Lonchyna, V. "To Resuscitate or Not . . . in the Operating Room: The Need for Hospital Policies for Surgeons Regarding DNR Orders." *Annals of Health Law* 6 (1997): 2.

Margolis, J., et al. "Do Not Resuscitate (DNR) Orders during Surgery: Ethical Foundations for Institutional Policies in the United States." *Anesthesiology and Analgesia* 80 (1995): 806.

Parri, R. "If I Call 911, Is My Living Will Any Good? The Living Will v. The DNRO." *Florida Bar Journal* 70 (1996): 82.

Rosin, A., and M. Sonnenblick, "Autonomy and Paternalism in Geriatric Medicine. The Jewish Ethical Approach to Issues of Feeding Terminally Ill Patients, and to Cardiopulmonary Resuscitation." *Journal of Medical Ethics* 24 (1998): 44.

Rushton, C., et al. "To Honor and Obey—DNR Orders and the School." *Pediatric Nursing* 20 (1994): 581.

Sabatino, C. "Survey of State EMS-DNR Laws and Protocols." *Journal of Law, Medicine & Ethics* 27 (1999): 297–315.

The SUPPORT Investigators. "The Stability of DNR Orders on Hospital Readmission." *Journal of Clinical Ethics* 7 (1996): 48.

Walker, L., et al. "Do-Not-Resuscitate Orders in Nursing Homes: Institutional Policies and Practices." *Journal of Ethics, Law and Aging* 1 (1995): 97.

Wenger, N., et al. "Patients with DNR Orders in the Operating Room: Surgery, Resuscitation, and Outcomes." *Journal of Clinical Ethics* 8 (1997): 250.

Pain Management and Palliative Care

AGS Ethics Committee. "The Care of Dying Patients: A Position Statement from the American Geriatrics Society." *Journal of the American Geriatrics Society* 43 (1995): 577.

Alpers, A. "Criminal Act or Palliative Care? Prosecutions Involving the Care of the Dying." *Journal of Law, Medicine and Ethics* 26 (1998): 308.

Campbell-Taylor, I., and R. Fisher. "The Clinical Case Against Tube Feeding in Palliative Care of the Elderly." *Journal of the American Geriatric Society* 35 (1987): 1100.

Cantor, N., and G. Thomas. "Pain Relief, Acceleration of Death, and Criminal Law." *Kennedy Institute of Ethics Journal* 6 (1996): 107.

Cavanaugh, T. "The Ethics of Death-Hastening or Death-Causing Palliative Analgesic Administration to the Terminally Ill." *Journal of Pain and Symptom Management* 12 (1996): 248.

BIBLIOGRAPHY

Eippert, T. "A Proposal to Recognize a Legal Obligation on Physicians to Provide Adequate Medication to Alleviate Pain." *Journal of Law and Health* 12 (1997–98): 381.

Emanuel, E. "Pain and Symptom Control—Patient Rights and Physician Responsibilities." *Pain and Palliative Care* 10 (1996): 41.

Haddox, J.D., and G. Aronoff. "Commentary: The Potential for Unintended Consequences from Public Policy Shifts in the Treatment of Pain." *Journal of Law, Medicine and Ethics* 26 (1998): 350.

Haugen, P. "Pain Relief for the Dying: The Unwelcome Intervention of the Criminal Law." *William Mitchell Law Review* 23 (1997): 325.

Hoffmann, D. "Pain Management and Palliative Care in the Era of Managed Care: Issues for Health Insurers." *Journal of Law, Medicine and Ethics* 26 (1998): 267.

Institute of Medicine. *Approaching Death: Improving Care at the End of Life*. M. Field & Co. C. Cassel, eds.Washington, DC: National Academy Press, 1997.

Jost, T. "Public Financing of Pain Management: Leaky Umbrellas and Ragged Safety Nets." *Journal of Law, Medicine and Ethics* 26 (1998): 290.

Martino, A. "In Search of a New Ethic for Treating Patients with Chronic Pain: What Can Medical Boards Do?" *Journal of Law, Medicine and Ethics* 26 (1998): 332.

Meier, D., et al. "Improving Palliative Care." *Annals of Internal Medicine* 127 (1997): 225.

Meisel, A. "Pharmacists, Physician-Assisted Suicide, and Pain Control." *University of Maryland Journal of Health Care Law and Policy* 2 (1999): 201.

Nuccetelli, S. and Seay, G. "Relieving Pain and Foreseeing Death: A Paradox About Accountability and Blame." *Journal of Law, Medicine & Ethics* 28 (2000): 19.

Quill, T., et al. "Palliative Options of Last Resort. A Comparison of Voluntarily Stopping Eating and Drinking, Terminal Sedation, Physician-Assisted Suicide, and Voluntary Active Euthanasia." *Journal of the American Medical Association* 278 (1997): 29.

Ralston, D. "Pain Management: Texas Legislative and Regulatory Update." *Journal of Law, Medicine & Ethics* 24 (1996): 328.

Report of the Medical Society of Virginia Pain Management Subcommittee. "Guidelines for the Use of Opioids in the Treatment of Chronic, Non-Cancer Pain." *BioLaw* 11 (1998): S175.

Rich, B. "A Prescription for the Pain: The Emerging Standard of Care for Pain Management." *William Mitchell Law Review* 26 (1999): 1.

Sachs, G., et al. "Good Care of Dying Patients: The Alternative to Physician-Assisted Suicide and Euthanasia." *Journal of the American Geriatrics Society* 43 (1995): 553.

Shapiro, R. "Liability Issues in the Management of Pain." *Journal of Pain and Symptom Management* 9 (1994): 146.

Smith, G. "Terminal Sedation as Palliative Care: Revalidating a Right to a Good Death." *Cambridge Quarterly of Healthcare Ethics* 7 (1998): 382.

Smith, W. Comment. "That Which Does Not Kill Us, Does It Make Us Stronger? Legal Aspects of Pain Management in Great Britain." *Pace International Law Review* 10 (1998): 649.

Sternberg, T. "Textbook of Pain." *Journal of the American Medical Association* 279 (1998): 331.

Sulmasy, D. "Commentary: Double Effect—Intention Is the Solution, Not the Problem." *Journal of Law, Medicine & Ethics* 28 (2000): 26.

Symposium. "Appropriate Management of Pain: Addressing the Clinical, Legal, and Regulatory Barriers." *Journal of Law, Medicine and Ethics* 24 (1997): 285.

Tucker, K. "Improving Pain Care: A Safe Harbor Is Not Enough, The Seas Outside the Harbor Must be Rough." *Health Lawyer* 11 (May 1999): 15.

Wheeler, W. "Hospice Philosophy: An Alternative to Assisted Suicide." *Ohio Northern University Law Review* 20 (1994): 755.

Zuckerman, C. and A. Mackinnon. *The Challenge of Caring for Patients near the End of Life: Findings from the Hospital Palliative Care Initiative*. New York: United Hospital Fund of New York, 1998.

Persistent Vegetative State

Andrews, K., et al. "Misdiagnosis of the Vegetative State: Retrospective Study in a Rehabilitation Unit." *British Medical Journal* 313 (1996): 13.

Cranford, R. "Beyond the Vegetative State." *Journal of Contemporary Health Law and Policy* 15 (1999): 427.

Cranford, R. "Misdiagnosing the Persistent Vegetative State: An Apparently High Rate of Misdiagnosis Demands Critical Review and Action." *British Medical Journal* 313 (1996): 5.

Fenwick, A. "Applying Best Interests Standard to Persistent Vegetative State—A Principled Distortion?" *Journal of Medical Ethics* 24 (1998): 86.

BIBLIOGRAPHY

Gillon, R. "Persistent Vegetative State, Withdrawal of Artificial Nutrition and Hydration, and the Patient's 'best interests.'" *Journal of Medical Ethics* 24 (1998): 75.

Steinbock, B. "Recovery from Persistent Vegetative State?: The Case of Carrie Coons." *Hastings Center Report* 19: (July/August 1989): 14.

Zeman, A. "Persistent Vegetative State." *Lancet* 350 (1997): 795.

Zuckerman, C., and A. Mackinnon. *The Challenge of Caring for Patients near the End of Life: Findings from the Hospital Palliative Care Initiative*. New York: United Hospital Fund of New York, 1998.

Pregnancy

Cole, H. "Legal Interventions During Pregnancy: Court-Ordered Medical Treatments and Legal Penalties for Potentially Harmful Behavior by Pregnant Women." *Journal of the American Medical Association* 264 (1990): 2663.

VOLUME 2

CHAPTER 10

LEGAL STATUS OF ADVANCE DIRECTIVES

§ 10.1   Scope of Part IV

Page 4, add to footnote 2:

See also Nancy P. Gordon & Starley B. Shade, *Advance Directives Are More Likely Among Seniors Asked About End-of-Life Care Preferences,* 159 Archives Internal Med. 701 (1999) (reporting one-third of over-age-65 members of HMO had advance directives, but only 15% had talked with clinician about end-of-life care preferences); Elizabeth Bradley et al., *The Patient Self-Determination Act and Advance Directive Completion in Nursing Homes,* 7 Archives Family Med. 417 (1998) (more than one-third of nursing home residents in study had documented in their medical record that they had advance directives).

§ 10.2   Background

Page 5, add after third sentence of second paragraph:

However, most advance directive *statutes* confine the use of advance directives to end-of-life decisionmaking. In fact, they are usually confined even more narrowly to patients who are terminally ill or in a persistent vegetative state.[3.1]

Page 5, add to footnote 9:

See Martin D. Goodman et al., *Effect of Advance Directives on the Management of Elderly Critically Ill Patients,* 26 Critical Care Med. 701 (1998).

§ 10.3   Purposes of Advance Directives

Page 6, add to footnote 10:

MA: *In re* Smith, 684 N.E. 2d 613, 616–17 (Mass. App. Ct. 1997).

[3.1]   See §§ **11.9** and **12.17** in the main volume and this supplement.

NJ: *In re* Roche, 687 A.2d 349, 352 (N.J. Super. Ct. Ch. Div. 1996).

Page 6, add to footnote 12:

But see J. Teno et al., *Do Advance Directives Provide Instructions That Direct Care?*, 45 J. Am. Geriatric Soc'y 508 (1997) (advance directives were helpful in naming a proxy but not in providing directions about care).

Page 6, add to footnote 14:

IL: Ill. Ann. Stat. ch. 755, § 40/20(b-5)(1) (unrevoked advance directive, invalid because of technical deficiency, may be used as evidence of patient's wishes).

Page 7, add note 18.1 reference at end of first sentence of last paragraph and add note 18.1:

18.1 *But see* Joan Teno et al., *The Illusion of End-of-Life Resource Savings with Advance Directives*, 45 J. Am. Geriatric Soc'y 513 (1997) (better documentation in hospital records of existence of advance directives does not lead to reduction in use of hospital resources).

§ 10.4   Types of Advance Directives

Page 9, add note 27.1 reference at end of third sentence of last paragraph and add note 27.1:

27.1**IL:**   Ficke v. Evangelical Health Sys., 674 N.E.2d 888, 890 (Ill. App. Ct. 1996) ("[L]iving wills soon proved too inflexible to adequately address the needs of individuals wishing to make advance health care decisions.").

§ 10.6   Background

Page 15, add to footnote 46:

DE: *Accord In re* Tavel, 661 A.2d 1061, 1069 (Del. 1995).

§ 10.7   Advance Directives and Informed Consent

Page 18, add to footnote 57:

DC: *But see In re* A.C., 573 A.2d 1235, 1249–50 (D.C. 1990) ("greatest weight" should be given to advance directives, whether written or oral, "even though the treatment alternatives at hand may not have been addressed," to protect patient's right to choose).

§ 10.12   — Nonconforming or Conflicting Advance Directives

Page 26, in footnote 97, replace West Virginia citation with:

WV: W. Va. Code § 16-30-6(c).

Page 28, in carryover footnote 100, replace West Virginia citation with:

WV :   W. Va. Code § 16-30-16(a).

Page 28, add to footnote 100:

GU: 10 Guam Code Ann. § 91,112(h) ("rights granted by this Act are in addition to, and not in derogation of, rights under any other statutory or case law").

MD: Wright v. Johns Hopkins Health Sys. Corp., 728 A.2d 166, 168–69 (Md. 1999).

NM: N.M. Stat. Ann. § 24-7A-16(B) ("does not impair a guardianship, living will, durable power of attorney, right-to-die statement or declaration or other advance directive for health-care decisions that is in effect before July 1, 1995").

Page 28, add to footnote 101:

MD: Wright v. Johns Hopkins Health Sys. Corp., 728 A.2d 166, 168 (Md. 1999) ("In addition to constitutional and common law rights to refuse life-sustaining medical procedures, an individual's ability to direct in advance his choice concerning whether to refuse life-sustaining procedures is based in" the advance directive statute.).

Page 29, add to footnote 104:

DND: *But cf.* Gabrynowicz v. Heitkamp, 904 F. Supp. 1061, 1064 (D.N.D. 1995) (in challenge to constitutionality of pregnancy provision of living will statute, state "indicated that a declaration without the pregnancy clause would not be 'substantially' in the statutory form, and thus not entitled to presumptive evidence of the patient's intent").

Page 30, add to footnote 107:

PA: *In re* Goldman, 18 Fiduc. Rep. 2d 79 (C.P. Northampton County, Pa. 1997) (durable power of attorney for health care executed in

California that does not conform to Pennsylvania advance directive statute is enforceable in Pennsylvania on common-law grounds).

§ 10.13 —Applicability of Advance Directive Legislation to Nondeclarants

Page 31, add to footnote 114:

DE: *In re* Tavel, 661 A.2d 1061, 1067 (Del. 1995) (living will statute "was not intended to affect the rights of persons who do not choose to take advantage of its provisions").

PA: *In re* Fiori, 673 A.2d 905, 911 (Pa. 1996) ("[T]he Act does not address the situation where no advance directives were left as to treatment.").

MI: Martin v. Martin, 538 N.W.2d 399, 406 n.11 (Mich. 1995) (court refused to determine how issue would be resolved by health care power of attorney statute because patient had not appointed a proxy).

VA: *In re* Baby "K," 16 F.3d 590, 597 n.10 (4th Cir. 1994).

Page 31, add to footnote 115:

CA: *See also* Duarte v. Chino Community Hosp., 85 Cal. Rptr. 2d 521 (Ct. App. 1999) (holding immunity provisions of health care power of attorney statute, but not of living will statute, applicable to decision made by surrogate not appointed pursuant to health care power of attorney), discussed in **§ 17.24** in this supplement.

Page 33, add to footnote 126:

Construed in In re Fiori, 673 A.2d 905, 911 n.7 (Pa. 1996).

Page 34, add at end of section:

A similar kind of situation can occur with respect to forgoing artificial nutrition and hydration. For example, the Ohio advance directive statute imposes certain requirements on forgoing artificial nutrition and hydration for nondeclarants—including a court order.[126.1] However, an Ohio trial court has held that this provision is not mandatory, binding neither a guardian nor a court.[126.2] The court drew this conclusion from the fact that the statute lacks sanctions and penalties, except for the provision that if the statute is not followed, statutory immunity is unavailable in civil or criminal litigation.

[126.1] Ohio Rev. Code Ann. § 2133.09.

[126.2] *In re* Myers, 610 N.E.2d 663 (P. Ct. Summit County, Ohio 1993).

The Georgia Supreme Court clearly stated in *Edwards v. Shumate*[126.3] that the provisions of the living will and health care power of attorney statutes making the falsification or forgery of an advance directive a crime were inapplicable when no statutory advance directives had been issued, that is, were inapplicable to oral advance directives. Strictly speaking, this was not part of the holding because there was no falsification or forgery, but it is almost certain that the court would have held that, had there been a falsification by the surrogate of the patient's orally expressed wishes or designation of a surrogate, there would have been no liability under the living will or health care power of attorney statute. The court did not discuss the possibility of criminal liability based on criminal statutes of more general application.

§ 10.14   — Applicability of Advance Directive Legislation to Declarants Possessing Decisionmaking Capacity

Page 34, add to footnote 127:

OH: Anderson v. St. Francis-St. George Hosp., 614 N.E.2d 841 (Ohio Ct. App. 1992), *opinion after remand,* No. C-930819, 1995 WL 109128, at *3 (Ohio Ct. App. Mar. 15, 1995), *rev'd on other grounds,* 671 N.E.2d 225 (Ohio 1996).

Page 34, add after note 128 reference:

Another situation in which an advance directive might be used even if the patient is still competent is exemplified by the *Gordy* case.[128.1] Mrs. Gordy was a 96-year-old woman who was experiencing the onset of Alzheimer's disease. She was having increasing difficulty eating, and the hospital staff wished to have a feeding tube implanted in her. On a number of occasions in discussions with "a psychiatrist, an attorney serving as her guardian ad litem, and a representative of the State Division of Aging, Ombudsman's office," she refused to consider the possibility. Although the court determined that she had not lost decisionmaking capacity, it considered the possibility that her decisionmaking capacity might be impaired. Nonetheless it honored her wishes in part because she had previously made a living will

> in which she expressly rejected the use of a feeding tube . . . [and] where she not only initialed that she did not want "artificial nutrition and hydration (nourishment provided by a feeding tube)" used, but took the further step of writing

---

[126.3] 468 S.E.2d 23 (Ga. 1996).

[128.1] **DE:** *In re* Gordy, 658 A.2d 613 (Del. Ch. 1994).

the word "No" next to her initials. . . . Even if for some reason one sought to give the living will a very narrow interpretation, it nevertheless would offer corroboration for the view that Mrs. Gordy's recent statements resisting a feeding tube were not the result of her diminished capacity.[128.2]

Thus, a living will may also be used in conjunction with a questionably competent patient's contemporaneous wishes to buttress those wishes and to provide further evidence of competence.

Page 35, add to footnote 133:

AL: Ala. Code § 22-8A-7(a).
GU: 10 Guam Code Ann. § 91,112(e).

Page 36, in footnote 135, replace West Virginia citation with:

WV: W. Va. Code § 16-30-6(a) ("Any capable adult may make his or her own health care decisions without regard to guidelines contained in this article.").

§ 10.15   —Immunity and Nonconforming Advance Directives

Page 38, add at end of section:

A California court of appeal held that the immunity provision of the health care power of attorney statute applied to a decision made by a surrogate who was *not* appointed by a health care power of attorney.[143.1]

§ 10.16   —Nonstatutory Oral Directives

Page 38, add to footnote 145:

GA: *See, e.g.,* Edwards v. Shumate, 468 S.E.2d 23 (Ga. 1996) (especially when patient-designated surrogate is a friend rather than a family member).
MI: Martin v. Martin, 538 N.W.2d 399, 410 (Mich. 1995) (preferable even in state not having advance directive statute).

[128.2] *Id.* at 615–16, 617.

[143.1] **CA:** *See* Duarte v. Chino Community Hosp., 85 Cal. Rptr. 2d 521 (Ct. App. 1999), discussed in § **17.24** in this supplement.

Page 40, add to footnote 150:

DE: *In re* Tavel, 661 A.2d 1061 (Del. 1995).
MD: Wright v. Johns Hopkins Health Sys. Corp., 728 A.2d 166, 169 (Md. 1999) (dictum).

Page 40, add to footnote 152:

MI: Martin v. Martin, 538 N.W.2d 399 (Mich. 1995) (oral expression of patient's wishes made before losing decisionmaking capacity did not address the circumstances that the patient was now in).

Page 40, add to footnote 154:

MD: Wright v. Johns Hopkins Health Sys. Corp., 728 A.2d 166, 169 (Md. 1999) (dictum).

Page 40, add at end of paragraph:

However, for an oral advance directive to be effective, it must be more specific than an expression of "'a generalized and open-ended desire to forgo life-sustaining procedures . . . in the indefinite future.'"[154.1]

§ 10.17   Uniform Acts

Page 44, replace last sentence of section with:

To date, only a small number of states have adopted the Uniform Health-Care Decisions Act.[172.1]

§ 10.18   —Uniform Health-Care Decisions Act (UHCDA)

Page 44, add to footnote 174:

See also Protection and Advocacy System, Inc. v. Presbyterian Healthcare Services, 989 P.2d 890, 894 (N.M. Ct. App. 1999) ("the UHCDA focuses primarily on the procedures for decision making rather than the content of decisions").

[154.1] **MD**: Wright v. Johns Hopkins Health Sys. Corp., 728 A.2d 166, 178 (Md. 1999), quoting 79 Md. Op. Att'y Gen. 137, 154 (1994).

[172.1] See § **10.18** in this supplement.

Page 44, add at end of second paragraph:

The UHCDA has been adopted in a small number of states.[176.1]

Page 45, add before last sentence of first full paragraph:

These requirements may also have the effect of constricting the imposition of liability on health care providers who ignore a patient's advance directive.[177.1] This, in turn, will undermine the incentives that health care providers have to honor advance directives.

Page 45, add reference to footnote 177.2 at end of last sentence of first full paragraph, and add new footnote 177.2:

[177.2] *See* Protection and Advocacy System, Inc. v. Presbyterian Healthcare Services, 989 P.2d 890, 893 (N.M. Ct. App. 1999) (the UHCDA "is not restricted to decisions regarding those who are terminally ill or in an irreversible coma").

§ 10.19 — Uniform Rights of the Terminally Ill Act (URTIA)

Page 46, add to footnote 187:

GU: 10 Guam Code Ann. §§ 91,100–91,117.

§ 10.21 Patient Self-Determination Act (PSDA)

Page 51, add to footnote 241:

superseded by U.S. Dep't of Health & Hum. Servs., Health Care Fin. Admin., Medicare and Medicaid Programs; Advance Directives, 60 Fed. Reg. 33262 (June 27, 1995) (final rule) (codified at 42 C.F.R. pts. 417, 430, 431, 434, 483, 484, & 489).

[176.1] *See* Me. Rev. Stat. Ann. tit. 18-A, §§ 5-801 to -817; 1998 Miss. Laws ch. 542 (H.B. 546); N.M. Stat. Ann. §§ 24-7A-1 to -18. The particular provisions of these statutes are discussed in **Chs. 11, 12,** and **14** in this supplement.

[177.1] **OH:** *Cf.* Anderson v. St. Francis-St. George Hosp., 671 N.E.2d 225 (Ohio 1996) (denying negligence liability for violation of DNR order and limiting battery liability to nominal damages); Allore v. Flower Hosp., No. L-96-329, 1997 WL 362465, at *3 (Ohio Ct. App. June 27, 1997) (implying that liability should be denied to estate of patient treated seemingly contrary to advance directive because he was not "terminally ill" though he died within an hour).

Page 51, add note 241.1 reference at end of second sentence of second paragraph and add note 241.1:

241.1 **DKS:** Asselin v. Shawnee Mission Medical Ctr., Inc., 894 F. Supp. 1479
(D. Kan. 1995) (PSDA does not create private right of action).

    IL: Ficke v. Evangelical Health Sys., 674 N.E.2d 888, 893 n.1 (Ill.
App. Ct. 1996) ("The federal Act only provides termination of federal revenue as a sanction for its violation. Omnibus Budget Reconciliation Act of 1990, Pub. L. No. 101-508, sec. 4206 (West 1992 & Supp.1995).").

Page 52, add to footnote 242:

RI: *See also* R.I. Gen. Laws §§ 23-17.15-1, -2 (requiring home health care clients to be provided with information about advance directives).

Page 52, add at end of page:

The requirement of the Patient Self-Determination act to provide patients with information does not require that patients be given information about actively hastening death.[248.1] However, where state law creates a right to adequate pain relief,[248.2] the Patient Self-Determination Act does require that patients be informed of this right.[248.3]

Page 54, add to footnote 264:

J. Teno et al., *Advance Directives for Seriously Ill Hospitalized Patients: Effectiveness with the Patient Self-Determination Act and the SUPPORT Intervention*, 45 J. Am. Geriatric Soc'y 500 (1997). *See also* Elizabeth Bradley et al., *Discussions About End-of-Life Care in Nursing Homes*, J. Am. Geriatric Soc'y 1235 (1998).

[248.1] Assisted Suicide Funding Restriction Act, 42 U.S.C.A. § 14406:

    [The PSDA] shall not be construed—

    (1) to require any provider, organization, or any employee to inform or counsel any individual regarding any right to obtain an item or service furnished for the purpose of causing, or the purpose of assisting in causing, the death of the individual, such as by assisted suicide, euthanasia, or mercy killing; or

    (2) to apply to or to affect any requirement with respect to a portion of an advance directive that directs the purposeful causing of, or the purposeful assisting in causing, the death of any individual, such as by assisted suicide, euthanasia, or mercy killing.

[248.2] See § **9.38** in the main volume and this supplement.

[248.3] *Federal Law Mandates Providers Inform Patients of Pain Treatment Options*, 8 BNA's Health L. Rep. 1157 (1999).

Page 54, add at end of section:

However, there is some evidence that the Act has increased the rate at which individuals execute advance directives.[264.1]

§ 10.22 Enforcement in Medical Emergencies

Page 55, add to footnote 266:

MA: *But cf. In re* Shine v. Vega, 709 N.E.2d 58 (Mass. 1999) (even in life-threatening emergency, repeated refusals of treatment by patient must be honored if patient is competent, or family's substituted judgment, if patient is not).

Page 55, add to footnote 269:

MA: *In re* Shine v. Vega, 709 N.E.2d 58, 64 n.20 (Mass. 1999) (relying on comment to Restatement (Second) Torts § 892D(b) (1977), stating that "'[i]f the actor knows or has reason to know, because of past refusals or other circumstances, that the consent would not be given, he is not privileged to act.'").

Page 57, replace Ohio citation in footnote 275 with:

OH: Anderson v. St. Francis-St. George Hosp., 614 N.E.2d 841 (Ohio Ct. App. 1992), *opinion on remand,* No. C-930819, 1995 WL 109128 (Ohio Ct. App. Mar. 15, 1995), *rev'd on other grounds,* 671 N.E.2d 225 (Ohio 1996).

§ 10.30 Probative Value (Weight)

Page 68, add to footnote 327:

ND: *See* Gabrynowicz v. Heitkamp, 904 F. Supp. 1061, 1062 n.1 (D.N.D. 1995) ("A declaration executed under the statute does not obligate a physician to do anything, but it is 'presumptive evidence of the declarant's desires . . . and must be given great weight by the physician in determining the intent of the incompetent declarant.'"; construing N.D. Cent. Code § 23-06.4-04).

[264.1] *See* Elizabeth Bradley et al., *The Patient Self-Determination Act and Advance Directive Completion in Nursing Homes,* 7 Archives Family Med. 417 (1998) (finding that more than one-third of nursing home records indicated existence of advance directive, in comparison with less than 5% prior to passage of PSDA).

Page 69, add to footnote 332:

MI: Martin v. Martin, 538 N.W.2d 399, 411 (Mich. 1995).

Page 69, add to footnote 334:

MI: Martin v. Martin, 538 N.W.2d 399, 411 (Mich. 1995).

Page 69, add to footnote 336:

MI: Martin v. Martin, 538 N.W.2d 399, 411 (Mich. 1995).

§ 10.31   —Specificity of the Directive

Page 70, add to footnote 338:

MI: Martin v. Martin, 538 N.W.2d 399, 411 (Mich. 1995).

Page 71, add note 342.1 reference at end of first sentence of first full paragraph and add note 342.1:

342.1 **MI:** *But see* Martin v. Martin, 538 N.W.2d 399 (Mich. 1995) ("Statements made in response to seeing or hearing about another's prolonged death do not fulfill the clear and convincing standard.").

NY: *But see In re* Westchester County Medical Ctr. (O'Connor), 531 N.E.2d 607 (N.Y. 1988) (same).

§ 10.34   Standard of Proof

Page 76, add to footnote 367:

MI: Martin v. Martin, 538 N.W.2d 399, 410 n.22 (Mich. 1995).

Bibliography

Ackerman, T. "Forsaking the Spirit for the Letter of Law: Advance Directives in Nursing Homes." *Journal of the American Geriatrics Society* 45 (1997): 114.

Benson, J., and R. Austin. "The Impact of Advance Medical Directives on Distribution of Estate Assets under the Simultaneous Death Act." *Elder Law Journal* 5 (1997): 1.

Bradley, E., et al. "The Patient Self-Determination Act and Advance Directive Completion in Nursing Homes." *Archives of Family Medicine* 7 (1998): 417.

Bradley, E., et al. "Assessing Capacity to Participate in Discussions of Advance Directives in Nursing Homes: Findings from a Study of the Patient Self Determination Act." *Journal of the American Geriatrics Society* 45 (1997): 79.

Brock, D. "Advance Directives: What Is It Reasonable to Expect from Them?" *Journal of Clinical Ethics* 5 (1994): 57.

Cantor, N. "Making Advance Directives Meaningful." *Psychology, Public Policy and Law* 4 (1998): 629.

Cerminara, K. "Eliciting Patient Preferences in Today's Health Care System." *Psychology, Public Policy and Law* 4 (1998): 688.

Culver, C. "Advance Directives." *Psychology, Public Policy and Law* 4 (1998): 676.

DeGrazia, D. "Advance Directives, Dementia, and 'The Someone Else Problem.'" *Bioethics* 13 (1999): 373.

Department of Health and Human Services, General Accounting Office. "Providers, HHS Focus on Living Wills, but Few Patients Have Arrangements." *BNA's Health Law Reporter* 4 (1995): 1377.

Dresser, R. "Confronting the 'Near Irrelevance' of Advance Directives." *Journal of Clinical Ethics* 5 (1994): 55.

Emanuel, L. "Advance Directives: What Have We Learned So Far?" *Journal of Clinical Ethics* 4 (1993): 8.

Ganzini, L., et al. "Is the Patient Self-Determination Act Appropriate for Elderly Persons Hospitalized for Depression?" *Journal of Clinical Ethics* 4 (1993): 46.

General Accounting Office, "Patient Self-Determination Act: Providers Offer Information on Advance Directives but Effectiveness Uncertain." Gaithersburg, Md. (info@www.gao.gov).

Goodman, K. "End-of-Life Algorithms." *Psychology, Public Policy and Law* 4 (1998): 719.

Hanson, L., and E. Rodgman. "The Use of Living Wills at the End of Life." *Archives of Internal Medicine* 156 (1996): 1018.

Hoffman, D., et al. "The Dangers of Directives or the False Security of Forms." *Journal of Law, Medicine and Ethics* 24 (1996): 5.

Hoffman, D., et al. "How Close Is Enough? Family Relationships and Attitudes Toward Advance Directives and Life-Sustaining Treatments." *Journal of Ethics, Law, and Aging* 3 (1997): 5.

BIBLIOGRAPHY

Horttor, B. "A Survey of Living Will and Advanced Health Care Directives." *North Dakota Law Review* 74 (1998): 233.

Howe, E. "The Vagaries of Patients' and Families' Discussing Advance Directives." *Journal of Clinical Ethics* 4 (1993): 3.

Iserson, K. "A Simplified Prehospital Advance Directive Law: Arizona's Approach." *Annals of Emergency Medicine* 22 (1993): 1703.

Kapp, M. "'A Place Like That': Advance Directives and Nursing Home Admissions." *Psychology, Public Policy and Law* 4 (1998): 805.

Larson, E., and T. Eaton. "The Limits of Advance Directives: A History and Assessment of the Patient Self-Determination Act." *Wake Forest Law Review* 32 (1997): 249.

Lieberson, A. "Commentary: Advance Medical Directives — 1998: A Medical View." *Quinnipiac Probate Law Journal* 12 (1998): 305.

Loue, S. "Living Wills, Durable Powers of Attorney for Health Care, and HIV Infection." *Journal of Legal Medicine* 16 (1995): 461.

Mackler, A., ed. *Jewish Medical Directives for Health Care*. New York: Rabbinical Assembly, 1994.

McIntyre, K. "Loosening Criteria for Witholding Prehospital Cardiopulmonary Resuscitation." *Archives of Internal Medicine* 153 (1993): 2189.

Mezey, M., et al. "Implementation of the Patient Self-Determination Act (PSDA) in Nursing Homes in New York City." *Journal of the American Geriatrics Society* 45 (1997): 43.

Miles, S., "Advance Directives to Limit Treatment: The Need for Portability." *Journal of the American Geriatric Society* 35 (1987): 74.

Miles, S., et al. "Advance End-of-Life Treatment Planning: A Research Review." *Archives of Internal Medicine* 156 (1996): 1062.

Miller, R. "Advance Directives for Psychiatric Treatment: A View from the Trenches." *Psychology, Public Policy and Law* 4 (1998): 728.

Parri, R. "If I Call 911, Is My Living Will Any Good? The Living Will v. The DNRO." *Florida Bar Journal* 70 (1996): 82.

Pope, T. "The Maladaptation of Miranda to Advance Directives: A Critique of the Patient Self Determination Act." *Health Matrix: Journal of Law-Medicine* 9 (1999): 139.

Rich, B. "Personhood, Patienthood, and Clinical Practice: Reassessing Advance Directives." *Psychology, Public Policy and Law* 4 (1998): 610.

Sachs, G. "Improving Advance Directives: More Dialogue, Not More Laws." *Journal of Clinical Ethics* 4 (1993): 171.

Sachs, G., et al. "Limiting Resuscitation: Emerging Policy in the Emergency Medical System." *Annals of Internal Medicine* 114 (1991): 151.

Sass, H-M, et al., eds. *Advance Directives and Surrogate Decision Making in Health Care: United States, Germany, and Japan.* Baltimore, MD: Johns Hopkins University Press, 1998.

Shewchuk, T. "Completing Advance Directives for Health Care Decisions: Getting to Yes." *Psychology, Public Policy and Law* 4 (1998): 703.

Silberfeld, M., et al. "Capacity to Complete an Advance Directive." *Journal of the American Geriatric Society* 41 (1993): 1141.

Steinberg, M.A., et al. *Patient Self-Determination in Terminal Care: Phase 2: Designing "Useful" Advance Directives and Proxies.* Herston, Queensland, Australia: Department of Social and Preventive Medicine, School of Medicine, University of Queensland, 1997.

The SUPPORT Principal Investigators. "A Controlled Trial to Improve Care for Seriously Ill Hospitalized Patients." *Journal of the American Medical Association* 274 (1995): 1591.

Tarantino, L. "Withdrawal of Life Support: Conflict Among Patient Wishes, Family, Physicians, Courts and Statutes, and the Law." *Buffalo Law Review* 42 (1994): 623.

Teno, J., et al. "Advance Directives for Seriously Ill Hospitalized Patients: Effectiveness with the Patient Self-Determination Act and the SUPPORT Intervention." *Journal of the American Geriatric Society* 45 (1997): 500.

Teno, J., et al. "Do Advance Directives Provide Instructions That Direct Care?" *Journal of the American Geriatric Society* 45 (1997): 508.

Teno, J., et al. "The Illusion of End-of-Life Resource Savings with Advance Directives." *Journal of the American Geriatrics Society* 45 (1997): 513.

Thomas, D. et al. "Advance Directives in a Correctional Setting." *Psychology, Public Policy and Law* 4 (1998): 878.

Ulrich, L. *The Patient Self-Determination Act: Meeting the Challenges in Patient Care.* Washington, DC: Georgetown University Press, 1999.

Waldman, E. "Application of PSDA to Psychiatric Facilities." *BioLaw* 11 (1992): S:857.

Winick, B. "Advance Directive Instruments for Those with Mental Illness." *University of Miami Law Review* 51 (1996): 57.

Winick, B. "Client Denial and Resistance in the Advance Directive Context: Reflections on How Attorneys Can Identify and Deal with a Psycholegal Soft Spot." *Psychology, Public Policy and Law* 4 (1998): 901.

BIBLIOGRAPHY

Winick, B. "Foreword: Planning for the Future Through Advance Directive Instruments." *Psychology, Public Policy and Law* 4 (1998): 579.

Wood, W. "Advance Directives: Religious, Moral, and Theological Aspects." *Elder Law Journal* 7 (1999): 457.

CHAPTER 11

STATUTORY LIVING WILLS

§ 11.1 Purpose

Page 83, replace Delaware and Maine citations in footnote 7 with:

DE: Del. Code Ann. tit. 16, § 2505 (form, part 2) (modification of UHCDA provision).

ME: *Accord* Me. Rev. Stat. Ann. tit. 18-A, § 5-804 (allows choice to prolong life as long as possible within limits of generally accepted health care standards).

Page 84, add to footnote 7:

NM: *Accord* N.M. Stat. Ann. § 24-7A-2 (adopting UHCDA).

OH: Anderson v. St. Francis-St. George Hosp., No. C-930819, 1995 WL 109128, at *4 (Ohio Ct. App. Mar. 15, 1995), *appeal allowed*, 652 N.E.2d 800 (Ohio 1995) ("[L]egislative enactments of the right to make advance directives about health care when terminally ill is not limited to the right to refuse treatment. The same laws give a person the right to choose extraordinary and heroic measures to preserve his or her life at any cost.").

Accord UHCDA § 4.

Page 84, add to footnote 8:

LA: *See, e.g., In re* Lebreton v. Rabito, 650 So. 2d 1245 (La. Ct. App. 1995) (adult daughter of patient from whom life-sustaining medical treatment had been removed alleged that she had authority to require continuation of treatment under surrogate decisionmaking provisions of living will statute).

Page 84, delete Maine citation from footnote 11.

Page 85, replace Texas citation in carryover footnote 11 with:

TX: *Accord* Tex. Health & Safety Code Ann. § 672.009 (for advance directives executed before Sept. 1, 1999); Tex. Health & Safety Code Ann. § 166.039 (for directives executed thereafter).

§ 11.3 Statutory Living Will Form

Page 85, delete "Delaware" and "New Mexico" in first sentence of section.

Pages 85–86, replace Alabama, Delaware, Florida, Hawaii, Maine, Mississippi, and Texas citations in footnote 13 with:

AL: Ala. Code § 22-8A-4(h) ("substantially in the following form").

DE: Del. Code Ann. tit. 16, § 2518 ("Nothing in this chapter shall be construed to limit the use of any . . . form which meets the requirements of this chapter.").

FL: Fla. Stat. Ann. § 765.303(1) ("may, BUT NEED NOT, be in the following form").

HI: 1999 Haw. Sess. Laws 169, Sec. 1, § 16 (form) ("may be used to create . . . may be modified . . . or a completely different form may be used") (modifying UHCDA).

ME: Me. Rev. Stat. Ann. tit. 18-A, § 5-804 (section titled optional form; "following form may, but need not, be used").

MS: Miss. Code Ann. § 41-41-209 ("form may be used") (adopting UHCDA).

TX: Tex. Health & Safety Code Ann. § 672.004 (for advance directives executed before Sept. 1, 1999); Tex. Health & Safety Code Ann. § 166.033 (for directives executed thereafter).

Page 86, add to footnote 13:

GU: 10 Guam Code Ann. § 91,103.

MN: Minn. Stat. Ann. § 145B.04, 145C.16.

RI: R.I. Gen. Laws § 23-4.11-3(d) (1998) ("declaration may, but need not, be in the following form").

Page 86, replace West Virginia citation in carryover footnote 13 with:

WV: W. Va. Code § 16-30-4(g).

§ 11.4 Execution by or for Incompetent
(New Title)

Page 87, add at end of section:

The same issue can arise with respect to a health care power of attorney.[16.1]

[16.1] See § **12.7** in this supplement, discussing *In re* Mason, 669 N.E.2d 1081 (Mass. App. Ct. 1996).

The fact that a statute provides—as most do[16.2]—that an advance directive may be revoked, suspended, or reinstated by a person who lacks decision-making capacity still does not permit an incompetent person to make an advance directive to begin with.[16.3] However, an advance directive executed by an incompetent may still be evidence of that person's wishes.[16.4]

§ 11.5   Execution by or for Minor

Page 87, delete New Mexico citation from footnote 17.

Page 87, replace Texas citation in footnote 17 with:

TX: Tex. Health & Safety Code Ann. § 672.006 (for advance directives executed before Sept. 1, 1999); Tex. Health & Safety Code Ann. § 166.035 (for directives executed thereafter).

§ 11.6   Witnesses

Page 88, replace Alabama and West Virginia citations in footnote 24 with:

AL: Ala. Code § 22-8A-4(c)(4) (related to the declarant neither by blood, adoption, nor marriage).
WV: W. Va. Code § 16-30-4(b)(2).

Page 88, delete Hawaii and Mississippi citations from footnote 24.

Page 88, replace Louisiana citation in footnote 24 with:

LA: La. Rev. Stat. Ann. § 40:1299.58.2(15) (related to declarant or qualified patient by blood or marriage).

Page 88, add to footnote 24:

RI: R.I. Gen. Laws § 23-4.11-3(a) (1998) (witnesses may not be related to declarant by blood or marriage).

Page 88, add to footnote 25:

HI: 1999 Haw. Sess. Laws 169, Sec. 1, § 3(d) (modifying UHCDA).

[16.2]   See § **11.4** in the main volume.

[16.3]   **NJ:** *In re* Roche, 687 A.2d 349 (N.J. Super. Ct. Ch. Div. 1996).

[16.4]   *Id*. See § **7.45** in the main volume and this supplement.

TX: Tex. Health & Safety Code Ann. § 6724.003(c)(2) (for advance directives executed before Sept. 1, 1999); Tex. Health & Safety Code Ann. § 166.003(2) (for directives executed thereafter).

Page 89, replace Alabama, Texas, and West Virginia citations in footnote 27 with:

AL: Ala. Code § 22-8A-4(c)(4).

TX: Tex. Health & Safety Code Ann. § 6724.003(c)(3) (for advance directives executed before Sept. 1, 1999); Tex. Health & Safety Code Ann. § 166.003(2) (for directives executed thereafter).

WV: W. Va. Code § 16-30-4(b)(3).

Page 89, replace Louisiana citation in footnote 27 with:

LA: La. Rev. Stat. Ann. § 40:1299.58.2(15).

Page 89, delete Mississippi citation from footnote 27.

Page 89, add to footnote 27:

GU: 10 Guam Code Ann. § 91,103.

Page 90, delete Mississippi citation from footnote 28.

Page 90, replace Hawaii, Texas, and West Virginia citations in footnote 28 with:

HI: 1999 Haw. Sess. Laws 169, Sec. 1, § 3(c) (modifying UHCDA).

TX: Tex. Health & Safety Code Ann. § 672.003(c)(4), (5) (for advance directives executed before Sept. 1, 1999); Tex. Health & Safety Code Ann. § 166.003(2) (for directives executed thereafter).

WV: W. Va. Code § 16-30-4(b)(5).

Page 90, add to footnote 28:

GU: 10 Guam Code Ann. § 91,103.

Page 90–91, replace Delaware, Hawaii, and Texas citations in footnote 29 with:

DE: Del. Code Ann. tit. 16, § 2503(b)(1)(D)(v) (modification of UHCDA provision).

HI: 1999 Haw. Sess. Laws 169, Sec. 1, § 3(c)(2) (modifying UHCDA).

TX: Tex. Health & Safety Code Ann. § 672.003(c)(6) (for advance directives executed before Sept. 1, 1999); Tex. Health & Safety Code Ann. § 166.003(2) (for directives executed thereafter).

Page 90, delete Mississippi citation from footnote 29.

Page 91, replace Delaware citation in footnote 30 with:

DE: Del. Code Ann. tit. 16, § 2503(b)(1)(D)(iv) (modification of UHCDA provision).

Page 91, delete West Virginia citation from footnote 30.

Page 91, add to footnote 31:

HI: 1999 Haw. Sess. Laws 169, Sec. 1, § 3(c)(3) (modifying UHCDA).
TX: Tex. Health & Safety Code Ann. § 672.003(c)(1) (for advance directives executed before Sept. 1, 1999); Tex. Health & Safety Code Ann. § 166.003(2) (for directives executed thereafter).

Page 92, add to footnote 33:

GU: *Accord* 10 Guam Code Ann. § 91,104.

§ 11.7   Notarization

Page 92, replace Hawaii and West Virginia citations in footnote 36 with:

HI: 1999 Haw. Sess. Laws 169, Sec. 1, § 3(b) (modifying UHCDA).
WV: W. Va. Code § 16-30-4(5).

§ 11.8   Recitals

Page 93, delete Hawaii and Mississippi citations from footnote 39.

Page 93, replace West Virginia and Texas citations in footnote 39 with:

TX: Tex. Health & Safety Code Ann. § 672.004 (for advance directives executed before Sept. 1, 1999); Tex. Health & Safety Code Ann. § 166.033 (for directives executed thereafter).
WV: W. Va. Code § 16-30-4.

Page 93, add to footnote 39:

GU: 10 Guam Code Ann. § 91,103(a).

Page 94, delete Maine and Mississippi citations from footnote 40.

Page 94, replace Hawaii citation in footnote 40 with:

HI: 1999 Haw. Sess. Laws 169, Sec. 1, § 16(14)(a) (form, part 4) (modifying UHCDA).

Page 94, add to footnote 40:

DE: Del. Code Ann. tit. 16, § 2505(12) (modification of UHCDA provision).

§ 11.9   Incompetence; Terminal Illness or Permanent Unconsciousness

Page 95, add note 41.1 reference at end of first full sentence and add note 41.1:

[41.1] *Cf.* Allore v. Flower Hosp., No. L-96-329, 1997 WL 362465, at *3 (Ohio Ct. App. June 27, 1997) (implying that liability should be denied to estate of patient treated seemingly contrary to advance directive because he was not "terminally ill" though he died within an hour).

Page 95, replace Alabama, Alaska, Louisiana, Texas, and West Virginia citations in footnote 42 with:

AL: Ala. Code § 22-8A-3(10).
AK: Alaska Stat. § 18.12.100(11).
LA: La. Rev. Stat. Ann. §§ 40:1299.58.2(12), .58.2(9).
TX: Tex. Health & Safety Code Ann. § 672.002(8) (for advance directives executed before Sept. 1, 1999); Tex. Health & Safety Code Ann. § 166.031(2) (for directives executed thereafter).
WV: W. Va. Code § 16-30-2(4).

Page 95, add to footnote 42:

DE: Del. Code Ann. tit. 16, § 2501(r) (modification of UHCDA provision) (living will is effective upon declarant's incapacity; however, declarant must have "qualifying condition" for living will to apply to forgoing life-sustaining treatment).
FL: Fla. Stat. Ann. § 765.302(1).
GU: 10 Guam Code Ann. § 91,102(j).
ME: *But see* Me. Rev. Stat. Ann. tit. 18-A, §§ 5-801 to -816 (contains no requirement of terminal illness or permanent unconsciousness).

NM: *But see* N.M. Stat. Ann. §§ 24-7A-1 to -18 (adopting UHCDA).
RI: R.I. Gen. Laws § 23-4.11-2 (1998).
SD: S.D. Codified Laws Ann. § 34-12D-1(8).

Page 95, delete Alabama citation from footnote 43.

Page 95, add at end of page:

Some statutes permit termination of treatment for a patient who is neither terminally ill nor permanently unconscious but is in an "end stage condition."[43.1]

Page 96, add to footnote 43:

GU: 10 Guam Code Ann. § 91,102(h).
SD: S.D. Codified Laws Ann. § 34-12D-1(7).

Page 96, replace Louisiana and Rhode Island citations in footnote 43 with:

LA: La. Rev. Stat. Ann. § 40:1299.58.2(12), .58.2(9).
RI: R.I. Gen. Laws § 23-4.11-2(11) (1998).

Page 96, add to footnote 44:

DE: *But see In re* Gordy, 658 A.2d 613 (Del. Ch. 1994) (when patient is competent but competence is diminished, living will offers corroboration for patient's recent statements concerning treatment refusal that did not result from her diminished capacity).
OH: Anderson v. St. Francis-St. George Hosp., 1995 WL 109128, at *3 (Ohio Ct. App. Mar. 15, 1995), *rev'd,* 671 N.E.2d 225 (Ohio 1996).
RI: R.I. Gen. Laws § 23-4.11-3(c) (1998) (declaration effective only when communicated to attending physician, attending physician determines declarant is in terminal condition, and declarant is unable to make treatment decisions).

Page 96, replace footnote 45 with:

AL: *See, e.g.,* Ala. Code § 22-8A-7(a) ("The desires of an individual shall at all times supersede the effect of an advance directive for health care.").

[43.1] **MD:** Md. Code Ann., Health-Gen. § 5-606(b) (defined by § 601(i) as "an advanced, progressive, irreversible condition caused by injury, disease, or illness: (1) That has caused severe and permanent deterioration indicated by incompetency and complete physical dependency; and (2) For which, to a reasonable degree of medical certainty, treatment of the irreversible condition would be medically ineffective.").

§ 11.9 INCOMPETENCE, TERMINAL ILLNESS

Page 96, replace Alabama, Alaska, Delaware, Louisiana, Maine, and Rhode Island citations in footnote 46 with:

AL: Ala. Code § 22-8A-3(14).
AK: Alaska Stat. § 18.12.100(11).
DE: Del. Code Ann. tit. 16, § 2501(r)(1) (modification of UHCDA provision).
LA: La. Rev. Stat. Ann. § 40:1299.58.2(14).
ME: Me. Rev. Stat. Ann. tit. 18-A, § 5-801(r).
RI: R.I. Gen. Laws § 23-4.11-2(13) (1998).

Page 96, delete Hawaii and Mississippi citations from footnote 46.

Page 97, add to footnote 46:

GU: 10 Guam Code Ann. § 91,102(j).
SD: S.D. Codified Laws Ann. § 34-12D-1(8).

Page 97, replace Texas and West Virginia citations in footnote 46 with:

TX: Tex. Health & Safety Code Ann. § 672.002(9) (for advance directives executed before Sept. 1, 1999); Tex. Health & Safety Code Ann. § 166.022(13) (for directives executed thereafter).
WV: W. Va. Code § 16-30-6(d).

Page 97, delete Florida and Hawaii citations from footnote 47.

Page 97, replace Louisiana citation in footnote 47 with:

LA: La. Rev. Stat. Ann. § 40:1299.58.2(14).

Page 97, add to footnote 47:

CA9: *See* Compassion in Dying v. Washington, 79 F.3d 790, 816 n.70 (9th Cir. 1996) (citing first edition of this treatise).
SD: S.D. Codified Laws Ann. § 34-12D-1(8).

Page 97, delete Arkansas and Maine citations from footnote 48.

Page 98, add to footnote 48:

DE: Del. Code Ann. tit. 16, § 2501(r) (modification of UHCDA provision).
GU: 10 Guam Code Ann. § 91,102(h).

Page 98, replace Texas citation in footnote 48 with:

TX : Tex. Health & Safety Code Ann. § 672.002(8) (for advance directives executed before Sept. 1, 1999); Tex. Health & Safety Code Ann. § 166.031(2) (for directives executed thereafter).

Page 97, delete last sentence and carryover sentence on page 98 and footnote 49.

Page 98, replace Arkansas and Maine citations in footnote 50 with:

AR: Ark. Code Ann. § 20-17-201(6).
ME: Me. Rev. Stat. Ann. tit. 18-A, § 5-801(s).

Page 98, add to footnote 50:

AL: Ala. Code § 22-8A-3(10).
DE: Del. Code Ann. tit. 16, § 2501(r)(2) (modification of UHCDA provision).
GU: 10 Guam Code Ann. § 91,102(e) (permanent unconscious condition).

Page 98, add to footnote 51:

ME: *Accord* Me. Rev. Stat. Ann. tit. 18-A, §§ 5-802(a), 5-804.
NM: *Accord* N.M. Stat. Ann. §§ 24-7A-2(a), -4.

Page 99, add at end of **"Terminal Condition"** *subsection:*

One court has implicitly acknowledged the very limitation that the terminal condition requirement imposes and worked its way around the requirement. In *In re* Gordy[58.1] the court was confronted with a living will executed by a woman suffering from Alzheimer's disease. The state attorney general opposed the implementation of the living will, which would have prevented the implantation of a feeding tube and led to the patient's death, on the ground that the patient was not in a terminal condition. Although the court accepted the evidence of one physician that the patient was in a terminal condition, it seemed willing to ignore the requirement on the ground that "Alzheimer's disease will cause her death"[58.2] regardless of how imminently it will do so.

Pages 99–100, replace Alabama, Alaska, Delaware, Florida, Louisiana, Maine, Rhode Island, and West Virginia citations in footnote 59 with:

AL: Ala. Code § 22-8A-3(8).
AK: Alaska Stat. § 18.12.100(8).

[58.1] **DE:** 658 A.2d 613 (Del. Ch. 1994).

[58.2] *Id.* at 617 n.6.

DE: *Cf.* Del. Code Ann. tit. 16, § 2501(l)(1) (life-sustaining procedure is any "medical procedure, treatment, or intervention [which] utilizes mechanical or other artificial means to sustain, restore, or supplant a spontaneous vital function and is of such a nature as to afford a patient no reasonable expectation of recovery") (modification of UHCDA provision).

FL: Fla. Stat. Ann. § 765.101(10).

LA: La. Rev. Stat. Ann. § 40:1299.58.2(9).

ME: Me. Rev. Stat. Ann. tit. 18-A, § 5-801(r).

RI: R.I. Gen. Laws § 23-4.11-2(8) (1998).

WV: W. Va. Code § 16-30-3(m).

Page 100, delete Hawaii, Mississippi, and Texas citations from footnote 59.

Page 100, delete New Mexico citation from carryover footnote 59.

Page 100, add to footnote 59:

GU: 10 Guam Code Ann. § 91,102(d).

SD: S.D. Codified Laws Ann. § 34-12D-1(4).

§ 11.11 Pregnancy

Page 102, replace Alabama, Delaware, and Texas citations in footnote 64 with:

AL: Ala. Code § 22-8A-4(e).

DE: Del. Code Ann. tit. 16, § 2503(j) (modification of UHCDA provision).

TX: Tex. Health & Safety Code Ann. § 672.019 (for advance directives executed before Sept. 1, 1999); Tex. Health & Safety Code Ann. § 166.049 (for directives executed thereafter).

Page 102, delete Mississippi citation from footnote 64.

Page 102, add to footnote 64:

GU: 10 Guam Code Ann. § 91,108(c).

ND: *Discussed in* Gabrynowicz v. Heitkamp, 904 F. Supp. 1061 (D.N.D. 1995).

SD: S.D. Codified Laws § 34-12D-10 (unless life-sustaining treatment or artificial nutrition and hydration would not permit continued development of unborn child, would be physically harmful to woman, or would prolong severe pain that cannot be alleviated by medication).

Page 102, add to footnote 65:

DND: *See* Gabrynowicz v. Heitkamp, 904 F. Supp. 1061, 1064 (D.N.D. 1995) (though not ripe for adjudication, statutory prohibition on enforcement of living will for pregnant patient "raise[s] constitutional questions").

Page 103, add to footnote 66:

DE: Del. Code Ann. tit. 16, § 2503(j) (if fetus could develop to viability if life-sustaining treatment were continued) (modification of UHCDA provision).

§ 11.12   Nutrition and Hydration

Page 103, add to footnote 69:

GU: *See also* 10 Guam Code Ann. § 91,102(d).

Pages 103–04, delete Arizona, Maine, and Nevada citations from footnote 70.

Page 104, add to footnote 70:

FL: Fla. Stat. Ann. § 765.101(10).
LA: La. Rev. Stat. Ann. § 40:1299.58.2.
WI: *Construed in* Edna M.F. v. Eisenberg, 563 N.W.2d 485, 490 (Wis. 1997) (dictum).

Page 104, add to footnote 76:

ME: Me. Rev. Stat. Ann. tit. 18-A, § 5-804 (form part 2, § 7).
NM: N.M. Stat. Ann. § 24-7A-4 (form part 2, § 7).
UHCDA § 4 (form part 2, § 7).

Pages 105, delete Hawaii citation from footnote 77.

Page 105, replace Louisiana and Maine citations in footnote 77 with:

LA: La. Rev. Stat. Ann. § 40:1299.58.2(9).
ME: Me. Rev. Stat. Ann. tit. 18-A, § 5-801(r).

Page 105, add to footnote 77:

DE: Del. C ode Ann. tit. 16, § 2501(h)(3) (modification of UHCDA provision).

NM: N.M. Stat. Ann. § 24-7A-1(G)(3).
UHCDA § 1(6)(iii).

Page 105, replace Hawaii and Maine citations in footnote 78 with:

HI: 1999 Haw. Sess. Laws 169, Sec. 1, § 16(7) (form, part 2) (modifying UHCDA).
ME: Me. Rev. Stat. Ann. tit. 18-A, § 5-804.

Page 105, add to footnote 78:

NM: N.M. Stat. Ann. § 24-7A-4.

Page 106, replace Delaware, Maine, and Mississippi citations in footnote 79 with:

DE: Del. Code Ann. tit. 16, § 2505 (sample form, part 2) (modification of UHCDA provision).
ME: Me. Rev. Stat. Ann. tit. 18-A, § 5-804 (form part 2, § 7).
MS: Miss. Code Ann. § 41-41-209 (form) (adopting UHCDA).

Page 106, add to footnote 79:

AL: Ala. Code § 22-8A-4 (sample form).
NM: N.M. Stat. Ann. § 24-7A-4 (form part 2, § 7).
UHCDA § 4 (form part 2, § 7).

Page 107, add to footnote 83:

CA9:   Compassion in Dying v. Washington, 79 F.3d 790, 816 n.70 (9th Cir. 1996) (citing first edition of this treatise).

§ 11.12A   Mental Health Treatment (New)

A number of states have enacted statutes, or amended existing advance directive statutes, authorizing advance directives for mental health treatment. These are discussed in § **12.29A.**

§ 11.13   Duration of Directive

Page 107, add to footnote 84:

FL: *But see* Fla. Stat. Ann. § 765.104(1) ("advance directive or designation of a surrogate may be amended or revoked at any time by a *competent* principal") (emphasis added).

ME: Me. Rev. Stat. Ann. tit. 18-A, § 5-803(b) (adopting UHCDA).
NM: N.M. Stat. Ann. § 24-7A-3(A) (adopting UHCDA).

Page 108, add to footnote 88:

ME: Me. Rev. Stat. Ann. tit. 18-A, § 5-802(h) (adopting UHCDA).
NM: *Accord* N.M. Stat. Ann. § 24-7A-16(A).

§ 11.14   Revocation

Page 108, replace Hawaii and Texas citations in footnote 91 with:

HI: 1999 Haw. Sess. Laws 169, Sec. 1, § 4(b) (modifying UHCDA).
TX: Tex. Health & Safety Code Ann. § 672.007 (for advance directives executed before Sept. 1, 1999); Tex. Health & Safety Code Ann. § 166.037 (for directives executed thereafter).

Page 108, add to footnote 91:

FL: *But see* Fla. Stat. Ann. § 765.104(1) ("advance directive or designation of a surrogate may be amended or revoked at any time by a *competent* principal") (emphasis added).
GU: 10 Guam Code Ann. § 91,106(a).

Page 109, add to footnote 93:

RI: R.I. Gen. Laws § 23-4.11-4(a)(1) (1998).

Page 109, add to footnote 94:

ME: *Accord* Me. Rev. Stat. Ann. tit. 18-A, § 5-803(b) (adopting UHCDA).
NM: *Accord* N.M. Stat. Ann. § 24-7A-3(B) (adopting UHCDA).
RI: R.I. Gen. Laws § 23-4.11-4(a)(1) (1998) (adopting language of UHCDA).

Page 109, add to footnote 95:

ME: Me. Rev. Stat. Ann. tit. 18-A, § 5-803(c) (adopting UHCDA).
NM: N.M. Stat. Ann. § 24-7A-3(E) (adopting UHCDA).
WI: *But see* Wis. Stat. Ann. § 154.05(1)(d) (subsequent declaration fully revokes earlier directive).

§ 11.14A   Conflict Between Living Will and Agent (New)

An issue that has not received much attention, either legislatively[95.1] or in the courts, is how to proceed when the instructions in a living will conflict with the decisions that a patient-appointed surrogate gives, in the absence of a direction in the advance directive itself as to how to resolve such conflicts. This same issue can arise when there is a judicially appointed guardian. As to the latter, a provision of the Virginia guardianship statute prohibits the guardian from overriding "a valid advance directive or durable power of attorney previously executed by the incapacitated person."[95.2]

§ 11.15   Notification to Attending Physician

Page 109, replace Alabama and Texas citations in footnote 96 with:

AL: Ala. Code § 22-8A-4(f).
TX   Tex. Health & Safety Code Ann. § 672.003(e) (for advance directives executed before Sept. 1, 1999); Tex. Health & Safety Code Ann. § 166.032(d) (for directives executed thereafter).

Page 109, delete Hawaii citation from footnote 96.

Page 110, add to footnote 96:

GU: 10 Guam Code Ann. § 91,105(a).

Page 110, replace West Virginia citation in carryover footnote 96 with:

WV: W. Va. Code § 16-30-3(d).

Page 110, replace Texas citaion in footnote 97 with:

TX: Tex. Health & Safety Code Ann. § 672.003(e) (for advance directives executed before Sept. 1, 1999); Tex. Health & Safety Code Ann. § 166.032(d) (for directives executed thereafter).

Page 110, delete first full sentence on page and footnote 98.

Page 110, delete Hawaii citation from footnote 99.

[95.1] **KS:**   Kan. Stat. Ann. § 58-629(b).
   MN: Minn. Stat. Ann. § 145C.01(5).
[95.2] **VA:**   Va. Code Ann. § 37.1-137.1. See also § 12.24 in the main volume and this supplement.

§ 11.16   Filing in Declarant's Medical Record

Pages 110–11, replace Alabama, Hawaii, Mississippi, Texas, West Virginia, and Wisconsin citations in footnote 101 with:

AL: Ala. Code § 22-8A-4(f).

HI: 1999 Haw. Sess. Laws 169, Sec. 1, § 7(b) (modifying UHCDA).

MS: 1998 Miss. Laws ch. 542 (H.B. 546) § 8(2),(3) (adopting UHCDA).

TX: Tex. Health & Safety Code Ann. § 672.003(e) (for advance directives executed before Sept. 1, 1999); Tex. Health & Safety Code Ann. § 166.032(e) (for directives executed thereafter).

WV: W. Va. Code § 16-30-3(d) (imposing duty on "attending physician or health care provider").

WI: Wis. Stat. Ann. §§ 154.03(1), .11(8).

Page 111, add to footnote 101:

DE: Del. Code Ann. tit. 16, § 2508(b) (modification of UHCDA provision).

GU: 10 Guam Code Ann. § 91,103(c).

SD: S.D. Codified Laws Ann. §§ 34-12D-7 to -8.

§ 11.17   Immunity

Page 111, add to footnote 102:

AZ: Ariz. Rev. Stat. Ann. § 36-3205(A).

DE: Del. Code Ann. tit. 16, § 2510(a) (modification of UHCDA provision).

GU: 10 Guam Code Ann. § 91,110(b).

ME: Me. Rev. Stat. Ann. tit. 18-A, § 5-809 (adopting UHCDA).

MS: 1998 Miss. Laws ch. 542 (H.B. 546) § 10(1) (adopting UHCDA).

NM: N.M. Stat. Ann. § 24-7A-9(A) (adopting UHCDA).

TX: Tex. Health & Safety Code Ann. § 672.016(b) (no good faith requirement), *construed in* Stolle v. Baylor College of Med., 981 S.W.2d 709 (Tex. Ct. App. 1998).

§ 11.18   Obligation to Comply or Transfer

Page 112, replace Florida, Hawaii, Maine, Mississippi, New Mexico, Texas, and West Virginia citations in footnote 104 with:

FL: Fla. Stat. Ann. § 765.1105.

HI: 1999 Haw. Sess. Laws 169, Sec. 1, § 7(g) (modifying UHCDA).

ME: Me. Rev. Stat. Ann. tit. 18-A, § 5-807(g)(3) (adopting UHCDA).

MS: 1998 Miss. Laws ch. 542 (H.B. 546) § 8(4), (7) (adopting UHCDA).

NM: N.M. Stat. Ann. § 24-7A-7(G) (adopting UHCDA).

TX: Tex. Health & Safety Code Ann. § 672.016(c) (for conduct before Jan. 1, 2000); *see* Tex. Health & Safety Code Ann. § 166.045(c) (regarding conduct occurring thereafter).

WV: *But see* W. Va. Code § 16-30-12(b)(2) ("The medical power of attorney representative or surrogate decision maker shall have responsibility for arranging the transfer of the person to another health care provider. The individual health care provider shall cooperate in facilitating such transfer.").

Page 113, add to footnote 104:

DE: Del. Code Ann. tit. 16, § 2508(g).

GU: 10 Guam Code Ann. § 91,109.

ME: Me. Rev. Stat. Ann. tit. 18-A, § 5-807(g) (adopting UHCDA).

ND: *Discussed in* Gabrynowicz v. Heitkamp, 904 F. Supp. 1061, 1062 n.1 (D.N.D. 1995) ("A declaration executed under the statute does not obligate a physician to do anything, but it is 'presumptive evidence of the declarant's desires . . . and must be given great weight by the physician in determining the intent of the incompetent declarant.'").

SD: S.D. Codified Laws Ann. § 34-12D-11.
        UHCDA § 7(g).

Page 113, add to footnote 105:

NC: *See, e.g.,* First Healthcare Corp. v. Rettinger, 456 S.E.2d 347 (N.C. Ct. App. 1995), *rev'd,* 467 S.E.2d 243 (N.C. 1996) (wife of patient in nursing home that would not honor patient's advance directive found it impossible to transfer patient).

Page 113, add at end of section:

Physicians and administrators of health care facilities, however, might not be required to comply with a statutorily based advance directive unless statutory formalities are met, especially confirmation of the patient's condition as terminal or permanently unconscious. Thus, in *First Healthcare Corp. v.*

Rettinger,[105.1] the court held that a patient's estate was liable for the costs of treatment rendered to him between the time that his wife attempted to apply his living will to terminate treatment and the issuance of a court order authorizing the termination of treatment. The nursing home was not obligated to terminate treatment until the attending physician and one other physician had complied with the provision of the living will statute requiring their certification that the patient was in a terminal condition.

This decision demonstrates the deficiencies, in some jurisdictions (though not in North Carolina), of statutory advance directives in comparison with nonstatutory advance directives and the deficiencies of living wills in comparison with health care powers of attorney. In many jurisdictions, a patient with a nonstatutory advance directive would not need to observe these formalities. Treatment could have been terminated with the agreement of the attending physician alone.[105.2] However, in North Carolina, the surrogate decisionmaking statute requires the same formalities as does the living will statute. Second, a patient can ignore the health care power of attorney statute and execute a power of attorney based on the general durable power of attorney statute, conferring authority on another to make health care decisions without any requirement that he be terminally ill and avoiding other statutory formalities.

§ 11.19 Penalties

Page 113, delete Maine citation from footnote 106.

Page 113, add to footnote 106:
GU: 10 Guam Code Ann. § 91,111(a) (felony of third degree).

Page 113, delete Hawaii citation from footnote 107.

Page 114, add to footnote 108:
MS: Miss. Code Ann. § 41-41-221(1) (adopting UHCDA).

Page 114, add to footnote 109:
ME: Me. Rev. Stat. Ann. tit. 18-A, § 5-810 (adopting UHCDA).
NM: N.M. Stat. Ann. § 24-7A-10 (adopting UHCDA).

[105.1] 467 S.E.2d 243 (N.C. 1996), *rev'g* 456 S.E.2d 347 (N.C. Ct. App. 1995).
[105.2] See § **10.13.**

Pages 114, replace Alabama, Florida, Hawaii, Minnesota, and Texas citations in footnote 110 with:

AL: Ala. Code § 22-8A-8(c).

FL: Fla. Stat. Ann. § 765.1115(1) (felony of third degree).

HI: 1999 Haw. Sess. Laws 169, Sec. 1, § 10(b) (damages of $2,500 or actual damages) (modifying UHCDA).

MN: Minn. Stat. Ann. § 145B.105(1) (gross misdemeanor).

TX: Tex. Health & Safety Code Ann. § 672.018(a) (for offense committed before Sept. 1, 1999); *see* Tex. Health & Safety Code Ann. § 166.048(a) (for offense committed thereafter).

Pages 114–15, delete Maine and New Mexico citations from footnote 110.

Pages 115–16, delete Maine, Mississippi, New Mexico, and West Virginia citations from footnote 112.

Pages 115–16, replace Alabama, Florida, Minnesota, and Texas citations in footnote 112 with:

AL: Ala. Code § 22-8A-8(d).

FL: Fla. Stat. Ann. § 765.1115(2) (felony of second degree).

MN: Minn. Stat. Ann. § 145B.105(2) (felony).

TX: Tex. Health & Safety Code Ann. § 672.018(b) (for offense committed before Sept. 1, 1999); *see* Tex. Health & Safety Code Ann. § 166.048(b) (for offense committed thereafter).

Page 116, delete Hawaii citation from footnote 113.

Page 116, add to footnote 113:

GU: 10 Guam Code Ann. § 91,111 (felony of third degree).

MS: Miss. Code Ann. § 41-41-221(2) (adopting UHCDA).

Page 116, replace footnote 114 with:

Del. Code Ann. tit. 16, § 2513(a), (b) (adopting UHCDA § 11).

Page 116, add at end of section:

For there to be liability, criminal or civil, for forging or falsifying an advance directive, if a patient dies after a forged instrument is honored, the advance directive should be the cause of the forgoing of treatment and thus the cause of death.[114.1]

[114.1] *See* Edwards v. Shumate, 468 S.E.2d 23, 26 (Ga. 1996).

§ 11.20   Execution as Condition of Medical Care
or Insurance

Page 116, add to footnote 115:

GU: 10 Guam Code Ann. § 91,112(b).

Page 117, replace Delaware, Hawaii, Mississippi, and New Mexico citations in footnote 116 with:

DE: Del. Code Ann. § 2512(c).
HI: 1999 Haw. Sess. Laws 169, Sec. 1, § 7(h) (modifying UHCDA).
MS: Miss. Code Ann. § 41-41-215(8) (adopting UHCDA).
NM: N.M. Stat. Ann. § 24-7A-7(H) (adopting UHCDA).

Page 117, delete Maine citation from footnote 116.

Page 117, add to footnote 116:

GU: 10 Guam Code Ann. § 91,112(c).
ME: Me. Rev. Stat. Ann. tit. 18-A, § 5-807(h) (adopting UHCDA).
RI: R.I. Gen. Laws § 23-4.11-10(c) (1998).
SD: S.D. Codified Laws Ann. § 34-12D-16.
          UHCDA § 7(h).

Pages 117–18, replace Delaware, Hawaii, Maine, New Mexico, Texas, and West Virginia citations in footnote 117 with:

DE: Del. Code Ann. § 2512(a).
HI: 1999 Haw. Sess. Laws 169, Sec. 1, § 13(b) (modifying UHCDA).
ME: Me. Rev. Stat. Ann. tit. 18-A, § 5-813(b) (adopting UHCDA).
NM: N.M. Stat. Ann. § 24-7A-13(B) (adopting UHCDA).
TX: Tex. Health & Safety Code Ann. § 672.017 (for actions before before Sept. 1, 1999); *see* Tex. Health & Safety Code Ann. § 166.047(2) (regarding later actions).
WV: W. Va. Code § 16-30-14(b)(c).

Page 117, delete Mississippi citation from footnote 117.

Page 118, add to footnote 117:

GU: 10 Guam Code Ann. § 91,112(a).
SD: S.D. Codified Laws Ann. § 34-12D-14.

§ 11.21 Portability

Page 119, add to footnote 118:

GU: 10 Guam Code Ann. § 91,114.
RI: R.I. Gen. Laws § 23-4.11-12 (1998).
WI: Wis. Stat. Ann. § 154.11(9) (to extent declaration is consistent with laws of Wisconsin).

Page 119, delete Hawaii and Maine citations from footnote 120.

Page 119, add to footnote 120:

DE: Del. Code Ann. § 2516.

Page 119, add to footnote 122:

DND: *See* Gabrynowicz v. Heitkamp, 904 F. Supp. 1061, 1062 n.1 (D.N.D. 1995) ("A declaration executed under the statute does not obligate a physician to do anything, but it is 'presumptive evidence of the declarant's desires . . . and must be given great weight by the physician in determining the intent of the incompetent declarant.'").

Page 119, add to footnote 123:

ME: Me. Rev. Stat. Ann. tit. 18-A, § 5-802(h) (adopting UHCDA).
NM: N.M. Stat. Ann. § 24-7A-16(A) (adopting UHCDA).

§ 11.22 Table of Living Will Statutes

*Page 120, replace **Table 11–1** with:*

Table 11–1

Living Will Statutes

AL:	Ala. Code §§ 22-8A-1 to -10
AK:	Alaska Stat. §§ 18.12.010–.100
AZ:	Ariz. Rev. Stat. Ann. §§ 36-3201 to -3262
AR:	Ark. Code Ann. §§ 20-17-201 to -218
CA:	Cal. Health & Safety Code §§ 7185–7194.5
CO:	Colo. Rev. Stat. §§ 15-18-101 to -113
CT:	Conn. Gen. Stat. Ann. §§ 19a-570 to -580c
DE:	Del. Code Ann. tit. 16, §§ 2501–2517
DC:	D.C. Code Ann. §§ 6-2421 to -2430
FL:	Fla. Stat. Ann. §§ 765.101–.401, .1105, .1115

GA:	Ga. Code Ann. §§ 31-32-1 to -12
GU:	10 Guam Code Ann. §§ 91,100–91,117
HI:	1999 Haw. Sess. Laws 169
ID:	Idaho Code §§ 39-4501 to -4509
IL:	Ill. Ann. Stat. ch. 755, §§ 35/1–10
IN:	Ind. Code Ann. §§ 16-36-4-1 to -21
IA:	Iowa Code Ann. §§ 144A.1–.12
KS:	Kan. Stat. Ann. §§ 65-28,101 to -28,109
KY:	Ky. Rev. Stat. Ann. §§ 311.621–.643
LA:	La. Rev. Stat. Ann. §§ 40:1299.58.1–.10, .60–64[1]
ME:	Me. Rev. Stat. Ann. tit. 18-A, §§ 5-801 to -817
MD:	Md. Code Ann., Health-Gen. §§ 5-601 to -618
MN:	Minn. Stat. Ann. §§ 145B.01–.17
MS:	Miss. Code Ann. § 41-41-201 to -229
MO:	Mo. Ann. Stat. §§ 459.010–.055
MT:	Mont. Code Ann. §§ 50-9-101 to -111, -201 to -206
NE:	Neb. Rev. Stat. §§ 20-401 to -416
NV:	Nev. Rev. Stat. Ann. §§ 449.535–.690
NH:	N.H. Rev. Stat. Ann. §§ 137-H:1–:15
NJ:	N.J. Stat. Ann. §§ 26:2H-53 to -78
NM:	N.M. Stat. Ann. §§ 24-7A-1 to -18
NC:	N.C. Gen. Stat. §§ 90-320 to -323
ND:	N.D. Cent. Code §§ 23-06.4-01 to -14
OH:	Ohio Rev. Code Ann. §§ 2133.01–.15
OK:	Okla. Stat. Ann. tit. 63, §§ 3101.1–.16
OR:	Or. Rev. Stat. §§ 127.505–.660, .995
PA:	Pa. Cons. Stat. Ann. tit. 20, §§ 5401–5416
RI:	R.I. Gen. Laws §§ 23-4.11-1 to -14
SC:	S.C. Code Ann. §§ 44-77-10 to -160
SD:	S.D. Codified Laws Ann. §§ 34-12D-1 to -22
TN:	Tenn. Code Ann. §§ 32-11-101 to -112
TX:	Tex. Health & Safety Code Ann. §§ 166.031-.051[2]
UT:	Utah Code Ann. §§ 75-2-1101 to -1119
VT:	Vt. Stat. Ann. tit. 18, §§ 5251–5262
	Vt. Stat. Ann. tit. 13, § 1801
VA:	Va. Code Ann. §§ 54.1-2981 to -2993
WA:	Wash. Rev. Code Ann. §§ 70.122.010–.920
WV:	W. Va. Code §§ 16-30-1 to -13
WI:	Wis. Stat. Ann. §§ 154.01–.15
WY:	Wyo. Stat. §§ 35-22-101 to -109

---

[1] Advance directive for members of the military

[2] Former law, Tex. Health & Safety Code. Ann. §§ 672.001-.021, continues to govern for any document executed or offense committed before Sept. 1, 1999. Any conduct under subsection (b) § 166.045 that occurs before Jan. 1, 2000, will continue to be governed by Tex. Health & Safety Code Ann. § 672.016.

Bibliography

General

Burch, T. "Incubator or Individual?: The Legal and Policy Deficiencies of Pregnancy Clauses in Living Will and Advance Health Care Directive Statutes." *Maryland Law Review* 54 (1995): 528.

Emanuel, L. "Advance Directives: What Have We Learned So Far?" *Journal of Clinical Ethics* 4 (1993): 8.

Fazel, S., et al. "Assessment of Competence to Complete Advance Directives: Validation of a Patient Centred Approach." *British Medical Journal* 318 (1999): 493.

Hoffmann, D., et al. "The Dangers of Directives or the False Security of Forms." *Journal of Law, Medicine and Ethics* 24 (1996): 5.

Iserson, K. "A Simplified Prehospital Advance Directive Law: Arizona's Approach." *Annals of Emergency Medicine* 22 (1993): 1703.

McIntyre, K. "Loosening Criteria for Withholding Prehospital Cardiopulmonary Resuscitation." *Archives of Internal Medicine* 153 (1993): 2189.

Miles, S. "Advance Directives to Limit Treatment: The Need for Portability." *Journal of the American Geriatric Society* 35 (1987): 74.

Miles, S., et al. "Advance End-of-Life Treatment Planning: A Research Review." *Archives of Internal Medicine* 156 (1996): 1062.

Robb, M. "Living Wills: The Right to Refuse Life Sustaining Medical Treatment—A Right Without a Remedy?" *University of Dayton Law Review* 23 (1997): 169.

Sachs, G., et al. "Limiting Resuscitation: Emerging Policy in the Emergency Medical System." *Annals of Internal Medicine* 114 (1991): 151.

Schonwetter, R., et al. "Life Values, Resuscitation Preferences, and the Applicability of Living Wills in an Older Population." *Journal of the American Geriatric Society* 44(8) (1996): 954.

Winick, B. "Advance Directive Instruments for Those with Mental Illness." *University of Miami Law Review* 51 (1996): 57.

Specific States

FL: Gustitus, T. "Note. A Comparative View of Advance Health Care Directives in Florida and North Carolina." *Quinnipiac Probate Law Journal* 11 (1997): 163; Parri, R. "If I Call 911, Is My Living Will Any Good? The Living Will v. The DNRO." *Florida Bar Journal* 70 (1996): 82.

LA: Neskora, T. "Living Wills and Health Care Powers of Attorney." *Louisiana Bar Journal* 44 (1997): 512.

MD: Hoffmann, D., et al. "The Dangers of Directives or the False Security of Forms." *Journal of Law, Medicine and Ethics* 24 (1996): 5.

NC: Gustitus, T. "Note. A Comparative View of Advance Health Care Directives in Florida and North Carolina." *Quinnipiac Probate Law Journal* 11 (1997): 163; Spargur, J. Note. "*First Healthcare Corp. v. Rettinger:* Are Living Wills Dead in North Carolina?" *Wake Forest Law Review* 32 (1997): 591.

OH: Lederman, A. "A Womb of My Own: A Moral Evaluation of Ohio's Treatment of Pregnant Patients with Living Wills." *Case Western Reserve Law Review* 45 (1994): 351.

TN: Fockler, J. "Should You Use One or Both? Durable Power of Attorney for Health Care and Living Will." *Tennessee Bar Journal* 31 (1995): 14.

CHAPTER 12

HEALTH CARE POWERS OF ATTORNEY (PROXY DIRECTIVES)

§ 12.1 Nature and Purpose of Proxy Directives

Page 127, replace Hawaii and West Virginia citations in footnote 1 with:

HI: 1999 Haw. Sess. Laws 169, Sec. 1, § 16(a) (modifying UHCDA).
WV: W. Va. Code § 16-30-2.

Page 127, add to footnote 1:

AL: Ala. Code § 22-8A-2.
AR: Ark. Stat. Ann. § 20-13-104(B).
MI: Mich. Comp. Laws § 700.5501.
NY: *In re* Lowe, 688 N.Y.S.2d 389, 391 (Sup. Ct. Queens County N.Y. 1999) ("[T]he law is . . . premised upon the same policy as the common law principles—to ensure that an individual's wishes concerning his own health care treatment are followed.").

Page 128, add to footnote 3:

ND: *Cf.* N.D. Cent. Code § 30.1-28-04 ("unless a court . . . decides otherwise, a durable power of attorney for health care . . . takes precedence of any authority to make medical decisions granted to a guardian").
PA: *Cf. In re* Ord, 16 Fiduc. Rep. 2d ___ (C.P. Blair County, Pa. 1994) (refusing to appoint guardian for 93-year-old man, in part because he had executed power of attorney).

Page 128, replace West Virginia citation in footnote 3 with:

WV: W. Va. Code § 16-30-2(a) ("The intent of the Legislature is to establish an effective method for private health care decision making for incapacitated adults, and to provide that the courts should not be the usual venue for making decisions.").

Page 128, delete West Virginia citation from footnote 4.

Page 128, add to footnote 7:

NY: *But see In re* Lowe, 688 N.Y.S.2d 389, 391 (Sup. Ct. Queens County 1999) ("[T]he health care proxy law is a departure from the common law prohibition against allowing health care decisions to be made on behalf of an incompetent person based upon the agent's substituted judgment and/or belief as to the incompetent's best interests").

§ 12.3 — Proxy Directives and Standards for Surrogate Decisionmaking

Page 130, add note 15.1 reference at end of second paragraph and add note 15.1:

Page 132, add to footnote 29:

NY: *Accord In re* Lowe, 688 N.Y.S.2d 389, 391 (Sup. Ct. Queens County 1999).

§ 12.4 Legal Basis for Proxy Directives

Page 133, delete "except Alabama" in second sentence of first paragraph.

§ 12.6 — Powers of Attorney and Durable Powers of Attorney

Page 135, add to carryover paragraph:

A durable power of attorney may also be used to designate a guardian,[36.1] and a court is ordinarily bound to honor that wish.[36.2]

[15.1] **US:** *But see* Cruzan v. Director, 497 U.S. 261, 290 (1990) (O'Connor, J., concurring) (failure to honor patient's intent could be avoided if states were to consider "the patient's appointment of a proxy to make health care decisions on her behalf" . . . "an equally probative source of evidence" as living will).

  MD: *But see* Mack v. Mack, 618 A.2d 744, 757–58 (Md. 1993) (health care power of attorney meets subjective standard or substituted judgment standard) (by implication).

  NY: *But see In re* Westchester County Medical Ctr. (O'Connor), 531 N.E.2d 607, 612 (N.Y. 1988) (same); *In re* Lowe, 688 N.Y.S.2d 389, 391 (Sup. Ct. Queens County 1999) (same).

[36.1] **MA:** *See In re* Smith, 684 N.E.2d 613 (Mass. App. Ct. 1997).

[36.2] *See* Uniform Durable Power of Attorney Act, 3(b), 8 U.L.A. 322 (West 1993).

Page 136, add to footnote 40:

MD: *See* Wright v. Johns Hopkins Health Sys. Corp., 728 A.2d 166, 171 (Md. 1999) (dictum).

§ 12.7   Who May Execute Health Care Power of Attorney

Page 136, add at end of section:

An interesting question is whether an attorney-in-fact under a durable power of attorney may execute an advance directive (that is, a living will and/or health care power of attorney) for the principal. Although this question probably arises with some frequency in actual practice, there is only one reported instance of its being attempted. In *In re Mason*,[41.1] a man who was acting as surrogate for his incompetent mother executed a health care power of attorney (referred to under Massachusetts law as a "health care proxy"[41.2]) for her. He did so after his judicial appointment as her temporary guardian for the purpose of health care decisionmaking had expired, and was probably motivated to do so by the extremely adversarial relationship between him and the health care personnel treating his mother.

Pursuant to this instrument and another similar instrument he produced that he claimed his mother had executed, he sought to block the entry of a DNR order. The court avoided determining the validity of either of the instruments, assuming that they were valid but upholding the authority of the hospital to enter a DNR order despite the son's objections and holding that he was not acting in his mother's best interests.

§ 12.8   —Age

Page 137, add to Arkansas citation in footnote 42:

AR: *But compare* 1999 Ark. Acts 1448, § 3(a) (under health care power of attorney statute, a "person may execute a power of attorney for health care").

Page 137, delete Maine citation from footnote 42.

[41.1] 669 N.E.2d 1081 (Mass. App. Ct. 1996).

[41.2] Mass. Gen. Laws Ann. ch. 201D, § 1.

Page 137, replace Michigan and West Virginia citations in footnote 42 with:

MI: Mich. Comp. Laws § 700.5506(1).
WV: W. Va. Code § 16-30-4(a).

Page 137, add to footnote 42:

AL: Ala. Code § 22-8A-3(1) (19 years of age or over).

Pages 137–38, replace Delaware, Florida, and New Mexico citations in footnote 43 with:

DE: Del. Code Ann. § 2503(a) (modification of UHCDA provision).
FL: Fla. Stat. Ann. § 765.101(14).
NM: N.M. Stat. Ann. § 24-7A-2 (adopting UHCDA).

Page 138, add to footnote 43:

ME: Me. Rev. Stat. Ann. tit. 18-A, § 5-802(b) (adult or emancipated minor). UHCDA § 2(b).

Page 138, replace California and Mississippi citations in footnote 44 with:

CA: Cal. Prob. Code §§ 4600–4806.
MS: Miss. Code Ann. § 41-41-205(2) (emancipated minor may execute a power of attorney for health care) (adopting UHCDA).

Page 138, delete Hawaii, Maine, and New Mexico citations from footnote 44.

Page 138, add to footnote 44:

AR: Ark. Stat. Ann. § 20-13-104(d)(1).

Page 138, add to footnote 48:

HI: *Accord* Haw. Rev. Stat. § 327E-3(a) ("An adult or emancipated minor may give individual instruction.").
ME: *Accord* Me. Rev. Stat. Ann. tit. 18-A, § 5-802(b) (adopting UHCDA).
NM: *Accord* N.M. Stat. Ann. § 24-7A-2(B) (adopting UHCDA).

§ 12.9 — Capacity

Page 138, delete Arkansas citation from footnote 49.

Page 139, delete Hawaii citation from carryover footnote 49.

Page 139, replace Minnesota and West Virginia citations in footnote 49 with:

MN: Minn. Stat. Ann. § 145B.03(4).
WV: W. Va. Code § 16-30-4(a).

Page 139, add to footnote 49:

AL: Ala. Code § 22-8A-4(b).
DE: Del. Code Ann. § 2503(a) (mentally competent) (modification of UHCDA provision).
ME: Me. Rev. Stat. Ann. tit. 18-A, § 5-802(b) (adopting UHCDA).
MI: Mich. Comp. Laws § 700.5506(1) (sound mind).
NM: N.M. Stat. Ann. § 24-7A-2(B) (adopting UHCDA).

Page 139, replace California, Georgia, and Illinois citations in footnote 51 with:

CA: *Accord* Cal. Prob. Code § 4771.
GA: Ga. Code Ann. § 31-36-10(a)(7).
IL: Ill. Ann. Stat. ch. 755, § 45/4-10(7).

Page 139, delete Hawaii citation from footnote 51.

Page 140, add to footnote 51:

AL: *Accord* Ala. Code § 22-8A-4.
DE: *Accord* Del. Code Ann. § 2505(11) (modification of UHCDA provision).

Page 140, replace Texas citation in footnote 51 with:

TX: *Accord* Tex. Civ. Prac. & Rem. Code Ann. § 135.016 (for advance directives executed before Sept. 1, 1999); Tex. Health & Safety Code Ann. § 166.164 (for directives executed thereafter).

§ 12.10 Disclosure Statement

Page 140, replace California, Mississippi, and Texas citations in footnote 52 with:

CA: Cal. Prob. Code §§ 4703, 4770, 4772 (a).
MS: Miss. Code Ann. § 41-41-209 (adopting UHCDA).

TX: Tex. Civ. Prac. & Rem. Code Ann. § 135.015 (for advance directives executed before Sept. 1, 1999); Tex. Health & Safety Code Ann. § 166.163 (for directives executed thereafter).

Page 140, add to footnote 52:

DE: Del. Code Ann. § 2505 (warning included in declaration form) (modification of UHCDA provision).
HI: Haw. Rev. Stat. § 327E-16 (notice in form) (modifying UHCDA).
ME: Me. Rev. Stat. Ann. tit. 18-A, § 5-804 (adopting UHCDA).
NM: N.M. Stat. Ann. § 24-7A-4 (adopting UHCDA).

§ 12.11 Statutorily Prescribed Form

Page 141, replace California, Hawaii, Maine, Mississippi, New Mexico, Texas, and West Virginia citations in footnote 54 with:

CA: Cal. Prob. Code § 4779.
HI: Haw. Rev. Stat. § 327E-16 (modifying UCHDA).
ME: Me. Rev. Stat. Ann. tit. 18-A, § 5-804 (adopting UHCDA).
MS: Miss. Code Ann. § 41-41-209 (adopting UHCDA).
NM: N.M. Stat. Ann. § 24-7A-4 (adopting UHCDA).
TX: Tex. Civ. Prac. & Rem. Code Ann. § 135.016 (for advance directives executed before Sept. 1, 1999); Tex. Health & Safety Code Ann. § 166.164 (for directives executed thereafter).
WV: W. Va. Code § 16-30-4(h).

Page 141, add to Minnesota citation in footnote 54:

Minn. Stat. Ann. § 145C.16.

Page 142, add to footnote 54:

AL: Ala. Code § 22-8A-4(h).
DE: Del. Code Ann. tit. 16, § 2505 (modification of UHCDA provision); Del. Code Ann. tit. 16, § 2518 ("Nothing in this chapter shall be construed to limit the use of any . . . form which meets the requirements of this chapter.").

Page 142, replace California citation in footnote 56 with:

CA: Cal. Prob. Code §§ 4703(a), 4771.

Page 142, replace California citation in footnote 57 with:

Cal. Prob. Code §§ 4704(a), 4772(b).

Page 142, replace footnote 58 with:

Id. §§ 4600–4806.

Page 142, replace footnote 59 with:

Id. § 4700(b) (referring to Cal. Prob. Code § 4121(c), which requires either two witnesses or notarization for general durable powers of attorney).

Page 142, replace footnote 60 with:

Id. § 4771.

Page 143, add at end of section:

The Florida legislature creates a working group of the Department of Elderly Affairs, health care professionals, health facilities, attorneys, consumers, clergy, academic institutions, and other interested parties to create a model advance directive form which is to be made available to the public.[62.1]

§ 12.12 Witnesses and Authentication

Page 143, replace Arkansas, California, Maine, Texas, and West Virginia citations in footnote 63 with:

AR: Ark. Stat. Ann. § 20-13-104(C).
CA: Cal. Prob. Code § 4773.
ME: Me. Rev. Stat. Ann. tit. 18-A, §§ 5-802(b), -804.
TX: Tex. Civ. Prac. & Rem. Code Ann. § 135.004(a) (for advance directives executed before Sept. 1, 1999); Tex. Health & Safety Code Ann. § 166.154(a) (for directives executed thereafter).
WV: W. Va. Code § 16-30-4(a)(4).

Page 143, delete Mississippi citation from footnote 63.

Page 143, add to footnote 63:

AL: Ala. Code § 22-8A-4(c)(4).
AR: 1999 Ark. Acts 1448, § 3(b)(3).
DE: Del. Code Ann. § 2503(b)(1) (modification of UHCDA provision).
MI: Mich. Comp. Laws § 700.5506(3).
NM: *But see* N.M. Stat. Ann. § 24-7A-4 (two witnesses recommended but not required).

[62.1] **FL:** S.B. 2228, 1999 Leg. (Fla. 1999), § 34.

Pages 143–44, replace California, Hawaii, Minnesota, Mississippi, and West Virginia citations in footnote 64 with:

CA: Cal. Prob. Code § 4700(b) (incorporating criteria for general durable powers of attorney set forth in Cal. Prob. Code § 4121).
HI: Haw. Rev. Stat. § 327E-3(b) (modifying UHCDA).
MN: Minn. Stat. Ann. § 145B.03(2); Minn. Stat. Ann. § 145C.03(5).
MS: Miss. Code Ann. § 41-41-205 (2) (adopting UHCDA).
WV: W. Va. Code § 16-30-4(a)(5) (two witnesses and notary).

Page 143, delete Delaware citation in footnote 64.

Page 144, replace California and Mississippi citations in footnote 66 with:

CA: Cal. Prob. Code §§ 4701(c)(1), 4771.
MS: Miss. Code Ann. § 41-41-205 (4)(a).

Page 144, add to footnote 66:

HI: Haw. Rev. Stat. § 327E-3(d)(1) (modifying UHCDA).

Page 144, replace California and Mississippi citations in footnote 67 with:

CA: Cal. Prob. Code §§ 4701(c)(2), 4771.
MS: Miss. Code Ann. § 41-41-205 (4)(b).

Page 144 add to footnote 67:

HI: Haw. Rev. Stat. § 327E-3(d)(2) (modifying UHCDA).

Page 145, delete Hawaii citation from footnote 68.

Page 145, replace Michigan, Texas, and West Virginia citations in footnote 68 with:

MI: Mich. Comp. Laws § 700.5506(3).
TX: Tex. Civ. Prac. & Rem. Code Ann. § 135.004(b)(3)(4) (for advance directives executed before Sept. 1, 1999); Tex. Health & Safety Code Ann. § 166.003 (for directives executed thereafter).
WV: W. Va. Code § 16-30-4(b).

Page 145, add to footnote 68:

AL: Ala. Code § 22-8A-4(c)(4).

Pages 145–46, replace California, Hawaii, Mississippi, and Texas citations in footnote 69 with:

CA: Cal. Prob. Code §§ 4701(b), 4771.
HI: Haw. Rev. Stat. § 327E-16.
MS: Miss. Code Ann. § 41-41-205(2)(a).
TX: Tex. Civ. Prac. & Rem. Code Ann. § 135.004 (for advance directives executed before Sept. 1, 1999); Tex. Health & Safety Code Ann. § 166.003 (for directives executed thereafter).

Page 146, delete Maine citation from carryover footnote 69.

Page 146, add to footnote 69:

AL: Ala. Code § 22-8A-4 (sample form).
MI: Mich. Comp. Laws § 700.5506(3).
MN: Minn. Stat. Ann. § 145C.03(5).

Page 146, add to footnote 70:

DE: Del. Code Ann. § 2513(b) (modification of UHCDA provision).
ME: Me. Rev. Stat. Ann. tit. 18-A, § 5-811(b) (adopting UHCDA).
MN: Minn. Stat. Ann. § 145C.10(a) (presumption of capacity "absent clear and convincing evidence to the contrary").
NM: N.M. Stat. Ann. § 24-7A-11(B) (adopting UHCDA).
UHCDA § 11(b) (principal presumed to have capacity to execute advance directive and designate surrogate).

Page 146, delete West Virginia citation from footnote 70.

§ 12.13 —Execution of Advance Directive in a Health Care Facility

Page 147, replace California, Michigan, Mississippi, and Texas citations in footnote 71 with:

CA: Cal. Prob. Code §§ 4701(a)(1), 4771.
MI: Mich. Comp. Laws § 700.5506(3).
MS: Miss. Code Ann. § 41-41-205 (3)(a).
TX: Tex. Civ. Prac. & Rem. Code Ann. § 135.004(b)(2) (for advance directives executed before Sept. 1, 1999); Tex. Health & Safety Code Ann. § 166.003 (for directives executed thereafter).

Page 147, add to Minnesota citation in footnote 71:

Minn. Stat. Ann. § 145C.03(3)(b) (one witness must not be health care provider).

Page 147, add to footnote 71:

HI: Haw. Rev. Stat. § 327E-3(c)(1) (modifying UHCDA).

Pages 147–48, replace California, Hawaii, Michigan, Mississippi, and Texas citations in footnote 72 with:

CA: Cal. Prob. Code §§ 4701(a)(1), 4771.
HI: Haw. Rev. Stat. § 327E-3(c)(2) (modifying UHCDA).
MI: Mich. Comp. Laws § 700.5506(3).
MS: Miss. Code Ann. § 41-41-205 (3)(a).
TX: Tex. Civ. Prac. & Rem. Code Ann. § 135.004(b)(2) (for advance directives executed before Sept. 1, 1999); Tex. Health & Safety Code Ann. § 166.003 (for directives executed thereafter).

Page 147, add to Minnesota citation in footnote 72:

Minn. Stat. Ann. § 145C.03(3)(b).

Page 148, replace California citation in footnote 73 with:

CA: Cal. Prob. Code §§ 4701(a)(2), 4701(a)(3), 4771 (community care facility or residential care facility for elderly).

Page 148, replace California, Hawaii, Michigan, and Mississippi citations in footnote 74 with:

CA: Cal. Prob. Code §§ 4701(a)(2), 4701(a)(3), 4771 (community care facility or residential care facility for elderly).
HI: Haw. Rev. Stat. § 327E-3(c)(2) (modifying UHCDA).
MI: Mich. Comp. Laws § 700.5506(3).
MS: Miss. Code Ann. § 41-41-205(3)(b) (modifying UHCDA).

Pages 148–49, replace California, Michigan, and West Virginia citations in footnote 75 with:

CA: Cal. Prob. Code §§ 4701(a)(1), 4771.
MI: Mich. Comp. Laws § 700.5506(3).
WV: W. Va. Code § 16-30-4(b)(5).

Page 148, delete Hawaii citation from footnote 75.

§ 12.16 LOSS OF DECISIONMAKING CAPACITY

Page 149, replace California, Michigan, second Minnesota, Mississippi, Texas, and West Virginia citations in footnote 76 with:

CA: Cal. Probe. Code §§ 4701(b), 4771.

MI: Mich. Comp. Laws § 700.5506(3).

MN: Minn. Stat. Ann. § 145C.03(a).

MS: Miss. Code Ann. § 41-41-205 (3)(c).

TX: Tex. Civ. Prac. & Rem. Code Ann. § 135.004(b)(1) (for advance directives executed before Sept. 1, 1999); Tex. Health & Safety Code Ann. § 166.003 (for directives executed thereafter).

WV: W. Va. Code § 16-30-4(b)(6).

Page 148, add to footnote 76:

AL: Ala. Code § 22-8A-4(c)(4).

HI: Haw. Rev. Stat. § 327E-3(c)(3) (modifying UHCDA).

Page 148, add to footnote 77:

AL: Ala. Code § 22-8A-4(c)(4).

Page 150, add to footnote 80:

CA: *Accord* Cal. Prob. Code §§ 4701(e), 4771.

§ 12.14 Notarization

Page 150, delete Hawaii and Maine citations from footnote 84.

Page 150, replace West Virginia citation in footnote 84 with:

WV: W. Va. Code § 16-30-4(a)(5).

Page 151, delete New Mexico citation from carryover footnote 85.

Page 151, add to footnote 85:

HI: Haw. Rev. Stat. § 327E-16 (form, Part 4) (modifying UHCDA).

MN: Minn. Stat. Ann. § 145C.16.

§ 12.16 —Loss of Decisionmaking Capacity

Page 152, replace Florida, Maryland, Texas, and West Virginia citations in footnote 90 with:

FL: Fla. Stat. Ann. § 765.101(8).

MD: Md. Code Ann., Health-Gen. § 5-601(l) (defining "incapable of making informed decision").

TX: Tex. Civ. Prac. & Rem. Code Ann. § 135.001(4) (for advance directives executed before Sept. 1, 1999); Tex. Health & Safety Code Ann. § 166.002(8) (for directives executed thereafter).

WV: W. Va. Code § 16-30-3(l).

Page 152, add to footnote 90:

HI: Haw. Rev. Stat. § 327E-2(7) (modifying UHCDA).

ME: Me. Rev. Stat. Ann. tit. 18-A, § 5-801(c) (adopting UHCDA).

MN: Minn. Stat. Ann. § 145C.01 (1b).

MS: Miss. Code Ann. § 41-41-203 (d) (defining capacity).

NM: N.M. Stat. Ann. § 24-7A-1(C) (adopting UHCDA).

Page 152, replace Maryland and New Mexico citations in footnote 91 with:

MD: Md. Code Ann., Health-Gen. § 5-603(§ II(A)(4) of sample form).

NM: N.M. Stat. Ann. § 24-7A-4(3) (adopting UHCDA).

Page 152, add to footnote 91:

ME: Me. Rev. Stat. Ann. tit. 18-A, §§ 5-802(C), 5-804(§ 3 of sample form).

MN: Minn. Stat. Ann. § 145C.06(2).
UHCDA § 4(3).

Page 153, replace Hawaii, Maine, and West Virginia citations in footnote 92 with:

HI: Haw. Rev. Stat. § 327E-3(e) (modifying UHCDA).

ME: Me. Rev. Stat. Ann. tit. 18-A, § 5-802(c) (adopting UHCDA).

WV: W. Va. Code § 16-30-6(d) ("The medical power of attorney representative or surrogate's authority shall commence upon a determination . . . of the incapacity of the adult.").

Page 153, add to footnote 92:

MI: Mich. Comp. Laws § 700.5508(1).

NM: N.M. Stat. Ann. § 24-7A-2(C) (adopting UHCDA).

Pages 153–54, replace Florida, Maine, Michigan, Texas, and West Virginia citations in carryover footnote 93 with:

FL: Fla. Stat. Ann. § 765.204(2) (requiring second opinion only where attending physician requests one).

ME: Me. Rev. Stat. Ann. tit. 18-A, § 5-802(d) (adopting UHCDA).

MI: Mich. Comp. Laws § 700.5508(1).
TX: Tex. Civ. Prac. & Rem. Code Ann. § 135.002(b)(for advance directives executed before Sept. 1, 1999); Tex. Health & Safety Code Ann. § 166.152(b) (for directives executed thereafter).
WV: W. Va. Code § 16-30-7(a).

Page 154, add to footnote 93:

DE: Del. Code Ann. § 2503(e) (modification of UHCDA provision).
MS: Miss. Code Ann. § 41-41-205 (6) (primary physician unless otherwise stated in health care power of attorney) (adopting UHCDA).
NM: N.M. Stat. Ann. § 24-7A-11(C) (two qualified physicians, one of whom is primary physician, must determine loss of capacity, unless otherwise specified).

Page 154, replace Maryland citation in footnote 94 with:

MD: Md. Code Ann., Health-Gen. § 5-603(II)(A)(4).

Page 154, add to footnote 94:

DE: Del. Code Ann. § 2503(e) (modification of UHCDA provision).
MI: Mich. Comp. Laws § 700.5508(1) ("If the patient's religious beliefs prohibit an examination and this is stated in the designation, the patient must indicate in the designation how it shall be determined when the patient advocate exercises powers concerning decisions on behalf of the patient").
MN: Minn. Stat. Ann. § 145C.05(2)(b)(1) ("A principal who in good faith generally selects and depends upon spiritual means or prayer for the treatment or care of disease or remedial care and does not have an attending physician, may include a statement appointing an individual who may determine the principal's decision-making capacity.").

§ 12.17   —Terminal Condition or Permanent Unconsciousness

Pages 155–56, delete Arkansas, Maine, and West Virginia citations from footnote 96.

Page 156, add to footnote 96:

MD: Wright v. Johns Hopkins Health Sys. Corp., 728 A.2d 166, 170 (Md. 1999) ("If a health care agent has been appointed, and if two physicians have certified as to the declarant's incapacity, [unlike a living will,] there is no express requirement for physician certification that the declarant is in one of the three defined diagnostic conditions prior to withholding or withdrawing life-sustaining procedures.").

OH: *Cf.* Allore v. Flower Hosp., No. L-96-329, 1997 WL 362465, at *3 (Ohio Ct. App. June 27, 1997) (implying that liability should be denied to estate of patient treated seemingly contrary to advance directive because he was not "terminally ill" though he died within an hour).

§ 12.18 Recordkeeping and Notification Requirements

Page 156, add to footnote 97:

ME: Me. Rev. Stat. Ann. tit. 18-A, § 5-804 (adopting UHCDA).
NM: N.M. Stat. Ann. § 24-7A-4 (adopting UHCDA).

Pages 156–57, replace Delaware, Maine, Michigan, and West Virginia citations in footnote 100 with:

DE: Del. Code Ann. § 2508(b) (modification of UHCDA provision).
ME: Me. Rev. Stat. Ann. tit. 18-A, § 5-807(b) (adopting UHCDA).
MI: Mich. Comp. Laws § 700.5506(2).
WV: W. Va. Code § 16-30-4(d).

Page 157, add to footnote 100:

AL: Ala. Code § 22-8A-4(f).
NM: N.M. Stat. Ann. § 24-7A-7(B) (adopting UHCDA).

§ 12.19 Designation of Successor or Concurrent Proxies

Pages 157–58, replace California, Maine, New Mexico, and Texas citations in footnote 101 with:

CA: Cal. Prob. Code § 4771(9).
ME: Me. Rev. Stat. Ann. tit. 18-A, § 5-804 (adopting UHCDA).
NM: N.M. Stat. Ann. § 24-7A-4(1) (adopting UHCDA).
TX: Tex. Civ. Prac. & Rem. Code Ann. § 135.016 (for advance directives executed before Sept. 1, 1999); Tex. Health & Safety Code Ann. § 166.164 (for directives executed thereafter).

Page 158, add to footnote 101:

AL: Ala. Code § 22-8A-4 (sample form).
DE: Del. Code Ann. § 2505 (form, part 1) (modification of UHCDA provision).
MI: Mich. Comp. Laws § 700.5507(1).

Page 158, delete West Virginia citation in carryover footnote 101.

Page 158, replace California and Texas citations in footnote 102 with:

CA: Cal. Prob. Code § 4771(9).
TX: Tex. Civ. Prac. & Rem. Code Ann. § 135.016 (for advance directives executed before Sept. 1, 1999); Tex. Health & Safety Code Ann. § 166.164 (for directives executed thereafter).

Page 158, delete Maine and West Virginia citations from footnote 102.

Page 158, add to footnote 102:

AL: Ala. Code § 22-8A-4 (sample form).

Page 159, delete New Mexico citation from footnote 103.

Page 159, delete New Mexico citation from footnote 104.

Page 159, delete New Mexico citation from footnote 105.

Page 159, add to footnote 107:

ME: Me. Rev. Stat. Ann. tit. 18-A, § 5-804 (adopting UHCDA).
NM: N.M. Stat. Ann. § 24-7A-4 (adopting UHCDA).
PA: *E.g., In re* Kauffman, 20 Fiduc. Rptr. 2d 223 (C.P. Montgomery County, Pa. 2000) (for three weeks, primary agent designated in power of attorney renounced willingness to make decisions).

Page 159, add to footnote 108:

In *In re* Kauffman, 20 Fiduc. Rptr. 2d 223 (C.P. Montgomery County, Pa. 2000), for example, a conflict arose when the primary agent under a patient's power of attorney renounced his willingness to make decisions but then retracted the renunciation three weeks later. The secondary agent under the power of attorney suggested the primary agent could not retract a renunciation, but the court determined that the primary agent had indeed regained authority. Key to the court's decision was the patient's designation of only the primary agent as her proxy decisionmaker in her living will. *Id.* at 225–26. Had the court decided that the secondary agent had authority under the patient's power of attorney, it would have been left with a situation in which the patient's power of attorney designated one surrogate decision-maker and her living will designated another.

Page 160, add at end of section:

A New York trial court ruled that it is not empowered, in the case of a person who is incompetent and has an operative health care power of attorney, to appoint a guardian with the authority to appoint a successor agent.[109.1] Furthermore, even if it did have the authority to appoint a guardian, the guardian would not have the authority to appoint a successor proxy, because "the selection of a health care agent is a strictly personal decision, which can only be made by the competent principal himself."[109.2]

§ 12.20 Persons Disqualified from Acting as Proxy

Pages 160–61, replace California, Texas, and West Virginia citations in footnote 111 with:

CA: Cal. Prob. Code §§ 4702(a)(1), 4771.
TX: Tex. Civ. Prac. & Rem. Code Ann. § 135.003(1) (for advance directives executed before Sept. 1, 1999); Tex. Health & Safety Code Ann. § 166.153 (for directives executed thereafter).
WV: W. Va. Code § 16-30-4(c)(1).

Page 160, delete Hawaii and Mississippi citations from footnote 111.

Page 161, add to footnote 111:

AL: Ala. Code §§ 22-8A-4(b)(iv), 26-1-2(g)(5).

Page 161, delete Mississippi citation from footnote 112.

Page 161, replace California, Texas, and West Virginia citations in footnote 113 with:

CA: Cal. Prob. Code §§ 4702(b), 4771 (allows employee who is relative of principal by blood, marriage, or adoption or who is employed by same health care facility as principal to serve).
TX: Tex. Civ. Prac. & Rem. Code Ann. § 135.003(2) (for advance directives executed before Sept. 1, 1999); Tex. Health & Safety Code Ann. § 166.153(2) (for directives executed thereafter).

[109.1] **NY:** *In re* Lowe, 688 N.Y.S.2d 389 (Sup. Ct. Queens County 1999).
[109.2] *Id.* at 391.

WV: W. Va. Code § 16-30-4(2).

Page 161, add to footnote 113:

AL: Ala. Code §§ 22-8A-4(b)(iv), 26-1-2(g)(5).
HI: 1999 Haw. Sess. Laws 169, Sec. 1, § 3(a) (modifying UHCDA).

Page 162, replace California, Texas, and West Virginia citations in footnote 114 with:

CA: Cal. Prob. Code §§ 4702(a)(2), 4702(a)(3), 4771.
TX: Tex. Civ. Prac. & Rem. Code Ann. § 135.003(3) (for advance directives executed before Sept. 1, 1999); Tex. Health & Safety Code Ann. § 166.153(3) (for directives executed thereafter).
WV: W. Va. Code § 16-30-4(3) ("an operator of a health facility serving the principal").

Page 162, add to footnote 114:

ME: Me. Rev. Stat. Ann. tit. 18-A, § 5-802(b) (adopting UHCDA).
MS: Miss. Code Ann. § 41-41-205(2) (adopting UHCDA).
NM: N.M. Stat. Ann. § 24-7A-2(B) (adopting UHCDA).

Page 161, add to footnote 115:

MS: Miss. Code Ann. § 41-41-205(2) (adopting UHCDA).

Pages 162–63, replace California, Texas, and West Virginia citations in footnote 116 with:

CA: Cal. Prob. Code §§ 4702(b), 4771 (allows employee who is relative of principal by blood, marriage, or adoption or who is employed by same health care facility as principal to serve).
TX: Tex. Civ. Prac. & Rem. Code Ann. § 135.003(4) (for advance directives executed before Sept. 1, 1999); Tex. Health & Safety Code Ann. § 166.153(4) (for directives executed thereafter).
WV: W. Va. Code § 16-30-4(4).

Page 163, add to footnote 116:

ME: Me. Rev. Stat. Ann. tit. 18-A, § 5-802(b) (adopting UHCDA).
MS: Miss. Code Ann. § 41-41-205(2) (adopting UHCDA).
NM: N.M. Stat. Ann. § 24-7A-2(B) (adopting UHCDA).

§ 12.21 Nomination of Guardian or Conservator

Page 163, replace California citation in footnote 117 with:

CA: Cal. Prob. Code §§ 4126, 4771(10).

Page 163, add to footnote 117:

AL: Ala. Code § 26-1-2(c)(2).
DE: Del. Code Ann. § 2503(i) (modification of UHCDA provision).
ME: Me. Rev. Stat. Ann. tit. 18-A, § 5-802(g) (adopting UHCDA).
NM: N.M. Stat. Ann. § 24-7A-2(G) (adopting UHCDA).

Page 163, delete West Virginia citation from footnote 117.

Page 163, delete last sentence in section and accompanying footnote 118.

Page 163, add at end of section:

These statutes reflect the modern trend. Most nineteenth- and early twentieth-century state statutes did not require courts to consider the preferences of the principal in the appointment of a guardian, and most courts held that they were not required to consider the incompetent's wishes.[118.1] However, in more recent years, state courts and legislatures have increasingly recognized that the principal's preferences should be given primacy.[118.2] Although a variety of different approaches have been used,[118.3] the dominant approach is that embodied originally in the 1969 Uniform Probate Code,[118.4] which intended for durable powers of attorney to be used as an alternative to court-facilitated protective procedures.[118.5] The Uniform Durable Power of Attorney Act, promulgated in 1979, includes the identical provision,[118.6] and has been adopted in 29 states.[118.7]

Under the Uniform Durable Power of Attorney Act, a court is to make its appointment of a guardian in accordance with the principal's most recent nomination, absent "good cause or disqualification."[118.8] This provision appears to

---

[118.1] Gerry W. Beyer, *Enhancing Self-Determination Through Guardian Self-Declaration,* 23 Ind. L. Rev. 71, 75–76 (1990).

[118.2] *Id.* at 77.

[118.3] *Id.* at 78–86.

[118.4] § 5-503(b), 8 U.L.A. pt. II, 418, 421 (West 1998).

[118.5] Uniform Durable Power of Attorney Act, 8A U.L.A. 309, 310 (West 1993) (prefatory note).

[118.6] *See id.* 3(b), at 322.

[118.7] *See* 8A U.L.A. 48, 48 (West Supp. 1997) (table of adoptions).

[118.8] 3(b), 8A U.L.A. 309, 322; *accord* Uniform Probate Code § 5-503(b), 8 U.L.A. pt. II, 418, 421 (1998).

have been judicially construed and applied in only one case, *In re Smith*,[118.9] in which the principal's family members challenged his designation through a durable power of attorney of his guardians. The court honored the principal's wishes, finding that no conflict existed between the guardians' interests and the principal's, and thus there was no reason to disqualify their designation.

§ 12.22 Scope of Proxy's Authority to Make Health Care Decisions

Pages 164–65, replace California, Delaware, Michigan, Mississippi, and West Virginia citations in footnote 119 with:

CA: Cal. Prob. Code §§ 4720(c), 4771 (duty to act consistent with desires of principal or, if principal's desires unknown, to act in best interests of principal).

DE: Del. Code Ann. § 2505(4) (modification of UHCDA provision).

MI: Mich. Comp. Laws § 700.5507(4)(6.) ("The known desires of the patient expressed or evidenced while the patient is able to participate in medical treatment decisions are presumed to be in the patient's best interests").

MS: Miss. Code Ann. § 41-41-205(7) (adopting UHCDA).

WV: W. Va. Code § 16-30-9(a)(1).

Page 165, add to Massachusetts citation in footnote 119:

MA: *See In re* Mason, 669 N.E.2d 1081, 1084–85 (Mass. App. Ct. 1996) (construing Mass. Gen. Laws Ann. ch. 201D, § 1, authorizing court to "have the agent removed on the ground that the agent is . . . competent to fulfill his or her obligations under this chapter or is acting in bad faith").

Page 165, add to footnote 119:

HI: Haw. Rev. Stat. § 327E(5)(g) (modifying UHCDA).

ME: Me. Rev. Stat. Ann. tit. 18-A, § 5-802(e) (adopting UHCDA).

NM: N.M. Stat. Ann. § 24-7A-2(E) (adopting UHCDA).

Page 164, add after first sentence:

Although not a conflict between the principal and the proxy per se, a proxy who borders on lacking decisionmaking capacity because he is unable to make decisions based on the manifest medical facts but is instead motivated

---

[118.9] 684 N.E.2d 613 (Mass. App. Ct. 1997), discussed in §§ **1A.5** and **1A.6** in this supplement.

by his own cognitive impairments or personality disorders is not acting in the principal's best interests and is subject to removal as proxy.[119.1]

Page 165, delete Hawaii citation from footnote 120.

Page 165, replace Michigan citation in footnote 120 with:

MI: Mich. Comp. Laws § 700.5507(4)(4.) ("patient advocate may make a decision to withhold or withdraw treatment that would allow a patient to die only if the patient has expressed in a clear and convincing manner that the patient advocate is authorized to make such a decision").

Page 165, add to footnote 120:

AL: Ala. Code §§ 22-8A-4(b)(i), 26-1-2(g)(2).

Page 165, add Arkansas citation in footnote 121:

1999 Ark. Acts 1448, § 4(a) (broadly defining *health care* for purposes of health care power of attorney).

Page 165, replace California, Hawaii, Maine, and Texas citations in footnote 121 with:

CA: Cal. Prob. Code § 4771(3).
HI: Haw. Rev. Stat. § 327E(5)(g) (modifying UHCDA).
ME: Me. Rev. Stat. Ann. tit. 18-A, § 5-804 (adopting UHCDA).
TX: Tex. Civ. Prac. & Rem. Code Ann. § 135.002(a) (for advance directives executed before Sept. 1, 1999); Tex. Health & Safety Code Ann. § 166.152(a) (for directives executed thereafter).

Page 165, replace parenthethical in Minnesota citation in footnote 121 with:

("Unless the principal has otherwise specified in the health care directive, the appointment of the health care agent in a health care directive is considered a nomination of a guardian or conservator of the person").

Page 166, add to footnote 121:

MS: Miss. Code Ann. § 41-41-209 (all health care decisions unless limited by principal) (adopting UHCDA).
NM: N.M. Stat. Ann. § 24-7A-4 (adopting UHCDA).

Page 166, delete West Virginia citation from footnote 121.

[119.1] *In re* Mason, 669 N.E.2d 1081 (Mass. App. Ct. 1996).

§ 12.22   SCOPE OF PROXY'S AUTHORITY

Page 166, add to footnote 123:

PA: *But see In re* Estate of Strickland, 44 Cumb. 357 (C.P. Cumberland County, Pa. 1995) (revoking power of attorney to patient's son, who refused to execute nursing home application for principal).

Page 167, replace California, Delaware, Florida, Mississippi, and Texas citations in footnote 124 with:

CA: Cal. Prob. Code §§ 4612, 4771(1) (includes "consent, refusal of consent, or withdrawal of consent to health care, or decision to begin, continue, increase, limit, discontinue, or not to begin any health care").
DE: Del. Code Ann. § 2501(h) (modification of UHCDA provision).
FL: Fla. Stat. Ann. § 765.101(5)(a).
MS: Miss. Code Ann. § 41-41-203(h)(iii) (adopting UHCDA).
TX: Tex. Civ. Prac. & Rem. Code Ann. § 135.001(6) (for advance directives executed before Sept. 1, 1999); Tex. Health & Safety Code Ann. § 166.002(7) (for directives executed thereafter).

Page 167, add to footnote 124:

ME: Me. Rev. Stat. Ann. tit. 18-A, § 5-801(f) (adopting UHCDA).
NM: N.M. Stat. Ann. § 24-7A-1(G) (adopting UHCDA).
WV: W. Va. Code § 16-30-3(i) (defining "health care decision" as "a decision to give, withhold or withdraw informed consent to any type of health care").

Pages 167–68, replace California, Michigan, and Mississippi citations in footnote 125 with:
CA: Cal. Prob. Code §§ 4720(b), 4771(3).
MI: Mich. Comp. Laws § 700.5507(1).
MS: Miss. Code Ann. § 41-41-205(2) (adopting UHCDA).

Page 168, replace second Minnesota citation in footnote 125 with:

Minn. Stat. Ann. § 145C.07(3) (health care agent has duty to act in "good faith").

Pages 167–68, delete Hawaii and New Mexico citations from footnote 125.

Page 168, add to footnote 125:
AL: Ala. Code §§ 22-8A-6, 26-1-2(g)(1).

§ 12.24 — Conflict Between Principal and Proxy

Page 169, replace New Mexico citation in footnote 130 with:

NM: N.M. Stat. Ann. § 24-7A-4 (adopting UHCDA).

Page 169, add to footnote 130:

AL: Ala. Code § 26-1-2(g)(1).
ME: Me. Rev. Stat. Ann. tit. 18-A, § 5-804 (adopting UHCDA).
MS: Miss. Code Ann. § 41-41-205(2) ("An adult or emancipated minor may execute a power of attorney for health care, which may authorize the agent to make any health-care decision the principal could have made while having capacity.") (modification of UHCDA).

Pages 169–70, replace California, Michigan, and Texas citations in footnote 132 with:

CA: Cal. Prob. Code §§ 4724, 4771(4).
MI: Mich. Comp. Laws § 700.5510(1)(d).
TX: Tex. Civ. Prac. & Rem. Code Ann. § 135.002(c) (for advance directives executed before Sept. 1, 1999); Tex. Health & Safety Code Ann. § 166.152(c) (for directives executed thereafter).

Page 169, delete Mississippi citation from footnote 132.

Page 170, replace California, Hawaii, Michigan, and Texas citations in footnote 134 with:

CA: Cal. Prob. Code § 4720(a) (attorney in fact does not have authority to make particular health care decision if principal is able to give informed consent with respect to that decision); Cal. Prob. Code § 4771.
HI: Haw. Rev. Stat. § 327E(5)(e) (modifying UHCDA).
MI: Mich. Comp. Laws § 700.5509(2).
TX: Tex. Civ. Prac. & Rem. Code Ann. § 135.002(b) (for advance directives executed before Sept. 1, 1999); Tex. Health & Safety Code Ann. § 166.152(b) (for directives executed thereafter).

Page 171, add to footnote 134:

ME: Me. Rev. Stat. Ann. tit. 18-A, § 5-802(c) (adopting UHCDA).
NM: N.M. Stat. Ann. § 24-7A-2(C) (adopting UHCDA).

§ 12.25 —Life-Sustaining Treatment

Pages 171-72, replace California, Delaware, Hawaii, Maine, Michigan, Mississippi, New Mexico, Texas, and West Virginia citations in footnote 135 with:

CA: Cal. Prob. Code §§ 4650, 4771.

DE: Del. Code Ann. § 2503(c) (modification of UHCDA provision).

HI: Haw. Rev. Stat. § 327E-16(d) (form) (modifying UHCDA).

ME: Me. Rev. Stat. Ann. tit. 18-A, § 5-804 (adopting UHCDA).

MI: Mich. Comp. Laws § 700.5507(4)(4.).

MS: Miss. Code Ann. § 41-41-203(h)(iii) (adopting UHCDA).

NM: N.M. Stat. Ann. § 24-7A-4 (adopting UHCDA).

TX: Tex. Civ. Prac. & Rem. Code Ann. § 135.015 (for advance directives executed before Sept. 1, 1999); Tex. Health & Safety Code Ann. § 166.163 (for directives executed thereafter).

WV: W. Va. Code § 16-30-4.

Page 171, delete second Minnesota citation from footnote 135.

Page 172, add to footnote 135:

AL: Ala. Code § 22-8A-2.

AR: *But see* 1999 Ark. Acts 1448 (containing no limitations on health care to which proxy may consent or refuse).

Page 172, delete Minnesota citation from footnote 138.

Page 173, add to footnote 139:

MN: Minn. Stat. Ann. §§ 145C.01–145C.16.

Page 173, add to footnote 140:

DE: Del. Code Ann. § 2503(c) (proxy may only make decisions regarding withholding or withdrawing life-sustaining treatment if declarant has a terminal condition or is permanently unconscious) (modification of UHCDA provision).

FL: *Cf.* Fla. Stat. Ann. § 765.401(3) (requiring proxy's decision to withhold or withdraw life-prolonging procedures to be supported by "clear and convincing evidence that the decision would have been the one the patient would have chosen had the patient been competent").

Page 173, add to footnote 141:

DE: Del. Code Ann. § 2505(2) (modification of UHCDA provision).

MI: Mich. Comp. Laws § 700.5511(1) ("Irrespective of a previously expressed or evidenced desire, a current desire by a patient to have provided and not withheld or withdrawn, a specific life-extending care, custody, or medical treatment is binding on the patient advocate").

Page 173, replace California and West Virginia citations in footnote 142 with:

CA: Cal. Prob. Code § 4771(4)(a).
WV: W. Va. Code § 16-30-4.

Page 173, delete Minnesota citation from footnote 142.

Page 173, add to footnote 142:

AL: Ala. Code § 22-8A-4 (sample form).
DE: Del. Code Ann. § 2505(2) (modification of UHCDA provision).

Page 174, add to footnote 145:

MN: Minn. Stat. Ann. § 145C.15(a).

§ 12.26   —Artificial Nutrition and Hydration

Pages 174–75, delete Hawaii, Maine, Minnesota, Utah, and West Virginia citations from footnote 147.

Page 176, add to footnote 151:

AL: Ala. Code § 26-1-2(g)(2) (proxy may make decisions regarding artificial nutrition and hydration only if "specifically authorized to do so in the durable power of attorney").

Page 176, replace Iowa citation in footnote 153 with:

IA: Iowa Code Ann. § 114B.1.3.

Page 176, delete Maine citation from footnote 153.

Page 177, add to footnote 156:

ME: Me. Rev. Stat. Ann. tit. 18-A, § 5-804 (adopting UHCDA).
MS: 1998 Miss. Laws ch. 542 (H.B. 546), § 3(7) (adopting UHCDA).
NM: N.M. Stat. Ann. § 24-7A-4 (adopting UHCDA).

§ 12.27   — Pregnancy

Page 177, add to footnote 157:

ND: Gabrynowicz v. Heitkamp, 904 F. Supp. 1061 (D.N.D. 1995) (questioning constitutionality of provision).

Page 177, replace Delaware and Michigan citations in footnote 158 with:

DE: Del. Code Ann. § 2503(j) (modification of UHCDA provision).
MI: Mich. Comp. Laws § 700.5507(4)(3.).

Page 177, add to footnote 158:

MN: Minn. Stat. Ann. § 145C.10(g) (creates rebuttable presumption that pregnant woman would want life-sustaining treatment).
ND: N. D. Cent. Code § 23-06.5-01 (prohibiting proxy's consent to abortion).

§ 12.28   — Active Euthanasia

Pages 178–79, replace California, Maine, and West Virginia citations in footnote 162 with:

CA: Cal. Prob. Code § 4723.
ME: Me. Rev. Stat. Ann. tit. 18-A, § 5-813(c) (adopting UHCDA).
WV: W. Va. Code § 16-30-14(b).

Page 179, add to footnote 162:

AL: Ala. Code § 22-8A-10.
MI: Mich. Comp. Laws § 700.5512(4).
MN: Minn. Stat. Ann. § 145C.01(4) (health care does not include any treatment or procedure amounting to assisted suicide) (adopting UHCDA).
MS: Miss. Code Ann. § 41-41-227(3).
NM: N.M. Stat. Ann. § 24-7A-13(C) (adopting UHCDA).
     UHCDA § 13(c).

§ 12.29   — Non-Life-Sustaining Treatments

Page 179, replace California and Texas citations in footnote 164 with:

CA: Cal. Prob. Code § 4722(a).

TX: Tex. Civ. Prac. & Rem. Code Ann. § 135.002(f)(1) (for advance directives executed before Sept. 1, 1999); Tex. Health & Safety Code Ann. § 166.152(f)(1) (for directives executed thereafter).

Page 179, delete Minnesota citation from footnote 164.

Page 179, add to footnote 164:

ME: Me. Rev. Stat. Ann. tit. 18-A, § 5-813(e) (adopting UHCDA).
MS: Miss. Code Ann. § 41-41-227(5) (adopting UHCDA).
NM: N.M. Stat. Ann. § 24-7A-13(E) (adopting UHCDA).

Page 180, replace California and Texas citations in footnote 165 with:

CA: Cal. Prob. Code § 4722(b).
TX: Tex. Civ. Prac. & Rem. Code Ann. § 135.002(f)(1) (for advance directives executed before Sept. 1, 1999); Tex. Health & Safety Code Ann. § 166.152(f)(1) (for directives executed thereafter).

Page 180, replace California citation in footnote 166 with:

CA: Cal. Prob. Code § 4722(c).

Page 180, add to footnote 166:

AL: Ala. Code § 26-1-2(g)(1).

Page 180, replace California citation in footnote 167 with:

CA: Cal. Prob. Code § 4722(d).

Page 179, add to footnote 167:

AL: Ala. Code § 26-1-2(g)(1).

Page 179, delete Minnesota citation from footnote 168.

Page 180, replace California and Texas citations in footnote 168 with:

CA: Cal. Prob. Code § 4722(e).
TX: Tex. Civ. Prac. & Rem. Code Ann. § 135.002(f)(4) (for advance directives executed before Sept. 1, 1999); Tex. Health & Safety Code Ann. § 166.152(f)(4) (for directives executed thereafter).

Page 180, add to footnote 168:

AL: Ala. Code § 26-1-2(g)(1).
MS: Miss. Code Ann. § 41-41-227(7).

§ 12.29A   — Mental Health Treatment (New)

In the 1990s, state legislatures began to enact statutes, or to amend existing advance directive statutes, permitting individuals to execute an advance directive to authorize treatment for mental illness. This has been a particularly vexing problem ever since courts and legislatures began to recognize a right on the part of patients, including involuntarily civilly committed patients, to refuse treatment for mental illness on terms similar to the right to refuse treatment for other kinds of illnesses or injuries. Although hedged with more limitations than the general right to refuse treatment, the underlying principles are the same, as are the problems created by the recognition of such a right. The most fundamental problem is that when chronically mentally ill individuals are suffering from an acute episode of mental illness, they sometimes refuse the treatment needed to put that episode of illness into remission, thereby prolonging its duration and possibly its intensity. When they eventually recover, they sometimes regret their refusal and indicate that the next time they have an acute episode of illness they wish to be treated— but then again refuse when they are in fact acutely ill.

This fact pattern is ideally suited to the use of an advance directive, but there has been question about whether, without a statutory basis, such an advance directive would be a valid defense if a patient, treated pursuant to an advance directive, were to bring an action for battery for nonconsensual treatment after treatment and recovery. This uncertainty arises in part from the fact that many advance directive statutes apply only to individuals who are terminally ill or permanently unconscious.[168.1] In addition, in some jurisdictions, a proxy operating under a health care power of attorney is specifically barred from authorizing or withholding a non-life-sustaining treatment, such as commitment to a mental health facility, electroconvulsive therapy, or psychosurgery.[168.2]

However, after many years of inaction, accompanied by complaints from mental health professionals and the families of chronically mentally ill individuals who are stymied by the right to refuse treatment, state legislatures have begun to provide a statutory basis for mental health advance directives.[168.3]

[168.1] See §§ **11.9** and **12.17** in the main volume.

[168.2] See § **12.29** in the main volume.

[168.3] **AK:**   Alaska Stat. § 47.30.950; Alaska Stat. § 13.26.335.

AZ: Ariz. Rev. Stat. Ann. § 36-3281.

ID: Idaho Code § 66-601.

IL: Ill. Ann. Stat. ch. 755, § 43/1. *But see* 755 Ill. Ann. Stat. ch. 755, § 40/60-(b).

MN: Minn. Stat. Ann. § 253B.03.

NC: N.C. Gen. Stat. § 32A-15; N.C. Gen. Stat. § 122C-71.

Types of Mental Health Advance Directives. Some mental health advance directive statutes provide for a directive that combines appointing an agent for health care decisionmaking and giving instructions,[168.4] in effect combining a health care power of attorney and a living will.[168.5]

Witnessing Requirements; Who May Serve as Proxy. The execution of a mental health advance directive raises concerns of decisionmaking capacity

---

OK: Okla. Stat. Ann. tit. 43A, § 11-101.

OR: Or. Rev. Stat. § 127-700.

TX: Tex. Civ. Prac. & Rem. Code Ann. § 137.

UT: Utah Code Ann. § 62A-12-502.

[168.4] **AK:** Alaska Stat. § 47.30.950(a) ("adult of sound mind may make a declaration of preferences or instructions regarding mental health treatment"); § 47.30.850(b) ("declaration may designate a competent adult to act as attorney-in-fact to make decisions about mental health treatment").

AZ: Ariz. Rev. Stat. Ann. § 36-3281(A), (B) ("An adult, known as the principal . . . may designate another adult or adults . . . to act as an agent and to make mental health care decisions on that person's behalf.").

ID: Idaho Code § 66-602(1) ("competent adult may make a declaration of preferences or instructions regarding mental health treatment . . . the declaration shall name an attorney-in-fact").

IL: Ill. Ann. Stat. ch. 755, § 43/10(1) ("adult of sound mind may make a declaration of preferences or instructions regarding mental health treatment"); § 43/15 ("declaration may designate a competent adult to act as attorney-in-fact to make decisions about mental health treatment").

MN: Minn. Stat. Ann. § 253B.03(6d)(a) ("competent adult may make a declaration of preferences or instructions regarding intrusive mental health treatment"); § 253B.03(6d)(b) ("declaration may designate a proxy to make decisions about intrusive mental health treatment").

NC: N.C. Gen. Stat. § 32A-19(a) ("principal, pursuant to a health care power of attorney, may grant to the health care agent full power and authority to make health care decisions . . . . A health care power of attorney may also contain or incorporate by reference any lawful guidelines or directions relating to the health care of the principal as the principal deems appropriate").

OK: Okla. Stat. Ann. tit. 43A, § 11-103(1) ("'Advance directive for mental health treatment' means a written document, voluntarily executed by a declarant in accordance with the requirements of this act and includes: a. a declaration, or b. the appointment of an attorney-in-fact").

OR: Or. Rev. Stat. § 127-702(1) ("adult of sound mind may make a declaration of preferences or instructions regarding mental health treatment"); § 127-705 ("declaration may designate a competent adult to act as attorney-in-fact to make decisions about mental health treatment").

UT: Utah Code Ann. § 62A-12-502(1) ("adult who is not incapable may make a declaration of preferences or instructions regarding his mental health treatment"); § 62A-12-502(2) ("declaration for mental health treatment shall designate a capable adult to act as attorney-in-fact to make decisions about mental health treatment for the declarant").

and voluntariness similar to those that exist for patients in a health care facility.[168.6] This may explain why mental health advance directive statutes contain many of the same precautions as those for patients in a health care facility. Both the proxy and witnesses must be competent adults.[168.7] For example, most statutes require the signatures of two witnesses and the mental health patient.[168.8] The statutes are hesitant to allow anyone associated with the provision of health care to serve as either a proxy or a witness. The proxy and witnesses cannot be the attending physician or mental health service provider or employee;[168.9] or the owner, operator, or employee of the health care facil-

---

[168.5] See § **12.1** in the main volume.

[168.6] See § **12.13** in the main volume.

[168.7] **AK:**   Alaska Stat. § 47.30.952 ("may designate a competent adult to make decisions"); § 47.30.954 ("two competent adult witnesses").

ID: Idaho Code § 66-603(1) ("may designate a competent adult to make decisions"); § 66-604(1) ("two competent adult witnesses").

IL: Ill. Ann. Stat. ch. 755, § 43/15 ("may designate a competent adult to make decisions"); § 43/20 ("two competent adult witnesses").

OR: Or. Rev. Stat. § 127-705 ("may designate a competent adult to act as attorney-in-fact"); § 127-707 ("two competent adult witnesses").

[168.8] **AK:**   Alaska Stat. § 47.30.954(a) ("effective only if signed by the principal and two competent adult witnesses").

ID: Idaho Code § 66-604(1) ("declaration effective only if signed by the principal and two competent adult witnesses").

IL: Ill. Ann. Stat. ch. 755, § 43/20 ("declaration effective only if signed by the principal and two competent adult witnesses").

MN: Minn. Stat. Ann. § 253B.03(6d)(c) ("declaration effective only if signed by the declarant and two witnesses").

OK: Okla. Stat. Ann. tit. 43A, § 11-105(A) ("advance directive for mental health treatment valid only if it is signed by the declarant and two capable witnesses").

OR: Or. Rev. Stat. § 127-707 ("declaration effective only if signed by the principal and two competent adult witnesses").

TX: Tex. Civ. Prac. & Rem. Code Ann. § 137.003(a) ("declaration . . . must be signed by the principal in presence of two or more subscribing witnesses").

UT: Utah Code Ann. § 62A-12-502(3) ("declaration effective only if signed by the declarant and two witnesses").

[168.9] **AK:**   Alaska Stat. § 47.30.952(b)(1) ("The following may not serve as attorney-in-fact; the attending physician or mental health service provider, or an employee of the physician or provider, if the physician, provider, or employee is unrelated to the principal by blood, marriage or adoption"); § 47.30.954(b)(1) ("the following may not serve as a witness . . . the attending physician or mental health service provider or a relative of the physician or provider").

AZ: *See also* Ariz. Rev. Stat. Ann. § 36-3281(C) ("An agent shall not be a person who is directly involved with the provision of health care to the principal at the time the mental health care power of attorney is executed.").

ity in which the principal is a patient or resident.[168.10] In addition, some statutes specify that the witnesses cannot be related to the principal by blood,

---

ID: Idaho Code § 66-603(2)(a) ("The following may not serve as agent; the attending physician or mental health service provider, or an employee of the physician or provider, if the physician, provider, or employee is unrelated to the principal by blood, marriage or adoption"); § 66-604(2)(a) ("the following may not serve as a witness; the attending physician or mental health service provider or a relative of the physician or provider").

IL: Ill. Ann. Stat. ch. 755, § 43/60(1) ("Restrictions on who may serve as attorney-in-fact—the attending physician or mental health service provider, or an employee of the physician or provider, if the physician, provider, or employee is unrelated to the principal by blood, marriage, or adoption"); § 43/65(1) ("Restrictions on who may serve as a witness—the attending physician or mental health service provider or a relative of the physician or provider").

OK: Okla. Stat. Ann. tit. 43A, § 11-105(B)(1) ("None of the following shall be eligible to serve as attorney-in-fact; the attending physician or psychologist or an employee of the physician or psychologist").

OR: Or. Rev. Stat. § 127-727(1) ("Who may not serve as attorney-in-fact; the attending physician or mental health service provider, or an employee of the physician or provider, if the physician, provider, or employee is unrelated to the principal by blood, marriage or adoption"); § 127-730(1) ("Who may not serve as a witness; the attending physician or mental health service provider or a relative of the physician or provider").

TX: Tex. Civ. Prac. & Rem. Code Ann. § 137.003(b)(1) ("[witness may not be] the principal's health or residential care provider or an employee of that provider").

[168.10] **AK:** Alaska Stat. § 47.30.952(b)(2) ("The following may not serve as attorney-in-fact; an owner, operator, or employee of a health care facility in which the principal is a patient or resident if the owner, operator, or employee is unrelated to the principal by blood, marriage, or adoption"); § 47.30.954(b)(2) ("The following may not serve as a witness; an owner, operator, or relative of an owner or operator of a health care facility in which the principal is a patient or resident").

ID: Idaho Code § 66-603(2)(b) ("The following may not serve as agent; an owner, operator, or employee of a health care facility in which the principal is a patient or resident if the owner, operator, or employee is unrelated to the principal by blood, marriage, or adoption"); § 66-604(2)(b) ("The following may not serve as a witness; an owner, operator, or relative of an owner or operator of a health care facility in which the principal is a patient or resident").

IL: Ill. Ann. Stat. ch. 755, § 43/60(2) ("Restrictions on who may serve as attorney-in-fact—an owner, operator, or employee of a health care facility in which the principal is a patient or resident if the owner, operator, or employee is unrelated to the principal by blood, marriage, or adoption"); § 43/65(2) ("Restrictions on who may serve as a witness-an owner, operator, or relative of an owner or operator of a health care facility in which the principal is a patient or resident").

OK: Okla. Stat. Ann. tit. 43A, § 11-105(B)(2)("None of the following shall be eligible to serve as attorney-in-fact; an owner operator or employee of a health care facility in which the declarant is a patient or resident").

marriage, or adoption.[168.11]

When Directive Becomes Effective.   The proxy's statutory authority becomes effective when the principal becomes incapable of making decisions,[168.12] and instruction directives also become effective when the principal

---

OR: Or. Rev. Stat. § 127-727(2) ("Who may not serve as attorney-in-fact; an owner, operator, or employee of a health care facility in which the principal is a patient or resident if the owner, operator, or employee is unrelated to the principal by blood, marriage, or adoption"); § 127-730(2)("Who may not serve as a witness; an owner, operator, or relative of an owner or operator of a health care facility in which the principal is a patient or resident").

TX: Tex. Civ. Prac. & Rem. Code Ann. § 137.003(b)(2) ("[witness may not be] the operator of a community health care facility providing care to the principal or an employee of an operator of the facility").

[168.11] **AK:** Alaska Stat. § 47.30.954(b)(3) ("The following may not serve as a witness; a person related to principal by blood, marriage, or adoption").

ID: Idaho Code § 66-604(2)(c) ("The following may not serve as a witness; a person related to principal by blood, marriage, or adoption").

IL: Ill. Ann. Stat. ch. 755, § 43/65(3) ("Restrictions on who may serve as a witness — a person related to principal by blood, marriage, or adoption").

OR: Or. Rev. Stat. § 127-730(3) ("Who may not serve as a witness; a person related to principal by blood, marriage, or adoption").

TX: Tex. Civ. Prac. & Rem. Code Ann. § 137.003(3) ("[witness may not be] a person related to the principal by blood , marriage, or adoption").

[168.12] **AK:** Alaska Stat. § 47.30.958(a) ("attorney-in-fact does not have authority to make mental health treatment decisions unless the principal is incapable").

AZ: Ariz. Rev. Stat. Ann. § 36-3281 ("[m]ay make decisions about mental health treatment on behalf of the principal if the principal is found incapable").

ID: Idaho Code § 66-605(1) ("physician or provider shall act in accordance with an operative declaration when the principal has been found to be incapable").

IL: Ill. Ann. Stat. ch. 755, § 43/30(1) ("attorney-in-fact does not have authority to make mental health treatment decisions unless the principal is incapable").

MN: Minn. Stat. Ann. § 253B.03(6d)(c) ("physician or provider shall continue to obtain declarant's informed consent to all intrusive mental health treatment decisions if declarant is capable of informed consent").

NC: N.C. Gen. Stat. § 122C-74(e) ("attending physician or mental health treatment provider shall continue to obtain the principal's informed consent to all mental health treatment decisions when the principal is capable of providing informed consent or refusal").

OK: Okla. Stat. Ann. tit. 43A, § 11-104(C)(1) ("advance directive . . . shall not affect the right of an individual to make decisions about mental health treatment, so long as the individual is capable").

OR: Or. Rev. Stat. § 127-712(1) ("attorney-in-fact does not have authority to make mental health treatment decisions unless the principal is incapable").

UT: Utah Code Ann. § 62A-12-502(5)(a) ("attorney-in-fact does not have authority to make mental health treatment decisions unless the principal is incapable").

loses decisionmaking capacity.[168.13] Some statutes specify how the determination that the principal lacks decisionmaking capacity is to be made.[168.14] Some statutes also specify that the directive does not go into effect until it has been given to the attending physician and made a part of the principal's medical record.[168.15] Of the statutes that require appointment of a proxy, some also

---

[168.13] **TX:** Tex. Civ. Prac. & Rem. Code Ann. § 137.004 ("physician or other provider shall continue to seek and act in accordance with the principal's informed consent to all mental health treatment decisions if the principal is capable of providing informed consent").

[168.14] **AK:** Alaska Stat. § 47.30.970 ("only if a court, two physicians that include a psychiatrist, or a physician and a professional mental health clinician believe that you are incapable of making treatment decisions").

ID: Idaho Code § 66-601(4) ("'Incapable' means that, by order of a court in a guardianship proceeding . . . or in the opinion of two physicians that include a psychiatrist, or in the opinion of a physician and a professional mental health clinician . . . the person currently lacks the capacity to make mental health treatment decisions").

IL: Ill. Ann. Stat. ch. 755, § 43/5(5) ("'Incapable' means that in the opinion of two physicians or the court . . . the person currently lacks the capacity to make mental health treatment decisions").

NC: N.C. Gen. Stat. § 122C-74(e) ("unless the principal is deemed incapable by the attending physician or eligible psychologist the instruction of the principal at the time of treatment shall supersede the declarations expressed in the principal's advance instruction").

[168.15] **AK:** Alaska Stat. § 47.30.956(a) ("declaration becomes operative when delivered to the principal's physician or other mental health treatment provider"); § 47.30.956(b) ("physician or other provider shall make the declaration a part of the principal's medical record").

ID: Idaho Code § 66-605(1) ("declaration becomes operative when delivered to the principal's physician or other mental health treatment provider"); § 66-605(2) ("physician or other provider shall make the declaration a part of the principal's medical record").

IL: Ill. Ann. Stat. ch. 755, § 43/25 ("declaration becomes operative when delivered to the principal's attending physician"); § 43/40 ("attending physician shall make the declaration a part of the principal's medical record").

MN: Minn. Stat. Ann. § 253B.03(6d)(c) ("declaration becomes operative when delivered to the principal's physician or other mental health treatment provider"); § 66-605(2) ("physician or other provider shall make the declaration a part of the principal's medical record").

NC: N.C. Gen. Stat. § 122C-74(g) ("attending physician or other mental health treatment provider shall make the advance instruction a part of the principal's medical record").

OR: Or. Rev. Stat. § 127-717 ("physician or other provider shall make the declaration a part of the principal's medical record").

TX: Tex. Civ. Prac. & Rem. Code Ann. § 137.007 ("physician or other health care provider shall make the declaration a part of the principal's medical record").

require acceptance in writing by the proxy before the directive will go into effect.[168.16]

Duration of Directive.   Under some statutes, a directive expires after a set period of time or until revoked by the principal.[168.17] If the declaration has been invoked, however, it remains effective until the principal regains decisionmaking capacity.[168.18] A mental health advance directive may be revoked by the principal at any time, as long as the principal possesses decisionmaking capacity,[168.19] which is unlike some ordinary advance directive statutes in

---

[168.16]**IL:**   Ill. Ann. Stat. ch. 755, § 43/15 ("attorney-in-fact who has accepted the appointment in writing may make decisions").

OR: Or. Rev. Stat. § 127-705 ("attorney-in-fact who has accepted the appointment in writing may make decisions").

UT: Utah Code Ann. § 62A-12-502(2) ("attorney-in-fact who has accepted the appointment in writing may make decisions").

[168.17]**AZ:**   Ariz. Rev. Stat. Ann. § 36-3284(A) (effective until revoked by the principal).

IL: Ill. Ann. Stat. ch. 755, § 43/10(2) ("A declaration for mental health treatment may be invoked within three years of its execution unless it is revoked.").

OR: Or. Rev. Stat. § 127-702(2) ("A declaration for mental health treatment continues in effect for three years or until revoked.").

TX: Tex. Civ. Prac. & Rem. Code Ann. § 137.002(b) ("A declaration for mental health treatment expires on the third anniversary of the date of its execution or when revoked by the principal, whichever is earlier.").

UT: Utah Code Ann. § 62A-12-502(6)(a) ("A declaration for mental health treatment remains effective for a period of three years or until revoked by the declarant.").

[168.18]**AK:**   Alaska Stat. § 47.30.950(b) ("If a declaration of mental health treatment has been invoked and is in effect at the expiration of three years after its execution, the declaration remains effective until the principal is no longer incapable").

IL: Ill. Ann. Stat. ch. 755, § 43/10(2) ("declaration may be invoked within three years of its execution . . . If a declaration of mental health treatment has been invoked and is in effect at the expiration of three years after its execution, the declaration remains effective until the principal is no longer incapable").

OR: Or. Rev. Stat. § 127-702(2) ("If a declaration of mental health treatment has been invoked and is in effect at the expiration of three years after its execution, the declaration remains effective until the principal is no longer incapable").

TX: Tex. Civ. Prac. & Rem. Code Ann. § 137.002(c) ("If the declaration for mental health treatment is in effect and the principal is incapacitated on the third anniversary . . . the declaration remains in effect until the principal is no longer incapacitated.").

UT: Utah Code Ann. § 62A-12-502(6)(a) ("declaration . . . remains effective for a period of three years . . . if invoked . . . declaration remains effective until declarant no longer is incapable").

[168.19]**AK:**   Alaska Stat. § 47.30.970 ("you may not revoke this declaration when you are considered incapable").

AZ: *But see* Ariz. Rev. Stat. Ann. § 36-3285(A) ("Unless limited by the express authority in the document, a principal even if incapable . . . may revoke all or any part of the principal's mental health care power of attorney.").

which the patient need not possess decisionmaking capacity to revoke.[168.20]

Once a proxy[168.21] or physician[168.22] agrees to follow a mental health advance directive, they may be able to withdraw from this duty as long as the other parties—principal, proxy, physician, and provider—are notified of the withdrawal.

ID: Idaho Code § 66-602(2) ("declaration may be revoked in whole or part at any time by the principal, if the principal is not incapable").

IL: Ill. Ann. Stat. ch. 755, § 43/50 ("declaration may be revoked in whole or part, by written statement at any time by the principal, if the principal is not incapable").

MN: Minn. Stat. Ann. § 253B.03(6d)(e) ("declaration . . . may be revoked in whole or in part at any time and in any manner by the declarant if the declarant is competent at the time of revocation").

NC: N.C. Gen. Stat. § 122C-74(j) ("An advance instruction may be revoked at any time by the principal so long as the principal is not incapable").

OK: Okla. Stat. Ann. tit. 43A, § 11-109(A) ("advance directive for mental health treatment may be revoked in whole or in part by the declarant at any time while the declarant is capable").

OR: Or. Rev. Stat. § 127-722 ("declaration may be revoked in whole or part at any time by the principal, if the principal is not incapable").

TX: Tex. Civ. Prac. & Rem. Code Ann. § 137.011 ("you may not revoke this when you are considered by a court to be incapacitated").

[168.20] See § **12.38.**

[168.21] **AK:** Alaska Stat. § 47.30.952(c) ("attorney-in-fact may withdraw by giving notice to the principal. If a principal is incapable . . . by giving notice to the attending physician, or provider").

ID: Idaho Code §§ 66-605(2), 66-607 ("agent may withdraw by giving notice to the principal. If a principal is incapable, the agent may withdraw by giving notice to the attending physician or provider").

IL: Ill. Ann. Stat. ch. 755, § 43/70 ("attorney-in-fact may withdraw by giving notice to the principal. If a principal is incapable . . . by giving notice to the attending physician").

OK: Okla. Stat. Ann. tit. 43A, § 11-106(D) ("attorney-in-fact may withdraw by giving notice to the declarant. If the declarant is incapable . . . by giving notice to the named alternative attorney-in-fact if any, and if none then to the attending physician or provider").

OR: Or. Rev. Stat. § 127-732(1) ("attorney-in-fact may withdraw by giving notice to the declarant. If the declarant is incapable . . . by giving notice to the attending physician, or provider").

[168.22] **AK:** Alaska Stat. § 47.30.956(b) ("If the physician or other provider is unwilling at any time to comply with the declaration, the physician or provider may withdraw from providing treatment consistent with the exercise of independent medical judgment and shall promptly notify the principal and the attorney-in-fact and document the notification in the principal's medical record").

ID: Idaho Code § 66-605(2) ("physician or provider may withdraw from providing treatment consistent with the exercise of independent medical judgment by promptly notifying the principal and the agent").

Standards for Decisionmaking.   The proxy must follow the principal's wishes as indicated in the declaration.[168.23] If the principal's wishes are unknown, the proxy must in good faith do what is in the patient's best interests.[168.24] Physicians are permitted to disregard the principal's wishes in emer-

---

IL: Ill. Ann. Stat. ch. 755, § 43/40 ("If the physician or other provider is unwilling at any time to comply with the declaration, the physician or provider may withdraw from providing treatment consistent with the exercise of independent medical judgment and must promptly notify the principal and the attorney-in-fact and document the notification in the principal's medical record").

OR: Or. Rev. Stat. § 127-717 ("If the physician or other provider is unwilling at any time to comply with the declaration, the physician or provider may withdraw from providing treatment consistent with the exercise of independent medical judgment and must promptly notify the principal and the attorney-in-fact and document the notification in the principal's medical record").

TX: Tex. Civ. Prac. & Rem. Code Ann. § 137.007 ("If the physician or other provider is unwilling at any time to comply with the declaration, the physician or provider may withdraw from providing treatment consistent with the exercise of independent medical judgment and must promptly: (1) notify the principal, or principal's guardian, if appropriate, of that action; and (2) document the notification in the principal's medical record").

[168.23]**AK:** Alaska Stat. § 47.30.970(2) ("person you appoint has a duty to act consistent with your desires as stated in this document").

AZ: Ariz. Rev. Stat. Ann. § 36-3283(E) ("agent shall act consistently with the wishes of the principal as expressed in the mental health care power of attorney").

ID: Idaho Code § 66-606(3)("duty to act consistently with the desires of the principal as expressed in the declaration").

IL: Ill. Ann. Stat. ch. 755, § 43/30(4) ("duty to act consistently with the desires of the principal as expressed in the declaration").

MN: Minn. Stat. Ann. § 253B.03(6d)(b) ("make decisions on behalf of declarant consistent with any desires the declarant expresses in the declaration").

NC: N.C. Gen. Stat. § 32A-19(b) ("health care agent's decisions about mental health treatment shall be consistent with any statements the principal has expressed in an advance instruction for mental health treatment").

OK: Okla. Stat. Ann. tit. 43A, § 11-106(C)(1) ("decisions shall be consistent with any wishes or instructions the declarant has expressed in the declaration").

OR: Or. Rev. Stat. § 127-712(4) ("duty to act consistently with the desires of the principal as expressed in the declaration").

UT: Utah Code Ann. § 62A-12-502(5)(d) ("the attorney-in-fact shall act consistently with the instructions and desires of the declarant, as expressed in the declaration").

[168.24]**AK:** Alaska Stat. § 47.30.970(2) ("The person you appoint has a duty to act consistent with your desires as stated in this document or, if your desires are not stated or otherwise made known to the attorney-in-fact, to act in a manner consistent with what the person in good faith believes to be in your best interest").

AZ: Ariz. Rev. Stat. Ann. § 36-3283(E) ("[i]f the principal's wishes are not expressed in the mental health care power of attorney and are not otherwise known by the agent, the agent shall act in accordance with what the agent in good faith believes to be in the principal's best interests").

gency situations endangering life or health.[168.25] When patients are civilly committed, mental health advance directives are, in effect, rendered inoperative,[168.26] and a mental health advance directive cannot be used by a declarant

---

ID: Idaho Code § 66-606(3) ("duty to act in what the agent in good faith believes to be in the best interests of the principal").

IL: Ill. Ann. Stat. ch. 755, § 43/30(4) ("duty to act in what the attorney-in-fact in good faith believes to be in the best interests of the principal").

NC: N.C. Gen. Stat. § 32A-19(b) ("if none exists [mental health instruction], [health care agent's decision] shall be consistent with what the agent believes in good faith to be the manner in which the principal would act if the principal did not lack sufficient understanding or capacity to make or communicate health care decision").

OK: Okla. Stat. Ann. tit. 43A, § 11-106(C)(1) ("If wishes or instructions of the declarant are not expressed, attorney-in-fact shall act in what attorney-in-fact believes to be in the best interest of the declarant").

OR: Or. Rev. Stat. § 127-712(4) ("If principal's desires are not expressed . . . duty to act in what attorney-in-fact in good faith believes to be the best interests of the principal").

UT: Utah Code Ann. § 62A-12-502(5)(d) ("If the declarant's desires are unknown, the attorney-in-fact shall act in what he, in good faith, believes to be the best interest of the declarant").

[168.25] **AK:** Alaska Stat. § 47.30.962(2) ("physician or provider may subject the principal to mental health treatment contrary to the principal's wishes . . . in cases of emergency endangering life or health").

ID: Idaho Code § 66-609(2) ("physician or provider may subject the principal to mental health treatment contrary to the principal's wishes . . . in cases of emergency endangering life or health").

IL: Ill. Ann. Stat. ch. 755, § 43/45(1)(b) ("physician or provider may subject the principal to mental health treatment contrary to the principal's wishes . . . in cases of emergency endangering life or health").

TX: Tex. Civ. Prac. & Rem. Code Ann. § 137.008(a)(2) ("physician or other health care provider may subject the principal to mental health treatment in a manner contrary to the principal's wishes . . . in case of an emergency . . . to prevent: (1) probable imminent death or serious bodily injury to the patient . . . (2) imminent physical or emotional harm to another").

[168.26] **AK:** Alaska Stat. § 47.30.962(1) ("physician or provider may subject the principal to mental health treatment contrary to the principal's wishes . . . if principal is committed to a treatment facility and treatment is authorized in compliance with AS 47.30.825-47.30.865").

ID: Idaho Code § 66-609(1) ("physician or provider may subject the principal to mental health treatment contrary to the principal's wishes . . . if principal is committed to a treatment facility under section 66-329 ID Code").

MN: Minn. Stat. Ann. § 253B.03(6d)(d) ("physician or provider may subject the declarant to intrusive mental health treatment contrary to the declarant's expressed wishes, only if declarant is committed as mentally ill or mentally ill and dangerous to public, and a court order authorizing the treatment has been issued").

NC: N.C. Gen. Stat. § 122C-74(g)(5) ("provider shall comply with the advance instruction unless . . . the principal is committed to a 24-hour facility pursuant to

to thwart civil commitment.[168.27]

Scope of Directive.   The scope of an advance directive for mental health treatment is limited to electroconvulsive therapy, psychoactive or psychotropic medications, and admission to a mental health facility.[168.28] In addi-

---

Article 5 of Chapter 122C of the General Statutes, and treatment is authorized in compliance with G.S. 122C-57").

OR: Or. Rev. Stat. § 127-720(1)(a) ("when physician or provider may disregard declaration; principal is committed . . . and treatment is authorized in compliance with ORS 426.385(2)").

TX: Tex. Civ. Prac. & Rem. Code Ann. § 137.008(a)(1) ("physician or other health care provider may subject the principal to mental health treatment in a manner contrary to the principal's wishes . . . if the principal is under an order for temporary or extended mental health services under section 574.034 or 544.035 Health and Safety Code and treatment is authorized in compliance with section 574.106 Health and Safety Code").

[168.27] **AK:**   Alaska Stat. § 47.30.964 ("declaration does not limit any authority provided in this chapter either to take a person into custody, or to admit, retain, or treat a person in a health care facility").

ID: Idaho Code § 66-610 ("declaration does not limit any authority provided in this chapter either to take a person into custody, or to admit, retain, or treat a person in a health care facility").

IL: Ill. Ann. Stat. ch. 755, § 43/45(2) ("declaration does not limit any authority provided in Sections 3-100 through 3-910 of the Mental Health and Developmental Disabilities Code either to take a person into custody or to admit, retain, or treat a person in a health care facility").

NC: N.C. Gen. Stat. § 122C-74(i) ("an advance instruction does not limit any authority provided in Article 5 of G.S. 122C either to take a person into custody, or to admit, retain or treat a person in a facility").

OR: Or. Rev. Stat. § 127-720(2) ("declaration does not limit any authority provided in ORS 426.005 TO 426.390 either to take a person into custody, or to admit, retain or treat a person in a facility").

TX: Tex. Civ. Prac. & Rem. Code Ann. § 137.008(c) ("declaration for mental health treatment does not limit any authority provided by Chapter 573 or 574 Health and Safety Code: (1) to take a person in custody; or (2) to admit or retain a person in a mental health treatment facility").

[168.28] **AK:**   Alaska Stat. § 47.30.970 ("'Mental health treatment' means electroconvulsive treatment, treatment of mental illness with psychotropic medication, and admission to and retention in a health care facility for a period up to 17 days").

ID: Idaho Code § 66-601(5) ("'Mental health treatment' means electroconvulsive treatment, treatment of mental illness with psychotropic medication, and admission to and retention in a health care facility for a period not to exceed 17 days").

IL: Ill. Ann. Stat. ch. 755, § 43/5(7) ("'Mental health treatment' means electroconvulsive treatment, treatment of mental illness with psychotropic medication, and admission to and retention in a health care facility for a period not to exceed 17 days").

tion, many statutes limit the number of days to which the patient may be admitted to a facility.[168.29]

Advance Directive Form. Some statutes include a form directive and require that the declaration be made in a form substantially similar to the statutory form.[168.30] Some form directives permit some flexibility to the principal. For example the Oklahoma statute sets a limit of 28 days retention in a mental health

---

OK: Okla. Stat. Ann. tit. 43A, § 11-103(8) ("'Mental health treatment' means convulsive treatment, treatment with psychoactive medication, and admission to and retention in a health care facility for a period of up to twenty-eight (28) days").

OR: Or. Rev. Stat. § 127-700(6) ("'Mental health treatment' means convulsive treatment, treatment . . . with psychoactive medication, and admission to and retention in a health care facility for a period not to exceed 17 days").

TX: Tex. Civ. Prac. & Rem. Code Ann. § 137.001(6) ("'Mental health treatment' means electroconvulsive or other convulsive treatment, treatment of mental illness with psychoactive medication . . . or emergency mental health treatment").

[168.29]**AK:** Alaska Stat. § 47.30.970 ("'Mental health treatment' means electroconvulsive treatment, treatment of mental illness with psychotropic medication, and admission to and retention in a health care facility for a period up to 17 days").

ID: Idaho Code § 66-601(5) ("'Mental health treatment' means electroconvulsive treatment, treatment of mental illness with psychotropic medication, and admission to and retention in a health care facility for a period up to 17 days").

IL: Ill. Ann. Stat. ch. 755, § 43/5(7) ("'Mental health treatment' means electroconvulsive treatment, treatment of mental illness with psychotropic medication, and admission to and retention in a health care facility for a period not to exceed 17 days").

OR: Or. Rev. Stat. § 127-700(6) ("'Mental health treatment' means convulsive treatment, treatment . . . with psychoactive medication, and admission to and retention in a health care facility for a period not to exceed 17 days").

[168.30]**AK:** Alaska Stat. § 47.30.970 ("declaration for mental health treatment shall be in substantially the following form").

AZ: *But see* Ariz. Rev. Stat. Ann. § 36-3286 (permitting use of "any writing that meets the requirements . . . to create a mental health care power of attorney" and offering a form as a sample only).

ID: Idaho Code § 66-613 ("declaration for mental health treatment shall contain the following language, or language substantially similar").

IL: Ill. Ann. Stat. ch. 755, § 43/75 ("declaration for mental health treatment shall be in substantially the following form").

NC: N.C. Gen. Stat. § 122C-77(b) ("use of the following or similar form . . . shall specifically meet the requirements and be construed in accordance with the provisions of this Part").

OK: Okla. Stat. Ann. tit. 43A, § 11-106(E) ("advance directive for mental health treatment shall be notarized and shall be in substantially the following form").

OR: Or. Rev. Stat. § 127-735 ("declaration for mental health treatment shall be in substantially the following form").

TX: Tex. Civ. Prac. & Rem. Code Ann. § 137.011 ("declaration must be in substantially the following form for mental health treatment").

facility, but allows the patient to make specific instructions within those limits.[168.31] The Illinois form allows the patient to specifically consent to or withhold consent for each type of treatment that falls under the scope of the statute.[168.32]

Immunity. If the proxy and physician follow this "good faith" standard, most statutes grant immunity from criminal and civil liability, and from professional disciplinary action.[168.33] Some statutes also specify that the proxy

---

[168.31] **AK:** Okla. Stat. Ann. tit. 43A, § 11-106 ("I understand that 'mental health treatment' means convulsive treatment, treatment with psychoactive medication, and admission to and retention in a health care facility for a period of up to twenty-eight (28) days. I direct the following concerning my mental health care: _____").

[168.32] **IL:** Ill. Ann. Stat. ch. 755, § 43/75 ("PSYCHOTROPIC MEDICATIONS . . . I consent to the administration of the following medications: . . . I do not consent to the administration of the following medications: . . . Conditions or limitations . . . ").

[168.33] **AK:** Alaska Stat. § 47.30.968 ("a physician or provider who administers or does not administer mental health treatment according to and in good faith reliance . . . is not subject to criminal prosecution, civil liability, or professional disciplinary action resulting from a subsequent finding of a declaration's invalidity").

AZ: Ariz. Rev. Stat. Ann. § 36-3283(G) ("An agent is not subject to criminal or civil liability for decisions made in good faith and pursuant to a mental health care power of attorney.").

ID: Idaho Code § 66-606(4) ("agent not subject to criminal prosecution, civil liability, or professional disciplinary action for an action taken in good faith pursuant to a declaration for mental health").

IL: Ill. Ann. Stat. ch. 755, § 43/30(5) ("attorney-in-fact not subject to criminal prosecution, civil liability, or professional disciplinary action for an action taken in good faith pursuant to a declaration for mental health").

MN: Minn. Stat. Ann. § 253B.03(6d)(f) ("provider who administers intrusive mental health treatment according to and in good faith reliance upon the validity of a declaration . . . is held harmless from any liability resulting from subsequent finding of invalidity").

NC: N.C. Gen. Stat. § 122C-75(a) ("attending physician or eligible psychologist who in good faith determines that the principal is not incapable for the purpose of deciding whether to proceed or not to proceed according to an advance instruction, is not subject to criminal prosecution, civil liability, or professional disciplinary action for action upon that determination").

OK: Okla. Stat. Ann. tit. 43A, § 11-112(B) ("physician or psychologist whose actions . . . are in accord with reasonable medical standards . . . is not subject to criminal or civil liability or discipline for unprofessional conduct with respect to those actions"); § 11-112(C) ("attorney-in-fact . . . whose decisions regarding declarant are made in good faith . . . is not subject to criminal or civil liability or discipline for unprofessional conduct with respect to those actions").

OR: Or. Rev. Stat. § 127-712(5) ("attorney-in-fact not subject to criminal prosecution, civil liability, or professional disciplinary action for an action taken in good faith pursuant to a declaration for mental health treatment"); § 127-725 ("a physician or provider who administers . . . in good faith reliance upon the validity of a declaration is not subject to criminal prosecution, civil liability, or professional disciplinary action").

will not be liable for costs of treatments administered in adherence to the principal's wishes.[168.34]

Execution or nonexecution of a mental health treatment advance directive cannot be made a prerequisite for insurance.[168.35]

§ 12.30 Proxy's Authority Supersedes That of Other Decisionmakers

Page 181, replace California and Hawaii citations in footnote 169 with:

CA: Cal. Prob. Code §§ 4720(a), 4727(d).

HI: 1999 Haw. Sess. Laws 169, Sec. 1, § 6(b) (modifying UHCDA) ("Absent a court order to the contrary, a health-care decision of agent takes precedence over that of a guardian").

TX: Tex. Civ. Prac. & Rem. Code Ann. § 137.005(a) ("attending physician, health or residential care provider . . . not subject to criminal or civil liability and has not engaged in professional misconduct for an act or omission if the act or omission is done in good faith under the terms of a declaration for mental health treatment").

UT: Utah Code Ann. § 62A-12-502(5)(e) ("attorney-in-fact not subject to criminal prosecution, civil liability, or professional disciplinary action for an action taken in good faith pursuant to a declaration for mental health treatment").

[168.34] **AK:**   Alaska Stat. § 47.30.958(b) ("attorney-in-fact is not . . . personally liable for costs of treatment provided to principal").

IL: Ill. Ann. Stat. ch. 755, § 43/30(2) ("attorney-in-fact is not . . . personally liable for costs of treatment provided to principal").

OR: Or. Rev. Stat. § 127-712(2) ("attorney-in-fact is not . . . personally liable for costs of treatment provided to principal").

[168.35] **AK:**   Alaska Stat. § 47.30.960 ("person may not be required to execute or to refrain from executing a declaration as a criterion for insurance").

ID: Idaho Code § 66-608 ("person may not be required to execute or to refrain from executing a declaration as a criterion for insurance").

IL: Ill. Ann. Stat. ch. 755, § 43/35 ("person may not be required to execute or to refrain from executing a declaration as a criterion for insurance").

NC: N.C. Gen. Stat. § 122C-73(c) ("person may not be required to execute or to refrain from executing a declaration as a condition for insurance").

OK: Okla. Stat. Ann. tit. 43A, § 11-104(E) ("person may not be required to execute or to refrain from executing a declaration as a criterion for insurance").

OR: Or. Rev. Stat. § 127-715 ("person may not be required to execute or to refrain from executing a declaration as a criterion for insurance").

TX: Tex. Civ. Prac. & Rem. Code Ann. § 137.006(2)(B) ("[may not] require a person to execute a declaration for mental health treatment before: . . . insuring the person").

UT: Utah Code Ann. § 62A-12-502(7) ("person may not be required to execute or to refrain from executing a declaration as a criterion for insurance").

Page 181, add to footnote 169:

ME: Me. Rev. Stat. Ann. tit. 18-A, § 5-806(b) (adopting UHCDA).

MS: Miss. Code Ann. § 41-41-213(2) (absent court order to contrary, agent's health-care decision takes precedence over that of guardian) (adopting UHCDA).

NM: N.M. Stat. Ann. § 24-7A-6(B) (adopting UHCDA).

ND: N.D. Cent. Code § 30.1-28-04 ("unless a court . . . decides otherwise, a durable power of attorney for health care . . . takes precedence of any authority to make medical decisions granted to a guardian").

PA: *But see In re* Bracco, 15 Fiduc. Rep. 2d 173 (C.P. Bucks County, Pa. 1995) (appointing guardian to supersede agent appointed by durable power of attorney "for good cause"). *Cf. In re* Ord, 16 Fiduc. Rep. 2d, (C.P. Blair County, Pa. 1994) (refusing to appoint guardian for 93-year-old man, in part because he had executed power of attorney).

VA: Va. Code Ann. § 37.1-137.1 ("A guardian's duties and authority shall not extend to decisions addressed in a valid advance directive or durable power of attorney previously executed by the incapacitated person.") (from Jan April 16, 1998).

Page 181, add to footnote 170:

MA: *Cf. In re* Smith, 684 N.E.2d 613 (Mass. App. Ct. 1997) (court must appoint persons designated in durable power of attorney as guardians except for good cause or statutory disqualification).

Page 181, delete Texas citation in footnote 171.

Page 181, replace West Virginia citation in footnote 171 with:

WV: W. Va. Code § 16-30-5(c) (only to the extent needed to resolve the inconsistency).

Page 182, add to footnote 172:

KY: Ky. Rev. Stat. Ann. §§ 311.621 to 311.643.

§ 12.31   Withdrawal of the Proxy

Page 182, replace Michigan citation in footnote 177 with:

MI: Mich. Comp. Laws § 700.5507(4)(8.).

Page 183, delete Maine citation from footnote 178.

§ 12.32   Powers Suspended in Emergency

Page 183, replace California citation in footnote 179 with:

CA: Cal. Prob. Code § 4652(b).

Page 183, add to footnote 179:

DE: Del. Code Ann. § 2504(f) (modification of UHCDA provision).

§ 12.34   —Medical Records

Pages 183–84, replace California, Mississippi, Texas, and West Virginia citations in footnote 181 with:

CA: Cal. Prob. Code §§ 4721, 4771(5).
MS: Miss. Code Ann. § 41-41-217 (adopting UHCDA).
TX: Tex. Civ. Prac. & Rem. Code Ann. § 135.007(1) (for advance directives executed before Sept. 1, 1999); Tex. Health & Safety Code Ann. § 166.157(1) (for directives executed thereafter).
WV: W. Va. Code §§ 16-30-4, 16-30-6.

Page 184, add to footnote 181:

AL: Ala. Code § 26-1-2(g)(4).
DE: Del. Code Ann. § 2509 (adopting UHCDA § 8).
ME: Me. Rev. Stat. Ann. tit. 18-A, § 5-808 (adopting UHCDA).
NM: N.M. Stat. Ann. § 24-7A-8 (adopting UHCDA).

§ 12.35   —Selection of Health Care Professionals

Page 184, replace California citation in footnote 182 with:

CA: Cal. Prob. Code § 4776 (if statutory form is followed).

Page 185, add to footnote 182:

DE: Del. Code Ann. § 2505 (modification of UHCDA provision).
ME: Me. Rev. Stat. Ann. tit. 18-A, §§ 5-801(f)(1), -804 (adopting UHCDA).
MN: Minn. Stat. Ann. § 145C.16 (form directive).

MS: Miss. Code Ann. § 41-41-205(7).
NM: N.M. Stat. Ann. §§ 24-7A-1(G)(1), -4 (adopting UHCDA).
UHCDA §§ 1(6)(i), 4 (proxy has authority to "select and discharge health care providers and institutions").

Page 185, delete West Virginia citation from carryover footnote 182.

Page 185, replace Michigan citation in footnote 184 with:

MI: Mich. Comp. Laws § 700.5512(6).

§ 12.36 —Releases of Liability

Page 185, replace California citation in footnote 185 with:

CA: Cal. Prob. Code § 4771(6)(b).

Page 185, delete Minnesota citation from footnote 185.

§ 12.38 Revocation by the Principal

Page 186, replace California and Texas citations in footnote 186 with:

CA: Cal. Prob. Code § 4654 (health care power of attorney executed after January 1, 1984, but before January 1, 1992, expires seven years after date of execution; power of attorney executed on or after January 1, 1992, exists for indefinite period unless principal expressly limits duration); Cal. Prob. Code § 4771(8) (powers given by health care power of attorney exist for indefinite period unless principal expressly limits duration).
TX: Tex. Civ. Prac. & Rem. Code Ann. § 135.002(g) (for advance directives executed before Sept. 1, 1999); Tex. Health & Safety Code Ann. § 166.152(g) (for directives executed thereafter).

Page 186, delete Florida and UHCDA citations from footnote 186.

Page 186, delete Maine citation from footnote 187.

Pages 186–87, replace Michigan, Texas, and West Virginia citations in footnote 187 with:

MI: Mich. Comp. Laws § 700.5510(d).

TX: Tex. Civ. Prac. & Rem. Code Ann. § 135.005 (for advance directives executed before Sept. 1, 1999); Tex. Health & Safety Code Ann. § 166.155 (for directives executed thereafter).

WV: W. Va. Code § 16-30-18.

Page 186, delete second Minnesota citation from footnote 187.

Page 187, add to footnote 187:

AL: Ala. Code §§ 22-8A-5, 26-1-2(g)(1).

MS: Miss. Code Ann. § 41-41-207(1) (designation of agent revocable only by signed writing or by personally informing the supervising health-care provider) (adopting UHCDA).

Page 187, replace California and Florida citations in footnote 188 with:

CA: Cal. Prob. Code § 4727(a).

FL: Fla. Stat. Ann. § 765.104(1).

Page 187, delete Mississippi citation from footnote 188.

UHCDA § 3(a) (individual may revoke designation of agent by signed writing or by personally informing health care provider).

Page 187, add to footnote 188:

DE: Del. Code Ann. § 2504(a) (declarant must be mentally competent to revoke directive) (modification of UHCDA provision).

FL: Fla. Stat. Ann. § 765.104(1).

ME: Me. Rev. Stat. Ann. tit. 18-A, § 5-803(A) (individual with capacity may revoke by signed writing or by personally informing health care provider).

MN: Minn. Stat. Ann. § 145C.09(1).

NM: N.M. Stat. Ann. § 24-7A-3(A) (person with capacity may revoke by signed writing or by personally informing health care provider).

Page 187, replace California and Mississippi citations in footnote 190 with:

CA: Cal. Prob. Code § 4727(c).

MS: Miss. Code Ann. § 41-41-223(2) (adopting UHCDA).

Page 187, add to footnote 190:

ME: Me. Rev. Stat. Ann. tit. 18-A, § 5-811(b) (adopting UHCDA).

NM: N.M. Stat. Ann. § 24-7A-11(B) (adopting UHCDA).
UHCDA § 11(b).

§ 12.39   WRITTEN OR ORAL STATEMENT

Page 187, delete Maine citation from footnote 191.

Page 188, replace Michigan and Texas citations in footnote 191 with:

MI: Mich. Comp. Laws § 700.5510(1) ("patient advocate designation is revoked by any of the following: . . .").

TX: Tex. Civ. Prac. & Rem. Code Ann. § 135.005(a)(1) (for advance directives executed before Sept. 1, 1999); Tex. Health & Safety Code Ann. § 166.155(a)(1) (for directives executed thereafter).

§ 12.39   —Revocation by Written or Oral Statement

Pages 188–89, replace California, Maine, Mississippi, Texas, and West Virginia citations in footnote 193 with:

CA: Cal. Prob. Code § 4727(a)(2) (revocation of agent's authority to make health care decisions made by notifying health care provider).

ME: Me. Rev. Stat. Ann. tit. 18-A, § 5-803(c) (adopting UHCDA).

MS: Miss. Code Ann. § 41-41-207(1) (revocation to be written unless principal personally informs supervising health care provider) (adopting UHCDA).

TX: Tex. Civ. Prac. & Rem. Code Ann. § 135.005(b) (for advance directives executed before Sept. 1, 1999); Tex. Health & Safety Code Ann. § 166.155(b) (for directives executed thereafter).

WV: W. Va. Code § 16-30-18 ("effective only upon delivery of the written revocation to the attending physician").

Page 189, add to footnote 193:

AL: Ala. Code § 22-8A-5(a)(3) (effective upon receipt by attending physician or health care provider).

DE: Del. Code Ann. § 2504 (oral revocation must be witnessed by two persons, one of whom must be a health care provider, who must inform the supervising health care provider or institution) (modification of UHCDA provision).

NM: N.M. Stat. Ann. § 24-7A-3(C) (adopting UHCDA).

Pages 189–90, replace California, Maine, Mississippi, Texas, and West Virginia citations in footnote 194 with:

CA: Cal. Prob. Code § 4727(b).

ME: Me. Rev. Stat. Ann. tit. 18-A, § 5-807(b) (adopting UHCDA).

MS: Miss. Code Ann. § 41-41-215(2) (adopting UHCDA).

TX: Tex. Civ. Prac. & Rem. Code Ann. § 135.005(b) (for advance directives executed before Sept. 1, 1999); Tex. Health & Safety Code Ann. § 166.155(b) (for directives executed thereafter).

WV: W. Va. Code § 16-30-18.

Page 190, add to footnote 194:

AL: Ala. Code § 22-8A-5(a)(3).

DE: Del. Code Ann. § 2504(b), (c) (modification of UHCDA provision).

MI: Mich. Comp. Laws § 700.5510(1)(d).

NM: N.M. Stat. Ann. § 24-7A-7(B) (adopting UHCDA).
UHCDA § 7(b).

Page 190, replace California, Texas, and West Virginia citations in footnote 195 with:

CA: Cal. Prob. Code § 4727(b).

TX: Tex. Civ. Prac. & Rem. Code Ann. § 135.005(b) (for advance directives executed before Sept. 1, 1999); Tex. Health & Safety Code Ann. § 166.155(b) (for directives executed thereafter).

WV: *But see* W. Va. Code § 16-30-18 (requiring attending physician to make record of revocation but not requiring notification of agent).

Page 190, add to footnote 195:

ME: Me. Rev. Stat. Ann. tit. 18-A, § 5-807(c) (adopting UHCDA).

MI: Mich. Comp. Laws § 700.5510(1)(d).

NM: N.M. Stat. Ann. § 24-7A-7(C) (adopting UHCDA).
UHCDA § 7(c) (if possible, primary physician must communicate to person authorized to make health care decisions for patient any condition that affects authority of agent).

Page 191, add to footnote 197:

MS: Miss. Code Ann. § 41-41-207(3) (health care provider, agent, guardian, or surrogate who is informed of revocation is required to promptly communicate revocation to supervising health care provider and health care institution) (adopting UHCDA).

Page 191, add to footnote 198:

MN: Minn. Stat. Ann. § 145C.09(1), (2) (written statement sufficient).

§ 12.40   —Revocation by Subsequent Power
of Attorney

Pages 191–92, replace California, Michigan, Mississippi, and Texas citations in footnote 202 with:

CA: Cal. Prob. Code § 4727(d).
MI: Mich. Comp. Laws § 700.5510(1)(e).
MS: Miss. Code Ann. § 41-41-207(5) (adopting UHCDA).
TX: Tex. Civ. Prac. & Rem. Code Ann. § 135.005(a)(2) (for advance directives executed before Sept. 1, 1999); Tex. Health & Safety Code Ann. § 166.155(a)(2) (for directives executed thereafter).

Page 191, delete Delaware citation in footnote 202.

Page 192, add to footnote 202:

ME: Me. Rev. Stat. Ann. tit. 18-A, § 5-803(e) (adopting UHCDA).
NM: N.M. Stat. Ann. § 24-7A-3(E) (adopting UHCDA).

§ 12.41   —Revocation by Destruction

Page 192, delete Delaware citation in footnote 203.

Page 192, add to footnote 203:

AL: *Accord* Ala. Code §§ 22-8A-5(a)(1), 26-1-2(g)(1).

§ 12.42   —Partial Revocation by Amendment

Page 193, add to footnote 204:

FL: Fla. Stat. Ann. § 765.104.
MN: Minn. Stat. Ann. § 145C.09(1).

§ 12.43   Termination by Operation of Law

Page 193, replace California citation in footnote 205 with:

Cal. Prob. Code § 4654 (applies only to health care power of attorney executed after January 1, 1984, but before January 1, 1992, or to one executed on or after January 1, 1992, containing statement expressly limiting duration).

Page 193, replace California and Texas citations in footnote 206 with:

CA: Cal. Prob. Code § 4654 (applies only to health care power of attorney executed after January 1, 1984, but before January 1, 1992, or to one executed on or after January 1, 1992, containing statement expressly limiting duration).

TX: *Accord* Tex. Civ. Prac. & Rem. Code Ann. § 135.002(g) (for advance directives executed before Sept. 1, 1999); Tex. Health & Safety Code Ann. § 166.152(g) (for directives executed thereafter).

Page 193, replace California citation in footnote 207 with:

CA: Cal. Prob. Code § 4654.

Page 193, delete Minnesota citation from footnote 207.

Page 194, replace Texas citation in footnote 208 with:

TX: Tex. Civ. Prac. & Rem. Code Ann. § 135.002(g) (for advance directives executed before Sept. 1, 1999); Tex. Health & Safety Code Ann. § 166.152(g) (for directives executed thereafter).

Page 194, replace California, Michigan, Texas, and West Virginia citations in footnote 209 with:

CA: Cal. Prob. Code § 4727(e).

MI: Mich. Comp. Laws § 700.5510(1)(g).

TX: Tex. Civ. Prac. & Rem. Code Ann. § 135.005(a)(3) (for advance directives executed before Sept. 1, 1999); Tex. Health & Safety Code Ann. § 166.155(a)(3) (for directives executed thereafter).

WV: W. Va. Code § 16-30-18(c).

Page 195, add to footnote 209:

AL: Ala. Code §§ 22-8A-4(b)(iii), 26-1-2(g)(3).

DE: Del. Code Ann. § 2504(d) (modification of UHCDA provision).

ME: Me. Rev. Stat. Ann. tit. 18-A, § 5-803(d) (adopting UHCDA).

MS: Miss. Code Ann. § 41-41-207(4) (adopting UHCDA).

NM: N.M. Stat. Ann. § 24-7A-3(D) (adopting UHCDA).

Page 195, replace California citation in footnote 210 with:

CA: Cal. Prob. Code § 4727(e).

Page 195, add to footnote 210:

NM: N.M. Stat. Ann. § 24-7A-3(D).

§ 12.44   Termination by Judicial Order

Page 195, replace Texas citation in footnote 211 with:

TX: *Accord* Tex. Civ. Prac. & Rem. Code Ann. § 135.017(a) (for advance directives executed before Sept. 1, 1999); Tex. Health & Safety Code Ann. § 166.165 (a) (for directives executed thereafter).

Page 195, replace California and Michigan citations in footnote 212 with:

CA: Cal. Prob. Code § 4771.
MI: Mich. Comp. Laws § 700.5511(4).

Page 195, add to footnote 213:

MA: *But see In re* Smith, 684 N.E.2d 613 (Mass. App. Ct. 1997) (in guardianship proceeding, court must appoint as guardians persons designated by principal in previously executed durable power of attorney).
MS: Miss. Code Ann. § 41-41-213 (adopting UHCDA).
NY: *In re* Lowe, 688 N.Y.S.2d 389, 390 (Sup. Ct. Queens County N.Y. 1999) (court should not appoint guardian for person who has valid health care power of attorney).
PA: *See In re* Estate of Strickland, 44 Cumb. 357 (C.P. Cumberland County, Pa. 1995) (revoking power of attorney to patient's son, who refused to execute nursing home application for principal).

§ 12.45   Termination by Guardian or Conservator

Page 195, delete New Mexico citation from footnote 214.

Page 196, add to footnote 214:

WI: Wis. Stat. Ann. § 243.07(1)(a) (guardian or conservator has same power to revoke or amend power of attorney that principal would have).

Page 196, replace Maine and Texas citations in footnote 215 with:

ME: Me. Rev. Stat. Ann. tit. 18-A, § 5-814 (adopting UHCDA).
TX: Tex. Civ. Prac. & Rem. Code Ann. § 135.006(a)(for advance directives executed before Sept. 1, 1999); Tex. Health & Safety Code Ann. § 166.156(a) (for directives executed thereafter).

Page 196, add to footnote 215:

NM: N.M. Stat. Ann. § 24-7A-14 (adopting UHCDA).
VA: Va. Code Ann. § 37.1-137.1.
WI: Wis. Stat. Ann. § 243.07(6r) (any interested party may petition for judicial review of agent's performance of duties). UHCDA § 14 (guardian may petition court to enjoin health care decision or order other equitable relief).

Page 196, add at end of section:

A New York trial court ruled that it is not empowered, in the case of a person who is incompetent and has an operative health care power of attorney, to appoint a guardian with the authority to appoint a successor agent.[215.1]

§ 12.46 Immunity of Health Care Providers

Pages 196–97, replace California, Maine, Mississippi, and Texas citations in footnote 216 with:

CA: Cal. Prob. Code § 4750(a), *construed in* Duarte v. Chino Community Hosp., 85 Cal. Rptr. 2d 521 (Ct. App. 1999).
ME: Me. Rev. Stat. Ann. tit. 18-A, § 5-809(a) (adopting UHCDA).
MS: Miss. Code Ann. § 41-41-213 (adopting UHCDA).
TX: Tex. Civ. Prac. & Rem. Code Ann. § 135.010(b) (for advance directives executed before Sept. 1, 1999); Tex. Health & Safety Code Ann. § 166.160(b) (for directives executed thereafter).

Page 196, delete Michigan citation in footnote 216.

Page 197, add to footnote 216:

AL: Ala. Code §§ 22-8A-7(c), 26-1-2(g)(6).
DE: Del. Code Ann. § 2510(a) (modification of UHCDA provision).
HI: 1999 Haw. Sess. Laws 169, Sec. 1, § 9(a) (modifying UHCDA).
NM: N.M. Stat. Ann. § 24-7A-9(A) (adopting UHCDA).

Page 197, add to footnote 217:

DE: Del. Code Ann. § 2510(a)(5) (modification of UHCDA provision).

[215.1] **NY:** *In re* Lowe, 688 N.Y.S.2d 389 (Sup. Ct. Queens County 1999).

Page 197, replace Texas citation in footnote 218 with:

TX: Tex. Civ. Prac. & Rem. Code Ann. § 135.008(c) (for advance directives executed before Sept. 1, 1999); Tex. Health & Safety Code Ann. § 166.158(c) (for directives executed thereafter).

Page 197, replace Florida citation in footnote 219 with:

FL: Fla. Stat. Ann. § 765.1105(2) (must transfer to another health care provider within seven days or carry out wishes of patient or patient's surrogate).

Page 197, delete Maine citation from footnote 219.

Page 197, add to footnote 219:

WV: W. Va. Code § 16-30-10(d).

Page 198, delete West Virginia citation from footnote 220.

Page 198, add to footnote 220:

ME: Me. Rev. Stat. Ann. tit. 18-A, § 5-807(g) (adopting UHCDA).
MS: Miss. Code Ann. § 41-41-215(7) (adopting UHCDA).
NM: N.M. Stat. Ann. § 24-7A-7(G) (adopting UHCDA).
  UHCDA § 7(g) (health care provider or institution must inform patient and make reasonable efforts to assist in patient's transfer).

Page 198, replace California citation in footnote 221 with:

CA: Cal. Prob. Code § 4750(c), *construed in* Duarte v. Chino Community Hosp., 85 Cal. Rptr. 2d 521 (Ct. App. 1999).

Page 198, delete Mississippi citation from footnote 221.

Page 198, add after first sentence:

(One court has even applied such statutory immunity to a decision made by surrogates not appointed pursuant to a health care power of attorney.)[221.1]

Page 199, add to footnote 224:

MS: *See also* Miss. Code Ann. § 41-41-221 (adopting UHCDA).

[221.1] **CA:** *See* Duarte v. Chino Community Hosp., 85 Cal. Rptr. 2d 521 (Ct. App. 1999), discussed in § **17.24** in this supplement.

§ 12.47   Immunity of Proxies

Page 199, replace Maine and Mississippi citations in footnote 226 with:

ME: Me. Rev. Stat. Ann. tit. 18-A, § 5-809(b) (adopting UHCDA).
MS: Miss. Code Ann. § 41-41-219(2) (adopting UHCDA).

Pages 199–200, delete Michigan and West Virginia citations from footnote 226.

Page 200, add to footnote 226:

AL: Ala. Code § 26-1-2(g)(8).
DE: Del. Code Ann. § 2510(b) (modification of UHCDA provision).
HI: 1999 Haw. Sess. Laws 169, Sec. 1, § 9(b) (modifying UHCDA).
NM: N.M. Stat. Ann. § 24-7A-9(B) (adopting UHCDA).
         UHCDA § 9(b).

Page 200, replace Arizona and Texas citations in footnote 227 with:

AZ: Ariz. Rev. Stat. Ann. § 36-3203(A).
TX: Tex. Civ. Prac. & Rem. Code Ann. § 135.010(a) (for advance directives executed before Sept. 1, 1999); Tex. Health & Safety Code Ann. § 166.160(a) (for directives executed thereafter).

Page 200, replace California and Texas citations in footnote 228 with:

CA: Cal. Prob. Code § 4727(f).
TX: Tex. Civ. Prac. & Rem. Code Ann. § 135.010(a) (for advance directives executed before Sept. 1, 1999); Tex. Health & Safety Code Ann. § 166.160(a) (for directives executed thereafter).

Page 200, delete Maine, Michigan, Mississippi, and West Virginia citations from footnote 228.

§ 12.48   Penalties

Page 201, replace California, Florida, and Rhode Island citations in footnote 229 with:

CA: Cal. Prob. Code § 4726 ("unlawful homicide").
FL: Fla. Stat. Ann. § 765.1115(2) (felony of second degree).
RI: R.I. Gen. Laws § 23-4.10-8(c) (imprisonment for no less than one year but no more than five years or fine of no less than $5,000 but no more than $10,000).

Page 201, delete Maine citation from footnote 229.

Page 201, add to footnote 229:

AL: Ala. Code § 22-8A-8(d) (class C felony).

Page 202, replace California and Rhode Island citations in footnote 230 with:

CA: Cal. Prob. Code § 4726 (no penalty unless forgery or alteration hastens principal's death).

RI: R.I. Gen. Laws § 23-4.10-8(b) (imprisonment for no less than six months but no more than one year or fine of no less than $2,000 but no more than $5,000).

Page 202, delete Hawaii citation from footnote 230.

Page 202, add to footnote 230:

AL: Ala. Code § 22-8A-8(c) (class A misdemeanor).

DE: Del. Code Ann. § 2513(b) ("Class C felony" "to create the false impression that another person has directed that health care be utilized for the prolongation of his life" as opposed to intending to shorten life) (modification of UHCDA provision).

Page 202, replace Hawaii citation in footnote 231 with:

HI: 1999 Haw. Sess. Laws 169, Sec. 1, § 10(a) (modifying UHCDA).

Page 202, add to footnote 231:

ME: Me. Rev. Stat. Ann. tit. 18-A, § 5-810(b) (adopting UHCDA).
MS: Miss. Code Ann. § 41-41-221(2) (adopting UHCDA).
NM: N.M. Stat. Ann. § 24-7A-10(B) (adopting UHCDA).

Page 202, add to carryover paragraph:

For there to be liability, criminal or civil, for forging or falsifying an advance directive, the advance directive should be the cause of the forgoing of treatment and thus the cause of death.[231.1]

Page 203, replace California, Florida, and Rhode Island citations in footnote 232 with:

CA: Cal. Prob. Code § 4726 ("unlawful homicide").

[231.1] *See* Edwards v. Shumate, 468 S.E.2d 23, 26 (Ga. 1996).

FL: Fla. Stat. Ann. § 765.1115(2) (felony of second degree).

RI: R.I. Gen. Laws § 23-4.10-8(c) (imprisonment for no less than one year but no more than five years or fine of no less than $5,000 but no more than $10,000).

Page 203, delete Maine citation from footnote 232.

Page 203, add to footnote 232:

AL: Ala. Code § 22-8A-8(d) (class C felony).

Page 203, delete Hawaii citation from footnote 233.

Page 203, replace Rhode Island citation in footnote 233 with:

RI: R.I. Gen. Laws § 23-4.10-8(b) (imprisonment for no less than six months but no more than one year or fine of no less than $2,000 but no more than $5,000).

Page 204, add to footnote 233:

AL: Ala. Code § 22-8A-8(c) (class A misdemeanor).

Page 204, replace Hawaii citation in footnote 234 with:

HI: 1999 Haw. Sess. Laws 169, Sec. 1, § 10(b) (modifying UHCDA).

Page 204, add to footnote 234:

ME: Me. Rev. Stat. Ann. tit. 18-A, § 5-810(b) (adopting UHCDA).
MS: Miss. Code Ann. § 41-41-221(2) (adopting UHCDA).
NM: N.M. Stat. Ann. § 24-7A-10(B) (adopting UHCDA).

Page 204, replace Florida citation in footnote 236 with:

FL: Fla. Stat. Ann. § 765.110(3) (subject to professional discipline, revocation of license or certification, and fine of not more than $1,000 per incident).

Page 204, delete Maine citation from footnote 236.

§ 12.49   Execution as Condition for Receipt of Services and Insurance

Pages 204–05, replace Florida, Michigan, Texas, and West Virginia citations in footnote 237 with:

FL: Fla. Stat. Ann. § 765.110(3).
MI: Mich. Comp. Laws § 700.5512(2).
TX: Tex. Civ. Prac. & Rem. Code Ann. § 135.009(2)(A) (for advance directives executed before Sept. 1, 1999); Tex. Health & Safety Code Ann. § 166.159(2)(A) (for directives executed thereafter).
WV: W. Va. Code § 16-30-4(e).

Page 205, replace Maine, Michigan, and Texas citations in footnote 238 with:

ME: Me. Rev. Stat. Ann. tit. 18-A, § 5-807(h) (adopting UHCDA).
MI: Mich. Comp. Laws § 700.5512(2).
TX: Tex. Civ. Prac. & Rem. Code Ann. § 135.009(2)(C) (for advance directives executed before Sept. 1, 1999); Tex. Health & Safety Code Ann. § 166.159(2)(C) (for directives executed thereafter).

Page 205, add to footnote 238:

AL: Ala. Code §§ 22-8A-9(c), 26-1-2(g)(10).
DE: Del. Code Ann. § 2512(c).
NM: N.M. Stat. Ann. § 24-7A-7(H) (adopting UHCDA).
UHCDA § 7(h).

Page 206, replace California, Delaware, Michigan, and Texas citations in footnote 239 with:

CA: Cal. Prob. Code § 4725.
DE: Del. Code Ann. § 2512(c).
MI: Mich. Comp. Laws § 700.5512(3).
TX: Tex. Civ. Prac. & Rem. Code Ann. § 135.009(2)(B) (for advance directives executed before Sept. 1, 1999); Tex. Health & Safety Code Ann. § 166.159(2)(B) (for directives executed thereafter).

Page 206, delete Maine and Mississippi citations from footnote 239.

Page 206, add to footnote 239:

AL: Ala. Code §§ 22-8A-9(c), 26-1-2(g)(10).
NM: N.M. Stat. Ann. § 24-7A-2.1.

Page 206, replace Delaware and Michigan citations in footnote 240 with:

DE: Del. Code Ann. § 2512(b).
MI: Mich. Comp. Laws § 700.5512(3).

Page 207, delete Maine, Mississippi, and West Virginia citations from foot-note 240.

Pages 208–09, replace California, Delaware, Maine, Michigan, and West Virginia citations in footnote 245 with:

CA: Cal. Prob. Code § 4723.
DE: Del. Code Ann. § 2512(a).
ME: Me. Rev. Stat. Ann. tit. 18-A, § 5-813(b) (adopting UHCDA).
MI: Mich. Comp. Laws § 700.5512(4).
WV: W. Va. Code § 16-30-14.

Page 209, add to footnote 245:

AL: Ala. Code § 22-8A-9(a).
NM: N.M. Stat. Ann. § 24-7A-13(B) (adopting UHCDA).

§ 12.50   Enforcement in Other Jurisdictions ("Portability")

Page 209, add to footnote 246:

PA: Pa. Cons. Stat. Ann. tit. 20, § 5611 ("A power of attorney executed in another state . . . and in conformity with the laws of that state . . . shall be considered valid . . . except to the extent that . . . [it] would allow an agent to make a decision inconsistent with the laws of this Commonwealth.").

Page 209, replace Texas citation in footnote 246 with:

TX: Tex. Civ. Prac. & Rem. Code Ann. § 135.013 (for advance directives executed before Sept. 1, 1999); Tex. Health & Safety Code Ann. § 166.161 (for directives executed thereafter).

Page 209, replace California, Maine, and West Virginia citations in footnote 248 with:

CA: Cal. Prob. Code § 4653.
ME: Me. Rev. Stat. Ann. tit. 18-A, § 5-802(h) (adopting UHCDA).
WV: W. Va. Code § 16-30-21.

Page 209, add to footnote 246:

PA: Pa. Cons. Stat. Ann. tit. 20, § 5611 ("A power of attorney executed in another state. . . and in conformity with the laws of that state. . . shall be considered valid. . . except to the extent that. . .[it] would allow an agent to make a decision inconsistent with the laws of this Commonwealth.").

Page 209, add to footnote 248:

AL: Ala. Code §§ 22-8A-10(3), 26-1-2(g)(13).
DE: Del. Code Ann. § 2516.
NM: N.M. Stat. Ann. § 24-7A-16(A).

§ 12.51   Role of the Courts

Page 210, add to footnote 252:

ME: *See also* Me. Rev. Stat. Ann. tit. 18-A, § 5-814 (adopting UHCDA).
NM: *See also* N.M. Stat. Ann. § 24-7A-14 (adopting UHCDA). *See* Protection and Advocacy System, Inc. v. Presbyterian Healthcare Services, 989 P.2d 890, 894 (N.M. Ct. App. 1999) (commenting on the UHCDA's "concern about excessive judicial involvement").

§ 12.52   Table of Health Care Power of Attorney Statutes

*Pages 211–13, replace **Table 12–1** with:*

Table 12–1

Health Care Power of Attorney Statutes

AL: Ala. Code §§ 22-8A-1 to -10⁺
AK: Alaska Stat. §§ 13.26.332–.358
AZ: Ariz. Rev. Stat. Ann. §§ 36-3221 to -3224
        Ariz. Rev. Stat. Ann. § 14-5501[1]
AR: Ark. Code Ann. § 20-17-202⁺, *as amended by* 1999 Ark. Acts 1448
        Ark. Stat. Ann. § 20-17-201
CA: Cal. Prob. Code §§ 4600–4806
CO: Colo. Rev. Stat. §§ 15-14-501 to -509
        Colo. Rev. Stat. §§ 15-18.5-101 to -103⁺
CT: Conn. Gen. Stat. Ann. §§ 19a-570 to -580c⁺
        Conn. Gen. Stat. Ann. §§ 1-42 to -56˙
DE: Del. Code Ann. tit. 16, §§ 2501–2517

DC:	D.C. Code Ann. §§ 21-2201 to -2213
FL:	Fla. Stat. Ann. §§ 765.101–.401, .1105, .1115
	Fla. Stat. Ann. § 709.08*
GA:	Ga. Code Ann. §§ 31-36-1 to -13
HI:	Haw. Rev. Stat. § 327E
ID:	Idaho Code §§ 39-4502 to -4509
IL:	Ill. Ann. Stat. ch. 755, §§ 45/4-1 to -12[3]
IN:	Ind. Code Ann. § 16-36-1-7
	Ind. Code Ann. §§ 30-5-1-1 to -10-4*
IA:	Iowa Code Ann. §§ 144B.1–.12[4]
	Iowa Code Ann. § 633.705*
	Iowa Code Ann. § 144A.7(1)+
KS:	Kan. Stat. Ann. §§ 58-625 to -632
KY:	Ky. Rev. Stat. Ann. §§ 311.621–.641+
LA:	La. Rev. Stat. Ann. § 40:1299.58.3(C)(1),+ .60–.64***
	La. Civ. Code Ann. art. 2997(A)(7)
ME:	Me. Rev. Stat. Ann. tit. 18-A, §§ 5-801 to -817
	Me. Rev. Stat. Ann. tit. 18-A, §§ 5-501 to -506*
MD:	Md. Code Ann., Health-Gen. §§ 5-601 to -618+
	Md. Code Ann., Est. & Trusts §§ 13-601 to -602[5]
MA:	Mass. Gen. Laws Ann. ch. 201D, §§ 1–17
MI:	Mich. Comp. Laws § 700.496
	Mich. Comp. Laws § 700.5501–.5513 (effective Apr. 1, 2000)
MN:	Minn. Stat. Ann. §§ 145C.01–.16
	Minn. Stat. Ann. §§ 145B.01–.17+
MS:	Miss. Code Ann. § 41-41-201 to -229
MO:	Mo. Ann. Stat. §§ 404.800–.872[6]
MT:	Mont. Code Ann. §§ 50-9-101 to -111, -201 to -206+
	Mont. Code Ann. §§ 72-5-501 to -502[7]
NE:	Neb. Rev. Stat. §§ 30-3401 to -3432
NV:	Nev. Rev. Stat. Ann. §§ 449.800–.860
	Nev. Rev. Stat. Ann. §§ 449.535–.690+
NH:	N.H. Rev. Stat. Ann. §§ 137-J:1–:16*
NJ:	N.J. Stat. Ann. §§ 26:2H-53 to -78
	N.J. Stat. Ann. § 46:2B-8[8]
NM:	N.M. Stat. Ann. §§ 45-5-501 to -502*
	N.M. Stat. Ann. §§ 24-7A-1 to -18
NY:	N.Y. Pub. Health Law §§ 2980–2994
NC:	N.C. Gen. Stat. §§ 32A-15 to -26
ND:	N.D. Cent. Code §§ 23-06.5-01 to -18
OH:	Ohio Rev. Code Ann. §§ 1337.11–.17
OK:	Okla. Stat. Ann. tit. 63, §§ 3101.1–.16+
OR:	Or. Rev. Stat. §§ 127.005–.660, .995
PA:	Pa. Cons. Stat. Ann. tit. 20 §§ 5401–5416
	Pa. Cons. Stat. Ann. tit. 20 §§ 5601–5607*
RI:	R.I. Gen. Laws §§ 23-4.10-1 to -12
SC:	S.C. Code Ann. §§ 62-5-501 to -505

	S.C. Code Ann. § 44-77-50[+]
SD:	S.D. Codified Laws Ann. §§ 59-7-2.1 to -8[*]
	S.D. Codified Laws Ann. §§ 34-12C-1 to -8[+]
TN:	Tenn. Code Ann. §§ 34-6-201 to -215
TX:	Tex. Health & Safety Code Ann. §§ 166.151-.166[9]
UT:	Utah Code Ann. §§ 75-2-1101 to -1118[+]
VT:	Vt. Stat. Ann. tit. 14, §§ 3451–3467
VA:	Va. Code Ann. §§ 37.1-134.6 to -144
	Va. Code Ann. §§ 54.1-2981 to -2993[+]
WA:	Wash. Rev. Code Ann. §§ 11.94.010–.900[*]
WV:	W. Va. Code § 16-30-2-30
WI:	Wis. Stat. Ann. §§ 155.01–.80
WY:	Wyo. Stat. §§ 3-5-201 to -213
	Wyo. Stat. § 35-22-102(d)[+]

[+] Proxy provision in living will statute.

[*] General durable power of attorney statute with health care decisionmaking provision.

[**] Advance directive for members of the military.

[1] Rasmussen v. Fleming, 741 P.2d 674, 689 n.21 (Ariz. 1987) (dictum), appears to authorize the use of the general durable power of attorney statute, Ariz. Rev. Stat. Ann. § 14-5501 (1975), for health care decisionmaking.

[2] As construed by *In re* Crabtree, No. 86-0031 (Haw. Fam. Ct. 1st Cir. Apr. 26, 1990).

[3] *See also* Ill. Ann. Stat. ch. 755, §§ 40/4-1 to -11 (Michie Supp. 1994) (general durable power of attorney statute authorizing appointment of agent to make health care decisions but not specifically mentioning life-sustaining treatment).

[4] Iowa Code Ann. §§ 144B.1–.12 is a health care power of attorney statute. In addition, the living will statute, Iowa Code Ann. § 144A.71, authorizes an agent appointed under the durable power of attorney statute, Iowa Code Ann. § 633.705, to make health care decisions.

[5] General durable power of attorney statute not expressly authorizing agent to make health care decisions. However, 73 Md. Op. Att'y Gen. 253 (Op. No. 88-046, Oct. 17, 1988) concludes that "although [this provision] does not expressly authorize the delegation of health care decisionmaking, nothing in the statute or other law prevents it." *Id.* at 275. Therefore, "[a] person (the principal) may use a durable power of attorney to direct an agent (the attorney in fact) to carry out the principal's specific directive concerning medical treatment, including the withholding or withdrawing of artificially administered sustenance under specified circumstances." *Id.* at 276. Furthermore, the surrogate decisionmaking statute implies that the general durable power of attorney statute may be used for health care decisionmaking. *See* Md. Code Ann., Health-Gen. § 20-107(d) ("[I]n the absence of a durable power of attorney that relates to medical care . . . any of the following individuals may give a substituted consent.").

[6] This statute incorporates the procedures and requirements of an enumerated list of provisions from Missouri's durable power of attorney statute, Mo. Ann. Stat. §§ 404.705, .707.1, .707.2, .710, .714, .717, .723.1, .723.2, .727, .731.

[7] The living will statute, Mont. Code Ann. §§ 50-9-101 to -206, permits the use of either the living will statute or the general durable power of attorney statute, Mont. Code Ann. §§ 72-5-501 to -502, to appoint a health care proxy.

[8] General durable power of attorney, as construed by *In re* Peter, 529 A.2d 419 (N.J. 1987).

[9] Former law, Tex. Civ. Prac. & Rem. Code Ann. §§ 135.001-.018, continues to govern for any document executed or offense committed before September 1, 1999.

Bibliography

General

Alexander, G. "Durable Powers of Attorney as a Substitute for Conservatorship: Lessons for Advance Directives." *Psychology, Public Policy and Law* 4 (1998): 653.

Backlar, P. "Anticipatory Planning for Research Participants with Psychotic Disorders Like Schizophrenia." *Psychology, Public Policy and Law* 4 (1998): 829.

Blustein, J. "Choosing for Others as Continuing a Life Story: The Problem of Personal Identity Revisited." *Journal of Law, Medicine and Ethics* 27 (1999): 20.

Burch, T. "Incubator or Individual?: The Legal and Policy Deficiencies of Pregnancy Clauses in Living Will and Advance Health Care Directive Statutes." *Maryland Law Review* 54 (1995): 528.

Choice in Dying. "Healthcare Agents: Appointing One and Being One." Washington, DC: 1998.

Collopy, B. "The Moral Underpinning of the Proxy-Provider Relationship: Issues of Trust and Distrust." *Journal of Law, Medicine and Ethics* 27 (1999): 37.

Dubler, N.N. "The Doctor-Proxy Relationship: The Neglected Connection." *Kennedy Institute of Ethics Journal* 5 (1995): 289.

Emanuel, L. "Advance Directives: What Have We Learned So Far?" *Journal of Clinical Ethics* 4 (1993): 8.

Fazel, S., et al. "Assessment of Competence to Complete Advance Directives: Validation of a Patient Centered Approach." *British Medical Journal* 318 (1999): 493.

Fins, J. "Commentary: From Contract to Covenant in Advance Care Planning." *Journal of Law, Medicine and Ethics* 27 (1999): 46.

Fleischner, R. "Advance Directives for Mental Health Care: An Analysis of State Statutes." *Psychology, Public Policy and Law* 4 (1998): 788.

Gallagher, E. "Advance Directives for Psychiatric Care: A Theoretical and Practical Overview for Legal Professionals." *Psychology, Public Policy and Law* 4 (1998): 746.

Gasner, M.R., and C.D. Finley. "What Should Be Done When a Proxy Is Reluctant to Carry Out the Wishes of an Incompetent Patient?" *Journal of Clinical Ethics* 3 (1992): 146.

Gillick, M., and T. Fried. "The Limits of Proxy Decision Making: Undertreatment." *Cambridge Quarterly on Health Care Ethics* 4(2) (1995): 172.

BIBLIOGRAPHY

Hardwig, J. "The Problem of Proxies with Interests of Their Own: Toward a Better Theory of Proxy Decisions." *Journal of Clinical Ethics* 4 (1993): 20.

Hoffmann, D., et al. "The Dangers of Directives or the False Security of Forms." *Journal of Law, Medicine and Ethics* 24 (1996): 5.

Iserson, K. "A Simplified Prehospital Advance Directive Law: Arizona's Approach." *Annals of Emergency Medicine* 22 (1993): 1703.

Kapp, M. "Commentary: Anxieties as a Legal Impediment to the Doctor-Proxy Relationship." *Journal of Law, Medicine and Ethics* 27 (1999): 69.

Kapp, M.B., et al. "Proxy Decision-making in Alzheimer's Disease Research: Durable Powers of Attorney, Guardianship, and Other Alternatives." *Alzheimer's Disease and Associated Disorders* 8 Supp. 4 (1994): 28.

Kuczewski, M. "Commentary: Narrative Views of Personal Identity and Substituted Judgment in Surrogate Decision Making." *Journal of Law, Medicine and Ethics* 27 (1999): 32.

McClung, J. "Time and Language in Bioethics: When Patient and Proxy Appear to Disagree." *Journal of Clinical Ethics* 6 (1995): 39.

McCrary, S.V., et al. "Questionable Competency of a Surrogate Decision Maker under a Durable Power of Attorney." *Journal of Clinical Ethics* 4 (1993): 166.

McIntyre, K. "Loosening Criteria for Withholding Prehospital Cardiopulmonary Resuscitation." *Archives of Internal Medicine* 153 (1993): 2189.

Miles, S. "Advance Directives to Limit Treatment: The Need for Portability." *Journal of the American Geriatric Society* 35 (1987): 74.

Miles, S., et al. "Advance End-of-Life Treatment Planning: A Research Review." *Archives of Internal Medicine* 156 (1996): 1062.

Miller, R. "Advance Directives for Psychiatric Treatment: A View from the Trenches." *Psychology, Public Policy and Law* 4 (1998): 728.

Moreno, J. "Health-Care Agents: Decisional Capacity and Legal Compliance." *Journal of Clinical Ethics* 4 (1993): 173.

Post, L., J. Blustein, and N. Dubler. "The Doctor-Proxy Relationship: An Untapped Resource." *Journal of Law, Medicine and Ethics* 27 (1999): 5.

Povar, G. "Second Guessing the Patient's Trust: Facing the Challenge of the Difficult Surrogate." *Journal of Clinical Ethics* 4 (1993): 168.

Powell, T. "Extubating Mrs. K: Psychological Aspects of Surrogate Decision Making." *Journal of Law, Medicine and Ethics* 27 (1999): 81.

Sabatino, C. "The Legal and Functional Status of the Medical Proxy: Suggestions for Statutory Reform." *Journal of Law, Medicine and Ethics* 27 (1999): 52.

Sachs, G., et al. "Limiting Resuscitation: Emerging Policy in the Emergency Medical System." *Annals of Internal Medicine* 114 (1991): 151.

Stolle, D. "Advance Directives, AIDS, and Mental Health: TJ Preventive Law for the HIV-Positive Client." *Psychology, Public Policy and Law* 4 (1998): 854.

Winick, B. "Advance Directive Instruments for Those with Mental Illness." *University of Miami Law Review* 51 (1996): 57.

Zeleznik, J., et al. "The Doctor-Proxy Relationship: Perception and Communication." *Journal of Law, Medicine and Ethics* 27 (1999): 13.

Specific States

FL: Gustitus, T. "Note. A Comparative View of Advance Health Care Directives in Florida and North Carolina." *Quinnipiac Probate Law Journal* 11 (1997): 163.

LA: Neskora, T. "Living Wills and Health Care Powers of Attorney." *Louisiana Bar Journal* 44 (1997): 512.

MD: Hoffmann, D., et al. "The Dangers of Directives or the False Security of Forms." *Journal of Law, Medicine and Ethics* 24 (1996): 5.

MI: Trainer, T. "Update on Medical Decision-Making at the End of Life." *Michigan Bar Journal* 72 (1993): 34.

NC: Gustitus, T. "Note. A Comparative View of Advance Health Care Directives in Florida and North Carolina." *Quinnipiac Probate Law Journal* 11 (1997): 163.

OH: Lederman, A. "A Womb of My Own: A Moral Evaluation of Ohio's Treatment of Pregnant Patients with Living Wills." *Case Western Reserve Law Review* 45 (1994): 351.

RI: Stachura, M.E. "The Rhode Island Health Care Power of Attorney and the Living Will: A Comparative Overview." *Rhode Island Bar Journal* 43 (1995): 15.

TN: Fockler, J. "Should You Use One or Both? Durable Power of Attorney for Health Care and Living Will." *Tennessee Bar Journal* 31 (1995): 14.

CHAPTER 13

DRAFTING AND ADMINISTRATION OF ADVANCE DIRECTIVES

§ 13.1 Introduction: Nonstatutory Advance Directives

Page 218, add to footnote 1:

NC: *See, e.g.,* First Healthcare Corp. v. Rettinger, 467 S.E.2d 243 (N.C. 1996), *rev'g* 456 S.E.2d 347 (N.C. Ct. App. 1995) (living will not enforceable until two physicians certified patient was in a terminal condition).

§ 13.5 —Designating a Proxy

Page 221, replace Nevada citation in footnote 7 with:

See, e.g., Nev. Rev. Stat. Ann. § 449.830(7) (Michie Supp. 1995).

§ 13.6 —Scope of Decisionmaking Authority

Page 221, add to footnote 9:

OH: *Cf.* Allore v. Flower Hosp., No. L-96-329, 1997 WL 362465, at *3 (Ohio Ct. App. June 27, 1997) (implying that liability should be denied to estate of patient treated seemingly contrary to advance directive because he was not "terminally ill" though he died within an hour).

§ 13.24 —Medical Condition

Page 236, add note 54.1 reference at end of first paragraph and add note 54.1:

[54.1]*See, e.g.,* Allore v. Flower Hosp., No. L-96-329, 1997 WL 362465, at *3 (Ohio Ct. App. June 27, 1997) (implying that liability should be denied to estate of patient treated seemingly contrary to advance directive because he was not "terminally ill" though he died within an hour).

§ 13.34   Limitations on Institutional Policy

Page 243, add to footnote 73:

FL: *See, e.g.,* Fla. Stat. Ann. § 765.110(2) ("A health care provider or health care facility may not require a patient to execute an advance directive or to execute a new advance directive using the facility's or provider's forms.").

§ 13.37   Maintenance of Registry

Page 246, replace California citation in footnote 84 with:

CA: Cal. Prob. Code § 4800 (requiring secretary of state to establish registry for health care powers of attorney).

Bibliography

Bush, J. "Who Will Ensure That a Patient's Living Will Is Enforced?" *Estate Planning* 24 (1997): 195.

Choice in Dying. "Healthcare Agents: Appointing One and Being One." Washington, DC: 1998.

Fockler, J. "Should You Use One or Both? Durable Power of Attorney for Health Care and Living Will." *Tennessee Bar Journal* 31 (1995): 14.

Layson, R., et al. "Discussions about the Use of Life-Sustaining Treatments: A Literature Review of Physicians' and Patients' Attitudes and Practices." *Journal of Clinical Ethics* 5 (1994): 195.

Steinberg, M.A., et al. *Patient Self-Determination in Terminal Care: Phase 2: Designing "Useful" Advance Directives and Proxies.* Herston, Queensland, Australia: Department of Social and Preventive Medicine, School of Medicine, University of Queensland, 1997.

CHAPTER 14

SURROGATE (FAMILY) DECISIONMAKING STATUTES

§ 14.1 Introduction

Page 249, add note 0.1 reference at end of second sentence of first paragraph and add note 0.1:

[0.1]*But see* Fla. Stat. Ann. § 765.101(15), (16) (using term "proxy" to refer to one "who has not been expressly designated to make health care decisions for a particular incapacitated individual, but who" is entitled to do so by virtue of Fla. Stat. Ann. § 765.401, and using "surrogate" to refer to a decisionmaker appointed by the patient under Fla. Stat. Ann. §§ 765.201–.205).

Page 250, add to footnote 4:

GA: *See also* Ga. Code Ann. § 31-36A-1-6(d) (separately providing authority solely for the purpose of "[t]ransfer, admission or discharge decision and responsibilities associated with such decision").

Page 250, replace California citation in footnote 7 with:

CA: Cal. Health & Safety Code § 1418.8 (automatically repealed as of Jan. 1, 1997, unless reenacted before that date).

§ 14.2 Coordination with Advance Directives

Page 251, replace West Virginia citations in carryover footnote 8 with:

WV: W. Va. Code § 16-30-8.

Page 251, add to footnote 8:

DE: Del. Code Ann. § 2507(1) (surrogate may make health care decisions when there is no guardian or appointed agent) (modification of UHCDA provision).

ME: Me. Rev. Stat. Ann. tit. 18-A, § 5-805(a) (surrogate may make decision if patient lacks capacity and no agent or guardian appointed).

NM: N.M. Stat. Ann. § 24-7A-5(A).
UHCDA § 5(a).

Page 251, replace Hawaii and Texas citations in footnote 9 with:

HI: 1999 Haw. Sess. Laws 169, Sec. 1, § 6(a) ("guardian shall comply with the ward's individual instructions and shall not revoke the ward's pre-incapacity advance health-care directive") (modifying UHCDA).

TX: Tex. Health & Safety Code Ann. § 672.007 (for advance directives executed before Sept. 1, 1999); Tex. Health & Safety Code Ann. § 166.037 (for directives executed thereafter).

Page 251, delete New Mexico citation from footnote 9.

Page 251, add to footnote 9:

DE: Del. Code Ann. § 2507(1) (surrogate may make health care decisions when directive does not address the specific issue) (modification of UHCDA provision).

Page 251, delete Maine citation from footnote 11.

Page 252, add to footnote 11:

AL: Ala. Code § 22-8A-10(2)(a).

GA: *See also* Ga. Code Ann. § 31-36A-3(a) (in listing in order of priority, potential surrogates to consent to the transfer of a patient from one medical facility to another, recognizing "that there may be occasions when an adult has not made advance arrangements for a situation when he or she is unable to consent").

§ 14.3 When Statute Becomes Operative

Page 252, add to footnote 13:

DE: Del. Code Ann. § 2507(1) (modification of UHCDA provision).
GA: Ga. Code Ann. § 31-36A-5 (patient relocation statute).
ME: Me. Rev. Stat. Ann. tit. 18-A, §§ 5-802, 5-805.
NM: N.M. Stat. Ann. § 24-7A-5(A).
WV: W. Va. Code § 16-30B-5(d) (incapacity).
UHCDA § 5(a).

Page 253, replace Texas citation in footnote 14 with:

TX: Tex. Health & Safety Code Ann. § 672.002(8) (for advance directives executed before Sept. 1, 1999); Tex. Health & Safety Code
Ann. § 166.031(2) (for directives executed thereafter).

Page 253, add to footnote 14:

IL: *Construed in* Ficke v. Evangelical Health Sys., 674 N.E.2d 888 (Ill.
App. Ct. 1996).

ME: Me. Rev. Stat. Ann. tit. 18-A, §§ 5-802, 5-805 (surrogate may not
make decision unless patient is in terminal condition or persistent
vegetative state; advance directive effective when condition specified
by declarant occurs).

Page 253, replace Maine citation in footnote 15 with:

ME: Me. Rev. Stat. Ann. tit. 18-A, § 5-805(a).

Page 253, delete New Mexico citation from footnote 15.

Page 253, add to footnote 15:

AL: Ala. Code § 22-8A-10(2)(a).
UT: Utah Code Ann. § 75-2-1107(1).

Page 253, add at end of section:

A person who would otherwise have statutory authority to act as surrogate
lacks such authority if the patient remains in possession of decisionmaking
capacity.[15.1]

§ 14.4   Priority of Persons Who May Serve
as Surrogates

*Page 253, add note 15.1 reference in second sentence of section after "prior-
ity," and add note 15.2:*

[15.2]**IL:**   Ficke v. Evangelical Health Sys., 674 N.E.2d 888, 891 (Ill. App. Ct.
1996) (surrogate decisionmaking statute "establishes . . . a hierarchical list of candidates [to serve as surrogate] to make life-sustaining
treatment decisions").

[15.1] *In re* Austwick, 656 N.E.2d 773, 776 (Ill. App. Ct. 1995).

Page 254, replace Maine, Texas, and West Virginia citations in footnote 16 with:

ME: Me. Rev. Stat. Ann. tit. 18-A, § 5-805(b) (adopts UHCDA but alters list, adding adult who shares an emotional, physical, and financial relationship with the patient similar to that of a spouse, adult grand-children, adult niece or nephew, adult aunt or uncle, another adult relative closely related, close friend if none other available).

TX: Tex. Health & Safety Code Ann. § 313.004(a), and Tex. Health & Safety Code Ann. § 672.009(b) (for advance directives executed before Sept. 1, 1999); Tex. Health & Safety Code Ann. § 166.039(b) (for directives executed thereafter).

WV: W. Va. Code § 16-30-8.

Page 254, add to footnote 16:

AL: Ala. Code § 22-8A-10(2)(d).
DE: Del. Code Ann. § 2507(2)(b) (modification of UHCDA provision).
GA: Ga. Code Ann. § 31-36A-6 (patient relocation statute).
NM: N.M. Stat. Ann. § 24-7A-5(B).
    UHCDA § 5(b).

Page 254, add after carryover paragraph:

At common law, the status of a friend of a patient acting as a surrogate in the absence of a health care power of attorney designating him as such is highly uncertain.[16.1] However, a small number of surrogate decisionmaking statutes specifically provide for a friend to act as surrogate. The statutes authorizing a patient's "friend" to serve as surrogate are

AZ: Ariz. Rev. Stat. Ann. § 36-3231(A)(6)
FL: Fla. Stat. Ann. § 765.401(1)(g)
IL: ILCS Ann. ch. 755, para. 40/25(a)(7)
MD: Md. Code. Ann., Health-Gen. § 5-605(a)(2)(vi)
NY: N.Y. Pub. Health § 2965(2)(a)(vi) (DNR statute)
WV: W. Va. Code § 16-30B-7(a)(6).

Each statute defines *friend*. Most of the definitions include the following requirements. The "friend"

1. must be 18 years or older (Florida, Illinois, New York, West Virginia) or an "adult" (Arizona) or a competent individual (Maryland);

[16.1] See § **5.21** in the main volume and in this supplement.

2. must have exhibited special care and concern for principal (Arizona, Florida, Illinois, West Virginia);

3. must be willing to make health care decisions for principal (Arizona, Florida, Illinois, West Virginia) to the satisfaction of the attending physician;

4. has presented an affidavit to the treating physician stating that he or she is a friend of the principal (Florida, Illinois, Maryland, New York), which must state facts and circumstances demonstrating the familiarity (Illinois, New York);

5. is familiar with principal's health care concerns (Arizona); and

6. has maintained regular contact with the principal so that he or she would be familiar with the principal's activities, health, and religious or moral beliefs (Florida, Illinois, Maryland, New York, West Virginia).

Page 255, add note 18.1 reference at end of first paragraph and add note 18.1:

[18.1] *But see* W. Va. Code § 16-30B-7(b) (physician may choose among surrogates at the same level or rely on a surrogate at a lower level if the physician believes that the individual is the most qualified, considering his regular contact with the patient, demonstrated care, and potential for full involvement in the decisionmaking process).

Page 255, replace Hawaii citation in footnote 21 with:

HI: 1999 Haw. Sess. Laws 169, Sec. 1, § 5(b) (modifying UHCDA).

Page 255, add to footnote 21:

GA: *Cf.* Ga. Code Ann. § 31-36A-6(6) (patient relocation statute).

Page 256, delete Maine citation from footnote 21.

Page 256, add to footnote 21:

ME: Me. Rev. Stat. Ann. tit. 18-A, § 5-805 (adopting UHCDA).
NM: N.M. Stat. Ann. § 24-7A-5 (adult or emancipated minor).
          UHCDA § 5 (adult or emancipated minor).

Page 256, replace Texas and West Virginia citations in carryover footnote 21 with:

TX: Tex. Health & Safety Code Ann. § 313.002(1) (adult or person who has had disabilities of minority removed); Tex. Health & Safety Code Ann. § 672.009 (for advance directives executed before Sept. 1,

1999); Tex. Health & Safety Code Ann. § 166.039(a) (for directives executed thereafter).

WV: W. Va. Code § 16-30-8(2).

Page 256, delete West Virginia citation from footnote 22.

§ 14.5   Unavailability of Potential Surrogates

Pages 256–57, replace Maine and West Virginia citations in footnote 23 with:

ME: Me. Rev. Stat. Ann. tit. 18-A, § 5-805(b), (c).
WV: W. Va. Code § 16-30-8(b).

Page 257, add to footnote 23:

DE: Del. Code Ann. § 2507(2)(b) (modification of UHCDA provision).
NM: N.M. Stat. Ann. § 24-7A-5(B) (reasonably available).
UT: Utah Code Ann. § 75-2-1107(2)(b).
        UHCDA § 5(b)–(c).

Page 257, add at end of carryover paragraph:

The Mississippi statute adopting the UHCDA allows the owner, operator, or employee of a residential long-term health care institution to make the necessary decisions if an agent, guardian, or surrogate is not reasonably available.[24.1]

§ 14.6   Resolution of Disputes Among
Potential Surrogates

Page 259, delete Maine citation from footnote 28.

Page 259, replace Maine citation in footnote 34 with:

ME: Me. Rev. Stat. Ann. tit. 18-A, § 5-805(e) (all members of class and all individuals of lower priority disqualified).

Page 259, add to footnote 34:

NM: N.M. Stat. Ann. § 24-7A-5(E).
        UHCDA § 5(e).

[24.1] **MS:** Miss. Code Ann. § 41-41-215(9).

Page 260, replace first paragraph with:

2. *Majority Governs.* Some statutes provide that the decision of the majority of a class of surrogates governs. Some statutes provide that if there is more than one adult child or adult sibling in the highest reasonably available decisionmaking class, the decision of a majority of the adult children governs.[35] Others provide that if there is disagreement within any decisionmaking class, the decision of a majority of the members of that class governs.[36] Many statutes also include grandparents or adult grandchildren as categories of surrogates but provide no direction for resolution if the members of these classes disagree about a health care decision.

Page 260, replace footnote 35 with:

AZ: Ariz. Rev. Stat. Ann. § 36-3231(A)(2) (adult child).
AR: Ark. Code Ann. § 20-17-214(4) (adult child).
FL: Fla. Stat. Ann. § 765.401(1)(c) (adult child).
IN: Ind. Code Ann. § 16-36-4-13(g)(4) (adult child).
IA: Iowa Code Ann. § 144A.7(1)(d) (adult child).
KY: Ky. Rev. Stat. Ann. § 311.631(1)(c) (adult child).
MT: Mont. Code Ann. § 41-41-3(2)(b) (adult child).
NV: Nev. Rev. Stat. Ann. § 449.626(2)(b) (adult child).
NC: N.C. Gen. Stat. § 90-322(b) (adult child).
OH: Ohio Rev. Code Ann. § 2133.08(B)(3), (5) (adult child or sibling).
OR: Or. Rev. Stat. § 127.635(2)(d), (f) (adult child or sibling).
TX: Tex. Health & Safety Code Ann. § 313.004(a)(3) (adult child); Tex. Health & Safety Code Ann. § 672.009(b)(2) (for advance directives executed before Sept. 1, 1999); Tex. Health & Safety Code Ann. § 166.039(b)(2) (for directives executed thereafter).
UT: Utah Code Ann. § 75-2-1105(2)(b)(v) (adult child).

Page 260, replace footnote 36 with:

IL: Ill. Ann. Stat. ch. 755, § 40/25(a).
ME: Me. Rev. Stat. Ann. tit. 18-A, § 5-805(e).
NM: N.M. Stat. Ann. § 24-7A-5(E).
VA: Va. Code Ann. § 54.1-2986(A).

Page 260, delete Maine and West Virginia citations from footnote 39.

Page 261, add to footnote 42:

DE: *Accord* Del. Code Ann. § 2507(i) (modification of UHCDA provision).

Page 261, add at end of section:

The West Virginia statute addresses the problem of the multiple decision-makers situation before conflicts arise. It authorizes the health care provider to choose among potential surrogates the one best qualified to serve as surrogate, considering their regular contact with the patient, demonstrated care and concern, and the potential for full involvement in the decisionmaking process.[43.1]

§ 14.7   Scope of Decisionmaking Authority

Page 261, add to footnote 44:

DE: Del. Code Ann. § 2507(1) (modification of UHCDA provision).
KY: Ky. Rev. Stat. Ann. § 311.631(1).
ME: Me. Rev. Stat. Ann. tit. 18-A, § 5-805 (adopting UHCDA).
NM: N.M. Stat. Ann. § 24-7A-5.
WV: W. Va. Code § 16-30B-3(h).
UHCDA § 5.

Page 261, replace Texas and West Virginia citations in footnote 44 with:

TX: Tex. Health & Safety Code Ann. § 672.009 (for advance directives executed before Sept. 1, 1999); Tex. Health & Safety Code Ann. § 166.039 (for directives executed thereafter).
WV: W. Va. Code § 16-30-3(I).

Page 261, add note 44.1 reference at end of first sentence and add note 44.1:

[44.1] **ME:** *See, e.g.,* Me. Rev. Stat. Ann. tit. 18-A, § 5-805(a) (surrogate may make all health care decisions but "may not deny surgery, procedures or other interventions that are lifesaving and medically necessary" unless patient is in terminal condition or persistent vegetative state).

Page 262, add to footnote 46:

DE: Del. Code Ann. § 2503(J) (life-sustaining treatment may not be withheld if fetus could develop to viability with continued treatment) (modification of UHCDA provision).
KY: Ky. Rev. Stat. Ann. § 311.629(4).

Page 262, replace Kentucky citation in footnote 47 with:

KY: Ky. Rev. Stat. Ann. § 311.631(4) (surrogate may only authorize withholding artificial nutrition and hydration if patient's death is

---

[43.1] W. Va. Code § 16-30-8(b)(1).

imminent, patient's advance directive so authorizes, the patient cannot assimilate the artificial nutrition and hydration, or the burden of
providing artificial nutrition and hydration outweighs the benefit).

Page 262, delete footnote 48.

Page 262, add to footnote 50:

AZ: *But see* Ariz. Rev. Stat. Ann. § 36-3231(E) ("A surrogate may make
decisions about mental health care treatment [,but] a surrogate who is
not the patient's agent or guardian shall not make decisions to admit
the patient to a level one behavioral health facility.").

IL: 755 Ill. Ann. Stat. ch. 755, § 40/60-(b) ("A surrogate decisionmaker,
other than a court-appointed guardian, may not consent to specific
mental health services for an adult patient.").

§ 14.8   Substantive Standards for Decisionmaking

Page 263, add to Georgia citation in footnote 54:

GA: Ga. Code Ann. § 31-36A-6(b) (substituted judgment standard; person authorized to consent to patient relocation from medical facility
must "[a]ct in good faith to consent to a transfer, admission, or discharge which the patient would have wanted had the patient been
able to consent").

Page 264, replace Maine citation in footnote 54 with:

ME: Me. Rev. Stat. Ann. tit. 18-A, § 5-805(f) (in accordance with
patient's instructions; if no instructions, in patient's best interest and
in good faith).

*Page 264, replace New Mexico, Texas, and West Virginia citations in foot-
note 54 with:*

NM: N.M. Stat. Ann. § 24-7A-5(F) (subjective or substituted judgment
standard/best interests standard; surrogate shall make decision based
on patient's individual instructions or other wishes, and if unknown,
based on patient's best interests considering patient's personal values).
UHCDA § 5(f).

TX: Tex. Health & Safety Code Ann. § 313.005(c) (substituted judgment
standard; treatment decision must be based on knowledge of what
patient would desire, if known); Tex. Health & Safety Code Ann.

§ 672.009(c) (for advance directives executed before Sept. 1, 1999); Tex. Health & Safety Code Ann. § 166.039(c) (for directives executed thereafter).

WV: W. Va. Code § 16-30-9 ("[s]urrogate shall make health care decisions in accordance with the person's wishes, including religious and moral beliefs").

Page 264, add to footnote 54:

DE: Del. Code Ann. § 2507 (subjective or substituted judgment standard; otherwise, based upon patient's best interests) (modification of UHCDA provision).

IL: *Construed in* Ficke v. Evangelical Health Sys., 674 N.E.2d 888 (Ill. App. Ct. 1996).

Page 265, delete Maine citation from footnote 56.

Page 265, add to footnote 56:

DE: Del. Code Ann. § 2507(g) ("[H]ealth care decision to treat, withdraw or withhold treatment" must be made "in accordance with the patient's individual instructions.") (modification of UHCDA provision).

Page 266, replace Maine and West Virginia citations in footnote 58 with:

ME: Me. Rev. Stat. Ann. tit. 18-A, § 5-805 (adopting UHCDA).
WV: W. Va. Code § 16-30-9.

Page 266, add to footnote 58:

NM: N.M. Stat. Ann. § 24-7A-5(F) (decision should be made based on best interests of patient, considering patient's personal values to extent known by surrogate).
UHCDA § 5(f).

Page 266, add to footnote 59:

AL: Ala. Code § 22-8A-10(2)(c) ("Where possible, the surrogate shall consider how the patient would have weighed the burdens and benefits of initiating or continuing life-sustaining treatment or artificially provided nutrition and hydration against the burdens and benefits to the patient of that treatment").

Page 266, replace Texas citation in footnote 59 with:

TX: Tex. Health & Safety Code Ann. § 672.009(c) (for advance directives executed before Sept. 1, 1999); Tex. Health & Safety Code
Ann. § 166.039(c) (for directives executed thereafter).

§ 14.9   Immunity

Page 267, replace West Virginia citation in footnote 65 with:

WV: W. Va. Code § 16-30B-9.

Page 267, add to footnote 65:

ME: Me. Rev. Stat. Ann. tit. 18-A, § 5-809(a).
NM: N.M. Stat. Ann. § 24-7-8.1(B).
         UHCDA § 9(a).

Page 267, add to footnote 66:

ME: Me. Rev. Stat. Ann. tit. 18-A, § 5-809(b) (if made in good faith).
NM: N.M. Stat. Ann. § 24-7A-9(B).
         UHCDA § 9(b).

§ 14.10   Table of Surrogate Decisionmaking Statutes

*Pages 268–69, replace **Table 14–1** with:*

Table 14–1

Surrogate Decisionmaking Statutes

AL:	Ala. Code § 22-8A-10[1]
AZ:	Ariz. Rev. Stat. Ann. § 36-3231[1]
AR:	Ark. Code Ann. § 20-17-214[2]
	Ark. Code Ann. § 20-9-602(2)[3,a]
CA:	Cal. Health & Safety Code § 1418.8[b]
CO:	Colo. Rev. Stat. §§ 15-18.5-101 to -103
CT:	Conn. Gen. Stat. Ann. § 19a-571[1]
DE:	Del. Code Ann., tit. 16, §§ 2501, 2507–2514
DC:	D.C. Code Ann. § 21-2210[4]
FL:	Fla. Stat. Ann. § 765.101–.401, .404[2]
GA:	Ga. Code Ann. §§ 31-36A-1-6-7
	Ga. Code Ann. §§ 31-39-1 to -9[5]
ID:	Idaho Code § 39-4303[3]

SURROGATE DECISIONMAKING STATUTES

IL: Ill. Cons. Stat. Ann. ch. 755, §§ 40/1–40/55

IN: Ind. Code Ann. §§ 16-36-1-1 to -14

         Ind. Code Ann. § 16-36-4-13[2]

IA: Iowa Code Ann. § 144A.7[2]

KY: Ky. Rev. Stat. Ann. § 311.631

LA: La. Rev. Stat. Ann. § 40:1299.53(A)[3]

         La. Rev. Stat. Ann. § 40:1299.58.5[2]

ME: Me. Rev. Stat. Ann. tit. 18-A, § 5-805[1]

         Me. Rev. Stat. Ann. tit. 24, § 2905[3]

MD: Md. Code Ann., Health-Gen. § 5-605(B)[1]

         Md. Code Ann., Health-Gen. § 20-107(f)(2)

MS: Miss. Code Ann. § 41-41-3[3]

MO: Mo. Ann. Stat. § 431.061[3]

MT: Mont. Code Ann. §§ 50-9-101 to 106[2]

NV: Nev. Rev. Stat. Ann. §§ 449.535–.690[2]

NM: N.M. Stat. Ann. §§ 24-7A-5, -6[1]

NY: N.Y. Pub. Health Law § 2965(4)[5]

NC: N.C. Gen. Stat. § 90-322[2]

         N.C. Gen. Stat. §§ 32A-28 to -34[c]

ND: N.D. Cent. Code § 23-12-13[3]

OH: Ohio Rev. Code Ann. § 2133.08[2]

OR: Or. Rev. Stat. § 127.635(2)[1]

SC: S.C. Code Ann. §§ 44-66-10 to -80

SD: S.D. Codified Laws Ann. § 34-12C-3[3]

TX: Tex. Health & Safety Code Ann. §§ 313.001-.007, as amended by S.B. 1260, 76th Leg., (Tex. 1999). Tex. Health & Safety Code Ann. §§ 166.035, -.039[6]

UT: Utah Code Ann. § 78-14-5(4)(b), (d)[3]

         Utah Code Ann. §§ 75-2-1105, -1107[2]

VA: Va. Code Ann. § 54.1-2986[1]

WA: Wash. Rev. Code Ann. § 7.70.065[3]

WV: W. Va. Code § 16-30-2-30

WY: Wyo. Stat. § 35-22-105(b)[2]

         Wyo. Stat. § 3-5-209(b)[4]

---

[a] Applies only to parent of minor adult child of unsound mind

[b] Applies only to residents in skilled nursing or intermediate care facilities

[c] Authorizes parents of minor children to delegate decisions relating to child's health care

[1] combined living will and health care power of attorney advance directive statute

[2] living will statute

[3] medical consent or informed consent statute

[4] health care power of attorney statute

[5] applicable only to cardiopulmonary resuscitation

[6] Former law, Tex. Health & Safety Code Ann. §§ 672.006, -.009, continues to govern for any document executed or offense committed before September 1, 1999.

BIBLIOGRAPHY

Bibliography

Bishop, M. "Crossing the Decisional Abyss: An Evaluation of Surrogate Decision-Making Statutes as a Means of Bridging the Gap Between Post-Quinlan Red Tape and the Realization of an Incompetent Patient's Right to Refuse Life-Sustaining Medical Treatment." *Elder Law Journal* 7 (1999): 153.

Brock, D.W. "What Is the Moral Authority of Family Members to Act as Surrogates for Incompetent Patients?" *Milbank Quarterly* 74 (1996): 599.

Dubler, N. "The Doctor-Proxy Relationship: The Neglected Connection." *Kennedy Institute of Ethics Journal* 5 (1995): 289.

Fraleigh, A. "An Alternative to Guardianship: Should Michigan Statutorily Allow Acute-Care Hospitals to Make Medical Treatment Decisions for Incompetent Patients Who Have Neither Identifiable Surrogates Nor Advance Directives?" *University of Detroit Mercy Law Review* 76 (1999): 1079.

Hamann, A. "Family Surrogate Laws: A Necessary Supplement to Living Wills and Durable Powers of Attorney." *Villanova Law Review* 38 (1993): 103.

Hoffmann, D., et al. "The Dangers of Directives or the False Security of Forms." *Journal of Law, Medicine and Ethics* 24 (1996): 5.

Krupp, A. "Health Care Surrogate Statutes: Ethics Pitfalls Threaten the Interests of Incompetent Patients." *West Virginia Law Review* 101 (1998): 99.

CHAPTER 15

DECISIONMAKING FOR CHILDREN AND NEWBORNS: COMMON-LAW APPROACH

§ 15.1   Introduction

Page 274, add to footnote 1:

DC: *In re* K.I., 735 A.2d 448 (D.C. Ct. App. 1999).

NY: *In re* Matthews, 650 N.Y.S.2d 373 (App. Div. 1996) (not a right-to-die case but a case involving choice among alternative treatments).

§ 15.2   Presumptions of Children's Incompetence and Parents as Natural Guardians

Page 276, add to footnote 8:

FL: M.N. v. Southern Baptist Hosp. of Fla., Inc., 648 So. 2d 769, 770 (Fla. Dist. Ct. App. 1994) (parents have constitutionally protected liberty interest).

§ 15.3   —Mature Minors: Rebuttability of Presumption of Incompetence

Page 277, add to footnote 14:

MA: *In re* Rena, 705 N.E.2d 1155 (Mass. App. Ct. 1999).

Page 277, add to footnote 15:

See, e.g., Novak v. Cobb County-Kennestone Hosp. Auth., 74 F.3d 1173, 1174 n.1 (11th Cir. 1996) ("As a minor, . . . Novak could not withhold his consent to medical treatment" citing Ga. Code Ann. § 31-9-7, which, however, merely states that "[n]othing contained in this chapter shall be construed to abridge any right of a person 18 years of age or over to refuse to consent to medical and surgical treatment as to his own person.").

Page 278, add to footnote 24:

MA: *Accord In re* Rena, 705 N.E.2d 1155, 1157 n.3 (Mass. App. Ct. 1999) ("We recognize that our laws provide no bright line as to when a minor reaches an age to make certain decisions in life.").

Page 279, add to footnote 27:

CA11: Novak v. Cobb County-Kennestone Hosp. Auth., 74 F.3d 1173 (11th Cir. 1996), *aff'g* 849 F. Supp. 1559 (N.D. Ga. 1994).

Page 280, add to footnote 31:

MA: *Cf. In re* Rena, 705 N.E.2d 1155 (Mass. App. Ct. 1999) ("In assessing the child's expressed preference, religious convictions, and present and future incompetency, it is appropriate for a judge to consider the maturity of the child to make an informed choice.").

§ 15.4   —Rebuttability of Presumption of Parental Decisionmaking Authority

Page 281, add to footnote 41:

DC: *See In re* K.I., 735 A.2d 448, 454 (D.C. Ct. App. 1999) (in case involving child previously adjudicated as neglected, ruling that parental interest is not absolute since "[t]he paramount concern is the child's welfare and all other considerations, including the rights of a parent to a child, must yield to its best interests and well-being").

ME: *In re* Nikolas E., 720 A.2d 562 (Me. 1998) (holding mother's decision to delay treatment of four-year-old child for AIDS did not constitute neglect).

Page 282, add to footnote 42:

ME: *Cf. In re* Nikolas E., 720 A.2d 562, 566 (Me. 1998) ("[T]he determination that the mother's decision was rational and reasoned assisted the court in evaluating the evidence, and resulted in no misapplication of the law.").

Page 282, add note 46.1 reference at end of section and add note 46.1:

[46.1] **ME:** *See, e.g., In re* Nikolas E., 720 A.2d 562 (Me. 1998).
   NV: Nev. Op. Att'y Gen. No. 97-08, 1997 WL 133532 (1997).

§ 15.5 Parental Informed Consent and Exceptions

Page 282, add to footnote 47:

WA: Branom v. State, 974 P.2d 335 (Wash. Ct. App. 1999) (obligation to obtain parental informed consent is obligation owed to child, not to parents).

§ 15.6 Parental Right to Refuse Treatment of Child

Page 286, add to footnote 65:

FL: *But see* M.N. v. Southern Baptist Hosp. of Fla., Inc., 648 So. 2d 769 (Fla. Dist. Ct. App. 1994) (parental interests prevail unless outweighed by compelling state interests).

MA: *See In re* Rena, 705 N.E.2d 1155 (Mass. App. Ct. 1999).

MN: *Cf.* Lundman v. McKown, 530 N.W.2d 807 (Minn. Ct. App. 1995), *cert. denied,* 116 S. Ct. 814 (1996) (imposing liability for negligence for wrongful death of child on mother, stepfather, and various Christian Science practitioners).

Page 286, add to footnote 66:

ME: *See, e.g., In re* Nikolas E., 720 A.2d 562 (Me. 1998) (approving mother's refusal of experimental treatment for AIDS in four-year-old child).

Page 286, add to footnote 69:

MN: *But see* State v. McKown, 475 N.W.2d 63 (Minn. 1991) (indictment of parents of child who died when given Christian Science treatment instead of accepted treatment violated parents' due process rights because statute failed to give fair notice of prohibited conduct).

Page 287, add to footnote 71:

ME: *See In re* Nikolas E., 720 A.2d 562 (Me. 1998) (approving mother's refusal of experimental treatment for AIDS in four-year-old child).

NY: *Accord In re* Matthews, 650 N.Y.S.2d 373, 378 (App. Div. 1996) ("[I]n cases where there is a division of medical opinion as to the appropriate treatment for a life-threatening condition, deference should be given to the decision of the parents as long as the chosen course of treatment is a reasonable one within medical standards.").

Page 287, add to footnote 72:

ME: *See In re* Nikolas E., 720 A.2d 562, 568 (Me. 1998) (approving mother's refusal of experimental treatment for AIDS in four-year-old child, but "if better treatment options should become available, that balance could shift in favor of treatment.").

NY: *Accord In re* Matthews, 650 N.Y.S.2d 373 (App. Div. 1996).

Page 287, add to footnote 74:

MN: Lundman v. McKown, 530 N.W.2d 807 (Minn. Ct. App. 1995) (imposing liability for wrongful death).

Page 287, add to footnote 75:

NV: Nev. Op. Att'y Gen. No. 97-08, 1997 WL 133532 (1997) (parental right to consent to DNR order).

Page 288, add to footnote 79:

MA: *See, e.g., In re* Rena, 705 N.E.2d 1155 (Mass. App. Ct. 1999).

Page 288, add to footnote 81:

ME: *See, e.g., In re* Nikolas E., 720 A.2d 562 (Me. 1998) (involving refusal of experimental treatment for AIDS).

Page 289, add to footnote 85:

FL: *Cf.* M.N. v. Southern Baptist Hosp. of Fla., Inc., 648 So. 2d 769 (Fla. Dist. Ct. App. 1994) (parental interests prevail unless outweighed by compelling state interests).

§ 15.7   Background

Page 290, add to footnote 91:

MN: Lundman v. McKown, 530 N.W.2d 807 (Minn. Ct. App. 1995), *cert. denied,* 116 S. Ct. 814 (1996) (religious beliefs).

§ 15.8   Substantive Rights: Source and Scope

Page 291, add to footnote 95:

FL: *Accord* M.N. v. Southern Baptist Hosp. of Fla., Inc., 648 So. 2d 769 (Fla. Dist. Ct. App. 1994).

Page 292, add to footnote 99:

FL: M.N. v. Southern Baptist Hosp. of Fla., Inc., 648 So. 2d 769 (Fla. Dist. Ct. App. 1994).

Page 292, add to footnote 101:

FL: M.N. v. Southern Baptist Hosp. of Fla., Inc., 648 So. 2d 769, 771 (Fla. Dist. Ct. App. 1994) ("[S]tate's interest diminishes as the severity of an affliction and the likelihood of death increase.").

Page 292, add at end of first sentence after carryover paragraph:

although one court has combined a more conventional constitutional analysis with this approach.[101.1]

§ 15.9 —Standards for Decisionmaking by Surrogates

Page 293, add to footnote 111:

ME: *But cf. In re* Nikolas E., 720 A.2d 562 (Me. 1998) (applying best interests standard to determination of whether to uphold decision of mother to refuse experimental treatment of four-year-old child for AIDS).

Page 294, add to footnote 112:

MA: *But see In re* Rena, 705 N.E.2d 1155, 1157 (Mass. App. Ct. 1999) ("The best interests of a child are determined by applying the same criteria applicable in substituted judgment cases").

Page 294, add to footnote 113:

DC: *In re* K.I., 735 A.2d 448, 455-56 (D.C. Ct. App. 1999) (unlike cases involving previously competent adults, when use of the substituted judgment standard is appropriate, "in cases involving minor respondents who have lacked, and will forever lack, the ability to express a preference regarding their course of medical treatment," and where the parents do not speak with the same voice but disagree as to the proper course of action, the best interests of the child standard shall be applied to determine whether to issue a DNR).

[101.1] *See* M.N. v. Southern Baptist Hosp. of Fla., Inc., 648 So. 2d 769, 771 (Fla. Dist. Ct. App. 1994) (only a compelling state interest will overcome right to refuse treatment, and only if means are narrowly tailored to achieve this interest).

Page 295, add new footnote reference 118.1 at end of carryover sentence, and add new footnote 118.1:

[118.1] *See In re* K.I., 735 A.2d 448, 455 (D.C. Ct. App. 1999). In *K.I.*, the mother of a brain-damaged child previously adjudicated as neglected argued that the court should apply the substituted judgment standard to determine whether to authorize entry of a DNR regarding the child. The court held:

> To attempt to apply the substituted judgment test in this case where [the child's mother] and [the child's putative father] disagree; where [the two-year-old child] has never been healthy; [and] has issued no oral or written directives as to medical matters or formed any opinions about anything, let alone a value system; not only would be impossible, but also would violate the spirit of the substituted judgment standard, the purpose of which is to implement the wishes of the incompetent individual.

Id.

Page 295, delete "The court's" *from beginning of first full sentence and substitute:*

The *Barry* court's

Page 295, delete "Id." in footnote 119 and substitute:

Barry, 445 So. 2d at 371.

Page 295, add to footnote 120:

MA: *See also In re* Rena, 705 N.E.2d 1155, 1157 (Mass. App. Ct. 1999):

> The best interests of a child are determined by applying the same criteria applicable in substituted judgment cases, namely (1) the patient's expressed preferences, if any; (2) the patient's religious convictions, if any; (3) the impact on the patient's family; (4) the probability of adverse side effects from the treatment; (5) the prognosis without treatment; and (6) the present and future incompetency of the patient in making that decision. Care & Protection of Beth, 412 Mass. 188, 195 & n. 11, 587 N.E.2d 1377 (1992).

Page 296, add to footnote 127:

FL: *See, e.g.,* M.N. v. Southern Baptist Hosp. of Fla., Inc., 648 So. 2d 769, 771 (Fla. Dist. Ct. App. 1994) (in addition to considering parents' "interest in making fundamental decisions regarding the care of their minor child, [and] the state's interest in preserving human life," trial court must consider "child's own welfare and best interests, in light of the severity of the child's illness, the likelihood as to whether the proposed treatment will be effective, the child's chances of survival with and without such treatment, and the invasiveness and nature of the treatment with regard to its effect on the child").

§ 15.12 — Designation of a Surrogate

Page 299, add to footnote 143:

ME: *In re* Nikolas E., 720 A.2d 562 (Me. 1998) (implying that if mother's decision to refuse experimental treatment of four-year-old child for AIDS had not been "rational" it should have been overridden).

Page 299, add to footnote 144:

ME: *In re* Nikolas E., 720 A.2d 562 (Me. 1998) (state and guardian ad litem contended that mother's decision to refuse experimental treatment of four-year-old child for AIDS constituted "serious abuse or neglect.").

Page 299, add to footnote 145:

DC: *In re* K.I., 735 A.2d 448 (D.C. Ct. App. 1999) (child received guardian ad litem and medical guardian ad litem in DNR proceeding after prior adjudication of neglect on part of mother, and when mother and putative father disagreed regarding entry of DNR).

Page 299, add to footnote 146:

NV: Nev. Op. Att'y Gen. No. 97-08, 1997 WL 133532 (1997) (judicial order needed to write DNR order for minor if parents disagree with doctor's recommendation).

Page 299, add at end of carryover paragraph:

Similarly, in cases in which a child has previously been adjudicated as neglected, so that child protective services authorities are responsible for his or her care, parental authority regarding medical decisions may be overridden.[147.1]

Page 299, add note 151.1 reference at end of page and add note 151.1:

[151.1]**ME:** *See, e.g., In re* Nikolas E., 720 A.2d 562 (Me. 1998) (report by physician to state Department of Human Services of mother's refusal of

---

[147.1] *See In re* K.I., 735 A.2d 448 (D.C. Ct. App. 1999) (involving not only prior adjudication of neglect but also disagreement between child's mother and putative father).

treatment of four-year-old child for AIDS led to filing of child protective services petition and appointment of guardian ad litem).

§ 15.14   —Judicial Review

Page 300, add to footnote 157:

NV: Nev. Op. Att'y Gen. No. 97-08, 1997 WL 133532 (1997) (court order needed for DNR order in absence of parental consent).

Page 301, add to footnote 158:

NE: Tabatha R. v. Rhonda R., 564 N.W.2d 598 (Neb. 1997).

Page 302, add to footnote 169:

CT: *Cf.* Stamford Hosp. v. Vega, 674 A.2d 821, 827 (Conn. 1996) (noting "extraordinary procedural history" of case in which "hearing before the trial court took place in the middle of the night, under extreme emergency conditions that were not conducive to the ability of either party to develop fully its arguments, . . . [patient] was not represented by counsel at the outset of the hearing and, of that portion of the hearing in which her attorney was present, most was not recorded").

NE: Tabatha R. v. Rhonda R., 564 N.W.2d 598 (Neb. 1997) (due process required under nonemergency circumstances to terminate life support because functional equivalent of termination of parental rights).

§ 15.15   ——Standard of Proof

Page 302, add to footnote 171:

DC: *In re* K.I., 735 A.2d 448, 456 (D.C. Ct. App. 1999) (holding that "the standard of proof required for the issuance of a DNR in the best interests of a child is clear and convincing evidence").

Page 302, add to footnote 172:

ME: *But see In re* Nikolas E., 720 A.2d 562 (Me. 1998) (applying clear and convincing evidence standard in child protection proceeding).

NE: Tabatha R. v. Ronda R., 564 N.W.2d 598 (Neb. 1997).

Bibliography

American Academy of Pediatrics, Committee on Bioethics. "Informed Consent, Parental Permission, and Assent in Pediatric Practice." *Pediatrics* 95 (1995): 314.

American Academy of Pediatrics, Committee on Bioethics. "Religious Objections to Medical Care." *Pediatrics* 99 (1997): 279.

Anderson, B., and B. Hall. "Parents' Perceptions of Decision Making for Children." *Journal of Law, Medicine and Ethics* 23 (1995): 15.

Fleming, M. "A Case Study of Child Abuse and a Parent's Refusal to Withdraw Life-Sustaining Treatment." SPG. *Human Rights* 26 (1999): 12.

Hartsell, J. "Mother May I . . . Live? Parental Refusal of Life-sustaining Medical Treatment for Children Based on Religious Objections." *Tennessee Law Review* 66 (1999): 499.

Hawkins, S. Note. "Protecting the Rights and Interests of Competent Minors in Litigated Medical Treatment Disputes." *Fordham Law Review* 64 (1996): 2075.

Kun, J. Note and Comment. "Rejecting the Adage 'Children Should Be Seen and Not Heard'—The Mature Minor Doctrine." *Pace Law Review* 16 (1996): 423.

Linge, E. "Treating Children by Faith—Colliding Constitutional Issues." *Journal of Legal Medicine* 17 (1996): 301.

Mlyniec, W. "A Judge's Ethical Dilemma: Assessing a Child's Capacity to Choose." *Fordham Law Review* 64 (1996): 1872.

Nelson, L., et al. "Forgoing Medically Provided Nutrition and Hydration in Pediatric Patients." *Journal of Law, Medicine and Ethics* 23 (1995): 33.

Oberman, M. "Minor Rights and Wrongs." *Journal of Law, Medicine, and Ethics* 24 (1996): 127.

Penkower, J. Comment. "The Potential Right of Chronically Ill Adolescents to Refuse Life-Saving Medical Treatment—Fatal Misuse of the Mature Minor Doctrine." *DePaul Law Review* 45 (1996): 1165.

Rosato, J. "The Ultimate Test of Autonomy: Should Minors Have a Right to Make Decisions Regarding Life-Sustaining Treatment?" *Rutgers Law Review* 49 (1996): 1.

Rosato, J. "Using Bioethics Discourse to Determine When Parents Should Make Health Care Decisions for Their Children: Is Deference Justified?" *Temple Law Review* 73 (2000):1.

BIBLIOGRAPHY

Ross, C. "An Emerging Right for Mature Minors to Receive Information." *University of Pennylvania Journal of Constitutional Law* 2 (1999): 223.

Ross, L. *Children, Families, and Health Care Decision Making.* Oxford/New York: Clarendon Press, 1998.

Ross, L. "Health Care Decisionmaking by Children: Is It in Their Best Interest?" *Hastings Center* Report 27 (November/December 1997): 41.

Royal College of Paediatrics and Child Health. *Withholding or Withdrawing Life Saving Treatment in Children—A Framework for Practice.* London: Royal College of Paediatrics and Child Health, 1997.

Sheldon, M. "Ethical Issues in the Forced Transfusion of Jehovah's Witness Children." *Journal of Emergency Medicine* 14 (1996): 251.

Traugott, I., and A. Alpers. "In Their Own Hands: Adolescents' Refusals of Medical Treatment." *Archives of Pediatric and Adolescent Medicine* 151 (1997): 922.

Walters, S. "Life-Sustaining Medical Decisions Involving Children: Father Knows Best." *Thomas M. Cooley Law Review* 15 (1998): 115.

Weir, R., and C. Peters. "Affirming the Decisions Adolescents Make about Life and Death." *Hastings Center Report* 27 (November/December 1997): 29.

CHAPTER 16

DECISIONMAKING FOR HANDICAPPED INFANTS

§ 16.9   Nature and Purpose of Child Abuse Amendments of 1984

Page 320, add at end of section:

It is difficult to gauge whether the Child Abuse Amendments have had a significant impact—or even any impact. Judging from the reported cases, the impact is nil. The only case to cite the Child Abuse Amendments does so in a dissenting opinion in which the judge criticizes the lower court for ignoring the Child Abuse Amendments in its decision to authorize entry of a DNR order for an infant.[98.1] In the only other reported cases in which the Child Abuse Amendments were relevant, they were not even mentioned.[98.2]

Bibliography

Carter, B., and J. Sandling. "Decision Making in the NICU: The Question of Medical Futility." *Journal of Clinical Ethics* 3 (1992): 142.

Clark, F. "Withdrawal of Life-Support in the Newborn: Whose Baby Is It?" *Southwestern University Law Review* 23 (1993): 1.

Clayton, E. "Commentary: What Is Really at Stake in *Baby K*? A Response to Ellen Flannery." *Journal of Law, Medicine and Ethics* 23 (1995):13.

Crossley, M. "Infants with Anencephaly, the ADA, and the Child Abuse Amendments." *Issues in Law and Medicine* 11 (1996): 379.

Fine, D. "Government as God: An Update on Federal Intervention in the Treatment of Critically Ill Newborns." *New England Law Review* 34 (2000): 343.

Flannery, E. "One Advocate's Viewpoint: Conflicts and Tensions in the *Baby K* Case." *Journal of Law, Medicine and Ethics* 23 (1995): 7.

[98.1] **IL:** *See* C.A. v. Morgan, 603 N.E.2d 1171, 1192 (Ill. App. Ct. 1992) (McMorrow, J., dissenting).

[98.2] **TX:** Stolle v. Baylor College of Med., 981 S.W.2d 709 (Tex. Ct. App. 1998).
    WA: *See* Branom v. State, 974 P.2d 335 (Wash. Ct. App. 1999).

BIBLIOGRAPHY

Kopelman, L., et al. "Neonatologists Judge the Baby Doe Regulations." *New England Journal of Medicine* 318 (1988): 677.

Nelson, L., et al. "Forgoing Medically Provided Nutrition and Hydration in Pediatric Patients." *Journal of Law, Medicine and Ethics* 23 (1995): 33.

Nelson, R., and R. Shapiro. "The Role of an Ethics Committee in Resolving Conflict in the Neonatal Intensive Care Unit." *Journal of Law, Medicine and Ethics* 23 (1995): 27.

Symposium. "From Baby Doe to Baby K: Evolving Challenges in Pediatric Ethics." *Journal of Law, Medicine and Ethics* 23 (1995): 5.

Van der Heide, A., et al. "Medical End-of-Life Decisions Made for Neonates and Infants in the Netherlands." *Lancet* 350 (1997): 251.

CHAPTER 17

CIVIL LIABILITY

§ 17.1 Introduction

Page 351, add to footnote 3:

IN: Estate of Taylor v. Muncie Medical Investors, L.P., 727 N.E.2d 466 (Ind. Ct. App. 2000) (suit against nursing home for physicians' actions in administering nutrition and hydration despite family's wishes).

MI: Osgood v. Genesys Regional Med. Ctr., No. 94-26731-NH (Cir. Ct. Genesee County, Mich.), discussed in Andrew Broder, *She Don't Want No Life Support,* 75 U. Det. Mercy L. Rev. 595 (1998).

NC: *Cf.* First Healthcare Corp. v. Rettinger, 456 S.E.2d 347 (N.C. Ct. App. 1995) (suit against wife of deceased patient for refusal to pay for unwanted treatment), *rev'd,* 467 S.E.2d 243 (N.C. 1996).

Page 351, add to footnote 4:

OH: *rev'd,* 671 N.E.2d 225 (Ohio 1996); Allore v. Flower Hosp., No. L-96-329, 1997 WL 362465 (Ohio Ct. App. June 27, 1997).

Page 352, add to footnote 7:

IL: *But cf.* Gragg v. Calandra, 696 N.E.2d 1282 (Ill. App. Ct. 1998) (reinstating cause of action arising out of nonconsensual treatment of terminally ill patient).

MD: *See* Wright v. Johns Hopkins Health Sys. Corp., 728 A.2d 166 (Md. 1999) (affirming dismissal of claims for unwanted resuscitation).

MA: *But cf. In re* Shine v. Vega, 709 N.E.2d 58 (Mass. 1999) (reinstating causes of action based on failure to honor request of allegedly competent patient not to be intubated).

Page 352, add to footnote 8:

MI: Osgood v. Genesys Regional Med. Ctr., No. 94-26731-NH (Cir. Ct. Genesee County, Mich.), discussed in Andrew Broder, *She Don't Want No Life Support,* 75 U. Det. Mercy L. Rev. 595 (1998).

§ 17.2 Battery

Page 353, add to "Anderson" citation in footnote 14:

OH: *rev'd on other grounds,* 671 N.E.2d 225 (Ohio 1996) (permitting only nominal damages), *followed in* Allore v. Flower Hosp., No. L-96-329, 1997 WL 362465 (Ohio Ct. App. June 27, 1997).

Page 353, add to footnote 14:

IL: *See* Gragg v. Calandra, 696 N.E.2d 1282 (Ill. App. Ct. 1998).

MA: *Cf. In re* Shine v. Vega, 709 N.E.2d 58 (Mass. 1999) (reinstating causes of action, including battery, based on failure to honor request of allegedly competent patient not to be intubated).

Page 353, add to footnote 15:

IL: *See* Gragg v. Calandra, 696 N.E.2d 1282, 1286 (Ill. App. Ct. 1998) ("[T]he violation of a plaintiff's right to bodily and personal integrity by an unconsented-to touching is the essence of the claim for battery.").

LA: Causey v. St. Francis Med. Ctr., 719 So. 2d 1072 (La. Ct. App. 1998) (physician's withdrawal of treatment, if actionable, is not actionable as battery).

OH: Anderson v. St. Francis-St. George Hosp., 614 N.E.2d 844, *rev'd on other grounds,* 671 N.E.2d 225 (Ohio 1996).

Page 353, add to footnote 16:

MA: *In re* Shine v. Vega, 709 N.E.2d 58 (Mass. 1999).

Page 354, add to footnote 17:

IL: *See* Gragg v. Calandra, 696 N.E.2d 1282, 1286 (Ill. App. Ct. 1998).

Page 354, add to footnote 20:

IL: Gragg v. Calandra, 696 N.E.2d 1282, 1286 (Ill. App. Ct. 1998) ("A defendant may be liable not only for contacts that do actual physical harm, but also for those relatively trivial ones that are merely offensive and insulting."); Cohen v. Smith, 648 N.E.2d 329 (Ill. App. Ct. 1995) (claim stated for battery when female patient's religiously based request not to be touched or viewed naked by male health care personnel even in the course of otherwise lawful treatment was violated).

Page 354, add to footnote 21:

IL: *See* Gragg v. Calandra, 696 N.E.2d 1282, 1287 (Ill. App. Ct. 1998) ("It is not the hostile intent of the defendant but rather the absence of consent by the plaintiff that is at the core of an action for battery.").

Page 354, add to footnote 22:

IL: Cohen v. Smith, 648 N.E.2d 329, 335 (Ill. App. Ct. 1995) (claim based on constructive intent survives motion to dismiss when patient, who holds views about what is offensive not widely held in community, allegedly communicated those views to defendants).

Page 354, add to footnote 23:

IL: *See* Gragg v. Calandra, 696 N.E.2d 1282 (Ill. App. Ct. 1998) (cause of action stated for failure to terminate life support pursuant to advance directive and at request of family).

§ 17.3   — Refusal of Treatment; Absence of Consent

Page 355, add to footnote 25:

MA: *In re* Shine v. Vega, 709 N.E.2d 58 (Mass. 1999) (reinstating causes of action, including battery, based on failure to honor repeated requests of allegedly competent patient not to be intubated).

§ 17.4   — Application to Right-to-Die Cases

Page 357, add at end of first full paragraph:

Nor can the emergency exception be used to avoid the unambiguous decision of a competent patient to decline treatment, even when the patient's condition is life-threatening and the refused treatment is likely to save the patient's life.[37.1]

Page 357, add to footnote 38:

rev'd, 671 N.E.2d 225 (Ohio 1996).

Page 357, add after third full paragraph:

After the case was remanded, the trial court granted the hospital's motion for summary judgment on the ground that the plaintiff "could not prove any

---

[37.1] **MA:** *See In re* Shine v. Vega, 709 N.E.2d 58 (Mass. 1999).

actual damages as a matter of law."[41.1] On the second appeal, the trial court's dismissal of the action was again reversed. The appellate court emphasized that although the plaintiff could not recover damages for "wrongful living"— "for finding himself still alive after unwanted resuscitative measures"[41.2]— there was a viable cause of action for negligence and battery. The court also emphasized that "damages arise from the violation of a competent adult patient's right to refuse treatment."[41.3] If actual damages can be proved, recovery can be obtained.[41.4] Plaintiff is also required to establish proximate cause—that it was "reasonably foreseeable that unwanted resuscitative measures would cause adverse health consequences to him."[41.5] Assuming that battery or negligence, and causation, can be proved, damages are available for medical expenses from the time of the unwanted resuscitation until the patient's death; for the costs of his nursing home care; for any "extraordinary expenses related to" his care; and for pain, suffering, and emotional distress arising from the stroke he suffered after the unwanted resuscitation.[41.6]

The Ohio Supreme Court granted review and reversed in a 4-3 decision.[41.7] The majority held that although a claim for battery could be pursued, the plaintiff is only entitled to nominal damages if the battery itself, as opposed to the consequences of the battery, is physically harmless. Thus, significant damages might be recovered only in negligence, but the court refused to permit recovery in negligence either.[41.8]

The court's analysis of the battery claim is questionable for a number of reasons. First, damages are allowable for a battery not only for harmful contact but also for offensive contact,[41.9] and a contact is offensive if "it offends a reasonable sense of personal dignity."[41.10] Second, the court applied a proximate cause test to the battery claim that is more appropriate, if at all, for negligence than for battery.[41.11]

[41.1] Anderson v. St. Francis-St. George Hosp., 1995 WL 109128, at *1 (Ohio Ct. App. Mar. 15, 1995).

[41.2] *Id.* at *3.

[41.3] *Id.*

[41.4] *Id.* at *5.

[41.5] *Id.*

[41.6] *Id.*

[41.7] Anderson v. St. Francis-St. George Hosp., 671 N.E.2d 225 (Ohio 1996), *followed in* Allore v. Flower Hosp., No. L-96-329, 1997 WL 362465 (Ohio Ct. App. June 27, 1997).

[41.8] See § **17.12** in this supplement.

[41.9] Restatement (Second) of Torts 18 (1965).

[41.10] *Id.* § 19. *See also* 1 F. Harper et al., The Law of Torts § 3.2, at 214–15 (1986) (at least when manifested by plaintiff, whether contact is offensive is measured by subjective test).

[41.11] W. Keeton et al., Prosser and Keeton on the Law of Torts § 9, at 40 (5th ed. 1984) ("The defendant's liability for the resulting harm extends, as in most other cases of

Page 361, add to footnote 65:

CA11: Novak v. Cobb County-Kennestone Hosp. Auth., 74 F.3d 1173 (11th Cir. 1996), *aff'g* 849 F. Supp. 1559 (N.D. Ga. 1994).

Page 362, add to footnote 71:

rev'd, 671 N.E.2d 225 (Ohio 1996).

Page 363, add at end of section:

In an interesting twist, a Pennsylvania trial court upheld a complaint alleging that the *termination* of ventilatory support could be a battery if the "disconnection . . . involved a surgical procedure," a matter which could not be resolved on the pleadings. However, the cause of action was sustained only as to the deceased minor patient, and it was dismissed as to her parents because they would not have been the "recipients of the unconsented touching."[71.1]

An Illinois case, *Gragg v. Calandra,*[71.2] may signal a new willingness on the part of courts to award damages for nonconsensual end-of-life treatment. One cautionary note, however, is that this case arose in a jurisdiction in which there is a substantial body of case and statutory law establishing the right to refuse end-of-life treatment, and thus there was no excuse for dismissing the case on the ground that the defendants did not have fair warning of the state of the law, as has happened in other jurisdictions. Nevertheless, the case held that the plaintiff's claims of liability for nonconsensual treatment and for intentional infliction of emotional distress stated a cause of action, without any reference by the court to this body of end-of-life case or statutory law; it relied exclusively on more conventional medical liability cases.

The patient in this case went to the defendant hospital's emergency room. His wife and daughter consented to cardiac catheterization, during which he suffered a cardiac arrest and became unconscious and nonresponsive. The plaintiffs alleged that there was no reasonable likelihood that the patient would survive, but that the defendant physicians performed open-heart bypass surgery without obtaining consent. They further alleged that as a result of the surgery, the patient sustained irreversible brain damage, remained nonresponsive, and became dependent on life support. The plaintiffs repeatedly attempted to have treatment discontinued in accordance with

---

intentional torts, to consequences which the defendant did not intend, and could not reasonably have foreseen, upon the obvious basis that it is better for unexpected losses to fall upon the intentional wrongdoer than upon the innocent victim.").

[71.1] Rideout v. Hershey Medical Ctr., 16 Fiduc. Rep. 2d 181, 191 (C.P. Dauphin County, Pa. 1995).

[71.2] 696 N.E.2d 1282 (Ill. App. Ct. 1998).

the patient's living will, which directed that he did not wish extraordinary measures. After the patient's regular physician became involved in the efforts to discontinue life support, a meeting was held with the family and some members of the health care team and an attorney for the resistant physician to discuss the living will. However, after the meeting, the hospital's medical director told the family that the hospital and doctors would not honor the living will. The patient never regained consciousness and died a few days later.

The patient's daughter, in her individual capacity and as administrator of her mother's estate, brought suit alleging battery, intentional infliction of emotional distress, and two statutory theories of recovery.[71.3] The court reinstated the dismissal of the complaint on the two common-law theories, but permitted one of the statutory claims to proceed.

The court took a view of the battery claim entirely consistent with traditional tort theory,[71.4] though one that is unusual not only in end-of-life cases but also in medical liability cases in general, where courts are so reluctant to impose liability on physicians for battery. The plaintiff's battery allegations were quite straightforward: that the defendants performed open-heart surgery on the patient without consent and that they continued to treat him postoperatively despite the refusal expressed in his living will and reiterated and substantiated by his wife and daughter and presumably by his personal physician. The reinstatement of the battery claim[71.5] (and the intentional infliction of emotional distress claim)[71.6] by the appeals court seem correct; what is difficult to understand is why they were dismissed by the trial court.

§ 17.5 Intentional Infliction of Emotional Distress

Page 363, add to footnote 72:

CA: *See* Duarte v. Chino Community Hosp., 85 Cal. Rptr. 2d 521 (Ct. App. 1999) (jury found by special verdict that defendant physician's conduct had not been outrageous; claim dropped on appeal).

[71.3] See § **17.19** in this supplement.

[71.4] 696 N.E.2d at 1286 ("Liability for battery emphasizes the plaintiff's lack of consent to a touching. [Citation omitted.] A defendant may be liable not only for contacts that do actual physical harm, but also for those relatively trivial ones that are merely offensive and insulting. [Citation omitted.] '[A] plaintiff is entitled to demand that the defendant refrain from the offensive touching, although the contact results in no visible injury.' W. Keeton, Prosser & Keeton on Torts § 9, at 41 (5th ed. 1984).").

[71.5] *Id.* at 1287 ("Here, the violation of a plaintiff's right to bodily and personal integrity by an unconsented-to touching is the essence of the claim for battery. By stating that surgery and treatment were performed without consent, plaintiff has stated a claim for medical battery.").

[71.6] See § **17.6** in this supplement.

IL: Gragg v. Calandra, 696 N.E.2d 1282 (Ill. App. Ct. 1998).

Page 363, add to footnote 75:

IL: Gragg v. Calandra, 696 N.E.2d 1282, 1289 (Ill. App. Ct. 1998).

Page 365, add to footnote 86:

IL: Gragg v. Calandra, 696 N.E.2d 1282 (Ill. App. Ct. 1998) (reinstating complaint and remanding for trial on claim of intentional infliction of emotional distress).

§ 17.6   — Application to Right-to-Die Cases

Page 365, add to footnote 87:

IL: *But see* Gragg v. Calandra, 696 N.E.2d 1282 (Ill. App. Ct. 1998) (reinstating complaint and remanding for trial on claim of intentional infliction of emotional distress).

Page 365, add to footnote 88:

IL: *But see* Gragg v. Calandra, 696 N.E.2d 1282 (Ill. App. Ct. 1998) (reinstating complaint and remanding for trial on claim of intentional infliction of emotional distress).

Page 369, add to footnote 109:

CA: *See also* Duarte v. Chino Community Hosp., 85 Cal. Rptr. 2d 521 (Ct. App. 1999) (failure to follow patient's oral advance directive requesting termination of life support found by jury not to be outrageous).

Page 371, add to footnote 118:

DKS: Asselin v. Shawnee Mission Medical Ctr., Inc., 894 F. Supp. 1479 (D. Kan. 1995) (PSDA does not create private right of action).

Page 371, add to footnote 119:

MI: *See also* Virk v. Detroit Receiving Hosp., No. 93-333085 (Cir. Ct. Wayne County, Mich.), discussed in Andrew Broder, *She Don't Want No Life Support,* 75 U. Det. Mercy L. Rev. 595 (1998).

Page 373, add after carryover quotation:

The applicability of the theory of intentional infliction of emotional distress will be put to a true test in *Gragg v. Calandra*,[126.1] in which the plaintiff alleged this theory among others.[126.2] After requesting that the patient's life support be terminated in accordance with his living will, the patient's wife and daughter allegedly were "'verbally abused' and 'repeatedly insult[ed] and injure[d]'" by defendants' "repeatedly accusing them in a public area in the presence of others of trying to kill [the patient]."[126.3] They also claimed that the defendants' refusal to honor the patient's living will and the family's requests to terminate life support and refusal "to perform an EEG test or to report the results of such a test, knowing that the test would likely confirm that there was no brain activity," to constitute severe emotional distress.[126.4] The court agreed with the plaintiff that this could be considered by a jury to be outrageous conduct, especially in light of the fact that the plaintiff was more susceptible to emotional distress because of the patient's severe condition, and reinstated the complaint on this count.

Page 373, add to footnote 129:

IL: *But see* Gragg v. Calandra, 696 N.E.2d 1282 (Ill. App. Ct. 1998) (reinstating complaint and remanding for trial on claim of intentional infliction of emotional distress).

Page 373, add to footnote 130:

PA: Rideout v. Hershey Med. Ctr., 16 Fiduc. Rep. 2d 181 (C.P. Dauphin County, Pa. 1995) (finding complaint stated cause of action for intentional infliction of emotional distress for termination of treatment over protests of patient's parents).

§ 17.7 —Recovery by Third Parties

Page 374, add to footnote 132:

WA: *But cf.* Branom v. State, 974 P.2d 335, 341 (Wash. Ct. App. 1999) (parents of child have no cause of action for *negligent* infliction of emotional distress under Washington statute authorizing claims arising out of provision of health care nor under common law, which requires that plaintiffs be placed in peril).

[126.1] 696 N.E.2d 1282 (Ill. App. Ct. 1998).

[126.2] See §§ **17.4** and **17.19** in this supplement.

[126.3] 696 N.E.2d at 1289.

[126.4] *Id.*

Page 375, add to footnote 137:

WA: *Cf.* Branom v. State, 974 P.2d 335, 341 (Wash. Ct. App. 1999).

Page 377, add at end of section:

The requirements of a cause of action for intentional infliction of emotional distress may be met for the unauthorized forgoing of life-sustaining treatment. On a motion to dismiss for failure to state a claim, a Pennsylvania trial court upheld a complaint for intentional infliction of emotional distress by the parents of a young, terminally ill child from whom a ventilator was disconnected over their opposition, and who learned of the termination when the hospital's chaplain, who was in the patient's room, announced over the hospital's intercom system that ventilatory support had been withdrawn.[150.1]

§ 17.9 Negligence

Page 379, add to "Anderson" citation in footnote 160:

aff'd & rev'd on other grounds, 671 N.E.2d 225 (Ohio 1996).

Page 379, add to footnote 160:

TX: *But see* Stolle v. Baylor College of Med., 981 S.W.2d 709 (Tex. Ct. App. 1998) (bringing suit for unauthorized treatment as negligence claim).

Page 379, add note 162.1 reference at end of second sentence of last paragraph and add note 162.1:

[162.1] **CA:** *See, e.g.,* Duarte v. Chino Community Hosp., 85 Cal. Rptr. 2d 521 (Ct. App. 1999).

Page 380, add to footnote 163:

NC: *But cf.* First Healthcare Corp. v. Rettinger, 456 S.E.2d 347 (N.C. Ct. App. 1995) (upholding nursing home's claim to be paid for care of patient who had a living will refusing the provided treatment), *rev'd,* 467 S.E.2d 243 (N.C. 1996).

[150.1] Rideout v. Hershey Med. Ctr., 16 Fiduc. Rep. 2d 181 (C.P. Dauphin County, Pa. 1995).

§ 17.10   —Negligence Liability in Administering Treatment

Page 380, add to footnote 165:

IN: *See, e.g.,* Estate of Taylor v. Muncie Medical Investors, L.P., 727 N.E.2d 466 (Ind. Ct. App. 2000) (involving the nursing home's receipt of conflicting signals from family members).

Page 380, add to footnote 166:

TX: *But see* Stolle v. Baylor College of Med., 981 S.W.2d 709 (Tex. Ct. App. 1998) (bringing suit for unauthorized treatment as negligence claim).

Page 380, add to footnote 167:

MA: *See In re* Shine v. Vega, 709 N.E.2d 58 (Mass. 1999).

Page 380, add to footnote 167, in "IN" section, after "e.g." but before citation to Payne:

Estate of Taylor v. Muncie Medical Investors, L.P., 727 N.E.2d 466 (Ind. Ct. App. 2000);

Page 380, add to footnote 168:

rev'd, 671 N.E.2d 225 (Ohio 1996), *and followed in* Allore v. Flower Hosp., No. L-96-329, 1997 WL 362465 (Ohio Ct. App. June 27, 1997).

Page 380, add at end of second paragraph:

However, on appeal, the Ohio Supreme Court reversed and dismissed the action. See §§ **17.4** and **17.12** in this supplement.

§ 17.11   —Informed Consent

Page 383, add to "Anderson" citation in footnote 183:

aff'd & rev'd on other grounds, 671 N.E.2d 225 (Ohio 1996).

§ 17.12 ——Application to Right-to-Die Cases

Page 385, add to "Anderson" citation in footnote 197:

aff'd in part & rev'd on other grounds, 671 N.E.2d 225 (Ohio 1996) (but permitting only nominal damages).

Page 386, add to footnote 199:

IN: *But see* Estate of Taylor v. Muncie Medical Investors, L.P., 727 N.E.2d 466, 471 (Ind. Ct. App. 2000) (affirming grant of summary judgment on multi-count complaint alleging, *inter alia*, lack of informed consent because court refused to recognize "a new cause of action for wrongful prolongation of life").

Page 386, add to footnote 200:

MI: *See also* Hendon v. William Beaumont Hosp., No. 176168 (Mich. Ct. App. May 28, 1996), *appeal denied,* 564 N.W.2d 901 (Mich. 1997), discussed in Andrew Broder, *She Don't Want No Life Support,* 75 U. Det. Mercy L. Rev. 595 (1998).

Page 388, add to footnote 206:

MD: *Cf.* Wright v. Johns Hopkins Health Sys. Corp., 728 A.2d 166 (Md. 1999) (affirming dismissal of suit, refusing to impose liability for ignoring a "'generalized and open-ended desire to forgo life-sustaining procedures'").

Page 390, add at end of section:

Anderson v. St. Francis-St. George Hospital[217.1] illustrates another way in which negligence can occur in end-of-life decisionmaking—namely, by not following a patient's decision not to be treated. Although such a claim may also be brought as one in battery,[217.2] some courts limit recovery only to nominal damages if the treatment itself—as distinguished from the consequences of the treatment—is not harmful, as was the case in *Anderson*.

The patient in *Anderson* had been administered CPR by a nurse despite the fact that, at his request, his attending physician had written a DNR order. The Ohio Supreme Court seemed willing to conclude, or at least to assume, that the defendants' conduct was either a negligent or intentional wrong.[217.3]

[217.1] 671 N.E.2d 225 (Ohio 1996), *followed in* Allore v. Flower Hosp., No. L-96-329, 1997 WL 362465 (Ohio Ct. App. June 27, 1997).

[217.2] See § **17.4** in the main volume and this supplement.

[217.3] 671 N.E.2d at 227 ("Whether intentional or negligent, interference with a person's legal right to die would constitute a breach of that duty to honor the wishes of the patient.").

Although styled a "wrongful living" cause of action, the court correctly observed that "[i]n reality, a claim of wrongful living is a damages concept, just as a claim for 'wrongful whiplash' or 'wrongful broken arm,' and must necessarily involve an underlying claim of negligence or battery."[217.4]

In the majority's view, the plaintiff's claim failed either on the issue of causation or on the issue of damages. On the court's first pass at these issues, it stated that causation is to be measured by a "but for" test, and "once it is established that but for the conduct of the medical professional, death would have resulted, the causation element of a 'wrongful living' claim is satisfied."[217.5] Then damages must be established, and the damages must be shown to "flow from the 'harm' caused the plaintiff."[217.6] In this regard, the plaintiff could not prevail because he was seeking damages for the stroke he suffered three days after being resuscitated against his wishes, and the bodily and psychic harms and financial expenses that were foreseeable results of the resuscitation. As almost all courts have concluded in cases involving "wrongful birth," damages such as these are not legally compensable because of "'the impossibility of a jury placing a price tag" on the benefit of life,'"[217.7] and the impossibility "of awarding damages on the relative merits of 'being versus nonbeing.'"[217.8] The Ohio Court of Appeals had, in effect, allowed an impermissible action for wrongful living, permitting recovery for "damages based upon the torts of negligence or battery for all the foreseeable consequences of the therapy, including the pain, suffering, and emotional distress beyond that which he normally would have suffered had the therapy not been initiated."[217.9]

The problems with this analysis are several. First, although it is true that plaintiffs have been startlingly unsuccessful in wrongful life cases, parents who are forced to pay expenses flowing from a birth resulting from wrongful conduct by a physician to prevent that birth have been almost equally successful in obtaining such damages. Second, in this case, the patient himself was competent and made clear that he considered continued life of a certain kind (post-CPR life) to be a detriment, not a benefit. Furthermore, in wrongful life cases, the existential comparison on which the cause of action has faltered is between not ever having come into existence and living. Here, however, the comparison is between living in a compromised fashion that one wishes to avoid and not living at all, a comparison made by the patient himself with knowledge of what living a good life has been.

[217.4] *Id.*

[217.5] *Id.*

[217.6] *Id.* at 227–28.

[217.7] *Id.* at 228 (quoting Johnson v. University Hosps. of Cleveland, 540 N.E.2d 1370, 1378 (Ohio 1989)).

[217.8] *Id.* (quoting Bowman v. Davis, 356 N.E.2d 496, 499 n.3 (Ohio 1976)).

[217.9] 671 N.E.2d at 228. For a case for "wrongful prolongation of life" based on the same type of allegations, *see* Estate of Taylor v. Muncie Medical Investors, L.P., 727 N.E.2d 466 (Ind. Ct. App. 2000) (discussed in **§ 17.17** of this treatise).

The court claimed that the plaintiff had, perhaps in anticipation of its unwillingness to entertain a cause of action for these kinds of damages, changed the nature of his claim:

> Winter's estate now argues that it is not asserting a "wrongful living" claim. Rather, it argues that it is entitled to damages for the stroke suffered by Winter . . . , and any injuries, other than continued living, that were the foreseeable results of the "wrongful" resuscitation of Winter.[217.10]

This prompted the court to return to an analysis of causation. Because of the patient's age and medical problems, even if he had survived the ventricular tachycardia without resuscitation, it was reasonably foreseeable that he would have suffered a stroke and the consequent damages for which he sought redress from the defendants. Thus, the resuscitation was not the legal cause of the stroke. The court then adds that plaintiff "never presented any evidence that the defibrillation itself caused or contributed to Winter's suffering a stroke in any way other than by simply prolonging his life."[217.11]

There are two problems with this, one procedural and the other substantive, both of which were noted in the dissent. Procedurally, the court overlooks the fact that to this point, all of the proceedings have been conducted on the basis of pleadings and discovery; there has been no trial. The trial court twice entered summary judgment and the intermediate appellate court twice reversed. The plaintiff had not yet had his day in court, and as the dissenting opinion commented:

> Medical experts were prepared to testify on behalf of the plaintiff that "it was medically foreseeable that he [Winter] would suffer a stroke during the days immediately following defibrillation." This statement strongly suggests that there was a factual dispute as to causation that ought to have survived summary judgment.[217.12]

From a substantive perspective, the majority persisted in the belief, and its opinion was grounded on the assumption, that the plaintiff was seeking damages for prolongation of life. He was not. He was seeking damages for a stroke and its consequences, such as financial expenses and pain and suffering, which would certainly have been avoided had defendants complied with the DNR order and allowed him to die. This is analogous to the situation in which a person suffers some devastating illness or injury, such as a heart attack, likely to cause death, and is brought to a hospital emergency room where he is negligently treated and dies. Since the patient probably would have died if he had been given appropriate medical care, the argument has been made that recov-

---

[217.10] 671 N.E.2d at 228.

[217.11] *Id.* at 229.

[217.12] *Id.* at 230.

ery should be denied for want of causation. However, this argument is increasingly rejected because the plaintiff has been negligently deprived of an opportunity to live, and recovery is permitted under the "loss-of-chance" doctrine of § 323(a) of the *Restatement (Second) of Torts*.[217.13]

This is, in effect, the situation in *Anderson*. The defendants' negligence increased the risk to the plaintiff of an unfavorable outcome. The defendants' wrongful (negligent or intentional) ignoring of the DNR order increased the risk to the patient of a stroke. What makes the *Anderson* holding difficult to understand is that the loss-of-chance doctrine was accepted by the Ohio Supreme Court less than two months before *Anderson* was decided. In *Roberts v. Ohio Permanente Medical Group, Inc.*,[217.14] the Ohio Supreme Court explicitly overruled an older precedent[217.15] that took the position that recovery must be denied in such cases. *Roberts* was a wrongful death action filed against a physician for failure to diagnose and treat lung cancer in a timely fashion. The court rejected the argument that because the deceased patient had a less than 50 percent chance of survival from the lung cancer even if the physician had not been negligent, the physician should not be liable. Rather, the court concluded that the time had come to discard the harsher proximate cause rule and join the majority of states that follow the loss-of-chance doctrine. Thus, the court held that it was "a jury question as to whether the defendant's negligence was a cause of the plaintiff's injury or death"[217.16] once "the plaintiff present[s] expert medical testimony showing that the health care provider's negligent act or omission increased the risk of harm to the plaintiff."[217.17] This is the rule that the court should have applied in *Anderson* as well.[217.18]

In *Branom v. State*,[217.19] the parents of a child born with a bowel obstruction and microcephaly claimed that the physician, when recommending surgery to correct the former, failed to inform them of the latter; had they been adequately informed, they claimed they would not have consented to the surgery. Their claim was dismissed because the doctor was held to owe a duty to parents to obtain informed consent for treatment of their child only in

---

[217.13] *See generally* John D. Hodson, Annotation, *Medical Malpractice: "Loss of Chance" Causality,* 54 A.L.R.4th 10, 17–18 (1988) ("When the results complained of are such as might normally be expected to follow from the original disease . . . the courts have . . . permitted the finding that medical malpractice was a proximate cause of results which proper treatment probably would have prevented, even though the effects on the patient were attributable to the patient's disease or injury.").

[217.14] 668 N.E.2d 480 (Ohio 1996).

[217.15] *See* Cooper v. Sisters of Charity of Cincinnati, Inc., 272 N.E.2d 97 (Ohio 1971).

[217.16] 668 N.E.2d at 483.

[217.17] *Id.*

[217.18] **IA:** *See* Wendland v. Superior Court, 56 Cal. Rptr. 2d 595 (Ct. App. 1996) (applying rule in DNR context when physician withheld CPR without order or consent to do so).

[217.19] 974 P.2d 335 (Wash. Ct. App. 1999).

their capacity as the child's representatives and not as parents qua parents, and the action before the court was the one brought in their own right.

§ 17.13 — Negligence Liability for Not Treating ("Futility" Cases)

Page 390, add to footnote 220:

IA: Wendland v. Sparks, 574 N.W.2d 327 (Iowa 1998) (claim for damages against physician who intentionally failed to resuscitate patient).

LA: *See* Causey v. St. Francis Med. Ctr., 719 So. 2d 1072 (La. Ct. App. 1998).

NE: *Cf.* Tabatha R. v. Ronda R., 564 N.W.2d 598 (Neb. 1997).

Page 391, add to footnote 221:

KS: *But cf.* State v. Naramore, 965 P.2d 211, 214 (Kan. Ct. App. 1998) ("[It has also been suggested that inadequate control of pain due to substandard treatment may constitute medical negligence. [Cherny and Catane, "Editorial: Professional Negligence in the Management of Cancer Pain," 76 *Cancer* 2181, 2183 (December 1, 1995)].""), citing amicus curiae brief of Kansas Medical Society).

See generally Robyn S. Shapiro, *Health Care Providers' Liability Exposure for Inappropriate Pain Management*, 24 J. L., Med. & Ethics 360 (1996).

§ 17.15 — —Application to Futility Cases

Page 395, add note 247.1 reference at end of first paragraph and add note 247.1:

[247.1] **GA:** Velez v. Bethune, 466 S.E.2d 627, 628 (Ga. Ct. App. 1995) (affirmance of denial of motion for summary judgment in part on claim that physician abandoned patient "by causing the 'termination[, deescalation,] and discontinuance of cardio pulmonary resuscitation, life support measures and medical treatment for her,' without the consent and approval of the infant's parents, and without their knowledge.").

Page 396, add to footnote 248:

CA4: Bryan v. Rectors & Visitors of the Univ. of Va., 95 F.3d 349 (4th Cir. 1996) (no cause of action under EMTALA for failure to treat once patient is stabilized).

PA: *But see* Rideout v. Hershey Medical Ctr., 16 Fiduc. Rep. 2d 181 (C.P. Dauphin County, Pa. 1995) (no cause of action stated under EMTALA for termination of treatment of terminally ill child over parental opposition).

Page 397, add to footnote 252:

LA: *See, e.g.*, Causey v. St. Francis Med. Ctr., 719 So. 2d 1072, 1073 (La. Ct. App. 1998) ("Because Mrs. Causey's family demanded aggressive life-sustaining care, Dr. Harter sought unsuccessfully to transfer her to another medical facility willing to provide this care.").

NC: *Cf.* First Healthcare Corp. v. Rettinger, 456 S.E.2d 347 (N.C. Ct. App. 1995) (impossible to transfer patient whose living will declined treatment that nursing home refused to discontinue), *rev'd,* 467 S.E.2d 243 (N.C. 1996).

Page 398, add to footnote 257:

GA: Velez v. Bethune, 466 S.E.2d 627, 633 (Ga. Ct. App. 1995) (Andrews, J., dissenting) (no evidence that discontinuation of medical treatment and life-support measures was proximate cause of the child's death within the meaning of wrongful death statutes).

Page 398, add to footnote 259:

GA: Velez v. Bethune, 466 S.E.2d 627 (Ga. Ct. App. 1995) (near end of life, measure of damages likely to be small).

Page 398, add to footnote 261:

NY: *Cf.* Afentakis v. Memorial Hosp., 667 N.Y.S.2d 602 (Sup. Ct. N.Y. County 1997).

§ 17.15A   — Negligent Infliction of Emotional Distress (New)

The implementation of a decision to withhold or withdraw life-sustaining medical treatment may give rise to a cause of action for negligent infliction of emotional distress. Whether it does or not will very much depend on the particular jurisdiction in which the events occur because the cause of action for negligent infliction of emotional distress has not been recognized in all jurisdictions and, more importantly, the rules for recovery vary considerably among jurisdictions.

The case of *Rideout v. Hershey Medical Center*[261.1] provides an illustration of the kinds of events that might give rise to such a cause of action. The attending physician, with the concurrence of the physician who was the chairman of the hospital's ethics committee, issued an order to terminate ventilatory support for a terminally ill child over the express opposition of the parents. At the time the ventilator was withdrawn, the parents were in the hospital, though not in the child's room, and

> [s]imultaneously, the hospital's Chaplain, who was located in [the patient's] room, announced to the Rideouts over the hospital's intercom system: "they turned her off, they turned her off!" The Rideouts heard the announcement and immediately rushed . . . to [her] room, hysterically crying and screaming that their child had been murdered.[261.2]

On the basis of these facts, the trial court denied the defendant's motion to dismiss the claim for negligent infliction of emotional distress, finding that the elements required by Pennsylvania law were met—namely, (1) the plaintiff's location near the scene of the events, (2) shock or emotional distress resulting from the emotional impact on the plaintiff from the sensory and contemporaneous observance of the traumatic events, and (3) a close relationship between the plaintiff and the victim.

However, the Court of Appeals of Washington dismissed a claim by the parents of a severely neurologically impaired infant against the physician who treated the infant, on the ground that under both the Washington statute authorizing claims arising out of provision of health care and the common law, the plaintiffs—i.e., the parents—must themselves be placed in peril in order to recover.[261.3]

§ 17.16   Defenses to Negligence Claims

Page 399, add to footnote 263:

cert. denied, 474 U.S. 827 (1985).

Page 400, replace last paragraph of section with:

Other cases come to the same conclusion as *Shorter* on similar facts and reasoning,[270] though some have viewed the defense not as contributory negli-

---

[261.1] 16 Fiduc. Rep. 2d 181 (C.P. Dauphin County, Pa. 1995).

[261.2] *Id.* at 184.

[261.3] **WA:** Branom v. State, 974 P.2d 335 (Wash. Ct. App. 1999).

[270] **IL:** Corlett v. Caserta, 562 N.E.2d 257 (Ill. App. Ct. 1990).

   NY: Estate of Rozewicz v. New York City Health & Hosps. Corp., 656 N.Y.S.2d 593 (Sup. Ct. N.Y. County 1997).

gence or assumption of risk, but as an application of the doctrine of "avoidable consequences."[270.1]

Emergency Exception.   A well-accepted defense to a claim of lack of informed consent (or medical battery) is that emergency conditions prevented the physician from obtaining the patient's informed consent.[270.2] Although well-accepted in theory, its contours are little explored in court decisions.

In re Shine v. Vega[270.3] takes a major step toward changing this. In this case, an emergency room physician invoked the emergency exception to intubate a patient who was having an acute asthmatic episode. However, the patient, who was conscious and probably competent throughout her time in the emergency room, had repeatedly and vociferously refused to be intubated, though she was willing to accept other treatment. To avoid intubation, she attempted to run out of the emergency room with her sister who had accompanied her to the hospital, but was detained by a security guard. She was then "'walked back' to her room where [the physician] immediately ordered that she be placed in four-point restraints, in part because she had refused treatment and attempted to leave the emergency room" and then intubated her.

She was so traumatized by this experience that during a later attack of asthma, she delayed going to the hospital so long that she died. Her estate brought suit on a variety of theories, including lack of informed consent, battery, and false imprisonment, to all of which the defendants defended on the ground that the situation was a life-threatening emergency and they were therefore privileged to take the actions they did without the patient's consent.[270.4] The trial judge so charged the jury, which brought back verdicts for the defendants.

However, the Massachusetts Supreme Judicial Court reversed and remanded for a new trial on the ground that the instructions were erroneous insofar as they related to the emergency exception. First, the court reiterated several important and reasonably well-established points. It made clear that the defendants had the burden of proof of establishing the applicability of the privilege. Competent patients have a right to refuse treatment even if that

---

[270.1] **CA5:** Munn v. Algee, 924 F.2d 568 (5th Cir. 1991).

  NY: Williams v. Bright, 658 N.Y.S.2d 910 (App. Div. 1997).

  See generally Gary Knapp, Annotation, *Refusal of Medical Treatment on Religious Grounds as Affecting Right to Recover for Personal Injury or Death,* 3 A.L.R.5th 721 (1993).

[270.2] See § **3.23** in the main volume and this supplement.

[270.3] 709 N.E.2d 58 (Mass. 1999).

[270.4] 709 N.E.2d at 61.

action is unwise from a medical perspective. The fact that the treatment is life-saving does not affect the patient's right to refuse treatment.

The court then turned to a discussion of the privilege based on the emergency exception:

> Consistent with other courts that have considered the issue, we recognize that the emergency-treatment exception cannot entirely subsume a patient's fundamental right to refuse medical treatment. The privilege does not and cannot override the refusal of treatment by a patient who is capable of providing consent. If the patient is competent, an emergency physician must obtain her consent before providing treatment, even if the physician is persuaded that, without the treatment, the patient's life is threatened.[270.5]

The holding seriously narrows the privilege from the more expansive readings that physicians are inclined to give it in practice, as illustrated by the actions of the physician in this case. The court's version of the privilege is also far more consistent with the value accorded self-determination in law than is a broader reading of the privilege. Quoting a comment to the *Restatement (Second) of Torts*, the court also stated that a physician is not privileged to treat in an emergency if he knows or has reason to know, as he did in this case, that the patient had previously refused treatment.[270.6] The court acknowledged that "[i]n the often chaotic setting of an emergency room, physicians and medical staff frequently must make split-second, life-saving decisions. Emergency medical personnel may not have the time necessary to obtain the consent of a family member when a patient is incapable of consenting without jeopardizing the well-being of the patient." However, it emphasized, "a competent patient's refusal to consent to medical treatment cannot be overridden whenever the patient faces a life-threatening situation."[270.7] Finally, the court really reduced the emergency exception to little more than a variation on the incompetency exception, by holding that "whether an 'emergency' existed sufficient to insulate" defendants from liability requires the jury to decide whether the plaintiff was "capable of consenting to treatment."[270.8]

[270.5] *Id*. at 64.

[270.6] *Id*. at 64 n.18, citing Restatement (Second) of Torts § 892D(b) (1977).

[270.7] *Id*. at 65.

[270.8] *Id*.

§ 17.17   Other Tort Theories

Page 401, delete first sentence of second paragraph (after heading) and replace with the following:

Three cases have attempted to assert liability under a new theory labeled by one as "wrongful living"[275] and the other two as "wrongful prolongation of life."[276]

Page 402, add after carryover paragraph:

In *Estate of Taylor v. Muncie Medical Investors, L.P.*,[280.1] the estate of a female, comatose, nursing home patient sued the nursing home after physicians and other personnel had provided artificial nutrition and hydration against the wishes of her children. The estate alleged gross negligence, negligence, battery, violation of the Indiana Health Care Consent Act, "failure to seek a guardian ad litem," violation of the patient's constitutional rights, "violation of the Federal Nursing Home Reform Law," constructive fraud, fraudulent misrepresentation, intentional infliction of emotional distress, and breach of contract.[280.2] The trial court granted summary judgment to the defendants, and the estate appealed.

On appeal, the Indiana Court of Appeals considered whether the trial court had erred in entering summary judgment on the estate's claim for wrongful prolongation of life without specifying which one or more of the listed claims constituted the claim for wrongful prolongation of life.[280.3] The court's opinion did not identify a claim the estate's attorney had titled as requesting relief for wrongful prolongation of life. At times, the court discussed the wrongful prolongation of life claim as if the estate had alleged it through the count alleging violation of the Indiana Health Care Consent Act.[280.4] At other

---

[275] Benoy v. Simons, 831 P.2d 167 (Wash. Ct. App. 1992).

[276] **IN:** Estate of Taylor v. Muncie Medical Investors, L.P., 727 N.E.2d 466 (Ind. Ct. App. 2000).

   OH: Anderson v. St. Francis-St. George Hosp., 614 N.E.2d 841 (Ohio Ct. App. 1992), *rev'd*, 671 N.E.2d 225 (Ohio 1996), discussed in §§ **17.4** and **17.12** in this supplement, *and followed in* Allore v. Flower Hosp., No. L-96-329, 1997 WL 362465 (Ohio Ct. App. June 27, 1997).

[280.1] 727 N.E.2d 466 (Ind. Ct. App. 2000).

[280.2] *Id.* at 469.

[280.3] *Id.* at 469, 471–72.

[280.4] *Id.* at 470–71 (noting that the estate asserted "that the 'rights' of families to make health care decisions created by the Health Care Consent Act . . . and recognized by our supreme court . . . are meaningless without a remedy to enforce them. . . . Consequently, the [e]state conclude[d] that families must have the right to file suit

413

times, however, it seemed as if the court was reading the estate's allegations of negligence as stating the claim.[280.5]

In any event, the court refused to recognize the cause of action, ruling, in essence, that the family should have gone to court earlier if it disagreed with the actions of the nursing home.[280.6] According to the court, the procedures set forth in the Indiana statutes sufficiently safeguarded the rights of the patient and of the patient's surrogates to refuse treatment. The patient's children in this case "could have challenged the actions of [her] physicians and [the nursing home] in court at any time to enforce their decisions regarding [her] care."[280.7] Because the estate did not lack the means to enforce the children's decisions with regard to the patient's medical treatment, the court affirmed the trial court's refusal to recognize a new cause of action for wrongful prolongation of life.[280.8]

In the aftermath of *Taylor*, a family in Indiana attempting to refuse life-sustaining treatment that is encountering resistance from physicians may have to seek concurrent court review of the dispute or remain stoic about the situation later. It appears from the court's wholesale approach that it treated all counts of the complaint, merged together, as a claim for wrongful prolongation of life rather than as discrete counts.[280.9] Because of this lack of clarity in the court's decision, later courts may be unclear whether claims such as battery or lack of informed consent can be asserted by such families after treatment has been administered against their wishes. Such a result would be unfortunate, for it surely could not have been contemplated by the legislature when it passed the statutes upon which the court in *Taylor* relied.

---

against health care providers, either before or after the incapacitated patient has died, in order to protect their decisionmaking authority."). *See also id.* at 471 (describing the estate's claim as an argument that the patient's children "should have been allowed their existing rights under Indiana law").

[280.5] *See, e.g., id.* at 470 (refusing to find that the estate had waived the claim because "the [e]state did clearly state in its complaint that it was raising a tort claim based upon the [defendant's] alleged breach of its duties to respect [the patient's] wishes and avoid unnecessarily prolonging her life).

[280.6] The estate's claims against the physicians involved were addressed in another appeal. 727 N.E.2d at 472 n.2.

[280.7] *Id.* at 472.

[280.8] *Id.*

[280.9] *See also id.* at 472–73 (in discussing claim that a dispute of material fact remained for trial regarding lack of informed consent, the court ruled in part that "[b]ecause the [wrongful prolongation of life] claim is invalid, any disputes of fact in regard to that claim are immaterial").

Page 403, add at end of section:

Criminal Negligence/Intentional Tort. In *Velez v. Bethune*,[288.1] the court held that termination of life-sustaining medical treatment without a surrogate's consent might constitute criminal negligence "equivalent to an intentional tort."[288.2] However, in reaching its decision, the court based its conclusion that the physician "had no right to decide, unilaterally, to discontinue medical treatment even if . . . the child was terminally ill and in the process of dying"[288.3] on the authority of *In re Doe*,[288.4] which was based on the Georgia DNR statute requiring that resuscitation be provided to a child unless both parents agreed that it should be withheld.[288.5] Thus, it is not clear that this theory of recovery would apply in a jurisdiction lacking a similar statute, or even in Georgia if the facts of the case did not fall within the statute.

Right of Dignity. In *Afentakis v. Memorial Hospital*,[288.6] the wife of a man who had died of brain cancer in the defendant hospital sued the hospital, contending that it had breached the patient's "right to dignity." The plaintiff alleged examples such as the hospital's "delay in treating a bruised arm caused by 'possibly sloppy IV infiltrated work,' until plaintiff complained," and "a doctor's thoughtless cruelty in allegedly expressing, in front of Afentakis, the doctor's belief that there was no longer any point in keeping Afentakis alive."[288.7]

Although not intended as a malpractice claim involving a departure from a recognized standard of medical practice, the court dismissed the claim in part because there was no evidence that the patient suffered physical injuries "which can be attributed to departures from standard good and accepted medical practice, and which are distinguishable from the ordinary discomfiture which often attend[s] a hospital stay."[288.8] Instead, the court treated the claim as, in plaintiff's counsel's words, "'quite similar to or may be just another way of articulating a claim for negligent infliction of emotional distress.'"[288.9]

While freely recognizing that "all patients . . . have the right to be treated with dignity and caring," the court dismissed this suit for failure to plead or prove any physical injuries or "proof of any emotional injury Afentakis actually sustained, beyond speculation as to what he must have been feeling or

---

[288.1] 466 S.E.2d 627 (Ga. Ct. App. 1995).

[288.2] *Id.* at 629.

[288.3] *Id.*

[288.4] 418 S.E.2d 3 (Ga. 1992).

[288.5] See **§ 19.18** in the main volume.

[288.6] 667 N.Y.S.2d 602 (Sup. Ct. N.Y. County 1997).

[288.7] *Id.* at 603.

[288.8] *Id.* at 604.

[288.9] *Id.*

thinking, and the evidence of [plaintiff's] own understandable distress as she watched her husband's decline."[288.10] It refused to loosen the requirements needed for proof of negligent infliction of emotional distress, because of the difficulty in drawing a line between "the ordinary assaults upon a patient's dignity which stem from the loss of power and control which is all too often the corollary to illness, and the loss of autonomy produced by even a short hospitalization, from those occasioned by the failure of a hospital and its staff to maintain a certain level of caring, respect and consideration for the feelings of its charges."[288.11]

False Imprisonment. Treatment of a competent patient against her will may constitute false imprisonment, even in an emergency. In *In re Shine v. Vega*,[288.12] the Massachusetts Supreme Judicial Court reinstated causes of action against a physician and hospital for intubating a patient who was suffering from severe asthma, who had repeatedly refused the treatment and had tried to leave the hospital, but was prevented from doing so and restrained in order to be treated. The court held that the emergency exception to the requirements of consent and informed consent did not automatically immunize physicians from liability, even in a life-threatening emergency, if there was a competent refusal of treatment.

§ 17.19   State Statutory Violations

Page 405, add at end of carryover paragraph:

In *Gragg v. Calandra*,[298.1] the plaintiff claimed damages under the Illinois Consumer Fraud and Deceptive Business Practices Act.[298.2] The patient underwent a cardiac catheterization during which he suffered a cardiac arrest and became unconscious and nonresponsive, which was followed by open-heart bypass surgery that allegedly was performed without consent. The plaintiff alleged that the hospital and physicians "represented to the public that patients for cardiology services would promptly receive care for cardiac patients who would be in surgery within an hour . . . [and] that defendants had a complete cardiovascular center with a catheterization lab and would help patients choose the right doctor."[298.3]

[288.10] *Id.*

[288.11] *Id.*

[288.12] 709 N.E.2d 58 (Mass. 1999).

[298.1] 696 N.E.2d 1282 (Ill. App. Ct. 1998).

[298.2] 815 Ill. Comp. Stat. Ann. 505/1 *et seq.* (West 1996).

[298.3] 696 N.E.2d at 1288.

The court affirmed the trial court's dismissal of this claim because, "under the Consumer Fraud Act, a complaint must set forth specific facts that show a deceptive act or misrepresentation of a material fact by the defendant, the defendant's intention that the plaintiff rely on the deception or misrepresentation, and that the deception or misrepresentation occur in the course of business,"[298.4] and this plaintiff did "not specify how the advertisements were false or deceptive or how the advertisements caused any damages . . . [or] a connection between those representations and the injury that surgery was performed without consent and that [the patient] was placed on life support against his permission.[298.5]

Page 405, add to footnote 300:

IL: *But see* Ficke v. Evangelical Health Sys., 674 N.E.2d 888, 891 (Ill. App. Ct. 1996) (surrogate decisionmaking statute "codifies Illinois' common law and constitutional rights to forego life-sustaining treatment").

Page 405, add after first full paragraph:

Another case in which liability was sought to be imposed for violation of the advance directive statute is *Wright v. Johns Hopkins Health Systems Corporation*.[300.1] The patient was resuscitated, allegedly against his prior express refusal. Although terminally ill with AIDS, he was not expected to die imminently. In fact, he suffered a cardiac arrest after being given a blood transfusion in anticipation of being discharged from the hospital. He had executed a living will some time before, requesting that life-sustaining procedures be withheld or withdrawn if he were terminally ill, but the court found the living will not to apply because the patient had not been certified by two physicians to meet the requirements of the statute for implementation of an advance directive.

The plaintiffs also argued that the patient had given an oral advance directive against resuscitation on admission to the hospital in the emergency room. The court also refused to find that this constituted a basis for liability because, although the advance directive statute recognizes the validity of oral advance directives, the statutory requirements for an oral advance directive—it "must be made in the presence of the attending physician and one witness and must be documented as part of the patient's medical record"[300.2]—were also not met. The court also rejected the claim that the

---

[298.4] *Id.*

[298.5] *Id.*

[300.1] 728 A.2d 166 (Md. 1999).

[300.2] *Id.* at 176, citing Md. Code Ann., Health-Gen. § 506(d).

defendants breached a duty to record the patient's "expressed desires" in his medical record, holding that "a 'generalized and open-ended desire' need not be recorded because it is not a DNR order."[300.3]

Page 406, add at end of section:

Surrogate Decisionmaking Statutes. In *Ficke v. Evangelical Health Systems*[303.1] a patient admitted to a hospital with a DNR order was nonetheless alleged to have been treated "contrary to her expressed wishes." It was also alleged that she lacked decisionmaking capacity and that her medical condition was such that the Illinois Health Care Surrogate Act[303.2] applied. The plaintiffs, who were surviving family members of the patient, claimed that they were not informed of the patient's rights under the statute, which resulted in her being treated and which caused her injuries, because, had they been aware of the statute's provisions, they would have exercised their authority to discontinue life-sustaining medical treatment.

The Illinois Appellate Court affirmed the dismissal of the complaint, though it appears to have left the door open for recovery had the action been brought against the physicians rather than against the hospital. In adjudicating both the survival claim brought on behalf of the patient's estate and the claim by the patient's family members who sued in their own right claiming that "they each suffered as witnesses to their mother's unnecessary suffering," the court held that the hospital had no responsibilities under the statute until the attending physician had first determined that the patient met the prerequisites for the application of the statute—namely, that the patient lacked decisionmaking capacity and suffered from a "qualifying condition."[303.3] The court emphasized that this was not a mere technicality, but rather the legislature sought to clearly distinguish between the responsibilities of physicians and other health care providers in order "to avoid potential conflicts" among them so as not to unduly "frustrate or prolong what was intended to be a swift, doctor-patient diagnosis."[303.4] The hospital's duty, which is "to inquire into the availability of a surrogate,"[303.5] does not arise until the physician determines that the statutory conditions have been met.

In a separate opinion, one justice correctly pointed out that in fact physicians and nurses, who are agents of the hospital, collaborate in treating patients, and therefore "the hospital has sufficient knowledge of the condition of its patients to determine whether it is probable that a surrogate decision maker is

---

[300.3] *Id.* at 178.

[303.1] 674 N.E.2d 888 (Ill. App. Ct. 1996).

[303.2] Ill. Ann. Stat. ch. 755, §§ 40/1–40/55.

[303.3] Ficke, 674 N.E.2d at 892.

[303.4] *Id.*

[303.5] *Id.*

needed."[303.6] As a result, "[h]ospitals should facilitate the process of surrogate decision making and should not be allowed to sit by and disregard the rights of a patient."[303.7]

Suit was also brought against the attending physician. There is no discussion of a cause of action by the patient's estate against the physician, which was probably incorporated in a count dismissed by the trial court and not pursued on appeal. The court affirmed the dismissal of the claim by the patient's family against the physician on the ground that the statute contains no express right of action allowing the family to sue for a violation of the Act, and that there is no implied right of action because the patient's family are not members of the class the statute was enacted to protect. Further, the court was troubled by the "practical concern" of determining who was a family member who might be able to maintain a cause of action. Because "[a]t best, this would prove to be an inexact process and one that conflicts with the traditional rule of limiting claims in the medical arena to the 'patient-hospital or patient-doctor relationship,'"[303.8] the court felt compelled to affirm the dismissal of this count.

As previously noted,[303.9] the court in *Estate of Taylor v. Muncie Medical Investors, L.P.*[303.10] considered a complaint in which the estate of a nursing home patient alleged, *inter alia*, violation of the Indiana Health Care Consent Act.[303.11] The court did not rule on that claim, instead apparently considering the estate's complaint generally as alleging a claim for wrongful prolongation of life.

Family Expense Act.   Illinois has a statute, the Rights of Married Persons Act, a portion of which is referred to as the Family Expense Act,[303.12] permitting a spouse to "maintain an action against a tortfeasor under the statute for family expenses incurred due to injuries the victim's spouse sustained."[303.13] In *Gragg v. Calandra*,[303.14] the plaintiff, administrator of the estate of the deceased patient's wife, brought a claim under this act for damages incurred when the defendant hospital and physician allegedly treated the patient without consent and against the patient's wishes as expressed in his advance directive. The court affirmed the dismissal of the administrator's claim because "only a spouse may maintain an action against a tortfeasor under the

---

[303.6] *Id.* at 894 (Cerda, J., concurring and dissenting).

[303.7] *Id.*

[303.8] *Id.* at 893.

[303.9] See § **17.17**.

[303.10] 727 N.E.2d 466 (Ind. Ct. App. 2000).

[303.11] Ind. Code Ann. §§ 16-36-1-1–16-36-1-14.

[303.12] 750 Ill. Comp. Stat. Ann. 65/15 (West 1996).

[303.13] Gragg v. Calandra, 696 N.E.2d 1282, 1286 (Ill. App. Ct. 1998).

[303.14] 696 N.E.2d 1282 (Ill. App. Ct. 1998).

statute for family expenses incurred due to injuries [to] the victim's spouse."[303.15] However, the court held that the patient's wife's estate's claim survived her death, and thus it reinstated that count of the complaint.

§ 17.20   Federal Civil Rights Actions

Page 407, add to footnote 307:

CA11: Novak v. Cobb County-Kennestone Hosp. Auth., 74 F.3d 1173 (11th Cir. 1996), *aff'g* 849 F. Supp. 1559 (N.D. Ga. 1994).

Page 407, add to footnote 308:

CA11: Novak v. Cobb County-Kennestone Hosp. Auth., 74 F.3d 1173 (11th Cir. 1996), *aff'g* 849 F. Supp. 1559 (N.D. Ga. 1994).

Page 407, add to footnote 310:

CA11: Novak v. Cobb County-Kennestone Hosp. Auth., 74 F.3d 1173 (11th Cir. 1996), *aff'g* 849 F. Supp. 1559 (N.D. Ga. 1994).

Page 407, add to footnote 311:

CA11: Novak v. Cobb County-Kennestone Hosp. Auth., 74 F.3d 1173 (11th Cir. 1996), *aff'g* 849 F. Supp. 1559 (N.D. Ga. 1994).

Page 407, add to footnote 312:

CA11: Novak v. Cobb County-Kennestone Hosp. Auth., 74 F.3d 1173 (11th Cir. 1996), *aff'g* 849 F. Supp. 1559 (N.D. Ga. 1994).

Page 408, add to footnote 314:

CA11: Novak v. Cobb County-Kennestone Hosp. Auth., 74 F.3d 1173 (11th Cir. 1996), *aff'g* 849 F. Supp. 1559 (N.D. Ga. 1994).

Page 410, add to footnote 329:

CA11: *Aff'd,* 74 F.3d 1173 (11th Cir. 1996).

Page 410, add to footnote 330:

CA11: *Aff'd,* 74 F.3d 1173 (11th Cir. 1996).

[303.15] *Id.* at 1286.

Page 412, add to footnote 341:

CA11: Novak v. Cobb County-Kennestone Hosp. Auth., 74 F.3d 1173 (11th Cir. 1996), *aff'g* 849 F. Supp. 1559 (N.D. Ga. 1994).

Page 412, add to footnote 342:

CA11: *Aff'd,* 74 F.3d 1173, 1177 (11th Cir. 1996) (no allegation or evidence to support existence of conspiracy).

Page 413, add after carryover paragraph:

Although most federal civil rights actions have been brought seeking damages for unwanted medical treatment, it may be possible to fashion a cause of action for nonconsensual withholding or withdrawal of treatment as well, as illustrated by *Rideout v. Hershey Medical Center.*[347.1] The patient in this case was a terminally ill child whose parents refused to accede to the attending physician's suggestions that further treatment was futile and that ventilatory support should be terminated. Eventually the physician, with the backing of the hospital's ethics committee, terminated ventilatory support over the parents' opposition, and although at first the child breathed without the ventilator, she died two days later.

The parents sued the hospital alleging a variety of causes of action. Ruling on the hospital's motion to dismiss, the court refused to dismiss the claim that the hospital violated the parents' right to free exercise of religion and parental autonomy, based on the state and federal constitutions, to make medical decisions on their child's behalf. The court concluded that although "a hospital and/or physician is not compelled to obtain parental approval in every aspect of treating a child," when "removal of life-sustaining medical treatment is involved," the patient's constitutional rights are implicated, and "a parents' *[sic]* constitutionally-protected privacy interest in making important decisions on behalf of their children must include among them the right to assert their child's right to life."[347.2] The court also held that the claim based on the parents' free exercise of religious belief in wishing to maintain medical treatment also survived the motion to dismiss.[347.3]

§ 17.21   Rehabilitation Act

Page 416, add to footnote 369:

PA: *See also* Rideout v. Hershey Med. Ctr., 16 Fiduc. Rep. 2d 181 (C.P. Dauphin County, Pa. 1995) (cause of action for violation of

---

[347.1] 16 Fiduc. Rep. 2d 181 (C.P. Dauphin County, Pa. 1995).

[347.2] *Id.* at 198.

[347.3] *Id.* at 200.

Rehabilitation Act not stated when doctors terminated life-sustaining medical treatment of child over parental objections).

§ 17.23   Conscientious Objection

Page 431, add at end of section:

Illinois has enacted comprehensive legislation that prohibits discrimination based on the exercise of ethical standards.[444.1] The broadly stated goal of the statute is to

> protect the right of conscience of all persons who refuse to obtain, receive or accept, or who are engaged in, the delivery of, arrangement for, or payment of health care services and medical care . . . and to prohibit all forms of discrimination, disqualification, coercion, disability or imposition of liability upon such persons or entities by reason of their refusing to act contrary to their conscience.[444.2]

The statute protects a wide variety of persons or organizations, including physicians and other health care personnel, health care facilities, and health care payors. It also bars employment discrimination of the basis of conscientiously held belief.[444.3] The statute protects against civil or criminal liability for any refusal to participate in a health care procedure because of ethical standards,[444.4] and it also bars discrimination on the basis of conscientiously held belief in admission to or participation in any health care program for which the applicant is eligible.[444.5] However, the statute does not permit a health care professional to withhold information from patients about treatment options, based on ethical standards.[444.6] These prohibitions and protections present a wide variety of people with the assurance that their personal beliefs will not affect their rights, as "people and organizations hold different beliefs about whether certain health care services are morally acceptable."[444.7]

[444.1] *See* Ill. Ann. Stat. ch. 755, §§ 70/1 – 70/14.

[444.2] *Id.* § 70/2.

[444.3] *Id.* § 70/7.

[444.4] *Id.* §§ 70/4, 70/9.

[444.5] *Id.* § 70/5.

[444.6] *Id.* § 70/6.

[444.7] *Id.*

§ 17.24   Immunity

Page 434, add at end of section:

The applicability of statutory immunity provisions contained in advance directive statutes was addressed in *Duarte v. Chino Community Hospital*,[461.1] but in an ultimately unsatisfying way. The patient in this case was in a persistent vegetative state as a result of an automobile accident. Based on statements she had made to family members, her husband and six adult children agreed that she should be taken off the ventilator. The attending physician refused to do so unless the family obtained a court order, because she was not brain-dead.[461.2] A few days later, the doctor requested permission to insert a feeding tube in order to transfer her to a long-term care facility. The family refused and repeated the request to have ventilatory support withdrawn. Within a month of the accident, the patient died, still on life support, as the family's attorney was preparing to obtain a court order.

After the patient's death, the family brought suit for damages for the doctor's failure to follow the patient's wishes to have life support terminated. The theories of recovery were negligence, negligent infliction of emotional distress, and intentional infliction of emotional distress. The jury found for the defendant hospital and physician on all counts.

On appeal, the court affirmed the trial court's refusal to grant a judgment notwithstanding the verdict, on the ground that the defendants were immune from liability under the statutory immunity provision of the California health care power of attorney statute,[462.3] despite the fact that the patient had not executed a health care power of attorney (nor a living will). The court reasoned that immunity applied even though there was no health care power of attorney because, if a health care provider may, with impunity, ignore instructions from one holding a durable power of attorney, it may do so from one not holding such an instrument. It reached this conclusion on the ground that

> the authority of the Duartes to speak on her behalf and the accuracy of their account of her wishes were inherently less reliable than that of an attorney-in-fact appointed through a power of attorney in compliance with the statutory requirements.[462.4]

Thus,

> [i]t would be anomalous to hold that a physician is immune from liability for damages suffered as the result of his or her failure or refusal to comply with

---

[461.1]   85 Cal. Rptr. 2d 521 (Ct. App. 1999).

[461.2]   See § **9.48** in the main volume and this supplement.

[462.3]   Cal. Prob. Code § 4750.

[462.4]   85 Cal. Rptr. 2d at 525.

the more authoritative and reliable instruction, but is not immune from liability for the failure to comply with an instruction from a less authoritative and reliable decision-maker.[462.5]

The court distinguished the immunity under the living will statute, stating that there would have been no immunity under that statute even in the absence of a directive.

> In short, the immunity for failure to comply with the patient's own declaration is circumscribed and conditional, but the immunity granted to those who fail to comply with instructions from the patient's attorney-in-fact is broad and unconditional.[462.6]

The court's reason for making this distinction is that there was an intention by the Legislature to measure the breadth of the immunity according to the source and form of the directive. When the order to withdraw life support comes directly from the patient and is recorded in the patient's declaration, the immunity for failing to comply with that order is narrow. In contrast, when the order comes not from the patient, but from the patient's attorney-in-fact, who may or may not have received any specific instructions on that subject from the patient, then the immunity for refusing to comply with that less reliable expression of the patient's intent is broader.[462.7]

One problem with the court's reasoning is its conclusion that the advance directive was a proxy directive rather than an instruction directive. The patient's oral statements, which the family reported, could just as easily have been said to be an oral living will rather than a health care power of attorney.

Perhaps, however, the most appropriate resolution would have been that the immunity provision of neither statute applied, because the patient had not executed either a living will under the living will statute or a health care power of attorney under the health care power of attorney statute.[462.8]

Statutory immunity was also determinative in *Stolle v. Baylor College of Medicine*,[462.9] in which the parents of a handicapped newborn infant brought an action against the hospital and physicians for resuscitating the infant against the expressed wishes of the parents. The court of appeals affirmed the trial court's dismissal of the action on the theory that the immunity provision of the state's living will statute barred the action. The parents had executed a "Directive To Physicians" based on the Texas Natural Death Act, which allows parents to execute a directive on behalf of a minor,[462.10] directing that

---

[462.5] *Id.* at 525.

[462.6] *Id.* at 524.

[462.7] *Id.* at 527.

[462.8] See § **10.13, 10.15,** and **10.16** in the main volume and this supplement.

[462.9] 981 S.W.2d 709 (Tex. Ct. App. 1998).

[462.10] Tex. Health & Safety Code Ann. § 672.006.

life-sustaining procedures be withheld or withdrawn and that she be permitted to die naturally if she had an incurable condition and was certified to be in a terminal condition by two physicians, as the statute requires.

This holding is problematic. The court ignored the fact that immunity bars an action when the physician *complies* with the directive and this is precisely what did not happen. Further, the court held that "immunity precludes common-law causes of action asserted by appellants arising out of the same facts,"[462.11] despite the fact that another provision of the living will statute[462.12] provides that "[t]his chapter does not impair or supersede any legal right or responsibility a person may have to effect the withholding or withdrawal of life-sustaining procedures in a lawful manner."[462.13]

Bibliography

Broder, A. "She Don't Want No Life Support." *University of Detroit Mercy Law Review* 75 (1998): 595.

Donohue, J. "'Wrongful Living': Recovery for a Physician's Infringement on an Individual's Right to Die." *Journal of Contemporary Health Law and Policy* 14 (1998): 391.

Hackleman, T. Comment. "Violation of an Individual's Right to Die: The Need for a Wrongful Living Cause of Action." *University of Cincinnati Law Review* 64 (1996): 1355.

Hanson, F.A. "Suits for Wrongful Life, Counterfactuals, and the Nonexistence Problem." *Southern California Interdisciplinary Law Journal* 5 (1996): 1.

Knapp, W., and F. Hamilton. "'Wrongful Living': Resuscitation as Tortious Interference with a Patient's Right to Give Informed Refusal." *Northern Kentucky Law Review* 19 (1992): 253.

Milani, A. "Better Off Dead Than Disabled?: Should Courts Recognize a 'Wrongful Living' Cause of Action When Doctors Fail to Honor Patients' Advance Directives?" *Washington & Lee Law Review* 54 (1997): 149.

Quill, T., and C. Cassel. "Nonabandonment: A Central Obligation for Physicians." *Annals of Internal Medicine* 122 (1995): 368.

Robb, M. "Living Wills: The Right to Refuse Life Sustaining Medical Treatment—A Right Without a Remedy?" *University of Dayton Law Review* 23 (1997): 169.

[462.11] 981 S.W.2d at 714.

[462.12] Tex. Health & Safety Code Ann. § 672.021.

[462.13] 981 S.W.2d at 714.

Rodriguez, K. "Suing Health Care Providers for Saving Lives: Liability for Providing Unwanted Life-Sustaining Treatment." *Journal of Legal Medicine* 20 (1999): 1.

Shapiro, R. "Health Care Providers' Liability Exposure for Inappropriate Pain Management." *Journal of Law, Medicine, and Ethics* 24 (1996): 360.

Shapiro, R. "Liability Issues in the Management of Pain." *Journal of Pain and Symptom Management* 9 (1994): 146.

Strasser, M. "A Jurisprudence in Disarray: On Battery, Wrongful Living, and the Right to Bodily Integrity." *San Diego Law Review* 36 (1999): 997.

Wilborn, S. "The Right to Refuse Medical Treatment: Where There Is a Right, There Ought to Be a Remedy." *Northern Kentucky Law Review* 25 (1998): 649.

CHAPTER 18

CRIMINAL LIABILITY: ASSISTED SUICIDE AND ACTIVE EUTHANASIA

§ 18.1 Two Types of Potential Criminal Liability: Active and Passive Euthanasia

Page 451, add note 7.1 reference at end of last full paragraph and add note 7.1:

[7.1] **CA:** People v. Cleaves, 280 Cal. Rptr. 146 (Ct. App. 1991).

  OK: Edinburgh v. State, 896 P.2d 1176, 1179–80 (Okla. Crim. App. 1995) ("Many states have distinguished between the direct killing involved in euthanasia and conduct characterizing mere suicide assistance. . . . Thus, where the defendant only furnishes the means by which the victim kills herself, he has merely assisted suicide. But, where the defendant proximately causes the defendant's death he can be held liable for homicide.").

Page 452, add at end of first full sentence:

This bright line is beginning to break down. Two federal courts of appeal have held statutes criminalizing assisted suicide to be unconstitutional when applied to physicians hastening the dying of terminally ill, competent patients.[8.1]

Page 452, add to footnote 12:

CA2: Quill v. Vacco, 80 F.3d 716 (2d Cir. 1996), *rev'd,* 117 S. Ct. 2293 (1997).

CA9: Compassion in Dying v. Washington, 79 F.3d 790 (9th Cir. 1996), *rev'd sub nom.* Washington v. Glucksberg, 117 S. Ct. 2258 (1997).

See Asch, *The Role of Critical Care Nurses in Euthanasia and Assisted Suicide,* 334 New Eng. J. Med. 1374, 1375 (1996) (17% of intensive care nurses reported receiving requests to actively hasten death); Kuhse & Singer, *Voluntary Euthanasia and the Nurse: An Australian Survey*, 30 Int'l J. Nursing

---

[8.1] See § **18.22** in this supplement, discussing Quill v. Vacco, 80 F.3d 716 (2d Cir. 1996), and Compassion in Dying v. Washington, 79 F.3d 790 (9th Cir. 1996).

Stud. 311 (1993) (2% of nurses actively hastened death with a patient's, but without a physician's, request).

§ 18.2   Suicide and Liability for Assisted Suicide

Page 454, add note 17.1 reference at end of carryover paragraph and add note 17.1:

17.1 **LA:** *See, e.g.,* Perrier v. Bistes, 650 So. 2d 786 (La. Ct. App.), *cert. denied,* 653 So. 2d 569 (La. 1995) (siblings of patient who died from termination of life support allege physician engaged, with patient's husband and his siblings, in conspiracy to commit murder).

Page 455, add to footnote 26:

CA: People v. Cleaves, 280 Cal. Rptr. 146, 151 (Ct. App. 1991) ("[W]here a person *actually performs, or actively assists in performing, the overt act resulting in death,* . . . it is wholly immaterial whether this act is committed pursuant to an agreement with the victim.'" quoting People v. Matlock, 336 P.2d 505 (Cal. 1959)).

OK: Edinburgh v. State, 896 P.2d 1176 (Okla. Crim. App. 1995) (person who pulls trigger on rifle, killing another, is guilty of homicide, not assisted suicide).

§ 18.3   Forgoing Treatment Distinguished from Assisted Suicide

Page 455, add to footnote 29:

CA9:   *Cf.* Compassion in Dying v. Washington, 79 F.3d 790, 824 (9th Cir. 1996) (even providing means to patient for patient to *actively* hasten his death should not be considered suicide), *rev'd sub nom.* Washington v. Glucksberg, 117 S. Ct. 2258 (1997).

Page 455, replace "People v. Kevorkian" citation in footnote 30 with:

MI: People v. Kevorkian, 527 N.W.2d 714 (Mich. 1994) (prosecution for murder for assisting a suicide not permissible), *rev'g* 517 N.W.2d 293 (Mich. Ct. App. 1994), *and overruling* People v. Roberts, 178 N.W. 690 (Mich. 1920).

Page 455, add to footnote 31:

RI: *But see* Laurie v. Senecal, 666 A.2d 806, 807 (R.I. 1995) (viewing nonphysically ill prisoner's refusal to eat as suicide and therefore ordering tube-feeding of the prisoner, who was refusing to eat because "he no longer desired to live because of the stigma of his conviction for first-degree sexual assault upon a minor female").

Page 456, add to footnote 33:

US: Washington v. Glucksberg, 117 S. Ct. 2258 (1997).
CA2:   *But cf.* Quill v. Vacco, 80 F.3d 716 (2d Cir. 1996) (forgoing life-sustaining treatment might be suicide, but permissible when performed pursuant to exercise of patient's right to refuse treatment), *rev'd,* 117 S. Ct. 2293 (1997).
FL: McIver v. Krischer, 697 So. 2d 97 (Fla. 1997).

§ 18.5   — Causation

Page 458, add to footnote 39:

MI: People v. Kevorkian, 527 N.W.2d 714, 728 (Mich. 1994) ("suicide frustrates the natural course by introducing an outside agent to accelerate death, whereas the refusal or withdrawal of life-sustaining medical treatment allows nature to proceed, i.e., death occurs because of the underlying condition.").

Page 458, add to footnote 41:

Overruled in part by *In re* Conroy, 486 A.2d 1209, 1244 (N.J. 1985).

Page 458, add to footnote 42:

CA9:   *But see* Compassion in Dying v. Washington, 79 F.3d 790, 824 (9th Cir. 1996) (denying that *actively* hastening one's own death constitutes suicide), *rev'd sub nom.* Washington v. Glucksberg, 117 S. Ct. 2258 (1997).

Page 458, add to footnote 43:

US: Vacco v. Quill, 117 S. Ct. 2293, 2298 (1997). *But see* Washington v. Glucksberg, 117 S. Ct. 2258, 2310 (1997) (Stevens, J., concurring in the judgment).

Page 459, add to footnote 45:

CA2: *But see* Quill v. Vacco, 80 F.3d 716, 729 (2d Cir. 1996) ("By ordering the discontinuance of these artificial life-sustaining processes or refusing to accept them in the first place, a patient hastens his death by means that are not natural in any sense. It certainly cannot be said that the death that immediately ensues is the natural result of the progression of the disease or condition from which the patient suffers.").

CA9: *But see* Compassion in Dying v. Washington, 79 F.3d 790, 822–23 (9th Cir. 1996) (claiming that in both forgoing life-sustaining treatment and actively hastening one's death the cause of death is the same—actions taken by the physician or patient—and that both are equally licit with consent of patient), *rev'd sub nom.* Washington v. Glucksberg, 117 S. Ct. 2258 (1997).

Page 459, add to footnote 46:

FL: *Accord* McIver v. Krischer, 697 So. 2d 97, 102 (Fla. 1997).

Page 460, add at end of section:

Moreover, if life support is necessitated by injuries intentionally inflicted on the patient by another, termination of treatment by the patient[50.1] or by a surrogate on behalf of the patient,[50.2] it is not a supervening cause of death and thus does not relieve the person who harmed the patient from criminal liability.

§ 18.6 — Act and Omission

Page 460, add to footnote 52:

US: Vacco v. Quill, 117 S. Ct. 2293, 2301–02 (1997).

CA9: *But see* Compassion in Dying v. Washington, 79 F.3d 790, 822 (9th Cir. 1996) (rejecting distinction as one without a difference because "[i]n disconnecting a respirator, or authorizing its disconnection, a doctor is unquestionably committing an act; he is taking an active role in bringing about the patient's death"), *rev'd sub nom.* Washington v. Glucksberg, 117 S. Ct. 2258 (1997).

FL: McIver v. Krischer, 697 So. 2d 97, 102 (Fla. 1997).

[50.1] **IL:** People v. Caldwell, 692 N.E.2d 448 (Ill. App. Ct. 1998).

   TN: State v. Ruane, 912 S.W.2d 766 (Tenn. Crim. App. 1995).

[50.2] **IL:** People v. Driver, 379 N.E.2d 840 (Ill. App. Ct. 1978).

§ 18.7   —Intent

Page 462, add to footnote 58:

US: Vacco v. Quill, 117 S. Ct. 2293, 2298 (1997). *But see* Washington v. Glucksberg, 117 S. Ct. 2258, 2310 (1997) (Stevens, J., concurring in the judgment).

CA: Bartling v. Superior Court, 209 Cal. Rptr. 220, 226 (Ct. App. 1984).

CT: McConnell v. Beverly Enter.-Conn., Inc., 553 A.2d 596, 608 (Conn. 1989).

FL: Singletary v. Costello, 665 So. 2d 1099, 1109 (Fla. Dist. Ct. App. 1996) (state interest in prevention of suicide not implicated where prisoner's hunger strike sought to bring about change rather than death even if death might result).

ME: *In re* Gardner, 534 A.2d 947, 955–56 (Me. 1987).

MA: Brophy v. New Eng. Sinai Hosp., Inc., 497 N.E.2d 626, 638, 642 (Mass. 1986); Superintendent of Belchertown State Sch. v. Saikewicz, 370 N.E.2d 417, 427 n.11 (Mass. 1977).

MI: Rosebush v. Oakland County Prosecutor, 491 N.W.2d 633, 636 n.2 (Mich. Ct. App. 1992).

NJ: *In re* Conroy, 486 A.2d 1209, 1226 (N.J. 1985).

§ 18.8   —Advance Directive Legislation

Page 465, add to footnote 69:

LA: *Cf.* La. Rev. Stat. Ann. § 40:1299.58.10(B)(5) ("The removal of life support systems or the failure to administer cardio-pulmonary resuscitation under this part shall not be deemed the cause of death.").

PA: *Cf.* Commonwealth v. Luczak, 16 Fiduc. Rep. 2d 333 (Snyder County, Pa. 1995) (advance directive statute does not render assisted suicide statute unconstitutional).

§ 18.9   Liability for Homicide

Page 465, add to footnote 72:

KS: *See also* State v. Naramore, 965 P.2d 211 (Kan. Ct. App. 1998) (reversing convictions of physician, for attempted murder for administration of pain relief medications, and for second-degree murder for withholding and withdrawing treatment).

Page 466, add to footnote 74:

MN: *But see* State v. McKown, 475 N.W.2d 63 (Minn. 1991) (indictment of parents of child who died when given Christian Science treatment instead of accepted treatment violated parents' due process rights because statute failed to give fair notice of prohibited conduct).

Page 467, add note 80.1 reference after second full sentence in carryover paragraph and add note 80.1:

[80.1] **KS:** *See* State v. Naramore, 965 P.2d 211 (Kan. Ct. App. 1998) (reversing conviction for second-degree murder for withholding and withdrawing treatment).

§ 18.11 —Legal Right to Forgo Life-Sustaining Treatment

Page 468, add to footnote 83:

CA: People v. Cleaves, 280 Cal. Rptr. 146, 151 (Ct. App. 1991) ("[W]here a person *actually performs, or actively assists in performing, the overt act resulting in death, . . .* it is wholly immaterial whether this act is committed pursuant to an agreement with the victim.'" quoting People v. Matlock, 336 P.2d 505 (Cal. 1959)).

OK: Edinburgh v. State, 896 P.2d 1176, 1180 & n.4 (Okla. Crim. App. 1995) (killing of terminally ill patient allegedly at his request; "'Murder is no less murder because the homicide is committed at the desire of the victim. He who kills another upon another's desire or command is, in the judgment of the law, as much a murderer as if he had done it merely of his own head.'").

§ 18.13 —Causation

Page 470, add to footnote 95:

CA2: *But see* Quill v. Vacco, 80 F.3d 716, 729 (2d Cir. 1996) ("By ordering the discontinuance of these artificial life-sustaining processes or refusing to accept them in the first place, a patient hastens his death by means that are not natural in any sense. It certainly cannot be said that the death that immediately ensues is the natural result of the progression of the disease or condition from which the patient suffers."), *rev'd,* 117 S. Ct. 2293 (1997).

CA9:   *But see* Compassion in Dying v. Washington, 79 F.3d 790, 822–23 (9th Cir. 1996) (claiming that in both forgoing life-sustaining treatment and actively hastening one's death the cause of death is the same—actions taken by the physician or patient—and that both are equally licit with consent of patient), *rev'd sub nom.* Washington v. Glucksberg, 117 S. Ct. 2258 (1997).

Page 470, add note 96.1 reference at end of first sentence of second paragraph and add note 96.1:

96.1 **CA9:** Compassion in Dying v. Washington, 79 F.3d 790 (9th Cir. 1996), *rev'd sub nom.* Washington v. Glucksberg, 117 S. Ct. 2258 (1997).

§ 18.14   —Intent

Page 472, add to footnote 102:

CA9:   *Cf.* Compassion in Dying v. Washington, 79 F.3d 790, 822 (9th Cir. 1996) (physician's intent in forgoing life-sustaining treatment is that "the patient will die an earlier death than he otherwise would," and such intent is licit with consent of patient or surrogate), *rev'd sub nom.* Washington v. Glucksberg, 117 S. Ct. 2258 (1997).

§ 18.15   —Passive Euthanasia

Page 472, add to footnote 107:

CA2:   *Accord* Quill v. Vacco, 80 F.3d 716 (2d Cir. 1996) (but holding that euthanasia, whether passive or active, is constitutionally protected under certain circumstances), *rev'd,* 117 S. Ct. 2293 (1997).

Page 473, add note 107.1 reference at end of second sentence of last paragraph and add note 107.1:

107.1 **CA2:** *But see* Quill v. Vacco, 80 F.3d 716, 729 (2d Cir. 1996) ("[T]here is nothing 'natural' about causing death by means other than the original illness or its complications. The withdrawal of nutrition brings on death by starvation, the withdrawal of hydration brings on death by dehydration, and the withdrawal of ventilation brings about respiratory failure."), *rev'd,* 117 S. Ct. 2293 (1997).

§ 18.17 What Constitutes Assisted Suicide and Homicide

Page 475, add to footnote 115:

See Alan Meisel, Stuart Youngner, & Jan Jernigan, *Prosecutors and End-of-Life Decision Making,* 159 Archives Internal Med. 1089 (1999) (approximately three-fifths of prosecutors responding to survey would not prosecute physician for providing terminally ill cancer patient with extra morphine tablets, knowing she would hoard them and use them to end her life).

Page 475, add to footnote 122:

See People *ex rel.* Oakland County Prosecuting Attorney v. Kevorkian, 534 N.W.2d 172 (Mich. Ct. App. 1995), *appeal denied,* 549 N.W.2d 566 (Mich.), *cert. denied sub nom.* Kevorkian v. Michigan, 117 S. Ct. 296 (1996) (affirming trial court's grant of injunction on ground that "[d]efendant's conduct before the injunction was entered and his threatened conduct in the future supports *[sic]* the people's claim that recourse to the criminal courts alone may not be adequate to restrain unlawful acts or threats thereof that constitute, at a minimum, a public nuisance that affects health, morals, or safety").

Page 477, add to footnote 134:

CA: People v. Cleaves, 280 Cal. Rptr. 146, 151 (Ct. App. 1991) (mercy killing performed at victim's request constitutes crime of aiding and abetting suicide and murder).

OK: *See also* Edinburgh v. State, 896 P.2d 1176 (Okla. Crim. App. 1995) (killing another cannot be construed as assisting in suicide, even if the other is incapable of killing himself).

Page 477, add to footnote 137:

See Kevorkian v. Thompson, 947 F. Supp. 1152, 1155–56 (E.D. Mich. 1997) (providing complete but concise summary of Michigan litigation and legislation).

*Page 478, replace **Table 18–1** with:*

Table 18–1

(A) Assisted Suicide Statutes

AK: Alaska Stat. § 11.41.120
AZ: Ariz. Rev. Stat. Ann. § 13-1103(A)(3)
AR: Ark. Code Ann. § 5-10-104(a)(2)
CA: Cal. Penal Code § 401
CO: Colo. Rev. Stat. § 18-3-104

CT:	Conn. Gen. Stat. Ann. §§ 53a–56
DE:	Del. Code Ann. tit. 11, § 645
FL:	Fla. Stat. Ann. § 782.08
GA:	Ga. Code Ann. § 16-5-5(b)
HI:	Haw. Rev. Stat. § 707-702
IL:	Ill. Ann. Stat. ch. 720, para. 5/12-31
IN:	Ind. Code Ann. § 35-42-1-2.5
IA:	Iowa Code Ann. § 707A.1-.3
KS:	Kan. Stat. Ann. § 21-3406
KY:	Ky. Rev. Stat. Ann. § 216.302
LA:	La. Rev. Stat. Ann. § 14:32.12
ME:	Me. Rev. Stat. Ann. tit. 17-A, § 204
MI:	1997 Mich. Pub. Acts S.B. 200
MN:	Minn. Stat. Ann. § 609.215
	Minn. Stat. Ann. §§ 147.091(w), 151.06(a)(7)(xiii)
MS:	Miss. Code Ann. § 97-3-49
MO:	Mo. Ann. Stat. § 565.023
MT:	Mont. Code Ann. § 45-5-105
NE:	Neb. Rev. Stat. § 28-307
NV:	Nev. Rev. Stat. Ann. § 449.670
NH:	N.H. Rev. Stat. Ann. § 630:4
NJ:	N.J. Stat. Ann. § 2C:11-6
NM:	N.M. Stat. Ann. § 30-2-4
NY:	N.Y. Penal Law § 120.15(3)
	N.Y. Penal Law § 125.30
ND:	N.D. Cent. Code § 12.1-16-04
OK:	Okla. Stat. Ann. tit. 21, §§ 813–818
OR:	Or. Rev. Stat. § 163.125(1)(b)
PA:	Pa. Stat. Ann. tit. 18, §§ 2505, 2506
PR:	P.R. Laws Ann. tit. 33, § 4009
RI:	R.I. Gen. Laws §§ 11-60-1 to -5
SC:	S.C. Code Ann. § 16-3-1090 (C)(1)
SD:	S.D. Codified Laws Ann. § 22-16-37
TN:	Tenn. Code Ann. § 39-13-216
TX:	Tex. Penal Code Ann. § 22.08
WA:	Wash. Rev. Code Ann. § 9A.36.060
WI:	Wis. Stat. Ann. § 940.12

(B) Assisted Suicide Prohibited as a Common-Law Crime

AL:	Ala. Code § 1-3-1
DC:	D.C. Code Ann. § 22-107
ID:	Idaho Code § 18-303
MD:	Md. Code Ann., Const. art. 5
NV:	Nev. Rev. Stat. Ann. § 192.050
SC:	S.C. Code Ann. § 16-1-10
VT:	Vt. Stat. Ann. tit. 1, § 271

§ 18.18   Criminal Liability for "Active"
Interventions to End Life

Page 480, add to footnote 147:

ND: *Accord* N.D. Cent. Code § 12.1-16-08 ("If the person who assists in a suicide . . . is a person who is licensed, certified, or otherwise authorized . . . the licensing agency . . . may suspend or revoke the license or certification of that person.").

Page 480, replace footnote 150 with:

MN: Minn. Stat. Ann. § 609.215(a).
See **Table 9-1A** in this supplement (collecting statutes).

Page 480, add to text after first full paragraph:

Similarly, a physician who engages in active euthanasia may be subject to professional discipline. In *Gallant v. Board of Medical Examiners*,[150.1] for example, the petitioner physician sought review of a final order of the Oregon Board of Medical Examiners finding that he had committed an "unprofessional or dishonorable" act in ordering administration of Succinylcholine to end a patient's life.[150.2] The patient, a 78-year-old woman, had suffered a severe brain hemorrhage and had unexpectedly continued to live after removal of respiratory support in accordance with her advance directive and her family's request. The patient's breathing was agonal, and family members had continued to request further measures to end the patient's life.[150.3] The Board of Medical Examiners suspended the physician's medical license for 60 days.

Page 480, add to footnote 151:

CA9:   Compassion in Dying v. Washington, 79 F.3d 790, 829 (9th Cir. 1996), *rev'd sub nom.* Washington v. Glucksberg, 117 S. Ct. 2258 (1997).

Page 480, add to footnote 152:

KS: *But see* State v. Naramore, 965 P.2d 211 (Kan. Ct. App. 1998) (reversing conviction of physician for attempted murder from administration of pain relief medications).

[150.1] 974 P.2d 814 (Ore. Ct. App. 1999).

[150.2] *Id.* at 814.

[150.3] *Id.* at 815–16.

Page 481, add to footnote 155:

CA9: Compassion in Dying v. Washington, 79 F.3d 790, 811 (9th Cir. 1996) ("According to a survey by the American Society of Internal Medicine, one doctor in five said he had assisted in a patient's suicide."), *rev'd sub nom.* Washington v. Glucksberg, 117 S. Ct. 2258 (1997).

Page 482, replace footnote 159 with:

MN: Minn. Stat. Ann. § 609.215(a).
See also **Table 9–1A** (collecting statutes).
    See generally Caswell, *Rejecting Criminal Liability for Life-Shortening Palliative Care,* 6 J. Contemp. Health L. & Pol'y 127 (1990) (discussing proposals of Law Reform Commission of Canada that would in part recognize principle of double effect).

Page 483, add to footnote 165:

US: *But see* Vacco v. Quill, 117 S. Ct. 2293, 2301 n.11 (1997) ("Just as a State may prohibit assisting suicide while permitting patients to refuse unwanted lifesaving treatment, it may permit palliative care related to that refusal, which may have the foreseen but unintended 'double effect' of hastening the patient's death.").

KS: *See also* State v. Naramore, 965 P.2d 211 (Kan. Ct. App. 1998) (reversing conviction of physician for attempted murder from administration of pain relief medications).

Page 484, add to footnote 167:

CA2: Quill v. Vacco, 80 F.3d 716, 730 (2d Cir. 1996) (state interest in preservation of life is "greatly reduced" in final stages of terminal illness), *rev'd,* 117 S. Ct. 2293 (1997).

Page 484, add note 169.1 reference at end of first sentence of second full paragraph and add note 169.1:

[169.1] **CA9:** Compassion in Dying v. Washington, 79 F.3d 790, 832 (9th Cir. 1996) ("[T]he critical line in right-to-die cases [is] the one between the voluntary and involuntary termination of an individual's life."), *rev'd sub nom.* Washington v. Glucksberg, 117 S. Ct. 2258 (1997).

§ 18.19   Terminology: Assisted Suicide and
Active Euthanasia

Page 486, add note 175.1 reference at end of second paragraph and add note 175.1:

[175.1] **CA:** People v. Cleaves, 280 Cal. Rptr. 146 (Ct. App. 1991).
OK: Edinburgh v. State, 896 P.2d 1176, 1179–80 (Okla. Crim. App. 1995) ("Many states have distinguished between the direct killing involved in euthanasia and conduct characterizing mere suicide assistance. . . . Thus, where the defendant only furnishes the means by which the victim kills herself, he has merely assisted suicide. But, where the defendant proximately causes the defendant's death he can be held liable for homicide.").

Page 486, add footnote 175.2 reference at end of fourth sentence in third paragraph and add footnote 175.2:

[175.2] *E.g.,*Gallant v. Board of Medical Examiners, 974 P.2d 814 (Ore. Ct. App. 1999) (administration of Succinylcholine to end patient's life after patient lived despite discontinuation of life support in accordance with patient's advance directive and patient's family's wishes).

§ 18.20   Public's Attitudes Toward Active
Euthanasia and Assisted Suicide

Page 487, add note 175.1 reference at end of first sentence of section and add note 175.1:

[175.1] *But see* American Medical Ass'n, News Release — AMA Poll: Most Americans Would Not Choose Physician-Assisted Suicide (Jan. 6, 1997) (although "52% approve of intentionally ending a patient's life to relieve suffering," "by a five-to-one margin, Americans would choose comfort care and natural death over physician-assisted suicide once given specific information on existing options for care at end of life").

Page 487, add to footnote 176:

See also Conn. Poll Shows Some Support for Assisted Suicide, Am. Med. News, May 4, 1998, at 11 ("70% would support legislation allowing doctors to assist in suicide if a patient were close to death and at least two doctors agreed").

Page 487, add to footnote 178:

Compassion in Dying v. Washington, 79 F.3d 790, 810 & nn.48–50 (9th Cir. 1996) (citing Robert Risley, *Voluntary Active Euthanasia: The Next Frontier, Impact on the Indigent*, 8 Issues L. & Med. 361, 365 (1992) (according to Roper Report of April 1990, 64% of Americans believed that terminally ill should have right to physician aid-in-dying); Sanford H. Kadish, *Letting Patients Die: Legal and Moral Reflections*, 80 Cal. L. Rev. 857, 861 n.22 (1992); *Euthanasia Favored in Poll*, N.Y. Times, Nov. 4, 1991, at A16 (October 1991 national poll found that almost two-thirds of Americans favor physician-assisted suicide and euthanasia when requested by terminally ill patients)); David Cannella, *Physician-Assisted Suicide, Fight Rages in Several States: Issue Expected to Go to the Supreme Court*, Ariz. Republic, May 13, 1995 (1994 Harris poll found 73% of Americans favor legalizing physician-assisted suicide); Sarah Henry, *The Battle over Assisted-Suicide*, 20 Cal. Law. 1, 35 (1995) (according to March 1995 Field poll in California, 70% of Californians thought terminally ill individuals should be able to obtain medication from their doctors to end their lives)).

See also Ezekiel J. Emanuel et al., *Euthanasia and Physician-Assisted Suicide: Attitudes and Experiences of Oncology Patients, Oncologists, and the Public*, 347 Lancet 1805 (1996) (about two-thirds of oncology patients and the public consider euthanasia and physician-assisted suicide acceptable for patients with unremitting pain); *Poll Examines Adults' Innermost Feelings About Life's End*, N.Y. Times, Dec. 6, 1997, at A8 (nat'l ed.) (approximately two-thirds of respondents in Gallup poll favored legalization of physician-assisted suicide "'under a wide variety of specific circumstances,'" and about one-third supported legalization "only 'in a few cases.'").

Page 488, add to footnote 184:

See also § **18.24** in the main volume and this supplement.

§ 18.21   Physicians' Attitudes Toward Active Euthanasia and Assisted Suicide

Page 489, add to footnote 190:

See also Linda Beecham, *BMA Opposes Legalisation of Euthanasia*, 315 Brit. Med. J. 80 (1997) (British Medical Association "overwhelmingly" opposed to legalization of active euthanasia or physician-assisted suicide); American Geriatrics Society Public Policy Committee, *Voluntary Active Euthanasia*, 39 J. Am. Geriatrics Soc'y 826 (1996).

In Oregon, for example, the Board of Medical Examiners in 1999 suspended a physician's medical license for 60 days for ordering that Succinylcholine be administered to end the life of a patient who had suffered a severe brain hemorrhage, was considered to be in a "terminal" condition, and had executed an advance directive and designated a surrogate decision-maker who requested withdrawal of treatment. The patient had continued to breathe despite withdrawal of respiratory support, and the patient's family members were "concerned that the patient was suffering needlessly." Gallant v. Board of Medical Examiners, 974 P.2d 814, 815 (Ore. Ct. App. 1999). The hospital at which the physician treated the patient contacted the Board of Medical Examiners, *id*. at 816, which suspended the physician's license for "committing an 'unprofessional or dishonorable' act" in authorizing the administration of the drug. *Id*. at 814.

Page 489, add to footnote 192:

Daniel Sulmasy, *Physician Resource Use and Willingness to Participate in Assisted Suicide*, 158 Arch. Internal Med. 974 (1998) ("[P]hysicians who tend to practice resource-conserving medicine are significantly more likely than their resource-intensive counterparts to provide a lethal prescription at the request of a terminally ill patient."). *See also* Ezekiel Emanuel, *Cost Savings at the End of Life*, 275 JAMA 1907 (1996) (existing studies of cost savings from hospice and advance directives at end of life suffer from serious methodologic defects, but suggest savings in the range of 25% to 40% in last month of life and 0% to 10% in last year of life). *Cf.* Joan Teno et al., *The Illusion of End-of-Life Resource Savings with Advance Directives*, 45 J. Am. Geriatric Soc'y 513 (1997) (better documentation in hospital records of existence of advance directives does not lead to reduction in use of hospital resources). *But see* Ezekiel J. Emanuel & Margaret P. Battin, *What Are the Potential Cost Savings from Legalizing Physician-Assisted Suicide?*, 339 New Eng. J. Med. 167 (1998) (savings from physician-assisted suicide "can be predicted to be very small—less than 0.1 percent of both total health care spending in the United States and an individual managed-care plan's budget").

Page 490, add to footnote 193:

Bachman et al., *Attitudes of Michigan Physicians and the Public Toward Legalizing Physician-Assisted Suicide and Voluntary Euthanasia*, 334 New Eng. J. Med. 303–09 (1996) (56% of responding Michigan doctors preferred legalizing assisted suicide to prohibiting it); Doukas et al., *Attitudes and Behaviors on Physician-Assisted Death: A Study of Michigan Oncologists*, 13 J. Clinical Oncology 1055 (1995) (18% of responding Michigan oncologists reported active participation in assisted suicide); Slome et al., *Physicians'*

Attitudes Toward Assisted Suicide in AIDS, 5 J. Acquired Immune Deficiency Syndromes 712 (1992) (24% of responding physicians treating AIDS patients would grant patient's request for assistance in hastening death); Lee et al., *Legalizing Assisted Suicide—Views of Physicians in Oregon,* 335 New Eng. J. Med. 310–15 (1996) (60% of responding Oregon doctors supported legalizing assisted suicide for terminally ill patients). *See also* Kuhse et al., *End-of-Life Decisions in Australian Medical Practice,* 166 Med. J. Austl. 191 (1997) (1.8% of Australian deaths resulted from euthanasia or physician-assisted suicide).

See Ezekiel J. Emanuel et al., *Euthanasia and Physician-Assisted Suicide: Attitudes and Experiences of Oncology Patients, Oncologists, and the Public,* 347 Lancet 1805 (1996) (about one-fifth of oncologists approve of euthanasia and slightly less than one-half approve of physician-assisted suicide for oncology patients with unremitting pain).

Page 490, add to footnote 194:

See Asch, *The Role of Critical Care Nurses in Euthanasia and Assisted Suicide,* 334 New Eng. J. Med. 1374, 1374 (1996) ("In surveys of British and Australian physicians, 7 to 29 percent admit having performed euthanasia."); Back *et al., Physician-Assisted Suicide and Euthanasia in Washington State: Patient Requests and Physician Responses,* 275 JAMA 919 (1996) (26% of physicians reported receiving requests for actively hastening death; 24% of those requested performed assisted suicide and 24% active euthanasia); Ezekiel J. Emanuel et al., *Euthanasia and Physician-Assisted Suicide: Attitudes and Experiences of Oncology Patients, Oncologists, and the Public,* 347 Lancet 1805 (1996) (13.6% of oncologists report having performed euthanasia or physician-assisted suicide). *But see* Diane E. Meier et al., *A National Survey of Physician-Assisted Suicide and Euthanasia in the United States,* 338 New Eng. J. Med. 1193 (1998) (less than 3% of physician have written lethal prescription and less than 5% have administered lethal injection to terminally ill patients).

Page 490, add to footnote 195:

Back et al., *Physician-Assisted Suicide and Euthanasia in Washington State,* 275 JAMA 919–25 (1996) (12% of Washington state physicians reported having been asked by terminally ill patients for prescriptions to hasten death; 24% of those asked complied with such requests in year prior to study); Dyer, *Two Doctors Confess to Helping Patients to Die,* 315 Brit. Med. J. 206 (1997).

Page 490, add at end of first paragraph:

Nurses also figure in the debate about active euthanasia and assisted suicide. A survey of oncology nurses reported that 47 percent vote to legalize physician aid-in-dying, and 16 percent responded that with a physician's order, they would perform voluntary active euthanasia on a competent, terminally ill patient.[198.1]

Page 491, add to footnote 203:

See Ezekiel J. Emanuel et al., *Euthanasia and Physician-Assisted Suicide: Attitudes and Experiences of Oncology Patients, Oncologists, and the Public,* 347 Lancet 1805 (1996) (13.6% of oncologists report having performed euthanasia or physician-assisted suicide). *But see* Diane E. Meier et al., *A National Survey of Physician-Assisted Suicide and Euthanasia in the United States,* 338 New Eng. J. Med. 1193 (1998) (less than 3% of physicians have written lethal prescription and less than 5% have administered lethal injections to terminally ill patients).

Page 491, add at end of first full paragraph:

A survey of 1,600 nurses practicing in hospital intensive care units reported that 16 percent had participated at least once in active euthanasia or assisted suicide, with requests approximately evenly divided between those from competent patients and those from patients' families.[203.1] At least 7 percent reported participating in actively hastening death at least once without a request from either the patient or a surrogate, although some of these may have occurred with the advance knowledge and tacit consent of patients or surrogates.[203.2] Figures from Australia are similar. Twenty-three percent of surveyed nurses reported being asked by a physician to actively hasten death, and 85 percent reported they had complied. Two percent actively hastened death with a patient's, but without a physician's, request.[203.3]

Page 492, add to footnote 210:

See Timothy E. Quill et al., *The Debate over Physician-Assisted   Suicide: Empirical Data and Convergent Views,* 128 Ann. Internal Med. 552 (1998); Jill A. Rhymes, *Barriers to Effective Palliative Care of Terminal Patients: An International Perspective,* 12 Clinics in Geriatric Med. 407 (1996).

[198.1] *See* Young *et al., Oncology Nurses' Attitudes Regarding Voluntary, Physician-Assisted Dying for Competent, Terminally Ill Patients,* 20 Oncology Nursing Forum 445 (1993).

[203.1] Asch, *The Role of Critical Care Nurses in Euthanasia and Assisted Suicide,* 334 New Eng. J. Med. 1374, 1375 (1996).

[203.2] *Id.* at 1376.

[203.3] Kuhse & Singer, *Voluntary Euthanasia and the Nurse: An Australian Survey,* 30 Int'l J. Nursing Studies 311 (1993).

§ 18.22   Constitutionality of Statutory Prohibitions on Assisted Suicide

Page 497, add to footnote 243:

OK: *See* Edinburgh v. State, 896 P.2d 1176 (Okla. Crim. App. 1995) (reviewing conflicting evidence about whether decedent, a terminally ill person, consented to his life being ended; court held that consent was not a defense anyway).

Page 498, add at end of "Compassion in Dying" subsection:

Court of Appeals' Decision:

Compassion in Dying v. Washington
79 F.3d 790 (9th Cir. 1996),
rev'd, 117 S. Ct. 2258 (1997)

Plaintiffs—a coalition of terminally ill patients, physicians who treat terminally ill patients, and Compassion in Dying, an organization providing counseling to terminally ill individuals considering suicide—brought an action to declare unconstitutional the Washington statutes making assisting suicide a crime. The trial court entered judgment on the plaintiffs' motion for summary judgment, holding that the challenged statutes violated the due process and equal protection clauses of the 14th Amendment.[250.1]

The state of Washington appealed, and a three-judge panel of the United States Court of Appeals for the Ninth Circuit reversed in a 2-1 decision.[250.2] The plaintiffs petitioned for a rehearing en banc, which was granted. The en banc panel of 11 judges, which because of the large number of judges on the Ninth Circuit is less than the full court, in an 8-3 decision vacated the three-judge panel's decision and affirmed the trial court's decision on due process grounds, but did not reach the equal protection aspects of the case.[250.3] Thereafter, the state of Washington petitioned for a rehearing by the full court en banc, which was denied.[250.4] The Supreme Court granted certiorari and eventually reversed.[250.5]

The en banc decision was authored by Judge Reinhardt, who was clearly sympathetic to the plight of the terminally ill. He cited public opinion polls

---

[250.1] *See* Compassion in Dying v. Washington, 850 F. Supp. 1454 (W.D. Wash. 1994), discussed in § **18.22** in the main volume.

[250.2] See Compassion in Dying v. Washington, 49 F.3d 586 (9th Cir. 1995).

[250.3] Compassion in Dying v. Washington, 79 F.3d 790 (9th Cir. 1996).

[250.4] 85 F.3d 1440 (9th Cir. 1996).

[250.5] See discussion below, this section.

showing that the majority of Americans favor making physician-assisted suicide available to those terminally ill persons who request it. He was motivated by the wish to "restore humanity and dignity to the process by which Americans die," which have succumbed to the "marvels of technology."[250.6] Despite the fact that "Americans are living longer, . . . when they finally succumb to illness, [they are] lingering longer, either in great pain or in a stuporous, semi-comatose condition that results from the infusion of vast amounts of pain killing medications."[250.7] He was deeply troubled by the fact that the criminalization of assisted suicide has led doctors to practice it covertly and to fear being branded and punished as criminals for relieving suffering, something which is a goal of the medical profession.[250.8] And he was clearly not impressed, as demonstrated by his analysis of act and omission, double effect, and causation, by the purported distinction between actively and passively hastening death.[250.9] In fact, he could see no warrant for referring to actively hastening the death of a terminally ill patient as suicide or assisted suicide, concluding "that there is a strong argument that a decision by a terminally ill patient to hasten by medical means a death that is already in process, should not be classified as suicide."[250.10]

Existence of Liberty Interest.   On the due process claim, the decision did not deviate significantly from the reasoning of the trial court, though the opinion did elaborate on many points to which the trial court paid little or no attention. The court substantially grounded its decision in *Casey* and *Cruzan*, determining, in brief, that there is a constitutionally protected liberty interest "in determining the time and manner of one's own death,"[250.11] what it referred to elsewhere as a "right to die."[250.12] Unlike the weak right to die of *Quinlan* and its progeny—which permits the withholding or withdrawing of life-sustaining medical treatment—this robust right to die makes no distinction between so-called passive and active hastening of death, treating them as equivalents for constitutional purposes.[250.13]

The court's reliance on *Cruzan* seems to be somewhat of a stretch, though if its reliance on *Casey* is sound, this may turn out to be beside the point. The court concluded that *Cruzan* "necessarily recognizes a liberty interest in has-

---

[250.6]   79 F.2d at 812.

[250.7]   *Id.*

[250.8]   *Id.* at 829.

[250.9]   *Id.* at 822–24.

[250.10] *Id.* at 824.

[250.11] 79 F.3d at 793.

[250.12] *Id.* at 799.

[250.13] *See id.* at 822–23.

tening one's own death."[250.14] It came to this conclusion because of the fact that the Supreme Court, in permitting the removal of life-sustaining medical treatment if the request to do so met state standards, "clearly recognized that granting the request to remove the tubes through which Cruzan received artificial nutrition and hydration would lead inexorably to her death."[250.15]

Does Prohibition Against Assisted Suicide Violate the Liberty Interest?
Having found that a liberty interest exists that encompasses hastening one's death, the court proceeded to determine whether the prohibition of assisted suicide violated that interest. The fact that there is such an interest "does not mean that there is a concomitant right to exercise that interest in all circumstances or to do so free from state regulation."[250.16] The court then proceeded to "identify the factors relevant to the case at hand, assess the state's interests and the individual's liberty interest in light of those factors, and then weigh and balance the competing interests"[250.17] in order to determine whether the state's action impairs the liberty interest—namely, the statutory prohibition against assisted suicide—violates an individual's substantive due process rights.

The State's Interests. The court examined the four conventionally cited state interests—preservation of life, prevention of suicide, protection of the interest of third parties, and protection of the ethical integrity of the medical profession[250.18]—as well as several others, to determine the weight to be accorded them in balancing them against the individual's liberty interest in hastening death.

(1) *Preservation of Life.* The court concluded that

> the laws in state after state demonstrate [that] even though the protection of life is one of the state's most important functions, the state's interest is dramatically diminished if the person it seeks to protect is terminally ill or permanently comatose and has expressed a wish that he be permitted to die without further medical treatment (or if a duly appointed representative has done so on his behalf).[250.19]

It based this conclusion on several factors. First is the fact that the state interest in life is not absolute. "Were it otherwise no state could administer capital punishment; similarly, the draft, as well as the defense budget, would

---

[250.14] *Id.* at 816.

[250.15] *Id.*

[250.16] *Id.*

[250.17] *Id.*

[250.18] See §§ **8.16–8.18** in the main volume and this supplement.

[250.19] 79 F.3d at 820.

be unconstitutional."[250.20] Rather, the strength of this interest depends on "the medical condition and the wishes of the person whose life is at stake."[250.21] Second, the state of Washington, as well as almost every other state, has recognized by statute—specifically, living will statutes—that "its interest in preserving life should ordinarily give way—at least in the case of competent, terminally ill adults who are dependent on medical treatment—to the wishes of the patients."[250.22] Third, the Washington legislature (and those of other states) has made a legislative finding in its living will statute that the right of terminally ill individuals to hasten their deaths is based on a due process liberty interest. Consequently, the state's interest is "substantially reduced," allowing it within bounds to regulate, but not to prohibit, "the manner in which decisions to hasten death are made."[250.23]

(2) *Preventing Suicide.* This, of course, is what the case is all about, at least from the state's perspective, and thus this is the state's asserted primary interest. The court dismissed the argument that because the state does not prohibit suicide, it has no interest in discouraging it. Earlier in the opinion, the court had observed that "[j]ust as the mere absence of criminal statutes prohibiting suicide or attempted suicide does not indicate societal approval so the mere presence of statutes criminalizing assisting in a suicide does not necessarily indicate societal disapproval."[250.24] However, the state's interest is not in preventing suicide per se, but in preventing irrational suicide—"a clear interest in preventing anyone, no matter what age, from taking his own life in a fit of desperation, depression, or loneliness or as a result of any other problem, physical or psychological, which can be significantly ameliorated."[250.25] Further, when the person *is* terminally ill, the state's interest is further diminished. Indeed, in such a situation, "its insistence on frustrating their wishes seems cruel."[250.26] In the final analysis, moreover, the court was unwilling to characterize actively hastening death as "suicide."[250.27]

Beyond this, however, the court was reluctant to even characterize physician aid-in-dying as assisting "suicide," primarily for the reason that the court could see only a distinction without a difference between so-called active and passive means to hasten death:

> In light of [the case law recognizing, on forgoing life-sustaining treatment,] these drastic changes regarding acceptable medical practices, opponents of

---

250.20 *Id.* at 817 n.72.

250.21 *Id.* at 817.

250.22 *Id.*

250.23 *Id.* at 820.

250.24 *Id.* at 810.

250.25 79 F.3d at 820.

250.26 *Id.* at 821.

250.27 *Id.* at 824.

physician-assisted suicide must now explain precisely what it is about the physician's conduct in assisted suicide cases that distinguishes it from the conduct that the state has explicitly authorized. The state responds by urging that physician-assisted suicide is different in kind, not degree, from the type of physician-life-ending conduct that is now authorized, for three separate reasons. It argues that "assisted suicide": 1) requires doctors to play an active role; 2) causes deaths that would not result from the patient's underlying disease; and 3) requires doctors to provide the causal agent of patients' deaths.[250.28]

The court summarily rejected all three of these purported distinctions, "individually [and] collectively." The first it called a "distinction without a difference" because in terminating, or authorizing the termination of, treatment, "a doctor is unquestionably committing an act; he is taking an active role in bringing about the patient's death. In fact, there can be no doubt that in such instances the doctor intends that, as the result of his action, the patient will die an earlier death than he otherwise would."[250.29]

For the court, neither did the distinction based on causation have any legitimacy.

> While the distinction may once have seemed tenable, at least from a metaphysical standpoint, it was not based on a valid or practical legal foundation and was therefore quickly abandoned. When Nancy Cruzan's feeding and hydration tube was removed, she did not die of an underlying disease. Rather, she was allowed to starve to death. . . . Similarly, when a doctor provides a conscious patient with medication to ease his discomfort while he starves himself to death—a practice that is not only legal but has been urged as an alternative to assisted suicide—the patient does not die of any underlying ailment. To the contrary, the doctor is helping the patient end his life by providing medication that makes it possible for the patient to achieve suicide by starvation.[250.30]

Finally, the court rejected a distinction between actively and passively hastening death based on an intent or motive rationale, usually discussed under the aegis of double effect.[250.31] The use of medication for the dying patient's comfort is "routinely and openly provide[d] . . . with the knowledge that it will have a 'double effect'—reduce the patient's pain and hasten his death," and it is accepted medical practice to do so.[250.32] From this, the court concludes that "the causation argument is simply 'another bridge crossed' in the journey to vindicate the liberty interests of the terminally ill, and the state's

---

[250.28] *Id*. at 822.

[250.29] *Id*.

[250.30] *Id*. at 822–23.

[250.31] See § **8.7** in the main volume and this supplement.

[250.32] 79 F.3d at 822.

third distinction has no more force than the other two."[250.33] The unarticulated assumption, which is of course correct, is that the patient is entitled to have adequate medication for the relief of pain.

(3) *Protection of the Interest of Third Parties.* This interest, which the court labeled "Effect on Children, Other Family Members, and Loved Ones," is a legitimate one for the state to seek to promote, but, as is the case with the other interests, the interest "is of almost negligible weight when the patient is terminally ill and his death is imminent and inevitable."[250.34] This is so because forcing the patient to die a longer and/or more painful death does not aid any third parties. "In fact," the court observed, "witnessing a loved one suffer a slow and agonizing death as a result of state compulsion is more likely to harm than further the interests of innocent third parties."[250.35]

(4) *Protecting the Integrity of the Medical Profession.* Just as other courts have turned this objection on its head in the context of *forgoing* treatment, so did the court in *Compassion in Dying.* Permitting physicians to assist terminally ill patients in actively hastening their deaths will not compromise the integrity of the medical profession, the court concluded; rather, it is the statutes that criminalize such assistance that threaten the medical profession's integrity by making "covert criminals out of honorable, dedicated, and compassionate individuals."[250.36]

Furthermore, this claim is contrary to the evidence because doctors have been actively hastening death for a long time "with the tacit approval of a substantial percentage of both the public and the medical profession, and without in any way diluting their commitment to their patients." Also, "[g]iven the similarity between what doctors are now permitted to do" under the aegis of "double effect" and forgoing life-sustaining treatment, "and what the plaintiffs assert they should be permitted to do," the court saw "no risk at all to the integrity of the profession."[250.37] The court also concluded that because, as polls demonstrate, many doctors support physician-assisted suicide, legalization would not run contrary to their ethical integrity.

Perhaps the central argument undermining this claim is that relief of suffering is a time-honored and well-accepted goal of medicine. Though the court did not accord it this position of centrality, it did acknowledge its role in legitimating physician-assisted suicide.

[250.33] *Id.* at 823.

[250.34] *Id.* at 827.

[250.35] *Id.*

[250.36] *Id.*

[250.37] *Id.* at 828.

Finally, the court took on the arguments of organized medicine proffered by the American Medical Association, an amicus curiae in the case. The court dismissed the AMA's claim that the Hippocratic Oath prohibited physician-assisted suicide with the observation that "[t]wenty years ago, the AMA contended that performing abortions violated the Hippocratic Oath," but that once the Supreme Court "held that a woman has a constitutional right to have an abortion, doctors began performing abortions routinely and the ethical integrity of the medical profession remained undiminished."[250.38] The court implicitly rejected the relevance of the Hippocratic Oath, referring to the fact that its "rigid language" also prohibits any type of surgery, "a position that would now be recognized as preposterous by even the most tradition-bound AMA members."[250.39] More fundamentally, the court concluded that the legalization of physician-assisted suicide would make its performance permissive, not mandatory, and thus no doctor's ethical integrity would be compromised.

In addition to these four well-accepted state interests, the court discussed two others. These are relevant not only to physician-assisted suicide but also to forgoing treatment though the court did not expressly discuss them in the latter context.

(5) *Avoiding the Involvement of Third Parties, and Precluding the Use of Arbitrary, Unfair, or Undue Influence.* With respect to the general population, the court rapidly dismissed this state interest with the observation that "[a]ll are at their minimums when the assistance is provided by or under the supervision or direction of a doctor and the recipient is a terminally ill patient."[250.40]

It then turned to consider this interest when patients are poor, members of minority groups, and/or handicapped. This is an argument that the majority of the three-judge panel that had declared the statute unconstitutional had heavily relied on—namely, that the statutory prohibition on assisted suicide protects these groups from being imposed on by others to accept suicide that they would otherwise not seek or would reject.[250.41] The court en banc concluded the opposite: that such individuals will receive

> more medical services than the remainder of the population in one, and only one, area—assisted suicide—is ludicrous on its face. So, too, is the argument that the poor and the minorities will rush to volunteer for physician-assisted suicide because of their inability to secure adequate medical treatment.[250.42]

[250.38] 79 F.3d at 830.

[250.39] *Id.* at 829.

[250.40] *Id.* at 825.

[250.41] *See* 49 F.3d at 592.

[250.42] 79 F.3d at 825.

A subpart of this argument is that the elderly will be pressured by their families to avail themselves of assisted suicide if it is not prohibited by statute. Here the court responded in a way that might cover almost all, if not all, of the alleged state interests in criminalizing assisted suicide: that the danger is no greater than it is in the realm of forgoing life-sustaining medical treatment, yet there is no legal prohibition against that practice, nor could there constitutionally be one. Further, the court observed that the *open* practice of assisted suicide, with physician involvement, would do more to prevent imposition on the elderly than its practice behind closed doors that occurs when it is criminal.

Yet another part of the argument is that the legalization of assisted suicide will lead to undue financial pressure on the terminally ill to end their lives. Accepting that this is a real possibility, the court concluded that it is not an illegitimate one because "we are reluctant to say that, in a society in which the costs of protracted health care can be so exorbitant, it is improper for competent, terminally ill adults to take the economic welfare of their families and loved ones into consideration."[250.43] In other words, it is proper for states to regulate assisted suicide to reduce the possibility that individuals will be *unduly influenced* by others to act for this reason, but it is perfectly proper for individuals to seek assisted suicide because of the high costs of health care if done *freely*.

Finally, the court considered the claim that legalization of assisted suicide would result in doctors treating requests to die routinely and impersonally. While not rejecting the possible validity of this claim, the court was willing to trust that doctors would not provide aid in dying if there were other reasonable ways to alleviate suffering or if there were significant doubt about a patient's wishes.

The appropriate response to these concerns is not to prohibit assisted suicide, but to regulate it and the medical profession. However, the court remained far more concerned about this claim than any others. Thus, it concluded that "[w]hile steps can be taken to minimize the danger substantially, the concerns cannot be wholly eliminated."[250.44] Therefore, it accorded "more than [the] minimal weight" to this concern than it had to others.[250.45]

(6) *Fear of Adverse Consequences*. The final interest asserted by the state to support the criminalization of assisted suicide was what the court characterized as "slippery slope" arguments; namely, that physician-assisted suicide would eventually lead to "putting people to death, not because they are desperately ill and want to die, but because they are deemed to pose an unjustifi-

---

[250.43] *Id*. at 826.

[250.44] *Id*. at 827.

[250.45] *Id*.

able burden on society,"[250.46] and that physician-assisted suicide would spread beyond terminally ill individuals.

The court dismissed these claims at both the general and specific level. It first rejected slippery slope arguments in general with the observation that "[t]his same nihilistic argument can be offered against any constitutionally-protected right or interest"[250.47] and that "[r]ecognition of any right creates the possibility of abuse."[250.48] In particular, such an argument did not deter the Supreme Court from recognizing and continually reaffirming a constitutional right to choose abortion, and it should have no more relevance with respect to physician-assisted suicide.

As to the feared slide from physician-assisted suicide to physicians more directly ending patients' lives than merely providing them with the means to do so themselves, the court acknowledged that it *will* be difficult to distinguish between physician-assisted suicide and mercy killing. However, the latter may become necessary because some patients may be in such a condition as to freely consent to hastening their deaths but not be able to administer the drugs necessary to do so. The court did not decide that such conduct would also be licit but determined that it was not necessary to address that issue in order to resolve the legitimacy of physician-assisted suicide. As to the more serious problem of the potential metamorphosis of voluntary into involuntary hastening of death, the court pointed out the obvious, namely, that "the critical line in right-to-die cases is the one between the voluntary and involuntary termination of an individual's life."[250.49]

As to the claim that physician-assisted suicide would inevitably be extended beyond terminally ill individuals because of the inability to define "terminal illness," the court identified two flaws. "First it presupposes a need for greater precision than is required in constitutional law. [Footnote omitted.] Second, it assumes that the terms 'terminal illness' or 'terminal condition' cannot be defined, even though those terms have in fact been defined repeatedly" in advance directive statutes.[250.50]

The Legitimacy of the Means by Which the State Furthers Its Interests. Another factor to be taken into account in striking a balance between the state's interests and the liberty interest in hastening one's death—besides the strength of the state's interests—is the *means* by which the state seeks to effectuate its interests. Washington has sought to do so through a total prohibition on the conduct in question. In this case, that is a constitutional over-broad means for so doing because it promotes not only the legitimate interest of preventing irrational suicide, but it also subjects physicians to potential

---

[250.46] *Id.* at 830.

[250.47] *Id.*

[250.48] 79 F.3d at 831.

[250.49] *Id.* at 832. See § **18.18** in the main volume.

[250.50] 79 F.3d at 832.

prosecution for making an honest mistake of judgment in the administration of medication for the relief of suffering without any intent to bring about death from that medication.

Instead, in order to ensure that the means are not constitutionally over-broad, the state must regulate, rather than prohibit, assisted suicide; it must narrowly tailor the regulation to accomplish its legitimate ends. First, and foremost, the court suggests, but does not hold, that this can be accomplished by placing the effectuation of assisted suicide in the hands of physicians—*physician*-assisted suicide—because they are a regulated profession (though this would possibly permit assisted suicide to be carried out by other qualified and regulated professionals such as pharmacists, nurses, and psychologists in those jurisdiction in which they are permitted to prescribe medications). The court suggested, but did not include in its holding, a variety of other procedural safeguards, in either legislation, regulation, or even private professional standards, such as

> witnesses to ensure voluntariness; reasonable, though short, waiting periods to prevent rash decisions; second medical opinions to confirm a patient's terminal status and also to confirm that the patient has been receiving proper treatment, including adequate comfort care; psychological examinations to ensure that the patient is not suffering from momentary or treatable depression; reporting procedures that will aid in the avoidance of abuse.[250.51]

The Application of the Balancing Test. The court was more frank than most in acknowledging that there is no mathematical formula that can be employed when applying a balancing test, that it is "quintessentially a judicial role."[250.52] The outcome was almost foreordained. On the one hand, "[t]he liberty interest at issue here is an important one and, in the case of the terminally ill, is at its peak." On the other hand, "the state interests, while equally important in the abstract, are for the most part at a low point here." The court was satisfied that the state's "particularly strong interest in avoiding undue influence and other forms of abuse . . . in the case of life and death decisions" is protected by limiting assisted suicide to administration by physicians "who have a strong bias in favor of preserving life, and because the process itself can be carefully regulated and rigorous safeguards adopted."[250.53]

Consequently, the court concluded that the balance must be struck in favor of the individual's liberty interest in actively hastening death:

[250.51] *Id.* at 833.
[250.52] *Id.* at 836.
[250.53] *Id.* at 837.

The state has chosen to pursue its interests by means of what for terminally ill patients is effectively a total prohibition, even though its most important interests could be adequately served by a far less burdensome measure. The consequences of rejecting the as-applied challenge would be disastrous for the terminally ill, while the adverse consequences for the state would be of a far lesser order. This, too, weighs in favor of upholding the liberty interest.[250.54]

Page 503, add at end of "Quill v. Koppell" subsection:

Court of Appeals' Decision:

Quill v. Vacco,
80 F.3d 716 (2d Cir. 1996),
rev'd, 117 S. Ct. 2293 (1997)

The plaintiffs were physicians who brought an action challenging the constitutionality of New York statutes making it a crime to assist another in committing suicide.[277.1] The trial court entered summary judgment in favor of the defendants. The United States Court of Appeals for the Second Circuit in a 3-0 decision affirmed in part, but substantially reversed.[277.2]

Like the decision in *Compassion in Dying v. Washington,*[277.3] discussed above in this section, *Quill* is a landmark case holding unconstitutional a state's statute making assisted suicide a crime. Despite the fact that it is a narrower and more cautious opinion, based on equal protection rather than due process grounds, it is likely, unless cut off by the United States Supreme Court, to become part of a larger trend recognizing the thinness of the distinction between "active" and "passive" means to hasten death, and that ultimately what validates both is informed consent.[277.4] Like *Compassion in Dying, Quill* is strongly grounded in the *Casey* and *Cruzan* decisions, but because it is equal-protection based, it is also firmly grounded in the 20-year legal consensus based primarily in state common law, and to a lesser extent state statutory law, recognizing the legally protected right of individuals to hasten their deaths.

The court's holding was that "physicians who are willing to do so may prescribe drugs to be self-administered by mentally competent patients who seek to end their lives during the final stages of a terminal illness."[277.5] Apart from

---

[250.54] *Id.*

[277.1] *See* Quill v. Koppell, 870 F. Supp. 78 (S.D.N.Y. 1994), discussed in § **18.22** in the main volume.

[277.2] *See* Quill v. Vacco, 80 F.3d 716 (2d Cir. 1996).

[277.3] 79 F.3d 790 (9th Cir. 1996).

[277.4] See § **18.18** in the main volume.

[277.5] 80 F.3d at 718.

whatever other limitations an equal-protection basis imposes in comparison with a due-process basis, this holding might also be somewhat narrower than the Ninth Circuit's in that it appears to be limited not merely to terminally ill persons, but also to terminally ill persons who are in the "final stages" of their illness. This limitation arose, however, because the plaintiffs sought in their complaint only to be permitted to hasten death free from state interference when the patient was at this stage of a terminal illness.[277.6]

Due Process Claim. Unlike the Ninth Circuit, the Second Circuit court felt compelled by the Supreme Court's unwillingness, albeit "shaky,"[277.7] to expand the category of fundamental rights protected by the due process clause. Based primarily on the Court's refusal in *Bowers v. Hardwick*[277.8] to recognize that the due process clause prohibits the states from criminalizing sodomy, the Second Circuit concluded that "the right contended for here cannot be considered so implicit in our understanding of ordered liberty that neither justice nor liberty would exist if it were sacrificed. Nor can it be said that the right to assisted suicide claimed by plaintiffs is deeply rooted in the nation's traditions and history."[277.9] In fact, the history of criminalization of assisted suicide both in England and the United States shows that "the very opposite is true."[277.10] Even had the strictures previously set down by the Supreme Court not been in place, the court expressed an independent unwillingness, albeit quoting from *Bowers v. Hardwick,* to find that the due process clause embodies a right to assistance in committing suicide because "[t]he Court is most vulnerable and comes nearest to illegitimacy when it deals with judge-made constitutional law having little or no cognizable roots in the language or design of the Constitution."[277.11]

Equal Protection Claim. On the equal protection claim, the court rejected the plaintiffs' assertion that either the strict or intermediate scrutiny standards should govern. It accepted the state's position that the minimal scrutiny standard should apply, as the "statutes in question fall within the category of social welfare legislation and therefore are subject to rational basis scrutiny upon judicial review,"[277.12] but rejected the state's argument as to how it should apply. Instead, the court held that the statutes "do not treat equally all competent persons who are in the final stages of fatal illness and wish to hasten their deaths;

[277.6] *Id*. at 731.

[277.7] *Id*. at 724.

[277.8] 478 U.S. 186 (1986).

[277.9] 80 F.3d at 724.

[277.10] *Id*.

[277.11] *Id*. at 725.

[277.12] *Id*. at 727.

[and] the distinctions made by New York law with regard to such persons do not further any legitimate state purpose."[277.13]

"Passively" Hastening Death as Basis for "Actively" Hastening Death. The basis for the court's finding that the statutes treat different competent persons differently arises from the prohibition against what the state terms "physician-assisted suicide" and its placing of its imprimatur, both statutorily and through case law, on forgoing life-sustaining treatment—that is, its differential treatment of so-called active and passive hastening of death. Citing familiar New York precedents including *Schloendorff v. Society of New York Hospital,*[277.14] and *Eichner v. Dillon,*[277.15] the New York DNR health care power of attorney statutes, and *Cruzan,* it concluded that

> New York does not treat similarly circumstanced persons alike: those in the final stages of terminal illness who are on life-support systems are allowed to hasten their deaths by directing the removal of such systems; but those who are similarly situated, except for the previous attachment of life-sustaining equipment, are not allowed to hasten death by self-administering prescribed drugs.[277.16]

As to the asserted difference between active and passive means of hastening death, the court chose Justice Scalia's words in *Cruzan* to put the argument to rest:

> Justice Scalia, for one, has remarked upon "the irrelevance of the action-inaction distinction," noting that "the cause of death in both cases is the suicide's conscious decision to 'pu[t] an end to his own existence.'"[277.17]

Although intended to illustrate why a state could prohibit forgoing life-sustaining treatment—not merely make it exceedingly difficult as Missouri had in *Cruzan*—Justice Scalia's words had had six years to ripen for the plucking for the completely opposite purpose, namely, to demonstrate why, if a state permitted "inaction," it was constitutionally compelled to sanction "action" (to use Justice Scalia's phrases).

Lack of Genuine Distinctions Between "Actively" and "Passively" Hastening Death. As the Ninth Circuit did, the Second Circuit court rejected purported distinctions between actively and passively hastening death, including the claim that forgoing treatment leads to "natural death":

[277.13] *Id.*

[277.14] 105 N.E. 92 (N.Y. 1914).

[277.15] 420 N.E.2d 64 (N.Y. 1981).

[277.16] 80 F.3d at 729.

[277.17] *Id.* (quoting Cruzan v. Director, 497 U.S. 261 (1990) (citations omitted and alteration in original) (Scalia, J., concurring)).

[T]here is nothing "natural" about causing death by means other than the original illness or its complications. The withdrawal of nutrition brings on death by starvation, the withdrawal of hydration brings on death by dehydration, and the withdrawal of ventilation brings about respiratory failure. By ordering the discontinuance of these artificial life-sustaining processes or refusing to accept them in the first place, a patient hastens his death by means that are not natural in any sense. It certainly cannot be said that the death that immediately ensues is the natural result of the progression of the disease or condition from which the patient suffers.[277.18]

The court dealt similarly with the claim that writing a prescription "actively" hastens death, essentially making a shambles of a long history of carefully constructed evasions:

[T]he writing of a prescription to hasten death, after consultation with a patient, involves a far less active role for the physician than is required in bringing about death through asphyxiation, starvation and/or dehydration. Withdrawal of life support requires physicians or those acting at their direction physically to remove equipment and, often, to administer palliative drugs which may themselves contribute to death. The ending of life by these means is nothing more nor less than assisted suicide.[277.19]

No Greater Dangers in "Actively" Hastening Death. It also addressed the contention that the dangers from physician-assisted suicide are greater than from forgoing life-sustaining treatment, specifically, that there will be psychological pressure on the elderly and infirm to commit suicide and that the poor and physically handicapped will be disparately adversely affected. First, the court observed, these pressures can be applied just as well to forgoing treatment as to more active means of ending life. But more essentially, the court concluded that "[t]here is no clear indication that there has been any problem in regard to the former, and there should be none as to the latter."[277.20] But regardless, the court concluded, as did the Ninth Circuit, that its ruling did not prohibit the state from regulating physicians in hastening death. To the contrary, "the state of New York may establish rules and procedures to assure that all choices are free of such pressures."[277.21] It also dismissed the purported abuses—specifically, nonvoluntary euthanasia—in the Netherlands as lacking in relevance.

Is the Distinction a Rational One?   Having found the treatment of terminally ill competent patients to be differential, the court proceeded to deter-

---

[277.18] 80 F.3d at 729.

[277.19] *Id.*

[277.20] *Id.*

[277.21] *Id.*

mine whether the distinction between actively and passively hastening death on which the differential treatment is founded is irrational. The state attempted to justify the distinction by arguing that it was "preserving the life of all its citizens at all times and under all conditions."[277.22] Aside from being untrue (which the court graciously overlooked), as evidenced by New York law permitting the forgoing of treatment under some circumstances, the court was singularly unimpressed with the application of this principle in this context, asking

> what interest can the state possibly have in requiring the prolongation of a life that is all but ended? . . . And what business is it of the state to require the continuation of agony when the result is imminent and inevitable? What concern prompts the state to interfere with a mentally competent patient's "right to define [his] own concept of existence, of meaning, of the universe, and of the mystery of human life," *Planned Parenthood v. Casey* . . . when the patient seeks to have drugs prescribed to end life during the final stages of a terminal illness?[277.23]

To the questions it posed, the court responded simply "None."

Other Objections to Actively Hastening Death.   There are two other important points to the majority opinion.

Actively Hastening Death in This Context Is Not Killing. First, just as the Ninth Circuit eschewed the language of "suicide," the Second Circuit eschewed the use of the equally prejudicial terminology of "killing," preferring like the Ninth Circuit to talk about hastening death.[277.24]

"Terminal" Illness Can Be Satisfactorily Defined. Second, also like the Ninth Circuit, the Second Circuit court was not troubled by the purported difficulties in defining a "terminal" illness. The court took comfort in the fact that the plaintiffs sought to hasten death only when a patient is in the "final stages" of terminal illness, a condition that to the court seemed to be one the existence of which would find physicians in substantial agreement. Further, physicians already proffer advice, making similar determinations, to patients about forgoing life-sustaining treatment. And finally, the state is free to "define that stage of illness with greater particularity, require the opinion of more than one physician or impose any other obligation upon patients and physicians who collaborate in hastening death."[277.25]

[277.22] *Id.*

[277.23] *Id.* at 729.

[277.24] 80 F.3d at 730 ("Physicians do not fulfill the role of 'killer' by prescribing drugs to hasten death any more than they do by disconnecting life-support systems.").

[277.25] *Id.* at 731.

Page 506, add at end of section:

The Supreme Court Cases:

Washington v. Glucksberg
117 S. Ct. 2258 (1997)
and
Vacco v. Quill
117 S. Ct. 2293 (1997)

The Supreme Court reversed the holding of the two Courts of Appeals' decisions that had declared unconstitutional the Washington and New York statutes making assisted suicide a crime. The Ninth Circuit case, *Compassion in Dying,* decided by the Supreme Court under the name of *Glucksberg v. Washington,* had held that the Washington statute violated the due process clause of the Fourteenth Amendment.[287.1] The Second Circuit had held that the New York statute violated the equal protection clause of the Fourteenth Amendment.[287.2]

The Due Process Claim:

Washington v. Glucksberg
117 S. Ct. 2258 (1997)

In *Glucksberg,* the Court held that the Washington statute making assisted suicide a crime "does not violate the Fourteenth Amendment, either on its face or 'as applied to competent, terminally ill adults who wish to hasten their deaths by obtaining medication prescribed by their doctors.'"[287.3] Because of the Court's "tradition of carefully formulating the interest at stake in substantive-due-process cases,"[287.4] Chief Justice Rehnquist rejected the way in which the Court of Appeals had framed the question in the case—whether the due process clause of the Fourteenth Amendment permits a competent, terminally ill individual to determine the manner and timing of his death—in favor of a more restrictive framing of the issue: "whether the 'liberty' specially protected by the Due Process Clause includes a right to commit suicide which itself includes a right to assistance in doing so."[287.5]

[287.1] See discussion in this section of the main volume and this supplement.

[287.2] See discussion in this section of the main volume and this supplement.

[287.3] Washington v. Glucksberg, 117 S. Ct. 2258, 2274 (1997) (quoting Compassion in Dying v. Washington, 79 F.3d 790, 838 (9th Cir. 1996)).

[287.4] 117 S. Ct. at 2269.

[287.5] *Id.* at 2260.

The court began with its "established method of substantive-due-process analysis"—namely, that "the Due Process Clause specially protects those fundamental rights and liberties which are, objectively, 'deeply rooted in this Nation's history and tradition.'"[287.6] Thus, the Court proceeded to examine the history of the way in which the law views suicide and assisted suicide, a history which demonstrates unalterable opposition to both, not only in the United States but also in other countries sharing the English legal tradition. Even when, about two centuries ago, the law began to move away from imposing penalties for suicide, it was not because of any increased tolerance of suicide but because of a recognition of the unfairness of punishing the suicide's family, and the "courts continued to condemn it as a grave public wrong."[287.7] And more recently, despite new attitudes toward dying occasioned by medical technology, assisted suicide remains a crime in most states,[287.8] and public attitudes still do not favor assisted suicide, as evidenced by defeat of a large number of legislative proposals to legalize physician-assisted suicide and the enactment in states not previously having them of statutes making assisted suicide a crime.

Cruzan and Casey. "Against this backdrop of history, tradition, and practice, [the Court] turn[ed] to respondents' constitutional claim."[287.9] Instead of finding support in *Cruzan* and *Casey* for such a claim as had the Court of Appeals, Chief Justice Rehnquist found it easy to distinguish these cases. *Cruzan* recognized no general "right to die" "deduced from abstract concepts of personal autonomy,"[287.10] but was rooted in the long-recognized legal protection of the individual to be free from nonconsensual touching—that is, to be free from battery. Thus, *Cruzan* provides no support for concluding that statutory prohibitions against assisted suicide are violative of due process.

> "The decision to commit suicide with the assistance of another may be just as personal and profound as the decision to refuse unwanted medical treatment, but it has never enjoyed similar legal protection. Indeed, the two acts are widely and reasonably regarded as quite distinct."[287.11]

Justice Stevens' opinion read *Cruzan* more broadly. For him, "the common-law right to protection from battery, which included the right to refuse medical treatment in most circumstances, did not mark 'the outer limits of the

---

[287.6] *Id.* at 2268 (quoting Moore v. East Cleveland, 431 U.S. 494, 502 (1977) (plurality opinion)).

[287.7] *Id.* at 2264.

[287.8] *Id.* at 2266 ("At the same time, however, voters and legislators continue for the most part to reaffirm their States' prohibitions on assisting suicide.").[287.9] *Id.* at 2267.

[287.10] 117 S. Ct. at 2267.

[287.11] *Id.* at 2270 (quoting Cruzan v. Director, 497 U.S. 261, 280 (1990)).

substantive sphere of liberty' that supported the Cruzan family's decision to hasten Nancy's death."[287.12]

The Court dismissed the reliance on *Casey* even more readily, concluding that just because "many of the rights and liberties protected by the Due Process Clause sound in personal autonomy does not warrant the sweeping conclusion that any and all important, intimate, and personal decisions are so protected, and *Casey* did not suggest otherwise."[287.13]

Rational Relationship and State Interests. The Court next discussed the constitutional requirement that a statute be rationally related to legitimate governmental interests. It then reviewed the various interests that the state has in prohibiting physician-assisted suicide that had been identified by the Court of Appeals:

1. *Protection of Life.* Quoting *Cruzan,* the Court observed that "Washington has an 'unqualified interest in the preservation of human life.'"[287.14] However, it rejected the Court of Appeals' conclusion that "this interest depends on the 'medical condition and the wishes of the person whose life is at stake.'"[287.15] The reason for this is that Washington itself had done so, and "States 'may properly decline to make judgments about the "quality" of life that a particular individual may enjoy.' This remains true, as *Cruzan* makes clear, even for those who are near death."[287.16]

2. *Prevention of Suicide.* In discussing the state's interest in the prevention of suicide, the Court seemed fixated by its assertion that those who attempt suicide are usually depressed,[287.17] by its acceptance of the ques-

---

[287.12] *Id.* at 2307 (Stevens, J., concurring in the judgment).

[287.13] *Id.* at 2270 (citing San Antonio Indep. Sch. Dist. v. Rodriguez, 411 U.S. 1, 33–35 (1973)).

[287.14] 117 S. Ct. at 2272 (quoting *Cruzan,* 497 U.S. at 282).

[287.15] *Id.* (quoting Compassion in Dying v. Washington, 79 F.3d 790, 817 (9th Cir. 1996)).

[287.16] *Id.* (quoting *Cruzan,* 497 U.S. at 282). But see *id.* at 2308 (Stevens, J., concurring in the judgment) ("Allowing the individual, rather than the State, to make judgments '"about the 'quality' of life that a particular individual may enjoy."' *ante,* at 25 (quoting *Cruzan,* 497 U.S., at 282), does not mean that the lives of terminally-ill, disabled people have less value than the lives of those who are healthy, see *ante,* at 28. Rather, it gives proper recognition to the individual's interest in choosing a final chapter that accords with her life story, rather than one that demeans her values and poisons memories of her.").

[287.17] 117 S. Ct. at 2272 (citing New York State Task Force on Life & the Law, When Death Is Sought: Assisted Suicide and Euthanasia in the Medical Context 13–22, 126–28 (1994) (more than 95% of those who commit suicide had a major psychiatric illness at the time of death; among the terminally ill, uncontrolled pain is a "risk factor" because it contributes to depression); Physician-Assisted Suicide and Euthanasia in the Netherlands: A Report of Chairman Charles T. Canady to the Subcommittee on the

tionable proposition that if the depression is treated, "many people who request physician-assisted suicide withdraw that request if their depression and pain are treated,"[287.18] and by the assertion that depression is difficult to diagnose and thus doctors treating terminally ill patients frequently fail to respond to patients' needs.[287.19]

In making the assertion that the treatment of depression will cause patients to withdraw their request for assisted suicide, the Court relies heavily on the work of Herbert Hendin, an outspoken, and hardly unbiased, opponent of physician-assisted suicide. Of course, in this area, it is hard to find any commentators or researchers who are not strongly biased, but the Court fails even to acknowledge that there are strong differences of opinion about whether terminally ill individuals who seek assisted suicide are seriously depressed, whether treatment of depression is effective, and the more fundamental issue of what depression is, especially in the case of people who are terminally ill and suffering greatly.

In taking this position on depression and assisted suicide, the Court succumbs to the very pitfall that it has frequently inveighed against in the abortion context, the judicial practice of medicine. An alternative, and probably better, way to have handled this issue would have been to require the evaluation of persons seeking assisted suicide by a mental health professional.[287.20] And if the Court had been willing to confront fundamental issues rather than choosing among loudly competing "experts," it would have followed Justice Stevens' advice that

> the State's legitimate interests in preventing suicide, protecting the vulnerable from coercion and abuse, and preventing euthanasia are less significant in this context . . . [and do] not apply to an individual who is not victimized by abuse, who is not suffering from depression, and who makes a rational and voluntary decision to seek assistance in dying.[287.21]

Constitution of the House Committee on the Judiciary, 104th Cong., 2d Sess., 10–11 (Comm. Print 1996); *cf.* Back, Wallace, Starks, & Pearlman, *Physician-Assisted Suicide and Euthanasia in Washington State,* 275 JAMA 919, 924 (1996) ("[I]ntolerable physical symptoms are not the reason most patients request physician-assisted suicide or euthanasia")).

[287.18] *Id.* at 2273.

[287.19] *Id.*

[287.20] *See id.* at 2308 (Stevens, J., concurring in the judgment) ("Although, as the New York Task Force report discusses, diagnosing depression and other mental illness is not always easy, mental health workers and other professionals expert in working with dying patients can help patients cope with depression and pain, and help patients assess their options. *See* Brief for Washington State Psychological Association et al. as Amici Curiae 8–10."). *See also* Oregon Death with Dignity Act, Or. Rev. Stat. §§ 127.800 *et seq.* (1996).

[287.21] 117 S. Ct. at 2308.

In other words, although the prevention of suicide—along with other legitimate state interests such as protecting the vulnerable from coercion and abuse—is an important issue in the abstract, it must not be assumed to exist in all cases. Rather, efforts must be made to determine whether it exists in a particular case and to provide protections against it if it does.

3. *The Protection of the Ethical Integrity of the Medical Profession.* The Court took the exceedingly simplistic, but simple, path to dealing with this issue by treating the position of the American Medical Association—"that '[p]hysician-assisted suicide is fundamentally incompatible with the physician's role as healer'"[287.22]—as conclusively true. In other words, if physicians are allowed to assist patients in ending their own lives, patients will forever after be uncertain whether their doctor seeks to heal them or kill them. Justice Stevens recognized, however, that the matter is more complicated and that the refusal of a physician to provide a patient with assistance in actively ending his life might also compromise the ethical integrity of the profession, as discussed below. To accept this position, however, the Court would have had to have been willing to acknowledge that the means by which the death of a terminally ill person is hastened is of little or no import. Had it been willing to do that, it would have undercut its own position in any number of other ways and probably would have had to have reached a holding opposite from the one it did.

4. *Protection of Vulnerable Groups.* The Court observed that "[i]f physician-assisted suicide were permitted, many might resort to it to spare their families the substantial financial burden of end-of-life health-care costs."[287.23] In addition to preventing financial coercion, the state also has an interest in "protecting disabled and terminally ill people from prejudice, negative and inaccurate stereotypes, and 'societal indifference.'"[287.24] Washington achieves this end in part through its prohibition against assisted suicide and its even-handed application of this prohibition to the terminally ill, the disabled, and the elderly as well as to others not so afflicted.

To this point, the state interests discussed are the same as those routinely raised and dismissed in cases of passively hastening death. However, protection of vulnerable groups "—the poor, the elderly, and disabled persons—from abuse, neglect, and mistakes"[287.25] is an interest not ordinarily considered in cases of forgoing life-sustaining treatment. More fundamental than the nature of the Court's analysis is the fact that it chose to address this concern and that it failed to consider, as

---

[287.22] *Id.* at 2273 (quoting American Medical Ass'n, Code of Ethics § 2.211 (1994)).
[287.23] *Id.*

[287.24] *Id.* (quoting Compassion in Dying v. Washington, 49 F.3d 586, 592 (9th Cir. 1995)).
[287.25] *Id.* at 2273.

Justice Stevens urged, the equal applicability of these previously unaddressed issues in the context of withholding and withdrawing treatment as well as in the context of assisted suicide. Although the Court mentioned that it had "recognized . . . the real risk of subtle coercion and undue influence in end-of-life situations"[287.26] in *Cruzan,* it did so only to counter the Court of Appeals' contention that "the State's concern that disadvantaged persons might be pressured into physician-assisted suicide [w]as 'ludicrous on its face'"[287.27] rather than suggesting that because these concerns had never posed any insurmountable barrier to forgoing life-sustaining treatment, neither should they to physician-assisted suicide.

5. *Protecting Against the "Slippery Slope."* Opponents of physician-assisted suicide have long objected that the legalization of physician-assisted suicide ought to be resisted because it would lead to even more abhorrent practices, such as voluntary, nonvoluntary, or involuntary euthanasia.[287.28] This is a realistic concern, and the Court correctly noted that "the Court of Appeals' decision, and its expansive reasoning, provide ample support for the State's concerns."[287.29]

However, this concern need not have been dealt with by prohibiting physician-assisted suicide, and indeed prohibition does not seem to be the least restrictive means necessary to accomplish the state's legitimate interest. Procedural safeguards, such as those contained in the Oregon Death with Dignity Act,[287.30] can help to ensure that the right as practiced is not more expansive than intended.

In addition, however, the Court was concerned that there was no "principled" way to distinguish physician-assisted suicide from related practices such as voluntary euthanasia.[287.31] However, the same could be said for forgoing life-sustaining treatment, yet this concern has caused no prohibition against this practice. Objections to withholding treatment could have been made—that it would lead to withdrawing treatment, and that acceptable omissions would be transformed into unacceptable acts; that voluntary choices by competent patients to forgo treatment would lead to forgoing treatment by a surrogate, just as

---

[287.26] *Id.*

[287.27] 117 S. Ct. at 2273 (quoting Compassion in Dying v. Washington, 79 F.3d 790, 825 (9th Cir. 1996)).

[287.28] See § **18.25** in the main volume.

[287.29] 117 S. Ct. at 2274.

[287.30] Or. Rev. Stat. §§ 127.800 *et seq.* (1996). *See also* Charles Baron et al., *A Model State Act to Authorize and Regulate Physician-Assisted Suicide,* 33 Harv. J. Legis. 1 (1996).

[287.31] 117 S. Ct. at 2274 (citing Brief for United States as Amicus Curiae 26 ("Once a legislature abandons a categorical prohibition against physician assisted suicide, there is no obvious stopping point.")).

the Court was concerned that a voluntary choice by a competent patient in favor of assisted suicide could easily slide into assisted suicide by a surrogate;[287.32] and that forgoing treatment on the basis of the patient's known or presumed wishes could evolve into forgoing treatment without any knowledge of the patient's wishes on the basis of a best interests standard. Yet, while these objections have been made to these various developments in the law of forgoing life-sustaining treatment, they have generally not prevailed because of the recognition that safeguards could be developed to prevent abuse.

Finally, the Court buttressed its concerns about the slippery slope by reference to the practice of euthanasia in the Netherlands, and its concerns about the reports of widespread abuse.[287.33] Again, however, the Court selectively read the evidence, choosing to give credence only to those reports purporting to document abuse and ignoring those purporting to show that there has not been widespread abuse.[287.34]

What Did the Court Hold?   Having previously concluded that no fundamental right was at stake, and now concluding that the state's interests were surely legitimate and that the statute was reasonably related to furthering those interests, the Court held that the statute did not violate the Fourteenth Amendment "either on its face or 'as applied to competent, terminally ill adults who wish to hasten their deaths by obtaining medication prescribed by their doctors.'"[287.35]

Just how expansive the holding is, however, is unclear, as illustrated by the jousting between the opinions of the majority and of Justice Stevens. In a footnote at the end of the opinion, Chief Justice Rehnquist emphasizes that the Court is reversing the Court of Appeals' "specific holding that the statute is unconstitutional 'as applied' to a particular class."[287.36] In his separate opinion, Justice Stevens states that he would not "foreclose the possibility that an individual plaintiff seeking to hasten her death, or a doctor whose assistance was sought, could prevail in a more particularized challenge."[287.37] Justice Rehnquist rejoins that the holding "does not absolutely foreclose such a claim," but that such a claim is unlikely to prevail—because of the Court's

---

[287.32] *Id.* ("The Court of Appeals' decision . . . noted, for example, that the 'decision of a duly appointed surrogate decision maker is for all legal purposes the decision of the patient himself.'").

[287.33] *Id.* at 2274–75.

[287.34] *See, e.g., id.* at 2292 (Souter, J., concurring) ("There is, however, a substantial dispute today about what the Dutch experience shows.").

[287.35] *Id.* at 2275 (quoting Compassion in Dying v. Washington, 79 F.3d 790, 838 (9th Cir. 1996)).

[287.36] *Id.* at 2275 n.24.

[287.37] 117 S. Ct. at 2309 (Stevens, J., concurring in the judgment).

refusal to find that a fundamental right is at stake, and thus the state must only provide a legitimate reason for its ban on assisted suicide—unless it is "quite different from the ones advanced by respondents here."[287.38]

Thus, the majority appears to be keeping the door open, but not very wide, to the possibility that it might sometime in the future invalidate a statute banning assisted suicide. Justice Stevens' opinion seems to be trying to determine how much the door is open and perhaps to pry it open somewhat further. One implication of both opinions is that any further challenges before the Supreme Court probably should not be brought as class actions. Beyond that, however, it is not clear what different facts would have to be alleged and proved and what different legal arguments would need to be made to invalidate a state prohibition against assisted suicide.

Rather than encourage further litigation, the Court actually seeks to deter it, as do some of the concurring opinions, in its concluding observation that "[t]hroughout the Nation, Americans are engaged in an earnest and profound debate about the morality, legality, and practicality of physician-assisted suicide" and that the "holding permits this debate to continue, as it should in a democratic society."[287.39]

Concurring Opinions.   Although the decision was 9-0, four justices did not concur in the majority opinion. Justices Stevens, Souter, and Breyer each wrote separate opinions stating their own reasons for concurrence. Justice Ginsburg concurred in the judgment alone and only for the reasons stated in Justice O'Connor's opinion. Justice O'Connor concurred in the majority opinion but also wrote a separate concurring opinion. In addition to concurring in the judgment for the reasons stated in his own opinion, Justice Breyer also concurred in the judgment for the reasons stated in Justice O'Connor's opinion "except insofar as it joins the majority."[287.40]

Justice Stevens' Concurrence.   In the first paragraph of his opinion, Justice Stevens explains why he was writing a separate opinion: "to make it clear that there is also room for further debate about the limits that the Constitution places on the power of the States to punish the practice."[287.41] In so doing, he seems to be responsible for footnote 24 at the end of the majority opinion in which the Chief Justice leaves the door open for the possibility that some other set of facts and arguments might persuade the Court at some later date that a statute banning assisted suicide might be unconstitutional as

---

[287.38] *Id.* at 2275.

[287.39] *Id.* at 2275. *See also id.* at 2303 (O'Connor, J., concurring); *Id.* at 2293 (Souter, J., concurring in the judgment).

[287.40] *Id.* at 2310.

[287.41] *Id.* at 2308.

applied to a terminally ill patient seeking a doctor's assistance, as discussed above.

1. *The Future of Physician-Assisted Suicide.* First, Justice Stevens "agree[s] with the Court that the 'liberty' protected by the Due Process Clause does not include a categorical 'right to commit suicide which itself includes a right to assistance in doing so.'"[287.42] However, upholding a general statutory prohibition against assisted suicide does not mean that every possible application of the statute would be invalid. He uses an analogy to capital punishment. The Court's holding "that capital punishment is not always unconstitutional did not preclude later decisions holding that it is sometimes impermissibly cruel."[287.43] But he goes further with his analogy to capital punishment and makes the substantive claim that a state that employs the death penalty already acknowledges that "there are situations in which an interest in hastening death is legitimate," and thus "there are times when [the interest in hastening death] is entitled to constitutional protection."[287.44]

2. *The Nature of the Liberty Interest.* Whereas the majority opinion insisted that the nature of the interest protected by the right to refuse treatment in general and *Cruzan* in particular was the common-law right to be free from battery, Justice Stevens took a more expansive view of the matter. Following the lead of many commentators on the right to be free from unwanted medical treatment whether at the end of life or otherwise, he viewed the right to refuse treatment as an incident of a larger right to human dignity:

> [T]he source of Nancy Cruzan's right to refuse treatment was not just a common-law rule. Rather, this right is an aspect of a far broader and more basic concept of freedom that is even older than the common law. [Footnote omitted.] This freedom embraces, not merely a person's right to refuse a particular kind of unwanted treatment, but also her interest in dignity, and in determining the character of the memories that will survive long after her death. [Footnote omitted.] In recognizing that the State's interests did not outweigh Nancy Cruzan's liberty interest in refusing medical treatment, *Cruzan* rested not simply on the common-law right to refuse medical treatment, but—at least implicitly—on the even more fundamental right to make this "deeply personal decision," 497 U.S., at 289 (O'Connor, J., concurring).
> . . . .

[287.42] *Id.* at 2305.

[287.43] 117 S. Ct. at 2305.

[287.44] *Id.*

Cruzan did give recognition, not just to vague, unbridled notions of autonomy, but to the more specific interest in making decisions about how to confront an imminent death.[287.45]

In reaching this conclusion, he also relied on *Casey* for the conclusion that "the common-law right to protection from battery, which included the right to refuse medical treatment in most circumstances, did not mark 'the outer limits of the substantive sphere of liberty' that supported the Cruzan family's decision to hasten Nancy's death."[287.46]

Justice Stevens' opinion inched toward the Ninth Circuit's opinion in its observation on the *Cruzan* case that "Nancy Cruzan's interest in refusing medical care was incidental to her more basic interest in controlling the manner and timing of her death."[287.47] Further, "physicians are already involved in making decisions that hasten the death of terminally ill patients—through termination of life support, withholding of medical treatment, and terminal sedation."[287.48] But at the last minute, he pulls back from the full implication of what he is saying in his "agree[ment] that the distinction between permitting death to ensue from an underlying fatal disease and causing it to occur by the administration of medication or other means provides a constitutionally sufficient basis for the State's classification."[287.49] Then, almost to underscore his ambivalence, he reverts to his original theme that "[u]nlike the Court, however, see *Vacco, ante,* . . . , I am not persuaded that in all cases there will in fact be a significant difference between the intent of the physicians, the patients or the families in the two situations."[287.50]

3. *Strength of the Liberty Interest.* Justice Stevens believed that the now-deceased patients, who were originally plaintiffs in this case, may have had a liberty interest stronger than Nancy Cruzan's because they, unlike she, were "suffering constant and severe pain." "Avoiding intolerable pain and the indignity of living one's final days incapacitated and in agony is certainly '[a]t the heart of [the] liberty . . . to define one's own concept of existence, of meaning, of the universe, and of the mystery of human life.'"[287.51] Thus, this interest is one in

---

[287.45] *Id.* at 2306, 2307.

[287.46] *Id.* (quoting Planned Parenthood of Southeastern Pa. v. Casey, 505 U.S. 833, 848 (1992)).

[287.47] *Id.* at 2306.

[287.48] *Id.* at 2309. *Accord* McIver v. Krischer, 697 So. 2d 97, 110–11 (Fla. 1997) (Kogan, C.J., dissenting).

[287.49] 117 S. Ct. at 2309.

[287.50] *Id.*

[287.51] *Id.* at 2307 (quoting *Casey,* 505 U.S. at 851).

"deciding how, rather than whether, a critical threshold shall be crossed."[287.52]

4. *State Interests.*

    a. *Interest in Life.* Justice Stevens' understanding of the state interests in preventing assisted suicide was much more consistent with the commonly accepted understanding of those interests in cases involving forgoing life-sustaining treatment than was the majority analysis. For him, the state is required to permit individuals to take their own quality of life into account in deciding whether to continue to live or to die, and the state may not place an absolute value on life, because of the rootedness of this interest in human dignity. Only in this way can "proper recognition [be given] to the individual's interest in choosing a final chapter that accords with her life story, rather than one that demeans her values and poisons memories of her."[287.53]

    b. *Preventing Suicide, Protecting the Vulnerable, Preventing Euthanasia.* Although the state has "a compelling interest in preventing persons from committing suicide because of depression, or coercion by third parties,"[287.54] this interest is inapplicable in cases in which there is no depression or coercion. Rather than assuming they are omnipresent phenomena in the case of the dying as does the majority (though strangely only when death is sought to be actively hastened but not passively hastened), Justice Stevens was content to rely on mental health and other health professionals who work with dying patients to help them deal with depression or coercion "and help patients assess their options."[287.55] Adequately informed patients might make a rational choice of assisted suicide because palliative care cannot provide relief for all terminally ill patients suffering from severe pain.

    c. *Integrity of the Medical Profession.* Unlike the majority, which viewed this issue in black and white, Justice Stevens' opinion recognized that the failure of physicians to provide patients with assistance in actively hastening their deaths could compromise the integrity of the medical profession just as surely as providing such assistance could:

> For some patients, it would be a physician's refusal to dispense medication to ease their suffering and make their death tolerable

---

[287.52] *Id.* at 2307.

[287.53] *Id.* at 2308.

[287.54] *Id.*

[287.55] 117 S. Ct. at 2308.

and dignified that would be inconsistent with the healing role. [Citation omitted.] For doctors who have long-standing relationships with their patients, who have given their patients advice on alternative treatments, who are attentive to their patient's individualized needs, and who are knowledgeable about pain symptom management and palliative care options, [citation omitted], heeding a patient's desire to assist in her suicide would not serve to harm the physician-patient relationship.[287.56]

But more fundamental is the fact that doctors are already legally authorized to aid patients in ending their lives by withholding or withdrawing life-sustaining medical treatment, and thus "there is in fact significant tension between the traditional view of the physician's role and the actual practice in a growing number of cases."[287.57]

In addition, Justice Stevens recognized that although the American Medical Association might oppose physician-assisted suicide, surveys indicate that there is a substantial amount of support for it among individual physicians.[287.58]

Justice Souter's Concurrence. Justice Souter's reason for writing a concurring opinion was quite different from Justice Stevens' but led to the same general place. He, too, is willing to reconsider the fundamental issue of the constitutionality of state prohibitions against assisted suicide in the case of the terminally ill. His opinion is primarily an argument for the use of Justice Harlan's dissent in *Poe v. Ullman* to analyze the substantive due process claim.

[287.56] *Id.*

[287.57] *Id.* at 2309.

[287.58] *Id.* at 2309 n.12 (citing Bachman et al., *Attitudes of Michigan Physicians and the Public Toward Legalizing Physician-Assisted Suicide and Voluntary Euthanasia,* 334 New Eng. J. Med. 303–09 (1996) ("56% of responding doctors in Michigan preferred legalizing assisted suicide to an explicit ban"); Lee et al., *Legalizing Assisted Suicide—Views of Physicians in Oregon,* 335 New Eng. J. Med. 310–15 (1996) ("60% of responding [Oregon] doctors supported legalizing assisted suicide for terminally ill patients"); Back, Wallace, Starks, & Perlman, *Physician-Assisted Suicide and Euthanasia in Washington State,* 275 JAMA 919–25 (1996) ("12% of physicians polled in Washington State reported that they had been asked by their terminally ill patients for prescriptions to hasten death, and that, in the year prior to the study, 24% of those physicians had complied with such requests"); Doukas, Waterhouse, Gorenflo, & Seld, *Attitudes and Behaviors on Physician-Assisted Death: A Study of Michigan Oncologists,* 13 J. Clinical Oncology 1055 (1995) ("18% of responding Michigan oncologists reported active participation in assisted suicide"); Slome, Moulton, Huffine, Gorter, & Abrams, *Physicians' Attitudes Toward Assisted Suicide in AIDS,* 5 J. Acquired Immune Deficiency Syndromes 712 (1992) ("24% of responding physicians who treat AIDS patients would likely grant a patient's request for assistance in hastening death")).

Under this analysis, "[t]he question is whether the statute sets up one of those 'arbitrary impositions' or 'purposeless restraints' at odds with the Due Process Clause of the Fourteenth Amendment."[287.59] Applying this analysis, however, leads him to conclude that at least at this time, the state interests in prohibiting assisted suicide are sufficiently strong to override the individual's due process interest. His conclusion is based primarily on the equivocal nature of the Dutch experience with mercy killing. Because of the "substantial dispute today about what the Dutch experience shows,"[287.60] he remains skeptical that respondents' proposed safeguards will protect individuals who do *not* wish to actively hasten their death. Thus, although "[t]he day may come when we can say with some assurance which side is right [about what the Dutch experience shows], . . . for now it is the substantiality of the factual disagreement, and the alternatives for resolving it, that matter."[287.61]

Justice O'Connor's Concurrence. Justice O'Connor agreed in substantial part with the majority's analysis but believed that that analysis was heavily dependent on the fact that Washington's statute prohibiting assisted suicide does not prohibit physicians from employing adequate amounts of medication for the treatment of the pain experienced by the terminally ill.

Justice Breyer's Concurrence. The essence of Justice Breyer's difference with the majority is the Court's formulation of the liberty interest claimed by the respondents. Whereas the majority opinion "describes it as a 'right to commit suicide with another's assistance,'" Justice Breyer "would use words roughly like a 'right to die with dignity.'" He continues: "[I]rrespective of the exact words used, at its core would lie personal control over the manner of death, professional medical assistance, and the avoidance of unnecessary and severe physical suffering—combined."[287.62] Under this formulation, "our legal tradition may provide greater support" for respondents' claim.[287.63] However, Justice Breyer plainly states, "the avoidance of severe physical pain (connected with death) would have to comprise an essential part of any successful claim," and the particular claim in this case fails because the Washington statutes prohibiting assisted suicide do not prohibit physicians from prescribing and administering adequate medication for the relief of pain.[287.64]

[287.59] *Id.* at 2268 (Souter, J., concurring in the judgment) (quoting Poe v. Ullman, 367 U.S. 497, 543 (1961) (Harlan, J., dissenting)).

[287.60] *Id.* at 2292.

[287.61] 117 S. Ct. at 2292.

[287.62] *Id.* at 2311 (Breyer, J., concurring in the judgment).

[287.63] *Id.*

[287.64] *Id.*

The Equal Protection Claim:

Vacco v. Quill
117 S. Ct. 2293 (1997)

Vacco was a challenge to the constitutionality of the New York statute prohibiting assisted suicide, and it succeeded in the Court of Appeals on equal protection grounds. The Supreme Court reversed, holding that the fact that terminally ill patients may refuse life-sustaining treatment but may not obtain assistance to commit suicide does not violate equal protection.

Standard of Review.   Having determined in *Glucksberg* that there is no fundamental right at stake, the Court needed only to apply a minimal scrutiny test and was able to accord the statute a "'strong presumption of validity.'"[287.65] Thus, the Court would "uphold [it] so long as it bears a rational relation to some legitimate end.'"[287.66]

The Court of Appeals had held that the statute in question did meet this test because it treated similarly situated terminally ill patients differently— namely, those who needed to be kept alive by life-sustaining treatment were entitled under New York law to die by having that treatment withheld or withdrawn, but patients who might be suffering equally or greater but did not require life-sustaining treatment were denied the right to die because New York statutory law made it a crime to provide them with the assistance necessary to die.

The Supreme Court saw the matter quite differently. In its view, New York law did not treat the same patients differently; rather, it treated similar patients the same and different patients differently. Specifically, all competent patients are entitled to forgo life-sustaining treatment, and no one is permitted assistance in committing suicide. "Generally speaking, laws that apply evenhandedly to all 'unquestionably comply' with the Equal Protection Clause."[287.67] It found the distinction between assisting suicide and withdrawing life-sustaining treatment to be a rational one because "it is a distinction widely recognized and endorsed in the medical profession and in our legal traditions."[287.68] As support for the wide recognition and endorsement accorded the distinction in the medical profession, it cited, as it did in *Glucksberg,* the American Medical Association's statements on this matter.[287.69]

[287.65] Vacco v. Quill, 117 S. Ct. 2293, 2297 (quoting Heller v. Doe, 509 U.S. 312, 319 (1993)).

[287.66] *Id.* (quoting Romer v. Evans, 116 S. Ct. 1620, 1627 (1996)).

[287.67] *Id.* at 2298.

[287.68] *Id.*

[287.69] *Id.* at 2298 n.6 (citing Council on Ethical & Judicial Affairs, American Medical Ass'n, *Physician-Assisted Suicide,* 10 Issues in L. & Med. 91, 93 (1994) ("fundamental

Causation and Intent. In concluding that there is a rational distinction between forgoing life-sustaining treatment and assisted suicide, the Court focused on causation and intent, observing that "[t]he distinction comports with fundamental legal principles of causation and intent."[287.70] Its explanation tracks the conventional wisdom of right-to-die cases, which, from the beginning in *Quinlan,* have had to explain why it was not criminal homicide for a physician to withhold or withdraw life-sustaining medical treatment and allow a patient to die. In offering up explanations, state courts have distinguished forgoing life-sustaining treatment from culpable homicide[287.71] on three or four different grounds, paralleling the elements of homicide crimes.[287.72] Like the state courts, on the issue of causation the Supreme Court concluded that in forgoing life-sustaining treatment, the physician is not the cause of death; rather, the patient "dies from an underlying fatal disease or pathology." By contrast, if a patient ingests lethal medication prescribed by a physician, he is killed by that medication.[287.73] Intent is also different in forgoing life-sustaining treatment and assisted suicide. In the former, the Court agreed that the physician "intends . . . only to respect his patient's wishes and 'to cease doing useless and futile or degrading things to the patient when [the patient] no longer stands to benefit from them.'"[287.74] The same is true even when the patient dies as a result of too large a dose of pain medication because "the physician's purpose and intent is, or may be, only to ease his patient's pain."[287.75] By contrast, "[a] doctor who assists a suicide, however, 'must, necessarily and indubitably, intend primarily that the patient be made dead.'"[287.76] In effect, the court endorsed the principle of double effect.

A problem with this analysis, however, is that it confuses intent with motive. The court quotes approvingly an example given in a dissenting opin-

---

difference between refusing life-sustaining treatment and demanding a life-ending treatment"); Council on Ethical & Judicial Affairs, American Medical Ass'n, *Decisions Near the End of Life,* 267 JAMA 2229, 2230–31, 2233 (1992) ("The withdrawing or withholding of life-sustaining treatment is not inherently contrary to the principles of beneficence and nonmaleficence," but assisted suicide "is contrary to the prohibition against using the tools of medicine to cause a patient's death.")).

[287.70] *Id*. at 2298.

[287.71] 117 S. Ct. at 2299 n.8 (collecting cases).

[287.72] See §§ **18.3–18.8** and **18.10–18.16.** *See also* Alan Meisel, *Physician-Assisted Suicide: A Roadmap for State Courts,* 24 Fordham Urban L.J. ____ (1997).

[287.73] 117 S. Ct. at 2298.

[287.74] *Id*. (quoting Assisted Suicide in the United States, Hearing Before the Subcomm. on the Constitution of the House Comm. on the Judiciary, 104th Cong., 2d Sess. 368 (1996) (testimony of Dr. Leon R. Kass)).

[287.75] *Id*. at 2298–99. *But see* Alan Meisel, *Physician-Assisted Suicide: A Roadmap for State Courts,* 24 Fordham Urban L.J. ____ (1997).

[287.76] 117 S. Ct. at 2299 (quoting Assisted Suicide in the United States, Hearing Before the Subcomm. on the Constitution of the House Comm. on the Judiciary, 104th Cong., 2d Sess. 367 (1996) (testimony of Dr. Leon R. Kass)).

ion in the *Compassion in Dying* case of the use of intent or purpose to distinguish between two acts that may have the same result. Judge Kleinfelt wrote that "'[w]hen General Eisenhower ordered American soldiers onto the beaches of Normandy, he knew that he was sending many American soldiers to certain death. . . . His purpose, though, was to . . . liberate Europe from the Nazis.'"[287.77] Nice rhetoric though it may be, the difficulty is that conventional legal analysis would say that the liberation of Europe was the general's *motive*. However, because he knew with substantial certainty that soldiers would die, there was legal intent that they die. He was not guilty of homicide, however, because the action was taken in the legitimate prosecution of military affairs.

Act and Omission (Killing and Letting Die). In concluding that there is a rational distinction between forgoing life-sustaining treatment and assisted suicide, the Court also addressed the distinction between killing and letting die, and in so doing provided further explanation about the meaning of its decision in *Cruzan v. Director*.[287.78] The Court's position was that there is a legally relevant distinction between killing and letting die[287.79] based on the fact that *Cruzan* recognized a distinction "between letting a patient die and making that patient die."[287.80] Although "in some cases, the line between the two may not be clear . . . certainty is not required, even were it possible."[287.81] According to *Vacco,* in *Cruzan* the court had based its assumption that there was a right to refuse life-sustaining medical treatment on the "well established, traditional rights to bodily integrity and freedom from unwanted touching,"[287.82] rather than on a broader and more abstract "'right to hasten death,'" as the Second Circuit had held. Consequently, *Cruzan* does not support a right of doctors to take actions to aid patients in actively ending their own lives, which the Court characterized as "'nothing more nor less than suicide.'"[287.83]

The Court did not, however, engage in any serious analysis of the issue. It was content to rest its conclusion that there is a difference between the two forms of hastening death on the fact that the "distinction [is] widely recognized and endorsed in the medical profession and in our legal traditions."[287.84] In support of this, it cited the fact that the "American Medical Association

---

[287.77] *Id.* (quoting Compassion in Dying v. Washington, 79 F.3d 790, 858 (9th Cir. 1996) (Kleinfeld, J., dissenting)).

[287.78] 497 U.S. 261 (1990).

[287.79] See §§ **8.5, 18.6,** and **18.15** in the main volume and this supplement.

[287.80] *Vacco,* 117 S. Ct. at 2301.

[287.81] *Id.* at 2302.

[287.82] *Id.* at 2301 (citing *Cruzan*, 497 U.S. at 278–79).

[287.83] *Id.* (quoting Quill v. Vacco, 80 F.3d 716, 729 (2d Cir. 1996)).

[287.84] *Id.* at 2298.

emphasizes the 'fundamental difference between refusing life-sustaining treatment and demanding a life-ending treatment.'"[287.85] Thus, the Court concluded that

> [l]ogic and contemporary practice support New York's judgment that the two acts are different, and New York may therefore, consistent with the Constitution, treat them differently. By permitting everyone to refuse unwanted medical treatment while prohibiting anyone from assisting a suicide, New York law follows a longstanding and rational distinction.[287.86]

Concurring Opinions.   With the exception of Justice Souter, the concurring opinions written in *Glucksberg* are also applicable to *Vacco*. Justice Souter's concurrence in *Vacco* merely states that the reasons for his concluding that the ban against assisted suicide was not arbitrary on due process grounds also support the distinction between assisted suicide on the one hand and forgoing life-sustaining treatment and the use of "death-hastening pain medication"[287.87] on the other.

Other Aspects of the Opinions

Pain Management, Palliative Care, Terminal Sedation, and Double Effect.
Several of the opinions in both *Glucksberg* and *Vacco* make the point that physician-assisted suicide is not a necessary option in the care of the terminally ill because there are alternatives to it. These alternatives include pain medication, palliative care, and terminal sedation. If medications for the relief of pain, which is a component of palliative care and terminal sedation, are given to the extent necessary to be effective, especially in patients who have developed a tolerance for large doses of these medications, they can themselves cause death.[287.88] This being the case, some proponents of physician-assisted suicide contend that there is no difference in outcome between physician-assisted suicide and the effective and proper practice of medicine reflected in palliative care and terminal sedation.

The Supreme Court, however, rejected this reasoning, emphasizing what in its view was an important difference between the two—namely, intent—and justified palliative care and terminal sedation on the basis of the principle of double effect. "Just as a State may prohibit assisting suicide while permitting patients to refuse unwanted lifesaving treatment, it may permit

---

[287.85] *Id*. at 2298 n.6 (citing Council on Ethical & Judicial Affairs, American Medical Ass'n, *Physician-Assisted Suicide,* 10 Issues in L. & Med. 91, 93 (1994)).

[287.86] 117 S. Ct. at 2302.

[287.87] *Id*. (Souter, J., concurring).

[287.88] See § **9.38** in the main volume and this supplement.

palliative care related to that refusal, which may have the foreseen but unintended 'double effect' of hastening the patient's death."[287.89]

Although the majority opinion in neither *Glucksberg* nor *Vacco* elaborates on palliative care, some of the concurring opinions do. Justice O'Connor's opinion expressly assumes that there are no legal barriers to adequate pain medication.[287.90] In the context in which these discussions occur—especially in the majority opinion in *Vacco*—the "legal barriers" that are assumed not to exist are criminal prohibitions. Although this may be true on its face, there are in fact several real barriers, some of which are "legal," to the use of adequate pain medication.

First, it is not at all clear that the Court's analysis of the double effect is correct. The Court reasons that because the physician's intent is to provide relief from pain but not to kill, there is no criminal liability; but this overlooks the fact that legal intent is not the same as factual intent, and that in criminal law, one is held to intend the natural and probable consequences of one's conduct. Furthermore, there can be liability for criminal negligence even in the absence of intent. Thus, it is not entirely certain that when a patient dies from too much pain medication, the physician is not at risk of criminal liability.[287.91]

In addition to criminal law barriers, physicians may be subject to loss of their license to practice medicine and/or to their DEA privileges to prescribe controlled substances.[287.91a] Even if there is little likelihood of this actually occurring, the perception by doctors that they may be subject to these penalties can create a barrier to patients' receiving adequate pain medication. Limitations in health insurance for hospice coverage (including Medicare) and doctors' lack of knowledge of adequate techniques for pain relief create other barriers to terminally ill patients' receiving the kind of medication (and other services) necessary to manage pain effectively.[287.92]

[287.89] 117 S. Ct. at 2302 (citing New York Task Force on Life & the Law, When Death Is Sought: Assisted Suicide and Euthanasia in the Medical Context 163 (1994) ("It is widely recognized that the provision of pain medication is ethically and professionally acceptable even when the treatment may hasten the patient's death, if the medication is intended to alleviate pain and severe discomfort, not to cause death.")). See § **8.7** in the main volume and this supplement.

[287.90] 117 S. Ct. at 2303 (O'Connor, J., concurring) ("There is no dispute that dying patients in Washington and New York can obtain palliative care, even when doing so would hasten their deaths.").

[287.91] See § **8.7** in the main volume.

[287.91a] *See, e.g.,* Joannie M. Schrof, *Caught in Pain's Vicious Cycle He Helped His Patients—and Lost His License,* U.S. News & World Rep., Mar. 17, 1997, at 64 ("Over 100 doctors who prescribe narcotics lose their licenses each year, and 40 percent of pain specialists admit that they undermedicate patients to avoid trouble.").

[287.92] See § **9.38** in the main volume and this supplement. *See also* John Seiler, *The Politics of Pain Medicine: Patients and Physicians Sometimes Have to Turn a Government Gauntlet to Get Effective Treatment for Chronic Pain,* Orange County Reg., Aug. 17, 1997, at G-1.

CRIMINAL LIABILITY

McIver v. Krischer
697 So. 2d 97 (Fla. 1997)

A decision of the Florida Supreme Court is especially noteworthy because it closes off, at least in Florida at this time, a possible route around the United States Supreme Court decisions. *McIver* was a challenge to the constitutionality on state constitutional grounds of the Florida statute making assisted suicide a crime. Specifically, the plaintiffs, a terminally ill man and the physician willing to aid him in ending his life, contended that the statute violated the state constitutional right of privacy.[287.93]

The trial court held the statute unconstitutional, but the Florida Supreme Court reversed. This was a somewhat surprising decision in light of the pivotal role that this constitutional provision had played in establishing and extending the right to refuse treatment—both life-sustaining and lifesaving—beginning with the first Florida right-to-die case in 1978,[287.94] and continuing virtually uninterrupted into the 1990s.[287.95]

The court's analysis was a straightforward rejection of the application of this constitutional provision to permit terminally ill patients to obtain the aid of a physician in actively ending their lives. Central to the holding was the court's acceptance of the conventional distinction between passive and active means of dying, reaffirming its commitment to the former while rejecting the latter. It followed the United States Supreme Court's analysis in *Glucksberg* of finding that important state interests justify the differential treatment of actively and passively hastening death. Specifically, the court held that "three of the four recognized state interests are so compelling as to clearly outweigh Mr. Hall's desire for assistance in committing suicide"[287.96]—specifically, preserving life,[287.97] preventing suicide,[287.98] and protecting the ethical integrity of the medical profession.[287.99]

[287.93] Fla. Const. art. I, § 23.

[287.94] *See* Satz v. Perlmutter, 362 So. 2d 160 (Fla. Dist. Ct. App. 1978), *aff'd,* 379 So. 2d 359 (Fla. 1980).

[287.95] *See In re* Dubreuil, 629 So. 2d 819 (Fla. 1993); Browning v. Herbert, 568 So. 2d 4 (Fla. 1990); Wons v. Public Health Trust, 541 So. 2d 96 (Fla. 1989); Harrell v. St. Mary's Hosp., Inc., 678 So. 2d 455 (Fla. Dist. Ct. App. 1996); Corbett v. D'Alessandro, 487 So. 2d 368 (Fla. Dist. Ct. App.), *review denied,* 492 So. 2d 1331 (Fla. 1986); St. Mary's Hosp. v. Ramsey, 465 So. 2d 666 (Fla. Dist. Ct. App. 1985); *In re* Barry, 445 So. 2d 365 (Fla. Dist. Ct. App. 1984).

[287.96] McIver v. Krischer, 697 So. 2d 97, 103 (Fla. 1997).

[287.97] *Id.* ("The state has a compelling interest in preventing such affirmative destructive act and in preserving Mr. Hall's life.").

[287.98] *Id.* ("[L]egal physician-assisted suicide could make it more difficult for the State to protect depressed or mentally ill persons, or those who are suffering from untreated pain, from suicidal impulses.").

[287.99] *Id.* at 104 ("Physician-assisted suicide directly contradicts these ethical standards [of the AMA] and compromises the integrity of the medical profession and the role of hospitals in caring for patients.").

The court also relied substantially on the conclusions of the New York State Task Force on Life and the Law, contained in its report on physician-assisted suicide.[287.100] The Task Force reaffirmed its adherence to the conventional (and, for a governmental agency, politically expedient) distinction between actively and passively hastening death, the central part of which was its insistence, like all the courts in the right-to-die cases seeking to legitimate forgoing life-sustaining treatment by distinguishing it from suicide and homicide, on the existence of a bright line between the two means of hastening death. Interestingly, the Florida Supreme Court quoted from a particularly telling portion of the report in which the Task Force stated, "In essence, we propose a clear line for public policies and medical practice between forgoing medical interventions and assistance to commit suicide or euthanasia."[287.101] That is exactly what the Task Force did: it "proposed" such a distinction as if wishing would make it so.

The Task Force had identified 10 risks that might follow from the legalization of assisted suicide (and active euthanasia):

> (1) undiagnosed or untreated mental illness; (2) improperly managed physical symptoms; (3) insufficient attention to the suffering and fears of dying patients; (4) vulnerability of socially marginalized groups; (5) devaluation of the lives of the disabled; (6) sense of obligation; (7) patient deference to physician recommendations; (8) increasing financial incentives to limit care; (9) arbitrariness of proposed limits; and (10) impossibility of developing effective regulation.[287.102]

But like the United States Supreme Court in *Glucksberg,* it failed to explain why these risks were more likely to occur, and thus were more to be feared, in the context of actively hastening death than in passively hastening death.

The dissenting opinion of Chief Justice Kogan recognized that merely proclaiming a bright line to be so does not make it so:

> The notion of "dying by natural causes" contrasts neatly with the word "suicide," suggesting two categories readily distinguishable from one another. How nice it would be if today's reality were so simple. No doubt there once was a time when, for all practical purposes, the distinction was clear enough to all.[287.103]

[287.100] New York State Task Force on Life & the Law, When Death Is Sought: Assisted Suicide and Euthanasia in the Medical Context (1994).

[287.101] 697 So. 2d at 101 (quoting When Death Is Sought: Assisted Suicide and Euthanasia in the Medical Context at vi–vii).

[287.102] *Id.* (quoting When Death Is Sought: Assisted Suicide and Euthanasia in the Medical Context 4–5 (Supp. 1997)).

[287.103] *Id.* at 109 (Kogan, C.J., dissenting).

The line between actively and passively hastening death, if it was ever bright, has forever been eroded by the "technology [that has] crept into medicine."[287.104] "Dying no longer falls into the neat categories our ancestors knew. In today's world, we demean the hard reality of terminal illness to say otherwise."[287.105]

Chief Justice Kogan attempted to grapple with the problem that is probably at the root of the unwillingness of many—judges, physicians, and others—to accept even a very restricted version of active physician aid-in-dying: the difficulty in drawing a new line. It is this difficulty that makes it easier to insist on the continued existence of an old line, despite the evidence that it has disappeared:

> Once Florida had set itself adrift from the common law definition, the problem that immediately arose—that has vexed our courts ever since—is where to draw the new dividing line between improper "suicide" and the emerging "right of self-determination" without simultaneously authorizing involuntary euthanasia.[287.106]

Rather than using, as have all the judges that have rejected physician-assisted suicide, the *means* of death to distinguish between legitimate and illegitimate practices, Chief Justice Kogan proposed that the focus be on terminal illness.[287.107] His reason for so doing is that society has no interest in saving a life "when there is nothing of life to save but a final convulsion of agony."[287.108]

Unfortunately, although his reasoning may provide a "dividing line between improper 'suicide' and the emerging 'right of self-determination,'" his reasoning fails to provide the stopping point against the other danger that he articulated: involuntary euthanasia. Perhaps it is implicit in his reasoning that the "terminal illness" requirement must be accompanied by the voluntary choice of a competent person, but it must be made explicit so that euthanasia is not chosen by others for those who are terminally ill but cannot choose for themselves.

Kevorkian v. Arnett

Dr. Jack Kevorkian and a terminally ill patient (John Doe) brought suit to declare the California statutory prohibition against assisted suicide, performed by a physician, to be unconstitutional under the federal and state con-

---

[287.104] *Id.*

[287.105] *Id.*

[287.106] *Id.*

[287.107] 697 So. 2d 111 ("[T]he right of privacy attaches with unusual force at the death bed.").

[287.108] *Id.*

stitutions.[287.109] The trial court held that because Dr. Kevorkian was not a licensed California physician, he did not have standing to bring the action.

However, on appeal the Ninth Circuit vacated the decision and dismissed the appeal[287.109a] in light of the United States Supreme Court's holding in *Vacco v. Quill*.[287.109b]

Federal Due Process Claim.   In deciding the federal constitutional claims, the court was substantially guided by the opinion of the Ninth Circuit in *Compassion in Dying v. Washington*,[287.110] and specifically on the issues of whether there is a protected liberty interest, what the proper standard of review is, and whether the statute imposes an undue burden on the constitutionally protected liberty interest. It therefore held the statute to be facially violative of the patient's liberty interest under the Fourteenth Amendment's due process clause.

Federal Equal Protection Claim.   The court declined to rule on the equal protection challenge to the statute because of "the volatility and complexity of these constitutional issues and the fact that Ninth Circuit has recently heard oral argument in the appeal of Lee v. State of Oregon," and fearing that it would "contribute to the growing confusion in this area of law."[287.111]

California Constitutional Privacy Claim.   The court pointed out that a California appellate court had previously ruled in *Donaldson v. Van de Kamp*[287.112] that there is no right to assisted suicide under the state constitutional right of privacy. Thus, it felt compelled to conclude that "there is no persuasive authority to believe that the California Supreme Court would hold otherwise if directly presented with the issue"[287.113] and that principles of federalism required the conclusion that the statute is not invalid under the California constitutional right to privacy.

California Equal Protection Claim.   The court concluded that because of its finding that "California's right to privacy does not encompass a right to assisted suicide, [the statutory prohibition] does not create a suspect classification or implicate a fundamental right under the California Constitution."[287.114]

[287.109] Kevorkian v. Arnett, 939 F. Supp. 725 (C.D. Cal.).

[287.109a] 136 F.3d 1360 (9th Cir. 1998).

[287.109b] 117 S. Ct. 2293 (1997).

[287.110] 79 F.3d 790 (9th Cir. 1996), *rev'd,* 117 S. Ct. 2258 (1997).

[287.111] 939 F. Supp at 731.

[287.112] 4 Cal. Rptr. 2d 59 (Ct. App. 1992) (discussed in this section in the main volume).

[287.113] 939 F. Supp. at 732.

[287.114] *Id.*

Thus, under the rational basis test, it cannot be said that the statutory prohibition does not bear "some rational relationship to a conceivable legitimate state purpose," and there is no violation of equal protection.[287.115]

Kevorkian v. Thompson

Dr. Jack Kevorkian and a terminally ill patient (Janet Good) brought suit to invalidate the Michigan prohibition against assisted suicide on a variety of theories.[287.116] The district court held that both plaintiffs had standing but that Dr. Kevorkian could not maintain his claims under the *Younger* abstention doctrine.[287.117] Abstention was not applicable to the terminally ill plaintiff because there were no past or present criminal proceedings against her in the county in which the injunction was sought.[287.118]

Relief was sought on four constitutional theories—namely, that the prosecution of those who assist a terminally ill person in ending her life violates due process, equal protection, the prohibition on vagueness and overbreadth in legislation, and the prohibition on ex post facto laws. The court rejected the due process and equal protection claims, granted a narrow injunction on the grounds of vagueness, and failed to discuss the ex post facto claim.

Due Process. The plaintiff's due process claim was similar to that made successfully in *Compassion in Dying v. Washington*,[287.119] discussed above in this section of this supplement. In holding that "no constitutionally-protected liberty interest is implicated by the prohibition of assisted suicide," the court hewed to a traditional analysis. Because there was no right "readily identifiable in the text of the Constitution," the court's inquiry focused on such a right as "'implicit in the concept of ordered liberty' so that 'neither liberty nor justice would exist if they were sacrificed.'"[287.120] The court held that a right to physician-assisted suicide is not implicit in the concept of ordered liberty because "[s]uicide has traditionally been a criminal offense,"[287.121] and although it no longer is a criminal offense, assisted suicide is a statutory or common-law offense in most jurisdictions.[287.122]

[287.115] *Id.*

[287.116] Kevorkian v. Thompson, 947 F. Supp. 1152 (E.D. Mich. 1997).

[287.117] Younger v. Harris, 401 U.S. 37 (1971).

[287.118] 947 F. Supp. at 1164–65.

[287.119] 79 F.3d 790 (9th Cir. 1996).

[287.120] 947 F. Supp. at 1167 (citing Palko v. Connecticut, 302 U.S. 319, 325–26 (1937)).

[287.121] *Id.*

[287.122] *Id.* at 1168.

Equal Protection.   The plaintiff's equal protection claim tracked that upheld by the court in *Quill v. Vacco*,[287.123] discussed above in this section of this supplement. Both courts having found that there was no constitutionally protected liberty interest implicated by legal prohibitions against physician-assisted suicide, the state only needed to establish a rational basis for criminalizing physician-assisted suicide while permitting passively hastening death by withholding or withdrawing life-sustaining medical treatment. However, the court rejected the holding of the Second Circuit, reasoning that the law acknowledges distinctions between action and inaction in a variety of other contexts and that there was a rational basis for Michigan to do so in this context. The court quoted the Michigan Supreme Court in *People v. Kevorkian* to the effect that "suicide frustrates the natural course by introducing an outside agent to accelerate death, whereas the refusal or withdrawal of life-sustaining medical treatment allows nature to proceed, i.e., death occurs because of the underlying condition."[287.124]

Vagueness.   The plaintiff's final claim was that the Michigan prohibition against physician-assisted suicide was unconstitutionally vague, and the court agreed in part. The basis for the holding is not generally applicable because the history of criminalization of assisted suicide in Michigan is *sui generis*. There was no statutory prohibition against assisted suicide until 1992, and that prohibition has expired. However, in December 1994, the Michigan Supreme Court issued a clear-cut declaration that assisted suicide was a crime, and thus prosecution for assisted suicide for acts occurring since 1992 is constitutional.[287.125] A 1920 Michigan Supreme Court case[287.126] made assisted suicide a crime (homicide), but a 1983 Court of Appeals decision and its per curiam affirmance by the Michigan Supreme Court put the continued viability of the 1920 ruling in considerable doubt.[287.127] Thus, prosecution for assisted suicide for acts occurring between 1983 and 1992 was "unconstitutionally vague, because the law as it existed from the date of the *Campbell* decision in 1983 until December 1992 would not have provided 'fair notice' that assisting in a suicide was a crime in Michigan."[287.128]

[287.123] 80 F.3d 716 (2d Cir. 1996).

[87.124] People v. Kevorkian, 527 N.W.2d 714, 728 (Mich. 1994).

[287.125] *See* People v. Kevorkian, 527 N.W.2d 714 (Mich. 1994).

[287.126] People v. Roberts, 178 N.W. 690 (Mich. 1920).

[287.127] *See* People v. Campbell, 335 N.W.2d 27 (Mich. Ct. App. 1983), *aff'd per curiam,* 342 N.W.2d 519 (Mich. 1984).

[287.128] 947 F. Supp. at 1179.

CRIMINAL LIABILITY

Sanderson v. State

Sanderson presents the only reported First Amendment challenge to date to a statute prohibiting assisted suicide. In *Sanderson*, the plaintiff, although in good health, wanted to execute an advance directive authorizing his wife "to end his life by euthanasia, provided that two physicians agree his medical condition is hopeless."[287.129] He sought a declaratory judgment to assure himself that neither his wife nor the physician who actually engaged in the euthanasia would be subject to criminal liability pursuant to the Colorado statute prohibiting assisted suicide. In his complaint, he asserted claims under multiple federal constitutional provisions, but on appeal to the Colorado Court of Appeals after his complaint was dismissed, he pursued only a claim under the free exercise clause of the First Amendment to the United States Constitution.

Sanderson described his personal religious beliefs as including beliefs that "God, or nature, intended that the free will of man be exercised in all circumstances according to his own best judgment with due consideration for others"; that such free will included an ability to direct euthanasia; and that the ability to do so could be delegated to another to authorize euthanasia if certain medical prerequisites had been met.[287.130]

In analyzing Sanderson's First Amendment claim, the court relied on *Employment Division, Department of Human Resources v. Smith*.[287.131] In *Smith*, two Native Americans were denied unemployment benefits after they were fired for ingesting peyote during a religious ceremony. The Court ruled that the free exercise clause did not exempt the plaintiffs from the state law criminalizing their conduct, in large part because the law was an "'across-the-board' criminal prohibition[] on a particular form of conduct."[287.132] Colorado's prohibition of assisted suicide, the court ruled, fell into the same category of laws and thus constituted a "valid, religiously-neutral, and generally-applicable criminal statute that prohibits conduct a state is free to regulate."[287.133]

In addition to its unique First Amendment argument, *Sanderson* is interesting—and differs from the other cases in this section—in that the plaintiff was asserting a right to choose death through an advance directive rather than a right to commit suicide with assistance. Thus, the plaintiff was arguing that, while competent, he could direct others to euthanize him later, when

---

[287.129] Sanderson v. State, No. 99CA0203, 2000 WL 729008, at *1 (Colo. Ct. App. June 8, 2000).

[287.130] *Id*. at *2.

[287.131] 494 U.S. 872 (1990).

[287.132] Sanderson v. State, No. 99CA0203, 2000 WL 729008, at *3 (Colo. Ct. App. June 8, 2000).

[287.133] *Id*.

he was incompetent, if certain medical preconditions had been met. Rather than asserting his own right to take action, the plaintiff in *Sanderson* sought to authorize others to take action, and he wanted to ensure that the state would not prosecute those who acted at his request. The court noted the incongruity by describing his claim as being weakened because

> he does not just seek a limited exemption from the assisted suicide statute for himself so that he may freely practice his religion without fear of criminal prosecution. He also seeks exemptions for third parties—his wife and his physician—based on his personal religious beliefs, which may or may not be shared by the others. Even assuming that Sanderson had standing to raise such claims on behalf of third persons, an issue not raised by the parties on appeal, we have found no precedent for such a broad application of the Free Exercise Clause in First Amendment jurisprudence.[287.134]

Another incongruity that arises in light of such a claim relates to the criminal statute at issue. If Sanderson's wife and physician were to comply with his advance directive authorizing euthanasia once he were incompetent, then the interesting question is whether they would indeed be assisting a suicide. It seems more likely that criminal prosecution, if it were to follow in the aftermath of his wife's and physician's complying with the advance directive, would be for homicide rather than for assisting suicide.

§ 18.23   Constitutionality of Statutes Legalizing Assisted Suicide

Page 508, replace footnote 298 with:

Oregon Death with Dignity Act, Or. Rev. Stat. §§ 127.800–897 (1996), *implementation enjoined by* Lee v. Oregon, 891 F. Supp. 1429 (D. Or. 1995), *vacated and remanded,* 107 F.3d 1382 (9th Cir. 1997) (lack of federal jurisdiction), *cert. denied sub nom.* Lee v. Harcleroad, 118 S. Ct. 328 (1997).

Page 508, replace text of footnote 299 with:

Id. §§ 2.01, 3.10.

Page 508, replace text of footnote 302 with:

Id. § 1.01(3).

Page 508, replace text of footnote 308 with:

Id. §§ 3.01(c), 3.04.

[287.134] *Id.*

Page 508, replace text of footnote 309 with:

Id. §§ 3.01(c), 3.04.

Page 509, add at end of second full paragraph:

As of mid-1997, the Oregon statute had still not gone into effect. Its implementation was delayed first by litigation. The Ninth Circuit vacated and remanded the district court's decision for lack of federal jurisdiction.[320.1] However, the state sought review by the United States Supreme Court which was denied.[320.2] While the litigation was in progress, the Oregon legislature approved legislation to permit the electorate to vote to repeal the Death with Dignity Act in the November 1997 election,[320.3] but repeal was defeated by a 60%–40% margin.[320.4]

Thereafter, the Oregon statute finally became operational.[320.5] The Oregon Health Division issued its first statutorily mandated report on the operation of the statute covering the period up until December 31, 1998.[320.6]

§ 18.24 Active Euthanasia and Assisted Suicide in Other Countries (New Title)

Page 510, add before first paragraph of section:

Australia

Finally, outside the United States, the Northern Territory of Australia enacted legislation in 1995, effective July 1, 1996, legalizing physician-assisted suicide. Litigation slowed the actual implementation of this legislation. The Northern Territory Supreme Court upheld the validity of the legislation in a July 24, 1996, decision, but the region's medical association appealed the ruling to the High Court of Australia. The final copy of the regulations for the Act have been posted to the NT Legislative Assembly website at http://www.nt.gov.au/lant/rotti/termill.html.

At least four deaths pursuant to the legislation are known to have occurred.[322.1] However, the Australian Parliament repealed the legislation, as

---

[320.1] Lee v. Oregon, 107 F.3d 1382 (9th Cir. 1997).

[320.2] 118 S. Ct. 328 (1997).

[320.3] William Claiborne, *"Death With Dignity" Measure May Make Oregon National Battleground,* Wash. Post, June 27, 1997, at A19.

[320.4] Gail Kinsey Hill, *Suicide Law Stands,* The Oregonian, Nov. 5, 1997, at 1.

[320.5] See § **1A.7** in this supplement.

[320.6] See § **1A.7** in this supplement.

[322.1] Bradley Perrett, *Australia Kills Off Pioneering Euthanasia Law,* Reuter News Serv., Mar. 24, 1997.

it has the constitutional authority to do in the case of territorial, but not state, legislation. Repealing territorial legislation, however, is considered to be an extraordinary measure.[322.2]

Dr. Philip Nitschke, the physician who assisted the four known suicides, has vowed to continue to assist terminally ill patients in committing suicide.[322.2a]

According to news reports, there has been agitation for the enactment of legislation approving physician-assisted suicide in some Australian states[322.3] and at the federal level subsequent to the repeal of the Northern Territory's legislation.[322.4]

Colombia

The Constitutional Court, a judicial body with quasi-legislative powers, approved a law that allows active voluntary euthanasia with the written consent of a terminally ill patient. Six of nine Constitutional Court justices approved the euthanasia law on May 20, 1997.[322.5] Three of the justices abstained from the vote because human life is "indispensable and an essential element of the constitution."[322.6] The Court was forced to reconsider its ruling when one of the three abstaining justices, Eduardo Cifuentes, complained that the final text of the ruling was dissimilar to what had actually been approved.[322.7] Cifuentes resigned June 3 in protest.[322.8] On reconsideration, the Court affirmed its earlier ruling.[322.9]

The Colombian Congress will now be forced to pass legislation regulating the practice of euthanasia.[322.10] The Congress is "likely to draw up a

---

[322.2] *Id.*

[322.2a] *Australia Has Its Own Kevorkian,* Associated Press, Jan. 11, 1998.

[322.3] *See* AAP Newsfeed, *Highlights of the AAP National Wire at 20:00 Aug. 1, 1997,* Aug. 3, 1997 (West Australia); AAP Newsfeed, *Tas Should Lead on Euthanasia Laws: Brown,* July 22, 1997 (Tasmania).

[322.4] Reuter News Service—Australia & New Zealand, *Australian Party Pushes for Mercy Killing Law,* Apr. 12, 1997 (Australian Democrats, based on opinion polls "showing overwhelming support for mercy killings," call for referendum).

[322.5] *See* Agence France-Presse, *Colombia Allows Euthanasia for Terminally Ill Patients,* AFP, May 21, 1997.

[322.6] *Id.*

[322.7] *See* Agence France-Presse, *Colombia's High Court to Reconsider Approval of Euthanasia,* AFP, June 5, 1997.

[322.8] *See* John Otis, *Euthanasia Movement Gains Speed in Colombia,* Wash. Times, June 22, 1997, at A10.

[322.9] Agence France-Presse, *Colombian Supreme Court Allows Euthanasia,* AFP, June 12, 1997.

[322.10] *See* Agence France-Presse, Colombia Allows Euthanasia for Terminally Ill Patients, AFP, May 21, 1997.

wide range of restrictions."[322.11] The Constitutional Court has already set forth the requirement of patient-provided consent.[322.12]

Before it was approved by the Constitutional Court, physician-assisted suicide carried with it a prison sentence of between six months and three years.[322.13] Despite substantial opposition from the Roman Catholic church, at the time of the Constitutional Court ruling 53 percent of Colombians believed that physicians should not be punished for helping incurably ill and suffering patients to die.[322.14] This rather rapid change in the law has raised a firestorm of controversy in this predominantly Roman Catholic country.[322.15]

Page 513, add to footnote 337:

See also Bregie D. Onwuteaka-Philipsen et al., *Active Voluntary Euthanasia or Physician-Assisted Suicide?*, 45 J. Am. Geriatric Soc'y 1208 (1997) (reporting proportion of doctors who performed active euthanasia versus assisted suicide and discussing reasons for the choices).

Page 515, add at end of section:

South Africa

The South African Law Commission discussed proposals for laws pertaining to end-of-life decisionmaking, including the circumstances under which a physician could terminate life support, alleviate a patient's pain even though it might hasten the patient's death, and administer a lethal agent to a mentally competent and well-informed patient.[352.1]

§ 18.26   Civil Legislation to Prevent Assisted Suicide (New)

State legislatures are beginning to turn to other measures besides criminal liability to deter assisted suicide by enacting civil "anti-suicide" legislation.[367] The purpose of this legislation is to "protect vulnerable persons

---

[322.11] *Id.*

[322.12] *Id.*

[322.13] El Espectador, May 16, 1997.

[322.14] *Id.*

[322.15] *See* Serge F. Kovaleski, *Colombia Debates Court Ruling That Legalizes Mercy Killing*, Wash. Post, Aug. 18, 1997, at A15.

[352.1] *See* South African Law Commission, Discussion Paper 71, Project 86, *Euthanasia and the Artificial Preservation of Life* (http://www.law.wits.ac.za/salc/discussn/dp71.html).

[367] **KS:** Kan. Stat. Ann. §§ 21-3406, 65-1120(a)(9), 65-1436(a)(20), 65-1627(a)(14), 65-2006(a)(14), 65-2836(cc), 60-4401 to 60-4407, *discussed in* Kevin J. Breer

from suicide and to reduce the cost of enforcing such laws by promoting civil enforcement."[368] A violation of these statutes occurs if a person provides the physical means to commit suicide or participates in the physical act of assisting suicide.[369]

First, these statutes provide for the issuance of an injunction against a person who is or would be in violation of the act.[370] The award of damages[371] and attorneys' fees are also authorized.[372] When the violator of the statute is a health care professional, the penalty of suspension or revocation of the professional license may be imposed.[373]

There are provisions exempting palliative care and its possible double effect from the definition of assisted suicide,[374] thereby complementing or

---

& Cherie Leigh Durst, Note, *Recent Developments in Kansas Bioethics Law: The Kansas Prevention of Assisted Suicide Act*, 38 Washburn L.J. 557 (1999).

MD: 1999 Md. H.B. 496 (effective Oct. 1, 1999), to be codified at Md. Code Ann., Crimes & Punishments, art. 27, § 416(D)–(F).

ND: *Cf.* N.D. Cent. Code § 12.1-16-07 (permitting recovery of civil damages against any person who violates the criminal prohibition on aiding suicide, and authorizing suspension or revocation of license of health care provider who violates criminal prohibition on aiding suicide).

OK: Okla. Stat. Ann. tit. 63, §§ 3141.1–.8.

VA: Va. Code Ann. § 8.01-622.1.

[368] **OK:** Okla. Stat. tit. 63, § 3141.1.

[369] **KS:** Kan. Stat. Ann. § 21-3406(2)(A), (B).

OK: Okla. Stat. tit. 63, § 3141.3.

VA: Va. Code Ann. § 8.01-622.1 (A)(i), (ii).

[370] **KS:** Kan. Stat. Ann. § 60-4404.

OK: Okla. Stat. tit. 63, § 3141.6.

VA: Va. Code Ann. § 8.01-622.1 (B).

[371] **KS:** Kan. Stat. Ann. § 60-4405 (cause of action for civil damages may be maintained against any person who violates or attempts to violate Kan. Stat. Ann. 21-3406).

OK: Okla. Stat. tit. 63, § 3141.6 (compensatory and punitive damages may be sought).

VA: Va. Code Ann. § 8.01-622.1(C); (allows recovery of compensatory and exemplary damages).

[372] **KS:** Kan. Stat. Ann. § 60-4406.

OK: Okla. Stat. tit. 63, § 3141.7.

[373] **KS:** Kan. Stat. Ann. §§ 65-1120(a)(9) (nurse), 65-1436(a)(20) (dentist), 65-1627(a)(14) (pharmacist), 65-2006(a)(14) (podiatrist), 65-2836(cc) (any licensee).

OK: Okla. Stat. tit. 63, § 3141.8.

VA: Va. Code Ann. 8.01-622.1 (D).

[374] **KS:** Kan. Stat. Ann. § 60-4403(a).

OK: Okla. Stat. tit. 63, § 3141.4(A).

VA: Va. Code Ann. § 8.01-622.1 (E)(i).

substituting for "intractable pain" statutes.[375] The withdrawal or withholding of life-sustaining medical treatment is specifically excluded from the definition of assisting suicide.[376]

Bibliography

"Of Life and Death: A Report of the Special Committee on Euthanasia and Assisted Suicide Senate of Canada." *Issues of Law and Medicine* 11 (1995): 209.

"Narratives from the Netherlands." *Cambridge Quarterly of Healthcare Ethics* 5 (1996): 77.

"The Supreme Court—1996 Term: Physician-Assisted Suicide." *Harvard Law Review* 111 (1997): 237.

"Symposium on Physician-Assisted Suicide." *Journal of Medicine and Law* 2 (1997): 85.

AGS Ethics Committee. "Physician-Assisted Suicide and Voluntary Active Euthanasia." *Journal of the American Geriatrics Society* 43 (1995): 579.

Alesandro, J. Comment. "Physician-Assisted Suicide and New York Law." *Albany Law Review* 57 (1994): 820.

Alesandro, M. "Exploring Physician-Assisted Suicide: An Examination of the Circuit Court Decisions and Public Policy Concerns." *St. John's Journal of Legal Commentary* 12 (1997): 634.

Allen, W., and D. Brushwood. "Pharmaceutically Assisted Death and the Pharmacist's Right of Conscience." *Journal of Pharmacy & Law* 5 (1995): 1.

Alpers, A., and B. Lo. "Physician-Assisted Suicide in Oregon: A Bold Experiment." *JAMA* 274 (1995): 483.

American Geriatrics Society Ethics Committee. "The Care of Dying Patients: A Position Statement." *Journal of the American Geriatrics Society* 43 (1995): 577.

American Geriatrics Society Ethics Committee. "Physician-Assisted Suicide and Voluntary Active Euthanasia." *Journal of the American Geriatrics Society* 43 (1995): 579.

---

[375] See **Table 9-1A** in this supplement.

[376] **KS:** Kan. Stat. Ann. § 60-4403(b). *See also id.* § 60-4403(c) ("Providing spiritual treatment through prayer alone, in lieu of medical treatment, does not violate K.S.A. 21-3406").

OK: Okla. Stat. tit. 63, § 3141.4(B).

VA: Va. Code Ann. § 8.01-622.1 (E)(ii) (providing spiritual care alone, in lieu of medical treatment, also exempted from assisted suicide prevention bill).

BIBLIOGRAPHY

Amundsen, D., and D. O'Mathuna. Symposium on the Beginning and End of Life. "Historical and Biblical References in Physician-Assisted Suicide Court Opinions." *Notre Dame Journal of Law, Ethics and Public Policy* 12 (1998): 473.

Angell, M. "The Supreme Court and Physician-Assisted Suicide: The Ultimate Right." *New England Journal of Medicine* 336 (1997): 50.

Angell, M. Editorial. "Euthanasia in the Netherlands—Good News or Bad?" *New England Journal of Medicine* 335(22) (1996): 1676.

Annas, G. "Physician-Assisted Suicide—Michigan's Temporary Solution." *Ohio Northern University Law Review* 20 (1994): 561.

Annas, G. "The Promised End—Physician-Assisted Suicide and Abortion." *Duquesne Law Review* 35 (1996): 183.

Appleton, S. "Assisted Suicide and Reproductive Freedom: Exploring Some Connections." *Washington University Law Quarterly* 76 (1998): 15.

Arras, J. "Physician-Assisted Suicide: A Tragic View." *Journal of Contemporary Health Law and Policy* 13 (1997): 361.

Bachman, J., et al. "Attitudes of Michigan Physicians and the Public Toward Legalizing Physician-Assisted Suicide and Voluntary Euthanasia." *New England Journal of Medicine* 334 (1996): 303.

Back, A., et al. "Physician-Assisted Suicide and Euthanasia in Washington State." *Journal of the American Medical Association* 275 (1996): 919.

Baron, C. "Pleading for Physician-Assisted Suicide in the Courts." Western *New England Law Review* 19 (1997): 371.

Baron, C., et al. "A Model State Act to Authorize and Regulate Physician-Assisted Suicide." *Harvard Journal on Legislation* 33 (1996): 1.

Batavia, A. "Disability and Physician-Assisted Suicide." *New England Journal of Medicine* 336 (1997): 1671.

Battin, M. *Ethical Issues in Suicide*. Englewood Cliffs, NJ: Prentice Hall, 1995.

Battin, M. "Seven Caveats Concerning the Discussion of Euthanasia in Holland." *Perspectives in Biology and Medicine* 34 (1990): 73.

Battin, M., and A. Lipman, eds. *Drug Use in Assisted Suicide and Euthanasia*. Binghamton, NY: Pharmaceutical Products Press, 1995.

Battin, M., Rhodes, R., and Silvers, A. eds. *Physician-Assisted Suicide: Expanding the Debate*. New York: Routledge, 1998.

Beauchamp, T. "The Justification of Physician-Assisted Deaths." *Indiana Law Review* 29 (1996): 1173.

Beauchamp, T., ed. *Intending Death: The Ethics of Assisted Suicide and Euthanasia*. Upper Saddle River, NJ: Prentice Hall, 1996.

Beauchamp, T., and R. Veatch, eds. *Ethical Issues in Death and Dying*. 2d ed. Englewood Cliffs, NJ: Prentice Hall, 1996.

Belian, J. Comment. "Deference to Doctors in Dutch Euthanasia Law." *Emory International Law Review* 10 (1996): 255.

Benton, A. "Personal Autonomy and Physician-Assisted Suicide: The Appropriate Response to a Modern Ethical Dilemma." *Ohio Northern University Law Review* 20 (1994): 769.

Beschle, D. "The Role of Courts in the Debate on Assisted Suicide: A Communitarian Approach." *Notre Dame Journal of Law, Ethics and Public Policy* 9 (1995): 367.

Billings, J.A., and S. Block. "Slow Euthanasia." *Journal of Palliative Care* 12 (1996): 21.

Bleich, J.D. "Is There a Right to Physician-Assisted Suicide?" *Fordham Urban Law Journal* 24 (1997): 795.

Bopp, J. "Just the Medical Facts: An Argument in Support of the Continued Ban on Physician-Assisted Suicide." *St. John's Journal of Legal Commentary* 12 (1997): 610.

Bopp, J., and R. Coleson. "The Constitutional Case Against Permitting Physician-Assisted Suicide for Competent Adults with 'Terminal Conditions'." *Issues in Law and Medicine* 11 (1995): 239.

Bopp, Jr., J. et. al. "Three Strikes: Is an Assisted Suicide Right Out?" *Issues in Law and Medicine* 15 (1999): 3.

Boyle, J. "Who Is Entitled to Double Effect?" *Journal of Medicine and Philosophy* 16 (1991): 475.

Branigan, J. Note. "Michigan's Struggle with Assisted Suicide and Related Issues as Illuminated by Current Case Law: An Overview of *People v. Kevorkian*." *University of Detroit Mercy Law Review* 72 (1995): 959.

Breer, K. and Durst, C. "A Symposium on Kansas Law and Legislation; Recent Developments in Kansas Bioethics Law: The Kansas Prevention of Assisted Suicide Act." *Washburn Law Journal* 38 (1999): 557.

Brennan, J. "A State Based Right to Physician Assisted Suicide." *Boston University Law Review* 79 (1999): 231.

Bristow, L. "Physician's Role as Healer: American Medical Association's Opposition to Physician-Assisted Suicide." *St. John's Journal of Legal Commentary* 12 (1997): 653.

Bristow, L. "Report of the Board of Trustees of the American Medical Association: Euthanasia/Physician-Assisted Suicide: Lessons in the Dutch Experience." *Issues of Law and Medicine* 10 (1994): 81.

Brock, D. "A Critique of Three Objections to Physician-Assisted Suicide." *Issues in Law & Medicine* 15 (2000): 339.

BIBLIOGRAPHY

Brock, D. *Life and Death: Philosophical Essays in Biomedical Ethics*. New York: Cambridge University Press, 1993.

Brodkowski, H., and M. Malloy. "Suffering Against Their Will: The Terminally Ill and Physician Assisted Suicide—A Constitutional Analysis." *Saint John's Journal of Legal Commentary* 12 (1996): 171.

Brody, H. "Causing, Intending, and Assisting Death." *Journal of Clinical Ethics* 4 (1993): 112.

Brody, H. "Commentary on Billings and Block's 'Slow Euthanasia.'" *Journal of Palliative Care* 12 (1996): 38.

Brody, H. "Legislative Ban on Assisted Suicide: Impact on Michigan's Medical Practice." *Michigan Medicine* 92 (February 1993): 32.

Brody, H. "Physician Assisted Suicide in the Courts: Moral Equivalence, Double Effect, and Clinical Practice." *Minnesota Law Review* 82 (1998): 939.

Bryce, M. "Introductory Remarks of Panel I: Is There a Constitutional Right to Die?" *St. John's Journal of Legal Commentary* 12 (1997): 593.

Burgess, S. et al. "Suicide, Euthanasia, and the Psychiatrist." *Issues in Law and Medicine* 15 (1999): 230.

Burt, R. "Constitutionalizing Physician-Assisted Suicide: Will Lightning Strike Thrice?" *Duquesne Law Review* 35 (1996): 159.

Burt, R. "Disorder in the Court: Physician-Assisted Suicide and the Constitution." *Minnesota Law Review* 82 (1998): 965.

Burt, R. "Rationality and Injustice in Physician-Assisted Suicide." Western *New England Law Review* 19 (1997): 353.

Burt, R. "Self-Determination and the Wrongfulness of Death." *Journal of Health Care Law & Policy* 2 (1999): 177.

Burt, R. "The Supreme Court Speaks: Not Assisted Suicide but a Constitutional Right to Palliative Care." *New England Journal of Medicine* 337 (1997): 1234.

Bushong, S., and T. Balmer. "Breathing Life into the Right to Die: Oregon's Death with Dignity Act." *Issues in Law and Medicine* 11 (1995): 269.

Calandrillo, S. "Corralling Kevorkian: Regulating Physician-Assisted Suicide in America." *Virginia Journal of Social Policy & the Law* 7 (1999): 41.

Callahan, D., and M. White. "The Legalization of Physician-Assisted Suicide: Creating a Regulatory Potemkin Village." *University of Richmond Law Review* 30 (1996): 1.

Campbell, C., et al. "Conflicts of Conscience: Hospice and Assisted Suicide." *Hastings Center Report* 25 (May-June 1995): 36.

Campbell, S. "Religious Ethics and Active Euthanasia in a Pluralistic Society." *Kennedy Institute of Ethics Journal* 2 (1992): 253.

Canick, S. "Constitutional Aspects of Physician-Assisted Suicide After *Lee v. Oregon.*" *American Journal of Law and Medicine* 23 (1997): 69.

Cantor, N. "Two Opinions in Search of a Justice: The Constitution and Physician-Assisted Suicide." *Rutgers Law Journal* 28 (1997): 435.

Cantor, N., and G. Thomas. "Pain Relief, Acceleration of Death, and Criminal Law." *Kennedy Institute of Ethics Journal* 6 (1996): 107.

Capron, A. "Constitutionalizing Death." *Hastings Center Report* 25(6) (1995): 23.

Capron, A. "Legalizing Physician-Aided Death." *Cambridge Quarterly of Healthcare Ethics* 5 (1996): 10.

Capron, A. "Euthanasia in the Netherlands: American Observations." *Hastings Center Report* 22 (March–April 1992): 30.

Capron, A. "Philosophy and Theory: Life's Sacred Value—Common Ground or Battleground?: Life's Dominion: An Argument about Abortion, Euthanasia, and Individual Freedom." *Michigan Law Review* 92 (1994): 1491.

Carter, D. "Knight in the Duel with Death: Physician Assisted Suicide and the Medical Necessity Defense." *Villanova Law Review* 41 (1996): 663.

Cavanaugh, T. "Currently Accepted Practices that Are Known to Lead to Death, and PAS: Is There an Ethically Relevant Difference?" *Cambridge Quarterly of Healthcare Ethics* 7 (1998): 375.

Cavanaugh, T. "The Ethics of Death-Hastening or Death-Causing Palliative Analgesic Administration to the Terminally Ill." *Journal of Pain and Symptom Management* 12 (1996): 248.

Chesterman, S. "Last Rights: Euthanasia, the Sanctity of Life, and the Law in the Netherlands and the Northern Territory of Australia." *International and Comparative Law Quarterly* 47 (1998): 362.

Chochinov, H., et al. "Desire for Death in the Terminally Ill." *American Journal of Psychiatry* 152 (1995): 1185.

Chopko, M. "Assisted Suicide: Still a Wonderful Life?" *Notre Dame Law Review* 70 (1995): 519.

Chopko, M. "Responsible Public Policy at the End of Life." *University of Detroit Mercy Law Review* 75 (1998): 557.

Clark, A. "Autonomy and Death." *Tulane Law Review* 71 (1996): 45–137.

Clark, N. *The Politics of Assisted Suicide.* New York: Garland, 1997.

Cohen, D., and J. Wareham. "An Analysis of Contemporary State Statutes about Assisted Suicide." *Journal of Mental Health and Aging* 3 (1997): 4.

BIBLIOGRAPHY

Cohen, L. "Suicide, Hastening Death, and Psychiatry." *Archives of Internal Medicine* 158 (1998): 1973.

Coleman, C. "The New York State Task Force on Life and the Law: Why It Concluded Physician-Assisted Suicide Should Not Be Legalized." *St. John's Journal of Legal Commentary* 12 (1997): 647.

Coleman, C., and T. Miller. "Stemming the Tide: Assisted Suicide and the Constitution." Journal of Law, Medicine & Ethics 23 (1995): 389.

Coleman, D. "Assisted Suicide and Disability: Another Perspective." *WTR Human Rights* 27 (2000): 6.

Coleson, R. "Contemporary Religious Viewpoints on Suicide, Physician-Assisted Suicide, and Voluntary Active Euthanasia." *Duquesne Law Review* 35 (1996): 43.

Coleson, R. "The *Glucksberg & Quill* Amicus Curiae Briefs: Verbatim Arguments Opposing Assisted Suicide." *Issues in Law and Medicine* 13 (1997): 3.

"Conference Bibliography." *Cornell Journal of Law and Public Policy* 7 (1998): 405.

Cuperus-Bosma, J., et al. "Physician-Assisted Death: Policy-Making by the Assembly of Prosecutors General in the Netherlands." *European Journal of Health Law* 4 (1997): 225.

Curran, Patrick M., Jr. "Regulating Death: Oregon's Death with Dignity Act and the Legalization of Physician-Assisted Suicide." *Georgetown Law Journal* 86 (1998): 725.

Daniels, P. "An Illinois Physician-Assisted Suicide Act: A Merciful End to a Terminally Ill Criminal Tradition." *Loyola University of Chicago Law Journal* 28 (1997): 763.

Davidson, S. "But Why Do We Shoot Horses?: An Analysis of the Right to Die and Euthanasia." *New York Law School Journal of Human Rights* 12 (1994): 115.

Deigh, J. "Physician Assisted Suicide and Voluntary Euthanasia: Some Relevant Differences." *Journal of Criminal Law and Criminology* 88 (1998): 1155.

Dickens, B. "Commentary on 'Slow Euthanasia.'" *Journal of Palliative Care* 12 (1996): 42.

Dillmann, R. "Euthanasia in the The Netherlands: The Role of the Dutch Medical Profession." *Cambridge Quarterly of Healthcare Ethics* 5 (1996): 100.

Dixon, K. "The Quality of Mercy: Reflections on Provider-Assisted Suicide." *Journal of Clinical Ethics* 8 (1997): 290.

493

Dixon, N. "On the Difference Between Physician-Assisted Suicide and Active Euthanasia." *Hastings Center Report* 28 (September-October 1998): 25.

Doerflinger, R. "The Good Samaritan and the 'Good Death': Catholic Reflections on Euthanasia." *Issues of Law and Medicine* 11 (1995): 149.

Dolan, J. "Is Physician-Assisted Suicide Possible?" *Duquesne Law Review* 35 (1996): 355.

Donahue, J. Note. "Physician-Assisted Suicide: A 'Right' Reserved for Only the Competent?" *Vermont Law Review* 19 (1995): 795.

Donchin, A. "Autonomy, Interdependence, and Assisted Suicide: Respecting Boundaries/Crossing Lines." *Bioethics* 14 ( ): 187.

Dorff, E. "Assisted Suicide." *Journal of Law and Religion* 13 (1998-99): 263.

Doukas, D., et al. "Attitudes and Behaviors on Physician-Assisted Death: A Study of Michigan Oncologists." *Journal of Clinical Oncology* 13 (1995): 1055.

Doyal, L. "The Moral Character of Clinicians or the Best Interests of Patients? Intention Alone Cannot Determine the Morality of Actions." *British Medical Journal* 318 (1999): 1432.

Drickamer, M., et al. "Practical Issues in Physician-Assisted Suicide." *Annals of Internal Medicine* 126 (1997): 146.

Duberstein, P., et al. "Attitudes Toward Self-Determined Death: A Survey of Primary Care Physicians." *Journal of the American Geriatrics Society* 43 (1995): 395.

DuBois, J. "Physican-Assisted Suicide and Public Virtue: A Reply to the Liberty Thesis of "The Philosopher's Brief." *Issues in Law and Medicine* 15 (1999): 159.

Dworkin, G., R.G. Frey, and S. Bok. *Euthanasia and Physician-Assisted Suicide, For and Against.* New York: Cambridge University Press, 1998.

Dworkin, R. "Assisted Suicide: What the Court Really Said." *New York Review of Books* 20 (September 25, 1997): 40.

Dworkin, R. "The Fifth Annual Fritz B. Burns Lecture: Euthanasia, Morality, and the Law." *Loyola of Los Angeles Law Review* 30 (1997): 1465.

Dworkin, R. *Life's Dominion: An Argument About Abortion, Euthanasia and Individual Freedom.* New York: Knopf, 1994.

Dworkin, R., and J. Finnis. "Fritz B. Burns Lecture: Euthanasia, Morality, and Law." *Loyola of Los Angeles Law Review* 31 (1998): 1147.

BIBLIOGRAPHY

Dyck, A. "Beyond Theological Conflict in the Courts: The Issue of Assisted Suicide." *Notre Dame Journal of Law, Ethics and Public Policy* 9 (1995): 503.

Edgerton, T. "Fundamental Rights and Physician-Assisted Suicide: Protecting Personal Autonomy." *Journal of Gender, Race and Justice* 1 (1997): 283.

Emanuel, E. "Empirical Studies on Euthanasia and Assisted Suicide." *Journal of Clinical Ethics* 6 (1995): 158.

Emanuel, E. "The Future of Euthanasia and Physician-Assisted Suicide: Beyond Rights Talk to Informed Public Policy." *Minnesota Law Review* 82 (1998): 983.

Emanuel, E. "The History of Euthanasia Debates in the United States and Britain." *Annals of Internal Medicine* 121 (1994): 793.

Emanuel, E. "Oregon's Physician-Assisted Suicide Law." *Archives of Internal Medicine* 156 (1996): 825.

Emanuel, E. "Pain and Symptom Control. Patient Rights and Physician Responsibilities." *Pain and Palliative Care* 10 (1996): 41.

Emanuel, E. "The Practice of Euthanasia and Physician-Assisted Suicide in the United States: Adherence to Proposed Safeguards and Effects on Physicians." *Journal of the American Medical Association* 280 (1998): 507.

Emanuel, E. "What Is the Great Benefit of Legalizing Euthanasia or Physician-Assisted Suicide?" *Ethics* 109 (1999): 629.

Emanuel, E., and M. Battin, "What Are the Potential Cost Savings from Legalizing Physician-Assisted Suicide?" *New England Journal of Medicine* 339 (1998): 167.

Emanuel, E., and E. Daniels. "Oregon's Physician-Assisted Suicide Law." *Archives of Internal Medicine* 156 (1996): 825.

Emanuel, L., ed. *Regulating How We Die: The Ethical, Medical, and Legal Issues Surrounding Physician-Assisted Suicide*. Cambridge, MA: Harvard University Press, 1998.

Engelhardt, Jr., H. "Physician-Assisted Suicide Reconsidered: Dying as a Christian in a Post-Christian Age." *Issues in Law and Medicine* 15 (1999): 108.

Engelhardt, H.T., et al. "Suicide and Assisting Suicide: A Critique of Legal Sanctions." *Southwestern Law Journal* 36 (1982): 1003.

England, E. Note and Comment. "The Debate on Physician-Assisted Suicide Reaches the Federal Courts. A Discussion of the Decisions of the District and Circuit Courts in *Compassion in Dying v. Washington State*." *Pace Law Review* 16 (1996): 359.

Euthanasia in the Netherlands. 3d ed. Utrecht: Royal Dutch Medical Association, 1994.

Falk, Z. "Jewish Perspectives on Assisted Suicide and Euthanasia." *Journal of Law and Religion* 13 (1998–99): 379.

Fenigsen, R. "Dutch Euthanasia Revisited." *Issues in Law and Medicine* 13 (1997): 301.

Finnis, J. "Fritz B. Burns Lecture—Euthanasia, Morality, and Law." *Loyola of Los Angeles Law Review* 31 (1998): 1123.

Fins, J., et al. "Framing the Physician-Assisted Suicide and Voluntary Active Euthanasia Debate: The Role of Deontology, Consequentialism, and Clinical Pragmatism." *Journal of the American Geriatrics Society* 43 (1995): 563.

FitzGibbon, S. "The Failure of the Freedom-Based and Utilitarian Arguments for Assisted Suicide." *American Journal of Jurisprudence* 42 (1997): 211.

FitzGibbon, S., and K. Lai. "The Model Physician-Assisted Suicide Act and the Jurisprudence of Death." *Harvard Journal of Law and Public Policy* 20 (1996): 127.

Flack, L. "Just Caring: Assisted Suicide and Health Care Rationing." *University of Detroit Mercy Law Review* 72 (1995): 873.

Fleming, J. "Constitutional Tragedy in Dying: Responses to Some Common Arguments Against the Constitutional Right to Die." *Fordham Urban Law Journal* 24 (1997): 881.

Fleming, J. "Death, Dying, and Euthanasia: Australia Versus the Northern Territory." *Issues in Law & Medicine* 15 (2000): 291.

Florida, R. "A Response to Damien Keown's Suicide, Assisted Suicide and Euthanasia: A Buddhist Perspective." *Journal of Law and Religion* 13 (1998–99): 413.

Foley, K. "Competent Care for the Dying Instead of Physician-Assisted Suicide." *New England Journal of Medicine* 336 (1997): 54.

Foley, K., and H. Hendin. "The Oregon Report: Don't Ask, Don't Tell." *Hastings Center Report* 29 (May-June 1999): 37.

Forsythe, C. "The Incentives and Disincentives Created by Legalizing Physician-Assisted Suicide." *St. John's Journal of Legal Commentary* 12 (1997): 680.

Franklin, C. "Physician-Assisted Suicide: Misconceptions and Implications from a Physician's Perspective." *DePaul Journal of Health Care Law* 1 (1997): 579.

Frederick, M. Comment. "Physician Assisted Suicide: A Personal Right?" *Southern University Law Review* 21 (1994): 59.

BIBLIOGRAPHY

Friedman, L. "Assisted Suicide." *Touro Law Review* 14 (1998): 415.

Friedman, R. Comment. "It's My Body and I'll Die If I Want To: A Property-Based Argument in Support of Assisted Suicide." *Journal of Contemporary Health Law and Policy* 13 (1995): 183.

Fuller, M. "Just Whose Life Is It?: Establishing a Constitutional Right for Physician-Assisted Euthanasia." *Southwestern University Law Review* 23 (1993): 103.

Furrow, B. "Setting Limits in the Dying Zone: Assisted Suicide, Scarce Resources, and Hard Cases." *University of Detroit Mercy Law Review* 72 (1995): 901.

Gabel, J. "Release from Terminal Suffering? The Impact of AIDS on Medically Assisted Suicide Legislation." *Florida State University Law Review* 22 (1994): 369.

Ganzini, L., et al. "Depression, Suicide, and the Right to Refuse Life-Sustaining Treatment." *Journal of Clinical Ethics* 4 (1993): 337.

Ganzini, L., et al. "The Effect of Depression Treatment on Elderly Patients' Preferences for Life-Sustaining Medical Therapy." *American Journal of Psychiatry* 151 (1994): 1631.

Ganzini, L., and M. Lee. "Psychiatry and Assisted Suicide in the United States." *New England Journal of Medicine* 336 (1997): 1824.

Garzino, F. "Undue Economic Influence on Physician-Assisted Suicide." *DePaul Journal of Health Care Law* 1 (1997): 537.

Gaumer, C., and P. Griffith. "Whose Life Is It Anyway?: An Analysis and Commentary on the Emerging Law of Physician-Assisted Suicide." *South Dakota Law Review* 42 (1997): 357.

Geis, S., and D. Messer, eds. *How Shall We Die? Helping Christians Debate Assisted Suicide*. Nashville, TN: Abingdon Press, 1997.

Gevers, J. "Physicians-Assisted Suicide and the Dutch Courts." *Cambridge Quarterly of Healthcare Ethics* 5 (1996): 93.

Gilbert, A. "The Legal Response to Assisted Suicide." *Ohio Northern University Law Review* 20 (1994): 673.

Gillon, R. "Forseeing Is Not Necessarily the Same as Intending." *British Medical Journal* 318 (1999): 1431.

Gillon, R. "Physician Assisted Suicide—Sympathy and Skepticism." *University of Detroit Mercy Law Review* 75 (1998): 499.

Girsh, F. "The Hemlock Society: What We Are, What We Aren't, and Why." *St. John's Journal of Legal Commentary* 12 (1997): 689.

Glasson, J. "Report of the Council on Ethical and Judicial Affairs of the American Medical Association: Physician-Assisted Suicide (Resolution 3, A-93)." *Issues of Law and Medicine* 10 (1994): 91.

Gleicher, E. "Legalized Physician-Assisted Suicide." *Michigan Bar Journal* 73 (1994): 184.

Glynn, K. "Turning to State Legislatures to Legalize Physician-Assisted Suicide for Seriously Ill, Non-Terminal Patients after *Vacco v. Quill* and *Washington v. Glucksberg.*" *Journal of Law and Policy* 6 (1997): 329.

Goebel, B. Note. "Who Decides If There Is 'Triumph in the Ultimate Agony?' Constitutional Theory and the Emerging Right to Die with Dignity." *William and Mary Law Review* 37 (1996): 827.

Goodwin, P. "Oregon's Physician-Assisted Suicide Law: An Alternative Positive Viewpoint." *Archives of Internal Medicine* 157 (1997): 1642.

Gostin, L. "The Constitutional Right to Die: Ethical Considerations." *St. John's Journal of Legal Commentary* 12 (1997): 599.

Graber, M.A., et al. "Patients' Views About Physician Participation in Assisted Suicide and Euthanasia." *Journal of General Internal Medicine* 11 (1996): 71.

Griffiths, J., A. Rood, and H. Weyers. *Euthanasia and Law in the Netherlands.* Ann Arbor: University of Michigan Press, 1998.

Griffiths, J. et al. *Euthanasia and Law in the Netherlands.* Amsterdam: Amsterdam University Press, 1998.

Groenewoud, J., et al. "Physician-Assisted Death in Psychiatric Practice in the Netherlands." *New England Journal of Medicine* 336 (1997): 1795.

Gunderson, M., and D. Mayo. "Altruism and Physician Assisted Death." *Journal of Medicine and Philosophy* 18 (1993): 281.

Haber, J. "Should Physicians Assist the Reaper?" *Cambridge Quarterly of Healthcare Ethics* 5 (1996): 44.

Haley, K., M. and Lee, eds. *The Oregon Death with Dignity Act: A Guidebook for Health Care Providers.* Portland: Oregon Health Sciences University Center for Ethics in Health Care (1998).

Hanser, M. "Why Are Killing and Letting Die Wrong?" *Philosophy and Public Affairs* 24 (1995): 175.

Hapward, C. "The 'Right to Die' Is Dead: A Constitutional Analysis of Physician-Assisted Suicide." *Seton Hall Constitutional Law Journal* 7 (1996): 165.

Hardaway, R., et al. "The Right to Die and the Ninth Amendment: Compassion and Dying After *Glucksberg* and *Vacco.*" *George Mason Law Review* 7 (1999): 313.

Harris, L. "Semantics and Policy in Physician-Assisted Death: Piercing the Verbal Veil." *Elder Law Journal* 5 (1997): 251-291.

BIBLIOGRAPHY

Harvey, P. "A Response to Damien Keown's Suicide, Assisted Suicide and Euthanasia: A Buddhist Perspective." *Journal of Law and Religion* 13 (1998–99): 407.

Haugen, P. "Pain Relief for the Dying: The Unwelcome Intervention of the Criminal Law." *William Mitchell Law Review* 23 (1997): 325.

Heilig, S., et al. "Physician-Hastened Death Advisory Guidelines for the San Francisco Bay Area from the Bay Area Network of Ethics Committees." *Western Journal of Medicine* 166 (1997): 370.

Heilig, S., and S. Jamison. "Physician Aid-In-Dying: Toward a Harm Reduction Approach." *Cambridge Quarterly of Healthcare Ethics* 5 (1996): 113.

Hemlock Society USA. "Mercy Killing: A Position Statement Regarding David Rodriguez." *Issues in Law and Medicine* 13 (1997): 341.

Hendin, H. "Euthanasia and Physician-Assisted Suicide in the Netherlands." *New England Journal of Medicine* 336 (1997): 1385.

Hendin, H. *Seduced by Death: Doctors, Patients, and Assisted Suicide*. New York: W.W. Norton, 1998.

Hendin, H. *Seduced by Death: Doctors, Patients and the Dutch Cure*. New York: W.W. Norton, 1997.

Hendin, H. "Selling Death and Dignity." *Hastings Center Report* 25 (May-June 1995): 19.

Hendin, H. "Suicide and the Request for Assisted Suicide: Meaning and Motivation." *Duquesne Law Review* 35 (1996): 285.

Hendin, H., K. Foley, and M. White. "Physician-Assisted Suicide: Reflections on Oregon's First Case." *Issues in Law and Medicine* 14 (1998): 243.

Hendin, H., and G. Klerman, "Physician-Assisted Suicide: The Dangers of Legalization." *American Journal of Psychiatry* 150 (1993): 143.

Hendin, H., et al. "Physician-Assisted Suicide and Euthanasia in the Netherlands: Lessons from the Dutch." *JAMA* 277 (1997): 1720.

Hickey, M. Symposium on the Beginning and End of Life. "Reading the Mystery Passage Narrowly: A Legal, Ethical and Practical Argument Against Physician Assisted Suicide." *Notre Dame Journal of Law, Ethics and Public Policy* 12 (1998): 567.

Hirschfeld, L. "Moral Dilemmas for the Judiciary at the Millenium: Partial-Birth Abortion and Physician-Assisted Suicide." *Cardozo Law Review* 19 (1997): 1061.

Hittinger, R. "Private Uses of Lethal Force: The Case of Assisted Suicide." *Loyola Law Review* 43 (1997): 151.

House, H. "The Parable of the Good Samaritan: Implications for the Euthanasia Debate." *Issues in Law and Medicine* 11 (1995): 159.

Humber, J., et al., eds. *Physician-Assisted Death*. Totowa, NJ: Humana Press, 1993.

Humphry, D. *Final Exit: The Practicalities of Self-Deliverance and Assisted Suicide for the Dying*. 2d ed. New York: Dell, 1997.

Humphry, D., and M. Clement. *Freedom to Die: People, Politics and the Right-to-Die Movement*. New York: St. Martin's Press, 1998.

Jamison, S. *Assisted Suicide: A Decision-Making Guide for Health Professionals*. San Francisco, CA: Jossey-Bass, 1997.

Jochemsen, H. "Dutch Court Decisions on Nonvoluntary Euthanasia Critically Reviewed." *Issues in Law and Medicine* 13 (1998): 447.

Johnson, J. "Setting Limits on Death: A View from the United States." *Cambridge Quarterly of Healthcare Ethics* 5 (1996): 24.

Jones, C. "Assistance in Dying: Accounting for Difference." *Western New England Law Review* 19 (1997): 405.

Jonsen, A. "Physician-Assisted Suicide." *Seattle University Law Review* 18 (1995): 459.

Kamisar, Y. "Against Assisted Suicide—Even a Very Limited Form." *University of Detroit Mercy Law Review* 72 (1995): 735.

Kamisar, Y. "Are Laws Against Assisted Suicide Unconstitutional?" *Hastings Center Report.* 23 (May-June 1993): 32.

Kamisar, Y. "On the Meaning and Impact of the Physician-Assisted Suicide Cases." *Minnesota Law Review* 82 (1998): 895.

Kamisar, Y. "Physician-Assisted Suicide: The Problems Presented by the Compelling, Heartwrenching Case." *Journal of Criminal Law and Criminology* 88 (1998): 1121.

Kamisar, Y. "The 'Right to Die': A Catchy But Confusing Slogan." *Michigan Bar Journal* 73 (1994): 184.

Kamisar, Y. "The Reasons So Many People Support Physician-Assisted Suicide—And Why These Reasons Are Not Convincing." *Issues in Law and Medicine* 12 (1996): 113.

Kamisar, Y. "The 'Right to Die': On Drawing (and Erasing) Lines." *Duquesne Law Review* 35 (1996): 481.

Kaniuk, R. "European Perspectives Towards Euthanasia and Physician-Assisted Suicide." *New York International Law Review* 9 (1996): 85.

Kapp, M. "Old Folks on the Slippery Slope: Elderly Patients and Physician-Assisted Suicide." *Duquesne Law Review* 35 (1996): 443.

BIBLIOGRAPHY

Kass, L., and N. Lund. "Physician-Assisted Suicide, Medical Ethics and the Future of the Medical Profession." *Duquesne Law Review* 35 (1996): 395.

Kaufman, G. "*State v. Chabot:* A Euthanasia Case from the Netherlands." *Ohio Northern University Law Review* 20 (1994): 815.

Kaveny, C. "Managed Care, Assisted Suicide, and Vulnerable Populations." *Notre Dame Law Review* 73 (May-July, 1998): 1275.

Kehoe, S. "Giving the Disabled and Terminally Ill a Voice: Mandating Mediation for All Physician-Assisted Suicide, Withdrawal of Life Support, or Life-Sustaining Treatment Requests." *Hamline Journal of Public Law and Policy* 20 (1999): 373.

Keown, D. "Suicide, Assisted Suicide and Euthanasia: A Buddhist Perspective." *Journal of Law and Religion* 13 (1998–99): 385.

Keown, J. "Euthanasia in the Netherlands: Sliding Down the Slippery Slope?" *Notre Dame Journal of Law, Ethics and Public Policy* 9 (1995): 407.

Keown, J., ed. *Euthanasia Examined: Ethical, Clinical and Legal Perspectives.* New York: Cambridge University Press, 1997.

Keown, J., and D. Callahan, eds. *Euthanasia Examined: Ethical, Legal and Clinical Perspectives.* New York: Cambridge University Press, 1995.

Kimsma, G., and B. van Duin. "Teaching Euthanasia: The Integration of the Practice of Euthanasia into the Grief, Death, and Dying Curricula of Postgraduate Family Medicine Training." *Cambridge Quarterly of Healthcare Ethics* 5 (1996): 107.

King, P., and L. Wolf, "Empower and Protecting Patients: Lessons for Physician-Assisted Suicide from the African-American Experience." *Minnesota Law Review* 82 (1998): 1015.

Kirk, K. "How Oregon's Death with Dignity Act Affects Practice." *American Journal of Nursing* 98 (1998): 54.

Kleinberg, R., and T. Mochizuki. "The Final Freedom: Maintaining Autonomy and Valuing Life in Physician-Assisted Suicide Cases." *Harvard Civil Rights-Civil Liberties Law Review* 32 (1997): 197.

Kline, R. "Give Me Liberty and Give Me Death: Assisted Suicide as a Fundamental Liberty Interest." *Boston University Public Interest Law Journal* 6 (1997): 527.

Kline, R. "The Right to Assisted Suicide in Washington and Oregon: The Courts Won't Allow a Northwest Passage." *Boston University Public Interest Law Journal* 5 (1996): 213.

Koch, T. "Living Versus Dying with Dignity': A New Perspective on the Euthanasia Debate." *Cambridge Quarterly of Healthcare Ethics* 5 (1996): 50.

Koenig, H., et al. "Attitudes of Elderly Patients and Their Families Toward Physician-Assisted Suicide." *Archives of Internal Medicine* 156 (1996): 2240.

Kohm, L. and B. Brigner. "Women and Assisted Suicide: Exposing the Gender Vulnerability to Acquiescent Death." *Cardozo Women's Law Journal* 4 (1998): 241.

Korobkin, Russell. "Physician-Assisted Suicide Legislation: Issues and Preliminary Responses." *Notre Dame Journal of Law, Ethics and Public Policy* 12 (1998): 449.

Kreimer, S. "Does Pro-Choice Mean Pro-Kevorkian? An Essay on *Roe, Casey,* and the Right to Die." *American University Law Review* 44 (1995): 803.

Kreimer, S. "The Second Time as Tragedy: The Assisted Suicide Cases and the Heritage of *Roe v. Wade.*" *Hastings Constitutional Law Quarterly* 24 (1997): 863.

Kuhse, H. "Critical Notice: Why Killing Is Not Always Worse—and Is Sometimes Better—Than Letting Die." *Cambridge Quarterly of Healthcare Ethics* 7 (1998): 371.

Larson, E. "The Foulston & Siefkin Lecture. Tales of Death: Storytelling in the Physician-Assisted Suicide Litigation." *Washburn Law Journal* 39 (2000): 159.

Larson, E. "Seeking Compassion in Dying: The Washington State Law Against Assisted Suicide." *Seattle University Law Review* 18 (1995): 509.

Latham, S. "Aquinas and Morphine: Notes on Double Effect at the End of Life." *DePaul Journal of Health Care Law* 1 (1997): 625-643.

Law, S. "Birth and Death: Doctor Control vs. Patient Choice." *Minnesota Law Review* 82 (1998): 1045.

Law, S. "Physician-Assisted Death: An Essay on Constitutional Rights and Remedies." *Maryland Law Review* 55 (1996): 292.

Leading Case. "Physician-Assisted Suicide." *Harvard Law Review* 111 (1997): 237.

Lee, M., et al. "Legalizing Assisted Suicide—Views of Physicians in Oregon." *New England Journal of Medicine* 334 (1996): 310.

Lee, M. "The Oregon Death With Dignity Act: Implementation Issues." *Western Journal of Medicine* 166 (1997): 398.

BIBLIOGRAPHY

Legemaate, J., and K.K.M. Gevers. "Physician-Assisted Suicide in Psychiatry: Developments in the Netherlands." *Cambridge Quarterly of Healthcare Ethics* 6 (1997): 175.

Lidz, J. "Medicine as Metaphor in Plato." *Journal of Medicine and Philosophy* 20 (1995): 527.

Little, T. "Protecting the Right to Live: International Comparison of Physician-Assisted Suicide Systems." *Indiana International and Comparative Law Review* 7 (1997): 433.

Linton, P. "Relief or Reproach?: Euthanasia Rights in the Wake of Measure 16." *Oregon Law Review* 74 (1995): 449.

Lu, C. "The Debate Over Physician-Assisted Suicide." *Human Rights* 24 (1997): 8.

Lund, N. "Two Precipices, One Chasm: The Economics of Physician-Assisted Suicide and Euthanasia." *Hastings Constitutional Law Quarterly* 24 (1997): 903.

MacBride, J. Comment. "A Death Without Dignity: How the Lower Courts Have Refused to Recognize That the Right of Privacy and the Fourteenth Amendment Liberty Interest Protect an Individual's Choice of Physician-assisted Suicide." *Temple Law Review* 68 (1995): 755.

Madorsky, J. "Is the Slippery Slope Steeper for People with Disabilities?" *Western Journal of Medicine* 166 (1997): 410.

Mangini, L. "To Help or Not to Help: Assisted Suicide and Its Moral, Ethical, and Legal Ramifications." *Seton Hall Legislative Journal* 18 (1994): 728.

Manning, C. "High Technology, Antitrust & the Regulation of Competition: Live and Let Die?: Physician-Assisted Suicide and the Right to Die." *Harvard Journal of Law and Technology* 9 (1996): 513.

Marcus, F. "The Northern California Conference for Guidelines on Aid-in-Dying: Introduction." *Western Journal of Medicine* 166 (1997): 379.

Marker, R. "Assisted Suicide: Legal, Medical & Ethical Considerations for the Future." *St. John's Journal of Legal Commentary* 12 (1997): 670.

Martyn, S., and H. Bourguignon. "Physician-Assisted Suicide: The Lethal Flaws of the Ninth and Second Circuit Decisions." *California Law Review* 85(2) (1997): 371–426.

Mayo, D. "The Concept of Rational Suicide." *Journal of Medicine and Philosophy* 11 (1986): 143.

Mayo, D., and M. Gunderson. "Physician Assisted Death and Hard Choices." *Journal of Medicine and Philosophy* 18 (1993): 329.

McConnell, M. "The Right to Die and the Jurisprudence of Tradition." *Utah Law Review* (1997): 665.

503

McCormick, R. "Physician-Assisted Suicide: Flight from Compassion." *Christian Century* 108 (1991): 1132.

McGonnigal, M. "This Is Who Will Die When Doctors Are Allowed to Kill Their Patients." *John Marshall Law Review* 31 (1997): 95.

McGough, P. "Medical Concerns About Physician-Assisted Suicide." *Seattle University Law Review* 18 (1995): 521.

McGough, P., et al. "Physician-Assisted Suicide: Finding Common Ground." *Western Journal of Medicine* 166 (1997): 394.

McKhann, C. *A Time to Die: The Place for Physician Assistance*. New Haven: Yale University Press, 1999.

Meier, D. "Physician-Assisted Dying: Theory and Reality." *Journal of Clinical Ethics* 3 (1992): 35.

Meier, D., et al. "A National Survey of Physician-Assisted Suicide and Euthanasia in the United States." *New England Journal of Medicine* 338 (1998): 1193.

Meisel, A. "Managed Care, Autonomy, and Decision-Making at the End-of-Life." *University of Houston Law Review* 35 (1999): 1393.

Meisel, A. "Pharmacists, Physician-Assisted Suicide, and Pain Control." *University of Maryland Journal of Health Care Law and Policy* 2 (1999): 201.

Meisel, A. "Physician-Assisted Suicide: A Common Law Roadmap for State Courts." *Fordham Urban Law Journal* 24 (1997): 817.

Mikochik, S. "Symposium: Assisted Suicide and Disabled People." *DePaul Law Review* 46 (1997): 987.

Miles, S. "Physician-Assisted Suicide and the Profession's Gyrocompass." *Hastings Center Report* 25 (May-June 1995): 17.

Miller, F., and H. Brody. "Professional Integrity and Physician-Assisted Suicide." *Hastings Center Report* 25 (May-June 1995): 8.

Miller, F., and D. Meier. "Voluntary Death: A Comparison of Terminal Dehydration and Physician-Assisted Suicide." *Annals of Internal Medicine* 128 (1998): 559.

Miller, F., et al. "Regulating Physician-Assisted Death." *New England Journal of Medicine* 331 (1994): 119.

Ministry of Health, Welfare and Sport. *Euthanasia and Physician-Assisted Suicide in the Netherlands: Bibliography 1984–1995*. Rijswijk, Netherlands: Ministry of Health, Welfare and Sport, 1995.

Minois, G. *History of Suicide: Voluntary Death in Western Culture*. Baltimore: Johns Hopkins University Press, 1999.

Minow, M. "Which Question? Which Lie? Reflections on the Physician-Assisted Suicide Cases." *Supreme Court Review* (1997): 1.

BIBLIOGRAPHY

Morris, B. "Physician-Assisted Suicide: The Abortion of the Nineties." *Law and Psychology Review* 20 (1996): 215.

Moskowitz, E. "Mental Illness, Physical Illness, and the Legalization of Physician-Assisted Suicide." *Fordham Urban Law Journal* 24 (1997): 781.

Moss, D. "Physician-Assisted Suicide: A Symposium." *Western New England Law Review* 19 (1997): 313.

Mount, B. "Morphine Drips, Terminal Sedation, and Slow Euthanasia: Definitions and Facts, Not Anecdotes." *Journal of Palliative Care* 12 (1996): 31.

Muckelbauer, J. "Recent Development—Senate Bill 319: Assisted Suicide—Prohibition." *University of Baltimore Law Forum* 29 (1999): 83.

Mwaria, C. "Physician-Assisted Suicide: An Anthropological Perspective." *Fordham Urban Law Journal* 24 (1997): 859.

Myers, R. "An Analysis of the Constitutionality of Laws Banning Assisted Suicide from the Perspective of Catholic Moral Teaching." *University of Detroit Mercy Law Review* 72 (1995): 771.

National Council on Disability. "Assisted Suicide: A Disability Perspective." *Issues in Law and Medicine* 14 (1998): 273.

Neeley, G.S. *The Constitutional Right to Suicide: A Legal and Philosophical Examination.* New York: P. Lang, 1996.

Neeley, G.S. "The Constitutional Right to Suicide, the Quality of Life, and the 'Slippery Slope': An Explicit Reply to Lingering Concerns." *Akron Law Review* 28 (1994): 53.

Newman, J. "Live Through This . . . Physician Assisted Suicide." *Seton Hall Legislative Journal* 21 (1997): 535.

Noonan, J. "Phillip Clarke Family Lectures in Medical Ethics. Dealing with Death." *Notre Dame Journal of Law, Ethics and Public Policy* 12 (1998): 387.

Nuccetelli, S. and G. Seay. "Relieving Pain and Foreseeing Death: A Paradox About Accountability and Blame." *Journal of Law, Medicine & Ethics* 28 (2000): 19.

O'Brien, C., and G. Madek. "Physician-Assisted Suicide: New Protocol for a Rightful Death." *Nebraska Law Review* 77 (1998): 229.

Ontwuteaka-Philipsen, B., et al. "Attitudes of Dutch General Practitioners and Nursing Home Physicians to Active Voluntary Euthanasia and Physician-Assisted Suicide." *Archives of Family Medicine* 4 (1995): 951.

Orentlicher, D. "The Alleged Distinction Between Euthanasia and the Withdrawal of Life-Sustaining Treatment: Conceptually Incoherent and

Impossible to Maintain." *University of Illinois Law Review* 1998 (1998): 837.

Orentlicher, D. "The Legalization of Physician-Assisted Suicide." *New England Journal of Medicine* 335 (1996): 663.

Orentlicher, D. "The Legalization of Physician Assisted Suicide: A Very Modest Revolution." *Boston College Law Review* 38 (1997): 443.

Orentlicher, D. "The Supreme Court and Physician Assisted Suicide: Rejecting Assisted Suicide but Embracing Euthanasia." *New England Journal of Medicine* 337 (1997): 1236.

Orentlicher, D. "The Supreme Court and Terminal Sedation: Rejecting Assisted Suicide, Embracing Euthanasia." *Hastings Constitutional Law Quarterly* 24 (1997): 947.

O'Rourke, K. "Physician Assisted Suicide, A Religious Perspective." *St. Louis University Public Law Review* 15 (1996): 433.

Osgood, N. "Assisted Suicide and Older People—A Deadly Combination: Ethical Problems in Permitting Assisted Suicide." *Issues of Law and Medicine* 10 (1995): 415.

Otlowski, M. *Voluntary Euthanasia and the Common Law.* New York: Clarendon Press, 1997.

Patel, R. "Physician-Assisted Suicide: Is It Time?" *California Western Law Review* 35 (1999): 333.

Paust, J. "The Human Right to Die with Dignity: A Policy-Oriented Essay." *Human Rights Quarterly* 17 (1995): 463.

Pellegrino, E. "Doctors Must Not Kill." *Journal of Clinical Ethics* 3 (1992): 95.

"Physician-Assisted Suicide and Euthanasia in the Netherlands: A Report to the House Judiciary Subcommittee on the Constitution, Executive Summary." *Issues in Law and Medicine* 14 (1998): 301.

Pittman, L. "Physician-Assisted Suicide in the Dark Ward: The Intersection of the Thirteenth Amendment and Health Care Treatments Having Disproportionate Impacts on Disfavored Groups." *Seton Hall Law Review* 28 (1998): 774.

Plattner, A. "Australia's Northern Territory: The First Jurisdiction to Legislate Voluntary Euthanasia, and the First to Repeal It." *DePaul Journal of Health Care Law* 1 (1997): 645.

Popick, J. "A Time to Die?: Deciding the Legality of Physician-Assisted Suicide." *Pepperdine Law Review* 24 (1997): 1327.

Popkin, M. "The Constitutional Litigation on Assisted Suicide: A Last Look Before the Supreme Court Decides." *St. John's Journal of Legal Commentary* 12 (1997): 701.

BIBLIOGRAPHY

Portenoy, R. "Morphine Infusions at the End of Life: The Pitfalls in Reasoning from Anecdote." *Journal of Palliative Care* 12 (1996): 44.

Prado, C. *Assisted Suicide: Theory and Practice in Elective Death*. Amherst, NY: Humanity Books, 1999.

Prado, C. "Effects of Gender Differences on Physician-Assisted Suicide: Practice and Regulation." *Southern California Review of Law and Women's Studies* 8 (1998): 101.

Pratt, C. "Efforts to Legalize Physician-Assisted Suicide in New York, Washington and Oregon: A Contrast Between Judicial and Initiative Approaches—Who Should Decide?" *Oregon Law Review* 77 (1998): 1027.

Pratt, D. "Too Many Physicians: Physician-Assisted Suicide After Glucksberg/Quill." *Albany Law Journal of Science and Technology* 9 (1999): 161.

Pratt, D., and B. Steinbock. "Death with Dignity or Unlawful Killing: The Ethical and Legal Debate over Physician Assisted Death." *Criminal Law Bulletin* 23 (1997): 226.

Preston, T. "Physician Involvement in Life-Ending Practices." *Seattle University Law Review* 18 (1995): 531.

Previn, M. Note. "Assisted Suicide and Religion: Conflicting Conceptions of the Sanctity of Human Life." *Georgetown Law Journal* 84 (1996): 589.

Quill, T. *Death and Dignity: Making Choices and Taking Charge*. New York: 1993.

Quill, T. "Physician Assisted Death: After the U.S. Supreme Court Ruling." *University of Detroit Mercy Law Review* 75 (1998): 481.

Quill, T., and G. Kimsa. "End-of-Life Care in the Netherlands and the United States: A Comparison of Values, Justifications, and Practices." *Cambridge Quarterly on Health Care Ethics* 6 (1997): 189.

Quill, T., et al. "Care of the Hopelessly Ill: Proposed Clinical Criteria for Physician-Assisted Suicide." *New England Journal of Medicine* 327 (1992): 1380.

Quill, T., et al. "The Debate over Physician-Assisted Suicide: Empirical Data and Convergent Views." *Annals of Internal Medicine* 128: (1998): 552.

Quinn, K. "Assisted Suicide and Equal Protection: In Defense of the Distinction Between Killing and Letting Die." *Issues in Law and Medicine* 13 (1997): 145.

Quirk, P. "Euthanasia in the Commonwealth of Australia." *Issues in Law and Medicine* 13 (1998): 425.

Rachels, J. *The End of Life: Euthanasia and Morality*. Oxford: Oxford University Press, 1986.

Ragon, S. Comment. "A Doctor's Dilemma: Resolving the Conflict Between Physician Participation in Executions and the AMA's Code of Medical Ethics." *Dayton Law Review* 20 (1995): 975.

Reardon, T. "American Medical Association perspective on physician assisted suicide." *University of Detroit Mercy Law Review* 75 (1998): 515.

Reitman, J. "The Debate on Assisted Suicide—Redefining Morally Appropriate Care for People with Intractable Suffering." *Issues of Law and Medicine* 11 (1995): 299.

Resnicoff, S. "Jewish Law Perspectives on Suicide and Physician-Assisted Dying." *Journal of Law and Religion* 13 (1998–99): 289.

Resnicoff, S. "Physician Assisted Suicide Under Jewish Law." *DePaul Journal of Health Care Law* 1 (1997): 589.

Rice, C. "Abortion, Euthanasia, and the Need to Build a New 'Culture of Life.'" *Notre Dame Journal of Law, Ethics and Public Policy* 12 (1998): 497.

Rizzo, P. "Religion-Based Arguments in the Public Arena: A Catholic Perspective on Euthanasia, *Compassion in Dying v. State of Washington* and *Quill v. Vacco.*" *DePaul Journal of Health Care Law* 1 (1996): 243.

Robertson, J. "Sixty-Fifth Cleveland-Marshall Fund Lecture. Respect for Life in Bioethical Dilemmas—The Case of Physician-Assisted Suicide." *Cleveland State Law Review* 45 (1997): 329.

Robinson, J. "Physician Assisted Suicide: A Constitutional Crisis Resolved." *Notre Dame Journal of Law, Ethics and Public Policy* 12 (1998): 369.

Robinson, J. "Physician Assisted Suicide: Its Challenge to the Prevailing Constitutional Paradigm." *Notre Dame Journal of Law, Ethics and Public Policy* 9 (1995): 345.

Rogers, J. "Punishing Assisted Suicide: Where Legislators Should Fear to Tread." *Ohio Northern University Law Review* 20 (1994): 647.

Roscoe, L. "Physician-Assisted Suicide: Does Gender Matter?" *Journal of Ethics, Law, and Aging* 5 (1999): 111.

Rosenn, J. "The Constitutionality of Statutes Prohibiting and Permitting Physician-Assisted Suicide." *University of Miami Law Review* 51 (1997): 875.

Ryan, C., and M. Kaye. "Euthanasia in Australia: The Northern Territory Rights of the Terminally Ill Act." *New England Journal of Medicine* 334(5) (1996): 326.

Sachs, G., et al. "Good Care of Dying Patients: The Alternative to Physician-Assisted Suicide and Euthanasia." *Journal of the American Geriatrics Society* 43 (1995): 553.

BIBLIOGRAPHY

Sacred Congregation for the Doctrine of the Faith. "Declaration on Euthanasia." *Vatican Council II* 2 (1982): 510.

Safranek, J. "Autonomy and Assisted Suicide." *Hastings Center Report* 28 (July-August 1998): 32.

Safranek, J., and S. Safranek. "Assisted Suicide: The State Versus the People." *Seattle University Law Review* 21 (1997): 261.

Salem, T. "Promoting Autonomy—Or Medicalizing Suicide?" *Hastings Center Report* 29 (May-June 1999): 30.

Scherer, J. and Simon, R. *Euthanasia and the Right to Die*. Lanham, Maryland: Rowman Littlefield, 1999.

Schindler, T. "Assisted Suicide and Euthanasia: Ethical Dimensions of the Public Debate." *University of Detroit Mercy Law Review* 72 (1995): 719.

Schneider, W. "One Step Forward, Two Steps Back: Second Circuit Finds No Fundamental Right to Physician-Assisted Suicide." *Suffolk University Law Review* 30 (1997): 671.

Schwartz, M. "Practical Reasons for Lifting Bans on Physician-Assisted Suicide." *St. John's Journal of Legal Commentary* 12 (1997): 626.

Schwartz, R., and T. Kushner. "The Role of Institutional and Community Based Ethics Committees in the Debate on Euthanasia and Physician-Assisted Suicide." *Cambridge Quarterly of Healthcare Ethics* 5 (1996): 121.

Schwartz, R. "Rights of the Terminally Ill Act of the Australia Northern Territory." *Cambridge Quarterly of Healthcare Ethics* 5 (1996): 157.

Scofield, G. "Exposing Some Myths About Physician-Assisted Suicide." *Seattle University Law Review* 18 (1995): 473.

Scofield, G. "Natural Causes, Unnatural Results, and the Least Restrictive Alternative." *Western New England Law Review* 19 (1997): 317.

Sedler, R. "Abortion, Physician-Assisted Suicide and the Constitution: The View from Without and Within." *Notre Dame Journal of Law, Ethics and Public Policy* 12 (1998): 529.

Sedler, R. "Are Absolute Bans on Assisted Suicide Constitutional? I Say No." *University of Detroit Mercy Law Review* 72 (1995): 725.

Sedler, R. "Constitutional Challenges to Bans on 'Assisted Suicide': The View from Without and Within." *Hastings Constitutional Law Quarterly* 21 (1994): 777.

Shapiro, R., et al. "Willingness to Perform Euthanasia—A Survey of Physician Attitudes." *Archives of Internal Medicine* 154 (1994): 575.

Sheldon, T. "Euthanasia Reporting Is Increasing but Is Still Low." *British Medical Journal* 313 (1996): 1423.

Shepherd, L. "Sophie's Choices: Medical and Legal Responses to Suffering." *Notre Dame Law Review* 72 (1996): 103.

Shih, W. Note. "Assisted Suicide, the Due Process Clause and 'Fidelity in Translation.'" *Fordham Law Review* 63 (1995): 1245.

Shneidman, E. "Rational Suicide and Psychiatric Disorders." *New England Journal of Medicine* 326 (1992): 889.

Sieger, C. "Addressing and Dispelling Misconceptions Surrounding the Physician-Assisted Suicide Controversy." *St. John's Journal of Legal Commentary* 12 (1997): 659.

Silvers, A. "Protecting the Innocents: People with Disabilities and Physician-Assisted Dying." *Western Journal of Medicine* 166 (1997): 407.

Smith, C. "Advising Clients on Assisted Suicide: What Are the Legal Problems and Ethics of Working with Clients Considering Assisted Suicide?" *Oregon State Bar Bulletin* 54 (1994): 9.

Smith, G. "Terminal Sedation as Palliative Care: Revalidating a Right to a Good Death." *Cambridge Quarterly of Healthcare Ethics* 7 (1998): 382.

Smith, W. *Forced Exit: The Slippery Slope from Assisted Suicide to Legalized Murder.* New York: Times Books, 1997.

Smolin, D. "The Free Exercise Clause, the Religious Freedom Restoration Act, and the Right to Active and Passive Euthanasia." *Issues of Law and Medicine* 10 (1994): 3.

Solum, L. "Fritz B. Burns Lecture—Euthanasia, Morality, and Law—Introduction." *Loyola of Los Angeles Law Review* 31 (1998): 1115.

Spencer, D. "Practical Implications for Health Care Providers in a Physician-Assisted Suicide Environment." *Seattle University Law Review* 18 (1995): 545.

Spritz, N. "Physician-Assisted Suicide: Three Crucial Distinctions." *Fordham Urban Law Journal* 24 (1997): 869.

Stacy, T. "Euthanasia and the Supreme Court's Conceptions of Religious Liberty." *Issues of Law and Medicine* 10 (1994): 55.

Stone, G. *Suicide and Attempted Suicide: Methods and Consequences.* New York, NY: Carroll & Graf Publishers, 1999.

Stone, T., and W. Winslade. "Physician-Assisted Suicide and Euthanasia in the United States: Legal and Ethical Observations." *Journal of Legal Medicine* 16 (1995): 481.

Strasser, M. "Assisted Suicide and the Competent Terminally Ill: On Ordinary Treatments and Extraordinary Policies." *Oregon Law Review* 74 (1995): 539.

BIBLIOGRAPHY

Strasser, M. "Wrongful Life, Wrongful Birth, Wrongful Death, and the Right to Refuse Treatment: Can Reasonable Jurisdictions Recognize All But One?" *Missouri Law Review* 64 (1999): 29.

Sullivan, M., et al. "Should Physicians Serve as Gatekeepers for Physician-Assisted Suicide?" *Hastings Center Report* 28 (July-August 1998): 24.

Sulmasy, D. "Commentary: Double Effect—Intention Is the Solution, Not the Problem." *Journal of Law, Medicine & Ethics* 28 (2000): 26.

Sulmasy, D. "Killing and Letting Die: Another Look." *Journal of Law, Medicine, and Ethics* 26 (1998): 48.

Sunstein, C. Essay. "The Right to Die." *Yale Law Journal* 106 (1997): 1123.

Task Force on Physician-Assisted Suicide of the Society for Health and Human Values. "Physician-Assisted Suicide: Toward a Comprehensive Understanding." *Academic Medicine* 70 (1995): 583.

Thomas, K. "Confronting End-of-Life Decisions: Should We Extend the Right to Die?" *Federal Lawyer* 44 (1997): 30.

Thomasma, D. "An Analysis of Arguments For and Against Euthanasia and Assisted Suicide: Part One." *Cambridge Quarterly of Healthcare Ethics* 5 (1996): 62.

Thomasma, D., et al. *Asking to Die: Inside the Dutch Debate About Euthanasia.* Dordrecht: Kluwer Academic, 1998.

Thomasma, D., "Assessing the Arguments for and against Euthanasia and Assisted Suicide: Part II." *Cambridge Quarterly of Healthcare Ethics* 7 (1998): 388.

Thomasma, D., and G. Graber. *Euthanasia: Toward an Ethical Social Policy.* New York: Continuum, 1990.

Thomasma, D., et al., eds. *Asking to Die—Inside the Dutch Debate about Euthanasia.* Boston: Kluwer Academic Publications, 1998.

Torr, J., ed. *Euthanasia: Opposing Viewpoints.* San Diego: Greenhaven Press, 2000.

Traina, C. "Religious Perspectives on Assisted Suicide." *Journal of Criminal Law and Criminology* 88 (1998): 1147.

Tsarouhas, A. "The Case Against Legal Assisted Suicide." *Ohio Northern University Law Review* 20 (1994): 793.

Tucker, K., and D. Burman. "Physician Aid in Dying: A Humane Option, a Constitutionally Protected Choice." *Seattle University Law Review* 18 (1995): 495.

Tulsky, J., et al. "A Middle Ground on Physician-Assisted Suicide." *Cambridge Quarterly of Healthcare Ethics* 5 (1996): 33.

Tushnet, M. "How to Deny a Constitutional Right: Reflections of the Assisted-Suicide Cases." *Green Bag* 1 (1997): 55.

Ubel, P., and R. Arnold. "The Euthanasia Debate and Empirical Evidence: Separating Burdens to Others from One's Own Quality of Life." *Journal of Clinical Ethics* 5 (1994): 155.

Uhlmann, M., ed. *Last Rights? Assisted Suicide and Euthanasia Debated.* Washington, DC: Ethics and Public Policy Center, 1997.

Underwood, J. "The Supreme Court's Assisted Suicide Opinions in International Perspective: Avoiding a Bureaucracy of Death." *North Dakota Law Review* 73 (1997): 641.

Urofsky, M. "Leaving the Door Ajar: The Supreme Court and Assisted Suicide." *University of Richmond Law Review* 32 (1998): 313.

Urofsky, M. *Lethal Judgments: Assisted Suicide and American Law* (Landmark Law Cases and American Society Series). Lawrance, Kansas: University Press, 2000

Van der Heide, A., et al. "Medical End-of-Life Decisions Made for Neonates and Infants in the Netherlands." *Lancet* 350 (1997): 251.

Van der Maas, P.J., et al. "Euthanasia, physician-assisted suicide, and other medical practices involving the end of life in the Netherlands, 1990–1995." *New England Journal of Medicine* 335(22) (1996): 1699.

Van der Wal, G., and B. Onwuteaka-Philipsen. "Cases of Euthanasia and Assisted Suicide Reported to the Public Prosecutor in North Holland over 10 Years." *British Medical Journal* 312 (1996): 612.

Van Thiel, G., et al. "Retrospective Study of Doctors' 'End of Life Decisions' in Caring for Mentally Handicapped People in Institutions in the Netherlands." *British Medical Journal* 315 (1997): 88.

Weir, R., ed. *Physician-Assisted Suicide.* Bloomington, IN: Indiana University Press, 1997.

Weithman, P. "Of Assisted Suicide and 'The Philosophers' Brief.'" *Issues in Law and Medicine* 15 (1999): 223.

Werth, J., ed. *Contemporary Perspectives on Rational Suicide.* Philadelphia: Brunner Mazel, 1999.

Wheeler, W. "Hospice Philosophy: An Alternative to Assisted Suicide." *Ohio Northern University Law Review* 20 (1994): 755.

Wildes, K. "Life as a Good and Our Obligations to Persistently Vegetative Patients." In Wildes, K. et al., eds. *Birth, Suffering, and Death: Catholic Perspectives at the Edges of Life.* Boston, MA: Kluwer Academic, 1992.

Wolf, S. "Physician-Assisted Suicide, Abortion and Treatment Refusal: Using Gender to Analyze the Difference." In R. Weir, ed., *Physician-Assisted Suicide* 167–201. Bloomington: Indiana University Press, 1997.

BIBLIOGRAPHY

Wolf, S. "Physician-Assisted Suicide in the Context of Managed Care." *Duquesne Law Review* 35 (1996): 455.

Wolf, S. "Pragmatism in the Face of Death: The Role of Facts in the Assisted Suicide Debate." *Minnesota Law Review* 82 (1998): 1063.

Woods, E. "The Right to Die with Dignity with the Assistance of a Physician: An Anglo, American and Australian International Perspective." *ILSA Journal of International and Comparative Law* 4 (1998): 817.

Young, E. "Physician-Assisted Suicide: Overview of the Ethical Debate." *Western Journal of Medicine* 166 (1997): 402.

Young, E., et al. "Report of the Northern California Conference for Guidelines on Aid-in-Dying: Definitions, Differences, Convergences, Conclusions." *Western Journal of Medicine* 166 (1997): 381.

Young, S. "Dead Wrong: The Problems with Assisted Suicide Statutes and Prosecutions." *Stanford Law and Policy Review* 6 (1994): 123.

Zalman, M., et al. "Michigan's Assisted Suicide Three Ring Circus—An Intersection of Law and Politics." *Ohio Northern University Law Review* 23 (1997): 863.

Zipursky, B. "The Pedigrees of Rights and Powers in Scalia's *Cruzan* Concurrence." *University of Pittsburgh Law Review* 56 (1994): 283.

CHAPTER 19

THE PROBLEM OF "FUTILE" MEDICAL TREATMENT

§ 19.1 Nature of "Futility Cases"; Relationship to "Conventional" Right-to-Die Cases

Page 530, add to footnote 5:

But see Daniel J. Cher & Leslie A. Lenert, *Method of Medicare Reimbursement and the Rate of Potentially Ineffective Care of Critically Ill Patients,* 278 JAMA 1001 (1997) (ineffective care at end of life less likely to be provided by HMOs than traditional fee-for-service health plans).

Page 531, add note 6.1 reference at end of first sentence of first full paragraph and add note 6.1:

[6.1] **LA:** *See* Causey v. St. Francis Med. Ctr., 719 So. 2d 1072, 1074 (La. Ct. App. 1998) ("In the Karen Quinlan case the court rejected a physician's adamant stand that he had a moral duty to treat to the last gasp. In that case, the father, not the physician, was given the power to decide whether his comatose daughter's life-prolonging care was beneficial. . . . Now the roles are reversed. Patients or, if incompetent, their surrogate decision-makers, are demanding life-sustaining treatment regardless of its perceived futility, while physicians are objecting to being compelled to prolong life with procedures they consider futile.").

§ 19.2 Current State of the Law

Page 533, add to footnote 18:

NY: *See also In re* Long Island Jewish Medical Ctr. (Baby Doe), 641 N.Y.S.2d 989 (Sup. Ct. Queens County 1996).

Page 533, add at end of section:

Summary of Futility Cases

A trickle of futility cases continues to be litigated, with few reaching, or yet to reach, the appellate level. Some of the trial court decisions are accompanied by opinions, but others are jury verdicts and thus without opinions.

Appellate Cases.   In addition to the cases discussed in the main volume,[18.1] the following cases are noteworthy.

Georgia

Velez v. Bethune
466 S.E.2d 627 (Ga. Ct. App. 1995).

In an interlocutory appeal, the Georgia Court of Appeals affirmed a trial court's decision to permit the case to go to trial. Stripped to the essentials, there was a dispute as to whether the physician had obtained the parents' informed consent not to resuscitate the plaintiffs' severely ill infant who almost inevitably would have soon died even if she had been resuscitated. Because of this dispute, it was proper for the courts not to grant summary judgment for the physician.

However, what is more interesting is whether the plaintiffs failed to state a claim for which relief could be granted assuming the facts as alleged by the plaintiffs could be proved. Because the Georgia DNR statute on its face requires the consent of both parents to the writing of a DNR order for a minor, and because of the Georgia Supreme Court's holding to that effect in *In re Doe*,[18.2] the answer to this question in Georgia is presumably in the affirmative. More fundamentally, however, is whether such a result would be required in the absence of the DNR statute and the judicial gloss on it.

The Georgia Court of Appeals, or at least its chief judge in a concurring opinion, seemed to think so. Judge Beasley reasoned that because "the constitutional right to refuse belonged to the child, and had to be exercised by her surrogates (her parents)," treatment could not be forgone without the parents' permission.[18.3] This reasoning betrays a serious flaw. It is not nearly as clear as the judge would have it that the existence of a right to refuse treatment—a negative right—necessarily implies a right to demand treatment—a positive right.[18.4]

[18.1] *In re* Baby "K," 16 F.3d 590 (4th Cir. 1994), discussed in **§ 19.17** in the main volume; *In re* Doe, 418 S.E.2d 3 (Ga. 1992), discussed in **§ 19.18** in the main volume.

[18.2] 418 S.E.2d 3 (Ga. 1992).

[18.3] Velez v. Bethune, 466 S.E.2d at 629.

[18.4] See **§§ 19.9–19.15** in the main volume.

It is more likely that there is a duty to offer (but not necessarily to provide) treatment and that the nature and scope of the duty depend on professional standards of reasonableness. Under the doctrine of informed consent, doctors are required to inform patients (or surrogates) of the alternative forms of treatment in existence for the treatment (or diagnosis) of a particular condition. The *extent* of this disclosure — that is, the "standard" of disclosure — however, varies among jurisdictions. In some, patients must be told what a reasonable patient would find material to making a decision, in others, what a reasonable physician would disclose.[18.5]

Ironically, Georgia has perhaps the most impoverished informed consent requirement in the nation. The original statute dealing with this subject states that "a consent" is "presumed to be valid" if it "discloses in general terms the treatment or course of treatment with which it is given."[18.6] A subsequent amendment requires that patients must be informed in "general terms" of some other things. One element of information that must be provided is "the practical alternatives to such proposed surgical or diagnostic procedure which are generally recognized and accepted by reasonably prudent physicians."[18.7] Thus, a physician need not disclose all alternative treatments but only those reasonable to do so according to accepted medical standards.[18.8] However, these requirements concerning disclosure of alternatives apply only to certain surgical procedures and a limited list of other procedures and do not apply to cardiopulmonary resuscitation or likely to any of the other life-sustaining procedures needed by the Bethune baby.

However, even if the informed consent requirement in a particular jurisdiction is, unlike Georgia's, a particularly liberal one, the informed consent doctrine does not require physicians to provide treatment; it merely requires them to provide information about treatment. Having provided information about a treatment, for a number of possible reasons a physician might be free not to actually offer to perform it. Certainly, a physician need not perform a treatment that he is not qualified to perform (though this does not appear to have been the case in *Velez*), and indeed it would be the basis for tort liability if he did so and his substandard performance caused harm to the patient. Second, a physician might wish, as a matter of conscience, not to perform a particular treatment. (In the context of end-of-life decisionmaking, the administration of increasing doses of analgesics that risk "actively" hastening a patient's death is one not uncommon reason.) Finally, under the common law of abandonment, it appears that a physician may decline to perform treatment for any reason (or no reason at all) unless the failure to do so

---

[18.5] See §§ **3.7** and **3.14** in the main volume.

[18.6] Ga. Code Ann. § 31-9-6(d).

[18.7] *Id.* § 31-9-6.1(a)(5).

[18.8] *See* Moore v. Baker, 989 F.2d 1129 (11th Cir. 1993).

would violate some statutory duty such as nondiscrimination. Under the law of abandonment, depending on the facts, it might be the physician's duty to make reasonable efforts to arrange for another physician to treat the patient, but having done so, the physician would not be required to treat the patient.[18.9]

Thus, the *Velez* case does not advance the debate on the issue of futility. It merely reaffirms the Georgia law on the subject, which is statutorily based and might possibly turn out to be idiosyncratic. In any event, it does not grapple with the fundamental issues that these cases raise.

Louisiana

Causey v. St. Francis Medical Ctr.
719 So. 2d 1072 (La. Ct. App. 1998)

Causey raises the issue of futility in a straightforward manner, both factually and legally. The patient was a 31-year-old woman who was "comatose, quadriplegic and in end-stage renal failure." The attending physician "believed that she would have only a slight (1% to 5%) chance of regaining consciousness," though with continued dialysis and ventilatory support he thought she could possibly live for another two years. He recommended the termination of dialysis and other life support, but the patient's family would not agree. He then sought the advice of the hospital's ethics committee, which agreed with his recommended course of action, and the patient was removed from life support and died of respiratory and cardiac failure.

Suit was brought alleging that this course of conduct constituted a battery. This theory was chosen to avoid the Louisiana statutory requirement that medical malpractice cases be submitted to a medical review panel before a malpractice action may be filed.[18.10] The court held that this did not constitute a battery but that the Medical Malpractice Act was applicable.[18.11]

In reaching this conclusion, the court entered into a rather sweeping discussion of futile medical treatment, at least for an appellate court. To hold that the plaintiff's allegations must be submitted to a medical review panel, the court needed to determine that the allegations, if true, constituted malpractice. First, the court rejected any analysis based on the concept of futility, because "focus[ing] on a definition of 'futility' is confusing and generates polemical discussions."[18.12] Instead, the court utilized "an approach emphasiz-

---

[18.9] See §§ **17.13** and **17.14** in the main volume.

[18.10] Causey v. St. Francis Med. Ctr., 719 So. 2d 1072, 1074 (La. Ct. App. 1998), *citing* La. Rev. Stat. § 40:1299.47.

[18.11] *Id.* at 1076.

[18.12] *Id.* at 1075.

ing the standard of medical care."[18.13] Physicians have no obligation to provide treatment that is "medically inappropriate."[18.14]

Massachusetts

In re Mason
669 N.E.2d 1081 (Mass. App. Ct. 1996)

It is perhaps stretching it a bit to consider Mason a futility case. The reason for doing so is that the incompetent patient's son objected to the entry of a DNR order for his mother. The case, however, was not decided on the basis of resolving this dispute between the health care providers and the patient's son; rather, the court concluded that the son was not qualified to act as surrogate and that the entry of the DNR order was appropriate. It did not discuss the issue of the appropriate course of action when there was intractable opposition to the termination of treatment by someone legitimately qualified to act as surrogate.

Nebraska

Tabatha R. v. Ronda R.
564 N.W.2d 598 (Neb. 1997), modified,
566 N.W.2d 782 (Neb. 1998)

Although this case primarily deals with Nebraska procedural and evidentiary requirements under the Juvenile Code, the substantive aspect of the case involves forgoing life-sustaining treatment for an infant against the wishes of the infant's parents. The juvenile court had removed custody of the infant from her parents based on a finding that they had abused her.

Unlike other reported cases of this type in which the parents had abused their child so badly that it had died,[18.15] this child was still alive, though in a persistent vegetative state. In the cases of abuse leading to death, the children had all been on ventilatory support when death was determined by brain-death criteria, and thus the courts' decisions to permit termination of life support were relatively uncomplicated.

By contrast, this case is more closely akin to the other futility cases in which family members have refused physicians' recommendations to terminate life support and the physician or hospital has either sought a judicial order allowing for the termination of treatment or has terminated treatment

---

[18.13] *Id.*

[18.14] *Id.*

[18.15] See § **19.1** in the main volume.

and then been sued by a family member for damages. This appears to be the first reported case in which a court has ordered the termination of treatment over family protests. However, on appeal, the Nebraska Supreme Court held that the order to terminate the infant's life support was the equivalent of a termination of parental rights, and it remanded the case so that the same due process could be afforded as would be required in a case terminating parental rights.

On remand, the juvenile court found that the infant should remain in the state's custody "for appropriate care and placement."[18.16] Thus, the futility issue ultimately remained unresolved. A subsequent decision by the Nebraska Supreme Court[18.17] dealt with issues unrelated to the treatment of the infant.

Virginia

Bryan v. Rectors & Visitors of the University of Virginia
95 F.3d 349 (4th Cir. 1996)

This case is discussed in § **19.17** in this supplement.

Trial Court Cases.   The best known of the trial court cases is the first litigated futility case, *In re Wanglie*.[18.18] Other significant trial court cases are the following cases:

Massachusetts

Gilgunn v. Massachusetts General Hospital
No. SUCV92-4820 (Super. Ct., Suffolk County,
Mass., Apr. 21, 1995)

Prior to hospitalization, Mrs. Gilgunn had been in very poor health with a variety of medical problems—diabetes, Parkinson's disease, some sequelae of a stroke, breast cancer, and the precipitating event, her third hip fracture. After she entered the hospital for treatment of the fracture, but before surgery could be performed, she suffered repeated uncontrollable seizures and lapsed into a coma.

Mrs. Gilgunn was married and had children, and all agreed that one daughter, Joan, should act as surrogate. Joan Gilgunn represented that her mother

---

[18.16] Tabatha R. v. Ronda R., 587 N.W.2d 109, 115 (Neb. 1998).

[18.17] *See id.*

[18.18] No. PX-91-283 (Minn. Dist. Ct. Hennepin County July 1, 1991), discussed in § **19.3** in the main volume.

wanted everything possible to be done in the way of medical treatment to keep her alive, and this was done for a while. But after a few weeks, the physicians became convinced that she would not recover from her comatose condition. The physician consulted the hospital's "Optimum Care Committee," which functioned as an ethics committee, and then wrote a DNR order. However, he revoked the order because of the family's intense opposition. When a new attending physician "rotated" on to the case, he sought and obtained further consultation from the committee's chairman, who again supported a DNR order, which the new attending physician wrote. He also received support from the hospital's legal counsel for this action and for "terminally weaning" Mrs. Gilgunn from the ventilator, that is, removing the ventilator and not replacing it if she was unable to spontaneously breathe. He proceeded to perform the terminal wean, Mrs. Gilgunn was not able to breathe adequately on her own, and she died three days later.[18.19]

Joan Gilgunn brought suit against this attending physician, the chair of the ethics committee, and the hospital, claiming damages for the emotional distress caused her by the termination of her mother's life support against Joan Gilgunn's wishes. The jury found that Mrs. Gilgunn did in fact want everything possible done, but it absolved the doctors and hospital from liability on the ground that they were not required to meet this demand.

This case offers the first ray of hope to the health care professions that they need not provide treatment that offers no hope of recovery to a patient. However, as an unappealed jury verdict, it is hardly authoritative. Furthermore, the core issue in the futility debate—whether a patient or one legally authorized to speak on her behalf—was not raised by the pleadings in this case. Rather, the issue that was litigated was whether the physicians had violated the daughter's right to be free from emotional distress from the unilateral termination of treatment of a close family member. Finally, it is not clear that Joan Gilgunn had the legal authority, as one of several children who were not in agreement with each other, to make decisions about her mother's treatment.

Pennsylvania

Rideout v. Hershey Medical Center
16 Fiduc. Rep. 2d 181 (C.P. Dauphin County, Pa. 1995)

The patient in *Rideout* was a two-year-old girl who was terminally ill with a type of brain tumor known as a glioblastoma. After surgery at one hospital, she was admitted to the defendant hospital for a diagnostic test. While there, she began to experience difficulty breathing and appeared stuporous, and so

---

[18.19] *See generally* Capron, *Abandoning a Waning Life,* 25 Hastings Ctr. Rep. 25 (July–Aug. 1995).

was admitted to the hospital. She remained in the hospital for about three months and died there after her life support was discontinued. During this entire period, her physicians presented her parents with an extremely bleak prognosis, devoid of any hope for any outcome other than death, and her parents continually advocated aggressive treatment.

Eventually, the attending physician determined that termination of life support was the appropriate course of action because "[i]t was [his] conclusion that continued ventilatory support constituted futile and inappropriate care."[18.20] He consulted the hospital's ethics committee before conveying this conclusion to the parents and then called them and advised them of what he planned to do, why, and the likely result—namely, that the child almost certainly would die. He "encouraged [them] to be in attendance to say goodbye to Brianne."[18.21] As the trial court wrote, "[t]he Rideouts were vehemently opposed to the plan and threatened legal action. The Rideouts believed that Brianne's recent deterioration was not permanent."[18.22] The chairman of the ethics committee met with them and provided further explanation. They spoke with the hospital's patient advocate, and she then "persuade[d the attending physician and chairman of the ethics committee] to delay discontinuation of the ventilator so that the hospital staff could further consult with its attorneys."[18.23] After this legal consultation, the doctors decided to discontinue life support the next morning. The hospital had requested police officers to be present in anticipation of a "disorderly situation." When the parents arrived at the hospital, they went to the Patient Advocate Office, while other family members went to the patient's bedside. When the attending physician learned of the parents' presence in the hospital, he "instructed his staff to inform them to come to Brianne's room immediately because they were discontinuing the ventilatory support."[18.24] After waiting awhile, the attending physician extubated the patient without the parents being present. What happened next is factually important, if not critical, to the outcome of the case:

> Simultaneously, the hospital's Chaplain, who was located in Brianne's room, announced to the Rideouts over the hospital intercom system: "they turned her off, they turned her off!" The Rideouts heard the announcement and immediately rushed from the Patient Advocate Office to Brianne's room, hysterically crying and screaming that their child had been murdered. Although Brianne had begun breathing on her own, they begged Dr. Lucking to place her back on the ventilator. Mr. Rideout was so upset that he suffered an acute asthma

---

[18.20] 16 Fiduc. Rep. 2d at 183.

[18.21] *Id.*

[18.22] *Id.*

[18.23] *Id.*

[18.24] *Id.* at 184.

attack. Because Brianne was breathing on her own, . . . her then-attending physician believed that reconnection would be unnecessary.[18.25]

The patient died two days later, still extubated, and in her parents' presence, from cardiopulmonary failure caused by insufficient oxygen. In addition to the foregoing, there is some evidence that the hospital was motivated by financial concerns to encourage the doctors to terminate life support.[18.26]

The parents filed a complaint alleging a variety of different causes of action, most of which survived a motion to dismiss that was the subject of this reported opinion. It cannot be emphasized too strongly, however, that none of the sustained causes of action was predicated on the theory that the hospital and physicians were under an obligation to continue to provide medical treatment to the patient simply because the parents demanded that it be continued.[18.27] Rather, all of the sustained causes of action were for injuries inflicted on the parents by the manner in which the decision was made—namely, negligent infliction of emotional distress,[18.28] intentional infliction of emotional distress,[18.29] and federal civil rights actions.[18.30] The court dismissed claims under EMTALA[18.31] and the Rehabilitation Act.[18.32] On the claim for battery, the court held that the termination of ventilatory support could be a battery to the patient if the "disconnection . . . involved a surgical procedure," a matter which could not be resolved on the pleadings, but that it could not be a battery as to the parents.[18.33]

Thus, although the fact pattern of the *Rideout* case suggests that it is a futility case, it does not appear that it will be litigated on the theory that the parents had a right to demand continued treatment of their daughter, but rather on far more conventional theories based on the manner in which the termination of life support occurred.

[18.25] *Id.*

[18.26] 16 Fiduc. Rep. 2d at 182 ("On May 20, 1992, the Rideouts were informed by the hospital's Social Services department that Brianne's health insurance coverage might soon be exhausted and that medical assistance would be needed to cover her medical costs. . . . On May 26, 1992, the hospital's Social Services department confirmed that Brianne's health coverage would soon be exhausted. . . . By June 2, 1992, the Rideouts were informed that Brianne had most likely exhausted her current insurance coverage and that they needed to apply for medical assistance as soon as possible.").

[18.27] *Id.* at 192 ("[T]he hospital maintains that the Rideouts are . . . asserting a constitutionally protected unilateral right to insist upon or demand continuation of mechanical ventilatory support on behalf of Brianne. . . . The Rideouts do not dispute that a constitutional right to receive medical treatment does not exist.").

[18.28] See § **17.15A** in this supplement.

[18.29] See § **17.7** in this supplement.

[18.30] See § **17.20** in this supplement.

[18.31] See § **17.15** in this supplement and § **19.17** in the main volume.

[18.32] See § **17.21** in the main volume and this supplement.

[18.33] 16 Fiduc. Rep. 2d at 191.

§ 19.4   Nature of the Debate About Futility;

Meaning of Futility

Page 535, add to footnote 26:

LA: Causey v. St. Francis Med. Ctr., 719 So. 2d 1072, 1074–75 (La. Ct. App. 1998) ("When the medical professional and the patient, through a surrogate, disagree on the worth of pursuing life, this is a conflict over values, i.e., whether extra days obtained through medical intervention are worth the burden and costs.").

Page 536, add note 30.1 reference in first sentence after "cruel" and add note 30.1:

[30.1] **LA:** Causey v. St. Francis Med. Ctr., 719 So. 2d 1072, 1076 n.3 (La. Ct. App. 1998) (surrogate's demand to continue medically inappropriate treatment constitutes abuse).

Page 536, add to footnote 31:

LA: Causey v. St. Francis Med. Ctr., 719 So. 2d 1072, 1075 (La. Ct. App. 1998) ("When the medical professional and the patient, through a surrogate, disagree on the worth of pursuing life, this is a conflict over values, i.e., whether extra days obtained through medical intervention are worth the burden and costs.").

Page 536, add to footnote 33:

LA: *See also* Causey v. St. Francis Med. Ctr., 719 So. 2d 1072 (La. Ct. App. 1998) (physician seeking to terminate dialysis of severely ill patient with no hope of recovery but who had life expectancy of perhaps two years).

Page 537, add to footnote 35:

LA: Causey v. St. Francis Med. Ctr., 719 So. 2d 1072, 1074 (La. Ct. App. 1998) ("[T]the problem is with care that has an effect on the dying process, but which the physician believes has no benefit. Such life-prolonging care is grounded in beliefs and values about which people disagree. Strictly speaking, if a physician can keep the patient alive, such care is not medically or physiologically 'futile'; however, it may be 'futile' on philosophical, religious or practical grounds. . . . When the medical professional and the patient, through a surrogate, disagree on the worth of pursuing life, this is a conflict over values . . . . Futility is a subjective and nebulous concept which, except in the strictest physiological sense, incorporates value judgments.").

Page 537, add to footnote 37:

LA: *But cf.* Causey v. St. Francis Med. Ctr., 719 So. 2d 1072 (La. Ct. App. 1998) (suggesting but not holding that physician has unilateral right to terminate care deemed not to be medically appropriate).

§ 19.5   Meaning of Common-Law Right to Self-Determination and Relationship to Futility

Page 538, add note 39.1 reference at end of second sentence of last paragraph:

[39.1] **LA:** Causey v. St. Francis Med. Ctr., 719 So. 2d 1072, 1074 (La. Ct. App. 1998) ("The right or autonomy of the patient to refuse treatment is simply a severing of the relationship with the physician. In this case, however, the patient (through her surrogate) is not severing a relationship, but demanding treatment the physician believes is 'inappropriate.'").

Page 539, add note 39.2 reference at end of section and add note 39.1:

[39.2] **LA:** *See* Causey v. St. Francis Med. Ctr., 719 So. 2d 1072, 1075 (La. Ct. App. 1998) ("To focus on a definition of 'futility' is confusing and generates polemical discussions. We turn instead to an approach emphasizing the standard of medical care.").

§ 19.6   —Right to Choose Encompasses a Right to Demand Treatment

Page 539, add note 39.3 reference at end of first paragraph and add note 39.3:

[39.3] **GA:** *See* Velez v. Bethune, 466 S.E.2d 627, 629 (Ga. Ct. App. 1995) (Beasley, C.J., concurring specially) (constitutional and common-law right to refuse treatment means that *termination* of treatment requires consent of the patient or surrogate, and failure to do so "could be either an intentional or a negligent act, depending on the facts found by the jury").

§ 19.7   —Right to Choose Is Merely a Right to Refuse

Page 540, add note 41.1 reference at end of first sentence of first full paragraph and add note 41.1:

[41.1]   See § **3.15** in the main volume.

Page 540, add to footnote 44:

LA: *See* Causey v. St. Francis Med. Ctr., 719 So. 2d 1072, 1075 (La. Ct. App. 1998) ("Physicians are professionals and occupy a special place in our community. They are licensed by society to perform this special role. No one else is permitted to use life-prolonging technology, which is considered by many as 'fundamental' health care. The physician has an obligation to present all medically acceptable treatment options for the patient or her surrogate to consider and either choose or reject; however, this does not compel a physician to provide interventions that in his view would be harmful, without effect or 'medically inappropriate.'").

Page 540, add note 44.1 reference at end of second sentence of second full paragraph and add note 44.1:

[44.1] **LA:** Causey v. St. Francis Med. Ctr., 719 So. 2d 1072, 1074 (La. Ct. App. 1998) ("The right or autonomy of the patient to refuse treatment is simply a severing of the relationship with the physician.").

Page 541, add to footnote 45:

LA: *See* Causey v. St. Francis Med. Ctr., 719 So. 2d 1072, 1076 (La. Ct. App. 1998) ("A finding that treatment is "medically inappropriate" by a consensus of physicians practicing in that speciality translates into a standard of care.").

§ 19.8   The Different Contexts of Right-to-Die and Futility Cases

Page 542, add note 49.1 reference at end of first paragraph of section and add note 49.1:

[49.1] **LA:** Causey v. St. Francis Med. Ctr., 719 So. 2d 1072, 1074 (La. Ct. App. 1998) ("The right or autonomy of the patient to refuse treatment is simply a severing of the relationship with the physician. In this case, however, the patient (through her surrogate) is not severing a relationship, but demanding treatment the physician believes is 'inappropriate.'").

§ 19.10 — Positive Constitutional Rights: Claims Against the State

Page 546, add to footnote 63:

See also Harris v. McRae, 448 U.S. 297, 317–18 (1980) (right to be free from governmental interference in abortion decision does not include entitlement to funds necessary to exercise that right).

§ 19.17 — — Federal Statutory Rights: The *Baby K* Case

Page 554, add to footnote 99:

PA: *Cf*. Rideout v. Hershey Medical Ctr., 16 Fiduc. Rep. 2d 181, 196 (C.P. Dauphin County, Pa. 1995) (no constitutional right to demand medical treatment, citing Johnson v. Thompson, 971 F.2d 1487 (10th Cir. 1992)).

Page 558, add at end of section:

In *Bryan v. Rectors & Visitors of the University of Virginia*,[124.1] the Fourth Circuit was faced with an effort to apply and, as it concluded, extend the reach of EMTALA as it was construed in *Baby "K"*. The full facts are difficult to discern from the reported case, but it appears as if the patient was transferred to the defendant hospital from another hospital under emergency circumstances for the treatment of respiratory distress. The complaint alleged that the patient's family consistently and clearly instructed the medical authorities to "take all necessary measures to keep her alive and trust in God's wisdom."[124.2] Nonetheless, a DNR order was written against the family's wishes, and as a result the patient died 12 days later. The trial court dismissedthe complaint because the hospital had stabilized the patient's condition at the time of transfer to the hospital under emergency circumstances as required by EMTALA.

The plaintiffs claimed that EMTALA not only requires the hospital to stabilize the patient's condition in the initial emergency, but also requires con-

---

[124.1] 95 F.3d 349 (4th Cir. 1996).

[124.2] *Id*. at 350.

tinuous "stabilization" of "her condition no matter how long treatment was required to maintain that condition."[124.3] The hospital's entry of a DNR order constituted "abandonment" of stabilizing treatment, as did its failure to offer stabilizing treatment in response to a heart attack the patient suffered.

The Fourth Circuit rejected these claims and affirmed because under the plaintiffs' theory of the obligations imposed by EMTALA, "every presentation of an emergency patient to a hospital covered by EMTALA obligates the hospital . . . to provide treatment indefinitely—perhaps for years."[124.4] The court further held that its decision in the *Baby "K"* case did not require a different conclusion because "[t]he holding in *Baby K* . . . turned entirely on the substantive nature of the stabilizing treatment that EMTALA required for a particular emergency medical condition. The case did not present the issue of the temporal duration of that obligation, and certainly did not hold that it was of indefinite duration."[124.5]

In *Baby "K,"* the hospital claimed that EMTALA's stabilization requirement should depend on the patient's general medical condition. Because the patient suffered from anencephaly, and the standard of professional conduct in such cases was not to treat, the hospital was not required to stabilize the patient who, as a result of the general medical condition of anencephaly, was suffering from emergency respiratory distress. The court, however, concluded that "[u]nder the circumstances, the requirement was to provide stabilizing treatment of the condition of respiratory distress, without regard to the fact that the patient was anencephalic or to the appropriate standards of care for that general condition."[124.6]

It is important to note, as the district court observed, that the holding that EMTALA does not constitute a basis for liability does not mean that there might not be a remedy under state tort law.

§ 19.18   — —"DNR" Statutes: The *Doe* Case

Page 558, add to footnote 128:

GA: *See also* Velez v. Bethune, 466 S.E.2d 627 (Ga. Ct. App. 1995), discussed in § **19.2** in this supplement.

[124.3] *Id.*

[124.4] *Id.* at 351.

> **LA:** *Accord* Causey v. St. Francis Med. Ctr., 719 So. 2d 1072, 1075 n.2 (La. Ct. App. 1998) (EMTALA applies only in immediate aftermath of emergency admission) (dictum).

[124.5] *Id.*

[124.6] *Id.*

§ 19.19   — —Advance Directive Statutes

Page 560, add note 142.1 reference after first sentence and add note 142.1:

[142.1] **LA:** *See, e.g., In re* Lebreton v. Rabito, 650 So. 2d 1245 (La. Ct. App. 1995) (adult daughter of patient from whom life-sustaining medical treatment had been removed alleged that she had authority to require continuation of treatment under surrogate decisionmaking provisions of living will statute).

Page 561, add to footnote 146:

DE: Del. Code Ann. § 2508(f) ("A health-care provider or institution may decline to comply with an individual instruction or health-care decision that requires medically ineffective treatment or health care contrary to generally accepted health-care standards.").

§ 19.21   The Future of Futility

Page 563, add to text at end of last paragraph:

The American Medical Association Council on Ethical and Judicial Affairs has not established firm guidelines for differentiating between treatments that may or may not be medically futile. It has, however, recommended a process-based approach to futility determinations and urged that healthcare institutions incorporate its approach, or a similar one, in adopting their policies or guidelines.[158.1]

Page 564, add to footnote 161:

But see Daniel J. Cher & Leslie A. Lenert, *Method of Medicare Reimbursement and the Rate of Potentially Ineffective Care of Critically Ill Patients,* 278 JAMA 1001 (1997) (ineffective care at end of life less likely to be provided by HMOs than traditional fee-for-service health plans).

Bibliography

Ackerman, T. "Futility Judgments and Therapeutic Conversation." *Journal of the American Geriatric Society* 42 (1994): 902.

[158.1] Council on Ethical and Judicial Affairs, American Medical Association, *Medical Futility in End-of-Life Care*, 281 JAMA 937 (1999).

BIBLIOGRAPHY

Alpers, A., and B. Lo. "Avoiding Family Feuds: Responding to Surrogate Demands for Life-Sustaining Interventions." *Journal of Law, Medicine and Ethics* 27 (1999): 74.

American Medical Association, Council on Ethical and Judicial Affairs. "Medical Futility in End-of-Life Care." *Journal of the American Medical Association* 281 (1999): 937.

Bennett, A. "When Is Medical Treatment Futile?" *Issues in Law and Medicine* 9 (1993): 35.

Brody, H. "The Multiple Facets of Futility." *Journal of Clinical Ethics* 5 (1994): 142.

Brody, H., and R. Gillon. "Futile Care Treatment: Perspectives from the United States and United Kingdom." *University of Detroit Mercy Law Review* 75 (1998): 529.

Cantor, N. "Can Healthcare Providers Obtain Judicial Intervention Against Surrogates Who Demand 'Medically Inappropriate' Life Support for Incompetent Patients?" *Critical Care Medicine* 24 (No. 5 1996): 883.

Caplan, A. "Odds and Ends: Trust and the Debate Over Medical Futility." *Annals of Internal Medicine* 125 (1996): 688.

Carter, B., and J. Sandling. "Decision Making in the NICU: The Question of Medical Futility." *Journal of Clinical Ethics* 3 (1992): 142.

Clayton, E. "Commentary: What Is Really at Stake in *Baby K*? A Response to Ellen Flannery." *Journal of Law, Medicine and Ethics* 23 (1995): 13.

Coleson, R. "Child Abuse by Whom?—Parental Rights and Judicial Competency Determinations: The Baby K and Baby Terry Cases." *Ohio Northern University Law Review* 20 (1994): 821.

Cultice, P. "Medical Futility: When Is Enough, Enough?" *Journal of Health and Hospital Law* 278 (1994): 225.

Daar, J. "A Clash at the Bedside: Patient Autonomy v. A Physician's Professional Conscience." *Hastings Law Journal* 44 (1993): 1241.

Ebell, M. "Lessons from Quantifying Futility." *Archives of Family Medicine* 4 (1995): 308.

Ebell, M. "When Everything Is Too Much: Quantitative Approaches to the Issue of Futility." *Archives of Family Medicine* 4 (1995): 352.

Emanuel, E. "Cost Savings at the End of Life." *Journal of the American Medical Association* 275 (1996): 1907.

Fins, J. "Futility in Clinical Practice: Report on a Congress of Clinical Societies." *Journal of American Geriatrics Society* 42 (1994): 861.

Flannery, E. "One Advocate's Viewpoint: Conflicts and Tensions in the *Baby K* Case." *Journal of Law, Medicine and Ethics* 23 (1995): 7.

Gazelle, G. "The Slow Code—Should Anyone Rush to Its Defense?" *New England Journal of Medicine* 338(7): (1998): 467–469.

Halevy, A., R. Neal, and B. Brody. "The Low Frequency of Futility in an Adult Intensive Care Unit Setting." *Archives of Internal Medicine* 156 (1996): 100.

Hardwig, J. "Is There a Duty to Die?" *Hastings Center Report* 27 (March-April 1997): 34.

Humber, J., et al. *Is There a Duty to Die?* Totowa, NJ: Humana Press, 2000.

Jecker, N. "Is Refusal of Futile Treatment Unjustified Paternalism?" *Journal of Clinical Ethics* 6 (1995): 133.

Johnson, S., et al. "Legal and Institutional Policy Responses to Medical Futility." *Journal of Health and Hospital Law* 30 (1997): 21.

Lantos, J. "Futility Assessments and the Doctor-Patient Relationship." *Journal of the American Geriatric Society* 42 (1994): 868.

Layson, R., and T. McConnell. "Must Consent Always Be Obtained for a Do-Not-Resuscitate Order?" *Archives of Internal Medicine* 156 (1996): 2617.

Levine, E. "A New Predicament for Physicians: The Concept of Medical Futility, the Physician's Obligation to Render Inappropriate Treatment, and the Interplay of the Medical Standard of Care." *Journal of Law and Health* 9 (1994–95): 69.

Levinsky, N. "The Purpose of Advance Medical Planning— Autonomy for Patients or Limitation of Care?" *New England Journal of Medicine* 335 (1996): 741.

McCrary, S.V., et al. "Physicians' Quantitative Assessments of Medical Futility." *Journal of Clinical Ethics* 5 (1995): 100.

Menikoff, J. "Demanded Medical Care." *Arizona State Law Journal* 30 (1998): 1091.

Middleditch, L., and J. Trotter. "The Right to Live." *Elder Law Journal* 5 (1997): 395.

Peters, P. "When Physicians Balk at Futile Care: Implications of the Disability Rights Laws." *Northwestern University Law Review* 91 (1997): 798.

Post, S. "*Baby K*: Medical Futility and the Free Exercise of Religion." *Journal of Law, Medicine and Ethics* 23 (1995): 20.

Rivin, A. "Futile Care Policy: Lessons Learned From Three Years' Experience in a Community Hospital." *Western Journal of Medicine* 166 (1997): 389.

Rubin, S. *When Doctors Say No*. Bloomington, IN: Indiana University Press, 1998.

BIBLIOGRAPHY

Schneiderman, L. *Wrong Medicine: Doctors, Patients, and Futile Treatment*. Baltimore: Johns Hopkins University Press, 1995.

Schneiderman, L., and S. Manning. "The *Baby K* Case: A Search for the Elusive Standard of Medical Care." *Cambridge Quarterly of Healthcare Ethics* 6 (1997): 9.

Schneiderman, L., et al. "Medical Futility: Response to Critiques." *Annals of Internal Medicine* 125 (1996): 669.

Speilman, B. "Bargaining about Futility." *Journal of Law, Medicine, and Ethics* 23 (1995): 136.

Spielman, B. "Futility and Bargaining Power." *Journal of Clinical Ethics* 6 (1995): 44.

Strasser, M. "The Futility of Futility?: On Life, Death, and Reasoned Public Policy." *Maryland Law Review* 57 (1998): 505.

Swanson, J.W., and S. Van McCrary. "Medical Futility Decisions and Physicians' Legal Defensiveness: The Impact of Anticipated Conflict on Thresholds for End-of-Life Treatment." *Social Science and Medicine* 42 (1996): 125.

Symposium. "From *Baby Doe* to *Baby K*: Evolving Challenges in Pediatric Ethics." *Journal of Law, Medicine and Ethics* 23 (1995): 5.

"Symposium on Medical Futility." *Seton Hall Law Review* 25 (1995): 873.

Teno, J., et al. "Prognosis-Based Futility Guidelines: Does Anyone Win?" *Journal of the American Geriatrics Society* 42 (1994): 1202.

Toms, S. "Outcome Predictors in the Early Withdrawal of Life Support: Issues of Justice and Allocation for the Severely Brain Injured." *Journal of Clinical Ethics* 4 (1993): 206.

Truog, R. "Beyond Futility." *Journal of Clinical Ethics* 3 (1992): 143.

Truog, R. "Progress in the Futility Debate." *Journal of Clinical Ethics* 6 (1995): 128.

Waisel, D., and R. Truog. "The Cardiopulmonary Resuscitation-Not-Indicated Order: Futility Revisited." *Annals of Internal Medicine* 122 (1995): 304.

Wear, S., and G. Loque. "The Problem of Medically Futile Treatment: Looking Back on a Preventive Ethics Approach." *Journal of Clinical Ethics* 6 (1995): 138.

White, K. "Crisis of Conscience: Reconciling Religious Health Care Providers' Beliefs and Patients' Rights." *Stanford Law Review* 51 (1999): 1703.

Zawacki, B. "The 'Futility Debate' and the Management of Gordian Knots." *Journal of Clinical Ethics* 6 (1995): 112.

"FUTILE" MEDICAL TREATMENT

Zucker, M.B. *Medical Futility: and the Evaluation of Life-Sustaining Interventions*. New York: Cambridge University Press, 1997.

TABLE OF CASES

TABLE OF CASES

TABLE OF CASES

TABLE OF CASES

TABLE OF CASES

TABLE OF CASES

INDEX

INDEX

INDEX

INDEX

INDEX